Lecture Notes in Computer Science 4661

Commenced Publication in 1973
Founding and Former Series Editors:
Gerhard Goos, Juris Hartmanis, and Jan van Leeuwen

Ugo Montanari   Donald Sannella
Roberto Bruni (Eds.)

Trustworthy
Global Computing

Second Symposium, TGC 2006
Lucca, Italy, November 7-9, 2006
Revised Selected Papers

 Springer

Volume Editors

Ugo Montanari
Roberto Bruni
University of Pisa
Dipartimento di Informatica
Largo Bruno Pontecorvo 3, 56127 Pisa, Italy
E-mail: {ugo, bruni}@di.unipi.it

Donald Sannella
University of Edinburgh
Laboratory for Foundations of Computer Science
Edinburgh EH9 3JZ, Scotland, UK
E-mail: dts@inf.ed.ac.uk

Library of Congress Control Number: 2007939452

CR Subject Classification (1998): C.2.4, D.1.3, D.2, D.4.6, F.2.1-2, D.3, F.3

LNCS Sublibrary: SL 1 – Theoretical Computer Science and General Issues

ISSN   0302-9743
ISBN-10   3-540-75333-8 Springer Berlin Heidelberg New York
ISBN-13   978-3-540-75333-9 Springer Berlin Heidelberg New York

Springer is a part of Springer Science+Business Media

springer.com

© Springer-Verlag Berlin Heidelberg 2007
Printed in Germany

Typesetting: Camera-ready by author, data conversion by Scientific Publishing Services, Chennai, India
Printed on acid-free paper   SPIN: 12166930   06/3180   5 4 3 2 1 0

Preface

Computing technology has become ubiquitous, from worldwide distributed applications to minuscule embedded devices. Trust in computing is vital to help protect public safety, national security, and economic prosperity.

A new area of research, known as global computing, has recently emerged. It aims at defining new models of computation based on code and data mobility over wide area networks with highly dynamic topologies, and to provide infrastructures to support coordination and control of components originating from different, possibly untrusted, sources.

Trustworthy global computing aims at guaranteeing safe and reliable network usage, also by providing tools and framework for reasoning about behavior and properties of applications.

This volume contains the proceedings of the 2nd International Symposium on Trustworthy Global Computing (TGC 2006), held in Lucca, Italy, November 7–9, 2006. The first edition took place in Edinburgh, UK, as part of ETAPS 2005. TGC 2005 was the evolution of the previous Global Computing I Workshops held in Rovereto, Italy, in 2003 and 2004 and of the Foundation of Global Computing Workshops held as satellite events of ICALP and Concur.

The themes of the workshop addressed issues like theories, models, and algorithms for global computing and service-oriented computing, language-based security, theories of trust, authentication and anonymity, secure protocol composition, resource usage and information flow policies, privacy, reliability and business integrity, models of disciplined interaction and dynamic components management, sharing information and computation, self configuration and adaptiveness, efficient communication, language concepts and abstraction mechanisms, model-driven development, test generators, symbolic interpreters, and type checkers.

The above themes were inspired by the activities of the IST/FET proactive Initiative on Global Computing I and II funded by the European Union. In fact the FP6 Programme of the European Union launched several projects dedicated to these themes, whose (first year activity) reviews were co-located with TGC 2006:

- AEOLUS: Algorithmic Principles for Building Efficient Overlay Computers
  http://www.ceid.upatras.gr/aeolus
- MOBIUS: Mobility, Ubiquity and Security
  http://mobius.inria.fr
- SENSORIA: Software Engineering for Service-Oriented Overlay Computers
  http://www.sensoria-ist.eu
- CATNETS: Catallaxy Paradigm for Decentralized Operation of Dynamic Application Networks
  http://www.iw.uni-karlsruhe.de/catnets

Three special sessions of TGC 2006 were devoted to presenting and discussing recent progress within these projects and to the presentation of three FP7 initiatives named "Internet of the future," "Pervasive adaptation" and "ICT forever yours." The format of the symposium was not that of a classical conference, but one structured to leave room for discussions stimulated by a conspicuous number of invited talks and by the papers selected after standard refereeing.

The Program Committee selected 14 contributed papers out of 32 submissions after a selective refereeing process (each paper was reviewed by three experts, at least). These were grouped in five sessions on "Types to discipline interactions," "Calculi for distributed systems," "Flexible modeling," "Algorithms and systems for global computing," and "Security, anonymity and type safety."

Additionally the program included four keynote speeches by:

- Jayadev Misra (University of Texas at Austin, USA)
  "Structured Concurrent Programming"
- Andrei Sabelfeld (University of Goteborg, Sweden)
  "Dimensions of Declassification in Theory and Practice"
- Paola Inverardi (University of Aquila, Italy)
  "Software of the Future Is the Future of Software?"
- Danny Krizanc (Wesleyan University, USA)
  "An Algorithmic Theory of Autonomous Mobile Agent Computing"

Beside regular papers, this volume contains the overviews of FP6 Projects AEOLUS, MOBIUS, SENSORIA and CATNETS and invited papers by Paola Inverardi and Danny Krizanc.

It is planned to dedicate a special issue of the *Journal of Theoretical Computer Science* to the theme of the workshop, with the extended versions of the best papers presented at TGC 2006.

We would like to thank all the members of the Program Committee, and their sub-referees, for their assistance with the selection process. In view of the importance and the strategic role of trustworthy global computing, the plans are to organize TGC regularly in the future, and we thank all the members of the Steering Committee for their past and future efforts.

We also want to thank all the people involved in the local organization of the event for their help and support, and in particular: Massimo Bartoletti and Laura Semini from the University of Pisa and Marzia Buscemi, Pietro Carubbi, Barbara Iacobino, Silvia Lucchesi, Hernán Melgratti and Roberta Zelari from IMT Alti Studi Lucca.

November 2006

Ugo Montanari
Don Sannella
Roberto Bruni

Organization

TGC Steering Committee

Gilles Barthe	INRIA Sophia Antipolis (France)
Rocco De Nicola	University of Florence (Italy)
Christos Kaklamanis	University of Patras (Greece)
Ugo Montanari (Co-chair)	University of Pisa (Italy)
Davide Sangiorgi	University of Bologna (Italy)
Don Sannella (Co-chair)	University of Edinburgh (Scotland, UK)
Vladimiro Sassone	University of Southampton (UK)
Martin Wirsing	LMU Munich (Germany)

Program Committee

Gilles Barthe	INRIA Sophia Antipolis (France)
Rocco De Nicola	University of Florence (Italy)
José Luiz Fiadeiro	University of Leicester (UK)
Stefania Gnesi	ISTI-CNR, Pisa (Italy)
Manuel Hermenegildo	Technical University of Madrid (Spain)
Christos Kaklamanis	University of Patras (Greece)
Elias Koutsoupias	University of Athens (Greece)
Burkhard Monien	University of Paderborn (Germany)
Giuseppe Persiano	University of Salerno (Italy)
Ugo Montanari (Co-chair)	University of Pisa (Italy)
David Rosenblum	University College London (UK)
Davide Sangiorgi	University of Bologna (Italy)
Don Sannella (Co-chair)	University of Edinburgh (Scotland, UK)
Vladimiro Sassone	University of Southampton (UK)
Paul Spirakis	University of Patras (Greece)
Martin Wirsing	LMU Munich (Germany)
Gianluigi Zavattaro	University of Bologna (Italy)

Secondary Referees

Elvira Albert	Roberto Bruni	Gianluigi Ferrari
Puri Arenas	Marzia Buscemi	Fabio Gadducci
Robert Atkey	Marco Carbone	Flavio Garcia
Maurice ter Beek	Manuel Carro	Klaus Havelund
Lorenzo Bettini	Andrea Corradini	Alexander Knapp
Michele Boreale	Guillaume Dufay	Ivan Lanese
Gerard Boudol	Alessandro Fantechi	Frederic Lang

Michele Loreti   Ana Almeida Matos   Rick Thomas
Kenneth MacKenzie   Catuscia Palamidessi   Emilio Tuosto
Damiano Macedonio   Marinella Petrocchi   Irek Ulidowski
Sergio Maffeis   Randy Pollack   Frank Valencia
Pasquale Malacaria   Bilel Remmache   Carmine Ventre
Patrick Maier   Davide Sangiorgi   Cris Walton
Mieke Massink   Paul Spirakis

Sponsoring Institutions

Fondazione Cassa di Risparmio di Lucca
Tagetik

Table of Contents

Project AEOLUS: An Overview

Christos Kaklamanis[*]

Department of Computer Engineering and Informatics
University of Patras, 26500 Rio, Greece
kakl@ceid.upatras.gr

Abstract. In this paper we give a short overview of the IST FET Integrated Project FP6-015964 AEOLUS "Algorithmic Principles for Building Efficient Overlay Computers" which is funded by the European Union as part of the Proactive Initiative on Global Computing. We present the motivation and our long-term vision behind it and its objectives. We also give a short description of the research workplan and current activities.

1 Motivation and Vision

The impact of the Internet in our social fabric exceeded even the most optimistic predictions of only a few years ago. Today, most people in the developed countries have access to this medium thanks to technological advances on devices such as the personal computers and wireless devices.

Its success is mainly due to the fact that it supports and makes accessible the Web, by far the widest data repository available worldwide. Indeed, historically, the Web has been the main reason for which people are connected to the Internet. The focus of economic and research activity has concentrated on how to mine the Web in efficient and user-friendly ways (e.g., search engines), or how to store and protect the published information from unauthorized access. However, the Internet should not only be viewed as a medium for information dissemination, but also as a computing machine: aggregating the computational power even of a small fraction of the devices connected to the Internet would give rise to a computing "device" with enormous capabilities which can greatly expand the concept of "computationally tractable". Such a system could open new horizons.

Presently there are two important research directions, orthogonal to each other: efficient resource usage and interoperability. Due to the system size and inherent complexity, it is practically impossible to completely optimize the usage of its resources. It is even a challenge to develop ways that improve the usage of resources at a global scale. To complicate the situation, we have to take into account that such a goal is usually achieved at the cost of increasing the complexity of the applications. On the other hand, by its own nature, the system is composed of heterogeneous devices with diverse characteristics and, sometimes, complementary limitations. In this scenario, the major challenge has been to allow a complete interoperability among such devices.

---

[*] AEOLUS Coordinator.

U. Montanari, D. Sannella, and R. Bruni (Eds.): TGC 2006, LNCS 4661, pp. 1–9, 2007.

Notwithstanding the problems related to inefficient resource usage and inter-operability, the increasing number of distributed applications currently developed and deployed on the Internet show both the success of such a technology and the increasing need of the society for a global information system which provides reliable services that can be accessed by diverse means.

In such a scenario, what is really missing is transparency for the user. Indeed, currently, there exists a variety of service providers providing their own services that, most of the time, require a sort of ad-hoc proprietary software. The access to each service is granted using different authorization mechanisms of which the user has to be aware, while the rules for accessing resources may vary.

The cause of these limitations is the lack of a unique infrastructure on which different entities may easily develop and deploy software that efficiently exploits the tremendous storage capacity, computational power, and reliability of large scale distributed and heterogeneous systems and that, at the same time, guarantees privacy of the information and fairness of the resource usage.

In order to obtain real impact from this new global instrument, a key requirement is transparency for system designers and developers. Currently, system implementations have to take into account all the issues related to the distributed nature of information and computation like resource discovery, fault tolerance, load balancing, security, and so on. All such problems must be tackled in a heterogeneous system where nodes are owned by different entities that try to optimize their own objectives and possibly with malicious users. From this very brief description, it is clear that developing a successful distributed application that efficiently exploits the capabilities of the Internet is an extremely difficult task.

The existence of a unique programmable platform virtually overlaid on top of the existing heterogeneous system, providing a set of functionalities that hide from the programmer details related to subtle and crucial issues like scalability and efficiency of resource management as well as automatically and efficiently solving problems like data replication or recovery would have a great and immediate impact on the way in which distributed applications are developed. System designers and programmers will be able to concentrate only on the application, while leaving to the platform the duty of controlling the underlying global "device". The possibility of securing sensitive data while allowing transparent access to them, according to per-site policies, would foster the spread of a global information system with tremendous effect on everyday life. In other words, applications will be transparently accessing a unique data repository and service provider, regardless of the actual device they are running on.

In the long term, we envision the unique infrastructure to be an overlay computer, based on a global computer of grand scale consisting of Internet-connected computers (possibly mobile, with varying computational capabilities, connected among them with different communication media including wireless, owned by different entities optimizing their own objectives, with diverse and even limited availability, etc.), globally available and able to provide to its users a rich menu of high-level integrated services that make transparent and efficient use of the aggregated computational power, storage space, and information resources. Based on the growth of the number of nodes of the Internet, the improvements of computational and communication capabilities of wireless devices and the spread of use of such devices, it is very likely that a global computer of this kind will be the main data repository/computational infrastructure that will be widely used in a few years.

2   Basic Concepts and Objectives

In the context of AEOLUS, we consider a global computer to be composed of Internet-connected computing entities (small/medium computers, i.e., PCs, laptops). Possibly, this global computer can be extended through wireless communication (e.g., WiFi, Bluetooth, etc.) to include other computing devices. These devices will mainly be of similar computing power (i.e., mobile laptops) but potentially also include others like satellites, palmtops, mobile phones, and smaller peripherals like sensing devices.

Overlay computers are logical definitions over this global computer and can be subsets of nodes of the global computer cooperating for providing a service or running a distributed application. So, the overlay computer is an abstraction of the global computer on top of which services and applications can be implemented using basic primitives; these primitives are provided by the overlay computer as "tools to the programmer". They handle and hide the actual characteristics of the global computer (e.g., topology, computational power of nodes, communication media, etc.).

The first step towards fulfilling the ambitious goal of realizing such an overlay computer is a deep understanding of the features that the basic functionalities of the overlay computer should have. A first, compelling characteristic is related to the efficiency of such primitives. In any worldwide-deployed architecture with thousands of heterogeneous nodes, the amplification of the effect of an inefficient solution could lead to the collapse of the whole system, especially if the inefficiency is related to a basic functionality, e.g., scheduling or routing. An algorithmic approach to the design of such an infrastructure brings into focus the issue of efficiency, by its very nature.

AEOLUS addresses the four issues of scalability, resource usage and management, security, and distribution transparency that have been stressed by the Global Computing Proactive Initiative as pivotal to realizing the aim of the initiative. Although a necessary condition, efficiency by itself does not guarantee scalability of the proposed solutions. The project participants will specifically address this issue during the four years of the project.

In a grand-scale overlay computer, resource usage and management become critical primitives to be addressed. Because of its highly distributed nature, it is impossible to consider centralized management of resources. In this setting, primitives for resource discovery become crucial for the viability of any algorithm on an overlay computer. On the other hand, the overlay computer should guarantee proper usage of resources by implementing appropriate algorithms for scheduling and load balancing. Notice that ensuring fairness of resource usage is a prerequisite to guaranteeing that end-users will provide their resources to the overlay computer since they will be guaranteed they will be allowed to use other users' resources when needed. Furthermore, in our vision an overlay computer is an open system. It is thus unrealistic to assume that users behave according to some predefined protocol. AEOLUS considers resource management also for the case in which users act selfishly and try to optimize their own objectives.

Particular attention has been devoted to the issue of security as it will be fundamental for determining whether or not the new technology will be accepted by the end-users. Basic primitives addressing trust management, anonymity, and privacy are crucial in a distributed open system. Unfortunately, most of the solutions in literature cannot be applied as is in the context of the overlay computer since either they are not scalable or they make strong assumptions that are not realistic in this setting.

Distribution transparency is also a crucial issue in AEOLUS for various reasons. First of all, a specific feature of the overlay computer is to hide the distributed nature of resources and computation. Furthermore, AEOLUS specifically addresses the possibility of having wireless devices being part of the global computer. As explained above, the overlay computer should hide from the application the specific communication means by which the node is connected. Related research in AEOLUS includes problems like stability, topology control, fault tolerance, etc.

Overall, the goal of this project is to investigate the principles and develop the algorithmic methods for building an overlay computer that enables efficient and transparent access to the resources of an Internet-based global computer. In particular, the main objectives are:

- To identify and study the important fundamental problems and investigate the corresponding algorithmic principles related to overlay computers running on global computers defined as above.
- To identify the important functionalities such an overlay computer should provide as tools to the programmer, and to develop, rigorously analyze and experimentally validate algorithmic methods that can make these functionalities efficient, scalable, fault-tolerant, and transparent to heterogeneity.
- To provide improved methods for communication and computing among wireless and possibly mobile nodes so that they can transparently become part of larger Internet-based overlay computers.
- To implement a set of functionalities, integrate them under a common software platform (the *Overlay Computing Platform*) in order to provide the basic primitives of an overlay computer, as well as build sample services on this overlay computer, thus providing a proof-of-concept for the theoretical results.

3   Description of Research Activities

Summarizing the discussion of the previous section, it is clear that in order to realize the overlay computer, there are several problem areas that have to be studied:

- Resource usage and management including CPU, disk space, bandwidth, information, and application-level resources.
- Security including trust management, authentication, privacy, anonymity, secure distributed computation, etc.
- Overlay computers built on top of the Internet-based global computer should also be able to deal with wireless devices. Such devices have several special characteristics. They may be mobile, their existence certainly imposes heterogeneity, their computation power is usually limited, their availability is varying, etc. So, several issues should be addressed in order to allow transparent access to/from these devices so that they can become part of the overlay computer.

In order to deal with the complexity of the objectives, the research work within AEOLUS is divided in several vertical and horizontal components. Horizontal components contain work either on the investigation of general fundamental aspects or on the development of the overlay computer. Vertical components focus on specific areas which are important to the realization of the overlay computer. These components are the following:

- A horizontal component addressing fundamental issues of global computing with special focus on efficiency, transparency and scalability.
- Four vertical components addressing the issues of resource management, sharing information and computation, security and trust management and transparent extensions of overlay computers to include wireless devices, respectively.
- A horizontal component devoted to the implementation of basic functionalities under a common software platform (the Overlay Computing Platform) and the development of an application on top of it.

These components correspondingly define six subprojects:

Subproject 1. "Paradigms and principles" is devoted to the development of innovative theories to cope with new algorithmic problems that arise in global computing. It studies the structural properties of global/overlay computers, fundamental techniques for coping with selfishness and for achieving stability and fault tolerance, and tackles the challenge of computing with partial (i.e., uncertain, distributed, or even incomplete) knowledge by blending theories from economics, game theory and algorithmic theory. A better understanding of these problems will have a strong impact on the ability to propose scalable, distributed and dynamic algorithms. That will also allow understanding the efficiency trade-off between undesirable centralized strategies and anticipated fully distributed strategies.

Subproject 2. "Resource management" focuses on specific aspects related to the management of critical resources (like bandwidth), resource discovery, as well as to the design of mechanisms for accessing resources owned by selfish entities. Resources can either be of a low-level (i.e., infrastructure-dependent like bandwidth) or application-level (e.g., currency).

Subproject 3. "Sharing information and computation" considers algorithmic problems related to the management of resources focusing on computational and information resources. Issues like distributed data management, load management and scheduling are addressed here.

Subproject 4. "Security and trust management" explores problems related to trust management, authentication mechanisms, privacy, anonymity, and secure distributed computation (including techniques to face malicious behavior). The main goal of the research work in Subproject 4 is to address fundamental issues that are crucial to a transparent security layer. In achieving this goal, AEOLUS adapts concepts from cryptography and economics that have recently shown to be very successful in modelling adversarial but rational behavior.

Subproject 5. "Extending global computing to wireless users" mainly aims to transparently include wireless nodes in an Internet-based overlay computer. It focuses on issues like resource management and quality of service in wireless sub-networks, network design and topology control under dynamic scenarios, mobility and fault tolerance. The main objective of this subproject is to provide efficient and practical algorithmic solutions for high-quality, reliable, stable end-users services on heterogeneous wireless networks. Due to the specific limitations of wireless devices, a particular attention is devoted to the efficient usage of critical resource like energy and spectrum (i.e., frequencies).

Subproject 6. "Design and implementation of components and applications for programmable overlay computers" is devoted to the implementation and integration of functionalities produced within Subprojects 1, 2, 3, 4, and 5 into a common software platform (the *Overlay Computing Platform*) that will provide the programmable interface of the overlay computer. Special attention is devoted to the efficiency of the implementations. An application will be implemented on top of this overlay computer. Since the Overlay Computing Platform is intended to be a general purpose programmable computational infrastructure, it should efficiently support any kind of distributed application. Nonetheless, some types of applications that would benefit the most include:

- data discovery and processing in scenaria where data is diffused and owned by different entities, or the object/information is complex and diffused by itself, or requires processing in order to be retrieved
- large scientific computations especially with unpredictable load running on unused or idle CPUs
- multi-party transactions (e.g., access on distributed databases, consensus) requiring distributed security and potentially multi-round transactions (like auctions and distributed games).

The Overlay Computing Platform and the demo application will serve as a proof-of-concept of AEOLUS.

The work within the several Subprojects is further refined into workpackages. Subproject 1 consists of the following workpackages:

- Workpackage 1.1: Structural Properties, addressing topological properties, substructures and organization, embeddings.
- Workpackage 1.2: Coping with Incomplete Knowledge, addressing distributed and robust data structures, transparency and information hiding and reputation mechanisms.
- Workpackage 1.3: Coping with Selfishness, addressing Price of anarchy, fairness versus efficiency and equilibria selection and mechanisms.
- Workpackage 1.4: Stability and Fault-Tolerance, addressing adversarial queuing theory and distributed systems.
- Workpackage 1.5: Generic Algorithms, addressing connectivity issues, multi-criteria optimization and sampling paradigms.

Subproject 2 consists of the following workpackages:

- Workpackage 2.1: Resource Discovery, addressing construction of overlay networks, query routing in overlay networks, query execution in overlay networks.
- Workpackage 2.2: Sharing Critical Resources, addressing the transparent bandwidth sharing in a heterogeneous large-scale global computer in order to match the quality of service expected by the overlay computer.
- Workpackage 2.3: Mechanism Design, addressing the impact of the user selfishness on improving the price of anarchy and in reaching a good global status in global and overlay computers.

Subproject 3 consists of the following workpackages:

- Workpackage 3.1: Distributed Data Management, addressing replication degrees and replica placement, and dynamic load-adaptive adjustments, replica maintenance and proactive dissemination.
- Workpackage 3.2: Load Management, addressing load balancing for overlay computers, adaptive software and peer-to-peer-based parallel computing.
- Workpackage 3.3: Scheduling, addressing scheduling computations in overlay computers and the dynamic situation of scheduling at the application level.
- Workpackage 3.4: Workflow and Services, addressing the use of services for accessing data in overlay computers, the use of workflow for the definition and execution of composite web services, and the capabilities of a global computer and its overlay structures for dynamic self-configuration and automatic adaptation to system, workload, and applications dynamics.

Subproject 4 consists of the following workpackages:

- Workpackage 4.1: Trust Management, addressing identity-based Authentication, trust negotiation mechanisms, reputation based authentication and authorization and access control models and mechanisms.

- Workpackage 4.2: Privacy, Identity and Anonymity, addressing pseudonym systems, private credentials / anonymous certificates, identity management, anonymous communications, privacy and individual databases and privacy-preserving data mining.
- Workpackage 4.3: Secure Distributed Computation, addressing secure distributed algorithmic mechanism design, composability and further applications including secure distributed protocols supporting fault-tolerance and heterogeneity of users and prevention of denial of service attacks.

Subproject 5 consists of the following workpackages:

- Workpackage 5.1: Resource Management and Quality-of-Service (QoS).
- Workpackage 5.2: Dynamical Aspects of Network Design and Topology Control.
- Workpackage 5.3: Mobility and Fault Tolerance.

Finally, Subproject 6 consists of the following workpackages:

- Workpackage 6.1: Specification and design of the platform.
- Workpackage 6.2: Implementation of platform components.
- Workpackage 6.3: Integration and testing of the platform.
- Workpackage 6.4: Design and implementation of a demo application.

4   Other Information

AEOLUS consortium consists of 21 participants from 10 countries. Grouped on a country basis, they are: University of Patras, Research Academic Computer Technology Institute, University of Ioannina, and University of Athens from Greece, Radiolabs, Università degli Studi di Salerno, Università degli Studi di Roma "La Sapienza", Università degli Studi di Roma "Tor Vergata", Università degli Studi di Padova from Italy, CNRS and INRIA from France, University of Paderborn, Max-Planck Institut für Informatik, and Christian-Albrechts-Universität zu Kiel from Germany, University of Geneva and ETH Zurich from Switzerland, Universitat Politecnica de Catalunya (UPC) from Spain, Katholieke Universiteit Leuven from Belgium, DIMATIA-Charles University from Czech Republic, University of Cyprus from Cyprus and Cybernetica from Estonia.

AEOLUS started in September 2005. It has already completed the first year and is now continuing in its second year, out of the four years totally scheduled. So far, at least two hundred publications or technical reports with project results related to Subprojects 1-6 have been produced. Furthermore, the project participants are already working towards the development of the Overlay Computing Platform. They have defined its architecture and main components and are currently implementing functionalities or stand-alone prototypes in order to demonstrate several of its components. These include a microbenchmarking software package, a prototype for process migration and load balancing in BSP-based P2P systems, a generic engine for specifying computations in overlay computers, a prototype for anonymous communication, a prototype for secure distributed protocols, and a prototype for protocol security verification.

The interested reader may visit the web site of AEOLUS for additional and up to date information (`http://aeolus.ceid.upatras.gr`).

MOBIUS: Mobility, Ubiquity, Security[*]

Objectives and Progress Report

Gilles Barthe[1], Lennart Beringer[2], Pierre Crégut[3],
Benjamin Grégoire[1], Martin Hofmann[2], Peter Müller[4],
Erik Poll[5], Germán Puebla[6], Ian Stark[7], and Eric Vétillard[8]

[1] INRIA Sophia-Antipolis, France
[2] Ludwig-Maximilians-Universität München, Germany
[3] France Télécom, France
[4] ETH Zürich, Switzerland
[5] Radboud University Nijmegen, the Netherlands
[6] Technical University of Madrid (UPM), Spain
[7] The University of Edinburgh, Scotland
[8] Trusted Labs, France

Abstract. Through their global, uniform provision of services and their distributed nature, global computers have the potential to profoundly enhance our daily life. However, they will not realize their full potential, unless the necessary levels of trust and security can be guaranteed.

The goal of the MOBIUS project is to develop a Proof Carrying Code architecture to secure global computers that consist of Java-enabled mobile devices. In this progress report, we detail its objectives and provide a snapshot of the project results during its first year of activity.

1   Introduction

Global computers are distributed computational infrastructures that aim at providing services globally and uniformly; examples include the Internet, banking networks, telephone networks, digital video infrastructures, peer-to-peer and ad hoc networks, virtual private networks, home area networks, and personal area networks. While global computers may deeply affect our quality of life, security is paramount for them to become pervasive infrastructures in our society, as envisioned in ambient intelligence. Indeed, numerous application domains, including e-government and e-health, involve sensitive data that must be protected from unauthorized parties. Malicious attackers spreading over the network and widely disconnecting or disrupting devices could have devastating economic and social consequences and would deeply affect end-users' confidence in e-society. In spite of clear risks, provisions to enforce security in global computers remain extremely primitive. Some global computers, for instance in the automotive industry, choose to enforce security by maintaining devices completely under the control

---

[*] Work partially supported by the Integrated Project MOBIUS, within the Global Computing II initiative.

U. Montanari, D. Sannella, and R. Bruni (Eds.): TGC 2006, LNCS 4661, pp. 10–29, 2007.

of the operator. Other models, building on the Java security architecture, choose to enforce security via a sandbox model that distinguishes between a fixed trusted computing base and untrusted applications. Unfortunately, these approaches are too restrictive to be serious options for the design of secure global computers. In fact, any security architecture for global computing must meet requirements that reach beyond the limits of currently deployed models.

The objective of the MOBIUS project is to develop the technology for establishing trust and security in global computers, using the Proof Carrying Code (PCC) paradigm [37,36]. The essential features of the MOBIUS security architecture are:

- *innovative trust management*, dispensing with centralized trust entities, and allowing individual components to gain trust by providing verifiable certificates of their innocuousness; and
- *static enforcement mechanisms*, sufficiently *flexible* to cover the wide range of security concerns arising in global computing, and sufficiently *resource-aware* and *configurable* to be applicable to the wide range of devices in global computers; and
- *support for system component downloading*, for compatibility with the view of a global computer as an evolving network of autonomous, heterogeneous and *extensible* devices.

MOBIUS targets are embedded execution frameworks that can run third party applications which must be checked against a platform security policy. In order to maximize its chances of success, the MOBIUS project focuses on global computers that consist of Java-enabled devices, and in particular on devices that support the Mobile Information Device Profile (MIDP, version 2) of the Connected Limited Device Configuration (CLDC) of the Java 2 Micro Edition.

2   MIDP

CLDC is a variant of Java for the embedded industry, and stands between JavaCard and Java Standard Edition. CLDC is a perfect setting for MOBIUS because it has all the characteristics of a real language: true memory management, object orientation, etc., but applications developed for it are still closed: there is no reflection API, no C interface (JNI) and no dynamic class loading (class loading is done at launch time). Furthermore, CLDC is widely accepted by the industry as a runtime environment for downloadable code: on mobile phones (MIDP), set-top-boxes (JSR 242) and smart card terminal equipment (STIP).

The MIDP profile is a set of libraries for the CLDC platform that provides a standardized environment for Java applications on mobile phones (so-called midlets). Its wide deployment (1.2 billion handsets) has lead to a consensus on security objectives. Moreover, MIDP promotes the idea of small generic mobile devices downloading services from the network and is an archetypal example of the global computing paradigm.

MIDP defines a simple connection framework for establishing communications over various technologies, with a single method to open a connection that takes as argument a URL which encodes the protocol, the target address, and some of the connection parameters. MIDP offers a graphical user interface implementing the view/controller paradigm and provides access to specific mobile phones resources (persistent store, players, camera, geolocalisation, etc.).

MIDP security policy is based on the approval by the end-user of every method call that can threaten the security of the user (such as opening a network connection). Depending on the API, the frequency of security screens varies (from once for all to once for every call).

This scheme, although simple, has several drawbacks: users accept dangerous calls one at a time and have no idea of the forthcoming calls necessary for the transaction; there can be too many screens to perform a simple transaction; moreover even a clearly malicious action will be statistically accepted by some users if the customer basis is large enough. To mitigate some of these risks, MIDP2.0 proposes to sign midlets. Signing changes the level of trust of the midlet and reduces the number of mandatory warning screens. Signing moves the decision of accepting an API call from the end-user to a trusted entity (the manufacturer, the operator or an entity endorsed by them), but it does not provide clues to take the decision. One goal of MOBIUS is to develop the necessary technology for allowing the developer to supply clues and proofs that can help operators to validate midlets developed by third parties.

Finally, MIDP dynamic security policy does not provide any control on the information flow. This is in contrast with the european legislation that puts information control at the heart of its requirements for computerized systems [38]. The information flow analysis reported in Section 5.3 provides a first step to provide a technical enforcement of those regulations.

Several factors such as handset bugs, different handset capabilities, operational environment (language, network), etc. lead to a fragmentation of MIDP implementations. As resources (cpu, memory for heap, code or persistent data) on device are scarce, code specialization is the only viable alternative to adapt application to handsets. It is not uncommon to have hundreds of versions of a single application. Whereas some solutions exist for automating the development, the management, and the provisioning to the handset of so many variants, in practice, validation [32] is still based on a technology which is unable to cope with multiple versions: black-box testing. Indeed, only the bytecode is available to test houses, as software companies refuse to disclose their source code to third parties to protect their intellectual property. MOBIUS outcome should help to automate the validation process for operators. PCC can be used on the most complex properties whereas type based techniques could be sufficient on simple ones.

3   PCC Scenarios

Figure 1 shows the basic structure of all certificate-based mobile code security models, including Proof Carrying Code. This basic model, or *scenario*, comprises a code *producer* and a code *consumer*. The basic idea in PCC is that the *code* is accompanied by a *certificate*. The certificate can be automatically and efficiently checked by the consumer and it provides verifiable evidence that the code abides by a given *security policy*. The main difference w.r.t. digital signatures is that the latter allows having certainty on the *origin* of the code, whereas PCC allows having certainty about the

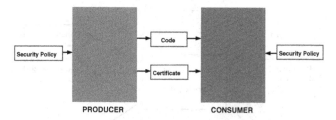

Fig. 1. Certificate-based Mobile Code Security

behaviour of the code. Different flavours of PCC exist which use different techniques for generating certificates, ranging from traditional logic-based verification to static analysis in general and type systems in particular.

In the context of global computing, this initial scenario needs to be extended in a number of ways to consider the presence of multiple producers, multiple consumers, multiple verifiers and intermediaries. We have identified a series of innovative scenarios for applying Proof Carrying Code in the context of global computers [23]; below we summarize the main scenarios and issues of interest within the context of MOBIUS.

3.1 Wholesale PCC for MIDP Devices

Figure 2 depicts the MOBIUS scenario for MIDP devices. It involves a trusted intermediary (typically the mobile phone operator), code producers that are external to the phone companies, and code consumers (the end users). PCC is used by developers to supply phone operators with proofs which establish that the application is secure. The operator then digitally signs the code before distributing it to the user.

This scenario for "wholesale" verification by a code distributor effectively combines the best of both PCC and trust, and brings important benefits to all participating actors. For the end user in particular, the scenario does not add PCC infrastructure complexity to the device, but still allows effective enforcement of advanced security policies.

From the point of view of phone operators, the proposed scenario enables achieving the required level of confidence in MIDP applications developed by third parties through formal verification. Although this process is very costly, which often results in third party code not being distributed, PCC enables operators to reproduce the program verification process performed by producers, but completely automatically and at a small fraction of the cost.

From the software producer perspective, the scenario removes the bottleneck of the manual approval/rejection of code by the operator. This results in a significant increase in market opportunity. Of course, this comes at a cost: producers have to verify their code and generate a certificate before shipping it to the operator, in return for access to a market with a large potential and which has remained rather closed to independent software companies.

3.2 Retail PCC and On-Device Checking

Although our main MOBIUS scenario is for wholesale proof-checking by a trusted intermediary, we are also exploring possibilities for "retail" PCC where checking

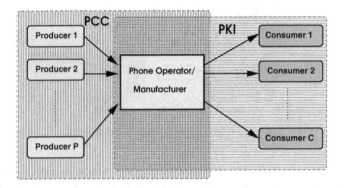

Fig. 2. The MOBIUS scenario

takes place on the device itself. Limited computing capabilities rule out full-blown proof-checking for the moment, but there are other kinds of certificates that support verification: MIDP already annotates code with basic type information for *lightweight bytecode verification* [40], and we aim to extend this with more sophisticated types to capture security properties, and with the results of other analyses as in *abstraction-carrying code* [1]. Complementary to digital signatures, these certificates maintain the PCC property that clients perform actual verification of received code, by providing rich type information to make it fast and cheap to do.

3.3 Beyond the MOBIUS Scenarios

Though the MOBIUS scenario concerns networks of mobile devices, we believe that the concept of trusted intermediary and the use of off-device PCC can have a significant impact in the quality of the applications developed in other contexts. For the case of general-purpose computers, we believe that our scenario is also applicable, since the role of trusted intermediary can be played by other organizations such as end-user organizations, governmental institutions, non-profit organizations, private companies, etc. Note that this scenario is radically different from the situation today: though some organizations play the role of trusted intermediaries, they do not have the technology for formally verifying code and they have to resort to other techniques such as manual code inspection. Thus, we argue that PCC holds the promise of bringing the benefits of software verification to everyone. The fact that verified code becomes available at low cost will increase the demand on verified code, which will in turn encourage software companies to produce verified code with certificates.

4   Security Requirements

A fundamental question in developing a security architecture for global computers is the inventory of the security requirements that we should be able to express and guarantee. This has been the one of the first step of the project.

The choice to focus on the MIDP framework was very helpful, as it allowed us to consider concrete examples of various kinds of security requirements. Moreover, as the framework has been actively used for some time, there is considerable experience with security requirements for MIDP applications. Although inspired by concrete MIDP setting, or even concrete MIDP ahpplications, the range of security requirements we have found is representative of the requirements that are important for any distributed computing infrastructure.

We have considered two, largely orthogonal ways to analyse and classify security requirements. In a first deliverable [19], we investigated two important classes of security requirements, namely *resource usage* and *information flow*. In a second one [20] we considered general security requirements that apply to all applications for the MIDP framework, so-called *framework-specific* security requirements, and security requirements specific to a given application, so-called *application-specific* security requirements. Here we summarise the main conclusions of those reports.

4.1 Resources

Any global computing infrastructure naturally raises issues about identifying and managing the resources required by mobile code. This is especially true on small devices, where resources are limited.

Central issues for resource policies are: what resources they should describe; how resource policies can contribute to security; and what kinds of formalism are appropriate. Surveying different possible kinds of "resource", we are looking to identify those that are both likely to be amenable to formal analysis by current technologies, and are also clearly useful to real-world MIDP applications. Some of these are classical instances of computational resources, namely *time*, where counting bytecodes executed can be a useful estimate of actual runtime, and *space*, of stack or heap, which may be rather limited on a mobile device. The focus on MIDP also allows us to address some platform-specific kinds of resource, namely *persistent store*, as file storage space will be limited, and *billable events* such as text messages (SMS) or network connections (HTTP), which have real-money costs for the user. Many of these platform-specific resources can be unified by treating particular system calls as the resource to be managed: how many times they are invoked, and with what arguments. This fits neatly into the existing MIDP security model, where certain APIs are only available to trusted applications.

Policies to control resources such as these are useful in themselves, but they also have a particular impact on security. First, some platform-specific resources are intrinsically valuable — for example, because an operator will charge money for them — and so we want to guard against their loss. Further, overuse of limited resources on the device itself may compromise *availability*, leading to denial of service vulnerabilities.

4.2 Information Flow

Information policies can track integrity or confidentiality. We concentrated on the second, as the former is essentially just its dual. The attacker model is a developer who leaks sensitive information to untrusted parties, either intentionally (in case of a malicious developer) or by accident. On the MIDP platform sensitive information is typically information related to the user: sources include the addressbook, audio or video capture, the permanent store, and textfields where the user typed in private data. Untrusted information sinks are network connections and the permanent store, especially if the store is shared between applications.

4.3 Framework-Specific Security Requirements

Framework-specific security requirements describe generic requirements applicable to all the applications running on a given framework. In industry there is already considerable experience with framework-specific security requirements for MIDP. [20] provides a comprehensive listing of all of these requirements.

Many of these requirements concern critical API methods: both the use of certain methods (does the application uses the network ?) and possibly also the arguments supplied to them (for example the URL supplied to open a connection defines the protocol used). Deciding these questions is already an issue in the current MIDP code-signing scheme: to decide if signing is safe, it is necessary to know statically which critical APIs are used and to compute an approximation of the possible values of their key parameters. There are already some dedicated static analysis techniques for this [16,24], but there is a limit to what such automated analyses can achieve.

More complicated requirements on API methods are temporal properties that involve the sequencing of actions, such as a requirement that every file that is opened must be closed before the program exits. Checking these properties requires a deeper insight of the control flow of a program, which can be complicated by the possibility of runtime exceptions, the dependency on dynamic data structures, and the influence of thread synchronization. Finite state automata are a convenient formalism for specifying temporal requirements. Such automata can be expressed in the program specification language JML that we plan to use. Moreover, they are easily understandable by non-experts.[1]

4.4 Application-Specific Security Requirements

An individual application may have specific security requirements beyond the generic requirements that apply to all the applications. These application-specific security requirements may simply be more specific instances of framework-specific security properties, but can also be radically different. Whereas framework-specific requirements are often about the absence of unwanted behaviour, security requirements for a particular application may include functional requirements, concerning the correctness of some functional behaviour. Application-specific properties are usually more complex than framework-specific properties and less likely to be certified by fully automatic techniques.

We have selected some archetypical applications representative of classical application domains for which interesting security requirements can be expressed. These applications include a secure private storage provider, an instant messenger client, an SSH

---

[1] In fact, the current industrial standard for testing MIDP applications, the Unified Testing Criteria [32] already uses finite automata for specification, albeit informally.

client, and an application for remote electronic voting. All of these have strong security requirements, including information flow requirements, that go beyond the framework-specific requirements.

The final two applications selected are in fact core services of the MIDP platform itself rather than applications that run on the platform, namely a bytecode verifier and a modified access controller. Note that for these components functional correctness is one of the security requirements. The specification language JML that we will use in logic-based verification is capable of expressing such functional requirements, although extensions to conveniently use mathematical structures in specification, as proposed in [15], may be needed to make this practical.

5 Enabling Technologies

A central component of the technology being developed by MOBIUS is a hierarchy of mechanisms that allow one to reason about intensional and extensional properties of MIDP-compliant programs executed on a Java Virtual Machine. The two enabling technologies that these mechanisms rely on are *typing* and *logic-based verification*. Depending on the security property, and the respective computational resources, code producer and consumer (or verifier in the case of wholesale PCC) may negotiate about the level at which the certificate is formulated. For example, the availability of a type system with an automated inference algorithm reduces the amount of code annotations, whereas expressive program logics may be applied in cases when type systems are insufficiently flexible, or when no static analysis is known that ensures the property of interest. In the sequel, we provide a short overview of the mechanisms developed during the first year of the project, namely the MOBIUS program logic for sequential bytecode, and type systems for resources, information flow, and aliasing.

In the following sections we summarise some of the formal systems which we have developed and outline possible verification approaches.

5.1 Operational Model

The lowest level of our hierarchy of formal systems consists of an operational model of the Java Virtual Machine that is appropriate for MOBIUS. In particular, as a consequence of the choice to target the MIDP prifile of the CLDC platform, features such as reflection and dynamic class loading may safely be ignored, as is the case for complex data types. In addition, our current model is restricted to the sequential fragment of the JVM and does not model garbage collection.

The operational model builds the basis for all program verification formalisms to be developed in MOBIUS: all formal systems considered within the MOBIUS project – and hence the validity of certificates – may in principle be given interpretations that only refer to the operational judgments defining the model. Like any mathematical proof, these interpretations may involve some abstractions and definitional layers, including some more abstract operational semantics which we have defined and formally proven compatible with the small-step relation.

In order to guarantee the utmost adherence to the official specification, we have implemented a small step semantics. The corresponding judgement relates two consecutive states during program execution. We keep the same level of detail as the official description, but with some simplifications due to the fact that we concentrate on the CLDC platform.

The correctness of an operational model can not be formally proved, we assert it axiomatically, and have developed a rigorous mathematical description of it, called Bicolano, in the Coq proof assistant [43]. In order to get more confidence in our axiomatization we have also developed an executable version of fragments of Bicolano which can be used to compare evaluation results with other implementations of the official specification.

5.2   Program Logic

The second layer of our reasoning infrastructure is built by a program logic. This allows proof patterns typically arising during the verification of recursive program structures to be treated in a uniform matter. Extending program logics with partial-correctness interpretations, the MOBIUS logic supports the verification of non-terminating program executions by incorporating strong invariants [28].

The global specification structure is given by a table M that associates a partial-correctness method specification Φ and a method invariant φ to each defined method, where the latter relates each state occurring throughout the (finite or infinite) execution of the method to its initial state. In order to support the modular verification of virtual methods, the method specification table is required to satisfy a *behavioural subtyping* condition which mandates that the specification of an overriding method declaration must be stronger (i.e. imply) the specification of the overwritten method. In addition, each program point in a method may be decorated with an assertion that is to be satisfied whenever the control flow passes through the decorated program point. All such annotations are collected in a global annotation table Q.

The program logic employs proof judgements of the form $G \vdash \{A\} \, \ell \, \{B\} \, (I)$ where the program point ℓ (comprising a method identifier M and a label in the definition of M's body) is associated with a (local) precondition A, a local postcondition B, a (strong) invariant I. The types and intended meanings of these components are as follows.

Whenever the execution of M, starting at label 0 and initial state s_0 reaches ℓ with current state s, and $A(s_0, s)$ holds, then

- $B(s_0, s, t)$ holds, provided that the method terminates with final state t,
- $I(s_0, s, H)$ holds, provided that H is the heap component of any state arising during the continuation of the current method invocation, including invocations of further methods, i.e. subframes,
- $Q(s_0, s')$ holds, provided that s' is reached at some label ℓ' during the continuation of the current method invocation, but not including subframes, where $Q(\ell') = Q$.

Moreover, the judgements are supplied with a proof context G. The latter contains assumptions typically associated with merge-points in the control flow graph. These assumptions are used by the logic rules in order to avoid infinite cycling in the proof derivation. For the technical details of this the reader is referred to [22,9].

In order to give a flavor of what the proof rules look like, we show the rule for basic instructions (arithmetic operations, load/store,...):

$$\text{INSTR} \frac{G \vdash \{Pre_{M,l}(A)\}\, M,\, suc_M(l)\, \{Post_{M,l}(B)\}\, (Inv_{M,l}(I)) \qquad \psi}{G \vdash \{A\}\, M, l\, \{B\}\, (I)}$$

Note that the correctness of l depends on the correctness of its successor. Also, the rule uses predicate transformers $Pre_{M,l}(A), Post_{M,l}(A)$, and $Inv_{M,l}(I)$ which relate the assertions for the successor instruction with the assertions of instruction l. For the definition of these transformers, see [9]. Finally, the side condition ψ states that the local precondition A implies the strong invariant I and any annotation that may be associated with M, l in the annotation table Q:

$$\psi = \forall\, s_0\, s.\ A(s_0, s) \to (I(s_0, s, heap(s)) \land \forall Q.\ \mathsf{Q}(M, l) = Q \to Q(s_0, s)).$$

In addition to rules of similar shape for all instruction forms, the logic is also supplied with logical rules, such as a consequence rule and an axiom rule that extracts assumptions from the proof context.

We have proven a soundness theorem for the proof system which ensures that the derivability of a judgement $G \vdash \{A\}\, \ell\, \{B\}\, (I)$ entails its semantic validity. The latter is obtained by formulating the above informal interpretation in terms of Bicolano's operational judgements.

This soundness result may subsequently be extended to programs. We first say that a program has been *verified* if each entry in the method specification table is justified by a derivation for the corresponding method body, and similarly for the entries of local proof contexts G. The soundness result for programs then asserts that all methods of a verified program satisfy their specifications: whenever $\mathsf{M}(M) = (\Phi, \varphi)$ holds, any invocation of M is guaranteed to fulfill the method invariant φ, with terminating invocations additionally satisfying the partial-correctness assertion Φ.

In order to evaluate our logic experimentally, we have implemented a verification condition generator (VCgen) that applies proof rules in an automatic fashion and emits verifications conditions stemming from side conditions such as ψ above, and from the application of the rule of consequence.

In the next period of the project, we will extend the logic by mechanisms for reasoning about the consumption of resources and incorporate ghost variables and associated concepts. This will provide a platform for the encoding of some type systems that defy the current version of the program logic. A typical example are type systems that track the number of calls to certain API-methods like sending of SMS messages or opening files.

5.3 Type Systems

In this section we describe **MOBIUS** work on types for information flow, resources, and alias control. Classically, types in programming languages are used to check data formats, but we envisage much broader type-based verification, with specialised systems to analyse individual security properties. Indeed, Java 5 has annotations that support just such *pluggable* type systems [11].

Information flow. Work on information flow has focused on the definition of an accurate information flow type system for sequential Java bytecode and on its relation with information flow typing for Java source code, as well as on flexible analyses for concurrency.

Policies. Our work mainly focuses on termination insensitive policies which assume that the attacker can only draw observations on the input/output behavior of methods. Formally, the observational power of the attacker is captured by its security level (taken from a lattice $\mathcal{S}$ of security levels) and by *indistinguishability* relations $\sim$ on the semantic domains of the JVM memory, including the heap and the output value of methods (normal values or exceptional values).

Then, policies are expressed as a combination of global policies, that attach levels to fields, and local policies, that attach to methods identifiers signatures of the form $k_v \xrightarrow{k_h} k_r$, where k_v sets the security level of local variables, k_h is the heap effect of the method, and k_r is a record of security levels of the form $\{n : k_n, e_1 : k_{e_1}, \ldots e_n : k_{e_n}\}$, where k_n is the security level of the return value (normal termination) and each e_i is an exception class that might be propagated by the method, and k_{e_i} is its corresponding security level.

A method is safe w.r.t. a signature $k_v \xrightarrow{k_h} k_r$ if:

1. two terminating runs of the method with $\sim_{k_v}$-equivalent inputs and equivalent heaps, yield $\sim_{k_r}$-equivalent results and equivalent heaps;
2. the heap effect of the method is greater than k_h, i.e. the method does not perform field updates on fields whose security level is below k_h.

The definition of heap equivalence adopted in existing works on information flow for heap-based language, including [8], often assumes that pointers are opaque, i.e. the only observations that an attacker can make about a reference are those about the object to which it points. However, Hedin and Sands [29] have recently observed that the assumption is unvalidated by methods from the Java API, and exhibited a Jif program that does not use declassification but leaks information through invoking API methods. Their attack relies on the assumption that the function that allocates new objects on the heap is deterministic; however, this assumption is perfectly reasonable and satisfied by many implementations of the JVM. In addition to demonstrating the attack, Hedin and Sands show how a refined information flow type system can thwart such attacks for a language that allows to cast references as integers. Intuitively, their type system tracks the security level of references as well as the security levels of the fields of the object its points to.

Bytecode verification for secure information flow. We have defined a lightweight bytecode verifier that enforces non-interference of JVM applications, and proved formally its soundness against Bicolano [8]. The lightweight bytecode verifier performs a one-pass analysis of programs, and checks for every program point that the instruction verifies the constraints imposed by transition rules of the form

$$\frac{P[i] = ins \qquad constraints(ins, st, st', \Gamma)}{\Gamma, i \vdash st \to st'}$$

where i is an index consisting of a method body and a program point for this body, and the environment Γ contains policies, a table of security signatures for each method identifier, a security environment that maps program points to security levels, as well as information about the branching structure of programs, that is verified independently in a preliminary analysis. For increased precision, the preliminary analysis checks null pointers (to predict unthrowable null pointer exceptions), classes (to predict target of throw instructions), array accesses (to predict unthrowable out-of-bounds exceptions), and exceptions (to over-approximate the set of throwable exceptions for each method); the information is then used by a CDR checker that verifies control dependence regions (cdr), using the results of the PA analyser to minimise the size of regions.

Relation with information flow type system for Java. JFlow [34] is an information flow aware extension of Java that enforces statically flexible and expressive information policies by a constraint-based algorithm. Although the expressiveness of JFlow makes it difficult to characterize the security properties enforced by its type system, sound information flow type systems inspired from JFlow have been proposed for exception-free fragments of Java.

JFlow offers a practical tool for developing secure applications but does not address mobile code security as envisioned in MOBIUS since it applies to source code. In order to show that applications written in (a variant of) JFlow can be deployed in a mobile code architecture that delivers the promises of JFlow in terms of confidentiality, [7] proves that a standard (non-optimizing) Java compiler translates programs that are typable in a type system inspired from [5], but extended to exceptions, into programs that are typable in our system.

Concurrency. Extending the results of [8] to multi-threaded JVM programs is necessary in order to cover MIDP applications, but notoriously difficult to achieve. Motivated by the desire to provide flexible and practical enforcement mechanisms for concurrent languages, Russo and Sabelfeld [41] develop a sound information flow type system that enforces termination-insensitive non-interference in for a simple concurrent imperative language. The originality of their approach resides in the use of pseudo-commands to constrain the behavior of the scheduler so as to avoid internal timing leaks. One objective of the project is to extend their ideas to the setting of the JVM.

Declassification. Information flow type systems have not found substantial applications in practice, in particular because information flow policies based on non-interference are too rigid and do not authorize information release. In contrast, many applications often release deliberately some amount of sensitive information. Typical examples of deliberate information release include sending an encrypted message through an untrusted network, or allowing confidential information to be used in statistics over large databases. In a recent survey [42], A. Sabelfeld and D. Sands provide an overview of relaxed policies that allow for some amount of information release, and a classification along several dimensions, for example who releases the information, and what information is released. Type-based enforcement mechanisms for declassification are presented in [12].

Resource analysis. In §4.1 we identified requirements for MOBIUS resource security policies, as well as some notions of "resource" relevant to the MIDP application domain. Here we survey work within the project on analyses to support such policies, with particular focus on the possibility of formally verifying their correctness: essential if they are to be a basis for proof-carrying code.

Memory usage. The Java platform has a mandatory memory allocation model: a stack for local variables, and an object heap. In [9] we introduce a bytecode type system for this, where each program point has a type giving an upper limit on the number of heap objects it allocates. Correctness is proved via a translation into the MOBIUS logic, and every well-typed program is verifiable [21, Thm. 3.1.1]. Using the technique of *type-preserving compilation* we can lift this above the JVM: we match the translation from a high-level program F to bytecode $[\![F]\!]$ with a corresponding translation of types; and again for every well-typed program its bytecode compilation is verifiable in the MOBIUS logic [21, Thm. 3.1.3]. Even without the original high-level source program and its types, this low-level proof can certify the bytecode for PCC.

Work in the MRG project [4] demonstrated more sophisticated space inference for a functional language, using Hofmann-Jost typing [30] to give space bounds dependent on argument size, and with these types used to generate resource proofs in a precursor of the MOBIUS logic. We have now developed this further, into a space type system for object oriented programming based on amortised complexity analysis [31].

Billable events. Existing MIDP security policies demand that users individually authorise text messages as they are sent. This is clearly awkward, and the series of confirmation pop-up screens is a soft target for social engineering attacks. We propose a Java library of *resource managers* that add flexibility without compromising safety[21, §3.3]: instead of individual confirmation, a program requests authorisation in advance for a series of activities. Resource security may be assured either by runtime checks, or a type system for resource accounting, such that any well-typed program will only attempt to use resources for which it already has authorisation.

We have also used abstract interpretation to model such external resources [10]. From a program control-flow graph, we infer constraints in a lattice of permissions: whenever some resourceful action takes place, the program must have acquired at least the permissions required. Automated constraint solving can then determine whether this condition is satisfiable.

Execution time. Static analysis to count instructions executed can be verified in bytecode logic using *resource algebras* [3]. We have recently developed a static analysis framework [?] which provides a basis for performing cost analysis directly at the bytecode level. This allows obtaining cost relations in terms of the size of input arguments to methods. In addition, platform-dependent factors are a significant challenge to predicting real execution time across varied mobile platforms. We have shown how parameterised cost models, calibrated to an individual platform by running a test program, can predict execution times on different architectures [33]. In a PCC framework, client devices would map certified platform-independent cost metrics into platform-dependent estimates, based on fixed calibration benchmarks.

Alias control. Alias characterisations simplify reasoning about programs [26]: they enable modular verification, facilitate thread synchronisation, and allow programmers to exchange internal representations of data structures. Ownership types [18,17] and Universe types [35] are mechanisms for *characterising* aliasing in object oriented programming languages. They organise the heap into a hierarchical structure of nested non-overlapping *contexts* where every object is contained in one such context. Each context is characterised by an *object*, which is said to *own* all the objects contained directly in that context. Figure 3 illustrates the ownership structure of a linked list with iterator.

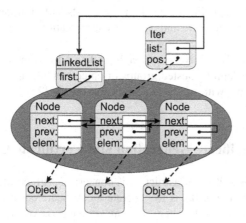

Fig. 3. Object structure of a linked list. The LinkedList object owns the nodes of the doubly-linked list. The iterator is in the same context as the list head. It has a peer reference to the list head and an any reference to the Node object at the iterator position.

In the Universe Type System [35,26], a context hierarchy is induced by extending types with Universe annotations, which range over rep, peer, and any. A field typed with a Universe modifier rep denotes that the object referenced by it must be within the context of the current object; a field typed with a Universe modifier peer denotes that the object referenced by it must be within the context that also contains the current object; a field typed with a Universe modifier any is agnostic about the context containing the object referenced by the field.

So far, we have concentrated on the following three areas:

- *Universe Java:* The formalisation and proof of soundness of a minimal object-oriented language with Universe Types.
- *Generic Universe Java:* The extension of Universe Java to Generic Java.
- *Concurrent Universe Java:* The use of Universe Types to administer race conditions and atomicity in a concurrent version of Universe Java.

UJ - Universe Java. As a basis for the other two work areas, we formalized Universe Java and proved the following key properties:

- *Type safety:* The Universe annotations rep and peer correctly indicate the owner of an object.
- *Encapsulation:* The fields of an object can only be modified through method calls made on the owner of that object (owner-as-modifier discipline).

GUJ - Generic Universe Java. We extended Universe Java to handle generics, which now form part of the official release of Java 1.5. In Generic Java, classes have parameters which can be bound by types: since in Universe Java, types are made up of a Universe modifier and a class, GUJ class parameters in generic class definitions are bound by Universe modifiers *and* classes. Generic Universe Java provide more static type safety then Universe Java by reducing the need for downcasts with runtime ownership checks. We proved that GUJ is type safe and enforces encapsulation.

UJ and Concurrency. The Universe ownership relation in UJ provides a natural way to characterise non-overlapping nested groups of objects in a heap. We therefore exploit this structure in a Java with multiple concurrent threads [25] to ensure atomcity and absence of data races.

6   Towards Certificate Generation and Certificate Checking

An important part of a PCC infrastructure is concerned with certificates. For the code producer one of the main tasks is to generate a certificate ensuring that his program meets the security policy of the client. In contrast, the code verifier/consumer needs to convince himself that the transmitted program respects his security policy.

In the scenario of Fig. 2 we assume that operators send compiled code, i.e. bytecode, to their customers, but this leaves the question of whether code producers will supply source code or bytecode to the operator. In MOBIUS, we concentrate on the latter, since this avoids the inclusion of the compiler in the trusted code base and does not require code producers to provide access to their source code.

6.1   Certificate Generation

The MOBIUS project focuses on two approaches for the generation of certificates, logic-based verification and type-based verification. By exploring both approaches, we hope to complement the rigorousness of our formalization by flexibility and automation.

The first technique (*logic-based verification*) is the concept of a proof transforming compiler [6], where properties can be specified and verified at the source code level and are then guaranteed to be preserved by the compilation, analogously to the way that *type-preserving compilation* guarantees the preservation of properties in the context of type systems. In addition to a program written in the source language, such a compiler expects a proof that the source program satisfies a (high-level) specification. Its output consist of the bytecode program and a proof (*certificate*) that this program satisfies the translation of the original specification into a formalism appropriate for bytecode. Logic-based verification is particularly suitable for functional correctness properties, but we have already shown in previous work how to generate JML annotations for a large class of high-level security properties [39]. Interactive usage of the proof assistant, for example in order to discharge side conditions emitted by the VCgen, is also admissible. To be able to write such a proof transforming compiler for Java programs annotated with JML, we have developed a dedicated annotation language for Java bytecode: the Bytecode Modeling Language (BML) [13].

The second technique for the generation of specifications and certificates, *type-based verification*, rests on automated (and in general conservatively approximate) program analysis. Here, certificates are derived from typing derivations or fixed-point solutions of abstract interpretations, as outlined in the previous section and in the philosophy of lightweight bytecode verification.

6.2   Certificate Checking

For the code verifier/consumer, the goal is to check that the received program meets its specification (i.e. check the validity of the certificate) and to ensure that the specification is compliant with his security policies. Both parts should be fully automatic, and the machinery employed for this task is part of the trusting computing base (TCB).

The size of TCB is one of the main difficulties in a PCC architecture. Foundational PCC [2] minimizes the TCB by modeling the operational semantics of the bytecode in a proof assistant, and by proving properties of programs w.r.t. the operational semantics. Then deductive reasoning is used to encode program logic rules or typing rules. FPCC allows to remove the VCgen and type checkers for the application type systems from the TCB, but the deductive reasoning to encode proof rules or typing rules leads to bigger certificates than using a VCgen or a type checker.

One ambitious goal is to merge both approaches, and to get a small TCB and small certificates. Ultimately, a **MOBIUS** certificate is always a Coq proof of desired property phrased in terms of semantics. Apart from the proof assistant itself, Bicolano represents the trusting computing base of **MOBIUS** reasoning infrastructure. By representing formal systems in a proof assistant, we firstly increase the confidence in the validity of our checkers. Secondly, these representations allow us to exploit the infrastructure of the proof assistant when verifying concrete programs and their certificates.

Based on this, and complementing FPCC, the following two proof methodologies for type-based verification are considered within **MOBIUS**.

Derived Assertions. The Derived Assertions-Approach pioneered in MRG associates with each typing judgement an assertion in the program logic, the derived assertion. For each (schematic) typing rule one then proves a derived program logic proof rule operating on these derived assertions and possibly involving semantic, e.g. arithmetic, side conditions to be discharged by the proof assistant. Given a concrete typing derivation, a proof of the derived assertion corresponding to its conclusion can then be obtained by a simple tactic which invokes these derived rules mirroring the typing derivation. The typing derivation itself will typically be obtained using an automatic type inference which then need not be part of the TCB.

Reflection. Recent versions of Coq come with a powerful computational engine [27] derived from the OCAML compiler. This allows computationally intensive tasks to be carried out within the proof assistant itself. A prominent example thereof is Gonthier-Werner's self-contained proof of the four-color theorem within Coq. This feature can be harnessed for our purposes in the following way using the reflection mechanism:

- we encode a type system T as a boolean-valued function $\mathsf{typable}_T$ on programs, and prove that the type system is sound in the sense that it enforces some expected semantic property interp_T. Formally, soundness is established by proving the lemma

$$\mathsf{TypeCorrect} : \forall P : \mathsf{prog}.\ \mathsf{typable}_T(P) = \mathsf{true} \implies \mathsf{interp}_T(P)$$

- to prove that $\mathsf{interp}_T(P_0)$ holds for a particular program P_0, we just have to apply the $\mathsf{TypeCorrect}$ lemma, and prove that $\mathsf{typable}_T(P_0) = \mathsf{true}$ holds.
- if your checker allows you to reason by computation (i.e. two propositions are equal if they are computationally equal) and if the program P_0 is typable, the proposition

$$\mathsf{typable}_T(P_0) = \mathsf{true}$$

is equal (i.e. reduces) to $\mathsf{true} = \mathsf{true}$ which is trivial to prove.

The Coq proof assistant allows such a reasoning mechanism. In Coq, the representation of such a proof is $\mathsf{TypeCorrect}\ P\ (\mathsf{refl\_equal\ true})$, where $(\mathsf{refl\_equal\ true})$ is a proof of $\mathsf{true} = \mathsf{true}$.

Similar to this reflectional approach to PCC is the technique we presented in [14], where lattice abstract interpretation is used to verify bounded memory use. Significantly, here both the algorithm and its correctness proof are expressed within the Coq proof assistant, such that we may extract a *certified checker* from the proof itself. This allows a novel realisation of proof-carrying code, where a fast program verifier is trusted because it is obtained from its own proof of correctness.

7   Next Steps

After a year activity, the MOBIUS project is well on tracks. Scientific progress is proceeding as expected: security requirements and the PCC scenarios for global computing have been defined, and significant advances in enabling technologies have been reported in deliverables and scientific publications. For further information, please consult http://mobius.inria.fr.

References

1. Albert, E., Puebla, G., Hermenegildo, M.V.: Abstraction-carrying code. In: Baader, F., Voronkov, A. (eds.) LPAR 2004. LNCS, vol. 3452, pp. 380–397. Springer, Heidelberg (2004)
2. Appel, A.W.: Foundational proof-carrying code. In: Halpern, J. (ed.) Proceedings of the Sixteenth Annual IEEE Symp. on Logic in Computer Science, LICS 2001 (Invited Talk), p. 247. IEEE Computer Society Press, Los Alamitos (2001)

3. Aspinall, D., Beringer, L., Hofmann, M., Loidl, H.-W., Momigliano, A.: A program logic for resource verification. In: TPHOLs 2004. LNCS, Springer, Heidelberg (2004)
4. Aspinall, D., Gilmore, S., Hofmann, M., Sannella, D., Stark, I.: Mobile Resource Guarantees for Smart Devices. In: Barthe, G., Burdy, L., Huisman, M., Lanet, J.-L., Muntean, T. (eds.) CASSIS 2004. LNCS, vol. 3362, pp. 1–27. Springer, Heidelberg (2005)
5. Banerjee, A., Naumann, D.: Stack-based access control for secure information flow. Journal of Functional Programming (Special Issue on Language-Based Security) 15, 131–177 (2005)
6. Barthe, G., Grégoire, B., Kunz, C., Rezk, T.: Certificate translation for optimizing compilers. In: SAS'06: Proceedings of Static Analysis Symposium. LNCS, Springer, Heidelberg (2006)
7. Barthe, G., Naumann, D., Rezk, T.: Deriving an information flow checker and certifying compiler for java. In: Symposium on Security and Privacy, 2006, IEEE Press, Orlando (2006)
8. Barthe, G., Pichardie, D., Rezk, T.: A certified lightweight non-interference java bytecode verifier. In: Niccola, R.D. (ed.) Proceedings of ESOP'07. LNCS, vol. 4xxx, Springer, Heidelberg (2007)
9. Beringer, L., Hofmann, M.: A bytecode logic for JML and types. In: Kobayashi, N. (ed.) APLAS 2006. LNCS, vol. 4279, pp. 389–405. Springer, Heidelberg (2006)
10. Besson, F., Dufay, G., Jensen, T.P.: A formal model of access control for mobile interactive devices. In: ESORICS 2006. LNCS, Springer, Heidelberg (2006)
11. Bracha, G.: Pluggable type systems. Presented at the OOPSLA 2004 Workshop on Revival of Dynamic Languages (October 2004)
12. Broberg, N., Sands, D.: Flow locks: Towards a core calculus for dynamic flow policies. In: Sestoft, P. (ed.) ESOP 2006 and ETAPS 2006. LNCS, vol. 3924, pp. 180–196. Springer, Heidelberg (2006)
13. Burdy, L., Huisman, M., Pavlova, M.: Preliminary design of BML: A behavioral interface specification language for Java bytecode. In: TSDM 2000. LNCS, Springer, Heidelberg (to appear)
14. Cachera, D., Jensen, D.P.T., Schneider, G.: Certified memory usage analysis. In: Fitzgerald, J.A., Hayes, I.J., Tarlecki, A. (eds.) FM 2005. LNCS, vol. 3582, pp. 91–106. Springer, Heidelberg (2005)
15. Charles, J.: Adding native specifications to JML. In: ECOOP workshop on Formal Techniques for Java-like Programs (FTfJP'2006) (2006)
16. Christensen, A.S., Møller, A., Schwartzbach, M.I.: Precise analysis of string expressions. In: Cousot, R. (ed.) SAS 2003. LNCS, vol. 2694, pp. 1–18. Springer, Heidelberg (2003), Available from http://www.brics.dk/JSA/
17. Clarke, D.G., Drossopoulou, S.: Ownership, Encapsulation and the Disjointness of Type and Effect. In: OOPSLA, pp. 292–310 (2002)
18. Clarke, D.G., Potter, J.M., Noble, J.: Ownership Types for Flexible Alias Protection. In: Proceedings of the 13th Conference on Object-Oriented Programming, Systems, Languages, and Applications (OOPSLA-98), ACM SIGPLAN Notices, vol. 33(10), pp. 48–64. ACM Press, New York (1998)
19. Consortium, M.: Deliverable 1.1: Resource and information flow security requirements (2006), Available online from http://mobius.inria.fr
20. Consortium, M.: Deliverable 1.2: Framework-specific and application-specific security requirements (2006), Available online from http://mobius.inria.fr
21. Consortium, M.: Deliverable 2.1: Intermediate report on type systems (2006), Available online from http://mobius.inria.fr
22. Consortium, M.: Deliverable 3.1: Bytecode specification language and program logic (2006), Available online from http://mobius.inria.fr

23. Consortium, M.: Deliverable 4.1: Scenarios for proof-carrying code (2006), Available online from http://mobius.inria.fr

24. Crégut, P., Alvarado, C.: Improving the security of downloadable Java applications with static analysis. In: Workshop on Bytecode Semantics, Verification, Analysis and Transformation (Bytecode 2005). Electronic Notes in Theoretical Computer Science, vol. 141, Elsevier Science, Inc, North-Holland (2005)

25. Cunningham, D., Drossopoulou, S., Eisenbach, S., Dietl, W., Müller, P.: CUJ: Universe Types for Race Safety. Preliminary version at http://slurp.doc.ic.ac.uk/pubs.html#cuj06

26. Dietl, W., Müller, P.: Universes: Lightweight ownership for JML. Journal of Object Technology (JOT) 4(8), 5–32 (2005)

27. Grégoire, B., Leroy, X.: A compiled implementation of strong reduction. In: ICFP'02: Proceedings of the International Conference on Functional Programming, pp. 235–246. ACM Press, New York (2002)

28. Hähnle, R., Mostowski, W.: Verification of safety properties in the presence of transactions. In: Barthe, G., Burdy, L., Huisman, M., Lanet, J.-L., Muntean, T. (eds.) CASSIS 2004. LNCS, vol. 3362, pp. 151–171. Springer, Heidelberg (2005)

29. Hedin, D., Sands, D.: Noninterference in the presence of non-opaque pointers. In: Proceedings of the 19th IEEE Computer Security Foundations Workshop, IEEE Computer Society Press, Los Alamitos (2006)

30. Hofmann, M., Jost, S.: Static prediction of heap space usage for first-order functional programs. In: POPL'03, Proceedings of the 30rd Annual. ACM SIGPLAN - SIGACT. Symposium. on Principles of Programming Languages, pp. 185–197. ACM Press, New York (2003)

31. Hofmann, M., Jost, S.: Type-based amortised heap-space analysis. In: Proceedings of ESOP2006, pp. 22–37 (2006)

32. U.T. Initiative Unified testing criteria for Java technology-based applications for mobile devices. Technical report, Sun Microsystems, Motorola, Nokia, Siemens, Sony Ericsson, Version 2.1 (May 2006)

33. Mera, E., López-García, P., Puebla, G., Carro, M., Hermenegildo, M.: Combining Static Analysis and Profiling for Estimating Execution Times. In: Hanus, M. (ed.) PADL 2007. LNCS, vol. 4354, Springer, Heidelberg (2006)

34. Myers, A.: JFlow: Practical mostly-static information flow control. In: Myers, A. (ed.) POPL'99, Proceedings of the 26rd Annual. ACM SIGPLAN - SIGACT. Symposium. on Principles of Programming Languages, pp. 228–241. ACM Press, New York (1999)

35. Müller, P.: Modular Specification and Verification of Object-Oriented Programs. PhD thesis, FernUniversität Hagen (2001)

36. Necula, G.C.: Proof-carrying code. In: POPL '97: Proceedings of the 24th ACM SIGPLAN-SIGACT Symposium on Principles of programming languages, pp. 106–119. ACM Press, New York (1997)

37. Necula, G.C., Lee, P.: Safe kernel extensions without run-time checking. In: Proceedings of Operating Systems Design and Implementation (OSDI), Seattle, WA, USENIX Assoc, pp. 229–243 (October 1996)

38. Parliement, E., Council, E.: Directive 95/46/ec of the european parliament and of the council of 24 october 1995 on the protection of individuals with regard to the processing of personal data and on the free movement of such data. Official Journal of the European Communities, number L 281, 31–50 (october 1995)

39. Pavlova, M., Barthe, G., Burdy, L., Huisman, M., Lanet, J.-L.: Enforcing high-level security properties for applets. In: Paradinas, P., Quisquater, J.-J. (eds.) Proceedings of CARDIS'04, Toulouse, France, August 2004, Kluwer Academic Publishers, Boston (2004)

40. Rose, E.: Lightweight bytecode verification. Journal of Automated Reasoning 31(3-4), 303–334 (2003)
41. Russo, A., Sabelfeld, A.: Securing interaction between threads and the scheduler. In: Proceedings of CSFW'06 (2006)
42. Sabelfeld, A., Sands, D.: Dimensions and principles of declassification. In: Proceedings of CSFW'05, IEEE Press, Orlando (2005)
43. The Coq development team. The coq proof assistant reference manual v8.0. Technical Report 255, INRIA, France, mars (2004), http://coq.inria.fr/doc/main.html

SENSORIA Process Calculi for Service-Oriented Computing*

Martin Wirsing[1], Rocco De Nicola[2], Stephen Gilmore[3], Matthias Hölzl[1], Roberto Lucchi[4,**], Mirco Tribastone[3], and Gianlugi Zavattaro[4]

[1] Ludwig-Maximilians-Universität München, Germany
[2] University of Florence, Italy
[3] University of Edinburgh, United Kingdom
[4] University of Bologna, Italy

Abstract. The IST-FET Integrated Project SENSORIA aims at developing a novel comprehensive approach to the engineering of service-oriented software systems where foundational theories, techniques and methods are fully integrated in a pragmatic software engineering approach. Process calculi and logical methods serve as the main mathematical basis of the SENSORIA approach.

In this paper we give first a short overview of SENSORIA and then focus on process calculi for service-oriented computing. The Service Centered Calculus SCC is a general purpose calculus which enriches traditional process calculi with an explicit notion of session; the Service Oriented Computing Kernel SOCK is inspired by the Web services protocol stack and consists of three layers for service description, service engines, and the service network; Performance Evaluation Process Algebra (PEPA) is an expressive formal language for modelling distributed systems which we use for quantitative analysis of services. The calculi and the analysis techniques are illustrated by a case study in the area of distributed e-learning systems.

1 Introduction

Service-oriented computing is an emerging paradigm where services are understood as autonomous, platform-independent computational entities that can be described, published, categorised, discovered, and dynamically assembled for developing massively distributed, interoperable, evolvable systems and applications. These characteristics push service-oriented computing towards nowadays widespread success, demonstrated by the fact that many large companies invest efforts and resources in promoting service delivery on a variety of computing platforms, mostly through the Internet in the form of Web services. Soon there will be a plethora of new services as required for e-government, e-business, and e-science, and other areas within the rapidly evolving Information Society.

---

* This work has been partially sponsored by the project SENSORIA, IST-2 005-016004 and by the DFG project MAEWA.
** Currently at European Commission, DG Joint Research Centre, Institute for Environment and Sustainability, Spatial Data Infrastructures Unit.

U. Montanari, D. Sannella, and R. Bruni (Eds.): TGC 2006, LNCS 4661, pp. 30–50, 2007.

However, service-oriented computing and development today is done in a pragmatic, mostly ad-hoc way. Theoretical foundations are missing, but they are badly needed for trusted interoperability, predictable compositionality, and for guaranteeing security, correctness, and appropriate resources usage. Service-oriented software development is not integrated in a controllable software development process based on powerful analysis and verification tools and it is not clear whether service-oriented software development scales up to the development of complete systems.

The IST-FET Integrated Project SENSORIA addresses the problems of service-oriented computing by building, from first-principles, novel theories, methods and tools supporting the *engineering of software systems for service-oriented overlay computers*. Its aim is to develop a novel comprehensive approach to the engineering of service-oriented software systems where foundational theories, techniques and methods are fully integrated in a pragmatic software engineering approach.

The results of SENSORIA will include a new generalised concept of service for global overlay computers, new semantically well-defined modelling and programming primitives for services, new powerful mathematical analysis and verification techniques and tools for system behaviour and quality of service properties, and novel model-based transformation and development techniques. The innovative methods of SENSORIA will be demonstrated by applying them in the service-intensive areas of e-business, automotive systems, and telecommunications.

A main research strand of SENSORIA is the development of adequate linguistic primitives for *modelling and programming global service-oriented systems*. This includes an ontology for service-oriented architectures, UML extensions (see e.g. [35]) and the declarative language SRML [16] for system modelling over service-oriented architectures. Process calculi serve as the mathematical basis for programming and modelling dynamic aspects of services and service-oriented systems and for analysing qualitative and quantitative properties of services such as quality of service, security, performance, resource usage, scalability. During the first year of SENSORIA a *family of process calculi for services* has been developed which supports complementary aspects of service-oriented computing and qualitative and quantitative analysis of service-oriented systems. The family comprises four core calculi for service description, invocation and orchestration [6,19,25,9], stochastic and probabilistic extensions of calculi for global computing [14,15,8], and process calculi and coordination languages with cost and priority [10,5,3].

In this paper we give first a short overview of SENSORIA and then focus on process calculi for service-oriented computing. For reasons of space we present only two of the SENSORIA core calculi and one stochastic process algebra for analysing quantitative properties of service-oriented systems. For the other SENSORIA calculi the reader is referred to the SENSORIA reports and publications available on the SENSORIA web site [32].

The *Service Centered Calculus* SCC is a general purpose calculus based on an abstract notion of service (independent of any specific technology) and aiming at a model suitable for different technologies and scenarios. SCC enriches the name passing communication mechanism of traditional process calculi, such as the π-calculus [27], with explicit notions of service definition, service invocation and bi-directional sessioning.

SCC's notion of service has been influenced by Cook and Misra's calculus Orc [28] for structured orchestration of services, where a service is a function returning a stream of values.

The *Service Oriented Computing Kernel* SOCK is a three-layered calculus inspired by the Web services protocol stack. The *service description* layer consists of a simple calculus for service interface description which takes inspiration from WSDL [34] and the abstract fragment of WS-BPEL [4]. At the *service engine* layer additional information can be added which indicates how a service is actually run; this layer is inspired by the full (executable) WS-BPEL language. The third *service network* layer, permits modeling an overall network of interacting services; the source of inspiration for this level has been the SOAP [7] protocol for message exchange among Web services.

Finally, we present Jane Hillston's stochastic *Performance Evaluation Process Algebra* (PEPA) [22,21]. This is an expressive formal language for modelling distributed systems which is supported by a flexible workbench [17]. We use PEPA for quantitative analysis of services. PEPA models are obtained by composing elements which perform individual activities or cooperate on shared ones. To each activity is attached an estimate of the rate at which it may be performed. The rates associated with activities are exponentially distributed random variables thus PEPA is a *stochastic process algebra* which describes the evolution of a process in continuous time. As an example for scalability analysis, we investigate with PEPA how models of Web service execution scale with increasing client population sizes.

All three presented calculi and analysis techniques are illustrated by a case study in the area of distributed e-learning systems.

The paper is organised as follows: In Sect. 2 we present shortly the SENSORIA project, its approach to service-oriented system development, and the running example, i.e., the case study of a distributed e-learning and course management system. We present the Service Centered Calculus SCC in Sect. 3.1 and the Service-Oriented Computing Kernel SOCK in Sect. 3.2. In Sect. 4 we use PEPA for scalability analysis: we investigate how models of Web service execution scale with increasing client population sizes. We conclude the paper in Sect. 5 with some remarks on further SENSORIA results.

2   SENSORIA

SENSORIA is one of the three Integrated Projects of the Global Computing Initiative of FET-IST, the Future and Emerging Technologies action of the European Commission. The SENSORIA Consortium consists of 12 universities, two research institutes and four companies (two SMEs) from seven countries[1].

---

[1] LMU München (coordinator), Germany; TU Denmark at Lyngby, Denmark; FAST GmbH München, S and N AG, Paderborn (both Germany); Budapest University of Technology and Economics, Hungary; Università di Bologna, Università di Firenze, Università di Pisa, Università di Trento, ISTI Pisa, Telecom Italia Lab Turino (all Italy); Warsaw University, Poland; ATX Software SA, Lisboa, Universidade de Lisboa (both Portugal); Imperial College London, University College London, University of Edinburgh, University of Leicester (all United Kingdom).

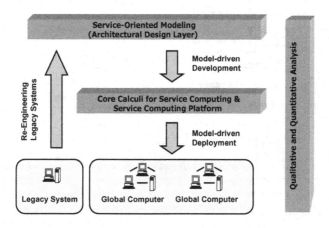

Fig. 1. The SENSORIA approach to service-oriented systems development

2.1   Aim and Approach of SENSORIA

The aim of the IST-FET Integrated Project SENSORIA is to develop a novel comprehensive approach to the engineering of service-oriented software systems where foundational theories, techniques and methods are fully integrated in a pragmatic software engineering approach. This includes a new generalised concept of service, new semantically well-defined modelling and programming primitives for services, new powerful mathematical analysis and verification techniques and tools for system behaviour and quality of service properties, and novel model-based transformation and development techniques.

The three main research themes of Sensoria concern

- **The definition of adequate linguistic primitives for modelling and programming global service-oriented systems**, by building on a category theoretic and process algebraic framework supporting architectural modelling and programming for mobile global computing and by formally connecting these linguistic primitives with UML in order to make the formal approaches available for practitioners;
- **The development of qualitative and quantitative analysis methods for global services**, by using powerful mathematical analysis techniques including program analysis techniques, type systems, logics, and process calculi for investigating the behaviour and the quality of service of properties of global services;
- **The development of sound engineering and deployment techniques for global services**, by providing new mathematical well-founded techniques for model-based transformation, deployment, and re-engineering, and integrating them into a novel engineering approach to service-oriented development.

In the envisaged software development process (cf. Fig. 1), services are modelled in a platform-independent architectural design layer. By using model transformations, these models are then transformed to the SENSORIA core calculi for qualitative and quantitative analysis; moreover, for constructing operational realisations they are transformed

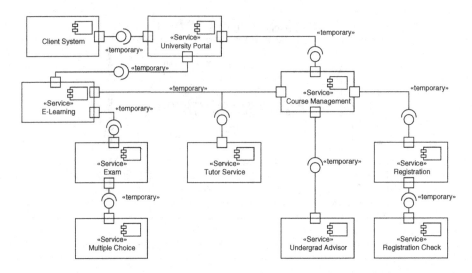

Fig. 2. Architecture of the SENSORIA distributed e-learning and course management system

and/or refined to the service computing platform of SENSORIA which, in turn, can be used for generating specific implementations over different global computing platforms in a (semi-)automated way. On the other hand, legacy code is transformed systematically into service oriented software models (see Fig. 1). In all phases of service-oriented development formal analysis techniques are used for validating and verifying qualitative and quantitative properties of services and their interactions.

2.2   The E-Learning and Course Management Case Study

Today's academic environment poses several challenges for administration, faculty, and students. Administration has to provide services for more and more students while the numbers of specialised subjects (e.g., bio-informatics and media informatics in addition to traditional computer science) increases steadily and hence more courses need to be scheduled. Faculty members are facing a higher workload and increasing demands from students, e.g., with regards to the availability of homework sheets, course slides and additional teaching aids. Furthermore students are expected to spend parts of their studies in foreign countries without delaying their exams. To manage these problems efficiently and cheaply, universities are beginning to use computerised course-management and e-learning systems. Some of the functionalities performed by typical university software systems are: management of curricula and students by a university, management of single courses by teaching personnel, management of degrees by students, and e-learning.

In SENSORIA we build a prototypical service-oriented distributed e-learning and course management system (DECMS) that satisfies these requirements and is used to guide SENSORIA research efforts. In order to support distribution, extensibility and dynamic composition, DECMS has a service-oriented architecture (cf. Fig. 2) consisting of services which are interconnected through ports that are typed by provided and required interfaces (written in a "ball-and-socket" notation). Fig. 2 shows a UML service diagram of the DECMS as a first simplified snapshot of an architecture model.

A client service connects to DECMS through a University Portal service which in turn holds connections to the e-learning and the course management services. A tutor service interacts with both, the e-learning and course management service. The e-learning service offers an examination facility with multiple choice questions. This is provided to the e-learning service by a dedicated examination service which in turn requires an auxiliary multiple choice service. Similarly, the course management service offers services for enrolling students in courses and querying and updating the current undergrad advisor. These services are provided by the corresponding auxiliary services.

In the following we use examples concerning the management of single courses and of degrees for illustrating the different process calculi presented in this article.

3   Core Calculi for Service-Oriented Computing

The core calculi for service specification permit focusing on the foundational aspects and properties of services, and drive (via operational semantics) the implementation of prototypes: Moreover they provide a common ground for experiments and for studying relative expressiveness and lay the basis for extensions to deal with issues such as linguistic primitives (e.g. compensation), quantitative properties (e.g. Quality of Service) and qualitative properties (e.g. logics and type systems).

During the first year of SENSORIA four core calculi have been developed which put different stress on and support complementary aspects of service-oriented computing:

SCC. The *Service Centered Calculus* [6] is a general purpose calculus for services which focuses on sessions, i.e. client-service bidirectional interactions,

SOCK. The *Service-Oriented Computing Kernel* [19] proposes a three-layered calculus inspired by the Web services protocol stack (WSDL, WS-BPEL, SOAP),

COWS. The *Calculus for Orchestration of Web services* [25] mirrors WS-BPEL constructs such as message correlations, fault and compensation handlers, and flow graphs,

SC. The *Signals Calculus* [9] considers publish/subscribe service interaction instead of message-based client-service communication and supports the prototype implementation of a middleware for programming Long Running Transactions as described by the SAGA-calculus.

Two different approaches have been followed in the design of core calculi for SOC: *technology-driven* and *theory-driven*. The technology-driven approach of SOCK and COWS consists of electing one specific service-oriented technology as the starting point, and extracting from it a corresponding core model. This permits to crosscheck whether the proposed general calculi adhere to the specificities of the currently available service oriented technologies. The opposite theory-driven approach of SCC and SC consists of designing an abstract model of services that is not bound to a specific technology; the resulting calculi are general enough to be applied to different global computers on which services run.

In the following we present informally two of the four calculi, namely SCC and SOCK.

$$
\begin{array}{lll}
P, Q ::= & \mathbf{0} & \text{Nil} \\
& |\ a.P & \text{Concretion} \\
& |\ (x)P & \text{Abstraction} \\
& |\ \text{return } a.P & \text{Return Value} \\
& |\ a \Rightarrow (x)P & \text{Service Definition} \\
& |\ a\{(x)P\} \Leftarrow Q & \text{Service Invocation} \\
& |\ r \rhd P & \text{Session} \\
& |\ P|Q & \text{Parallel Composition} \\
& |\ (\nu a)P & \text{New Name}
\end{array}
$$

Fig. 3. SCC: syntax of processes

3.1   A Session-Oriented Process Calculus for Service-Oriented Systems

SCC is a calculus developed around the notions of *service definition*, *service invocation* and *bi-directional sessioning*; it has been influenced by Cook and Misra's Orc [28], a basic programming model for structured orchestration of services. Orc is particularly appealing due to its simplicity and yet great generality; its three basic composition operators are sufficient to model the most common workflow patterns, identified by van der Aalst et al. in [33].

SCC has novel features for programming and composing services, while taking into account their dynamic behaviour. In particular, SCC supports explicit modeling of sessions both on the client and on the service side, and provides mechanisms for session naming and scoping, by relying on the constructs of π-calculus [27]. Sessions permit describing and reasoning about interaction modalities more structured than the simple *one-way* and *request-response* modalities provided by Orc and typical of a producer / consumer pattern. Moreover, in SCC, sessions can be closed thus providing a mechanism for process interruption and service cancellation and update which has no counterpart in most process calculi.

Summarising, SCC combines the service oriented flavour of Orc with the name passing communication mechanism of the π-calculus.

Calculus description. Within SCC, services are seen as interacting functions (and even stream processing functions) that can be invoked by clients. The syntax of (the kill-free fragment of) SCC is reported in Figure 3. The operational semantics is not reported for space constraints, it can be found in [6].

Service definitions take the form $a \Rightarrow (x)P$, where a is the service name, x is a formal parameter, and P is the actual implementation of the service. As an example, consider the service double defined as follows:

$$\text{double} \Rightarrow (x)x + x$$

(Here and in the following we omit the trailing $\mathbf{0}$.) This service receives the value x and computes its double $x + x$. Service invocations are written as $a\{(x)R\} \Leftarrow Q$: each new value v produced by the client Q will trigger a new invocation of service a; for each invocation, an instance of the process R, with x bound to the actual invocation value

v, implements the client-side protocol for interacting with the new instance of a. As an example, a client for the simple service described above will be written in SCC as

$$\texttt{double}\{(x)(y)\texttt{return } y\} \Leftarrow 5$$

After the invocation x is bound to the argument 5, the client waits for a value from the server and the received value 10 is substituted for y and hence returned as the result of the service invocation.

This is only the simplest pattern of interaction in the context of service oriented computing, the so-called *request-response* pattern. Differently from object oriented computing, in service oriented computing clients and services can interact via more complex patterns activating *sessions* after the first invocation. Within a session several values can be exchanged from the service to the client and vice versa. Moreover, also other services can be involved giving rise to a multi-party *conversation*.

A service invocation causes activation of a new session. A pair of dual fresh names, r and $\bar{r}$, identifies the two sides of the session. Client and service protocols are instantiated each at the proper side of the session. For instance, interaction of the client and of the service described above triggers the session

$$(\nu r)\big(r \rhd 5 + 5 \,|\, \bar{r} \rhd (y)\texttt{return } y\big)$$

(in this case, the client side makes no use of the formal parameter). The value 10 is computed on the service-side and then received at the client side, that reduces first to $\bar{r} \rhd \texttt{return } 10$ and then to $10 \,|\, \bar{r} \rhd \mathbf{0}$ (where $\mathbf{0}$ denotes the nil process).

More generally, communication within sessions is bi-directional, in the sense that the interacting partners can exchange data in both directions. Values returned outside the session to the enclosing environment can be used to invoke other services. For instance, a client may invoke the service `double` and then print the obtained result as follows:

$$\texttt{print}\{(z)\mathbf{0}\} \Leftarrow \big(\texttt{double}\{(x)(y)\texttt{return } y\} \Leftarrow 5\big)$$

(in this case, the service `print` is invoked with vacuous protocol $(z)\mathbf{0}$).

As a more significant example than those reported above, we present a simple orchestrator used in the course management system whose aim is to invoke a service which collects the results of two other services.

Example 1 (Service orchestration: email service for course events). A student wants to be notified via email of all important events for two courses in which he is enrolled. Assume that the course management system of the university provides the following services: services *Course1Events* and *Course2Events* provide announcements for the respective courses; the service *email* expects a value and then sends it to a student's address. Then the following process

$$
\begin{aligned}
email\{(-)\mathbf{0}\} \Leftarrow \big(\ & Course1Events\{(x)(y)\texttt{return } y\} \Leftarrow \bullet \\
| \ & Course2Events\{(x)(y)\texttt{return } y\} \Leftarrow \bullet \\
\big)
\end{aligned}
$$

will send an email for each announcement from either *Course1* or *Course2* to the student. Note that we use the names $\bullet$ and $-$ to denote unused names and binders for unused names, respectively.

As already anticipated above, another interesting aspect of SCC is that other services can be invoked during the execution of a session thus giving rise to a multi-party conversation. As an example, let us consider the following Course-Registration Check.

Example 2 (Multi-party conversation: registration service). Using a syntax enriched with the boolean *and* operator and an **if-else** construct, we can specify that a course registration might require the student to satisfy certain requirements, e.g., having completed a lab in the previous term and passing a selection test.

$$regCheck \Rightarrow (x) \, \textbf{if}((completedLab \Leftarrow x) \; and \; (passedTest \Leftarrow x))$$
$$allow$$
$$\textbf{else} \; deny$$

This example demonstrates the invocation of other services (`completedLab` and `passedTest`) during the execution of one service.

The full SCC comprises also other more specific operators that permit, for instance, to interrupt the execution of a session or to cancel/update service definitions. The full syntax is not reported here for space constraints, but can be found in [6]. Nevertheless we describe informally how the interruption mechanism can be used.

A protocol, both on client-side and on service-side, can be interrupted (e.g. due to the occurrence of an unexpected event), and interruption can be notified to the environment. More generally, the keyword close can be used to terminate a protocol on one side and to notify the termination to a suitable handler at the partner site. For example, the above client is extended below for exploiting a suitable service `fault` that can handle printer failures:

$$\texttt{print}\{(z)\textbf{0}\} \Leftarrow_{\texttt{fault}} (\,\texttt{double}\{(x)(y)\texttt{return}\,y\} \Leftarrow 5\,) \,|\, \texttt{fault} \Rightarrow (code)Handler$$

where $Handler$ is a protocol able to manage printer errors according to their identifier *code*.

Suppose that P is the printer protocol and that the keyword close occurs in P. When invoked by the above client, a service-side session of the form $r \triangleright_{\texttt{fault}} P[\texttt{fault}/\texttt{close}]$ is created, where `fault` is substituted for close. In case of printer failure the protocol P should invoke the service close (instantiated to `fault`), with an error code *err* as a parameter. As effect of this invocation, the whole service-side session r is destroyed. The invocation will instantiate an error recovery session that executes $Handler[\texttt{err}/code]$.

Example 3 (Undergrad advisor service update). Session closing can be used also for service update. Consider, for instance, the following service from a university management system

$$undergradAdvisor \Rightarrow (-)\texttt{Prof. A}$$

that returns the name of current advisor for undergraduates. The service must be updated as soon as the occupancy of this position changes. In the kill-free fragment of SCC reported in Figure 3 there is no way to cancel a definition and replace it with a new one. By contrast, in the full calculus, we can exploit session closing in order to remove services and the interruption handler service can be used to instantiate a new version of the same service. Consider, for instance,

$$r \rhd_{new} \left(\begin{array}{l} undergradAdvisor \Rightarrow (-)\texttt{Prof.A} \mid \\ new\{(-)\mathbf{0}\} \Leftarrow_{new} (update \Rightarrow (y)\textsf{return}\, y) \end{array} \right) \mid$$

$$new \Rightarrow (z) \left(\begin{array}{l} undergradAdvisor \Rightarrow (-)z \mid \\ new\{(-)\mathbf{0}\} \Leftarrow_{new} (update \Rightarrow (y)\textsf{return}\, y) \end{array} \right)$$

The service *update*, when invoked with a new name z, permits to cancel the currently active instance of service *undergradAdvisor* and replace it with a new one that returns the name z. Notice that the service *update* is located within the same session r of the service *undergradAdvisor*; this ensures that when it invokes the interruption handler service *new* the initial instance of the service *undergradAdvisor* is removed.

Other examples that assess the expressive power of SCC can be found in [6] and include also a mapping of Orc into SCC and applications to hotel booking and blog management.

3.2   SOCK: Service Oriented Computing Kernel

SOCK is a three-layered calculus which addresses all the basic mechanisms for service interaction and composition. In particular, SOCK permits to separately deal with all the service design issues, that are decomposed into three fundamental parts: the *behaviour*, the *declaration* and the *composition*. In a few words, the behaviour represents the workflow of a service instance (session), the service declaration introduces the aspects pertaining to execution modalities and, finally, composition allows us to reason about the behaviour of the whole system composed by all the involved services.

One of the main aims of SOCK is to deal with current standards and in particular with the ones related to Web services technologies (WS-BPEL, WSDL and SOAP). Indeed SOCK extends more simple calculi [11,12,18] whose aim was to capture and model the peculiarities of orchestration languages for Web services and, in particular, of WS-BPEL. Consequently, according to WSDL specification, the basic building blocks for service interaction are the two interaction forms supported by Web services: the one-way and the request-response ones. On top of these two simple interaction modalities we can build more complex interactions among participants by means of correlation sets. Such a mechanism follows a data-driven approach to correlate many interactions, thus making it possible to program communication sessions among participants. It is worth noting that communication sessions may involve more than two peers; by communicating correlation sets new participants can enter the communication session. Activities in SOCK can be composed by means of well known WS-BPEL workflow operators like parallel, sequence and two forms of choice, the external one depending on the behaviour of the other services and the internal one where the selected activity depends only on the internal state of the service instance. Finally, as in WS-BPEL, variables are used to track the internal state of SOCK processes.

Example 4 (Course registration service). The following service allows students to register for courses. To this end it accepts `register` messages that contain identifiers for the student and the course. The service replies to the client with either a `cancel` message (if the course is already fully booked or if the student is not eligible to take this course), or with a confirmation. If the course was confirmed the student chooses an exercise group; finally, the registration service notifies the student that he is enrolled for the course and the exercise group. The interface of the Registration service is specified in SOCK as follows:

$$\text{REGISTRATION} = register(\langle student, courseNr\rangle);$$
$$(\overline{cancel}@student(\langle student, courseNr\rangle) +$$
$$(\overline{confirm}@student(\langle student, courseNr\rangle);$$
$$exerciseGroup(\langle student, courseNr, groupNr\rangle);$$
$$\overline{enrolled}@student(\langle student, courseNr\rangle)))$$

The above specification is intended to be non-executable. This because further information must be added in order to indicate how the service interface is actually run by an actual service executor. The information that must be added specifies if different instances of the same service are run either in parallel or sequentially, and how the variables are managed (they can be either persistent, that is they are kept also after the execution of a service instance, or they are volatile).

An actual executor of the Registration service can be specified as follows

$$\text{RegistrationExec} = !(\{student, courseNr\} \triangleright \text{Registration}_\times)$$

where ! (the equivalent of the bang operator of the π-calculus) denotes that different service instances can be run in parallel and the subscript $\times$ indicates that variables are not persistent.

Another relevant information in the specification of the RegistrationExec is the correlation set, given by $\{student, courseNr\}$. Correlation sets are a fundamental information in case of parallel execution of different instances of the same service. In fact, when messages are received by the executor of the service, they must be delivered to the corresponding instance. The correlation set indicates which part of the message is used to identify the correct instance.

Calculus description. The idea in SOCK is that the service design is divided into three steps; the service behaviour defines a process describing the behaviour of a service instance, while the service declaration enriches such a process with some additional information about the execution modality of the service. Such parameters, that are exploited by the service engines, describe whether to allow concurrent execution of service instances or to support persistent state of service instances. Finally, the composition is used to observe the behaviour of services when interacting each other. The SOCK calculus is equipped with an operational semantics expressed by means of a labelled transition system. For space constraints we do not report here the semantics rules that are described in [19]. In the following we report the syntax and an informal description of how SOCK works.

The layer devoted to describe the service behaviour is programmed by using the syntax reported in Fig. 4. **0** is the nil process. Outputs can be a signal $\bar{s}$, the invocation of an operation that can be one-way $\bar{o}@k(\vec{x})$ or request-response $\overline{o_r}@k(\vec{x}, \vec{y})$, where s

$$P, Q ::= \qquad\qquad\qquad\mathbf{0} \qquad\qquad\quad \text{(Nil)}$$
$$\mid \bar{\epsilon} \qquad\qquad\quad \text{(Output)}$$
$$\mid \epsilon \qquad\qquad\quad \text{(Input)}$$
$$\mid x := e \qquad\quad\ \text{(Assign)}$$
$$\mid \chi?P : Q \qquad \text{(If-then-else)}$$
$$\mid P; P \qquad\qquad \text{(Sequence)}$$
$$\mid P \mid P \qquad\qquad \text{(Parallel)}$$
$$\mid \textstyle\sum_{i \in W}^{+} \epsilon_i; P_i \ \text{(Choice)}$$
$$\mid \chi \rightleftharpoons P \qquad\quad \text{(Loop)}$$

$$\epsilon ::= s \mid o(\vec{x}) \mid o_r(\vec{x}, \vec{y}, P)$$
$$\bar{\epsilon} ::= \bar{s} \mid \bar{o}@k(\vec{x}) \mid \overline{o_r}@k(\vec{x}, \vec{y})$$

Fig. 4. SOCK: syntax of processes

is a signal name, o and o_r are operation names, k represents the receiver location and, finally, $\vec{x}$ and $\vec{y}$ are vectors of variables used to store the information passed during the request and the response phase, respectively. Dually, inputs can be an input signal s, a one-way $o(\vec{x})$ or a request-response $o_r(\vec{x}, \vec{y}, P)$ invocation where s is a signal name, o and o_r are operation names, $\vec{x}$ and $\vec{y}$ are, respectively, the vectors of variables used to store the received information and the response and, finally, P is the process that has to be executed between the request and the response. The process $x := e$ assigns the result of the expression e to the variable x. Also, $\chi?P : Q$ is the *if-then-else* process, where χ is a logic condition on variables; if it holds then the process P is executed, otherwise, the process behaves as Q. The processes $P; Q$ and $P \mid Q$ are the standard sequential and concurrent composition of processes P and Q, respectively. $\sum_{i \in W}^{+} \epsilon_i; P_i$ represents the choice operator among input guarded processes and, finally, $\chi \rightleftharpoons P$ is the conditional loop that stops looping on P when the guard χ does not hold. In order to illustrate how SOCK works we use some examples (in the following we complete the services with their corresponding service declaration).

Example 5 (Service behaviour of multiple choice test evaluator). Let us consider the case of a service which keeps track of the score in a multiple choice test. The service suppplies a one-way operation *update* which is invoked every time a question is answered and a request-response operation *cres* that returns the current number of correctly and incorrectly answered questions. The operation *update* expects a parameter indicating whether the question was answered correctly or incorrectly, while *cres* has no parameter. We also introduce a one-way operation *reset* that resets the test results. The service behaviour is defined by the $MultipleChoice$ process:

$$MultipleChoice ::=$$
$$(update(answer);$$
$$(answer = correct) ? nrCorrect := nrCorrect + 1$$
$$: nrFalse := nrFalse + 1)$$
$$+$$
$$cres(\langle\ \rangle, \langle nrCorrect, nrFalse \rangle, \mathbf{0})$$
$$+$$
$$reset(\langle\ \rangle); nrCorrect := 0; nrFalse := 0$$

$$U ::= P_\times \mid P_\bullet \qquad W ::= c \triangleright U \qquad D ::= !W \mid W^* \qquad \text{(Service declaration)}$$

$$Y ::= D[H] \qquad H ::= c \triangleright P_S \qquad P_S ::= (P, \mathcal{S}) \mid P_S \mid P_S \qquad \text{(Service engine)}$$

Fig. 5. SOCK: syntax of service declaration and service engine

As previously mentioned the service behaviour programs session instances, in this case *MultipleChoice* supports three possible behaviours depending on the operation that is invoked: i) *update*: one of the variables used to count the number of correct or false answers is updated, the parameter *answer* determines which one, ii) *cres*: the variables $nrCorrect$ and $nrFalse$, that contain the numbers of correct or false answers, are returned to the invoker, and iii) *reset*: the variables $nrCorrect$ and $nrFalse$ are set to 0.

Example 6 (Service behaviour of orchestration: tutor service). We consider the case of a matchmaking service for private tuition: This service can be used in a course management system to match tutors willing to offer private tuition with students requesting extra tuition. Each offer is identified by an offer id (oId). The process *TutorService*, whose definition follows, defines the skeleton of the service behaviour that orchestrates tutors and students:

$$\begin{aligned}
TutorService ::= \\
requestTuition(oId, accept, offerTuition(oId, accept, \mathbf{0})) \\
+ \\
offerTuition(oId, accept, requestTuition(oId, accept, \mathbf{0}))
\end{aligned}$$

In this process two request-response operations are supported, namely *requestTuition* and *offerTuition*. If the *requestTuition* (resp. the *offerTuition*) operation is selected, the process responds to the invoker when the *offerTuition* (resp. the *requestTuition*) operation is performed and completed. As we will see in the following we exploit oId as a correlation set, in the service declaration, to drive the sessions and join the student and the tutor.

The service declaration consists of the service behaviour and of some parameters describing how to execute the service instances. The syntax is reported in Fig. 5. The term D represents a service declaration while Y represents a service engine. Service declarations are composed by a service behaviour, a flag describing how to manage the internal states of service instances, the set of variables which play the role of correlation set and a flag used to allow concurrent or sequential execution of service instances. In particular, flag $\times$ denotes that P is equipped with a non-persistent state while $\bullet$ denotes the opposite. Also, c is the correlation set which guards the execution of the sessions and, finally, $!W$ denotes a concurrent execution of the sessions while W^* denotes that sessions are executed sequentially. Service engines are used to describe the behaviour of the service during the execution. In particular, they are characterized by a service declaration and by the process H which represents the execution state of the service instances that, if the persistent state is not supported, are equipped with their own state $\mathcal{S}$ while, in the opposite case, they refer to a unique state shared among the instances.

Example 7 (Service declaration of multiple choice service). Now we recall the *MultipleChoice* service behaviour of Example 5 and we conclude its design by describing the service declaration which follows:

$$MultipleChoiceDec ::= \{\; \} \rhd MultipleChoice^*_\bullet$$

In this case the service supports the sequential execution of service instances, the persistent state and does not exploit correlation sets. The persistent state makes it possible to use variables to keep track of the test results; this is because service instances inherit the variables state of the previous service instance execution. It is worth noting that the sequential execution guarantees that variables $nrCorrect$ and $nrFalse$ are managed in a consistent way. Indeed, in the case of concurrent *update* invocations the variables updates are sequentially performed. When we intend to support the concurrent execution of service instances, the service behaviour must be refined by controlling the access to the critical section which updates the variables. This could be done by exploiting, for instance, the internal synchronization primitives.

Example 8 (Service declaration of tutor service orchestration). Now we recall the *TutorService* service behaviour of Example 6 and we conclude its design by describing the service declaration which follows:

$$TutorServiceDec ::= \{oId\} \rhd \; !TutorService_\times$$

In this case the service supports the concurrent execution of service instances and non-persistent state. The correlation set contains oId which is instantiated by the first operation invocation and is exploited in the second one to select the right invocation call (i.e. the one associated to the same offer id). As it emerges by this example, the correlation set mechanism allows to involve a number of peers (in this case the service itself, the student and the tutor clients) within a service instance.

Concluding, the third layer of the calculus allows us to reason about the behaviour of the whole system that, essentially, consists of the parallel composition of service engines. For example, this layer could be used to investigate the behaviour of the system composed by the tutor and student clients and by a *TradingService* orchestration service. Interested readers can find all the details in [19].

4   Stochastic Analysis of Nonfunctional Properties of Service-Oriented Systems

Well-engineered, safe systems need to deliver reliable services in a timely fashion with good availability. For this reason, we view quantitative analysis techniques as being as important as qualitative ones. The quantitative analysis of computer systems through construction and solution of descriptive models is a hugely profitable activity: brief analysis of a model can provide as much insight as hours of simulation and measurement. Jane Hillston's Performance Evaluation Process Algebra (PEPA) [22] is an expressive formal language for modelling distributed systems. PEPA models are constructed by the composition of components which perform individual activities or cooperate on shared ones. To each activity is attached an estimate of the rate at which it may be performed. The rates associated with activities are exponentially distributed random variables thus PEPA is a *stochastic process algebra* which describes the evolution of a process in continuous time.

Using such a model, a system designer can determine whether a candidate design meets both the behavioural and the temporal requirements demanded of it. That is: the service may be secure, but can it be executed quickly enough to perform its function within a specified time bound, with a given probability of success?

4.1   An Application: Scalability Analysis

A growing concern of Web service providers is *scalability*. An implementation of a Web service may be able at present to support its user base, but how can a provider judge what will happen if that user base grows? We present a modelling approach supported by the PEPA process algebra which allows service providers to investigate how models of Web service execution scale with increasing client population sizes. The method has the benefit of allowing a simple model of the service to be scaled to realistic population sizes without the modeller needing to aggregate or re-model the system.

One of the most severe problems a Distributed E-learning and Course Management System (DECMS) has to deal with is the performance degradation occurring when many users are requesting the service simultaneously. Let us imagine a DECMS is available for collecting final course projects of a class. Teaching staff usually put a deadline on those activities, and students are likely to get their projects ready very close to the due date. The DECMS has to cope with a flash crowd-like effect, as server resources (i.e. memory, CPU and bandwidth) have to be shared among a large number of users, thus paving the way for performance penalties experienced by users.

4.2   Setup of the Model

We consider the model in the optimistic scenario where hardware and software failures are assumed to occur sufficiently infrequently that we will not represent them. Further, the server is sufficiently well-provisioned that we may also neglect the possibility failures caused by out-of-memory errors or overrunning the thread limit on the JVM hosting the Web container. We will return to review these optimistic assumptions after we compute performance results from our model.

We conducted experiments to estimate the appropriate numerical values for the parameters used in our model. We implemented a simple Web Service in which SwA was enabled to allow it to save a binary file attached by the client. The implementation of the server interface as well as the method for processing attachments are timed methods, in order to let us gather measurement data on their invocation.

The client makes a designer-tunable number of service calls, the attachment file size being passed as application argument. The designer may also set an inter-message idle period; however, our results were not affected by changes in this parameter.

We restrict our analysis to a case where one single course is being managed. We assume that no other services simultaneously run on the server; thus, the server download capacity c_s as well as server upload capacity μ_s are fully available for the Web Service. The clients' (i.e. students) arrival process is assumed to be well-described by a Poisson distribution with rate λ. The system allows a maximum number of students (course size) N. We assume that all students have the same values for download capacity c_c and upload capacity μ_c. Like the server, we also suppose that no other process but the Web Service client-side application consumes network resources.

When multiple clients are involved, the server has to share its bandwidth among them. A model of the behaviour of the network is therefore necessary. We address this issue by developing a simple model for characterising service performance of the system. In this model we assume an ideal network in which no loss occurs and network nominal *capacity* means *available bandwidth*. We also suppose that transmissions are established on top of TCP connections where fairness against concurrent requests is perfect.

Given the above assumptions, if we denote i $(i > 0)$ as the number of uploading clients at any point in time, the uploading rate of each connection *request* is:

$$request = \min\left\{\frac{c_s}{i}, \mu_c\right\} \tag{1}$$

Similarly, if j is the number of downloading clients (i.e., clients who are receiving the response message), the downloading rate of each connection *response* is:

$$response = \min\left\{\frac{\mu_s}{j}, c_c\right\} \tag{2}$$

4.3   Model Analysis

Model analysis has been carried out by setting local activity rates as they were obtained in our experimental tests. Table 1 shows the complete parameter set. It is worthwhile to observe that network parameters represent bandwidths normalised by the message size being sent. For instance, $c_s = 0.001$ means that the server is able to get the entire message completed in $1000\,\mathrm{s}$; this value resembles a realistic situation where a server equipped with a $10\,\mathrm{Mbps}$ connection has to download a file about $1\,\mathrm{GB}$ long. We also would like to point out that server upload capacity is much faster than its download

Table 1. Parameter set for model analysis

Parameter	Meaning	Rate (s^{-1})
α	*create*	1689.20
β	*attach*	25000.00
γ	*processResponse*	6493.50
θ	*save*	12.33
η	*processRequest*	1290.32
λ	*queue*	20.00
N	Population size	100
c_s	Server download bandwidth	0.001
μ_s	Server upload bandwidth	$c_s/3$
c_c	Client download bandwidth	$(c_s/10) \cdot 10^6$
μ_c	Client upload bandwidth	$c_c/30$

capacity because of the size of the message being transmitted: here we have assumed 1 KB long SOAP response messages in our parameter set. The value of λ is to consider flash crowd-like effect, such that triggered for instance by simultaneous service requests when a deadline is due.

As our model considers client components which perform only one request, transient analysis has to be carried out for evaluating the performance of the system. The traditional approach to attempt this numerical evaluation via transient analysis of a continuous-time Markov chain will not succeed here because the state space of the system is too large. However, as shown in [21], the ODE-based representation of the model offers excellent scalability because the size of the space vector does not change for N varying. The model is shown in Fig. 6.

$$ClientIdle \stackrel{def}{=} (queue, \lambda).ClientUploading$$
$$ClientUploading \stackrel{def}{=} (request, \top).Stop$$
$$Server_0 \stackrel{def}{=} (queue, \top).Server_1$$
$$Server_i \stackrel{def}{=} (queue, \top).Server_{i+1} + (request, \min\{\tfrac{c_s}{i}, \mu_c\}).Server_{i-1}$$
$$(0 < i < N)$$
$$Server_N \stackrel{def}{=} (request, \min\{\tfrac{c_s}{N}, \mu_c\}).Server_{N-1}$$

$$\left(\underbrace{ClientIdle \parallel ClientIdle \parallel \cdots \parallel ClientIdle}_{N} \right) \underset{\{queue, request, response\}}{\bowtie} Server_0$$

Fig. 6. Simplified PEPA model of the DECMS

4.4 Numerical Results

We used the PEPA Workbench [17] to compile the PEPA model to a differential equation form which we could solve using a fifth-order Runge Kutta numerical integrator. In the continuous-space representation performance results could be evaluated at low computational cost. In particular, we required only 0.03 seconds of compute time to obtain a 10^6 seconds time series analysis. We considered a maximum number of users $N = 100$, requesting service according to a flash crowd-like effect at rate $\lambda = 20$. Server download capacity c_s was set to 0.001, and client upload capacity $\mu_c = c_s/30$.

Figure 7 (a) shows a time series plot of the number of client uploading to the server and Figure 7 (b) the initial burstiness of requests. Figure 7 (c) plots service durations for different server bandwidths (i.e., $c_s = 0.01, 0.02$, and 0.1) and Figure 7 (d) plots service durations for different values of N, when $c_s = 0.1$ and $\mu_c = c_s/30$.

Commentary on the results: We note that the system requires a significant amount of time to get every client request completed. Earlier we outlined a series of assumptions about the model setup which included the optimistic assumptions of absence of failure of various kinds, and did not include the possibility of users aborting long-running file uploads only to restart them again later. Since unsuccessful file transfers (of whatever kind) will only tend to delay things more we can safely interpret the results presented

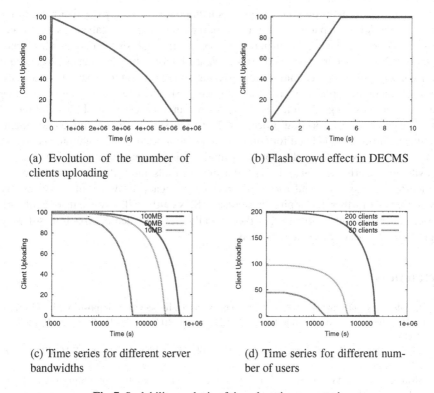

(a) Evolution of the number of clients uploading

(b) Flash crowd effect in DECMS

(c) Time series for different server bandwidths

(d) Time series for different number of users

Fig. 7. Scalability analysis of the e-learning case study

above as saying that even in this very optimistic setting the system is impractical for use and that an alternative design must be tried to support the expected number of student users.

5 Concluding Remarks

In this paper we have presented some of the first results of the SENSORIA project on software Engineering for Service-oriented Overlay Computers. We have focused on process calculi for service-oriented computing and informally explained the session-oriented general purpose calculus SCC for service description, the three layered calculus SOCK inspired by the Web Services protocol stack (WSDL, WS-BPEL, SOAP), and a technique for scalability analysis using the stochastic process calculus PEPA.

But these results represent only a small part of the SENSORIA project. In addition, the SENSORIA project is developing a comprehensive service ontology and a (SENSORIA) Reference Modelling Language (SRML) [16] for supporting service-oriented modelling at high levels of abstraction of "business" or "domain" architectures (similar to the aims of the service component architecture SCA [31]). Other research strands of SENSORIA comprise a probabilistic extension of a Linda-like language for service-oriented computing [8], stochastic extensions of KLAIM [30], and beta-binders [15].

SENSORIA addresses qualitative analysis techniques for security and control of resource usage. A first step towards a framework for modelling and analysing security and trust for services includes trust management and static analysis techniques for crypto-protocols [26,36], security issues on shared space coordination languages [20], secure service composition [1], techniques for ensuring constraints on interfaces between services [29], and autonomic security mechanisms [23]. The results for control resource usage by services range from a flow logic for resource access control [20] and model checking properties of workflow processes [24] to type systems for confining movements of data and processes [13] and for composing incomplete software components [2].

Moreover, SENSORIA is developing a model-driven approach for service-oriented software engineering (see also [35]) and a suite of tools and techniques for deploying service-oriented systems and for re-engineering of legacy software into services. By integrating and further developing these results SENSORIA will achieve its overall aim: a comprehensive and pragmatic but theoretically well founded approach to software engineering for service-oriented systems.

References

1. Bartoletti, M., Degano, P., Ferrari, G.: Security Issues in Service Composition. In: Gorrieri, R., Wehrheim, H. (eds.) FMOODS 2006. LNCS, vol. 4037, pp. 1–16. Springer, Heidelberg (2006)
2. Bettini, L., Bono, V., Likavec, S.: Safe and flexible objects with subtyping. SAC 2005 4(10), 5–29 (2005)
3. Bistarelli, S., Gadducci, F.: Enhancing constraints manipulation in semiring-based formalisms. In: Brewka, G., Coradeschi, S., Perini, A., Traverso, P. (eds.) Proceedings of ECAI 2006, 17th European Conference on Artificial Intelligence. Frontiers in Artificial Intelligence and Applications, vol. 141, pp. 63–67. IOS Press, Amsterdam (2006)
4. Bloch, B., Curbera, F., Goland, Y., Kartha, N., Liu, C.K., Thatte, S., Yendluri, P., Yiu, A.: Web services business process execution language version 2.0. Technical report, WS-BPEL TC OASIS (2005), http://www.oasis-open.org/
5. Bonchi, F., Koenig, B., Montanari, U.: Saturated semantics for reactive systems. In: Proceedings of LICS 2006, 21st Annual IEEE Symposium on Logic in Computer Science, IEEE Computer Society, Los Alamitos (to appear, 2006)
6. Boreale, M., Bruni, R., Caires, L., De Nicola, R., Lanese, I., Loreti, M., Martins, F., Montanari, U., Ravara, A., Sangiorgi, D., Vasconcelos, V., Zavattaro, G.: SCC: a service centered calculus. In: Bravetti, M., Núñez, M., Zavattaro, G. (eds.) WS-FM 2006. LNCS, vol. 4184, pp. 38–57. Springer, Heidelberg (2006)
7. Box, D., Ehnebuske, D., Kakivaya, G., Layman, A., Mendelsohn, N., Nielsen, H.F., Thatte, S., Winer, D.: Simple Object Access Protocol (SOAP) 1.2. W3C Recommendation (June 24, 2003), http://www.w3.org/TR/SOAP/
8. Bravetti, M., Zavattaro, G.: Service Oriented Computing from a Process Algebraic Perspective. Journal of Logic and Algebraic Programming 70(1), 3–14 (2006)
9. Bruni, R., Ferrari, G., Melgratti, H., Montanari, U., Strollo, D., Tuosto, E.: From theory to practice in transactional composition of web services. In: Bravetti, M., Kloul, L., Zavattaro, G. (eds.) Formal Techniques for Computer Systems and Business Processes. LNCS, vol. 3670, pp. 272–286. Springer, Heidelberg (2005)
10. Buscemi, M.G., Montanari, U.: Cc-pi: A constraint-based language for specifying service level agreements. In: Proc. ESOP'07, volume to appear of LNCS (2007)

11. Busi, N., Gorrieri, R., Guidi, C., Lucchi, R., Zavattaro, G.: Choreography and Orchestration: a synergic approach for system design. In: Benatallah, B., Casati, F., Traverso, P. (eds.) ICSOC 2005. LNCS, vol. 3826, pp. 228–240. Springer, Heidelberg (2005)
12. Busi, N., Gorrieri, R., Guidi, C., Lucchi, R., Zavattaro, G.: Choreography and Orchestration conformance for system design. In: Ciancarini, P., Wiklicky, H. (eds.) COORDINATION 2006. LNCS, vol. 4038, pp. 63–81. Springer, Heidelberg (2006)
13. De Nicola, R., Gorla, D., Pugliese, R.: Confining data and processes in global computing applications. Science of Computer Programming 63(1), 57–87 (2006)
14. De Nicola, R., Katoen, J.-P., Latella, D., Massink, M.: STOKLAIM: A Stochastic Extension of KLAIM. TR 2006-TR-01, ISTI (2006)
15. Degano, P., Prandi, D., Priami, C., Quaglia, P.: Beta-binders for biological quantitative experiments. In: ENTCS - Proceedings of QAPL, 4th Workshop on Quantitative Aspects of Programming Languages, 2006 (to appear, 2006)
16. Fiadeiro, J.L., Lopes, A., Bocchi, L.: A formal approach to service component architecture. In: Bravetti, M., Núñez, M., Zavattaro, G. (eds.) WS-FM 2006. LNCS, vol. 4184, pp. 193–213. Springer, Heidelberg (2006)
17. Gilmore, S., Hillston, J.: The PEPA Workbench: A Tool to Support a Process Algebra-based Approach to Performance Modelling. In: Haring, G., Kotsis, G. (eds.) Computer Performance Evaluation. LNCS, vol. 794, pp. 353–368. Springer, Heidelberg (1994)
18. Guidi, C., Lucchi, R.: Mobility mechanisms in service oriented computing. In: Gorrieri, R., Wehrheim, H. (eds.) FMOODS 2006. LNCS, vol. 4037, pp. 233–250. Springer, Heidelberg (2006)
19. Guidi, C., Lucchi, R., Busi, N., Gorrieri, R., Zavattaro, G.: SOCK: a calculus for service oriented computing. In: Dan, A., Lamersdorf, W. (eds.) ICSOC 2006. LNCS, vol. 4294, pp. 327–338. Springer, Heidelberg (2006)
20. Hansen, R.R., Probst, C.W., Nielson, F.: Sandboxing in myKlaim. In: The First Internat. Conference on Availability, Reliability and Security, ARES 2006 (2006)
21. Hillston, J.: Fluid flow approximation of PEPA models. In: Proceedings of the Second International Conference on the Quantitative Evaluation of Systems, Torino, Italy, September 2005, pp. 33–43. IEEE Computer Society Press, Los Alamitos (2005)
22. Hillston, J.: A Compositional Approach to Performance Modelling. Cambridge University Press, Cambridge (1996)
23. Koshutanski, H., Martinelli, F., Mori, P., Vaccarelli, A.: Fine-grained and history-based access control with trust management for autonomic grid services. In: Proceedings of the 2nd International Conference on Automatic and Autonomous Systems (ICAS'06), Silicon Valley, California, July 2006, IEEE Press, Orlando (2006)
24. Kovács, M., Gönczy, L.: Simulation and formal analysis of workflow models. In: Bruni, R., Varro, D. (eds.) Proc. of the Fifth International Workshop on Graph Transformation and Visual Modeling Techniques. ENTCS, Elsevier, Amsterdam (2006)
25. Lapadula, A., Pugliese, R., Tiezzi, F.: A calculus for orchestration of web services. In: Proc. of ESOP'07, volume to appear of LNCS (2007)
26. Martinelli, F., Petrocchi, M.: A uniform framework for the modeling and analysis of security and trust. In: Proc. of 1st Workshop on Information and Computer Security- ICS 2006. ENTCS, Elsevier, North-Holland (to appear, 2006)
27. Milner, R., Parrow, J., Walker, D.: A calculus of mobile processes. Inform. and Comput. 100(1), 1–40 (1992)
28. Misra, J., Cook, W.R.: Computation orchestration: A basis for wide-area computing. Journal of Software and Systems Modeling (to appear, 2006)
29. Nielson, H.R., Nielson, F.: Data flow analysis for CCS. Festschrift dedicated to Reinhard Wilhelm's 60. birthday (2006)

30. De Nicola, R., Katoen, J.P., Latella, D., Massink, M.: STOKLAIM: A Stochastic Extension of KLAIM. TR 2006-TR-01, ISTI (2006)
31. SCA Consortium. Service Component Architecture, version 0.9. Specification, 2005 (Last visited: June 2006), download.boulder.ibm.com/ibmdl/pub/software/dw/specs/ws-sca/SCA_White_Paper1_09.pdf
32. SENSORIA. Software Engineering for Service-Oriented Overlay Computers. Web site at http://www.sensoria-ist.eu
33. van der Aalst, W.M.P., ter Hofstede, A.H.M., Kiepuszewski, B., Barros, A.P.: Workflow patterns. Distributed and Parallel Databases 14(1), 5–51 (2003)
34. W3C. Web Services Description Language (WSDL) 1.1. http://www.w3.org/TR/wsdl
35. Wirsing, M., Clark, A., Gilmore, S., Hölzl, M., Knapp, A., Koch, N., Schroeder, A.: Semantic-Based Development of Service-Oriented Systems. In: Najm, E., Pradat-Peyre, J.F., Donzeau-Gouge, V.V. (eds.) FORTE 2006. LNCS, vol. 4229, pp. 24–45. Springer, Heidelberg (2006)
36. Zunino, R., Degano, P.: Handling exp, × (and timestamps) in protocol analysis. In: Aceto, L., Ingólfsdóttir, A. (eds.) FOSSACS 2006 and ETAPS 2006. LNCS, vol. 3921, pp. 413–427. Springer, Heidelberg (2006)

Global Grids - Making a Case for Self-organization in Large-Scale Overlay Networks

Torsten Eymann, Werner Streitberger, and Sebastian Hudert

Chair of Information Systems Management
Universitätsstrasse 30
University of Bayreuth, Germany
{eymann,streitberger,hudert}@uni-bayreuth.de

Abstract. Grid computing has recently become an important paradigm for managing computationally demanding applications, composed of a collection of services. The dynamic discovery of services, and the selection of a particular service instance providing the best value out of the discovered alternatives, poses a complex multi-attribute n:m allocation decision problem, which is often solved using a centralized resource broker. To manage complexity, this article proposes a two-layered architecture for *decentralized* service discovery in such Application Layer Networks (ALN). The first layer consists of a service market in which complex services are translated to a set of basic services, which are distinguished by price and availability. The second layer provides an allocation of services to appropriate resources in order to enact the specified services. This framework comprises the foundations for a later comparison of centralized and decentralized market mechanisms for allocation of services and resources in ALNs and Grids in general.

1 Introduction

This article describes an investigation in implementing an electronic Grid market based on the "Catallaxy" concept of F.A. von Hayek. Catallaxy describes a "free market" economic self-organization approach for electronic services brokerage, which can be implemented for realizing resource allocation in ALNs. The term ALN comprises network concepts, such as Grid and Peer-2-Peer (P2P) systems, which overlay the existing physical Internet topology. In ALNs, participants offer and request application services and computing resources of different complexity and value - creating interdependent markets.

In this article, the complex interdependencies are broken down into two types of interrelated markets:

- a service market - which involves trading of application services, and
- a resource market - which involves trading of computational and data resources, such as processors, memory, etc.

U. Montanari, D. Sannella, and R. Bruni (Eds.): TGC 2006, LNCS 4661, pp. 51–68, 2007.

This distinction between resource and service is necessary to allow different instances of the same service to be hosted on different resources. It also enables a given service to be priced based on the particular resource capabilities that are being made available by some hosting environment. In such interrelated markets, allocating resources and services on one market inevitably influences the outcome on the other market.

A common approach of many other Grid market concepts is to allocate resources and services by relying on the presence of centralized resource/service brokers. However, the complex reality could turn such approaches useless, as the underlying problem is computationally demanding and the number of participants in a worldwide ALN can be huge. The research question taken up in this article is *how* to develop a Grid realization of an economic concept, which describes the ability to trade electronic services in a decentralized fashion, a free-market economy to adjudicate and satisfy the needs of participants who are self-organized and follow their own interest.

The Catallaxy concept represents a coordination approach for systems consisting of such autonomous decentralized agents, and is based on constant negotiation and price signalling between agents [7]. Every individual (agent) assigns a value to service access information, and by exchanging bids for service access, the price signals carry information between individuals (agents) about the knowledge of others [9]. This exchange of information applies even across markets, as changing availability on the resource market will be reflected by cascading price changes for those basic services which rely on such resources. Hayek called this feature a "tele-communication" system in its literal sense. The huge size of Grids to be controlled, and the availability of software agent technology, makes implementing Hayek's Catallaxy an alternative to a centralized allocation approach, using the ensuing "spontaneous order" as a concrete proposal for both the design and coordination of information systems. The resulting multi-agent system will be highly dynamic, thereby leading to Grid networks which behave in a P2P fashion. The term P2P should be interpreted not as a specific system architecture, but as a general approach for distributed system design that can be realized under very different architectures and topologies, ranging from unstructured distributed networks to very centralized systems [16]. P2P systems exhibit a set of characteristics that are relevant from the architectural point of view [23]:

- Decentralization: there is no single or centralized coordination or administration point.
- Symmetric interaction between peers: all peers are simultaneously clients and servers requesting service of, and providing service to, their network peers.
- Non-deterministic topology: At any moment in time, the set of member nodes and overall topology of the network is unpredictable.
- Heterogeneity: The devices contributing applications can differ in many properties such as resource characteristics, performance or trustworthiness.

– Communication paths between peers are created dynamically based on various factors, like network conjunction or intermediate peers' state.

These characteristics, when considered together, lead to a set of stringent architectural requirements for self-organization. The dynamic nature of the network prevents an a priori configuration of the peers, or the maintenance of centralized configuration files. The peers need to continuously discover the network characteristics and adapt accordingly. This requires a distribution of some important system functions like resource and topology management, traditionally reserved to specialized nodes.

2   Principles of the Catallaxy

Friedrich August von Hayek [10] and other Neo-Austrian economists understood markets as decentralized coordination mechanisms, as opposed to a centralized command economy control. In addition to macroeconomic thoughts, Hayek's work also provides concrete insight into the working mechanisms of economic coordination. However, a formal description of this self-organizing market mechanism does not exist so far. The Catallaxy concept is based on the explicit assumption of self-interested actions of the participants, who try to maximize their own utility and choose their actions under incomplete information and bounded rationality [24]. The term Catallaxy originates from the Greek word "katallatein", which means to barter and at the same time to join a community. The goal of Catallaxy is to arrive at a state of coordinated actions, through the bartering and communicating of members, to achieve a community goal that no single user has planned for. The main characteristics of the Catallaxy [11] are enumerated below. Each property imposes several requirements upon the design of an information system embodying a Catallactic approach:

– Participants work for their own interest to gain income. Every system element is a utility maximizing entity, supporting means to measure and compare income and utility, and to express a desire to reach a defined goal.
– Participants can only estimate the effect of action alternatives on an income or utility maximization goal, as nobody has total knowledge and foresight of the environment. Instead, "constitutional ignorance" of the rationally bounded participants makes it inevitably impossible to know the exact environment state. For large and very dynamic information systems, this observation leads to a design shift. Instead of trying to overcome this limitation by central means, e.g. through synchronization of the system by introducing round-based brokerage, the focus shifts to improving the computational intelligence of the actions to decide under uncertainty, and to adapt to constantly changing signals from the outside.
– Participants communicate using commonly accessible markets, where they barter about access to resources held by other participants. The development of prices for a specific good, relative to alternatives, and whether they are increasing or decreasing, leads buyers to look for alternative sources of

procurement and thus enhances the dynamics of the market. In that view, a market is simply a communication bus; not a central optimization component, or a mechanism or a protocol.

Hayek's Catallaxy concept is the result of descriptive, qualitative research about economic decision-making of human participants. In the following section, its results are taken literally to construct ALN markets with software participants, who reason about economic decisions using artificial intelligence.

3   Prototyping the Catallaxy

This section will pick up the requirements of the Catallaxy described above and will present fundamental components to satisfy these requests in ALNs. Starting with a decomposition of the application scenario into two distinctive markets, needed functionality and components are identified. A formal model is given describing how to achieve Catallaxy in a global Grid environment. Subsequently, a Grid middleware architecture for trading services and resources and a corresponding application scenario are presented.

3.1   A Two Layer ALN of Services and Resources

ALNs encompass heterogeneous resources, computational and data services in different administrative domains, which are logically coupled. ALNs will depend on basic services that are dynamically combined to form value-added complex services [12]. For their enactment, these basic services require a set of resources, which need to be co-allocated to provide the necessary computing power (like in computational Grids). The orchestration and configuration of these basic services and resources itself can be understood as an inherent service. Such orchestration should be hidden from the application, and managed through the middleware. The environment is thus divided into two layers, the application layer and the resource layer presented in Figure 1. These two layers contain three different roles, which are:

- complex services (application layer),
- basic services (application layer and resource layer), and
- resources (resource layer).

Complex services act as service consumers. They request one or more basic services for the fulfillment of their tasks. Basic services are service providers at the application layer. They also provide an interface to access computational resources used by complex services. Finally, resource providers offer resources, which basic services acting as resource consumers use for executing their services. In both layers, the participants have varying objectives which change dynamically and unpredictably over time.

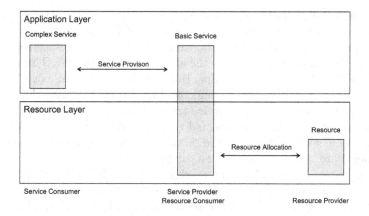

Fig. 1. An application layer network - layers and roles

3.2   Market Model

Current Grid Computing architectures exhibit a fairly static resource infrastructure, connected by physically stable links. The shift to a pervasive, ubiquitously accessible Grid demands for a more dynamic consideration of resources and connections. Figure 2 shows a perspective on a two-layered Grid Market, encompassing a distinct service and a resource market corresponding to the two-layer model above.

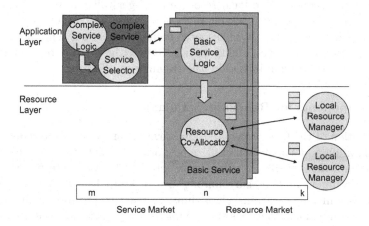

Fig. 2. Catallaxy-based Grid Market Model

A complex service is represented by a proxy who needs basic service capabilities for execution - supporting a service selector instance. Complex services are therefore shielded from details of the resource layer implementation. A basic service is split into the basic service logic and a resource allocator. The logic is able to negotiate with the complex service and to translate the requirements for service execution to resource instances (e.g. CPU, storage and quality of service requirements). A resource allocator gets the resource specification and broadcasts the respective demand to the local resource managers. This comprises bundles and co-allocative negotiations. Bundles are understood as an n-tuple of resource types (e.g. CPU, storage, and bandwidth); co-allocation describes obtaining resources for one single service transaction from various local resource managers simultaneously. It is expected that a local resource manager hides all details of the local allocation. On the service market, complex service and basic service negotiate; an agent managing a complex service acts as a buyer, the basic service agent as a seller. The same market roles can be found at the resource layer, the resource allocator is the buyer agent, the local resource manager acts as a seller agent. Contemplating the second market, it is a n:k market; n basic service copies are able to bargain with k resource services. This takes dynamic resources into account. Resources, like basic services, can fail and are subject to maintenance and inspection procedures.

Integration of the Markets. Offering a basic service within a Catallaxy-based Grid market, it is necessary to contract the required resources. First the basic service bargains with the complex service and in a second step, the basic service negotiates for resources. For service execution the basic service logic requests a resource bundle. The further process of contracting/allocating the resource is done by the resource co-allocator. The selection of a resource bundle is analogous to the selection of a service on the service market, with the exception that a bundle is requested, whereas on the service market only one service can be negotiated per request. The local resource managers offer resource bundles. A resource bundle is a tuple consisting of resources such as bandwidth, CPU, and storage (for instance). The local resource manager acts as a seller agent of the resource market, having the ability to negotiate with the resource co-allocator. The negotiation itself is initiated by the resource co-allocator.

3.3   Components for Realizing Catallaxy

For realization of the Catallaxy paradigm, several components are required. For the preparation and calculation of price proposals, a negotiation module is modelled and implemented that constitutes the interface between internal perception of the environment and the surrounding (sensor and effector). The negotiation strategy uses machine learning algorithms, to react to changes in the environment and to implement methods that adapt to the behaviour of the surrounding agents.

Negotiation. As a basic principle, the negotiation strategy constitutes a search process in a space of potential agreements. The number of search dimensions is identical to the number of negotiation attributes. Thus, a negotiation comprising quality of service, delivery time, and price, spans a 3-dimensional search space. In several cases, it is possible to collapse various attributes into the one criteria "price", for example when delivery time affects the buyer's usage and therefore justifies a change of price.

An automatic negotiation in an electronic market is shaped by an interaction of two or more software agents. These negotiations can be accomplished by integrative or distributive negotiation [13][18]. In integrative negotiations, participants exchange information about objectives and priorities to seek a common solution. This concept is recommended if the opponents have to accept the negotiation dimensions which cannot be represented by prices. This postulates a cooperation of the opponents for reaching the agreed target. Distributive negotiations imply a participant's step-by-step acceptance of concessions, bringing both opponents closer in their expectations in every negotiation round. Distributive negotiations are marked by existence of a common utility space [18] that can be represented by a price. Thus, distributive negotiations give the option to reduce the negotiation dimensions and are therefore selected for this work. This should result in a zero-sum game, where the utility one looses can be gained by the opponents and the global utility in the systems remains constant. The goal is a system wide pareto-optimum that can be defined as an acceptable doctrine of general goodness [20]: A solution X is pareto-optimal if no agent can further ameliorate the achieved result without discriminating an opponent. That implies that if solution X is not pareto-optimal, both agents could negotiate a deviating solution that promises pareto-optimality. Sandholm [21] extends this approach by introducing various additional criteria for the optimality determination: from game theory he uses the Nash-equilibrium that emerges if no agent has an incentive to diverge from its chosen selection. Translated to prices, this means that Pareto-optimality is a state in which no agent can increase its budget without decreasing the budget of other agents (compare zero-sum game). Utility can be understood as budget increase per transaction and per period, sales volume or other metrics are taken from Economics.

The implementation of Catallaxy uses efforts from both agent technology and economics, notably agent-based computational economics [26]. Autonomous software agents negotiate with each other using an alternating offers protocol [20] and adapt their negotiation strategies using feedback learning algorithms (evolutionary algorithms, Numerical optimization e. g. Nelder/Meads simplex method [17], hybrid methods e.g. Brenners VID model [3]). Ongoing communication by using price signalling leads to constant adaptation of the system as a whole and propagates changes in the scarcity of resources throughout the system. The resulting patterns are comparable to those witnessed in human market negotiation experiments [14][18][25].

Setup and Variables Definition. The negotiation strategy described here is based on the AVALANCHE strategy [5][6]. The strategy consists of 5 basic parameters, which define the individual behavior (genotype) of each agent.

For every tradeable good there are two types of agents, buyers and sellers. Let agent k be a buyer and agent v a seller of a tradeable good.

Let i_k be the number of negotiations that agent k has started and i_v the number of negotiations that agent v has started. It is irrelevant how many negotiations were finished successfully.

A genotype defines the behavior of the agents in the negotiation strategy. Let the genotype of agent k during his negotiation i_k be

$$G_k^{i_k} \in [0; 1]^5$$

with

$$G_k^{i_k} = (G_{k,1}^{i_k}, \ldots, G_{k,5}^{i_k})^\tau = (a_k^{i_k}, s_k^{i_k}, t_k^{i_k}, b_k^{i_k}, w_k^{i_k})^\tau$$

where

$a_k^{i_k}$	acquisitiveness
$s_k^{i_k}$	satisfaction
$t_k^{i_k}$	priceStep
$b_k^{i_k}$	priceNext
$w_k^{i_k}$	weightMemory.

Acquisitiveness defines the probability of sticking with the last offer made, and not to make an unilateral concession in the following negotiation step. The value interval is between 0 and 1, and will be challenged by a stochastic probe in every negotiation step. A value of 0.7 means a probability of 70% that the agent will not make a concession – a highly competitive strategy. An agent with acquisitiveness value 1.0 will never change his price and an agent with *acquisitiveness* value 0.0 will always make an unilateral concession. If the probe succeeds, a buyer agent will rise his offer, a seller agent will lower his price.

The exact change of the bid value is defined by the concession level (*priceStep*). The concession level is represented by a percentage of the difference between the initial starting prices. A value of *priceStep* = 0.25 means a computation of the concession level as 1/4 of the first stated difference. If both opponents are homogenously negotiating and always concede, they meet each other on the half way in the third negotiation round under the assumption of no negotiation abortion.

Obviously, with an *Acquisitiveness* level set high, and a *priceStep* set low enough, the opponents might never reach an agreement. The *Satisfaction* parameter determines if an agent will drop out from an ongoing negotiation. The more steps the negotiation takes, or the more excessive the partner's offers are, the sooner the negotiation will be discontinued. Effectively, this parameter creates time pressure. Like for *Acquisitiveness*, it does this by doing a stochastic probe against a set value between 0 and 1. A *satisfaction* value of 0.75 means, that the agent has a chance of 75% to continue the negotiation process. An agent with *satisfaction* = 0.0 will abort all negotiation at once and an agent with *satisfaction* = 1.0 will never abort.

The next piece of the strategy is an expression of selfishness. Behind each successful negotiation lies a future opportunity for gaining more of the utility share, by negotiating harder. *priceNext* thus modifies the starting bid. A successful seller will increase his offer price, a successful bidder will start with a lower bid next time.

For a viable strategy, the participants will have a close eye on what others deem to be the market price. If not, they risk being tagged as "excessive" and their bids will fail the *satisfaction* probe. They thus weigh current price information and historic price information in a specified ratio *weightMemory*, balancing short-time price fluctuation and longer-term opportunities.

In a formal representation, the genotype of an agent v during his negotiation i_v is

$$G_v^{i_v} \in [0;1]^5$$

with

$$G_v^{i_v} = (G_{v,1}^{i_v}, \ldots, G_{v,5}^{i_v})^\tau = (a_v^{i_v}, s_v^{i_v}, t_v^{i_v}, b_v^{i_v}, w_v^{i_v})^\tau.$$

At the beginning of the simulation the genes $G_{*,j}^{i_*}$ for $* = k, v$ and $j \in \{1, \ldots, 5\}$ are distributed according to the probabilities:

$$\mathrm{Ufo}([m_j - \delta_j ; m_j + \delta_j])$$

Thereby, the constants m_j and δ_j for $j \in \{1, \ldots, 5\}$ are defined so that $[m_j - \delta_j ; m_j + \delta_j] \subset [0;1]$.

Additionally, the agent k has the following variables:

$M_k^{i_k}$ is the market price, which is estimated by agent k during his negotiation i_k.

$P_k^{i_k}$ is the price of the the the last *successful* negotiation $1, 2, \ldots, i_k$ of agent k.

$O_k^{i_k}$ is the last offer, which the negotiation opponent has made in negotiation number i_k the agent k before the negotiation ended.

$p_k^{i_k}$ is the number of stored plumages of agent k direct after his negotiation i_k.

The related variables of agent v are defined in the same way. These variables build the basis for decision making during a negotiation.

The Negotiation Strategy. When agent k and agent v negotiate, agent k is the buyer and agent v the seller. The sequence $(P_j)_{j \in \mathbb{N}_0} \subset [0, \infty[$ constitutes the offer in chronological order. The buyer always makes the first offer. This means, all offers

$$P_{2m} \qquad \forall m \in \mathbb{N}_0$$

originate from the buyer and the offers

$$P_{2m+1} \qquad \forall m \in \mathbb{N}_0$$

come from the seller, where

$$m$$

is the negotiation round.

At the beginning of a negotiation the buyer k determines his initial price $\underline{K}$ and his maximum price $\overline{K}$:

$$\underline{K} = M_k^{i_k} \cdot (1 - b_k^{i_k}), \qquad \overline{K} = M_k^{i_k}$$

The seller v determines his starting price $\overline{V}$ and his minimum price $\underline{V}$:

$$\overline{V} = M_v^{i_v} \cdot (1 + b_v^{i_v}), \qquad \underline{V} = M_v^{i_v}$$

The buyer starts with the first bid:

$$P_0 = \underline{K}$$

First Case: $\underline{K} \geq \overline{V}$
Then v offers also

$$P_1 = \underline{K}$$

and the negotiation will be closed successfully to the price P_1.

Second Case: $\underline{K} < \overline{V}$
Then v offers his initial price

$$P_1 = \overline{V} .$$

Both agents determine now her steps δ_*^{j*} for price concessions:

$$\delta_*^{i*} = (\overline{V} - \underline{K}) \cdot t_*^{i*} \qquad \text{for} \quad * = k, v$$

In the subsequent negotiation rounds, let $A_1, A_2, A_3, \ldots$ and $S_1, S_2, S_3, \ldots$ be stochastic independent random variables with the following binomial distributions:

$$A_{2m} = \begin{cases} 1 \text{ with probability } a_k^{i_k} \\ 0 \text{ with probability } 1 - a_k^{i_k} \end{cases} \qquad \forall\, m \in \mathbb{N}$$

$$A_{2m+1} = \begin{cases} 1 \text{ with probability } a_v^{i_v} \\ 0 \text{ with probability } 1 - a_v^{i_v} \end{cases} \qquad \forall\, m \in \mathbb{N}$$

$$S_{2m} = \begin{cases} 1 \text{ with probability } s_k^{i_k} \\ 0 \text{ with probability } 1 - s_k^{i_k} \end{cases} \qquad \forall\, m \in \mathbb{N}$$

$$S_{2m+1} = \begin{cases} 1 \text{ with probability } s_v^{i_v} \\ 0 \text{ with probability } 1 - s_v^{i_v} \end{cases} \qquad \forall\, m \in \mathbb{N}$$

- Offer number $2m$; it is the buyer's k turn:
  If $S_{2m} = 0$ and $P_{2m-1} \geq P_{2(m-1)-1}$ with $m \neq 1$, then the buyer k cancels the negotiation. This means, $O_k^{i_k} = P_{2m-1}$ and $O_v^{i_v} = P_{2(m-1)}$.
  Otherwise, the buyer k makes the following offer:

$$P_{2m} = \left(\min \{\overline{K}, (P_{2(m-1)} + \delta_k^{i_k}), P_{2m-1}\} \right)^{1 - A_{2m}} .$$

$$\left(P_{2(m-1)} \right)^{A_{2m}}$$

- Bid number $2m + 1$; it is the seller's v turn:

If $S_{2m+1} = 0$ and $P_{2m} \leq P_{2(m-1)}$, then the seller v cancels the negotiation. That means, $O_v^{i_v} = P_{2m}$ and $O_k^{i_k} = P_{2(m-1)+1}$.

Otherwise the seller v makes the following offer:

$$P_{2m+1} = \left(\min \left\{ \underline{V}, \ (P_{2(m-1)+1} - \delta_v^{i_v}), \ P_{2m} \right\} \right)^{A_{2m+1}} \cdot$$

$$\left(P_{2(m-1)} \right)^{1 - A_{2m+1}}$$

The negotiation ends if either one of the agents cancels the negotiation or the negotiation ends successfully with

$$P_j = P_{j+1}$$

for a $j \in \mathbb{N}$. In this case, it holds $O_k^{i_k} = P_j = O_v^{i_v}$.

With the end of a *successful* negotiation to the price P_j the negotiation compute their estimated *profit*

$$\Pi_k^{i_k} = M_k^{i_k} - P_j \qquad \text{respectively} \qquad \Pi_v^{i_v} = P_j - M_v^{i_v} . \qquad (1)$$

Additionally, both agents update after *every* negotiation their estimated market price using

$$M_k^{i_k+1} = w_k^{i_k} \cdot O_k^{i_k} + (1 - w_k^{i_k}) \cdot M_k^{i_k}$$

respectively

$$M_v^{i_v+1} = w_v^{i_v} \cdot O_v^{i_v} + (1 - w_v^{i_v}) \cdot M_v^{i_v} .$$

This last step is independent of the success of a negotiation.

Gossip Learning. The learning concept used in this simulation is derived from so-called gossip learning. This means that the agents learn from received information about other transactions in the market. This information may not be accurate or complete, but serves as an indication about the gross direction of the market. In our implementation, this gossip information is created and broadcast by a successful agent, in analogy to issuing an ad-hoc information in stock market periodicals.

Let n be an agent and

$$g_1, \ldots, g_d$$

the tradeable goods. The agent n has finished his negotiation i_n successfully with an estimated profit of $\Pi_n^{i_n}(g)$ for the good $g \in \{g_1, \ldots, g_d\}$. A *learning* step according to the learning algorithm (see next paragraph) is performed by agent n last time at the end of his negotiation j_k. This means

$$G_n^{j_n+1} = G_n^{j_n+2} = \cdots = G_n^{i_n} .$$

If agent n with the negotiation numbers

$$j_n + 1, j_n + 2, \ldots, i_n$$

has successfully completed at least 10 negotiations for every good, he sends a *Plumage*

$$(G_n^{i_n}, F_n^{i_n})$$

to all other agents of his type. Then, his updated *fitness* is $F_n^{i_n}$, which is computed like the following:

(a) For every good $g_j \in \{g_1, \ldots, g_d\}$ the next profit value $\Pi(g_j)$ is determined t: Let be

$$\Pi_1(g_j), \ldots, \Pi_{10}(g_j)$$

the estimated profits of the last 10 successful negotiations of agent n for the good g_j. Then, the fitness is

$$F_n^{i_n}(g_j) = \frac{1}{10}\Big(\Pi_1(g_j) + \cdots + \Pi_{10}(g_j)\Big).$$

(b) The updated fitness $F_n^{i_n}$ finally is

$$F_n^{i_n} = \frac{1}{d}\Big(\Pi(g_1) + \cdots + \Pi(g_d)\Big).$$

The agents used in the simulations for this report are only able to negotiate one type of good ($d = 1$).

The Learning Algorithm. It is assumed that the agents show a cooperative behavior. This means, the agents report truthfully their learning information.

After having received some gossip information message, an agent may modify his own strategy. Comparing his own results with those of the strategy received, can lead to recognizing that the other strategy is much better than his own. In this case, the agent will try to cross both strategies to gain competitive advantage. In practice, out of a list of received genotype/performance-tuples, the agent will choose the best performing external genotype, and then mix, cross and mutate with his own genotype.

Let be n an arbitrary agent at the end of his negotiation i_n and let be $p_n^{i_n}$ the number of plumages, the agent n has stored directly after his negotiation i_n. The last *learning* step was performed by agent n after his negotiation j_k. Let be $e_n^{i_n}$ the number of negotiations, an agent n of the negotiation numbers

$$j_n + 1, j_n + 2, \ldots, i_n$$

has successfully finished.

Let be

$$p = 1. \tag{2}$$

If

$$p_n^{i_n} < p \qquad \text{or} \qquad e_n^{i_n} < 10$$

applies for agent n after his negotiation i_n, no *learning* step will be performed. This means, his genotype will not change:

$$G_n^{i_n+1} = G_n^{i_n}.$$

Hence, if

$$p_n^{in} \geq p \quad \text{and} \quad e_n^{in} \geq 10$$

applies, the agent n performs a *learning* step. The genotype of agent n changes like the following:

First, the stored plumage of agent n with the highest fitness is selected. Let be

$$G_f = (G_{f,1}, \ldots, G_{f,5})^\tau = (a_f, s_f, t_f, b_f, w_f)^\tau$$

the related genotype. Second, a *crossover* is performed. In doing so, a new genotype $\tilde{G}_n^{in+1}$ is created, which contains a random mixture of genes of the genotypes G_n^{in} and G_f. This process follows a *mutation* step third: Using the genotype $\tilde{G}_n^{in+1}$ and changing its genes slightly will result in the genotype G_n^{in+1}.

Crossover. Let be $C_1, \ldots, C_5$ stochastic independent random variables with the following binomial distribution:

$$C_j = \begin{cases} 1 \text{ with probability} \quad 0,5 \\ 0 \text{ with probability} \quad 0,5 \end{cases} \quad \forall j \in \{1, \ldots, 5\}$$

Then it is imperative

$$\tilde{G}_{n,j}^{in+1} = (1 - C_j) \cdot G_{n,j}^{in} + C_j \cdot G_{f,j} \quad \forall j \in \{1, \ldots, 5\}.$$

Mutation. Let be $M_1, \ldots, M_5, X_1, \ldots, X_5$ stochastic independent random variables with the following distributions:

$$M_j = \begin{cases} 1 \text{ with probability} \quad 0,05 \\ 0 \text{ with probability} \quad 0,05 \end{cases} \forall j \in \{1, \ldots, 5\}$$

$$X_j \sim \mathcal{N}(0, 1) \quad \forall j \in \{1, \ldots, 5\}$$

That means, X_j is $\forall j \in \{1, \ldots, 5\}$ standard normal distributed. Then, it holds

$$G_{n,j}^{in+1} = \max \left\{ 0 \, ; \, \min \left\{ \tilde{G}_{n,j}^{in+1} + \right. \right.$$

$$\left. \left. M_j \cdot ((\frac{1}{10} X_j) \bmod(1)) \, ; \, 1 \right\} \right\}$$

$\forall j \in \{1, \ldots, 5\}.$

3.4   Middleware Implementation

The Catallactic Grid market middleware has been envisioned as a set of economic agents that interact with each other using the strategy presented before, and the software components of the underlying ALN. This acts as a coordination technique and makes use of economic criteria for the assignment of resources, as can be seen in Figure 3.

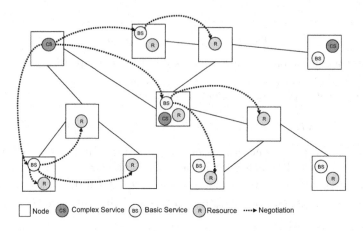

Fig. 3. Catallactic Grid market middleware as a network of agents

This high-level middleware structure would be applicable to all P2P network architectures. Instead of implementing Catallactic agents responsible for both the self-organization of the system and the management of the negotiation process, a layered architecture is implemented (see Figure 4). In this architecture, economic agents are responsible for implementing high level behaviour (negotiation, learning, adaptation to environment signals, strategies of other agents). Application services delegate activities such as negotiation to the economic agents. Economic agents rely on a lower P2P agent layer for self-organization of the system, and the interaction with the base platform that ultimately manages the resources being traded.

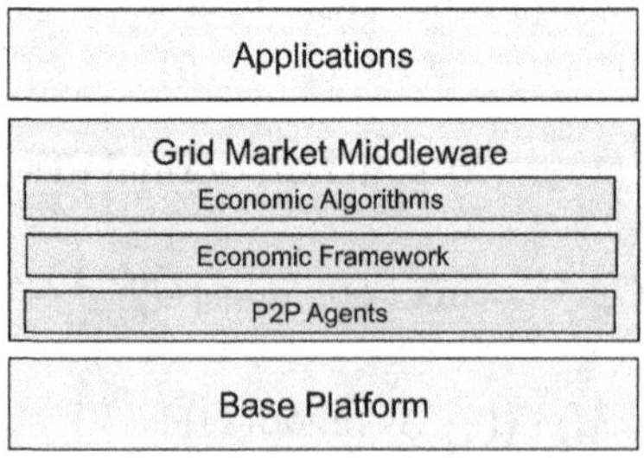

> **Applications**
>
> **Grid Market Middleware**
> Economic Algorithms
> Economic Framework
> P2P Agents
>
> **Base Platform**

Fig. 4. Grid market middleware - Layered architecture

This architectural approach offers the direct benefit of a clear separation of concerns between the layers, helping in tackling the complexity of the system and facilitating the construction of a more adaptable system as the upper layers can be progressively specialized (by means of rules and strategies used in the negotiations) to specific application domains. A detailed description of the middleware architecture can be found in [1][8].

4 Engineering the Market Scenario

The decentralized negotiation protocols following the Catallaxy paradigm will be compared with centralized auction protocols. Two extreme scenarios serve as benchmarks. One scenario is characterized by standardized commodities, whereas the other allows for highly heterogeneous goods. For a reasonable benchmark in the centralized approach, one has to find adequate auction protocols for both scenarios. Unfortunately, the environment and the underlying auction protocol exert crucial effects on the outcome. For instance, in a sealed bid auction the bidders simultaneously submit bids to the auctioneer without knowledge of the amount bid by other participants. In contrast, all bids under an open cry auction are available for everyone to see. Thus, in a sealed bid auction the participants do not learn as much about the valuations of the other participants as in an open cry auction. The higher information feedback may affect the bidding behaviour of the market participants and could therefore lead to different outcomes. As such, designing a market mechanism that achieves a desired outcome is extremely difficult, because it entails the anticipation of agent behaviour. In order to approach this task, a systematic Market Engineering approach guides the design of tailored market mechanisms by providing a structured and theoretically profound procedure. This approach provides a process model which is divided into four stages:

In the first stage - the environmental analysis - the requirements of the new market mechanism (i.e. which are the potential participants, what are their preferences, endowments, and constraints?) are deduced. On base of the requirements, a market mechanism is designed and implemented in the second stage. Having deployed the appropriate market mechanism, it is tested upon its economic properties and its operational functionality in the third stage and finally introduced within the fourth stage. While the market engineering approach has originally been invented for designing auction markets, many of its findings also apply for bargaining markets, especially the environmental analysis. The main difference lies in the second stage, the design of the allocation mechanism.

4.1 A Mechanism for the Service Market

Applying the Market Engineering approach to the service market, the environment has to be analyzed in the first step. Subsequently, the corresponding requirements have to be extracted. The environment comprises the market participants. Basically, buyers and sellers are services, such as basic services acting as sellers and complex services acting as buyers. The basic services offer one or more specific auxiliary services. Hence, they are responsible for providing the auxiliary services to the buyers as well as for acquiring the required resources for the services on the resource market. The products traded on the service market are completely standardized. For example, an instance of a PDF creator traded once does not differ from a PDF creator instance traded at a later time. Based upon the environment definition, the requirements for a market mechanism can be summarized as follows:

- Simultaneous trading: The mechanism requires that multiple sellers and multiple buyers can trade simultaneously.
- Immediate execution: It requires that suitable buyer orders are executed immediately against suitable seller orders.
- No partial execution: It requires that orders are not partially executed.

Following these requirements, a continuous double auction fits these requirements for the centralized market and serves as a comparable mechanism for the decentralized negotiation schema.

4.2   A Mechanism for the Resource Market

In a resource market, participants are the basic services as resource consumers (buyers) and resource services (sellers) offering computer resources. The transaction objects are computational resources with specific capacity, e.g. processing power. Capacity is allocated based on time slots, and the same resources (e.g. CPUs) can differ in their quality attributes, e.g. a hard disk can have 30GB or 200GB of space. Requirements for the resource market are [22]:

- Simultaneous trading: In analogy to the service market, the mechanism has to support simultaneous trading of multiple buyers and sellers, as well as an immediate resource allocation.
- Bundle orders: The mechanism has to support bundle orders - i.e. all-or-nothing orders on multiple resources - as basic services usually demand a combination of computer resources. This is based on the fact that computer resources (e.g. in the Computational Grid) are complementarities. Complementarities are resources with super additive valuations, as the sum of the valuations for the single resources is less than the valuation for the whole bundle.
- Multi-attribute orders: For comprising the different capacities of the resources (i.e. resources can differ in their quality), the mechanism has to support bids on multi-attribute resources. Reviewing the requirements and surveying the literature, no classical auction mechanism is directly applicable to the centralized resource market. Instead, there is a need for a multi-attribute combinatorial exchange that satisfies the described requirements.

When comparing to the service market, the challenges for the bargaining mechanism are the high number of messages needed to establish a bundle trade - this is going to be part of the evaluation, whether the higher communication overhead will outperform the lacking scalability of the centralized mechanism.

5   Conclusion

This paper has introduced the components of a decentralized market mechanisms for dynamic application layer networks. The Catallaxy by F.A. von Hayek serves as a basic principle for a decentralized market approach. This approach is translated into the decentralized market model for the CATNETS project. The comparison of both approaches is on one hand supported by applying a structured Market Engineering approach to both market designs. On the other hand, the foundation for the implementation techniques and the middleware are layered in order to achieve comparable results from both approaches in the future. The work is accompanied by reference and application scenarios. Future work includes the full implementation of both market approaches and a profound evaluation of the results of both markets. Critical questions are the scalability of market mechanisms and the allocation efficiency under constraints of the number of participating entities. As an acceptable system-wide performance matrix is impossible to define, an economics-based paradigm for the management or resource allocation and orchestration will be used.

Acknowledgments

This work has partially been funded by the EU in the IST programme "Future and Emerging Technologies" under grant FP6-003769 "CATNETS".

References

1. Ardaiz, O., Chacin, P., Chao, I., Freitag, F., Navarro, L.: An Architecture for Incorporating Decentralized Economic Models in Application Layer Networks. In: Proceedings of the International Workshop in Smart Grid Technologies, Utrecht, Nederlads (July 25 - 29 2005)
2. Balakrishnan, I., Kaashoek, M.F., Karger, D., Morris, R., Stoica, I.: Looking up data in P2P systems. Communications of the ACM 46(2), 43–48 (2003)
3. Brenner, T.: A behavioural learning approach to the dynamics of prices. Computational Economics, pp. 67–94 (2002)
4. Buyya, R.: Economic-based Distributed Resource Management and Scheduling for Grid Computing; Ph.D. Thesis, Monash University, Melbourne, Australia (2002)
5. Eymann, T., Schoder, D., Padovan, B.: Avalanche - an agent based value chain coordination experiment. In: Workshop on Artificial Societies and Computational Markets (ASCMA 98), Minneapolis, pp. 48–53 (1998)
6. Eymann, T.: Decentralized economic coordination in multi-agent systems. In: Buhl, H.-U., Huther, F., Reitwiesner, A. (eds.) Information Age Economy. Proceedings WI-2001, pp. 575–588. Physica Verlag, Heidelberg (2001)
7. Eymann, T., Sackmann, S., Müller, G., Pippow, I.: Hayek's Catallaxy: A Forward-looking Concept for Information Systems. In: Proc. of American Conference on Information Systems (AMCIS'03), Tampa, FL (2003)
8. Freitag, F., Navarro, L., Chacin, P., Ardaiz, O., Chao, I.: Integration of Decentralized Economic Models for Resource Self-Management in Application Layer Networks. In: Proceedings of the Second IFIP TC6 International Workshop on Autonomic Communication, Athens, Greece (October 3-5, 2005)
9. Hayek, F.A.V.: The Use of Knowledge in Society. American Economic Review XXXV(4), 519–530 (1945)
10. Hayek, F.A.V., Bartley, W.W., Klein, P.G., Caldwell, B.: The collected works of F.A. Hayek. University of Chicago Press, Chicago (1989)

11. Hoppmann, E.: Unwissenheit, Wirtschaftsordnung und Staatsgewalt. In: Freiheit, Wettbewerb und Wirtschaftsordnung, Vanberg, V. (eds.) Haufe Verlag, Freiburg, pp. 135–169 (1999)
12. Huhns, M.N., Singh, M.P.: Service-oriented computing: Key concepts and principles. IEEE Internet Computing 9(1), 75–81 (2005)
13. Jennings, N.R., Faratin, P., Lomuscio, A.R., Sierra, C., Wooldridge, M.J.: Automated negotiation: prospects, methods and challenges. International Journal of Group Decision and Negotiation 10(2), 199–215 (2001)
14. Kagel, J.H., Roth, A.E.: The handbook of experimental economics. Princeton University Press, Princeton (1995)
15. Krauter, K., Buyya, R., Maheswaran, M.: A taxonomy and survey of grid resource management systems for distributed computing. Software-Practice & Experience 32(2), 135–164 (2002)
16. Milojicic, D.S., Kalogeraki, V., Lukose, R., Nagaraja, K., Pruyne, J., Richard, B., Rollins, S., Xu, Z.: Peer-to-Peer Computing; Hewlett Packard Labs, Palo Alto HPL-2002-57 (2002)
17. Press, W.H., Teukolsky, W.H.: Numerical Recipes in C++ - The Art of Scientific Computing. Cambridge University Press, Cambridge, MA (2002)
18. Pruitt, D.G.: Negotiation behavior. Academic Press, New York (1981)
19. Ripeanu, M., Iamnitchi, A., Foster, I.: Mapping the Gnutella network. Ieee Internet Computing 6(1), 50–57 (2002)
20. Rosenschein, J.S., Zlotkin, G.: Rules of encounter - designing conventions for automated negotiation among computers. MIT Press, Cambridge (1994)
21. Sandholm, T.W.: Negotiation Among Self-Interested Computationally Limited Agents, Ph.D. Thesis. University of Massachusetts, Amherst (1996)
22. Schnizler, B., Neumann, D., Weinhardt, C.: Resource Allocation in Computational Grids - A Market Engineering Approach. In: Proc. of The 3rd Workshop on e-Business (WeB), Washington, D.C., US (2004)
23. Sewell, P., Leifer, J., Nestmann, U., Serjantov, A., Wansbrough, K.: Required foundations for peer-to-peer systems; PEPITO Project IST-2001-33234, Cambridge, UK D1.1, 01.06.2003 (2003)
24. Simon, H.A.: Models of Man - Social and Rational. John Wiley & Sons, New York (1957)
25. Smith, V.L.: An experimental study of competitive market behavior. Journal of Political Economy 70, 111–137 (1962)
26. Tesfatsion, L.: How economists can get alife. In: The Economy as a Evolving Complex System II. Arthur, W.B., Durlauf, S., Lane, D.A. (Hrsg.), pp. 533–564 (1997)
27. Weinhardt, C., Holtmann, C., Neumann, D.: Market Engineering. Wirtschaftsinformatik 45(6), 635–640 (2003)
28. Zhao, B.Y., Kubiatowicz, J.D., Joseph, A.D.: Tapestry: A fault-tolerant wide-area application infrastructure. Computer Communication Review 32(1), 81–81 (2002)

Software of the Future Is the Future of Software?

Paola Inverardi

Dipartimento di Informatica,
Università dell'Aquila
inverard@univaq.it

Abstract. Software in the near ubiquitous future (Softure) will need to
cope with variability, as software systems get deployed on an increasingly
large diversity of computing platforms and operates in different execution environments. Heterogeneity of the underlying communication and
computing infrastructure, mobility inducing changes to the execution
environments and therefore changes to the availability of resources and
continuously evolving requirements require software systems to be adaptable according to the context changes. Softure should also be reliable and
meet the user's performance requirements and needs. Moreover, due to its
pervasiveness, Softure must be dependable, which is made more complex
given the highly dynamic nature of service provision. Supporting the development and execution of Softure systems raises numerous challenges
that involve languages, methods and tools for the systems thorough design and validation in order to ensure dependability of the self-adaptive
systems that are targeted. However these challenges, taken in isolation
are not new in the software domain. In this paper I will discuss some
of these challenges, what is new and possible solutions making reference
to the approach undertaken in the IST PLASTIC project for a specific
instance of Softure focused on software for Beyond 3G (B3G) networks.

1 Introduction

Software in the near ubiquitous future (Softure) will need to cope with variability,
as software systems get deployed on an increasingly large diversity of computing
platforms and operates in different execution environments. Heterogeneity of
the underlying communication and computing infrastructure, mobility inducing
changes to the execution environments and therefore changes to the availability
of resources and continuously evolving requirements require software systems
to be adaptable according to the context changes. At the same time, Softure
should be reliable and meet the user's performance requirements and needs.
Moreover, due to its pervasiveness, Softure must be dependable, which is made
more complex given the highly dynamic nature of service provision.

Supporting the development and execution of Softure systems raises numerous
challenges that involve languages, methods and tools for the systems thorough
design and validation in order to ensure dependability of the self-adaptive systems that are targeted.

U. Montanari, D. Sannella, and R. Bruni (Eds.): TGC 2006, LNCS 4661, pp. 69–85, 2007.

However these challenges, taken in isolation are not new in the software domain. Adaptable and re-configurable systems do exist in many software application domains from tele-communication to the software domain itself, e.g. operating systems. Dependable systems have been intensively investigated and methods and tools exist to develop them. Hence what are the new challenges for Softure? In this paper I will discuss some of these challenges and possible solutions making reference to the approach undertaken in the IST PLASTIC [1] project for the specific instance of Softure as software for Beyond 3G (B3G) networks. I will try to highlight what I consider innovative and futurist for software and what I simply consider software for the future. The ultimate thesis of this paper is that Softure requires to rethink the whole software engineering process and in particular it needs to reconcile the static view with the dynamic view.

The paper is structured as follows. In the following section I discuss the Softure characteristics in order to identify the two key challenges: *adaptability* and *dependability*. Section 3 discusses and compares different notions of adaptability with different degrees of dependability. This discussion will bring me to consider the Softure issues in a software process perspective. Section 4 proposes a new software process and discusses it in the scope of the PLASTIC project [1].

2   Softure Challenges: Setting the Context

Softure is supposed to execute in an ubiquitous, heterogeneous infrastructure under mobility constraints. This means that the software must be able to carry on operations while changing different execution environments or *contexts*. Execution contexts offer a variability of resources that can affect the software operation. *Context awareness* refers to the ability of an application to *sense* the context in which it is executing and therefore it is the base to consider (Self-) adaptive applications, i.e. software systems that have the ability to change their *behavior* in response of external changes.

It is worthwhile stressing that although a change of context is measured in terms of availability of resources, that is in quantitative terms, an application can only be adapted by changing its behavior, i.e. its functional/qualitative specification. In particular, (Physical) Mobility allows a user to move out of his proper context, traveling across different contexts. To our purposes the difference among contexts is determined in terms of available resources like connectivity, energy, software, etc. However other dimensions of contexts can exist relevant to the user, system and physical domains, which are the main context domains identified in the literature [2]. In the software development practice when building a system the context is determined and it is part of the (non-functional) requirements (operational, social, organizational constraints). If context changes, requirements change therefore the system needs to change. Context changes occur due to physical mobility, thus while the system is in operation. This means that if the system needs to change this should happen dynamically. This notion leads to consider different ways to modify a system at run time that can happen in different forms namely *(Self-)adaptiveness/dynamicity/evolution* and at different levels of granularity, from software architecture to line of code.

Softure needs also to be dependable. *Dependability* is an orthogonal issue that depends on Quality of Service (QoS) attributes, like performance and all other—bilities. Dependability impacts all the software life cycle.

In general dependability is an attribute for software systems that operate in specific application domains. For Softure I consider dependability in its original meaning as defined in [3], that is *the trustworthiness of a computing system which allows reliance to be justifiably placed on the service it delivers ... Dependability includes such attributes as reliability, availability, safety, security.* Softure encompasses any kind of software system that can operate in the future ubiquitous infrastructure. The dependability requirement is therefore extended also to applications that traditionally have not this requirement. Dependability in this case represents the user requirement that states that the application must operate in the unknown world (i.e. out of a confined execution environment) with the same level of reliance it has when operating at home. At home means in the controlled execution environment where there is complete knowledge of the system behavior and the context is fixed. In the unknown world, the knowledge of the system is undermined by the absence of knowledge on contexts, thus the dependability requirement arises also for conventional applications. Traditionally dependability is achieved with a comprehensive approach all along the software life cycle from requirements to operation to maintenance by analyzing models, testing code, monitor and repair execution.

Therefore the overall challenge is to provide dependable assurance for highly adaptable applications. Since dependability is achieved throughout the life cycle many software artifacts are involved, from requirements specification to code. In the rest of this paper I will consider as such artifacts only *models* that is idealized view of the system suitable for reasoning, developing, validating a real system. Models can be functional and non-functional and can represent different level of abstractions of the real system, from requirements to code. My research bias is on Software Architecture, therefore I will often consider software architectural systems' models. An architectural model allows the description of the static and dynamic components of the system and explains how they interact. Software architectures support early analysis, verification and validation of software systems. Software architectures are the earliest comprehensive system model along the software lifecycle built from requirements specification. They are increasingly part of standardized software development processes because they represent a system abstraction in which design choices relevant to the correctness of the final system are taken. This is particularly evident for dependability requirements like security and reliability and quantitative ones like performance.

3   Adaptability: 3 Examples from My Own Bag

In this section I discuss the notion of adaptability. According to what presented so far, adaptability is the ability to change a system according to context variations, e.g. driven by QoS requirements. However, the change should maintain the *essence* of the system that from now on I will call *invariant*.

In Sections 3.2, 3.3, and 3.4, I will focus on evolving systems that change through adaptation. In order to classify them I propose to use a 4 dimension metric: the four *Ws*.

3.1   The Four Ws

The systems I consider can change through adaptability either their *structure* and/or their *behavior*. The four Ws characterize the nature of the change along the following four dimensions:

- *Why* there is the need to change?
- *What* does (not) change?
- *When* does the change happen?
- *What/Who* manages the change?

Why: This dimension makes explicit the need for the change. In a Software Engineering perspective this change is always done to meet requirements. It can be because the requirements evolved or it can be that the system does not behave properly according to the stated requirements. It is also worthwhile mentioning that requirements can be functional and non functional requirements. The former class captures the qualitative behavior of a software system, its functional specification. The latter defines the systems's quantitative attributes like, performance, reliability, security, etc. In the following I will provide 3 examples of functional and non functional adaptation that have been developed in the Software Engineering research group at University of L'Aquila.

What: Here we discuss the part of the system that is affected by the change. Referring to architectural models, changes can affect the structure and/or the behavior. For the structure, components can get in and out, new connectors can be added and removed. For the behavior components can change their functionality and connectors can change their interaction protocols.

When: This dimension captures the moment during the systems lifetime in which the change occurs. It does not mean that the change happens necessarily at run time. This dimension is related with the Static versus Dynamic issue.

What/Who: This is the description of the mechanisms to achieve the change. It can be a configuration manager or it can be the system itself. Involves monitoring the system to collect relevant data, evaluating this data, make a decision about the change alternatives and then perform the actual change.

3.2   Synthesis

Synthesis is a technique equipped with a tool that permits to assemble a component based application in a deadlock free way [35,21,34]. Starting from a set of Commercial Off The Shelf (COTS) components, Synthesis assembles them together according to a so called connector-based architecture by synthesizing a connector that guarantees deadlock-free interactions among components. The code that implements the new component representing the connector is derived, in an automatic way, directly from the COTS (black-box) components interfaces. Synthesis assumes a partial knowledge of the components' interaction behavior described as finite state automata plus the knowledge of a specification of the system to assemble given in terms of Message Sequence Charts [18,19,20].

Furthermore it is possible to go beyond deadlock if we have a specification of the behavioral integration failure to be avoided. This specification is an implicit failure specification. Actually we assume to specify all the assembled system behaviors which are failure-free rather than to explicitly specify the failure. Under these hypotheses Synthesis automatically derives the assembling code of the connector for a set of components. The connector is derived in such a way to obtain a failure-free system. It is shown that the connector-based system is *equivalent* according to a suitable equivalence relation to the initial one once depurated of all the failure behaviors.

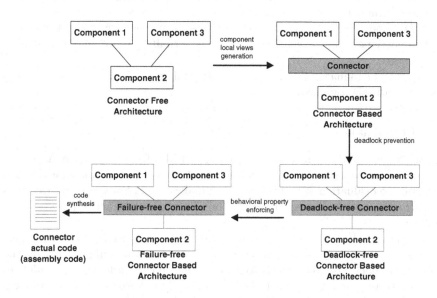

Fig. 1. The Synthesis Application Adaptation

As illustrated in Figure 1, the Synthesis framework realizes a form of system adaptation. The initial software system is *changed* by inserting a new component, the connector, in order to prevent interactions failures.

The framework makes use of the following models and formalisms. An architectural model, the connector-based architecture that constrains the way components can interact, by forcing interaction to go through the connector. A set of behavioral models for the components that describe each single component's interaction behavior with the external context in the form of label transition systems (LTS). A behavioral equivalence on LTS to establish the equivalence among the original system and the adapted one. Temporal logic to specify the behavioral integration failure to be avoided, and then Buchi Automata and model checking to synthesize the failure-free connector specification. From the connector specification the actual code can then be automatically derived.

Let us now analyze the Synthesis approach to adaptation by means of the four *Ws* metric:

- *Why* there is the need to change? Here the purpose of the change is to correct functional behavior. That is to avoid interaction deadlocks and/or enforce a certain interaction property P. This adaptation is not due to change of context, since it is not driven by quantitative parameters. The change here aims at correcting a functional misbehavior.
- *What* does (not) change? It changes the topological structure and the interaction behavior. A new component is inserted in the system and the overall interaction behavior is changed. The invariant part of the system is represented by all the correct behaviors. The proof that the adaptation preserves the invariant is by construction.
- *When* does the change happen? It happens at assembly time, thus prior to deployment and execution. Thus it is actually part of the development process.
- *What/Who* manages the change? An external entity: The developer through the Synthesis framework.

3.3   Performance

The work presented in this section, discusses PFM a framework to manage performance of software system at runtime based on monitoring and model-based performance evaluation [17]. The approach makes use of Software Architectures as abstractions of the managed application also at run time when the system is operating.

The framework monitors the performance of the application and, when a performance problem occurs, it decides the new application configuration on the basis of feedback provided by the on-line evaluation of performance models of several reconfiguration alternatives. The main characteristic of this approach is the way such alternatives are generated. In fact, differently from other approaches we do not rely on a fixed repository of predefined configurations but, starting from the data retrieved by the on-line monitoring (that represents a snapshot of the system current state), we generate a number of new configurations by applying the rules defined within the reconfiguration policy. Once such alternatives have been generated we proceed to the on-line evaluation by predicting which one of them is most suitable for resolving the problem occurred. In particular, the choice of the new system configuration might consider several factors, such as, for example, security and reliability of the application, and resources needed to implement the new configuration.

In this approach performance evaluation models are used to predict the system performance of the next system reconfiguration alternative. To this aim, each eligible system configuration is described by means of a predictive model instantiated with the actual values observed over the system until the moment of the performance alarm. The models are then evaluated and on the basis of the obtained results the framework decides the reconfiguration to perform over the software system. Therefore, the predictive models representing the software system alternatives are evaluated at run time and this poses strong requirements on the models themselves. PMF has been experimented to manage the performance of the SIENA publish/subscribe middleware [7,6]. The experiment shows that the usage of predictive models improves the decision step. The system reconfigured with the chosen alternative has better performance than the other alternatives generated during the reconfiguration process. The configuration alternatives we experimented all deal with structural changes of the SIENA network topology in order to improve messages routing.

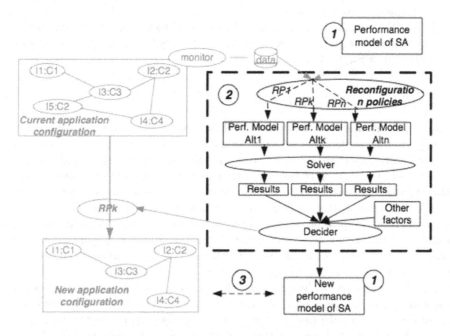

(b) Flow of the activities in an adaptation step

Fig. 2. Adaptation for performance

In Figure 2 the PMF components are represented. It is worthwhile stressing that all the described 4 steps are carried on at run time, while the system is operating. Note that predictive models are commonly used to carry on quantitative analysis at development time, while the system is under construction [9]. Their use at execution time raises a number of challenging research issues like: what data are relevant to collect? The collected data is more fine-grained than the performance model parameters, how can data be used? Models have to be modified and evaluated online this means that they must require fast solution techniques. However fast solution techniques usually apply for simple predictive models, then which performance model should be used? How is the decision on the next configuration taken? The answers to all these questions should consider different aspects like security, resources availability, and so on.

Let us now consider PMF with the four Ws metric:

- *Why* there is the need to change? The change aims to correct non-functional behavior, i.e. adjust Performance. This change is context dependent.
- What does (not) change? In the SIENA experiment the topological structure is going to be modified, while the overall behavior is kept equivalent. That is the change does not affects the routing capabilities of the SIENA network.
- When does the change happen? The change happens at run time, while the system is operating and it is enacted trough run time monitoring of performance parameters.
- What/Who manages the change? An external to the system entity, that is the PMF framework provides support to the whole re-configuration process as shown in Figure 2.

3.4   Resource Aware Applications

This framework aims at developing and deploying (Java) adaptable application. It supports the development of applications that are *generic* and can be correctly adapted with respect to a dynamically provided context, which is characterized in terms of available (hardware or software) resources, each one with its own characteristics. To attack this problem we use a declarative and deductive approach that enables the construction of a generic adaptable application code and its correct adaptation with respect to a given execution context [8,10,11]. Inspired by Proof Carrying Code (PCC) [12,15] techniques, we have defined a formal setting which enables us to reason about Java program adaptability with respect to resource usage. We use first-order logic formulas to model the code behavior with respect to the resources which characterize the execution context. The adaptation process is carried out by using theorem proving techniques that try to derive a formal proof that the code behavior can be correctly adapted to the given context. Provided that the proof exists, by construction it gives information on how the adaptation has to be done. The adapted code is thus by construction certified to correctly work with respect to the execution context resources availability. In Figure 3 we show the components of the framework's architecture.

The *Development Environment* is a standard Java development environment where the developer can write applications. We only assume that the applications are written according to some framework programming guidelines that easy their (generic) management. The output of this step is an extended Java program representing a generic program.

The *Abstract Resource Analyzer* produces from the application written in the *Development Environment* a declarative description of its characteristics in terms

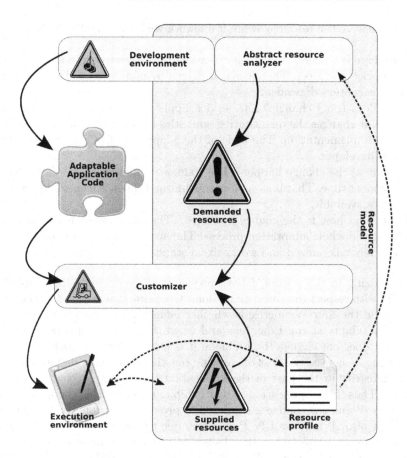

Fig. 3. Adaptation for resource consumption

of resource demands. It is an abstract semantics that interprets the applications with respect to a well defined *Resource Model*, and extracts the information according to that model.

The *Customizer* carries out the actual adaptation of the application before deploying it in the target environment for execution. This step produces a standard Java application.

The *Execution Environment* can be any device that will host the execution of the application. Typically the *Execution Environment* will be provided by Personal Digital Assistants (PDA), mobile phones, smart phones, etc. From this point of view, the *Execution Environment* is not strictly part of the framework we are presenting here. However it must be characterized by a declarative description of the resources it provides that we assume to be provided by the component itself.

The *Resource Model* characterizes resources and provides metrics to allow reasoning on the adaptation in order to be able to choose the *"best"* one according to the adaptation policy.

Let us analyze the resource aware framework with the four Ws metric:

- Why there is the need to change? The change allows to correctly utilize the host device resources. Therefore it is driven by non functional requirements and it is context dependent.
- What does (not) change? The service/application core behavior does not change. It changes the quantitative semantics (resource consumption) of the service implementation. The logic of the adaptation has been programmed by the developer.
- When does the change happen? The framework manages the adaptation at deployment time. That is as soon as the information on the execution context becomes available.
- What/Who how is the change managed? The deployment framework carries out the whole adaptation process. The application when in execution is completely customized and works like a standard Java application.

Summarizing in this section I have presented three examples of adaptation that differ with respect to several dimensions. One issue that is raised by the *when* dimension in the four Ws metric is whether *adaptability* is static or dynamic. The system adapts at run time, how and when the adaptation is computed or carried out does not change the problem, it is just a matter of *cost*. The cost I am referring to here is the cost of carrying out the adaptation maintaining the original integrity of the part of the application that does not change, i.e. the *invariant*. Thus if the application A that exhibits property P is changed into an application A' and the change is supposed to preserve the property P, then this means that also A' must satisfy P. For example the property P could be type integrity, thus we require that the change does not undermines type integrity in the changed application. Obviously, in this case, carrying out the change statically, i.e. before the system is running permits to prove type integrity of A' in a less expensive way than if done at run time.

4 Softure: The Process View

In this section I cast the above discussed challenges in a process view. The process view focusses on the set of activities that characterize the production and the operation of a software system. These activities are traditionally divided into activities related to the actual production of the software system and activities that are performed when the system can be executed and goes into operation. Specification, Design, Validation, and Evolution activities vary depending on the organization and the type of system being developed. Each Activity requires its Language, Methods and Tools and works on suitable artifacts of the system. For validation purposes each artifact can be coupled with a *model*. Models are an idealized view of the system suitable for reasoning, developing, validating a real system. To achieve dependability a large variety of models are used from behavioral to stochastic. These models represent the systems at very different levels of abstraction from requirements specification to code. The ever growing complexity of software has exacerbated the dichotomy development/static/compile time versus execution/dynamic/interpreter time concentrating as many analysis and validation activities as possible at development time.

Softure puts new requirements on this standard process. The evolutionary nature of Softure makes unfeasible a standard approach to validation since it would require before the system is in execution to predict the system behavior with respect to virtually any possible change. Therefore in the literature most approaches, that try to deal with the validation of dynamic software systems, concentrate the changes to the structure by using graph and graph grammars formalisms or topological constraints [25,23,22,24,26,27]. As far as changes to behavior are concerned, only few approaches exist that make use either of behavioral equivalence checks or of the type system [4,28,29] or through code certification [12,30]. If dependability has to be preserved through adaptation whatever the change mechanism is, at the time the change occurs, a validation check must be performed. This means that all the models necessary to carry on the validation step must be available at run time and that the actual validation time becomes now part of the execution time.

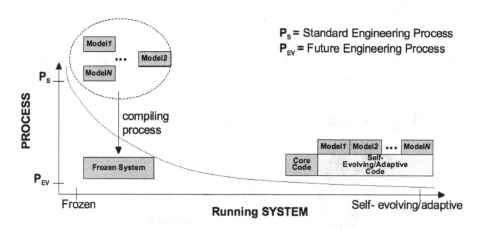

Fig. 4. The Future Engineering Process

The Future development process therefore has to explicitly account for complex validation steps at run time when all the necessary information are available. Figure 4 represents the process development plane delimited on one side by the standard process and on the other side by the future development one. The vertical dimension represents the static versus dynamic time with respect to the analysis and validation activities involved in the development process. The horizontal axis represents the amount of adaptability of the system, that is its ability to cope with evolution still maintaining dependability. The standard development process carries out most of the development and validation activities before the system is running that is during development. The result is a running system that, at run time, is frozen with respect to evolution. Considering development processes that allow increasingly degrees of adaptability permits to move along the horizontal axis thus ideally tending to a development process that is entirely managed at run time. In the middle we can place development processes that allow larger and larger portions of the system to change at run time and that make use for validation purposes of artifacts that can be produced statically. In the following section I introduce an instance of the Future Engineering Process that has been proposed in the scope of the PLASTIC project.

4.1 PLASTIC

The PLASTIC project aims to offer a comprehensive provisioning platform for software services deployed over B3G networks (see Figure 5). A characteristic of this kind of infrastructure is its heterogeneity, that is it is not possible to assume that the variety of its components' QoS is homogenized through a uniform layer. PLASTIC aims at offering B3G users a variety of application services exploiting the network's diversity and richness, without requiring systematic availability of an integrated network infrastructure. Therefore the PLASTIC platform needs to enable dynamic adaptation of services to the environment with respect to resource availability and delivered QoS, via a development paradigm based on Service Level Agreements and resource-aware programming.

The provided services should meet the user demand and perception of the delivered QoS, which varies along several dimensions, including: type of service, type of user, type of access device, and type of execution network environment.

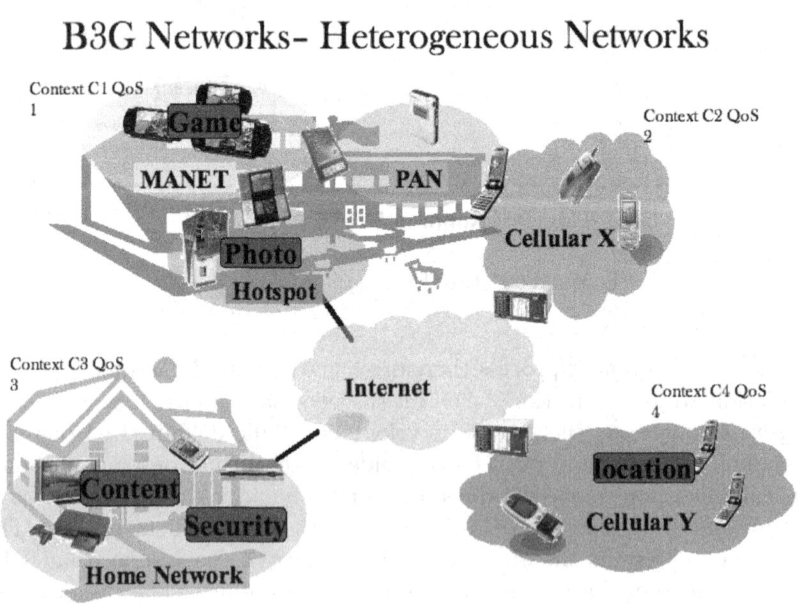

Fig. 5. B3G Networks

Referring to the challenges discussed in Section 2, this means that services must be *dependable* according to the users expected QoS.

This demands for a software engineering approach to the provisioning of services, which encompasses the full service life cycle, from development to validation, and from deployment to execution.

The PLASTIC answer to the above needs is to offer a comprehensive platform for the creation and provisioning of lightweight, adaptable services for the open wireless environment. Supporting the development of resource-aware and self-adapting components composing adaptable services requires focusing on the QoS properties offered by services besides the functional ones. The whole development environment is based on the PLASTIC Conceptual Model [1]. Recently, several approaches to conceptualize the world of services have been proposed. The PLASTIC model takes the move from the SeCSE conceptual model [31,32] that it has been suitably extended to reflect all the concepts related to B3G networks and service provision in B3G networks. In particular it focusses on the following key concepts:

— *Service level agreement* that clearly set commitment assumed by consumers and providers and builds on services descriptions that are characterized functionally, via a service interface and non-functionally via a Service Level Specification *SLS*.

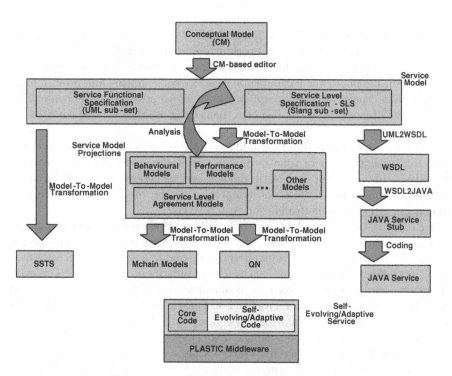

Fig. 6. The PLASTIC Development Process

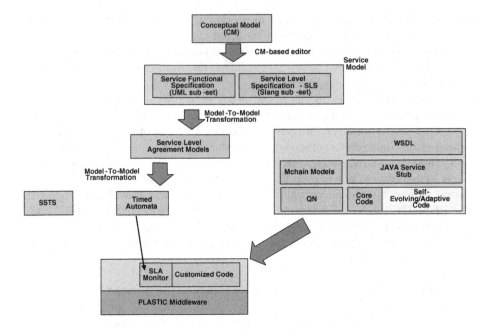

Fig. 7. The PLASTIC Deployment Process

– *Context awareness and adaptation* as the context is a key feature distinguishing services in the vast B3G networking environment. B3G networking leads to have diverse user populations, changing availability in system resources, and multiple physical environments of service consumption and provisioning. It is then crucial that services adapt as much as possible to the context for the sake of robustness and to make themselves usable for given contexts.

As illustrated in Figure 6 adaptability is achieved by transferring some of the validation activities at run time by making available models for different kind of analysis. In particular stochastic models and behavioral ones will be made available at run time to allow the adaptation of the service to the execution context and service on line validation, respectively.

In PLASTIC all the development tools will be based on the conceptual model exploiting as much as possible model-to-model transformations. The definition of a service will consists of a functional description and of a Service Level Specifications that defines the Quality of Service characteristics of the service. The overall service description is obtained by means of an iterative analysis specification phase that makes use of behavioral and stochastic models. These models suitably refined with pieces of information coming from the implementation chain, will then be made available as artifacts associated to the service specification.

With respect to the spectrum presented in Figure 4 the PLASTIC development process will present a limited form of adaptability as shown in Figure 7. The components implementing PLASTIC services will be programmed using the resource aware programming approach presented in Section 3 by using Java. In PLASTIC adaptation happens at the time the service request is matched with a service provision. This match has to take into account the user's QoS request and the service SLS and the result of the match will produce the Service Level Agreement (SLA) that defines the QoS constraints of the service provision. During this matching process in order to reach an SLA the service code might need to be adapted, according to the resource aware approach, thus resulting in a customized service code that satisfies the user's QoS request and results in a SLA.

5   Conclusions

In this paper I have discussed my point of view on software in the future. Adaptability and Dependability will play a key role in influencing models, languages and methodologies to develop and execute future software applications. In a broader software engineering perspective it is therefore mandatory to reconcile the static/compile time development approach to the dynamic/interpreter oriented one thus making models and validation technique manageable lightweight tools for run time use. There are several challenges in this domain. Programming Language must account in a rigorous way of *quantitative* concerns, allowing programmers to deal with these concerns declaratively. Models must become simpler and lighter by exploiting compositionality and partial evaluation techniques. Innovative development processes should be defined to properly reflect these new concerns arising from software for ubiquitous computing. I presented the PLASTIC approach to service development and provision in B3G networks as a concrete instance of the problem raised by Softure. The solutions we are experimenting in PLASTIC are not entirely innovative *per se* rather they are used in a completely new and non trivial fashion. Summarizing my message is that in the Softure domain it is important to think and research *point to point* theories and techniques but it is mandatory to re-think the whole development process in order to cope with the complexity of Softure and its requirements.

Acknowledgments

The author would like to acknowledge the IST project PLASTIC that partially supported this work and all the members of the PLASTIC Consortium and of the SEALab at University of L'Aquila for joint efforts on all the research efforts reported in this paper.

References

1. PLASTIC IST STREP Project: Home page on line at:
   http://www-c.inria.fr:9098/plastic
2. Schilit, B., Adams, N., Want, R.: Context-aware computing applications. In: IEEE Workshop on Mobile Computing Systems and Applications, Santa Cruz, CA, US (1994)

3. IFIP WG 10.4 on Dependable Computing And Fault Tolerancs
   http://www.dependability.org/wg10.4/
4. Allen, R., Garlan, D.: A Formal Basis for Architectural Connection. ACM Transactions on Software Engineering and Methodology 6(3), 213–249 (1997)
5. Magee, J., Kramer, J.: Concurrency: State models & java programs. Wiley publisher, Chichester (1999)
6. Caporuscio, M., Carzaniga, A., Wolf, A.L.: Design and evaluation of a support service for mobile, wireless publish/subscribe applications. IEEE Transactions on Software Engineering (December 2003)
7. Carzaniga, A., Rosenblum, D.S., Wolf, A.L.: Design and Evaluation of a Wide-Area Event Notification Service. ACM Transactions on Computer Systems 19(3), 332–383 (2001)
8. Inverardi, P., Mancinelli, F., Nesi, M.: A Declarative Framework for adaptable applications in heterogeneous environments. In: Proceedings of the 19th ACM Symposium on Applied Computing (2004)
9. Balsamo, S., Di Marco, A., Inverardi, P., Simeoni, M.: Model-based Performance Prediction in Software Development: A Survey IEEE Transaction on Software Engineering (May 2004)
10. Inverardi, P., Mancinelli, F., Marinelli, G.: Correct Deployment and Adaptation of Software Applications on Heterogenous (Mobile) Devices. In: ACM Proceedings Workshop on Self-Healing Software (2002)
11. Mancinelli, F., Inverardi, P.: Quantitative resource-oriented analysis of Java (adaptable) application. In: ACM Proceedings Workshop on Software Performance (2007)
12. Necula, G.C.: Proof-Carrying Code. In: Jones, N.D. (ed.) Proceedings of the Symposium on Principles of Programming Languages, pp. 106–119. ACM Press, Paris, France (1997)
13. Necula, G.C., Lee, P.: Proof-Carrying Code. Technical Report CMU-CS-96-165, School of Computer Science, Carnegie Mellon University (September 1996)
14. Necula, G.C., Lee, P.: Safe kernel extensions without run-time checking. In: Proceedings of the Symposium on Operating System Design and Implementation, Seattle, Washington, pp. 229–243 (October 1996)
15. Necula, G.C., Lee, P.: Efficient Representation and Validation of Logical Proofs. In: Pratt, V. (ed.) Proceedings of the Symposium on Logic in Computer Science, pp. 93–104. IEEE Computer Society Press, Indianapolis, Indiana (1998)
16. Necula, G.C., Lee, P.: Safe, untrusted agents using proof-carrying code. In: Vigna, G. (ed.) Mobile Agents and Security. LNCS, vol. 1419, pp. 61–91. Springer, Heidelberg (1998)
17. Caporuscio, M., Di Marco, A., Inverardi, P.: Model-based system reconfiguration for dynamic performance management. Journal of Systems and Software (to appear, 2006)
18. Itu telecommunication standardisation sector, itu-t reccomendation z.120. Message Sequence Charts (msc'96), Geneva
19. Uchitel, S., Kramer, J., Magee, J.: Detecting implied scenarios in message sequence chart specifications. In: ACM Proceedings of the joint 8th ESEC and 9th FSE, ACM Press, Vienna (2001)
20. Uchitel, S., Kramer, J.: A workbench for synthesising behaviour models from scenarios. In: proceeding of the 23rd IEEE International Conference on Software Engineering (ICSE'01), Toronto, Canada (May 2001)

21. Inverardi, P., Tivoli, M.: A compositional synthesis of failure-free connectors for correct components assembly. In: proceedings of the 6th ICSE Workshop on Component-Based Software Engineering (CBSE6): Automated Reasoning and Prediction at 25th ICSE 2003, Portland, Oregon, USA (May 3-10, 2003)

22. Georgiadis, I., Magee, J., Kramer, J.: Self-organising software architectures for distributed systems. In: Proc. of the 1st Work. on Self-Healing Systems (WOSS02), pp. 33–38. ACM Press, New York (2002)

23. Hirsch, D., Inverardi, P., Montanari, U.: Graph grammars and constraint solving for software architecture styles. In: Proc. of the 3rd Int. Software Architecture Workshop (ISAW-3), pp. 69–72. ACM Press, New York (1998)

24. Magee, J., Kramer, J.: Dynamic structure in software architectures. In: Proc. of the 4th ACM SIGSOFT Symp. On Foundations of Software Engineering (FSE-4), pp. 3–14. ACM Press, New York (1996)

25. Metayer, D.L.: Describing software architecture styles using graph grammars. IEEE Trans. Software Engineering 24(7), 521–533 (1998)

26. Taentzer, G., Goedicke, M., Meyer, T.: Dynamic change management by distributed graph transformation: Towards onfigurable distributed systems. In: Ehrig, H., Engels, G., Kreowski, H.-J., Rozenberg, G. (eds.) TAGT 1998. LNCS, vol. 1764, Springer, Heidelberg (2000)

27. Baresi, L., Heckel, R., Thne, S., Varr, D.: Style-Based Refinement of Dynamic Software Architectures. WICSA, 155–166 (2004)

28. Aldrich, J., Chambers, C., Notkin, D.: ArchJava: Connecting Software Architecture to Implementation. In: proceedings of ICSE 2002 (May 2002)

29. Aldrich, J.: Using Types to Enforce Architectural Structure. University of Washington Ph.D. Dissertation (August 2003)

30. Barthe, G.: Mobius, securing the next generation of java-based global computers. ERCIM News (2005)

31. SeCSE Project, http://secse.eng.it

32. Colombo, M., Di Nitto, E., Di Penta, M., Distante, D., Zuccalá, M.: Speaking a Common Language: A Conceptual Model for Describing Service-Oriented Systems. In: Benatallah, B., Casati, F., Traverso, P. (eds.) ICSOC 2005. LNCS, vol. 3826, Springer, Heidelberg (2005)

33. Autili, M., Cortellessa, V., Marco, A.D., Inverardi, P.: A conceptual model for adaptable context-aware services. In: Proc. of International Workshop on Web Services Modeling and Testing (WS-MaTe2006) (2006)

34. Autili, M., Inverardi, P., Navarra, A., Tivoli, M.: SYNTHESIS: a tool for automatically assembling correct and distributed component-based systems Proc. of International Conference on Software Engineering (ICSE 2007) - Tool Demos Session (to appear)

35. Inverardi, P., Tivoli, M.: Formal Methods for the Design of Computer, Communication and Software Systems: Software Architecture. In: Bernardo, M., Inverardi, P. (eds.) SFM 2003. LNCS, vol. 2804, Springer, Heidelberg (2003)

An Algorithmic Theory of Mobile Agents

Evangelos Kranakis[1] and Danny Krizanc[2]

[1] School of Computer Science, Carleton University, Ottawa, ON, Canada
[2] Department of Mathematics and Computer Science, Wesleyan University,
Middletown, Connecticut 06459, USA

Abstract. Mobile agents are an extension of multiagent systems in which the agents are provided with the ability to move from node to node in a distributed system. While it has been shown that mobility can be used to provide simple, efficient, fault-tolerant solutions to a number of problems in distributed computing, mobile agents have yet to become common in mainstream applications. One of the reasons for this may be the lack of an algorithmic theory which would provide a framework in which different approaches can be analyzed and the limits of mobile agent computing explored. In this paper we attempt to provide such an algorithmic theory.

1   Introduction

The concept of an agent working on behalf of another entity is a simple yet powerful abstraction that has been found useful in many areas of computing. In certain applications adding the capability of movement to an agent can lead to further simplifications and efficiencies. Consider, for example, the following scenarios:

- *Network Maintenance.* In a heterogeneous network it is necessary to regularly provide nodes with software updates, check for security vulnerabilities, etc. A simple approach to this would be to have an agent (or team of agents) regularly visit the nodes to determine what maintenance is required and to perform it.
- *Electronic Commerce.* In some situations the success of a given transaction requires the near simultaneous success of multiple transactions. For example, when preparing for a trip one may be purchasing airline tickets, making hotel reservations and scheduling meetings. A mobile agent can move between applications making sure that all transactions are ready before committing to any.
- *Intelligent Search.* When searching for information across multiple sources it is often the case that queries must be adapted depending on the answers received. An agent with the ability to filter information locally and adapt its behavior while moving between sources is potentially more efficient than one that always has to return to the user for guidance.

U. Montanari, D. Sannella, and R. Bruni (Eds.): TGC 2006, LNCS 4661, pp. 86–97, 2007.
© Springer-Verlag Berlin Heidelberg 2007

- *Robotic Exploration.* In a potentially dangerous environment it makes sense for robots to be the first to explore a region. A simple and potentially cheap solution is to have a team of small communicating robots (agents) cooperatively explore rather than one expensive human-controlled robot.

In this paper we concentrate on modeling agents as developed in distributed systems research (see Chapter 13 of [9]) though much of what we discuss could be applied in other domains such as artificial intelligence (e.g., intelligent multiagent systems [20]), robotics (e.g., autonomous mobile robots [13]), computational economics (e.g., agent-based economic modelling [17]) and networking (e.g., active networks [16]). We first informally describe what we mean by a mobile agent system and discuss the potential advantages and disadvantages of such systems. We then develop a framework for an algorithmic theory of mobile agents. Finally, we show how the theory can be applied to analyze the problem of achieving agent rendezvous in a network.

1.1 What Is a Mobile Agent?

We imagine a mobile agent to be a software entity endowed with the following properties:

- *Autonomy.* As is the case for real world agents such as travel agents, software agents should work with some degree of independence from their creator. They should be able to make at least some decisions without the need to consult a central authority.
- *Mobility.* In the case of mobile agents we insist that they have the ability to move from node to node in a distributed system. When such an agent moves it is assumed that it encapsulates some or all of its state to move with it.

Beyond the above, a number of researchers include the following attributes in their definition of a mobile agent:

- *Interactivity.* Obviously a agent must be able to interact with its environment, to make queries of nodes it visits, to report its findings, etc. But in many (possibly most) applications we imagine that more than one agent is present and the agents themselves are able to interact. Again in most instances this is likely to be cooperative behavior but competitive behavior is also possible. The exact form of this interaction depends upon the system but usually involves some sort of communication either by means of message passing or shared memory.
- *Intelligence.* The usefulness of an agent increases significantly with its ability to adapt to new situations, to learn from previous experience and to model correctly the intentions of the user who created it as well as those of the agents it encounters.

It is our goal to develop a flexible framework in which systems exhibiting any subset of the above properties can be analyzed.

1.2 Why Mobile Agents?

The applications one has in mind for mobile agents can generally be solved by traditional distributed computing approaches so why use them? While not a panacea, it can be argued that they offer a number of advantages over the standard solutions including:

- *Efficiency.* Assuming that the agents are sufficiently compact (program plus state) they offer potential savings in both latency and network bandwidth. In a situation where n sites must be visited in sequential order, where for instance the output from one site is used as part of the input to the next, a mobile agent can perform the task by moving along an n edge cycle incurring the cost of n communication steps whereas the communication pattern of a centrally located agent would be a star with $2n$ communication steps (to and from each site) required. In a situation where parallel access to the sites is possible then a team of mobile agents (in this case sometimes referred to as *clones*) can visit all of the sites faster than a single stationary agent.
- *Fault-tolerance.* In situations where a user has limited or even intermittent connectivity to the network (e.g., mobile devices) a mobile agent may overcome this deficit by acting on behalf of the user during blackout periods and returning useful information when connectivity returns. In situations where nodes may go down on a regular basis with limited notice a mobile agent can potentially move to another node and continue operating.
- *Flexibility.* It is generally easy to add features to agents that allow them to adapt their behavior to new conditions. More sophisticated agents may be designed to incorporate learning from past experience.
- *Ease of Use.* In many situations it is natural both from the perspective of the user and the programmer to imagine that they are dealing with autonomous agents. In some instances this improves the user's experience of the application. In other instances an agent-based paradigm makes the system's design and implementation easier to perform. While these benefits are hard to quantify they can be as important as the above.

In order to evaluate (at least theoretically) the above claims, especially those concerning efficiency and fault-tolerance, a model for analyzing the behavior of mobile agent algorithms is needed.

1.3 Whither Mobile Agents?

While many have touted the advantages of mobile agents and numerous mobile agent systems have been developed [3,10,12,18,19], they have yet to become a ubiquitous element of distributed systems. The reasons cited for this are many. They are said to lack a so-called "killer app" or to suffer from the "who goes first" phenomenon. A common objection to introducing mobile agents is security. There are many who believe that opening up your network to the "invasion" of potentially harmful mobile agents is not worth the advantages they may provide.

On the other hand, much work has been done to insure that mobile agents can be implemented in a secure fashion [15].

But perhaps the most common objection to mobile agent systems is that anything that can be achieved by mobile agents can just as easily be achieved using traditional means such as static agents. The counter argument to this is that no one has ever claimed that mobile agents were required to solve any particular problem only that they would provide a potentially more efficient and fault-tolerant solution to many common problems. But still some object that the resulting mobile agents will be too complex to realize the possible savings. While there has been some experimental work that attempts to verify that such savings exist [3,4,5], it is our contention that at least in part what is needed is an algorithmic model in which one can prove that a mobile agent solution achieves given complexity bounds and can thus provably provide the claimed efficiencies.

2   An Algorithmic Model for Mobile Agents

Work on the design and analysis of algorithms proceeds within the confines of a given algorithmic model. For example a popular model in which sequential algorithms are analyzed is the standard RAM model of computing. For parallel algorithm analysis a number of models, such as the PRAM, are used. For each paradigm an appropriate algorithmic model is developed. In general, a model is an abstraction which attempts to capture the most important aspects of a computational process. It consists of a description of allowable operations (or transitions) that can be performed by the process. For example the RAM model allows for read/write operations, arithmetic operations, etc. Once this is established one generally defines a set of measurable resources of interest, e.g., time (number of primitive operations), space (number of registers or potential states), etc. At this point one is ready to analyze algorithms for well-defined problems (often expressed as input-output conditions). Assuming the model captures the computation sufficiently accurately it can be used to:

- analyze the complexity (the amount of a given resource used) of different algorithms for a problem in order to determine which is most efficient, and
- determine lower bounds on the complexity of any algorithm for a given problem or relate the complexities of different problems.

In order to model mobile agents we must model both the agents themselves and the networks that host them. Rather than describe one model we present a framework for a class of related models for both hosts and agents among which one may choose a model to be used depending upon the application one has mind.

2.1   Mobile Agents

We are interested in modeling a set of software entities that act more or less autonomously from their originator and have the ability to move from node to node in a distributed network maintaining some sort of state with the nodes of the network providing some amount of (possibly longterm) storage and computational support. Either explicitly or implicitly such a mobile (software) agent is most often modeled using a finite automaton consisting of a set of states and a transition function. The transition function takes as input the agent's current state as well as possibly the state of the node it resides in and outputs a new agent state, possible modifications to the current node's state and a possible move to another node. In some instances we consider probabilistic automata which have available a source of randomness that is used as part of their input. Such agents are referred to as *randomized* agents.

An important property to consider is whether or not the agents are distinguishable, i.e., if they have distinct labels or identities. Agents without identities are referred to as *anonymous* agents. Anonymous agents are limited to running precisely the same program, i.e., they are identical finite automata. As the identity is assumed to be part of the starting state of the automaton, agents with identities have the potential to run different programs.

The knowledge the agent has about the network it is on and about the other agents can make a difference in the solvability and efficiency of many problems. For example, knowledge of the size of the network or its topology or the number of and identities of the other agents may be used as part of the agent's program. If available to the agents, this information is assumed to be part of its starting state. (One could imagine situations where the information is made available by the nodes of the network and not necessarily encoded in the agent.)

An important consideration for the case of teams of agents is how they interact. For example, are agents able to detect the presence of other agents at a given node? Assuming that the agents are designed to interact, the method through which they communicate is an important aspect of any model. For example one might consider a case where agents have the ability to read the state of other agents residing at the same node. Or one might only allow communication via a shared memory space or via message passing. Other properties that may be considered include whether or not the agents have the ability to "clone" themselves, i.e., produce new copies of themselves with the same functionality and whether or not they have the ability to "merge" upon meeting (sometimes referred to as "sticky" agents).

2.2 Distributed Networks

The model of a distributed network is essentially inherited directly from the algorithmic theory of distributed computing (see for example [14]). We model the network by a graph whose vertices comprise the computing nodes and edges correspond to communication links.

The nodes of the network may or may not have distinct identities. In an *anonymous* network the nodes have no identities. In particular this means that an agent can not distinguish two nodes except perhaps by their degree. The outgoing edges of a node are usually thought of as distinguishable but an important distinction is made between a globally consistent edge-labeling versus a locally independent edge-labeling. A simple example is the case of a ring where clockwise and counterclockwise edges are marked consistently around the ring in one case, and the edges are arbitrarily - say by an adversary - marked 1 and 2 in the other case. If the labeling satisfies certain coding properties it is called a *sense of direction* [7]. Sense of direction has turned out to greatly effect the solvability and efficiency of solution of a number of problems in distributed computing and has been shown to be important for the study of mobile agents as well.

Networks are also classified by how they deal with time. In a synchronous network there exists a global clock available to all nodes. This global clock is inherited by the agents. In particular it is usually assumed that in a single step an agent arrives at a node, performs some calculation, and exits the node and that all agents are performing these tasks "in sync". In an asynchronous network such a global clock is not available. The speed with which an agent computes or moves between nodes, while guaranteed to be finite, is not a priori determined.

We have to consider the resources provided by the nodes to the agents. All nodes are assumed to provide enough space to store the agent temporarily and computing power for it to perform its tasks. (The case of malicious nodes refusing agents or even worse destroying agents - so-called *blackholes* - is also sometimes considered.) It is also assumed that the nodes will transport the agents to other nodes upon request. Beyond these basic services one considers nodes that might provide some form of long-term storage, i.e., state that is left behind when the agent leaves. This long-term storage may or may not be shared among all agents using the services of the node. So for example this memory might be best thought of as a *whiteboard* on which an agent can leave messages for themselves or for other agents. A further service the node may provide to the agents is mechanism for sending and/or receiving messages via message passing.

Finally, when analyzing fault-tolerance one has to consider how a host network component might fail. Again, here we inherit the standard network fault models considered in distributed computing such as crash failures, omission failures, Byzantine failures, etc. One might also consider failures that do not effect the working of the network but only the agent subsystem, e.g., loss of shared data.

2.3   Resource Measures

For a given choice of agent plus network model there are a number of resources of interest for which one can define a complexity measure. Of paramount concern are measures that reflect the time and bandwidth efficiency of a given algorithm. In the synchronous setting it is clear that to measure time one should use the assumed global clock. In an asynchronous setting things are not so clear though in most instances authors choose to evaluate what the worst case time would be assuming that time proceeded synchronously. The total bandwidth consumed by the agent depends upon its size as well as the number of moves it makes during an execution of its algorithm. Generally the size of an agent is identified with the number of bits required to encode its states, i.e, it is proportional to the log base two of the number of possible states. If the agent sends messages then the size and number of these messages must also count towards any measure of its bandwidth. Other complexity measurements of interest include the size of shared memory required at each node assuming the agents communicate via shared memory, the number of random bits used by a randomized agent and the number of and kind of faults an algorithm can successfully deal with.

3   An Example: Randomized Rendezvous on the Ring

A natural problem to study for any multiagent mobile system is that of rendezvous. Given a particular agent model and network model a set of agents distributed arbitrarily over the nodes of the network are said to *rendezvous* if after running their programs after some finite time they all occupy the same node of the network at the same time. As is often the case, researchers are interested in examining cases that expose the limits of the problem being studied. For rendezvous the simplest interesting case is that of two agents attempting to rendezvous on a ring network. Of special interest is the highly symmetric case of anonymous agents on an anonymous network. In particular below we consider the standard model for an anonymous synchronous oriented ring [2] where

1. the nodes have no identities, i.e., the agents can not distinguish between the nodes,
2. the computation proceeds in synchronous steps,
3. the edges of each node are labeled left and right in a consistent fashion.

We model the agents as probabilistic finite automata $A = < S, \delta, s_0 >$ where S is the set of states of the automata including s_0 the initial state and the special state halt, and $\delta : S \times C \times P \to S \times M$ where $C = \{H, T\}$ represents a random coin flip, $P = \{\text{present}, \text{notpresent}\}$ represents a predicate indicating the presence of the other agent at a node, and $M = \{\text{left}, \text{right}\}$ represents the potential moves the agent may make. During each synchronous step, depending upon its current state, the answer to a query for the presence of the other agent, and the value of a independent random coin flip with probability of heads equal to .5, the agent uses δ in order to change its state and either move across the edge labeled left or right. We assume that the agent halts once it detects the presence of the other agent at a node.

The first question one may ask concerning this instance of rendezvous is whether or not it is solvable. It is fairly easy to see that if the two agents start at an odd distance apart on an even size ring they can never rendezvous in the above model as they are forced to move on each step and therefore will remain an odd distance apart forever. There are number of ways to fix this, the easiest perhaps being to add a third option to M of stay. For simplicity in the analysis below we will instead assume that they are an even distance apart on an even size ring.

For solvable instances of rendezvous one is interested in comparing the efficiency of different solutions. Much of the research focuses on the number of moves required to rendezvous or the expected number in the case of randomized agents (where the expectation is taken over the possible sequences of coin flips).

In the synchronous setting the number of moves is equivalent to the time and is measured via the global clock. (In some situations, it makes a difference if the agents begin their rendezvous procedure at the same time or there is possible delay between start times. Here we will assume a synchronous start.) Also of interest is the size of the program required by the agents to solve the problem. This is referred to as the memory requirement of the agents and is considered to be proportional to the base two logarithm of the number of states required by the finite state machine encoding the agent. Ideally one would like to design an agent whose size is constant independent of the size of the ring and which performs rendezvous in expected linear time (as in the worst case the agents are linear distance apart initially). As we shall see, achieving both goals simultaneously is not possible in this case.

3.1   Random Walk Algorithm

Many authors have observed that rendezvous may be solved by anonymous agents on an anonymous network by having the agents perform a random walk. The expected time to rendezvous can be shown to be a (polynomial) function of the (size of the) network and is related to the cover time of the network. (See [11] for definitions relating to random walks. See [6] for an analysis of the meeting time for random walks.)

For example consider the following algorithm for rendezvous on the ring:

1. **Repeat until** other agent **present**:
2. **If heads** move **right else** move **left**

If we let E_d be the expected time for two agents starting at an (even) distance d on an a ring of (even) size n to rendezvous using the above algorithm it is easy to see that $E_0 = 0$, and $E_{n/2} = 1 + (1/2)E_{n/2} + (1/2)E_{n/2-2}$. The latter equation gives rise to the recurrence

$$E_{n/2} = 2 + E_{n/2-2}. \tag{1}$$

More generally, in executing the algorithm one of the following three cases may occur. The two mobile agents make a single step and either move in the same direction with probability $1/2$, or in opposite direction either towards each other with probability $1/4$ or away from each other with probability $1/4$. From this we derive the identity

$$E_d = 1 + (1/2)E_d + (1/4)E_{d-2} + (1/4)E_{d+2}, \tag{2}$$

for $d = 2, 4, \ldots, n/2 - 2$. (Note that the case $d = n/2$ is special in that they are always at most distance $n/2$ apart.) Substituting $d + 2$ for d in Identity 2 and solving the resulting equation in terms of E_d we derive that for $d \geq 4$,

$$E_d = 2E_{d-2} - E_{d-4} - 4. \tag{3}$$

The initial condition $E_0 = 0$ and Identity 3 yield $E_4 = 2E_2 - 4$. More generally, we can prove the following identity for $2d \leq n/2$,

$$E_{2d} = dE_2 - 2d(d-1). \tag{4}$$

We prove by induction that there are sequences a_d, b_d such that

$$E_{2d} = a_d E_2 - 4b_d.$$

Indeed,

$$
\begin{aligned}
E_{2d} &= 2E_{2d-2} - E_{2d-4} - 4 \\
&= 2\left(a_{d-1}E_2 - 4b_{d-1}\right) - \left(a_{d-2}E_2 - 4b_{d-2}\right) - 4 \\
&= (2a_{d-1} - a_{d-2})E_2 - 4(2b_{d-1} - b_{d-2} + 1),
\end{aligned}
$$

which gives rise to the recurrences $a_d = 2a_{d-1} - a_{d-2}$ and $b_d = 2b_{d-1} - b_{d-2} + 1$ with initial conditions $a_0 = b_0 = 0, a_1 = 1, b_1 = 0$. Solving the recurrences we obtain easily that $a_d = d$ and $b_d = -\frac{1}{2}d + \frac{1}{2}d^2$, which proves Identity 4. To derive a formula for E_{2d}, it remains to compute E_2. Identity 4 yields the values

$$
\begin{aligned}
E_{n/2} &= \frac{n}{4}E_2 - 2\frac{n}{4}\left(\frac{n}{4} - 1\right) \\
E_{n/2-2} &= \left(\frac{n}{4} - 1\right)E_2 - 2\left(\frac{n}{4} - 1\right)\left(\frac{n}{4} - 2\right),
\end{aligned}
$$

which when substituted into Identity 1 shows that $E_2 = n - 2$. Finally, substituting this last value into Identity 4 we derive

$$E_{2d} = d(n - 2d). \tag{5}$$

Obviously the above algorithm translates into a finite automaton with a constant number of states and thus we have demonstrated:

Theorem 1. *Consider an n node ring. Two agents with $O(1)$ memory, starting at even distance $d \leq n/2$ can rendezvous in expected $\frac{d}{2}(n - d)$ steps.*

The agents in this algorithm are of optimal (to within a multiplicative constant) size but in the worst case $d = \Theta(n)$ and the expected number of steps is quadratic. One might ask if it is possible to achieve linear time.

3.2   Coin Half Tour Algorithm

It is fairly easy to achieve a linear upper bound on the expected number of steps using the following algorithm referred to as the "coin half tour" algorithm by Alpern [1].

1. **Repeat until** other agent **present**:
2. **If** heads move **right** for $n/2$ steps **else** move **left** for $n/2$ steps

If we refer to each execution of step 2 as a phase and consider a phase to be a success if the two agents choose to travel in opposite directions and a failure otherwise then it is easy to see that (a) the expected number of failed phases before obtaining a success is one (b) the number steps in a failed steps is $n/2$ and (c) the expected number of steps in a successful phase is $\frac{n}{2}$. Therefore the expected number of steps until the agents rendezvous is n since they are guaranteed to rendezvous on a successful phase. Note that this is independent of their starting positions assuming $d > 0$. Further note that a finite automaton implementing the above algorithm requires $n/2 + O(1)$ states and thus we have shown:

Theorem 2. *Two agents with $O(\log n)$ memory, starting at even distance $d > 0$ on an even n node ring can rendezvous in expected n steps.*

The above algorithm is optimal (to within a multiplicative constant) in its running time but requires $O(\log n)$ bits of memory. Is it possible to achieve linear running time with less memory?

3.3   Approximate Counting Algorithm

By replacing the exact $n/2$ steps taken in step 2 of the coin half tour algorithm with an approximate expected $O(n)$ steps one can reduce the memory requirements for rendezvous in this instance. Consider the following algorithm for an agent with k bits of memory:

1. **Repeat until** other agent `present`:
2. (a) **If heads** set $dir = $ `right` **else** set $dir = $ `left`
   (b) **Repeat until** 2^k heads observed in a row: Move in direction dir

By defining a phase correctly and with some analysis it is possible to show that the phases have expected length $O(2^{2^k})$ and have constant probability of success and thus we can show (see [8]):

Theorem 3. *Two agents with k bits of memory, starting at even distance $d > 0$ on an even n node ring can rendezvous in expected $O\left(\left\lceil \frac{n}{2^{2^k}} \right\rceil^2 \cdot 2^{2^k}\right)$ steps.*

In particular, the above theorem implies that with $\log \log n$ bits of memory rendezvous can be achieved in linear time. It turns out that this is optimal as it can be shown that [8]:

Theorem 4. *Any algorithm that achieves two agent rendezvous in expected $\Theta(n)$ steps on an n node ring (satisfying the constraints of the model above) requires $\Omega(\log \log n)$ bits of memory.*

4   Conclusions

Distributed applications have relied heavily on the "client/server" paradigm, whereby a client is making requests from a user machine to a server which services the requests across the network. Although this model works well for certain applications it breaks down in highly distributed systems when network connections are poor, multiple clients and servers are involved, and the application requires a predictable response time. By using mobile agents, nodes can have the dual role of either client or server and the resulting networks scale better since the flow of control moves across the whole system. An algorithmic theory of mobile agents, as proposed in the present paper, helps not only to illuminate these advantages but also understand better the limitations of mobile agents by looking at, for example, memory/time trade-offs in randomized algorithms for the rendezvous problem. We believe this theory has the potential to expose both the effectiveness and the limits of using mobile agents for a host of other problems.

Acknowledgments

Research of the first author was supported in part by NSERC (Natural Sciences and Engineering Research Council of Canada) and MITACS (Mathematics of Information Technology and Complex Systems) grants. The authors would like to thank the participants of the Workshop on Mobile Computing held on Elba Island, May 2004. The ideas presented here were developed in cooperation with all those involved in the meeting.

References

1. Alpern, S.: The Rendezvous Search Problem. SIAM Journal of Control and Optimization 33, 673–683 (1995)
2. Attiya, H., Snir, M., Warmuth, M.: Computing on an anonymous ring. Journal of the ACM 35, 845–875 (1988)
3. Baumann, J., Hohl, F., Rothermel, K., Strasser, M.: Mole: Concepts of a Mobile Agent System. World Wide Web 1, 123–137 (1998)
4. Carzaniga, A., Picco, G., Vigna, G.: Designing Distributed Applications with Mobile Code Paradigm. In: Proc. 19th Int. Conf. on Software Engineering, pp. 22–32 (1997)
5. Chia, T., Kannapan, S.: Strategically Mobile Agents. In: Proc. of first Int. Workshop on Mobile Agents, pp. 149–161 (1997)
6. Coppersmith, D., Tetali, P., Winkler, P.: Collisions among ramdom walks on a graph. SIAM Journal of Discrete Mathematics 6, 363–374 (1993)
7. Flocchini, P., Mans, B., Santoro, N.: Sense of direction: definition, properties and classes, Networks 32 (1998), 29–53. 653–664 (2006)
8. Kranakis, E., Krizanc, D., Morin, P.: Randomized Rendezvous on the Ring, in preparation
9. Milojicic, D., Douglis, F., Wheeler, R. (eds.): Mobility: Processes, Computers and Agents. ACM Press, New York (1999)
10. Milojicic, D., Chauhan, D., LaForge, W.: Mobile Objects and Agents (MOA). In: Proc. of 4th USENIX Conf. on Object-Oriented Technologies, pp. 1–14 (1998)
11. Motwani, R., Raghavan, P.: Randomized Algorithms. Cambridge University Press, New York (1995)

12. Peine, H., Stolpmann, T.: The Architecture of the Ara Platform for Mobile Agents. In: Proc. of First Int. Workshop on Mobile Agents, pp. 50–61 (1997)
13. Roy, N., Dudek, G.: Collaborative robot exploration and rendezvous: Algorithms, performance bounds and observations. Autonomous Robots 11, 117–136 (2001)
14. Santoro, N.: Design and Analysis of Distributed Algorithms. John Wiley and Sons, West Sussex (2007)
15. Singelee, D., Preneel, B.: Secure E-commerce using Mobile Agents on Untrusted Hosts, Computer Security and Industrial Cryptography (COSIC) Internal Report (May 2004)
16. Tennenhouse, D., Smith, J., Sincoskie, W., Wetherall, D., Minden, G.: A Survey of Active Network Research. IEEE Communications Magazine 35, 80–86 (1997)
17. Tesfatsion, L.: Agent-Based Computational Economics: Growing Economies From the Bottom Up. Artificial Life 8, 55–82 (2002)
18. Walsh, T., Paciorek, N., Wong, D.: Security and Reliability in Concordia. In: Proc. of 31st Hawaii Int. Conf. on System Sciences, pp. 44–53 (1998)
19. White, J.E.: Telescript Technology: Mobile Agents, in Software Agents. MIT Press, Cambridge (1996)
20. Wooldridge, M. (ed.): Intelligent Agents, in Multiagent Systems: A Modern Approach to Distributed Artificial Intelligence, Weiss, G (ed.), pp. 27–77. MIT Press, Cambridge (1999)

Spatial-Behavioral Types,
Distributed Services, and Resources

Luís Caires

CITI / Departamento de Informática, Universidade Nova de Lisboa, Portugal

Abstract. We develop a notion of spatial-behavioral typing suitable to discipline interactions in service-based systems modeled in a distributed object calculus. Our type structure reflects a resource aware model of behavior, where a parallel composition type operator expresses resource independence, a sequential composition type operator expresses implicit synchronization, and a modal operator expresses resource ownership. Soundness of our type system is established using a logical relations technique, building on a interpretation of types as properties expressible in a spatial logic.

1 Introduction

The aim of this work is to study typing disciplines for service-based systems, with a particular concern with the key aspects of safety, resource control, and compositionality. For our current purposes, we consider service-based systems to be certain kinds of distributed object systems, but where binding between parties is dynamic rather than static, system assembly is performed on-the-fly depending on discoverable resources, interactions between parties may involve long duration protocols, and the fundamental abstraction mechanism is task composition, rather than just remote method invocation. In this paper, we approach the issue of compositional analysis of distributed services and resources using a new notion of typing inspired by spatial logics. Technically, we proceed by introducing a core calculus for distributed services, where clients and servers are represented by concurrent "objects" (aggregates of operations and state). Services are called by reference, and references (names) to services may be passed around, as in π-calculi. New services may also be dynamically instantiated. We then develop and study a fairly expressive type system aimed at disciplining, in a compositional way, interactions and resource usage in such systems.

Our type structure is motivated by fundamental features and properties of our intended model. We conceive a service-based system as a layered distributed system, where service provider objects execute tasks in behalf of client objects, in a coordinated way. Even if the same object may act as client and server, we do not expect intrinsic cyclic dependencies to occur in such a system. The main coordination abstractions for assembling tasks into services are probably parallel (independent) and sequential composition. Tasks are independent when they never get to compete for resources; independent tasks appear to run simultaneously, this is the default behavior of the "global computer". On the other hand, causality, data flow, and resource competition introduce constraints in the control flow of computations. We will thus consider tasks and resources as the basic building blocks of service based systems.

U. Montanari, D. Sannella, and R. Bruni (Eds.): TGC 2006, LNCS 4661, pp. 98–115, 2007.

Models of concurrent programming usually introduce two kinds of entities in their universe of concepts: processes (active) and resources (passive). While processes are the main subject of analysis, resources are considered atomic, further unspecified entities besides being unshareable by definition (with objects such as as files, channels, etc, memory cells, given as classical examples). We adopt a view where resources and objects are not modeled a priori by different sorts of entities: but where *everything is an object*. Our distinction criteria is observational, and not strict: what distinguishes a resource among other objects is that resources must be used with care so to avoid meaningless or disrupted computations. For example, a massively replicated service such as Google behaves pretty much as if every client owned its own private copy of it. On the other hand, an object handling an e-commerce session with a user, is certainly not supposed to be shared: if other user gets in the middle and interferes with the session things may go wrong! We then consider the latter more "resource-like" than the former. Thus, instead of thinking of resources as external entities, for which usage policies are postulated, we consider a resource to be any object expressible in our model that *must* be used according to a strict discipline to avoid getting into illegal states. Our semantics realizes such illegal states concretely, as standard "message not understood" errors, rather than as violations of extraneously imposed policies, as *e.g.*, in [14,17,2].

Adopting a deep model of resources as fragile objects brings generality to our approach. Just as sequentiality in a workflow results from resource competition, resource competition is problematic in the sense that if a system does not respect precise sharing constraints on objects, illegal computation states may arise. This view allows us to conceive more general sharing constraints than the special cases usually considered: *e.g.*, at certain stage of a protocol a resource might be shareable, while at other stage it may be not. Such an uniform approach also naturally supports a computational model where resources may be passed around in transactions, buffered in pools, while ensuring that their capabilities are used consistently, by means of typing. Our type system, we believe, captures the fundamental constraints on resource access present in general concurrent systems. It is based on the following constructors

$$U,V ::= \textbf{stop} \mid U \mid V \mid U \wedge V \mid U;V \mid U^\circ \mid U \vartriangleright V \mid 1(U)V$$

to which we add a recursion operator (and type variables). The spatial composition type $U \mid V$ states that a service may be used accordingly to U and V by independent clients, one using it as specified by U, the other as specified by V. This implies, in particular, that the tasks U and V may be activated concurrently. For example, an object typed with

$$Travel \triangleq (\texttt{flight} \mid \texttt{hotel});\texttt{order}$$

will be able to service the `flight` (we abbreviate $1(\textbf{stop})\textbf{stop}$ by 1, and so on) and `hotel` tasks simultaneously and after that (and only after that), the `order` task. The spatial reading of $U \mid V$ implies further consequences, namely that the (distributed) resources used by U and V do not interfere; this property is important to ensure closure under composition of certain safety properties of typed systems. Owned types, of the form U°, state not only that the service is usable as specified by U, but also that such usage is completely owned (so that a object possessing a reference of owned type may, for example, store it for later use). Owned types allow one to distinguish between services that *must* be used according to U, and services that *may* be used according to U;

this distinction is crucial to control delegation of resources or services between partners. More familiar behavioral types may also be easily expressed. For example, using sequential composition and conjunction, the usage protocol of a file might be specified

$$File(V) \triangleq (\texttt{open};(\texttt{read}()V \wedge \texttt{write}(V))^{\star};\texttt{close})^{\star}$$

where $U^{\star} \triangleq \textbf{rec}\ \alpha.(\textbf{stop} \wedge (U;\alpha))$ expresses iteration. By combining recursion with spatial types, we then define shared types. A shared type $U!$ states of an object that it may be used according to an unbounded number of independent sessions, each one conforming to type U. By combining such operators, we may specify fine grained shared access protocols, such as standard "multiple readers/unique writer" access pattern:

$$RW(V) \triangleq ((\texttt{read}()V)!;\texttt{write}(V^{\circ}))^{\star}$$

Finally, and crucially, guarantee types, of the form $U \triangleright V$, allows us to compose subsystems into systems while preserving the properties ensured by their typings.

The paper is structured as follows. In Section 2, we present our core language and its operational semantics, and some examples. In Section 3 we introduce our basic type system, and prove its soundness. Our proof combines syntactical and semantical reasoning, in the spirit of the logical relations technique, where types are interpreted as properties expressed in a spatial logic. In Section 4, we show how to extend our basic system to cover more general forms of sharing. Finally, Section 5 discusses related work and draws some conclusions.

2   A Distributed Service Calculus

In this section we present the syntax and operational semantics of our distributed service calculus. We assume given an infinite set $\mathcal{N}$ of *names*. Names are used to identify objects (n,m,p), threads (b,c,d) and state elements (a). We also assume given an infinite set X of *variables* (x,y,z), and an infinite set L of *method labels* $(\texttt{j},\texttt{k},\texttt{l})$. We note $X = \mathcal{N} \cup \mathcal{V}$ and let η range over X (variables and names). We start by introducing expressions. In the definition of systems, expressions may syntactically occur either in the body of a method definition, or in a thread.

Definition 2.1 (Values, Expressions, Methods). *The sets $\mathcal{V}$ of values, $\mathcal{E}$ of expressions, and $\mathcal{M}$ of methods are defined by the abstract syntax in Fig. 1 (top).*

We use the notation $\bar{\varsigma}$ to denote a sequence of syntactical elements of class ς. The value **nil** is an atomic value that stands for the null reference. The *call* expression $n.\texttt{l}(v)$ denotes the invocation of the method $\texttt{l}$ of object n, where the value v is passed as argument. The *wait* expression $n.c()$ denotes waiting for a reply to a previously issued method invocation of the form $n.\texttt{l}(v)$, where c is the identifier of the thread which is serving the request (remotely). The wait construct plays a key technical role in our formulation of the dynamic and static semantics of our language, even if it is not expected to appear in source programs. The *composition* construct **let** $\overline{x=e}$ **in** f denotes the parallel evaluation of the expressions e_i, followed by the evaluation of the body f,

$$e, f, h ::= \in \mathcal{E} \quad \text{(Expressions)}$$

v	(Value)
$\mid v.\mathbf{1}(v)$	(Call)
$\mid n.c()$	(Wait)
$\mid a?$	(Read)
$\mid a!(v)$	(Write)
$\mid \mathbf{new}\ [M]$	(Object Creation)
$\mid \mathbf{let}\ \overline{x = e}\ \mathbf{in}\ e$	(Composition)
$\mid \mathbf{rec}\ x.e$	(Recursion)

$$v, r ::= \in \mathcal{V} \quad \text{(Values)}$$

n	(Name)
$\mid x$	(Identifier)
$\mid \mathbf{nil}$	(Termination)

$$M ::= \in \mathcal{M} \quad \text{(Methods)}$$

$\mathbf{0}$	(Empty)
$\mid \mathbf{1}(x) = e$	(Method)
$\mid M \mid M$	(Methods)

$$s ::= \in \mathcal{S}\ \text{(Stores)} \quad t ::= \in \mathcal{T}\ \text{(Threads)} \quad P, Q, R ::= \in \mathcal{P} \quad \text{(Network)}$$

$\mathbf{0}$	$\mathbf{0}$	$\mathbf{0}$ (Empty)
$\mid a\langle v\rangle$	$\mid t \mid t$	$\mid (\nu n)P$ (Restriction)
$\mid s \mid s$	$\mid c\langle e\rangle$	$\mid P \mid Q$ (Composition)
		$\mid n[M\ ;\ s\ ;\ t]$ (Object)

Fig. 1. Values, Expressions, Methods, Stores, Threads, Networks

$$n.\mathbf{1}(v) \xrightarrow{\overline{n.\mathbf{1}_c(v)}} n.c() \qquad\qquad \mathbf{new}\,[M] \xrightarrow{n[M]} n$$

$$n.c() \xrightarrow{n.c(v)} v \qquad\qquad \frac{e\{x \leftarrow \mathbf{rec}\ x.e\} \xrightarrow{\alpha} e'}{\mathbf{rec}\ x.e \xrightarrow{\alpha} e'}\ \text{(Rec)}$$

$$a? \xrightarrow{a?(v)} v \qquad \frac{e \xrightarrow{\alpha} e'}{\mathbf{let}\ \cdots, x = e, \cdots\ \mathbf{in}\ f \xrightarrow{\alpha} \mathbf{let}\ \cdots, x = e', \cdots\ \mathbf{in}\ f}$$

$$a!(v) \xrightarrow{a!(v)} \mathbf{nil} \qquad\qquad \mathbf{let}\ \overline{x = v}\ \mathbf{in}\ e \xrightarrow{\tau} e\{x \leftarrow v\}$$

Fig. 2. Evaluation (Expressions)

$$\frac{e \xrightarrow{\overline{n.\mathbf{1}_c(v)}} e'\quad [c\ fresh]}{n[\mathbf{1}(x) = h\ ;\ \ ;\ ] \mid m[\ ;\ ; b\langle e\rangle] \to (\nu c)(n[\mathbf{1}(x) = h\ ;\ \ ; c\langle h\{x \leftarrow v\}\rangle] \mid m[\ ;\ ; b\langle e'\rangle])}$$

$$\frac{e \xrightarrow{n.c(r)} e'}{n[\ ;\ ; c\langle r\rangle] \mid m[\ ;\ ; b\langle e\rangle] \to m[\ ;\ ; b\langle e'\rangle]} \qquad \frac{e \xrightarrow{\tau} e'}{n[\ ;\ ; c\langle e\rangle] \to n[\ ;\ ; c\langle e'\rangle]}$$

$$\frac{e \xrightarrow{a?(v)} e'}{n[\ ; a(v)\ ; c\langle e\rangle] \to n[\ ;\ ; c\langle e'\rangle]} \qquad \frac{e \xrightarrow{a!(v)} e'}{n[\ ;\ ; c\langle e\rangle] \to n[\ ; a(v)\ ; c\langle e'\rangle]}$$

$$\frac{e \xrightarrow{m[M]} e'\quad [m\ fresh]}{n[\ ;\ ; c\langle e\rangle] \to (\nu m)(m[M\ ;\ \ ;\ ] \mid n[\ ;\ ; c\langle e'\rangle])} \qquad \frac{P \equiv P'\quad P' \to Q'\quad Q' \equiv Q}{P \to Q}$$

$$\frac{P \to Q}{(\nu n)P \to (\nu n)Q} \qquad \frac{P \to Q}{P \mid R \to Q \mid R}$$

Fig. 3. Reduction (Networks)

where the result of evaluating each e_i is bound to the corresponding x_i. The x_i are distinct bound variables, with scope the body f. The **let** construct allows us to express arbitrary parallel / sequential control flow graphs, in which values may be propagated between parallel and sequential subcomputations. We use the following abbreviations (where x_1 and x_2 do not occur in e_1 and e_2):

$$(e_1 \mid e_2) \triangleq \textbf{let } x_1 = e_1, x_2 = e_2 \textbf{ in nil} \qquad (e_1;e_2) \triangleq \textbf{let } x_1 = e_1 \textbf{ in } e_2$$

The $a?$ and $a!(v)$ constructs allow objects to manipulate their local store. The *read* expression $a?$ picks and returns a value stored under tag a, while the *write* expression $a!(v)$ stores value v in the store under tag a. The store conforms to a data space model, where reading consumes data, and writing adds new data elements. Evaluation of **new**$[M]$ results in the allocation of a new object, with set of methods M, and whose identity (a fresh name) is returned. In the *method* $1(x) = e$ the parameter x is bound in the scope of the method body e (for the sake of simplicity, we just consider single parameter methods). Finally, the **rec** construct introduces recursion. To keep our language "small", we refrain from introducing other useful ingredients, such as basic data types and related operators, for instance booleans and conditionals. Since it should be straightforward to formally extend our language with such constructs, we will sometimes use them, mostly in examples. Having defined expressions, we introduce:

Definition 2.2 (Stores, Threads, Networks). *The sets S of stores, T of threads, and P of networks are given in Fig. 1 (bottom).*

A network is a (possibly empty) composition of objects, where composition $P \mid Q$ and restriction $(\nu n)P$ are introduced with their usual meaning (cf., the π-calculus). An object $n[M ; s ; t]$ encapsulates, under the object name n, some methods M (passive code), a store s (that holds the object local state), and some threads t (active, running code). A store s is a bag of pairs tag - value. Each value is recorded in a store under an access tag (a name), represented by $a\langle v \rangle$, where a is the tag and v is the value. A store may possibly record several values under the same name a, so that e.g., $a\langle 1 \rangle \mid a\langle 2 \rangle$ is a valid store. A thread $c\langle e \rangle$ is uniquely identified by its identifier c and holds a running piece of code, namely the expression e. Threads are spawned when methods are called, and may run concurrently with other independent threads in the same object or network.

Objects in a system are given unique names, so that, for instance, the network $n[M ; s ; t] \mid n[M' ; s' ; t']$ denotes the same network as $n[M \mid M' ; s \mid s' ; t \mid t']$. Identities between networks such as this one (the **Split** law) are formally captured by structural congruence, defined below. By $fn(P)$ (resp. $fn(t)$, $fn(s)$, etc.) we denote the set of free names in process P (resp. thread t, store s, etc.), defined as expected. We use A, B, C to range over $M \cup S \cup T \cup P$ (the $\mid$-"composable" entities).

Definition 2.3 (Structural Congruence). *Structural congruence, noted $\equiv$, is the least congruence relation on networks, methods, and threads, such that*

$$A \equiv A \mid \mathbf{0} \qquad n[M ; s ; t] \mid n[N ; r ; u] \equiv n[M \mid N ; s \mid r ; t \mid u]$$
$$A \mid (B \mid C) \equiv (A \mid B) \mid C \qquad n[M ; s ; t] \equiv n[N ; r ; u] \textbf{ if } M \equiv N, s \equiv r, t \equiv u$$
$$B \mid A \equiv A \mid B \qquad (\nu m)(\nu n)P \equiv (\nu n)(\nu m)P$$
$$(\nu n)\mathbf{0} \equiv \mathbf{0} \qquad (\nu n)(P \mid Q) \equiv P \mid (\nu n)Q \textbf{ if } n\#fn(P)$$

We use $n\#S$ (resp. $S\#S'$) to denote that $n \notin S$ (resp. that S and S' are disjoint). To lighten our notation, we avoid writing $\mathbf{0}$ in objects slots, leaving the corresponding place holder blank. For example, $n[M ; \mathbf{0} ; \mathbf{0}]$ will be frequently written simply as $n[M ; ;]$.

The operational semantics of networks is defined by suitable transition relations. The labeled transition system in Fig. 2 specifies evaluation of expressions. A remote method call reduces to a wait expression on a fresh (thread) name c. Such wait expression will reduce to the returned value, upon thread completion. Notice also how **let** introduced expressions are evaluated concurrently, until each one reduces to a value. For object networks, the operational semantics specifies a remote method invocation mechanism by means of the transition system in Fig. 3. Servicing a method call causes a new thread to be spawned at the callee object's location, to execute the method's body. Meanwhile, the thread that originated the call suspends, waiting for a reply. Such a reply will be sent back to the caller, after the handling thread terminates. A $n[M]$ labeled transition, caused by the evaluation of a **new** $[M]$ expression, triggers the creation of a new object. Thus, labels in transitions express the actions that objects may engage into.

Definition 2.4. *Labels $\mathcal{L}$ are given by:* $\alpha ::= \tau \mid \overline{n.1_c(v)} \mid n.c(v) \mid a?(v) \mid a!(v) \mid n[M]$.

Definition 2.5 (Evaluation and Reduction). Evaluation, *noted* $e \xrightarrow{\alpha} e'$, *is the relation defined on expressions by the labeled transition system in Figure 2. Reduction, noted* $P \rightarrow Q$, *is the relation defined on networks by the transition system in Figure 3.*

We use $\Rightarrow$ for the the reflexive transitive closure of $\rightarrow$. Notice the role of $\equiv$ in reduction, in particular the **Split** law, so that each rule may mention just the parts of objects that are relevant for each interaction. An idle object may only become active as effect of an incoming method call, issued by a running thread. An object $n[M ; s ; t]$ such that $t \equiv \mathbf{0}$, is said to be *idle*, since it contains no running threads. Likewise, a network is idle if all of its objects are idle. We set: idle$(P) \triangleq$ *For all Q.if $P \equiv (\nu\overline{m})(n[; ;t] \mid Q)$ then $t \equiv \mathbf{0}$.*

Example 2.6. We sketch a toy scenario of service composition, where several sites co-operate to provide a travel booking service. First, there is an object F implementing a service for finding and booking flights. It provides three methods: **flight** to look for and reserve a flight, **book** to commit the booking, and **free** to release a reservation. A similar service is provided by object H, used for booking hotel rooms.

$$F \triangleq f[\, \texttt{flight}() = \cdots \mid \texttt{book}() = \cdots \mid \texttt{free}() = \cdots ; ;]$$
$$H \triangleq h[\, \texttt{hotel}() = \cdots \mid \texttt{book}() = \cdots \mid \texttt{free}() = \cdots ; ;]$$

$$G \triangleq gw[\, \texttt{pay}(s) = \textbf{if } bk.\texttt{debit}() \textbf{ then } s.\texttt{book}() \textbf{ else } s.\texttt{free}() ; ;]$$

$$B \triangleq br[\, \texttt{flight}() = f.\texttt{flight}() \mid \texttt{hotel}() = h.\texttt{hotel}() \mid$$
$$\texttt{order}() = (gw.\texttt{pay}(f); gw.\texttt{pay}(h)) ; ;]$$

We elide method implementations in F and G, but assume that the operations must be called in good order to avoid disruption, namely that after calling **flight**, a client is supposed to call either **book** or **free**. The broker B, that implements the front-end of the whole system, is client of F and H, and also of a payment gateway G. The gateway books items if succeeds in processing their payment through a remote bank service named *bk*. Our travel booking service, available at *br*, is used by first invoking the `flight` and `hotel` operations in any order. In fact, these operations may be called concurrently, since they trigger separate computations. Afterwards, the `order` operation may be invoked to book and pay for both items, delegating access to *f* and *h* to the gateway. The session will then terminate, and the broker becomes ready for another round. We will see below how these usage patterns may be specified by typing, and the type of the whole system compositionally defined from the types of its components.

The operational semantics assumes and preserves some constraints on networks. In an object $n[M ; s ; t]$ no more than a method with the same label may occur in M, and no more than a thread with the same name may occur in t. Objects in a network are uniquely named, also all threads in a system are uniquely named. In general, a network P is *well-defined* if all threads occurring in P have distinct names, all methods in objects have distinct labels, and for each thread name c there is at most one occurrence in P of a wait expression $n.c()$. It is immediate that if P is well-defined and $P \equiv Q \mid R$ then both Q and R are well-defined. On the other direction, the same does not hold in general, e.g., P and Q might clash in method and thread names. We then define by $ft(P)$ the set of free thread names in P, and by $lab(P,n)$ the set of method labels of object n in P:

$$c \in ft(P) \qquad iff\ P \equiv (v\overline{m})(n[\; ; \; ; c\langle e \rangle] \mid Q)\ and\ c\#\overline{m}$$
$$1 \in lab(P,n) \qquad iff\ P \equiv (v\overline{m})(n[1(x) = e ; \; ; \;] \mid Q)\ and\ n\#\overline{m}$$

Definition 2.7. *We assert* $P\|Q \triangleq ft(Q)\#ft(P)$ *and for all* $n.\ lab(P,n)\#lab(Q,n)$.

$P\|Q$ means that P and Q are composable, in the sense that if $P\|Q$, and both P and Q are well-defined, so is $P \mid Q$. Notice that $P\|Q$ *does not* imply $fn(P)\#fn(Q)$. We also have

Lemma 2.8. *If P is a well-defined network and $P \to Q$ then Q is a well-defined network.*

Henceforth, we assume networks to be always well-defined. It is useful to introduce external action transitions, that extend the reduction semantics with labels $n.1_c(m)$ and $n.c(r)$, to capture incoming method calls from the environment, and their replies.

Definition 2.9. *External actions of networks are defined by the labeled transitions:*

$$(v\overline{m})(n[1(x) = e ; \; ; \;] \mid R) \xrightarrow{n.1_c(u)} (v\overline{m})(n[1(x) = e ; \; ; c\langle e\{x \leftarrow u\}\rangle] \mid R) \quad [c\ fresh\ and\ n, u\#\overline{m}]$$

$$(v\overline{m})(n[\; ; \; ; c\langle r \rangle] \mid R) \xrightarrow{\overline{n.c(r)}} (v\overline{m} \backslash r)(n[\; ; \; ; \;] \mid R) \qquad\qquad [c, n\#\overline{m}]$$

Even well-defined networks may get *stuck* if a method call is being issued, but the called object does not offer the requested method. We say P is stuck if stuck(P) holds, where

$$\text{stuck}(P) \triangleq Exists\ \overline{m}, Q, e, e'.\ P \equiv (v\overline{m})(p[\; ; \; ; c\langle e \rangle] \mid Q)\ and\ e \xrightarrow{n.1_c(v)} e'\ and\ 1 \notin lab(Q,n)$$

Service based systems, as we are modeling here, may easily get stuck, if not carefully designed. As in (untyped) object oriented languages, *message-not-understood* errors may arise whenever an object does not implement an invoked method. However, in our present context stuck states may also arise if method calls are not coordinated (do not respect protocols) and timing errors occur (for example, due to races, *e.g.*, competing calls to the same non-shareable method). The presence of state in objects creates history dependencies on resource usage, and introduces a grain of resource sensitiveness in our model, as discussed in the Introduction, and illustrated in the next example.

Example 2.10. Consider the object S defined thus

$$S \triangleq server[\; \mathtt{init}() = s!(\mathtt{nil})$$
$$\mathtt{open}() = \mathbf{let}\; r = pool.\mathtt{alloc}()\; \mathbf{in}\; (s?;s!(r))$$
$$\mathtt{use}() = \mathbf{let}\; r = s?\; \mathbf{in}\; (r.\mathtt{use}();s!(r))$$
$$\mathtt{close}() = \mathbf{let}\; x = s?\; \mathbf{in}\; (pool.\mathtt{free}(x);s!(\mathtt{nil}))\; ; \;\;]$$

Our server S is a spooler that offers certain specific service by relying on a remote resource pool to fetch appropriate providers. All resources (*e.g.*, printers) in the pool (*pool*) are supposed to implement the operation of interest (use). The server provides the use service repeatedly to clients, by forwarding it through a locally cached reference. First, the server is initialized: by calling the init method the local reference is set to nil. Afterwards, a client must open the service by calling the open method before using it (so that the server can acquire an available resource), and close it after use by calling the close method (so that the server may release the resource). The server implements these operations by accessing the pool through its alloc and free methods. The internal state of the server, hidden to clients, will always be either of the form $s(\mathtt{nil})$, or $s(r)$ where r is a reference to an allocated resource. Notice how the idiom $\mathbf{let}\; r = s?\; \mathbf{in}\; (\cdots;s!(r))$ expresses retrieving r from the local state, using it (in the $\cdots$ part), and storing it back again. The protocols described above must be strictly followed to avoid runtime errors, due to resource non-availability. This would occur, *e.g.*, if the use operation is invoked right after close, an attempt to call the use method on a nil reference will cause the system to crash. Our type system, presented in detail below, prevents erroneous behaviors of this sort to happen, by ensuring that all services in a network conform to well-defined resource usage protocols.

3 Spatial-Behavioral Types

In this section, we present a type system to discipline interactions on networks of objects, as motivated above. A type T in our system describes a usage pattern for an object. Typically, an assertion of the form $n : T$ states that the object n may be safely used as specified by the type T. In general, the type of a composite system is expressed by an assertion $n_1 : T_1 \mid \ldots \mid n_k : T_k$, specifying types of various objects. Such an assertion (or typing environment) states that the system provides *independent* services at the names n_i, each one able to be safely used as specified by the type T_i respectively.

Definition 3.1 (Types). *The set $\mathcal{T}$ of types is defined by the following abstract syntax:*

$T,U,V ::= \in \mathcal{T}$	(Types)		
$\mathbf{stop}$	(Stop)	$\mid T \mid U$	(Spatial Composition)
$\mid T \wedge U$	(Conjunction)	$\mid T;U$	(Sequential Composition)
$\mid T^{\circ}$	(Owned)	$\mid 1(U)V$	(Method)
$\mid \alpha$	(Variable)	$\mid c(n:U)V$	(Thread)
$\mid \mathbf{rec}\; \alpha.T$	(Recursion)		

We may intuitively explain the meaning of the various kinds of types, by interpreting them as certain properties of objects. An object satisfies **stop** if it is idle. An object satisfies $n : T \mid U$ if it can independently (in terms of resource separation) satisfy both $n : T$ and $n : U$. We may also understood such a typing as the specification of two independent views for the object n. An object satisfies $n : T \wedge U$ if it may satisfy both $n : T$ and $n : U$, although not concurrently. Such an object may be used either as specified by $n : T$ or as specified by $n : U$, being the choice made by the client. An object satisfies $n : T; U$ if can satisfy both $n : T$ and $n : U$, in sequence. In particular, it will only be obliged to satisfy $n : U$ after being used as specified by $n : T$. The owned type $n : T^{\circ}$ means that the object may be used as specified by T, and furthermore that this T view is *exclusively owned*. For example, a reference of type $n : T^{\circ}$ may be stored in the local state of an object, or returned by a method call, although a reference of type $n : T$ may not, because of possible liveness constraints associated to the type T. This will become clearer in the precise semantic definitions below.

An object satisfies $n : \mathtt{l}(U)V$ if it offers a method $\mathtt{l}$ that whenever passed an argument of type U is ensured to return back a result of type V, and exercise, during the call, an use of the argument conforming to type U. Thus, method types specify both safety and liveness properties. The $c(n : U)V$ types talk about running threads, and are not expected to type source programs, but are useful to define the semantics of method types, as explained below. Recursive types are interpreted as usual. We will not address in detail recursive types in our technical development, for their treatment is fairly independent from the features we want to focus, and should not raise special difficulties.

A typing environment $(\mathbf{A}, \mathbf{B}, \mathbf{C}, \sigma, \delta)$ is a finite partial mapping from $\mathcal{N} \cup \mathcal{V}$ to $\mathcal{T}$. We write $\eta_1 : T_1, \ldots, \eta_n : T_n$ for the typing environment $\mathbf{A}$ with domain $\mathfrak{D}(\mathbf{A}) = \{\eta_1, \ldots, \eta_n\}$ such that $\mathbf{A}(\eta_i) = T_i$, for $i = 1, \ldots, n$. Type operations $\mathbf{stop}$, $(T \mid U)$, $(T \wedge U)$, $(T; U)$ and T° extend to typing environments as follows. $\mathbf{stop}$ denotes any typing environment (including the empty one) that assigns $\mathbf{stop}$ to any element in its domain. Given $\mathbf{A}$ and $\mathbf{B}$ such that $\mathfrak{D}(\mathbf{A}) = \mathfrak{D}(\mathbf{B})$, we define environments $\mathbf{stop}$, $(\mathbf{A} \mid \mathbf{B})$, $(\mathbf{A}; \mathbf{B})$, $(\mathbf{A} \wedge \mathbf{B})$, and $\mathbf{A}^{\circ}$, all with domain $\mathfrak{D}(\mathbf{A})$, such that, for all $\eta \in \mathfrak{D}(\mathbf{A})$, we have

$$\mathbf{stop}(\eta) \triangleq \mathbf{stop} \quad (\mathbf{A} \mid \mathbf{B})(\eta) \triangleq \mathbf{A}(\eta) \mid \mathbf{B}(\eta) \quad (\mathbf{A}; \mathbf{B})(\eta) \triangleq \mathbf{A}(\eta); \mathbf{B}(\eta)$$
$$(\mathbf{A} \wedge \mathbf{B})(\eta) \triangleq \mathbf{A}(\eta) \wedge \mathbf{B}(\eta) \quad \mathbf{A}^{\circ}(\eta) \triangleq \mathbf{A}(\eta)^{\circ}$$

Given a sequence $\overline{T} = T_1, \ldots, T_n$ of types (or typing environments) we denote by $\Pi(\overline{T})$ the type (or typing environment) $(T_1 \mid \cdots \mid T_n)$. Our type system is based on the following forms of formal judgments:

$\mathbf{A} <: \mathbf{B}$	(Subtyping)	$e :: \mathbf{A} \mid \sigma \triangleright \mathbf{B} \mid \delta[U]$	(Expressions)
$[M; t] :: \mathbf{A} \mid \sigma \triangleright \mathbf{B} \mid \delta[U]$	(Objects)	$P :: \mathbf{A} \triangleright \mathbf{B}$	(Networks)

In an expression typing judgment, e is the expression to be typed, $\mathbf{A}$ and $\mathbf{B}$ are typing environments, and U is a type. The auxiliary type environments σ and δ keep information about effects on the local state of objects, and will be further explained below (notice the $\mid$ symbol separating the global environments $\mathbf{A}$ and $\mathbf{B}$ from the state environments σ and δ in judgments, not to be confused with the $\mid$ type constructor). For networks, the typing judgment assigns to the network P an "assume-guarantee" assertion of the form $\mathbf{A} \triangleright \mathbf{B}$, cf. the adjunct of the composition operator of spatial logics [8]. If a judgment $P :: \mathbf{A} \triangleright \mathbf{B}$ is valid, then if P is composed with any network that satisfies the typing $\mathbf{A}$, one is guaranteed to obtain a network that satisfies the typing $\mathbf{B}$.

$$A \mid B <: B \mid A$$
$$(A \mid B) \mid C <:> A \mid (B \mid C)$$
$$(A;B) \mid (C;D) <: (A \mid C);(B \mid D)$$
$$A;(B;C) <:> (A;B);C$$

$$\mathbf{stop};A <:> A$$
$$A;\mathbf{stop} <:> A$$

$$\mathbf{stop} \mid A <:> A$$
$$A \wedge B <: A$$
$$A \wedge B <: B$$

$$\eta : \mathbf{rec}\ \alpha.U <:> \eta : U\{\alpha \leftarrow \mathbf{rec}\ \alpha.U\}$$

$$A <: A$$

$$A^\circ <: \mathbf{stop}$$
$$A^\circ <: A$$
$$A^\circ <: A^{\circ\circ}$$

$$\mathbf{stop} <: \mathbf{stop}^\circ$$
$$(A \mid B)^\circ <:> A^\circ \mid B^\circ$$
$$A^\circ;B <: A^\circ \mid B$$

$$\frac{A <: B}{A^\circ <: B^\circ}$$

$$\frac{A <: B \quad A <: C}{A <: B \wedge C}$$

$$\frac{A <: B \quad B <: C}{A <: C}$$

$$\frac{A <: B}{A \mid C <: B \mid C}$$

$$\frac{A <: B}{A;C <: B;C}$$

$$\frac{A <: B}{C;A <: C;B}$$

$$\frac{\eta : U <: \eta : V}{\eta : \mathbf{rec}\ \alpha.U <: \eta : \mathbf{rec}\ \alpha.V}$$

Fig. 4. Subtyping Rules

$$\mathbf{nil} :: A \mid \sigma \rhd A \mid \sigma[\mathbf{stop}]$$

$$v :: v : T^\circ \mid \sigma \rhd \ \mid \sigma[T]$$

$$a? :: \ \mid \sigma, a : T \rhd \ \mid \sigma[T]$$

$$a!(v) :: v : T^\circ \mid \sigma \rhd \ \mid \sigma, a : T\, [\mathbf{stop}]$$

$$v.\mathtt{l}(u) :: v : \mathtt{l}(U)V \mid u : U \mid \sigma \rhd \ \mid \sigma[V]$$

$$n.c(v) :: n : c(U)V \mid v : U \mid \sigma \rhd \ \mid \sigma[V]$$

$$\frac{[M;0] :: A^\circ \mid \ \rhd \ \mid [T]}{\mathbf{new}[M] :: A^\circ \mid \ \rhd \ \mid [T^\circ]}$$

$$\frac{A <: A' \quad e :: A' \mid \sigma \rhd B' \mid \delta[V'] \quad B' <: B \quad V' <: V}{e :: A \mid \sigma \rhd B \mid \delta[V]}$$

$$\frac{e :: A \mid \sigma \rhd B \mid \delta[U] \quad e :: A \mid \sigma \rhd B \mid \delta[V]}{e :: A \mid \sigma \rhd B \mid \delta[U \wedge V]}$$

$$\frac{e :: A \mid \sigma \rhd B \mid \delta[V]}{e :: A \mid C \mid \sigma, \phi \rhd B \mid C \mid \delta, \phi[V]}$$

$$\frac{e :: A \mid \sigma \rhd B \mid \delta[V]}{e :: A;C \mid \sigma \rhd B;C \mid \delta[V]}$$

$$\frac{e_i :: B_i \mid \sigma_i \ \rhd \ \mid \delta_i[V_i] \quad e_i \#_{\mathfrak{D}(\Pi(\overline{\sigma}))} e_j\ (i \neq j)}{f :: C, \overline{x} : \overline{V}^\circ \mid \Pi(\overline{\delta}) \ \rhd \ E, \overline{x} : \mathbf{stop} \mid \phi[U]}$$
$$\overline{\mathbf{let}\ \overline{x} = \overline{e}\ \mathbf{in} f :: \Pi(\overline{B});C \mid \Pi(\overline{\sigma}) \rhd E \mid \phi[U]}$$

Fig. 5. Typing Rules (Expressions)

$$[M;0] :: A \mid \sigma \rhd A \mid \sigma[\mathbf{stop}] \qquad\qquad 0 :: A \rhd A$$

$$\frac{M \equiv (N \mid \mathtt{l}(x) = e) \quad e :: A, x : U \mid \sigma \rhd B, x : \mathbf{stop} \mid \delta[V]}{[M;0] :: A \mid \sigma \rhd B \mid \delta[\mathtt{l}(U)V]}$$

$$\frac{[M;t] :: A \mid \overline{s_i : V_i} \rhd B \mid \delta[T]}{n[M; \overline{s_i\langle n_i\rangle};t] :: A \mid \Pi(n_i : V_i^\circ) \rhd n : T}$$

$$\frac{e :: A, x : U \mid \sigma \rhd B, x : \mathbf{stop} \mid \delta[V]}{[M;c\langle e\{x \leftarrow m\}\rangle] :: A \mid \sigma \rhd B \mid \delta[c(m : U)V]}$$

$$\frac{P :: A \rhd B \quad Q :: C \rhd D \quad P\|Q}{P \mid Q :: A \mid C \rhd B \mid C}$$

$$\frac{[M';t'] :: A \mid \sigma \rhd B \mid \delta[U] \quad [M'';t''] :: C \mid \sigma' \rhd D \mid \delta'[V]}{[M' \mid M'';t' \mid t''] :: A \mid C \mid \sigma, \sigma' \rhd B \mid D \mid \delta, \delta'[U \mid V]}$$

$$\frac{P :: A \rhd B \quad Q :: B \rhd C \quad P\|Q}{P \mid Q :: A \rhd C}$$

$$\frac{[M;t] :: A \mid \sigma \rhd B \mid \delta[U] \quad [M;0] :: B \mid \delta \rhd C \mid \phi[V]}{[M;t] :: A \mid \sigma \rhd C \mid \phi[U;V]}$$

$$\frac{P :: A \rhd B \quad n\#A,B}{(\nu n)P :: A \rhd B}$$

$$\frac{[M;0] :: A^\circ \mid \ \rhd \ \mid [T]}{[M;0] :: A^\circ \mid \ \rhd \ \mid [T^\circ]}$$

$$\frac{A <: A' \quad P :: A' \rhd B' \quad B' <: B}{P :: A \rhd B}$$

Fig. 6. Typing Rules (Objects and Networks)

What does it mean for a network to satisfy a typing? As discussed above, types are interpreted as properties (sets of networks) expressible in a spatial logic. In Section 3.1 below we will present in detail a logical semantics of types, around which our soundness proofs are organized. First, we present our type system as a formal system, and explain from an intuitive perspective the various rules and main results. Our type system is composed by four sets of rules, to derive judgments of the four forms listed above. In Fig. 4 we present the subtyping rules. Subtyping, which holds between typing environments, is motivated by selected natural properties of types, and reflect valid semantic entailments in our logic (cf. Proposition 3.4). A first set of rules states that $(- \mid -)$ and **stop** define a commutative monoid. The rule $(\mathbf{A}; \mathbf{B}) \mid (\mathbf{C}; \mathbf{D}) \mathrel{<\!\mathbf{:}} (\mathbf{A} \mid \mathbf{C}); (\mathbf{B} \mid \mathbf{D})$ expresses the basic interaction principle between sequential and independent composition, allowing us to derive, $e.g.$, $\mathbf{A} \mid \mathbf{B} \mathrel{<\!\mathbf{:}} \mathbf{A}; \mathbf{B}$, expressing interleaving. The rules for $(-)^{\circ}$ are quite interesting, notice that $(-)^{\circ}$ and $(- \mid -)$ reveal a familiar algebraic structure. No so familiar is the rule $\mathbf{A}^{\circ}; \mathbf{B} \mathrel{<\!\mathbf{:}} \mathbf{A}^{\circ} \mid \mathbf{B}$, asserting a key principle involving sequential composition and ownership: the owned usage $\mathbf{A}^{\circ}$ is not active (yet), and thus $\mathbf{B}$ cannot causally depend on it. A further set of rules express congruence principles, and unfolding of recursion.

Fig. 5 presents the typing rules for expressions. Intuitively, a expression typing judgment $e :: \mathbf{A} \mid \sigma \triangleright \mathbf{B} \mid \delta [U]$ means that e, when given a services conforming to $\mathbf{A}$, in a store conforming to σ will, after termination, yield a value of type U, while leaving a store conforming to δ, and the used services in a state where they may be still used as specified by $\mathbf{B}$. Notice that typing of expressions depends on typing of objects, through the rule for $\mathbf{new}[M]$. To intuitively grasp the meaning of our rules, we should keep in mind that in a judgment $e :: \mathbf{A} \mid \sigma \triangleright \mathbf{B} \mid \delta [U]$, the return type U, as well as the stored types σ, δ, are implicitly owned (we avoid writing, $e.g.$, U° in the return type $[U]$). So, in the rule for a value (name or variable), the value v may be returned only if its type is owned (T°). The same happens in the rule for a write $a!(v)$, where ownership of a T view of v is handed over from the thread to the store. Notice how read / write effects are recorded in the left (σ) and right (δ) environments. The rule for method call $v.1(u)$ requires separation between the method server v and the argument u. However, it does not force them to be different objects: a general form of non-interference is here ensured by the spatial typing, stating that the method part and the argument part do not share resources. We also have some congruence rules, a subtyping rule, and a rule for **let**. In the **let** rule, each expression e_i is required not to interfere with a concurrent e_j ($e_i \# e_j$), by reading and writing in the local store. We assert $e \#_N e'$ whenever e and e' do not write ($a!(v)$) or read ($a?$) using a common tag name a in N ($e.g.$, we have $a!(); b? \#_{\{a\}} b!(); c?$). This condition will be relaxed in Section 4, after the introduction of shared variables and types. Notice that the values returned from each e_i, whose evaluation depends on separate resources $\mathbf{B}_i$, are separate owned values, each one of type V_i°.

In Fig. 6, we present the typing rules for objects and networks. Intuitively, if the judgement $[M ; t] :: \mathbf{A} \mid \sigma \triangleright \mathbf{B} \mid \delta [U]$ is valid, it states that any object $n[M ; s ; t]$ where the store s satisfies σ, may be composed with any system satisfying $\mathbf{A}$ and be safely used according to type U. The residuals $\mathbf{B}$ and δ reflect the state of the external and local resources after U has been exercised. Under this intuitive reading, all the rules for objects are already quite transparent, and the same remark also applies to the rules for networks. We discuss a bit the rule for object introduction. The rule requires that all state elements are distinctly named, and that each of the stored values n_i is actually owned by the object (typed by V_i°). Although in a perhaps subtle way, subtyping plays a key role in the derivation of expression, objects and network judgments, the factorization of a substantial amount of structural reasoning in the subtyping relation contributed to keep our typing rules reasonably clean (we omit the obvious rule for subtyping object judgments).

Example 2.6 (*continued*). We now assign types to the system components. For F and H we may expect the typings $F :: \; \triangleright f : T_f$ and $H :: \; \triangleright h : T_h$, where we consider $T_f \triangleq$ $\mathbf{rec}\ \alpha.\mathtt{flight}();(\mathtt{book}() \wedge \mathtt{free}());\alpha$ and $T_h \triangleq \mathbf{rec}\ \alpha.\mathtt{hotel}();(\mathtt{book}() \wedge \mathtt{free}());\alpha$. For the gateway G, let $G :: bk : T_{bank} \; \triangleright \; gw : T_{gw}$ where $T_{bk} \triangleq \mathbf{rec}\ \alpha.\mathtt{debit}()\mathbf{bool};\alpha$ and $T_{gw} \triangleq \mathbf{rec}\ \alpha.\mathtt{pay}(\mathtt{book}() \wedge \mathtt{free}());\alpha$. Set $T_{br} \triangleq \mathbf{rec}\ \alpha.(\mathtt{flight}() \mid \mathtt{hotel}())$; $\mathtt{order}();\alpha$. Now, the following judgment is derivable: $(F \mid H \mid G \mid B) :: bk : T_{bk} \; \triangleright \; br :$ T_{br}. It asserts that $(F \mid H \mid G \mid B)$, when composed with any system providing the T_{bk} type at bk, will be safe for use at br as specified by T_{br}. Such typing may be obtained compositionally in many ways. A possible factoring is between broker $B :: gw : T_{gw}, f :$ $T_f, h : T_h \; \triangleright \; br : T_{br}$ and back-end $(G \mid H \mid F) :: bk : T_{bk} \; \triangleright \; gw : T_{gw}, f : T_f, h : T_h$.

We define the following variant of the Kleene iterator: $T^\otimes \triangleq \mathbf{rec}\ \alpha.(T;\alpha)^\circ$. Notice that we have $T^\otimes \; \mathtt{<:>} \; (T;T^\otimes)^\circ \; \mathtt{<:} \; \mathbf{stop} \wedge (T;T^\otimes)$. Hence, $T^\otimes$ can be unfolded infinitely many times into copies of T (as T^* does), but also be stored and returned by method calls, since it is an owned type (while T^* may not).

Example 2.10 (*continued*). For the spooler S, we propose the following typings. First, we abbreviate $T_{res} \triangleq (\mathbf{use}())^\otimes$, $T_{rm} \triangleq \mathbf{rec}\ \alpha.\mathtt{alloc}()T_{res};\mathtt{free}(T_{res}^\circ);\alpha$ and $T_{srv} \triangleq$ $\mathbf{rec}\ \alpha.\mathtt{open}();T_{res};\mathtt{close}();\alpha$. Then the following is derivable: $S :: pool : T_{rm} \; \triangleright \; server :$ T_{srv}. Notice how owner types (T_{res}°) are used to express ownership transfer of resources from the pool to the spooler and back. In general, we would expect a resource pool such as the one expected at *pool* to be shared by multiple users, while here the T_{rm} type just captures a very particular sequential usage. We will return to this in Section 4 below.

The safety properties ensured by our type system may be formally expressed in many ways. The fundamental consequences of typing are stuck-freeness, from which, as discussed in Section 2, other properties follows, such as race absence for unshareable resources, and conformance to usage protocols. We can thus already hint to our main soundness result, in a somewhat specific form.

Claim. Let $P :: \; \triangleright \; n : \mathtt{l}(\mathbf{stop})\mathbf{stop}$. Then there is Q such that $P \xrightarrow{n.\mathtt{l}_c(\mathbf{nil})} Q$ and for all R such that $Q \Rightarrow R$ it is not the case that $stuck(R)$.

This states that any network typed by $n : \mathtt{l}(\mathbf{stop})\mathbf{stop}$ offers a method $\mathtt{l}$ at object n that, after invoked, is ensured to induce a well-behaved distributed computation. More general soundness results follow as direct consequence of the semantics of types developed in the next section.

3.1 Logical Semantics of Types

The intended semantics for a typing environment $\mathbf{A}$ is that it denotes a certain property $[\![\mathbf{A}]\!]$, in the sense that if P is assigned type $\mathbf{A}$, then soundness of our type system ensures that $P \in [\![\mathbf{A}]\!]$, or, in terms of logical satisfaction, that $P \models \mathbf{A}$. In fact, we will not interpret

$$
\begin{aligned}
&P \models \mathcal{A} \wedge \mathcal{B} &&\text{iff} && P \models \mathcal{A} \text{ and } P \models \mathcal{B} \\
&P \models \mathcal{A} \mid \mathcal{B} &&\text{iff} && \text{exists } Q, R.\ P \equiv Q \mid R \text{ and } Q \models \mathcal{A} \text{ and } R \models \mathcal{B} \\
&P \models \mathcal{A} \rhd \mathcal{B} &&\text{iff} && \text{for all } Q.\ \text{if } (P\|Q) \text{ and } Q \models \mathcal{A} \text{ then } P \mid Q \models \mathcal{B} \\
&P \models \forall x.\mathcal{A} &&\text{iff} && \text{for all } n.\ P \models \mathcal{A}\{x\leftarrow n\} \\
&P \models \textbf{stop} &&\text{iff} && idle(P) \\
&P \models \mathcal{A}^{\circ} &&\text{iff} && P \models \mathcal{A} \text{ and } P \models \textbf{stop} \\
&P \models \mathcal{A}; \mathcal{B} &&\text{iff} && \text{exists } Q, R.\ P \equiv Q \mid R \text{ and } Q \models \mathcal{A} \text{ and} \\
& && && \text{for all } Q'.\ \text{if } Q \xmapsto{\mathcal{A}} Q' \text{ then } Q' \mid R \models \mathcal{B} \\
&P \models n : 1(m) &&\text{iff} && \text{exists } Q.\ P \xmapsto{n.1_c(m)} Q \\
&P \models (\mathsf{v})\mathcal{A} &&\text{iff} && \text{exists } Q.\ P \equiv (\mathsf{v}\overline{m})Q \text{ and } Q \models \mathcal{A} \text{ and } \overline{m}\#fn(\mathcal{A}) \\
&P \models n : c(\mathcal{A}, r) &&\text{iff} && \text{for all } R, Q.\ \text{if } R\|P \text{ and } R \models \mathcal{A} \text{ and } P \mid R \Rightarrow Q \text{ then} \\
& && && \neg stuck(Q) \text{ and} \\
& && && \text{for all } Q', r.\ \text{if } Q \xmapsto{n.c(r)} Q' \text{ then exists } R', P'.\ Q' \equiv R' \mid P' \text{ and } R \xrightarrow{\mathcal{A}} R'
\end{aligned}
$$

$$P \xmapsto{\textbf{stop}} P \qquad \dfrac{P \xmapsto{\mathcal{U}} Q}{P \xmapsto{\mathcal{U}\wedge\mathcal{V}} Q} \qquad \dfrac{P \xmapsto{\mathcal{V}} Q}{P \xmapsto{\mathcal{U}\wedge\mathcal{V}} Q} \qquad \dfrac{P \xmapsto{\mathcal{U}\{x\leftarrow n\}} Q}{P \xmapsto{\forall x.\mathcal{U}} Q} \qquad \dfrac{P \xmapsto{n.1_c(m)} Q}{P \xmapsto{n:1(m)} Q}$$

$$\dfrac{P \equiv (\mathsf{v}\overline{m})R \quad R \xmapsto{\mathcal{U}} Q}{P \xmapsto{(\mathsf{v})\mathcal{U}} Q} \qquad \dfrac{P \equiv P_1 \mid P_2 \quad P_1 \xmapsto{\mathcal{U}} Q_1 \quad P_2 \xmapsto{\mathcal{V}} Q_2 \quad Q_1 \mid Q_2 \equiv Q}{P \xmapsto{\mathcal{U}\mid\mathcal{V}} Q}$$

$$\dfrac{P \xmapsto{\mathcal{U}} R \quad R \xmapsto{\mathcal{V}} Q}{P \xmapsto{\mathcal{U};\mathcal{V}} Q} \qquad \dfrac{P \equiv R \mid Q \quad R \models \mathcal{U}}{P \xmapsto{\mathcal{U}} Q} \qquad \dfrac{R \models \mathcal{U} \quad P \mid R \Rightarrow \xmapsto{n.c(r)} Q \mid R' \quad R \xmapsto{\mathcal{U}} R'}{P \xmapsto{n:c(\mathcal{U},r)} Q}$$

Fig. 7. Satisfaction and Typed Usage

types as properties directly, but will rather embed types in a more primitive spatial logic, so that each typing environment **A** is interpreted by a certain formula $\mathcal{A}$. The satisfaction predicate $\models$ is inductively defined on the structure of formulas, in such a way that $P \models \mathcal{A}$ implies that P enjoys certain general safety properties, in particular, stuck-freeness.

Definition 3.2 (Spatial Logic). *The set $\mathcal{F}$ of formulas is defined by:*

$$\mathcal{A}, \mathcal{B}, \mathcal{C}, \mathcal{U}, \mathcal{V} ::= \mathcal{A} \wedge \mathcal{B} \mid \forall x.\mathcal{A} \mid \mathcal{A} \mid \mathcal{B} \mid \mathcal{A} \rhd \mathcal{B} \mid \textbf{stop} \mid \mathcal{A}; \mathcal{B} \mid \mathcal{A}^{\circ} \mid n : c(\mathcal{A}, r) \mid n : 1(m) \mid (\mathsf{v})\mathcal{A}$$

As in [6,7,5], our logic includes (positive) first-order logic, the basic spatial operators of composition and its adjunct with their standard meanings, and certain specific operators, in particular some behavioral modalities. Instead of including action prefixing modalities, we introduce a general sequential composition formula of the form $\mathcal{A}; \mathcal{B}$, where $\mathcal{A}$ is interpreted both a property, and a *usage pattern*. Usage patterns are modeled by *typed usage*, a transition relation between networks and labeled by formulas, noted $P \xmapsto{\mathcal{A}} Q$. The intuitive meaning of $P \xmapsto{\mathcal{A}} Q$ is that if P is used as specified by $\mathcal{A}$, it may evolve to Q. Since satisfaction and typed usage are defined by mutual recursion, we present them in a single definition, for the sake of clarity.

Definition 3.3. Satisfaction, $P \models \mathcal{A}$, and typed usage, $P \xmapsto{\mathcal{A}} Q$ are defined in Fig. 7.

To avoid clashes between fresh names introduced in the subsidiary transitions, the rule for $P \xmapsto{\mathcal{U}\mid\mathcal{V}} Q$ is subject to the proviso $(fn(Q_1) \setminus fn(P_1)) \# (fn(Q_2) \setminus fn(P_2))$.

The semantics of $n : \mathtt{l}(m)$ and $n : c(\mathcal{A}, r)$ are defined from external actions of networks (Def 2.9). Intuitively, a network P satisfies formula $n : c(\mathcal{A}, r)$ if it contains a thread c that whenever passed a resource R satisfying $\mathcal{A}$, is guaranteed to always evolve in a stuck free way until a value r is returned, while exercising on R an usage as specified by $\mathcal{A}$. Thus, $n : c(\mathcal{A}, r)$ enforces both safety and liveness properties. Using these ingredients, we now define our interpretation of types. Given a type environment $\mathbf{A}$, we define a formula $\lceil \mathbf{A} \rceil$ by considering the embedding:

$$
\begin{aligned}
\lceil n : \mathbf{stop} \rceil &\triangleq \mathbf{stop} & \lceil n : U \mid V \rceil &\triangleq (\nu)(\lceil n : U \rceil \mid \lceil n : V \rceil) \\
\lceil n : U^\circ \rceil &\triangleq (\nu)\lceil n : U \rceil^\circ & \lceil n : U; V \rceil &\triangleq (\nu)(\lceil n : U \rceil; \lceil n : V \rceil) \\
\lceil n : \mathtt{l}(U)V \rceil &\triangleq \mathbf{stop} \wedge \forall u . n : \mathtt{l}(u); \lceil n : c(u : U)V \rceil & \lceil n : U \wedge V \rceil &\triangleq \lceil n : U \rceil \wedge \lceil n : V \rceil \\
\lceil n : c(u : U)V \rceil &\triangleq \forall r. c(\lceil u : U \rceil, r); \lceil r : V^\circ \rceil & \lceil \mathbf{A}, \mathbf{B} \rceil &\triangleq \lceil \mathbf{A} \rceil \mid \lceil \mathbf{B} \rceil
\end{aligned}
$$

Notice that all types are interpreted quite directly, except method and thread types, which are interpreted in terms of finer grain primitives. Building on this interpretation, we define validity of subtyping and typing judgments as follows:

$$
valid(\mathbf{A} <: \mathbf{B}) \triangleq \llbracket \mathbf{A} \rrbracket \subseteq \llbracket \mathbf{B} \rrbracket \qquad valid(P :: \mathbf{A} \rhd \mathbf{B}) \triangleq P \in \llbracket \mathbf{A} \rhd \mathbf{B} \rrbracket
$$

From now on, we will sometimes write typing environments where formulas are expected, having in mind the interpretation just presented. Our interpretation enjoys several nice properties. For example, the property stated in the *Claim* above (right before Section 3.1) is a direct consequence of the definition of the logical predicate $\models$. We can now state our main results:

Proposition 3.4 (Soundness of Subtyping). *For all* $\mathbf{A}$, $\mathbf{B}$, *if* $\mathbf{A} <: \mathbf{B}$ *then* $\llbracket \mathbf{A} \rrbracket \subseteq \llbracket \mathbf{B} \rrbracket$.

Proof. We may show the result for all properties, not just encodings of types, with the exception of congruence on the left for sequential composition. For that, we consider a stronger statement and prove, by induction on the derivation of $\mathbf{A} <: \mathbf{B}$, that if $\mathbf{A} <: \mathbf{B}$ and $\llbracket C \rrbracket \subseteq \llbracket \mathcal{D} \rrbracket$ then $\llbracket \mathbf{A}; C \rrbracket \subseteq \llbracket \mathbf{B}; \mathcal{D} \rrbracket$. ∎

Theorem 3.5 (Soundness of Typing). *If* $P :: \mathbf{A} \rhd \mathbf{B}$ *is derivable then* $P \models \mathbf{A} \rhd \mathbf{B}$.

Proof. The proof requires establishing a few facts about the satisfaction and typed usage relations, and some Lemmas stating soundness of typing for expressions and objects with respect to the intended notions of validity, which are given thus:

$$
valid([M; \overline{s_i \langle n_i \rangle}; t] :: \mathbf{A} \mid \sigma \rhd \mathbf{B} \mid \delta[T]) \triangleq
$$
$$
ForAll\ n .\ n[M ; \overline{s_i \langle n_i \rangle} ; t] \models (\mathbf{A} \mid \Pi(n_i : \sigma(n_i)^\circ) \rhd (n : T); (\mathbf{B} \mid \Pi(n_i : \delta(n_i)^\circ))
$$

$$
valid(e :: \mathbf{A}, \overline{x : T} \mid \sigma \rhd \mathbf{B}, \overline{x : S} \mid \delta[V]) \triangleq
$$
$$
Exists\ \mathbf{C}, \mathbf{U} .\ \mathbf{A} <: \mathbf{C}; \mathbf{B} .\ \overline{x : T} <: \mathbf{U}; \overline{x : S} .\ ForAll\ n, \overline{s}, v, \overline{p} .
$$
$$
n[; \overline{s_i \langle n_i \rangle} ; c \langle e\{x_1 \leftarrow p_1\} \cdots \{x_k \leftarrow p_k\} \rangle] \models
$$
$$
(\mathbf{A} \mid \overline{p : T} \mid \Pi(n_i : \sigma(n_i)^\circ) \rhd c(\mathbf{C} \mid \mathbf{U}, v); (\mathbf{B} \mid \overline{p : S} \mid \Pi(n_i : \delta(n_i)^\circ) \mid v : V^\circ)
$$

The definition of validity for expression judgments is a bit more involved, as it requires closure under substitution. Notice how our logic provides a suitable metalanguage in which the properties of interest, explained above in intuitive terms, may be formally expressed rather succinctly. As in typical semantical soundness proofs of logical systems, the proof proceeds by checking that each rule preserves validity. ∎

The proof technique we have developed here may be seen as an instance of the general method of logical relations, well understood in the setting of functional programming, but still quite unexplored in concurrency. In a similar way, we build on a semantic interpretation of typed terms, which is defined by induction on types (as formulas), and then prove soundness by induction on typing derivations. Our result establishing validity under substitution for derivable expression typing judgments then plays the role of the so-called Basic Lemma in the logical relations method. Because types are directly interpreted as properties of networks, our soundness results allows us to conclude:

Proposition 3.6. *Let* $P \models \mathbf{A}$ *and* $\mathbf{A} <: \mathbf{B}; \mathbf{C}$. *For all* Q. *if* $P \overset{\mathbf{B}}{\longmapsto} Q$ *then* $Q \models \mathbf{C}$.

Proposition 3.6 is a semantic counterpart of the more familiar syntactic subject reduction property. In our case, it is an immediate consequence of the soundness of subtyping and the semantics of $\mathbf{B}; \mathbf{C}$. By interpreting the type $n : \mathtt{l}(U)V$, we also have:

Proposition 3.7 (Stuck Freeness). *Let* $P :: \; \triangleright \; n : \mathtt{l}(U)V$ *be derivable. Let* R *be such that* $R \models m : U$ *and* $R\|P$. *Then, for all* Q *such that* $P \mid R \overset{n.\mathtt{l}_c(m)}{\Longrightarrow} Q$ *it is not the case that* $\mathrm{stuck}(Q)$. *Moreover, if* $Q \overset{\overline{n.c(r)}}{\longrightarrow} Q'$ *for some* Q', *then* $Q' \models r : V^\circ$.

4   Resource Sharing and Shared Types

Although our framework already seems fairly powerful, it still prevents useful forms of sharing to be typable. While race absence may be a desirable correctness property of concurrent programming in general, in many situations, races are not problematic if the involved resources may be safely shared (*e.g.*, read only variables). Moreover, many system resources are deliberately assumed to be raceful (*e.g.*, semaphores, buffers). Sharing is also particularly useful to allow local communication between different threads. In this section, we sketch how sharing is accommodated in our framework. No major extensions to the calculus are needed, we just add replicated methods to the basic syntax, and enrich structural congruence accordingly:

$$M ::= \cdots \mid *\mathtt{l}(x) = e \qquad \begin{aligned} *\mathtt{l}(x) = e &\equiv (*\mathtt{l}(x) = e \mid *\mathtt{l}(x) = e) \\ *\mathtt{l}(x) = e &\equiv (*\mathtt{l}(x) = e \mid \; \mathtt{l}(x) = e) \end{aligned}$$

The operational semantics in kept unmodified. Not surprisingly, more fundamental extensions relate to typing, and to the need to discipline shared access to the local store of objects. To that end, we assume that the local state of every object is classified in a unshared part (as in our basic model), and a shared part. The intent is that while the types of the values stored under a given tag in the unshared part may dynamically change (cf. the spooler example 2.10), values stored under a given tag in the shared part must satisfy a fixed invariant. Since the shared part may suffer interference from parallel running threads, we rely on this invariant to ensure soundness. To type such shared usages it is then useful to introduce shared types, defined $U! \overset{\triangle}{=} \mathbf{rec} \; \alpha.(\mathbf{stop} \wedge U \wedge (\alpha \mid \alpha))$.

Shared types satisfy interesting subtyping principles, namely $U! \mathrel{<:>} U! \mid U!, U! \mathrel{<:} U$ and $U! \mathrel{<:} \mathbf{stop}$. The first principle allows a service of type $U!$ to be used simultaneously by an unbounded number of clients. We may also derive $U! \mathrel{<:} U; (U!)$.

For a first (trivial) example, consider the object $NL \triangleq nl[\, *\mathtt{null}() = \mathbf{nil}\,;\ ;\,]$. It offers a method $\mathtt{null}$ that whenever called returns $\mathbf{nil}$. Clearly, the service provided by NL may be shared by an arbitrary number of clients, without incurring in any execution error (stuck state). So we expect the typing $NL :: \,\triangleright\, (\mathtt{null}()\mathbf{stop})!$ to be acceptable. For another example, consider the code: $BF \triangleq buf[\, *\mathtt{put}(x) = a!(x) \mid *\mathtt{get}() = a?;\ ;\,]$. Object BF implements a resource pool, that keeps in its local state a bunch of references for resources of a given type, say R°. Provided that the invariant $buf.a : R$ is maintained, we expect to assign a typing $BF :: \,\triangleright\, buf : (\mathtt{put}(R^\circ) \wedge \mathtt{get}()R)!$. This type allows any number of clients to share the pool, while using both methods, possibly concurrently. Another possible typing for BF is $BF :: \,\triangleright\, buf : \mathtt{put}(R^\circ)! \mid (\mathtt{get}()R)!$. This latter typing allows BF to be used as an (unordered) queue, in a context where a bunch of writers use the $buf : \mathtt{put}(R^\circ)!$ view, while a bunch of readers use the $buf : (\mathtt{get}()R)!$ view of BF. Notice that although the methods $\mathtt{put}$ and $\mathtt{get}$ interfere through the store, according to our intended semantics their are still separable by $(- \mid -)$ (up to changes in the store conforming to the sharing invariant $buf.a : R$).

Example 2.10 *(continued)*. Given an implementation of a resource pool RP similar to BF above, typed by $RP :: \,\triangleright\, pool : T_p$ where $T_p \triangleq (\mathtt{free}(T_{res}{}^\circ) \wedge \mathtt{alloc}()R)!$, we expect then to type S with $S :: pool : T_p \,\triangleright\, server : T_{\mathtt{srv}}$.

We now illustrate the technical development needed to introduce sharing in our type system. Basically, we extend typing judgments with a further extra component (ε), that specifies (by typing) the invariants on admissible interferences through the stores. We illustrate our general approach with a few key rules.

$$a? :: \; |\sigma|\varepsilon, a : T \,\triangleright\, |\sigma[T] \qquad\qquad a!(v) :: v : T^\circ \,|\sigma|\varepsilon, a : T \,\triangleright\, |\sigma[T]$$

$$\frac{[M;t] :: \mathbf{A} \,|\, \overline{s_i : V_i} \,|\, \overline{p_i : U_i} \,\triangleright\, \mathbf{B}; \delta[T]}{n[M; \overline{s_i\langle n_i\rangle} \,|\, \overline{p_{i_j}\langle r_{i_j}\rangle}; t] :: \mathbf{A} \,|\, \Pi(n_i : V_i^\circ) \,|\, \Pi(r_{i_j} : U_i^\circ) \,|\, \overline{n.p_i : U_i} \,\triangleright\, n : T}$$

The $\overline{n.p_i : U_i}$ (or $\overline{p_i : U_i}$) slot in the judgments specifies admissible interference from the environment, meaning that the store of object n may well be modified on cells $p_i\langle-\rangle$ provided that they will always contain values of type U_i°. To interpret the extended judgments, the logical predicate $\models$ is modified so that the interpretation of $c(\mathcal{A}, v)$ also takes into account interferences through the local store. Soundness proofs then follow the same lines of those above; a full treatment of these issues is left for an extended version of this paper.

5 Related Work and Discussion

We have presented a distributed object calculus able to model some essential aspects of service-based systems. However, the main focus of this work is on notions of spatial-behavioral typing, and their use to discipline interactions in distributed systems. Although the design of our calculus was influenced by several object calculi and related models [1,3,13], the distributed remote method invocation semantics adopted has not been much explored, even if it seems a natural choice when modeling distributed services [12,18]. In our case, such a model seemed to be fundamental for our spatial interpretation of types. Our type system enforces several safety properties, in particular availability (method calls are always served), and race absence with respect to unshareable resource access. Such properties result from the fact that our types are able to specify constraints on sequentiality of behavior, separation of resources, and dynamic propagation of ownership, in a compositional way. Compositionality is certainly a desirable property of any verification method, but it seems absolutely critical when one considers distributed service based systems, which are by nature open-ended, and dynamically assembled by relying on local interface specifications.

Formally, our type system can be seen as a fragment of a spatial logic for concurrency [6,7,5], where the composition operator plays a key role in ensuring resource control and non-interference. In our model, separation, up to structural congruence, cuts across the structure of objects, in order to separate both global and local resources. Our work draws inspiration on some specification techniques for the separation logics [20,19], in particular our use of | to talk about a form of resource separation, even if in the case of dynamic spatial logics the "resources" are active processes, quite unlike with the separation logics, that talk about the passive state (the heap). We have also introduced a sequential type composition operator and a owned type operator in our type structure. The owned type constructor, as we have studied here, seems to be new. Different notions of ownership and associated type systems have been proposed [4,11], where ownership is considered a structural rather than a dynamic capability. The spatial interpretation of composition, together with owned types, also distinguishes our approach from other type systems for concurrent calculi that also include a composition operation [16,10]. In those approaches, parallel composition is interpreted behaviorally, rather than as spatial separation, and subtyping corresponds to behavioral simulation, rather than to logical entailment; the same observation applies to [17]. Protocols definable in our type system are also reminiscent of session types [15], it would be interesting to see how sessions might be represented in this setting.

Unlike most works on type systems for concurrent and distributed calculi, we have adopted a semantic view of typing, and build on a logical relations technique to prove soundness. The (original) understanding of types as properties has not always been a common guiding principle in the design of types for concurrent calculi, where a syntactical view seems to be dominant (for an exception, we must refer to [9]). It would be also challenging to investigate how the compositional approach we have followed might also be applicable to (at least) certain kinds of security properties [2].

Acknowledgments. This work was supported by IST Sensoria IP (IST-3-016004-IP-09 2005-2008), SpaceTimeTypes (POSI/EIA/55582/2004), and CITI.

References

1. Abadi, M., Cardelli, L.: A theory of primitive objects: Untyped and first-order systems. Inf. Comput. 125(2) (1996)
2. Bartoletti, M., Degano, P., Ferrari, G.: Enforcing secure service composition. In: 18th IEEE Computer Security Foundations Workshop (CSFW-18 2005), pp. 211–223. IEEE Computer Society, Los Alamitos (2005)

3. Di Blasio, P., Fisher, K.: A calculus for concurrent objects. In: Sassone, V., Montanari, U. (eds.) CONCUR 1996. LNCS, vol. 1119, pp. 655–670. Springer, Heidelberg (1996)
4. Boyapati, C., Liskov, B., Shrira, L.: Ownership types for object encapsulation. In: Conference Record of POPL 2003: The 30th SIGPLAN-SIGACT Symposium on Principles of Programming Languages (2003)
5. Caires, L.: Behavioral and Spatial Properties in a Logic for the Pi-Calculus. In: Walukiewicz, I. (ed.) FOSSACS 2004. LNCS, vol. 2987, Springer, Heidelberg (2004)
6. Caires, L., Cardelli, L.: A Spatial Logic for Concurrency (Part I). Information and Computation 186(2), 194–235 (2003)
7. Caires, L., Cardelli, L.: A Spatial Logic for Concurrency (Part II). Theoretical Computer Science 3(322), 517–565 (2004)
8. Cardelli, L., Gordon, A.D.: Anytime, Anywhere. Modal Logics for Mobile Ambients. In: 27th ACM Symp. on Principles of Programming Languages, pp. 365–377. ACM, New York (2000)
9. Castagna, G., De Nicola, R., Varacca, D.: Semantic subtyping for the π-calculus. In: 20th IEEE Symposium on Logic in Computer Science (LICS 2005), pp. 92–101. IEEE Computer Society, Los Alamitos (2005)
10. Chaki, S., Rajamani, S.K., Rehof, J.: Types as models: model checking message-passing programs. In: Conference Record of POPL 2002: The 29th SIGPLAN-SIGACT Symposium on Principles of Programming Languages, pp. 45–57 (2002)
11. Clarke, D.G., Drossopoulou, S.: Ownership, encapsulation and the disjointness of type and effect. In: Proceedings of the 2002 ACM SIGPLAN Conference on Object-Oriented Programming Systems, Languages and Applications, OOPSLA 2002, pp. 292–310 (2002)
12. Boreale, M., et al.: SCC: a Service Centered Calculus. In: WS-FM 2006. LNCS, Springer, Heidelberg (2006)
13. Gordon, A.D., Hankin, P.D.: A concurrent object calculus: Reduction and typing. Electr. Notes Theor. Comput. Sci. 16(3) (1998)
14. Hennessy, M., Riely, J.: Resource access control in systems of mobile agents. Inf. Comput. 173(1), 82–120 (2002)
15. Honda, K., Vasconcelos, V.T., Kubo, M.: Language primitives and type discipline for structured communication-based programming. In: Hankin, C. (ed.) ESOP 1998 and ETAPS 1998. LNCS, vol. 1381, pp. 122–138. Springer, Heidelberg (1998)
16. Igarashi, A., Kobayashi, N.: A generic type system for the pi-calculus. In: POPL 2001: 28th Annual Symposium on Principles of Programming Languages (2001)
17. Igarashi, A., Kobayashi, N.: Resource usage analysis. In: POPL 2002: The 29th SIGPLAN-SIGACT Symposium on Principles of Programming Languages, pp. 331–342 (2002)
18. Misra, J., Cook, W.R.: Computation orchestration: A basis for wide-area computing. Journal of Software and Systems Modeling (2006)
19. O'Hearn, P.W.: Resources, concurrency and local reasoning. In: Gardner, P., Yoshida, N. (eds.) CONCUR 2004. LNCS, vol. 3170, pp. 49–67. Springer, Heidelberg (2004)
20. Reynolds, J.C.: Separation Logic: A Logic for Shared Mutable Data Structures. In: Third Annual Symposium on Logic in Computer Science, Copenhagen, Denmark, IEEE Computer Society, Los Alamitos (2002)

Integration of a Security Type System into a Program Logic*

Reiner Hähnle[1], Jing Pan[2], Philipp Rümmer[1], and Dennis Walter[1]

[1] Department of Computer Science and Engineering,
Chalmers University of Technology and Göteborg University
[2] Department of Mathematics and Computer Science,
Eindhoven University of Technology

Abstract. Type systems and program logics are often conceived to be at opposing ends of the spectrum of formal software analyses. In this paper we show that a flow-sensitive type system ensuring non-interference in a simple while language can be expressed through specialised rules of a program logic. In our framework, the structure of non-interference proofs resembles the corresponding derivations in a recent security type system, meaning that the algorithmic version of the type system can be used as a proof procedure for the logic. We argue that this is important for obtaining uniform proof certificates in a proof-carrying code framework. We discuss in which cases the interleaving of approximative and precise reasoning allows us to deal with delimited information release. Finally, we present ideas on how our results can be extended to encompass features of realistic programming languages like Java.

1 Introduction

Formal verification of software properties has recently attracted a lot of interest. An important factor in this trend is the enormously increased need for secure applications, particularly in mobile environments. Confidentiality policies can often be expressed in terms of information flow properties. Existing approaches to verification of such properties mainly fall into two categories: the first are type-based security analyses ([20] gives an overview), whereas the second are deduction-based employing program logics (e.g. [13, 5, 9]).

It is often noted that type-based analyses have a very logic-like character: A language for judgements is provided, a semantics that determines the set of *valid* judgments, and finally type rules to approximate the semantics mechanically. Type systems typically can trade a precise reflection of the semantics of judgments for automation and efficiency: many valid judgments are rejected.

* This work was funded in part by a STINT institutional grant and by the Information Society Technologies programme of the European Commission, Future and Emerging Technologies under the IST-2005-015905 MOBIUS project. This article reflects only the authors' views and the Community is not liable for any use that may be made of the information contained therein.

U. Montanari, D. Sannella, and R. Bruni (Eds.): TGC 2006, LNCS 4661, pp. 116–131, 2007.
© Springer-Verlag Berlin Heidelberg 2007

For program logics, the situation is quite the opposite: Calculi try to capture the semantics as precisely as possible and therefore have significantly higher complexity than type systems. Furthermore, due to the richer syntax of program logics – compared to the judgments in the type world – the framework is more general and the same program logic can be used to express and reason about different kinds of program properties.

The main contributions of this paper are: we construct a calculus for a program logic that naturally simulates the rules of a flow-sensitive type system for secure information flow. We prove soundness of the program logic calculus with respect to the type system. The so obtained interpretation of the type system in dynamic logic yields increased precision and opens up ways of expressing properties beyond pure non-interference. Concretely, we are able to prove the absence of exceptions in certain cases, and we can express delimited information release. Therefore, we can speak of an integration of a security type system into program logic.

A crucial benefit of the integration is that we obtain an automatic proof procedure for non-interference formulae: because of the similarity between the program logic calculus and the type rules, it is possible to mechanically translate type derivations to deduction proofs in the program logic. At the same time, certain advantages over the type system in terms of precision (Sect. 5) come for free without sacrificing automation.

The paper is organised as follows. In Section 2 we argue that a formal connection between type systems and program logics fits nicely into a verification strategy for advanced security policies of mobile JAVA programs based on proof-carrying-code (PCC). Section 3 introduces the terminology used in the rest of the paper. In Section 4 we define and discuss our program logic tailored to non-interference analysis. Our ideas for increasing the precision of the calculus and for covering delimited information release are given in Section 5. Due to lack of space, we could not include proofs in this paper. An extended version with all proofs is provided at [10].

2   Integrating Type Systems and Program Logics

We think that the integration of type systems and program logics is an important ingredient to make security policy checks scale up to mobile code written in modern industrial programming languages.

Certificates for Proof-Carrying Code. For the security infrastructure of mobile, ubiquituous computing it is essential that security policies can be enforced locally on the end-user device without requiring a secure internet connection to a trusted authentication authority. In the EU project MOBIUS[1] this infrastructure is based on the proof-carrying code (PCC) technology [16]. The basic idea of PCC is to provide a formal proof that a security policy holds for a given application, and then to hand down to the code consumer (end user) not only the

---

[1] mobius.inria.fr/twiki/bin/view/Mobius

application code, but also a certificate that allows to reconstruct the security proof locally with low overhead. Therefore, the end user device must run a proof checker, and, in a standard PCC architecture [16], also a verification condition generator, because certificates do not contain aspects of programs. The latter makes the approach unpractical for devices with limited resources. In addition, the security policies considered in MOBIUS [14] are substantially more complex than the safety policies originally envisioned in PCC. In foundational PCC [4] this is dispensed with at the price of including the formal semantics of the target language in the proof checker. The size of the resulting proof certificates makes this approach impractical so far. In the case of an axiomatic semantics as used in the verification system employed in the present paper [1], it seems possible to arrive at a *trusted code base* that is small enough. In the type-based version of PCC the trusted code base consists of a type checker instead of a proof checker. The integration of a type system for secure information flow into a program logic makes it possible to construct uniformly logic-based certificates, and no hybrid certificates need to be maintained. As a consequence, the PCC architecture is simplified and the trusted code base is significantly reduced. Efforts that go into similar directions in the sense that the scope of certificates is extended include Configurable PCC [17] and Temporal Logic PCC [8].

Synergies from Combining Type-Based and Deduction-Based Verification. The possibility to combine type-based and deduction-based reasoning in one framework leads to a number of synergies. In an integrated type- and deduction-based framework it is possible to increase the precision of the analysis dynamically on demand. Type systems ignore the values of variables. In a deduction framework, however, one can, e.g., prove that in the program "**if** (b) $y = x$; **if** $(\neg b)$ $z = y$;" the variables z and x are independent, because the value of b always excludes the path through one of the conditionals. Note that it is not necessary to track the values of all variables to determine this: only the value of b matters in the example. More realistic examples are in Sect. 5.

A further opportunity offered by the integration of type-based analysis into an expressive logical framework is the formulation of additional security properties without the need for substantial changes in the underlying rule system or the deduction engine. To illustrate this point we show in Sect. 5 that it is possible to express delimited information release in our program logic.

3   Background and Terminology

3.1   Non-interference Analysis

Generally speaking, a program has secure information flow if no knowledge about some given secret data can be gained by executing this program. Whether or not a program has secure information flow can hence only be decided according to a given security policy discriminating secret from public data. In our considerations we adopt the common model where all input and output channels are taken to be program variables. The semantic concept underlying secure information flow then is that of non-interference: nothing can be learned about a secret initially stored in variable h, by observing variable l after program execution, if the initial value of h *does not interfere with* the final value of l. Put differently, the final value of l must be *independent* of the initial value of h.

This non-interference property is commonly established via security type systems [20, 12, 21, 2], where a program is deemed secure if it is typable according to some given policy. Type systems are used to perform flow-sensitive as well as flow-insensitive analyses. Flow-insensitive approaches (e.g. [21]) require every subprogram to be well-typed according to the *same* policy. Recent flow-sensitive analyses [12, 2] allow the types of variables to change along the execution path, thereby providing more flexibility for the programmer. Like these type systems, the program logic developed in this paper will be termination insensitive, meaning that a security guarantee is only made about terminating runs of the program under consideration.

The type system of Hunt & Sands [12] is depicted in Fig. 1. The type p represents the security level of the program counter and serves to eliminate indirect information flow. The remaining components of typing judgments are a program α and two typing functions $\nabla, \nabla' : \text{PVar} \to \mathcal{L}$ mapping program variables to their respective pre- and post-types. The type system is parametric with respect to the choice of security types; it only requires them to form a (complete) lattice $\mathcal{L}$. In this paper, we will only consider the most general[2] lattice $\mathcal{P}(\text{PVar})$. One may thus think of the type $\nabla(v)$ of a variable v as the set of all variables that v's value may depend on at a given point in the program. A judgment $p \vdash^{\text{HS}} \nabla \{ \alpha \} \nabla'$ states that in context p the program α transforms the typing (or dependency approximation) ∇ into ∇'. We note that rule $\text{ASSIGN}^{\text{HS}}$ gives the system its flow-sensitive character, stating that variable v's type is changed by an assignment $v = E$ to E's type as given by the pre-typing ∇ joined with the context type p. The type t of an expression E in a typing ∇ can simply be taken to be the join of the types $\nabla(v)$ of all free variables v occurring in E, which we denote by $\nabla \vdash E : t$. Joining with the context p is required to accomodate for leakage through the program context, as in the program "$\textbf{if } (h) \{l = 1\} \{l = 0)\}$", where the initial value of h is revealed in the final value of l. A modification of the context p can be observed, e.g., in rule IF^{HS}, where the subderivation of the two branches of an if statement must be conducted in a context lifted by the type of the conditional.

3.2 Dynamic Logic with Updates

Following [9], the program logic that we investigate is a simplified version of dynamic logic (DL) for JavaCard [6]. The most notable difference to standard first-order dynamic logic for the simple while-language [11] is the presence of an explicit operator for simultaneous substitutions (called *updates* [19]). While updates become particularly useful when more complicated programming languages (with arrays or object-oriented features) are considered, in any case, they enable a more direct relation between program logic and type systems.

---

[2] In the sense that any other type lattice is subsumed by it, see [12, Lem. 6.8].

$$\frac{}{p \vdash^{\mathrm{HS}} \nabla \{ \ \} \nabla} \ \mathrm{SKIP}^{\mathrm{HS}}$$

$$\frac{\nabla \vdash E : t}{p \vdash^{\mathrm{HS}} \nabla \{ v = E \} \nabla[v \mapsto p \sqcup t]} \ \mathrm{ASSIGN}^{\mathrm{HS}}$$

$$\frac{p \vdash^{\mathrm{HS}} \nabla \{ \alpha_1 \} \nabla' \qquad p \vdash^{\mathrm{HS}} \nabla' \{ \alpha_2 \} \nabla''}{p \vdash^{\mathrm{HS}} \nabla \{ \alpha_1 \ ; \ \alpha_2 \} \nabla''} \ \mathrm{SEQ}^{\mathrm{HS}}$$

$$\frac{\nabla \vdash b : t \qquad p \sqcup t \vdash^{\mathrm{HS}} \nabla \{ \alpha_i \} \nabla' \ (i = 1,2)}{p \vdash^{\mathrm{HS}} \nabla \{ \mathbf{if} \ b \ \alpha_1 \ \alpha_2 \} \nabla'} \ \mathrm{IF}^{\mathrm{HS}}$$

$$\frac{\nabla \vdash b : t \qquad p \sqcup t \vdash^{\mathrm{HS}} \nabla \{ \alpha \} \nabla}{p \vdash^{\mathrm{HS}} \nabla \{ \mathbf{while} \ b \ \alpha \} \nabla} \ \mathrm{WHILE}^{\mathrm{HS}}$$

$$\frac{p_1 \vdash^{\mathrm{HS}} \nabla_1 \{ \alpha \} \nabla_1'}{p_2 \vdash^{\mathrm{HS}} \nabla_2 \{ \alpha \} \nabla_2'} \ \mathrm{SUB}^{\mathrm{HS}} \qquad\qquad p_2 \sqsubseteq p_1, \nabla_2 \sqsubseteq \nabla_1, \nabla_1' \sqsubseteq \nabla_2'$$

Fig. 1. Hunt & Sands' flow-sensitive type system for information flow analysis

A *signature* of DL is a tuple $(\Sigma, \mathrm{PVar}, \mathrm{LVar})$ consisting of a set Σ of *function symbols* with fixed, non-negative arity, a set PVar of *program variables* and of a countably infinite set LVar of *logical variables*. Σ, PVar, LVar are pairwise disjoint. Because some of our rules need to introduce fresh function symbols, we assume that Σ contains infinitely many symbols for each arity n. Further, we require that a distinguished nullary symbol $TRUE \in \Sigma$ exists. *Rigid terms* t_r, *ground terms* t_g, *terms* t,[3] *programs* α, *updates* U and *formulae* ϕ are then defined by the following grammar, where $f \in \Sigma$ ranges over functions, $x \in \mathrm{LVar}$ over logical variables and $v \in \mathrm{PVar}$ over program variables:

$$
\begin{aligned}
t_r &::= x \mid f(t_r, \ldots, t_r) & t_g &::= v \mid f(t_g, \ldots, t_g) \\
t &::= t_r \mid t_g \mid f(t, \ldots, t) \mid \{U\} t & U &::= \epsilon \mid v := t, U \\
\phi &::= \phi \wedge \phi \mid \forall x. \ \phi \mid \ldots \mid t = t \mid [\alpha]\phi \mid \{U\} \phi \\
\alpha &::= \alpha \ ; \ \ldots \ ; \ \alpha \mid v = t_g \mid \mathbf{if} \ t_g \ \alpha \ \alpha \mid \mathbf{while} \ t_g \ \alpha
\end{aligned}
$$

For the whole paper, we assume a fixed signature $(\Sigma, \mathrm{PVar}, \mathrm{LVar})$ in which the set $\mathrm{PVar} = \{v_1, \ldots, v_n\}$ is finite, containing exactly those variables occurring in the progam under investigation.

A *structure* is a pair $S = (D, I)$ consisting of a non-empty *universe* D and an *interpretation* I of function symbols, where $I(f) : D^n \to D$ if $f \in \Sigma$ has arity n. *Program variable assignments* and *variable assignments* are mappings $\delta : \mathrm{PVar} \to D$ and $\beta : \mathrm{LVar} \to D$. The space of all program variable assignments over the universe D is denoted by $PA^D = \mathrm{PVar} \to D$, and the corresponding flat domain by $PA_\perp^D = PA^D \cup \{\perp\}$, where $\delta \sqsubseteq \delta'$ iff $\delta = \perp$ or $\delta = \delta'$.

---

[3] Both rigid terms and ground terms are terms.

While-programs α are evaluated in structures and operate on program variable assignments. We use a standard denotational semantics for such programs

$$[\alpha]^S : PA^D \to PA^D_\perp$$

and define, for instance, the meaning of a loop "**while** b α" through

$$[\textbf{while } b \ \alpha]^S =_{\text{def}} \bigsqcup_i w_i, \qquad w_i : PA^D \to PA^D_\perp$$

$$w_0(\delta) =_{\text{def}} \perp, \quad w_{i+1}(\delta) =_{\text{def}} \begin{cases} (w_i)_\perp ([\alpha]^S(\delta)) & \text{for } val_{S,\delta}(b) = val_S(TRUE) \\ \delta & \text{otherwise} \end{cases}$$

where we make use of a 'bottom lifting': $(f)_\perp(x) = \textit{if } (x = \perp) \textit{ then } \perp \textit{ else } f(x)$.

Likewise, updates are given a denotation as total operations on program variable assignments. The statements of an update are executed in parallel and statements that literally occur later can override the effects of earlier statements:

$$[U]^{S,\beta} : PA^D \to PA^D$$
$$[w_1 := t_1, \ldots, w_k := t_k]^{S,\beta}(\delta) =_{\text{def}}$$
$$(\cdots ((\delta[w_1 \mapsto val_{S,\beta,\delta}(t_1)])[w_2 \mapsto val_{S,\beta,\delta}(t_2)]) \cdots)[w_k \mapsto val_{S,\beta,\delta}(t_k)]$$

where $(\delta[w \mapsto a])(v) = \textit{if } (v = w) \textit{ then } a \textit{ else } \delta(v)$ are ordinary function updates.

Evaluation $val_{S,\beta,\delta}$ of terms and formulae is mostly defined as it is common for first-order predicate logic. Formulas are mapped into a Boolean domain, where tt stands for semantic truth. The cases for programs and updates are

$$val_{S,\beta,\delta}([\alpha]\phi) =_{\text{def}} \begin{cases} val_{S,\beta,[\alpha]^S(\delta)}(\phi) & \text{for } [\alpha]^S(\delta) \neq \perp \\ \text{tt} & \text{otherwise} \end{cases}$$

$$val_{S,\beta,\delta}(\{U\}\phi) =_{\text{def}} val_{S,\beta,[U]^{S,\beta}(\delta)}(\phi)$$

We interpret free logical variables $x \in$ LVar existentially: a formula ϕ is *valid* iff for each structure $S = (D, I)$ and each program variable assignment $\delta \in PA^D$ there is a variable assignment $\beta : \text{LVar} \to D$ such that $val_{S,\beta,\delta}(\phi) = \text{tt}$. Likewise, a sequent $\Gamma \vdash^{\text{dl}} \Delta$ is called valid iff $\bigwedge \Gamma \to \bigvee \Delta$ is valid.

The set of unbound variables occurring in a term or a formula t is denoted by $\text{vars}(t) \subseteq \text{PVar} \cup \text{LVar}$. For program variables $v \in \text{PVar}$, this means $v \in \text{vars}(t)$ iff v turns up anywhere in t. For logical variables $x \in \text{LVar}$, we define $x \in \text{vars}(t)$ iff x occurs in t and is not in the scope of $\forall x$ or $\exists x$.

We note that the semantic notion of non-interference can easily be expressed in the formalism of dynamic logic: One possibility [9] is to express the variable independence property introduced above as follows. Assuming the set of program variables is $\text{PVar} = \{v_1, \ldots, v_n\}$, then v_j only depends on $v_1, \ldots, v_i$ if variation of $v_{i+1}, \ldots, v_n$ does not affect the final value of v_j:

$$\forall u_1, \ldots, u_i. \ \exists r. \ \forall u_{i+1}, \ldots, u_n. \ \{v_i := u_i\}_{1 \leq i \leq n} [\alpha](v_j = r) \ . \tag{1}$$

The particular use of updates in this formula is a standard trick to quantify over program variables which is not allowed directly: in order to quantify over all values that a program variable v occurring in a formula ϕ can assume, we introduce a fresh logical variable u and quantify over the latter. In the following we use quantification over program variables as a shorthand, writing $\dot{\forall}v.\ \phi$ for $\forall u.\ \{\, v := u\,\}\ \phi$. One result of this paper is that simple, easily automated proofs of formulae such as (1) are viable in at least those cases where a corresponding derivation in the type system of Hunt and Sands exists.

4   Interpreting the Type System in Dynamic Logic

We now present a calculus for dynamic logic in which the rules involving program statements employ abstraction instead of precise evaluation. The calculus facilitates automatic proofs of secure information flow. In particular, when proving loops the burden of finding invariants is reduced to the task of providing a dependency approximation between program variables. There is a close correspondence to the type system of [12] (Fig. 1). Intuitively, state updates in the DL calculus resemble security typings in the type system: updates arising during a proof will essentially take the form $\{\, v := f(\ldots vars \ldots)\,\}$, where the *vars* form the type of v in a corresponding derivation in the type system. To put our observation on a formal basis, we prove the soundness of the calculus and show that every derivation in the type system has a corresponding proof in our calculus.

The Abstraction-based Calculus. We introduce *extended type environments* as pairs (∇, I) consisting of a typing function $\nabla : \text{PVar} \to \mathcal{P}(\text{PVar})$ and an *invariance set* $I \subseteq \text{PVar}$ used to indicate those variables whose value does not change after execution of the program. We write ∇_v for the syntactic sequence of variables $w_1, \ldots, w_k$ with arbitrary ordering when $\nabla(v) = \{w_1, \ldots, w_k\}$ and ∇_v^C for a sequence of all variables *not* in $\nabla(v)$. Ultimately, we want to prove non-interference properties of the form

$$\{\, \alpha\,\} \Downarrow (\nabla, I) \quad \equiv_{\text{def}} \quad \bigwedge_{v \in \text{PVar}} \begin{cases} \dot{\forall}v_1 \cdots v_n.\ \forall u.\ \{\, v := u\,\}[\alpha]\, v = u &, v \in I \\ \dot{\forall}\nabla_v.\ \exists r.\ \dot{\forall}\nabla_v^C.\ [\alpha]\, v = r &, v \notin I \end{cases} \quad (2)$$

where we assume $\text{PVar} = \{v_1, \ldots, v_n\}$. Validity of a judgment $\{\, \alpha\,\} \Downarrow (\nabla, I)$ ensures that all variables in the invariance set I remain unchanged after execution of the program α, and that any variable v of the rest only depends on variables in $\nabla(v)$. The invariance set I corresponds to the context p that turns up in judgments $p \vdash^{\text{HS}} \nabla \{\, \alpha\,\} \nabla'$: while the type system ensures that p is a lower bound of the post-type $\nabla'(v)$ of variables v assigned in α, the set I can be used to ensure that variables with low post-type are not assigned (or, more precisely, not changed). The equivalence is formally stated in Lem. 2.

In the proof process we want to abstract program statements "**while** $b\ \alpha$" and "**if** $b\ \alpha_1\ \alpha_2$" into updates modelling the effects of these statements. Thus we avoid having to split up the proof for the two branches of an if-statement, or having to find an invariant for a while-loop. Extended type environments capture the essence of these updates: the arguments for the abstraction functions and the unmodified variables. They are translated into updates as follows:

$$\mathrm{upd}(\nabla, I) \quad =_{\mathrm{def}} \quad \{\, v := f_v(\nabla_v)\,\}_{v \in \mathrm{PVar} \setminus I}$$
$$\mathrm{ifUpd}(b, \nabla, I) \quad =_{\mathrm{def}} \quad \{\, v := f_v(b, \nabla_v)\,\}_{v \in \mathrm{PVar} \setminus I}$$

The above updates assign to each v not in the invariance set I a *fresh* function symbol f_v whose arguments are exactly the variables given by the type $\nabla(v)$. In a program "if b α_1 α_2" the final state may depend on the branch condition b, so the translation ifUpd 'injects' the condition into the update. This is the analogon of the context lifting present in $\mathrm{IF}^{\mathrm{HS}}$. For the while-rule, we transform the loop body into a conditional, so that we must handle the context lifting only in the if-rule.

Figs. 2 and 3 contain the rules for a sequent calculus. We have only included those propositional and first-order rules (the first four rules of Fig. 2) that are necessary for proving the results in this section; more rules are required to make the calculus usable in practice. The calculus uses free logical variables $X \in \mathrm{LVar}$ ($\mathrm{EX\text{-}RIGHT}^{\mathrm{dl}}$) and unification ($\mathrm{CLOSE\text{-}EQ}^{\mathrm{dl}}$) for handling existential quantification, where the latter rule works by applying the unifier of terms s and t to the whole proof tree. We have to demand that only rigid terms (not containing program variables) are substituted for free variables, because free variables can also occur in the scope of updates or the box modal operator. Skolemisation ($\mathrm{ALL\text{-}RIGHT}^{\mathrm{dl}}$) has to collect the free variables that occur in a quantified formula to ensure soundness. By definition of the non-interference properties (2) and by the design of the rules of the dynamic logic calculus it is sufficient to define update rules for terms, quantifier-free formulae, and other updates. Such rules can be used at any point in a proof to simplify expressions containing updates.

Rule $\mathrm{ABSTRACT}^{\mathrm{dl}}$ can be used to normalise terms occuring in updates to the form $f(\ldots vars \ldots)$. In rules $\mathrm{IF}^{\mathrm{dl}}$ and $\mathrm{WHILE}^{\mathrm{dl}}$ the second premiss represents the actual abstraction of the program statement for a suitably chosen typing ∇ and invariance set I. This abstraction is justified through the first premiss in terms of another non-interference proof obligation. The concretisation operator γ^* (cf. [12]) of rule $\mathrm{WHILE}^{\mathrm{dl}}$ is generally defined as

$$\gamma^*_{\nabla_1}(\nabla_2)(x) =_{\mathrm{def}} \{y \in \mathrm{PVar} \mid \nabla_1(y) \subseteq \nabla_2(x)\} \qquad (x \in \mathrm{PVar}) . \qquad (3)$$

Together with the side condition that for all v we require $v \in \nabla(v)$, a closure property on dependencies is ensured: $w \in \gamma^*_\nabla(\nabla)(v)$ implies $\gamma^*_\nabla(\nabla)(w) \subseteq \gamma^*_\nabla(\nabla)(v)$: if a variable depends on another, the latter's dependencies are included in the former's. This accounts for the fact that the loop body can be executed more than once, which, in general, causes transitive dependencies.

Function Arguments Ensure Soundness. A recurring proof obligation in a non-interference proof is a statement of the form $\dot{\forall}\nabla_v. \exists r. \dot{\forall}\nabla_v^C. [\alpha] v = r$. To prove this statement without abstraction essentially is to find a function of the variables

$$\frac{\Gamma \vdash^{\mathrm{dl}} \phi, \Delta \quad \Gamma \vdash^{\mathrm{dl}} \psi, \Delta}{\Gamma \vdash^{\mathrm{dl}} \phi \wedge \psi, \Delta} \ \text{AND-RIGHT}^{\mathrm{dl}}$$

$$\frac{\Gamma \vdash^{\mathrm{dl}} \phi[x/f(X_1, \ldots, X_n)], \Delta}{\Gamma \vdash^{\mathrm{dl}} \forall x. \ \phi, \Delta} \ \text{ALL-RIGHT}^{\mathrm{dl}} \qquad \{X_1, \ldots, X_n\} = \mathrm{vars}(\phi) \cap \mathrm{LVar}\backslash\{x\},$$
$$f \text{ fresh}$$

$$\frac{\Gamma \vdash^{\mathrm{dl}} \phi[x/X], \exists x. \ \phi, \Delta}{\Gamma \vdash^{\mathrm{dl}} \exists x. \ \phi, \Delta} \ \text{EX-RIGHT}^{\mathrm{dl}} \qquad X \text{ fresh}$$

$$\frac{\overset{*}{[s \equiv t]}}{\Gamma \vdash^{\mathrm{dl}} s = t, \Delta} \ \text{CLOSE-EQ}^{\mathrm{dl}} \qquad s, t \text{ unifiable (with rigid unifier)}$$

$$\frac{(\Gamma \vdash^{\mathrm{dl}} \Delta)[x/f(\mathrm{vars}(t))]}{(\Gamma \vdash^{\mathrm{dl}} \Delta)[x/t]} \ \text{ABSTRACT}^{\mathrm{dl}} \qquad f \text{ fresh}$$

$$\frac{\Gamma \vdash^{\mathrm{dl}} \{U\}\phi, \Delta}{\Gamma \vdash^{\mathrm{dl}} \{U\}[\,]\phi, \Delta} \ \text{SKIP}^{\mathrm{dl}} \qquad \frac{\Gamma \vdash^{\mathrm{dl}} \{U\}\{v := E\}[\ldots]\phi, \Delta}{\Gamma \vdash^{\mathrm{dl}} \{U\}[v = E;\ \ldots]\phi, \Delta} \ \text{ASSIGN}^{\mathrm{dl}}$$

$$\frac{\vdash^{\mathrm{dl}} \{\alpha_i\} \Downarrow (\nabla, I) \quad (i = 1, 2)}{\Gamma \vdash^{\mathrm{dl}} \{U\}\{\mathrm{ifUpd}(b, \nabla, I)\}[\ldots]\phi, \Delta}{\Gamma \vdash^{\mathrm{dl}} \{U\}[\textbf{if } b\ \alpha_1\ \alpha_2;\ \ldots]\phi, \Delta} \ \text{IF}^{\mathrm{dl}}$$

$$\frac{\vdash^{\mathrm{dl}} \{\textbf{if } b\ \alpha\ \{\}\} \Downarrow (\gamma_\nabla^*(\nabla), I)}{\Gamma \vdash^{\mathrm{dl}} \{U\}\{\mathrm{upd}(\nabla, I)\}[\ldots]\phi, \Delta}{\Gamma \vdash^{\mathrm{dl}} \{U\}[\textbf{while } b\ \alpha;\ \ldots]\phi, \Delta} \ \text{WHILE}^{\mathrm{dl}} \qquad v \in \nabla(v) \text{ for all } v \in \mathrm{PVar}$$

Fig. 2. A dynamic logic calculus for information flow security. In the last four rules the update $\{U\}$ can also be empty and disappear.

∇_v that yields the value of v under α for every given pre-state: one must find the strongest post-condition w.r.t. v's value. Logically, one must create this function as a term for the existentially quantified variable r in which the ∇_v^C do not occur. In a unification-based calculus the occurs check will let all those proofs fail where an actual information flow takes places from ∇_v^C to v. The purpose of function arguments for f_v is exactly to retain this crucial property in the abstract version of the calculus. We must make sure that a function f_v – abstracting the effect of α on v – gets at least those variables as arguments that are parts of the term representing the final value of v after α.

Theorem 1 (Soundness). *The rules of the DL calculus given in Figs. 2 and 3 are sound: the root of a closed proof tree is a valid sequent.*

Simulating Type Derivations in the DL Calculus. In order to show subsumption of the type system in the logic, we first put the connection between invariance sets and context on solid ground. It suffices to approximate the

$$\{\, w_1 := t_1, \ldots, w_k := t_k \,\} \, w_i \;\to^{\mathrm{dl}}\; t_i \qquad\qquad\qquad\quad \text{if } w_j \neq w_i \text{ for } i < j \leq k$$

$$\{\, w_1 := t_1, \ldots, w_k := t_k \,\} \, t \;\to^{\mathrm{dl}}\; t \qquad\qquad\qquad\quad \text{if } w_1, \ldots, w_k \notin \mathrm{vars}(t)$$

$$\{\, U \,\} \, f(t_1, \ldots, t_n) \;\to^{\mathrm{dl}}\; f(\{\, U \,\} \, t_1, \ldots, \{\, U \,\} \, t_n)$$

$$\{\, U \,\} \, (t_1 = t_2) \;\to^{\mathrm{dl}}\; \{\, U \,\} \, t_1 = \{\, U \,\} \, t_2$$

$$\{\, U \,\} \, \neg \phi \;\to^{\mathrm{dl}}\; \neg \{\, U \,\} \, \phi$$

$$\{\, U \,\} \, (\phi_1 * \phi_2) \;\to^{\mathrm{dl}}\; \{\, U \,\} \, \phi_1 * \{\, U \,\} \, \phi_2 \qquad\qquad \text{for } * \in \{\vee, \wedge\}$$

$$\{\, U \,\} \, \{\, w_1 := t_1, \ldots, w_k := t_k \,\} \, \phi \;\to^{\mathrm{dl}}\; \{\, U,\, w_1 := \{\, U \,\} \, t_1, \ldots, w_k := \{\, U \,\} \, t_k \,\} \, \phi$$

Fig. 3. Application rules for updates in dynamic logic, as far as they are required for Lem. 6. Further application and simplification rules are necessary in general.

invariance of variables v with the requirement that v must not occur as left-hand side of assignments ($Lhs(\alpha)$ is the set of all left-hand sides of assignments in α).

Lemma 2. *In the type system of [12], see Fig. 1, the following equivalence holds:*

$$p \vdash^{\mathrm{HS}} \nabla \{\, \alpha \,\} \nabla' \quad \text{iff} \quad \bot \vdash^{\mathrm{HS}} \nabla \{\, \alpha \,\} \nabla' \quad \text{and} \quad f.a.\ v \in Lhs(\alpha) : \; p \sqsubseteq \nabla'(v)$$

Furthermore, we can normalize type derivations thanks to the Canonical Derivations Lemma of [12]. The crucial ingredient is the concretisation operator γ^* defined in (3).

Lemma 3 (Canonical Derivations)

$$\bot \vdash^{\mathrm{HS}} \nabla \{\, \alpha \,\} \nabla' \quad \text{iff} \quad \bot \vdash^{\mathrm{HS}} \Delta_0 \{\, \alpha \,\} \gamma^*_\nabla(\nabla') \qquad \text{where } \Delta_0 = \lambda x.\, \{x\}$$

For brevity, we must refer to Hunt and Sands' paper for details, but in the setting at hand one can intuitively take Lemma 3 as stating that any typing judgment can also be understood as a dependency judgment: the typing on the left-hand side is equivalent to the statement that the final value of x *may depend on* the initial value of y only if y appears in the post-type, or dependence set, $\gamma^*_\nabla(\nabla')(x)$.

The type system of Fig. 4 only mentions judgments with a pre-type Δ_0 as depicted on the right-hand side of the equivalence in Lemma 3. Further, the context p has been replaced by equivalent side conditions (Lemma 2), and rule $\mathrm{SEQ}^{\mathrm{HS}}$ is built into the other rules, i.e., the rules always work on the initial statement of a program. Likewise, rule $\mathrm{SUB}^{\mathrm{HS}}$ has been integrated in $\mathrm{SKIP}^{\mathrm{cf}}$ and $\mathrm{WHILE}^{\mathrm{cf}}$. The type system is equivalent to Hunt and Sands' system (Fig. 1):

Lemma 4

$$\bot \vdash^{\mathrm{HS}} \Delta_0 \{\, \alpha \,\} \nabla \qquad \text{if and only if} \qquad \vdash^{\mathrm{cf}} \Delta_0 \{\, \alpha \,\} \nabla$$

The proof proceeds in multiple steps by devising intermediate type systems, each of which adds a modification towards the system in Fig. 4 and which is equivalent to Hunt and Sands' system.

Obviously, due to the approximating character of IF^{dl} and WHILE^{dl} (and the lack of arithmetic), our DL calculus is not (relatively) complete in the sense of [11]. For the particular judgements $\{\alpha\} \Downarrow (\nabla, I)$ the calculus is, however, not more incomplete than the type system of Fig. 1: every typable program can also be proven secure using the DL calculus[4].

Theorem 5

$$\perp \vdash^{\text{HS}} \Delta_0 \{\alpha\} \nabla \qquad \textit{implies} \qquad \vdash^{\text{dl}} \{\alpha\} \Downarrow (\nabla, \emptyset)$$

The proof of the theorem is constructive: A method for translating type derivations into DL proofs is given. The existence of this translation mapping shows that proving in the DL calculus is in principle not more difficult than typing programs using the system of Fig. 1.

The first part of the translation is accomplished by Lem. 4, which covers structural differences between type derivations and DL proofs. Applications of the rules of Fig. 4 can then almost directly be replaced with the corresponding rules of the DL calculus:

Lemma 6

$$\vdash^{\text{cf}} \Delta_0 \{\alpha\} \nabla \qquad \textit{implies} \qquad \vdash^{\text{dl}} \{\alpha\} \Downarrow (\nabla, \emptyset)$$

5   Higher Precision and Delimited Information Release

Many realistic languages feature exceptions as a means to indicate failure. The occurrence of an exception can also lead to information leakage. Therefore, an information flow analysis for such a language must, at each point where an exception might possibly occur, either ensure that this will indeed not happen at runtime or verify that the induced information flow is benign. The Jif system [15] which implements a security type system for a large subset of the Java language employs a simple data flow analysis to retain a practically acceptable precision w.r.t. exceptions. The data flow analysis can verify the absence of null pointer exceptions and class cast exceptions in certain cases. However, to enhance the precision of this analysis to an acceptable level one is forced to apply a slightly cumbersome programming style.

The need for treatment of exceptions is an example showing that we actually gain something from the fact that our analysis is embedded in a more general program logic: there is no need to stack one analysis on top of the other to scale the approach up to larger languages, but we can coherently deal with added features, in this case exceptions, within one calculus. In the precise version of the calculus for JavaCard – as implemented in the KeY system [1] – exceptions are handled like conditional statements by branching on the condition under which

---

[4] The converse of Theorem 5 does not hold. In the basic version of the calculus of Fig. 2, untypable programs like "**if** (h) $\{l = 1\}$ $\{l = 0\}$" can be proven secure. Sect. 5 discusses how the precision of the DL calculus can be further augmented.

$$\frac{}{\vdash^{\mathrm{cf}} \Delta_0 \{\ \} \nabla} \ \mathrm{SKIP}^{\mathrm{cf}} \qquad\qquad v \in \nabla(v) \text{ for all } v \in \mathrm{PVar}$$

$$\frac{\Delta_0 \vdash E : t \qquad \vdash^{\mathrm{cf}} \Delta_0 \{\ldots\} \gamma^*_{\Delta_0[v \mapsto t]}(\nabla)}{\vdash^{\mathrm{cf}} \Delta_0 \{ v = E ;\ \ldots \} \nabla} \ \mathrm{ASSIGN}^{\mathrm{cf}}$$

$$\frac{\begin{array}{c} \Delta_0 \vdash b : t \qquad \vdash^{\mathrm{cf}} \Delta_0 \{\ldots\} \gamma^*_\nabla(\nabla') \\ \vdash^{\mathrm{cf}} \Delta_0 \{ \alpha_i \} \nabla \ \ (i = 1, 2) \end{array}}{\vdash^{\mathrm{cf}} \Delta_0 \{ \text{if } b\ \alpha_1\ \alpha_2 ;\ \ldots \} \nabla'} \ \mathrm{IF}^{\mathrm{cf}} \qquad \begin{array}{l} \text{f.a. } v \in Lhs(\alpha_1).\ t \sqsubseteq \nabla(v) \\ \text{f.a. } v \in Lhs(\alpha_2).\ t \sqsubseteq \nabla(v) \end{array}$$

$$\frac{\begin{array}{c} \Delta_0 \vdash b : t \qquad \vdash^{\mathrm{cf}} \Delta_0 \{\ldots\} \gamma^*_\nabla(\nabla') \\ \vdash^{\mathrm{cf}} \Delta_0 \{ \alpha \} \gamma^*_\nabla(\nabla) \end{array}}{\vdash^{\mathrm{cf}} \Delta_0 \{ \text{while } b\ \alpha ;\ \ldots \} \nabla'} \ \mathrm{WHILE}^{\mathrm{cf}} \qquad \begin{array}{l} v \in \nabla(v) \text{ for all } v \in \mathrm{PVar} \\ \text{f.a. } v \in Lhs(\alpha).\ t \sqsubseteq \gamma^*_\nabla(\nabla)(v) \end{array}$$

Fig. 4. Intermediate flow-sensitive type system for information flow analysis

$$\frac{\dfrac{\dfrac{*}{[f'_l(TRUE) \equiv R]}}{odd(f_h(R)) \vdash^{\mathrm{dl}} f'_l(TRUE) = R} \ \mathrm{CLOSE\text{-}EQ}^{\mathrm{dl}}}{\dfrac{odd(f_h(R)) \vdash^{\mathrm{dl}} f'_l(odd(f_h(R))) = R}{odd(f_h(R)) \vdash^{\mathrm{dl}} \{ l := f_l(R), h := f_h(R) \} \{ l := f'_l(odd(h)) \} l = R}} \begin{array}{l} \mathrm{APPLY\text{-}EQ}^{\mathrm{dl}} \\[6pt] \xrightarrow{*}^{\mathrm{dl}} \end{array}$$

$$\mathcal{D}$$

$$\frac{\dfrac{\dfrac{*}{\vdash^{\mathrm{dl}} \{ l = 0 \} \Downarrow (\nabla, \{h\})} \quad \dfrac{*}{\vdash^{\mathrm{dl}} \{ l = 1 \} \Downarrow (\nabla, \{h\})} \quad \mathcal{D}}{odd(f_h(R)) \vdash^{\mathrm{dl}} \{ l := f_l(R), h := f_h(R) \} [\alpha] l = R}}{\dfrac{\vdash^{\mathrm{dl}} \{ l := f_l(R), h := f_h(R) \} (odd(h) \to [\alpha] l = R)}{\dfrac{\vdash^{\mathrm{dl}} \exists r.\ \dot{\forall} l.\ \dot{\forall} h.\ (odd(h) \to [\alpha] l = r)}{\vdash^{\mathrm{dl}} \{ \alpha \} \Downarrow (\nabla, \{h\}, odd(h))}}} \begin{array}{l} \mathrm{IF}^{\mathrm{dl}} \\[4pt] \xrightarrow{*}^{\mathrm{dl}}, \mathrm{IMP\text{-}RIGHT}^{\mathrm{dl}} \\[4pt] \mathrm{EX\text{-}RIGHT}^{\mathrm{dl}}, \mathrm{ALL\text{-}RIGHT}^{\mathrm{dl}} \\[4pt] (\mathrm{Def}), \mathrm{AND\text{-}RIGHT}^{\mathrm{dl}} \end{array}$$

$\ldots$

Fig. 5. Non-interference proof with delimited information release: The precondition $odd(h)$ entails that (only) the parity of h is allowed to leak into l. A similar proof is required for $\neg odd(h)$. For sake of brevity, we use odd both as function and predicate, and only in one step ($\mathrm{APPLY\text{-}EQ}^{\mathrm{dl}}$) make use of the fact that $odd(f_h(R))$ actually represents the equation $odd(f_h(R)) = TRUE$.

an exception would occur. An uncaught exception is treated as non-termination. As an example, the division v_1/v_2 would have the condition that v_2 is zero (".. ..." denotes a context possibly containing exception handlers):

$$\frac{v_2 \neq 0 \vdash^{\mathrm{dl}} \{ w := v_1/v_2 \} [..\ ...] \phi \qquad v_2 = 0 \vdash^{\mathrm{dl}} [..\ \text{throw } E\ ...] \phi}{\vdash^{\mathrm{dl}} [..\ w = v_1/v_2\ ...] \phi} \quad .$$

If we knew $v_2 \neq 0$ at this point of the proof, implying that the division does in fact not raise an exception, the right branch could be closed immediately.

Because our DL calculus stores the values of variables (instead of only the type) as long as no abstraction occurs, this information is often available: (i) rule $\text{ASSIGN}^{\text{dl}}$ does not involve abstraction, which means that sequential programs can be executed without loss of information, and (ii) invariance sets I in non-interference judgments allow to retain information about unchanged variables also across conditional statements and loops.

This can be seen for a program like "$v = 2$; **while** b α ; $w = w/v$" in which α does not assign to v. By including v in the invariance set for "**while** b α" we can deduce $v = 2$ also after the loop, and thus be sure that the division will succeed. This is a typical example for a program containing an initialisation part that establishes invariants, and a use part that relies on the invariants. The pattern recurs in many flavours: examples are the initialisation and use of libraries and the well-definedness of references after object creation. We are optimistic to gather empirical evidence of our claim that the increased precision is useful in practice through future experiments.

Increasing Precision. While our DL calculus is able to maintain state information *across* statements, the rules IF^{dl} and WHILE^{dl} lose this information in the first premisses, containing non-interference proofs for the statement *bodies*. This makes it impossible to deduce that no exceptions can occur in the program "$v = 2$; **while** b $\{w = w/v\}$". As another shortcoming, the branch predicate is not taken into account, so that absence of exceptions cannot be shown for a program like "**if** $(v \neq 0)$ $\{w = 1/v\}$ ".

One way to remedy these issues might be to relax the first premisses in IF^{dl} and WHILE^{dl}. The idea is to generalise non-interference judgments and introduce *preconditions* ϕ under which the program must satisfy non-interference.

$$\{\,\alpha\,\} \Downarrow (\nabla, I, \phi) \quad \equiv_{\text{def}} \quad \bigwedge_{v \in \text{PVar}} \begin{cases} \dot{\forall} v_1 \cdots v_n.\,(\phi \to [\alpha]\,v = u) & , v \in I \\ \dot{\forall} \nabla_v.\,\exists r.\,\dot{\forall} \nabla_v^C.\,(\phi \to [\alpha]\,v = r) & , v \notin I \end{cases}$$

In an extended rule for if-statements, for instance, such a precondition can be used to 'carry through' side formulae and state information contained in the update U, as well as to integrate the branch predicates: we may assume arbitrary preconditions ϕ_1, ϕ_2 in the branches if we can show that they hold before the if-statement:

$$\frac{\vdash^{\text{dl}} \{\,\alpha_1\,\} \Downarrow (\nabla, I, \phi_1) \qquad \qquad \vdash^{\text{dl}} \{\,\alpha_2\,\} \Downarrow (\nabla, I, \phi_2)}{\Gamma, \{U\}\,b = TRUE \vdash^{\text{dl}} \{U\}\,\phi_1, \Delta \qquad \Gamma, \{U\}\,b \neq TRUE \vdash^{\text{dl}} \{U\}\,\phi_2, \Delta}$$
$$\frac{\Gamma \vdash^{\text{dl}} \{U\}\,\{\,\text{ifUpd}(b, \nabla, I)\,\}\,[\ldots]\,\phi, \Delta}{\Gamma \vdash^{\text{dl}} \{U\}\,[\text{if } b\ \alpha_1\ \alpha_2 ;\ \ldots]\,\phi, \Delta}$$

Probably more interestingly, preconditions allow us to handle delimited information release in the style of [9], i.e. situations in which non-interference does not strictly hold and some well-defined information about secret values may be released. Fig. 5 shows parts of a non-interference proof with delimited information release for the program "$\alpha = \text{if } (odd(h))\ \{l = 0\}\ \{l = 1\}$", in which one can learn the parity of h by reading l. The typing ∇ is given by $\nabla(l) = \emptyset, \nabla(h) = \{h\}$, indicating that only declassified information flows into l.

6   Conclusion, Related and Future Work

In this paper we made a formal connection between type-based and logic-based approaches to information flow analysis. We proved that every program that is typeable in Hunt & Sands' type system [12] has a proof in an abstract version of dynamic logic whose construction is not more expensive than the type check. We argued that an integrated logic-based approach fits well into a proof-carrying code framework for establishing security policies of mobile software. In order to support this claim we showed how to increase the precision of the program logic, for example, to express declassification.

Related Work. The background for our work are a number of recent type-based and logic-based approaches to information flow [20, 2, 9, 12]. Our concrete starting points were the flow-sensitive type system of Hunt & Sands [12] and the characterisation of non-interference in [9]. Amtoft & Banerjee [2] devised an analysis with a very logic-like structure, that is however not more precise than the type system by Hunt & Sands. In an early paper Andrews & Reitman [3] developed a flow logic – one may also consider it a security type system – for proving information flow properties of concurrent Pascal programs. They outline a combination of their flow logic with regular Hoare logic, but keep the formulae for both logics separated. Joshi & Leino [13] give logical characterisations of the semantic notion of information flow, and their presentation in terms of Hoare triples is similar in spirit to our basic formulation. Their results do, however, not provide means to aid automated proofs of these triples. Finally, Beringer et al. [7] presented a logic for resource consumption whose proof rules and judgements are derived from a more general program logic; both logics are formalised in the Isabelle/HOL proof assistant. Their approach is similar in spirit to the one presented here, since the preciseness of their derived logic is compared to an extant type system for resource comsumption.

Future Work. On a technical level, we have not investigated the complexity of the translation of HS type derivations to DL proofs (Theorem 5) and the size of resulting proofs in detail. We believe that both can be linear in the size of type derivations, although this requires a more efficient version of proof obligations $\{\,\alpha\,\}\Downarrow(\nabla, I)$. Conceptually, the present work is only a starting point in the integration of type-based and logic-based information-flow analysis. In addition to non-interference and declassification, more complex security policies need to be looked at. It has to be seen how well the notion of abstraction presented in this paper is suited to express these. We also want to extend the program logic to cover at least JavaCard, based on the axiomatisation in [6], as implemented in our program verifier KeY. Ideas towards this goal have been worked out in [18], parts of which are also presented in [10]. Finally, a suitable notion of proof certificate and proof checking for proof-carrying code must be derived for dynamic logic proofs of security policies. This is a substantial task to which a whole Work Package within MOBIUS is devoted.

Acknowledgments

We would like to thank Dave Sands for inspiring discussions and Andrei Sabelfeld for reminding us of declassification. Thanks to Tarmo Uustalu for pointing out [3].

References

[1] Ahrendt, W., Baar, T., Beckert, B., Bubel, R., Giese, M., Hähnle, R., Menzel, W., Mostowski, W., Roth, A., Schlager, S., Schmitt, P.H.: The KeY tool: integrating object oriented design and formal verification. Software and System Modeling 4(1), 32–54 (2005)

[2] Amtoft, T., Banerjee, A.: Information flow analysis in logical form. In: Giacobazzi, R. (ed.) SAS 2004. LNCS, vol. 3148, pp. 100–115. Springer, Heidelberg (2004)

[3] Andrews, G.R., Reitman, R.P.: An axiomatic approach to information flow in programs. ACM Transactions on Programming Languages and Systems 2(1), 56–76 (1980)

[4] Appel, A.W.: Foundational Proof-Carrying code. In: Proc. 16th Annual IEEE Symposium on Logic in Computer Science, pp. 247–258. IEEE Computer Society, Los Alamitos, CA (2001)

[5] Barthe, G., D'Argenio, P.R., Rezk, T.: Secure Information Flow by Self-Composition. In: Foccardi, R. (ed.) Proceedings of CSFW'04, pp. 100–114. IEEE Press, Pacific Grove, USA (2004)

[6] Beckert, B.: A dynamic logic for the formal verification of Java Card programs. In: Attali, I., Jensen, T. (eds.) JavaCard 2000. LNCS, vol. 2041, pp. 6–24. Springer, Heidelberg (2001)

[7] Beringer, L., Hofmann, M., Momigliano, A., Shkaravska, O.: Automatic certification of heap consumption. In: Baader, F., Voronkov, A. (eds.) LPAR 2004. LNCS (LNAI), vol. 3452, pp. 347–362. Springer, Heidelberg (2005)

[8] Bernard, A., Lee, P.: Temporal logic for proof-carrying code. In: Voronkov, A. (ed.) CADE-18. LNCS (LNAI), vol. 2392, pp. 31–46. Springer, Heidelberg (2002)

[9] Darvas, A., Hähnle, R., Sands, D.: A theorem proving approach to analysis of secure information flow. In: Hutter, D., Ullmann, M. (eds.) SPC 2005. LNCS, vol. 3450, pp. 193–209. Springer, Heidelberg (2005)

[10] Hähnle, R., Pan, J., Rümmer, P., Walter, D.: On the integration of security type systems into program logics. Technical report, Chalmers University of Technology (2006), Preliminary version at www.cs.chalmers.se/~philipp/IflowPaper.pdf

[11] Harel, D., Kozen, D., Tiuryn, J.: Dynamic Logic. In: Foundations of Computing, MIT Press, Cambridge (2000)

[12] Hunt, S., Sands, D.: On flow-sensitive security types. In: Symp. on Principles of Programming Languages (POPL), ACM Press, New York (2006)

[13] Joshi, R., Leino, K.R.M.: A semantic approach to secure information flow. Science of Computer Programming 37(1-3), 113–138 (2000)

[14] MOBIUS Project Deliverable D 1.1, Resource and Information Flow Security Requirements (March 2006),
URL mobius.inria.fr/twiki/pub/DeliverablesList/WebHome/Deliv1-1.pdf

[15] Myers, A.C.: JFlow: Practical mostly-static information flow control. In: Symposium on Principles of Programming Languages, pp. 228–241 (1999)

[16] Necula, G.C., Lee, P.: Safe, untrusted agents using proof-carrying code. In: Vigna, G. (ed.) Mobile Agents and Security. LNCS, vol. 1419, pp. 61–91. Springer, Heidelberg (1998)

[17] Necula, G.C., Schneck, R.R.: A sound framework for untrusted verification-condition generators. In: Proc. IEEE Symposium on Logic in Computer Science LICS, Ottawa, Canada, pp. 248–260. IEEE Computer Society, Los Alamitos (2003)

[18] Pan, J.: A theorem proving approach to analysis of secure information flow using data abstraction. Master's thesis, Chalmers University of Technology (2005)

[19] Rümmer, P.: Sequential, parallel, and quantified updates of first-order structures. In: Hermann, M., Voronkov, A. (eds.) LPAR 2006. LNCS (LNAI), vol. 4246, pp. 422–436. Springer, Heidelberg (2006)

[20] Sabelfeld, A., Myers, A.C.: Language-based information-flow security. IEEE Journal on Selected Areas in Communications 21(1), 5–19 (2003)

[21] Volpano, D., Smith, G., Irvine, C.: A sound type system for secure flow analysis. Journal of Computer Security 4(3), 167–187 (1996)

PRISMA: A Mobile Calculus with Parametric Synchronization[*]

Roberto Bruni[1] and Ivan Lanese[2]

[1] Computer Science Department, University of Pisa, Pisa, Italy
bruni@di.unipi.it
[2] Computer Science Department, University of Bologna, Bologna, Italy
lanese@cs.unibo.it

Abstract. We present PRISMA, a parametric calculus that can be instantiated with different interaction policies, defined as synchronization algebras with mobility of names (SAMs). We define both operational semantics and observational semantics of PRISMA, showing that the second one is compositional *for any* SAM. We give examples based on heterogeneous SAMs, a case study on Fusion Calculus and some simple applications. Finally, we show that basic categorical tools can help to relate and to compose SAMs and PRISMA processes in an elegant way.

1 Introduction

Since the pioneering papers by Robin Milner [16] and Tony Hoare [10], the use of process description languages has kept proliferating at an impressive rate. Though nowadays the most prominent calculus is the π-calculus [17], many variants of it exist (see, e.g., the nice commented survey in [4]), exploiting different communication primitives and focusing on different aspects, but where interaction is a key issue [18,8,3,1].

While process calculi are used for modeling different kinds of systems, ranging from computer networks to biological systems, at different levels of abstraction, typically each calculus relies on just one fixed communication mechanism. When a different communication protocol is needed, either it is encoded using the available mechanism, and this may be quite difficult and may obfuscate the model, or a new ad hoc calculus providing this primitive is developed. For instance, [7] introduces a broadcast variant of π-calculus, while [6] proves that there is no uniform encoding of it into the π-calculus.

In Service Oriented Computing (SOC) it is commonly understood that services come with their own invocation policies (e.g., one-way or request-response), so that calculi for SOC should face the coexistence of several interaction policies within the same model. We want to overcome the limitation of previous proposals by allowing processes to interact using synchronization models tailored to the specific application in mind. For instance, take a news server S that interacts with news providers using a message passing protocol, but then

---

[*] Research supported by the Project FET-GC II IST 16004 SENSORIA.

U. Montanari, D. Sannella, and R. Bruni (Eds.): TGC 2006, LNCS 4661, pp. 132–149, 2007.

uses broadcast to send the news to subscribed recipients. We consider basic actions of the form $xa\vec{y}$ where x is the channel where the interaction is performed, a an action specifying the contribution to the interaction and $\vec{y}$ a tuple of parameters. Note the separation between the channel name and the action executed on it, which is a distinctive feature of our approach. In particular, we consider actions *in* and *out* respectively as input and output primitives for message passing, and in_b and out_b for broadcast. Also, we use *publish* and *news* as communication channels: the first is used for the interaction between the news provider and the server, and the latter for sending news to their recipients. Channel *info* is used as news value instead. Thus the server can be modeled as $S = !(x)publish\ in\langle x\rangle.(news\ out_b\langle x\rangle|S'[x])$ where $(-)$ is name restriction, | is parallel composition, . is prefixing and ! is replication. Here $S'[x]$ is a generic context exploiting x. A news provider instead has the form $P = (info)publish\ out\langle info\rangle$. Consider the system $P|S|C_1|C_2$, where $C_i = (y)news\ in_b\langle y\rangle.Use_i[y]$ is a suitable client, for each i. The components P and S can interact on channel *publish*, leading to $S|(info)(news\ out_b\langle info\rangle|S'[info])|C_1|C_2$. Then, a broadcast interaction among three different components (a sender and two receivers) delivers the news to the clients, leading in one step to $S|(info)(S'[info]|Use_1[info]|Use_2[info])$.

In the paper we show that many different protocols can be formalized as *synchronization algebras with mobility* (SAMs) and how the above defined interactions can be specified in a general framework. For the sake of presentation, the set of primitives is kept to a minimal extent, but we conjecture that other features (e.g., locations, ambients, encryption, probability) can be likely transferred from the literature. The main advantage of having a uniform framework for expressing high-level synchronization mechanisms is that their formalization becomes simpler, since SAMs are tools dedicated to that purpose, and there is no need of, e.g., introducing special processes implementing the required synchronization patterns on top of the available ones. Also, PRISMA allows for developing general theories and tools (i.e., independent from the synchronization model). Finally, when expressed in a uniform framework, different synchronization models can be more easily compared and integrated (e.g., the compound use of different policies is rather straightforward). The name PRISMA (the Italian for *prism*) is intended to expose the many communication facets of our calculus.

Although PRISMA is based on name fusion, it is reductive to see it just as an extension of Fusion Calculus [18], because much more general interactions are allowed in PRISMA. We have chosen fusion as the key primitive for mobility since Fusion Calculus inherits the expressive power of π-calculus, while making the communication primitive more symmetric and easy to generalize. In fact, in π-calculus, input and output are treated ad hoc, and this gives no hint on how to deal with actions that are neither inputs nor outputs, such as in the Hoare SAM (Example 2). Anyway we think that our approach can capture most interaction calculi, and in particular the π-calculus, but this complicates the technicalities of the approach (see e.g. the approach in [3] to deal with distinctions).

SAMs improve in a crucial way *synchronization algebras* [19] (which stem from ACP communication functions [2]), which were tailored for calculi such as

CCS and CSP, to keep them in line with more sophisticated mobile calculi for scenarios such as Global Computing.

SAMs were first defined in [13], in the context of a graph transformation framework called Synchronized Hyperedge Replacement (SHR) [5,9], to provide a uniform presentation of two existing synchronization models. PRISMA is not a mere translation of SHR. Like PRISMA, also SHR is a unifying framework for modeling systems, but SHR is more suitable for architectural models since the structure of the system is explicitly represented. Instead, PRISMA focuses on the linguistic aspect of interaction, and is more useful to analyze the interactions between synchronization patterns and other primitives, since process calculi can be easily extended with specific features (e.g., probabilities, pattern matching). Our presentation of SAMs is also more general and polished w.r.t. the one in [13].

As main results: (i) we prove that the observational semantics of PRISMA, called *hyperbisimilarity*, is a congruence under any SAM, (ii) we discuss how to build complex SAMs by composing basic ones and (iii) we show how to prove properties for general classes of synchronization protocols. The expressiveness of our calculus is demonstrated via original examples on a news server (already outlined), on communications with accounting, on interoperability between different synchronization policies, and via the case study on Fusion Calculus.

Structure of the paper. § 2 recalls SAMs and shows some examples. In § 3 we define the PRISMA calculus, analyze its operational and abstract semantics and prove the congruence theorem for hyperbisimilarity. The case study on Fusion Calculus is detailed in § 4, while § 5 analyzes the relationships among different SAMs using basic concepts from category theory, which can be found, e.g., in [15]. All the material in § 3–5 is original to this contribution. Finally, § 6 contains some conclusions and plans for future work. A full discussion on PRISMA calculus and related topics can be found in the Ph.D. thesis of the second author [12].

2   Synchronization Algebra with Mobility (SAM)

Notation. We write $A \uplus B$ to denote the disjoint union of A and B, with $\mathrm{inj}_1 : A \to A \uplus B$ and $\mathrm{inj}_2 : B \to A \uplus B$ the left and right inclusions, respectively. When no confusion can arise we write $\mathrm{inj}_i(x)$ simply as x. If $\mathrm{inj}_i(x) \in A \uplus B$ we denote with $comp(\mathrm{inj}_i(x))$ the element $\mathrm{inj}_{3-i}(x)$ in $B \uplus A$. We denote with $\underline{n}$ the set $\{1, \ldots, n\}$ (where $\underline{0} \stackrel{\text{def}}{=} \emptyset$), while id_n is the identity function on it. Given two functions $f : A \to C$ and $g : B \to D$ we denote with $[f, g] : A \uplus B \to C \uplus D$ the function that applies f to the elements in A and g to the ones in B. Given a function f, the function $f|_S$ (resp. $f|_{\backslash S}$) is obtained by restricting f to S (resp. to $dom(f) \setminus S$). Also, when set operations (e.g., $\cup$) are used on function f, it is implicitly assumed that f is seen as a set of pairs $(a, f(a))$. We use $\circ$ to denote the standard composition of functions, i.e. $(g \circ f)(x) = g(f(x))$. Given a vector $\vec{v}$ and an integer i we denote with $\vec{v}[i]$ the i-th element of $\vec{v}$ while $Set(\vec{v})$ is the set of elements in $\vec{v}$. Finally, we denote with $mgu(E)$ any idempotent substitution resulting from computing the most general unifier on the set of equations E, when it exists.

In this section we present SAMs, which are an extension of Winskel's synchronization algebras (SAs) [19] able to deal with name mobility, local resource handling and nondeterminism. SAMs can be used to specify the interactions among different actions, each carrying a tuple of arguments which are names of channels. Each allowed synchronization pattern is modeled by an action synchronization triple, whose first and second components are the interacting actions and whose third component is the result of the synchronization. This is composed by three different fields: (1) the resulting action, (2) a function specifying how the arguments attached to the resulting action are computed (the component Mob in Definition 2), (3) a relation determining which names are merged (the component $\doteq$ in Definition 2).

Definition 1 (Action signature). *An* action signature **A** *is a tuple* $(Act, \mathrm{ar}, \epsilon)$ *where Act is the set of actions,* $\mathrm{ar} : Act \to \mathbb{N}$ *is the* arity function *specifying the number of arguments of each action and* $\epsilon \in Act$ *has* $\mathrm{ar}(\epsilon) = 0$.

The action ϵ stands for "not taking part in synchronization", and it allows to deal in a uniform way with synchronization and with asynchronous execution of actions, the latter being modeled as synchronization with ϵ.

Definition 2 (Action synchronization set). *An* action synchronization set *AS on* **A** *is a set of triples of the form* $(a, b, (c, \mathrm{Mob}, \doteq))$ *where* $a, b, c \in Act$, $\mathrm{Mob} : \mathrm{ar}(c) \to \mathrm{ar}(a) \uplus \mathrm{ar}(b)$ *and* $\doteq$ *is an equivalence relation on* $\mathrm{ar}(a) \uplus \mathrm{ar}(b)$.

The Mob component assigns to each argument of c an argument of either a or b, i.e. it specifies how the arguments of the resulting action are obtained from the arguments of the component actions. Since actual arguments are not known at SAM-definition time, the correspondence is defined according to the positions in the tuple: for instance $\mathrm{Mob}(1) = \mathrm{inj}_2(1)$ means that the first parameter of the resulting action comes from the first parameter of the second action, as it is in the left part of Figure 1, that represents the action synchronization $(a, \overline{a}, (\overline{a}, \mathrm{Mob}_1, \doteq))$.

For $\doteq$, the idea is to define equivalence classes over incoming parameters: parameters in the same class are then merged. Again, a positional notation is used. For instance, according to the action synchronization in the left part of Figure 1, $a\langle x \rangle$ can interact with $\overline{a}\langle y \rangle$. Then x and y are merged, and the result is $\overline{a}\langle y \rangle$ (if y is chosen as representative of the equivalence class).

Action synchronizations $(a, b, (c, \mathrm{Mob}_1, \doteq))$ and $(a, b, (c, \mathrm{Mob}_2, \doteq))$ such that $\mathrm{Mob}_1(n) \doteq \mathrm{Mob}_2(n)$ for each n (see the example in Figure 1) are semantically equivalent (we will show in § 5 that they are isomorphic).

Next definition introduces a notion of composition on action synchronizations. In the general case, synchronization among n different processes must be specified. However, SAMs guarantee that the order in which synchronization is achieved is not important. Our approach allows to specify synchronization in a compositional way, i.e. by considering the interaction between two processes at the time. In particular, in order to express associativity we find it convenient to consider the synchronization of three actions, which arises as the composition of two binary synchronizations.

Fig. 1. Action synchronization

Definition 3 (Action synchronization composition)

Given $\alpha = (a_1, b_1, (c_1, \mathrm{Mob}_1, \doteq_1))$ and $\beta = (a_2, b_2, (c_2, \mathrm{Mob}_2, \doteq_2))$ with $c_1 = a_2$, the composition $\alpha \star_L \beta$ of α and β is the tuple $(a_1, b_1, b_2, (c_2, \mathrm{Mob}_3, \doteq_3))$ where $\mathrm{Mob}_3 = [\mathrm{Mob}_1, id_{\mathrm{ar}(b_2)}] \circ \mathrm{Mob}_2 : \mathrm{ar}(c_2) \rightarrow \mathrm{ar}(a_1) \uplus \mathrm{ar}(b_1) \uplus \mathrm{ar}(b_2)$, and the equivalence relation $\doteq_3$ on $\mathrm{ar}(a_1) \uplus \mathrm{ar}(b_1) \uplus \mathrm{ar}(b_2)$ is defined as the projection on the above specified domain of the least equivalence relation R on $\mathrm{ar}(a_1) \uplus \mathrm{ar}(b_1) \uplus \mathrm{ar}(c_1) \uplus \mathrm{ar}(b_2)$ such that $x\,R\,y$ if $x \doteq_1 y \vee x \doteq_2 y \vee \mathrm{Mob}_1(x) = y$. A similar composition $\alpha \star_R \beta$ is defined when $c_1 = b_2$ instead of $c_1 = a_2$.

Definition 4 (Action synchronization relation)

Given an action signature $\mathbf{A} = (Act, \mathrm{ar}, \epsilon)$, an action synchronization relation AS on $\mathbf{A}$ is an action synchronization set such that:

1. $(a, b, (\epsilon, \mathrm{Mob}, \doteq)) \in AS \Rightarrow a = b = \epsilon$;
2. $(a, \epsilon, (c, \mathrm{Mob}, \doteq)) \in AS \Rightarrow (c = a \wedge \mathrm{Mob} = \mathrm{inj}_1 \wedge \doteq = \mathrm{id})$;
3. $(a, b, (c, \mathrm{Mob}, \doteq)) \in AS \Rightarrow (b, a, (c, \mathrm{Mob}', \doteq')) \in AS$, where for each x, y $\mathrm{Mob}'(x) = comp(\mathrm{Mob}(x))$ and $x \doteq' y$ iff $comp(x) \doteq comp(y)$;
4. *if* $\alpha_1 = (a, b, (c, \mathrm{Mob}, \doteq)) \in AS$ *and* $\alpha_2 = (c, d, (e, \mathrm{Mob}', \doteq')) \in AS$ *then* $\exists f \in Act$, $\exists \beta_1 = (b, d, (f, \mathrm{Mob}'', \doteq'')), \beta_2 = (a, f, (e, \mathrm{Mob}''', \doteq''')) \in AS$ *such that* $\alpha_1 \star_L \alpha_2 = \beta_1 \star_R \beta_2$.

Condition 1 (already present in SAs) specifies that no action can disappear producing ϵ. Also, interaction of ϵ with any action just propagates the other action (condition 2). Conditions 3 and 4 ensure commutativity and associativity of synchronization respectively, by specifying that the composed actions take the same parameters and force the same merges.

Definition 5 (SAM).

A synchronization algebra with mobility is a triple $S = (\mathbf{A}, Fin, AS)$ which includes an action signature $\mathbf{A} = (Act, \mathrm{ar}, \epsilon)$, a set $Fin \subseteq Act$ of final actions and an action synchronization relation AS on $\mathbf{A}$.

Final actions are used to deal with local channels: since no process from outside can interact with a bound channel, only actions corresponding to successful interactions that do not require additional contributions can take place on bound channels. Those actions are in *Fin*. For instance in message passing synchronization an input is not in *Fin*, while the result of the synchronization between one input and one output is in *Fin*.

We present three simple examples of SAMs, taken from [13,14] (albeit with different notation). Below, $MP_{i,j}$ (for message passing) is a shorthand for the function from $\max(i,j)$ to (any superset of) $\underline{i} \uplus \underline{j}$ such that $MP_{i,j}(m) = \mathrm{inj}_1(m)$ if $m \leq i$, and $\mathrm{inj}_2(m)$ otherwise, while EQ_i denotes the least equivalence relation on (any superset of) $\underline{i} \uplus \underline{i}$ containing $\{(\mathrm{inj}_1(m), \mathrm{inj}_2(m)) | m \leq i\}$.

Remark 1. From now on, to simplify the presentation, we will not write explicitly the triples obtained by commutativity and we assume that the triple $(\epsilon, \epsilon, (\epsilon, MP_{0,0}, EQ_0))$ is omnipresent. We also assume that a ranked set of labels L is given such that $L \cap \{\epsilon, \tau\} = \emptyset$, with rank ar $: L \to \mathbb{N}$.

Example 1 (Milner SAM). The SAM *Milner$_L$* is given by:

- $Act = \{\tau, \epsilon\} \cup \bigcup_{a \in L} \{a, \overline{a}\}$, $\mathrm{ar}(\overline{a}) = \mathrm{ar}(a)$ for each $a \in L$, $\mathrm{ar}(\tau) = 0$;
- $Fin = \{\tau\}$;
- $(\lambda, \epsilon, (\lambda, MP_{\mathrm{ar}(\lambda),0}, EQ_0)) \in AS$ for each $\lambda \in Act$,
  $(a, \overline{a}, (\tau, MP_{0,0}, EQ_{\mathrm{ar}(a)})) \in AS$ for each $a \in L$.

Milner$_L$ represents message passing *à la* π-calculus: one input a interacts with one output $\overline{a}$, and parameters in the same position are merged. Action τ represents a complete message exchange, and thus belongs to *Fin*. Here we are more general than π-calculus, since it allows just one output action, while we allow many (each with corresponding input), and this corresponds to introducing a simple form of typing.

Example 2 (Hoare SAM). The SAM *Hoare$_L$* is given by:

- $Act = Fin = \{\epsilon\} \cup L$;
- $(\lambda, \lambda, (\lambda, MP_{\mathrm{ar}(\lambda),\mathrm{ar}(\lambda)}, EQ_{\mathrm{ar}(\lambda)})) \in AS$ for each $\lambda \in Act$.

Hoare synchronization models a global agreement on the action to perform. As before, corresponding parameters are merged, but now they are carried over the result of the interaction.

Example 3 (Broadcast SAM). The SAM *Bdc$_L$* is given by:

- $Act = \{\epsilon\} \cup \bigcup_{a \in L} \{a, \overline{a}\}$, $\mathrm{ar}(\overline{a}) = \mathrm{ar}(a)$ for each $a \in L$;
- $Fin = \bigcup_{a \in L} \{\overline{a}\}$;
- $(a, \overline{a}, (\overline{a}, MP_{\mathrm{ar}(a),\mathrm{ar}(\overline{a})}, EQ_{\mathrm{ar}(a)})) \in AS$ for each $a \in L$,
  $(a, a, (a, MP_{\mathrm{ar}(a),\mathrm{ar}(a)}, EQ_{\mathrm{ar}(a)})) \in AS$ for each $a \in L$.

The above SAM models broadcast. When used in PRISMA, it forces an output $\overline{a}$ from a sequential PRISMA process to synchronize with *all* the listening sequential processes in parallel, which have to perform an input a. Notice that, if one wants to have a multicast *Mul$_L$*, where some listening process may not synchronize with the output, it is enough to add the triples $(\lambda, \epsilon, (\lambda, MP_{\mathrm{ar}(\lambda),0}, EQ_0))$ for each $\lambda \in Act$ to AS.

We present now a more complex (and original) example: a SAM for *communication with priority* that allows many senders to synchronize with just one receiver, which takes only the message with the highest priority. This SAM can be used, e.g., to model communication in sensor networks, where the base station acquires at each step the most important available information. In the example we consider just one input action *in* of arity 1, but the generalizations to many actions and different arities are straightforward.

- $Act = \{in, \epsilon\} \cup \{(out, n)|n \in \mathbb{N}\} \cup \{(out+, n)|n \in \mathbb{N}\} \cup \{(out-, n)|n \in \mathbb{N}\}$;
- $ar(a) = 0$ for all $a \in \{\epsilon\} \cup \{(out+, n)|n \in \mathbb{N}\}$, and $ar(a) = 1$ otherwise;
- $Fin = \{(out+, n)|n \in \mathbb{N}\}$;
- $(a, \epsilon, (a, MP_{ar(a),0}, EQ_0)) \in AS$ for each $a \in Act$,
  $(in, (out, n), ((out+, n), MP_{0,0}, EQ_1)) \in AS$ for each n,
  $(in, (out, n), ((out-, n), MP_{1,0}, EQ_0)) \in AS$ for each n,
  $((out, n), (out, m), ((out, n), MP_{1,0}, EQ_0)) \in AS$ for each $n \geq m$,
  $((out, n), (out-, m), ((out+, n), MP_{0,0}, EQ_1)) \in AS$ for each $n \geq m$,
  $((out, n), (out-, m), ((out-, n), MP_{0,1}, EQ_0)) \in AS$ for each $n \geq m$,
  $((out, m), (out-, n), ((out-, n), MP_{0,1}, EQ_0)) \in AS$ for each $n \geq m$,
  $((out+, n), (out, m), ((out+, n), MP_{0,0}, EQ_0)) \in AS$ for each $n \geq m$.

Fig. 2. The priority SAM *Pri*

Example 4 (Priority SAM). The SAM *Pri* is defined in Figure 2. The basic idea is that the result of the synchronization of an action *in* and an action (out, n), i.e. an output with priority n, is guessed: either we guess that n is the highest priority, we merge the parameters and the result is $(out+, n)$, or we guess the opposite, we propagate the input variable and the result is $(out-, n)$. The first guess, if wrong, is discarded when an output with higher priority is found, the second one is checked when the channel is declared local, since $(out-, n) \notin Fin$. Here nondeterminism is useful for the guess, but also needed to choose which output to propagate when two with the same priority interact.

3   The PRISMA Calculus

We can now present the syntax and the semantics of PRISMA. Action prefixes in PRISMA are parametric on a given SAM $S = ((Act, ar, \epsilon), Fin, AS)$.

Definition 6 (PRISMA). *The syntax for PRISMA processes is:*

$$
\begin{array}{llll}
P ::= & 0 & \textit{(Inaction)} & \quad x a \vec{y}.P \quad \textit{(Prefix)} \\
& P_1 | P_2 & \textit{(Parallel composition)} & \quad P_1 + P_2 \quad \textit{(Nondeterministic sum)} \\
& (x)P & \textit{(Restriction)} & \quad !P \quad \textit{(Replication)}
\end{array}
$$

where x is a channel name, $a \in Act$ is an action and $\vec{y}$ is a vector of channel names whose length is $ar(a)$. Channel x is the subject of $x a \vec{y}$.

In PRISMA, restriction (x) is the only binder for x. As usual, processes are taken up to α-conversion of restricted names, and $fn(P)$ denotes the set of free names in P. The intrinsic compositionality of action synchronization in SAMs makes the LTS operational semantics more natural for PRISMA than semantics in the reduction style, where all possible global synchronizations, involving an unbound number of processes, should be considered explicitly (think, e.g., of broadcast). Roughly, reductions would correspond to "closed" synchronizations, according to *Fin*.

Table 1. Rule for synchronization

$$P_1 \xrightarrow{(Y_1)xa_1\vec{y}_1,\pi_1} P_1' \qquad P_2 \xrightarrow{(Y_2)xa_2\vec{y}_2,\pi_2} P_2' \qquad (a_1,a_2,(c,\mathrm{Mob},\doteq)) \in AS \qquad \Phi$$
$$\overline{P_1|P_2 \xrightarrow{(W)xc\vec{w},\pi|_{\backslash(Y_1\cup Y_2)}} (\vec{s})(P_1'|P_2')\pi} \tag{2}$$

where the premise Φ is the conjunction of the following five side conditions:

freshness of extruded names: $Y_1 \cap Y_2 = \emptyset$, $(Y_1 \cup Y_2) \cap (\mathrm{fn}(P_1) \cup \mathrm{fn}(P_2)) = \emptyset$;

forced fusions: $\pi = \mathrm{mgu}(\{\vec{y}_{i_1}[j_1] = \vec{y}_{i_2}[j_2]|\, \mathrm{inj}_{i_1}(j_1) \doteq \mathrm{inj}_{i_2}(j_2)\} \cup \{x = y|x\pi_1 = y\pi_1 \vee x\pi_2 = y\pi_2\})$ where we choose elements not in $Y_1 \cup Y_2$ as representatives for the equivalence classes of names in π, whenever possible;

arguments of c: $\vec{w}[k] = (\vec{y}_i[j])\pi$ iff $\mathrm{Mob}(k) = \mathrm{inj}_i(j)$;

names extruded by c: $W = \mathrm{Set}(\vec{w}) \cap (Y_1 \cup Y_2)$;

closed names: $\mathrm{Set}(\vec{s}) = (Y_1 \cup Y_2)\pi \setminus W$ (any order can be chosen for $\vec{s}$).

We present now the inference rules defining the semantics of PRISMA processes, in an incremental way. The rules are parametric on the SAM S that fixes the allowed interaction policies. Interestingly the rules exploit just α-conversion as structural law, and this simplifies the proofs of process properties. However, the kind of axioms usually used in structural congruence equate processes which are also equivalent according to our observational semantics (see Lemma 1). One could avoid α-conversion too, but this would unnecessarily complicate the inference rules. The first rule we examine is the one for prefix:

$$xa\vec{y}.P \xrightarrow{xa\vec{y},\mathrm{id}} P \tag{1}$$

The transition simply executes the corresponding action. Note that the label contains a substitution too (the identity substitution in this case): this is used to trace fusions of global names performed by the synchronization, since they must be applied to parallel processes (see, e.g., rule 9).

The most important, but also the most complex, rule allows to synchronize two actions performed by parallel processes (rule 2 in Table 1). Its complexity is due to the great degree of flexibility of PRISMA, which allows to specify both action synchronization and (name) mobility patterns. Also, we deal with slightly more complex actions than the ones seen so far, since a set of extruded names appears (when empty, such as in rule 1, it is deleted from the label). Extruded names are names that were bound before, but become global after being used as parameters in the label. Extruded names must be traced, since when they are removed from the tuple of parameters, restrictions for them have to be reintroduced (as in π-calculus (close) rule).

The rule for synchronization allows two actions a_1 and a_2 performed on the same channel x to synchronize. The main effect of the synchronization is to produce a new substitution π, which combines the previous substitutions traced by π_1 and π_2 with the new substitution π determined by taking into account the equivalence classes defined by $\doteq$. The substitution π is applied to the two interacting processes P_1' and P_2' and to the tuple $\vec{w}$ of parameters of the resulting action c, and, as far as global names are concerned, it is traced in the label as

$\pi|_{\backslash (Y_1 \cup Y_2)}$. The set W is the new set of extruded names. Finally, names that were extruded $(Y_1 \cup Y_2)$, still exist $((Y_1 \cup Y_2)\pi)$ and are no longer appearing in the label $((Y_1 \cup Y_2)\pi \backslash W)$ must be closed by inserting them into $\vec{s}$ (in any order).

Two additional aspects must be considered to deal with parallel composition. In some SAMs, such as the Milner one, no process is forced to participate to the synchronization, while in others, such as in broadcast, the processes in a given set *must* participate. This is specified in SAMs by allowing or disallowing the interaction with ϵ, which can be executed for free by any process using rule:

$$\frac{x \in \mathcal{N}}{P \xrightarrow{x\epsilon\langle\rangle, \mathrm{id}} P} \tag{3}$$

However, also in broadcast, we want to allow processes which are not interested in the synchronization to stay idle. We consider that a process is interested in a synchronization at x if it has an active prefix with subject x. Thus, following the approach of [7], we introduce a label $\neg x$ which can be executed by any process which has no active prefix with subject x. This can be modeled with:

$$\frac{x \text{ is not an active subject of } P}{P \xrightarrow{\neg x} P} \tag{4}$$

It is easy to give an inductive definition of this rule to allow proofs by induction (not shown here just for space constraints). A dedicated rule (and its symmetric) are required to allow this action to interact with a normal action:

$$\frac{P_1 \xrightarrow{(Y)xa\vec{y}, \pi} P_1' \quad P_2 \xrightarrow{\neg x} P_2 \quad Y \cap \mathrm{fn}(P_2) = \emptyset}{P_1 | P_2 \xrightarrow{(Y)xa\vec{y}, \pi} P_1' | P_2\pi} \tag{5}$$

Restriction is dealt with rules 6–10 in Table 2. Rule 6 says that restriction on channel z does not influence actions where z is neither the subject nor a parameter. If the equivalence class of z according to π is not a singleton, we have to remove z from π, since it is not visible outside its scope. If z is one of

Table 2. Rules for restriction

$$\frac{P \xrightarrow{(Y)xa\vec{y}, \pi} P' \quad z \notin \mathrm{Set}(\vec{y}) \cup \{x\} \quad z \notin \mathrm{Im}(\pi)}{(z)P \xrightarrow{(Y)xa\vec{y}, \pi|_{\backslash\{z\}}} (z)P'} \tag{6}$$

$$\frac{P \xrightarrow{(Y)xa\vec{y}, \pi} P' \quad z \in \mathrm{Set}(\vec{y}) \backslash \{x\} \backslash Y \quad z \notin \mathrm{Im}(\pi)}{(z)P \xrightarrow{(\{z\} \cup Y)xa\vec{y}, \pi|_{\backslash\{z\}}} P'} \tag{7}$$

$$\frac{P \xrightarrow{(Z)xa\vec{y}, \pi} P' \quad a \in Fin \quad x \notin \mathrm{Im}(\pi) \quad \mathrm{Set}(\vec{z}) = Z}{(x)P \xrightarrow{\sqrt{}, \pi|_{\backslash\{x\}}} (x\vec{z})P'} \tag{8}$$

$$\frac{P \xrightarrow{\sqrt{}, \pi} P'}{P|Q \xrightarrow{\sqrt{}, \pi} P'|Q\pi} \tag{9} \qquad \frac{P \xrightarrow{\sqrt{}, \pi} P' \quad x \notin \mathrm{Im}(\pi)}{(x)P \xrightarrow{\sqrt{}, \pi|_{\backslash\{x\}}} (x)P'} \tag{10}$$

the parameters instead (rule 7), then it is marked as extruded in the label (as in π-calculus rule (open)). Rule 8 closes the channel on which the action a is done, reintroducing the restriction for names that were extruded by a. This is allowed only if $a \in Fin$. This rule introduces a further form of label, namely $(\sqrt{}, \pi)$, which states that an action has been performed on a bound channel, and that substitution π is its effect on global names. The simpler rules 9 (and its symmetric) and 10 deal with this kind of labels.

Finally, (almost) standard rules can be added to deal with nondeterministic sum (rule 11 and its symmetric) and replication (rule 12):

$$\frac{P_1 \xrightarrow{\lambda} P_1' \quad \lambda \neq x\epsilon\langle\rangle, \mathrm{id} \quad \lambda \neq \neg x}{P_1 + P_2 \xrightarrow{\lambda} P_1'} \quad (11) \qquad \frac{P\|!P \xrightarrow{\lambda} P'}{!P \xrightarrow{\lambda} P'} \quad (12)$$

In the above rules, λ denotes a general label. The only peculiarity is that actions ϵ and $\neg x$, which can be executed for free and thus do not represent real process activities, should not force the choice of one branch of a sum.

Example 5. Take the priority SAM *Pri* of Example 4. The $\sqrt{}$-labeled transitions for the process $S = (x)(x\ in\langle y\rangle.P \mid x\langle out, 3\rangle\langle z\rangle.Q \mid x\langle out, 2\rangle\langle w\rangle.R)$ are:

$$S \xrightarrow{\sqrt{}, \{z/y\}} (x)(P \mid Q \mid x\langle out, 2\rangle\langle w\rangle.R)\{z/y\}$$
$$S \xrightarrow{\sqrt{}, \{w/y\}} (x)(P \mid x\langle out, 3\rangle\langle z\rangle.Q \mid R)\{w/y\}$$
$$S \xrightarrow{\sqrt{}, \{z/y\}} (x)(P \mid Q \mid R)\{z/y\}$$

together with a transition where y is chosen as representative instead of z or w. Here the last transition is the most interesting, since it features an interaction between two outputs and one input, with the output with the lowest priority, (out,2), being discarded. The only other admissible transitions are from S to itself with labels of the form $u\epsilon\langle\rangle$, id or $\neg u$ for any u.

Example 6 (News server and PRISMA). The transitions described in the Introduction for the news server can be derived, with suitable labels, in PRISMA by considering a SAM with six actions: *in* and *out* interacting using Milner synchronization and producing τ as a result, in_b and out_b interacting using broadcast synchronization, and ϵ. Such a SAM can also be built using a coproduct construction in the category of SAMs, as we will show in Section 5.

Also, more complex scenarios can be considered. For instance the broadcast action can be tagged with some additional information on the content of the news, and different input actions can be chosen to receive only some of them. For instance we can have actions $out - CS$ for computer science news and $out - math$ for mathematical news. Correspondingly we can have actions $in - CS$ and $in - math$, retrieving the corresponding news, and $in - all$ retrieving both of them. A process interested only in some kind of news must however explicitly use actions to discard the others, since broadcast enforces reception of the information by all the listening processes.

We study the observational properties of processes using hyperbisimilarity, as done in Fusion Calculus. This is required since standard bisimilarity is not a congruence w.r.t. composition operators.

Definition 7 (Hyperbisimilarity). *A* bisimulation *is a relation* $\sim_S$ *such that* $P \sim_S Q$ *implies:*

$$- \; P \xrightarrow{\neg x} P \Rightarrow Q \xrightarrow{\neg x} Q,$$
$$- \; P \xrightarrow{\sqrt{},\pi} P' \Rightarrow Q \xrightarrow{\sqrt{},\pi} Q' \wedge P' \sim_S Q',$$
$$- \; P \xrightarrow{(Y)x a\vec{y},\pi} P' \wedge Y \cap \mathrm{fn}(Q) = \emptyset \Rightarrow Q \xrightarrow{(Y)x a\vec{y},\pi} Q' \wedge P' \sim_S Q'$$

and vice versa, where all the transitions are derived using SAM S. A hyperbisimulation *is a substitution-closed bisimulation. We denote with* $\approx_S$ *the maximal hyperbisimulation. If* $P \approx_S Q$, *we say that* P *and* Q *are* hyperbisimilar. *We shall drop S from the notation when clear from the context.*

We present now some properties of hyperbisimilarity. Note that properties that hold for any SAM (or for any SAM satisfying suitable requirements, see, e.g., Lemma 2) can be proved once and for all. Next lemma, in particular, shows that hyperbisimilarity abstracts away from certain syntactic features of processes which are intuitively not important from an observational point of view. (We say that an axiom $P = Q$ on processes *bisimulates* if, for each instance of the axiom, the two equated processes are hyperbisimilar.)

Lemma 1. *The axioms below bisimulate for any SAM and for any* P, Q, R:
$$P|Q = Q|P \qquad (P|Q)|R = P|(Q|R) \qquad P|0 = P \qquad P + P = P$$
$$P + Q = Q + P \qquad (P+Q) + R = P + (Q + R) \qquad P + 0 = P$$
$$(x)(y)P = (y)(x)P \qquad (x)P|Q = (x)(P|Q) \; if \; x \notin \mathrm{fn}(Q)$$

Proof (Sketch). Each axiom requires a coinductive proof. Axioms concerning parallel composition exploit the properties of SAMs. The proof for $P + 0 = P$ uses the fact that transitions with source 0 cannot force a branch of the sum to be taken. Proofs for other axioms are standard. □

Lemma 2. *The axiom* $(x)0 = 0$ *bisimulates iff* $\epsilon \notin Fin$.

In fact, including ϵ in Fin corresponds to observe internal idle steps as $\sqrt{}$.

Next theorem proves that abstract semantics is compositional. This result is fundamental to compute the abstract semantics of large complex systems from the abstract semantics of their components. It extends in a non-trivial way an analogous result for Fusion Calculus [18]: the interesting point is that it holds for PRISMA over any SAM.

Theorem 1. *Hyperbisimilarity* $\approx_S$ *is a congruence for any SAM S w.r.t. all the operators in PRISMA.*

Proof (Sketch). For each unary (resp. binary) operator op, we have to prove that for each SAM S and for each P_1, P_2, Q_1, Q_2 processes, $P_1 \approx_S Q_1$ and $P_2 \approx_S Q_2$ implies $\mathrm{op}(P_1) \approx_S \mathrm{op}(Q_1)$ (resp. $\mathrm{op}(P_1, P_2) \approx_S \mathrm{op}(Q_1, Q_2)$). The proof is by rule induction on the derivation of the transition of $\mathrm{op}(P_1)$ (resp. $\mathrm{op}(P_1, P_2)$), and each step requires a coinductive proof. However, rule induction is needed just for replication, while in the other cases it is enough to consider each operator in isolation.

We show the proofs for prefix, parallel composition and replication as examples. The other cases are similar. We will not consider transitions with labels ϵ and $\neg x$ since they can always be trivially simulated.

Case prefix): We have to prove that for each SAM S, each prefix $xa\vec{y}$ and each pair of processes P and Q such that $P \approx_S Q$ we also have $xa\vec{y}.P \approx_S xa\vec{y}.Q$. Thus we have to prove that, for each substitution σ, $(xa\vec{y}.P)\sigma$ and $(xa\vec{y}.Q)\sigma$ can perform the same transitions, going into hyperbisimilar states. The only transitions to consider are the ones from rule 1, which have the same label as required and lead to states $P\sigma$ and $Q\sigma$ which are hyperbisimilar by hypothesis. In general, we have not to consider explicitly the substitution σ, since this corresponds to choosing $P' = P\sigma$ and $Q' = Q\sigma$.

Case |): Suppose that $P_1 \approx_S Q_1$ and $P_2 \approx_S Q_2$. To show $P_1|P_2 \approx_S Q_1|Q_2$ we have three rules to check. Let us consider rule 2. Most of the conditions deal only with the labels, thus they are verified for P_1 and P_2 iff they are verified for Q_1 and Q_2. The only condition to check is $(Y_1 \cup Y_2) \cap (\mathrm{fn}(P_1) \cup \mathrm{fn}(P_2)) = \emptyset$. This can be satisfied since names in $Y_1 \cup Y_2$ are bound, thus they can be α-converted if necessary. We have to prove that the two resulting processes, namely $(\vec{s})(P_1'|P_2')\sigma$ and $(\vec{s})(Q_1'|Q_2')\sigma$ are hyperbisimilar. Thanks to α-conversion, we can suppose that $\vec{s}$ is the same in both the cases. By hypothesis $P_1' \approx_S Q_1'$ and $P_2' \approx_S Q_2'$. By coinductive hypothesis, $P_1'|P_2' \approx_S Q_1'|Q_2'$. Thanks to the closure under substitutions of hyperbisimilarity $(P_1'|P_2')\sigma \approx_S (Q_1'|Q_2')\sigma$. Finally, using closure under restriction contexts, $(\vec{s})(P_1'|P_2')\sigma \approx_S (\vec{s})(Q_1'|Q_2')\sigma$. The cases for rules 5 and 9 are simpler than the one just shown.

Case !): We have to prove that if $P \approx_S Q$, then $!P \approx_S !Q$. We have to use rule induction for that case. If $!P \xrightarrow{\lambda} P'$, then we also have $P|!P \xrightarrow{\lambda} P'$, which is a premise. By inductive hypothesis on the context $\bullet|!\bullet$, $Q|!Q \xrightarrow{\lambda} Q'$ with $Q' \approx_S P'$. Since also $!Q$ has the same transition, the thesis follows. $\qquad\square$

4   A Case Study: Fusion Calculus

Let $L = \{\mathrm{in}_n | n \in \mathbb{N}\}$ with $\mathrm{ar}(\mathrm{in}_n) = n$. We will show that PRISMA over $Milner_L$ is essentially Fusion Calculus [18] (as expected), and we suggest a new channel-located semantics for it. We consider the subset of Fusion Calculus whose processes are defined by:

$$P ::= 0 \mid u\vec{x}.P \mid \overline{u}\vec{x}.P \mid P_1|P_2 \mid P_1 + P_2 \mid (u)P \mid !P$$

We do not allow fusion prefixes, but $\{\vec{x} = \vec{y}\}.P$ can be encoded as $(z)(z\vec{x}.P|\overline{z}\vec{y}.0)$ for $z \notin \mathrm{fn}(P)$. We denote with $\equiv$ the structural congruence on Fusion processes and with $\approx_f$ Fusion hyperbisimilarity. We refer to [18] for full details on Fusion Calculus and on its semantics.

We define the uniform encoding function $[\![-]\!]$ from Fusion processes into PRISMA processes as the homomorphic extension to the whole calculus of $[\![u\vec{x}.P]\!] = u\ \mathrm{in}_{|\vec{x}|}\ \vec{x}.[\![P]\!]$ and $[\![\overline{u}\vec{x}.P]\!] = u\ \mathrm{out}_{|\vec{x}|}\ \vec{x}.[\![P]\!]$ where in_n and $\mathrm{out}_n = \overline{\mathrm{in}_n}$

are complementary actions. The mapping can be extended to communication labels by defining $[\![(\vec{y})u\vec{x}]\!] = (\mathrm{Set}(\vec{y}))u\ \mathrm{in}_{|\vec{x}|}\ \vec{x}, \mathrm{id}$ and similarly for outputs. The translation loses the order of extruded names, but this is unimportant, since in Fusion all different orderings can be obtained thanks to structural congruence.

The following theorem shows the relationship between the behaviors of Fusion processes and of their translations into PRISMA.

Theorem 2. *Let P be a Fusion process. $P \xrightarrow{\alpha} P'$ iff:*

1. *α is a communication action, $[\![P]\!] \xrightarrow{[\alpha]} [\![P_1]\!]$ and $P_1 \equiv P'$ or;*
2. *α is a fusion action, $[\![P]\!] \xrightarrow{\lambda} [\![P_1\pi]\!]$ and $P_1\pi \equiv P'\pi$ where λ can be either $(\surd, \pi)$ or $(x\tau\langle\rangle, \pi)$ for some $x \in \mathrm{fn}([\![P]\!])$ and where π is a mgu of α.*

Proof (Sketch). The proof is by structural induction on Fusion processes, and has a case for each operator. One must prove that Fusion transitions correspond to PRISMA transitions of the two forms above (but PRISMA can have transitions with labels ϵ and $\neg x$ too, since these ones have no Fusion correspondence).

Notably, Fusion structural congruence can be simulated since translations of structural congruent processes are hyperbisimilar (see lemmas 1 and 2).

As far as parallel composition is concerned, Fusion synchronization is simulated by rule 2 using synchronization $(a, \bar{a}, (\tau, MP_{0,0}, EQ_{\mathrm{ar}(a)}))$. Asynchronous execution of Fusion actions can be simulated instead using synchronization $(a, \epsilon, (a, MP_{\mathrm{ar}(a),0}, EQ_0))$. Finally fusion propagation can be simulated by rule 9.

For restriction operator different rules have to be chosen according to the kind of actions: rule 6 to deal with actions on other channels, rule 7 for extrusions, rule 8 to move from the representation of fusions as $x\tau\langle\rangle, \pi$ to $(\surd, \pi)$ (note in fact that $\tau \in Fin$) and 10 if the label is already in this form.

The proofs for other operators are similar. Likewise, PRISMA rules can be simulated by Fusion rules for labels which are translations of Fusion labels.   □

In PRISMA each process can always do idle steps to itself, with labels of the form $x\epsilon\langle\rangle$ or $\neg x$, which have no Fusion correspondence. In particular, the second kind of labels allows to identify the active names of a process.

Corollary 1. $[\![P]\!] \approx_{Milner_L} [\![P']\!] \Rightarrow P \approx_f P'$.

The main difference between Fusion Calculus and PRISMA over $Milner_L$ is that in our more general form the τ is a normal action and thus it is located. The corresponding semantics can be defined also for Fusion Calculus, by adding located fusions $x\phi$ to the set of transition labels. Rules can be updated to take care of these labels.

The corresponding hyperbisimilarity is in general finer than the standard one, as the following examples illustrate (the examples are written in the Fusion Calculus syntax, but one can use the translation $[\![-]\!]$ to have them in the PRISMA setting).

Example 7. One can easily find two processes that are bisimilar with the standard (non-located) semantics, but not with the PRISMA one, e.g.:

$$x \mid \bar{x} \approx_f (y)(x+y) \mid (\bar{x}+\bar{y})$$

The right process can perform unlocated actions $\sqrt{}$ by making y and $\overline{y}$ react, while the left one cannot. A similar example can be written using replication:

$$\overline{x} \mid !x.\overline{x} \approx_f (y)y \mid \overline{y} \mid \overline{x} \mid !x.\overline{x}$$

(In both the examples the two members have the same set of active names.)

We think that the located semantics for τ can be useful, since, for accounting or performance reasons, synchronizations performed on different free channels may not be equivalent. Suppose for instance that channel x is provided by some company while channel y is local and owned by the user: a process performing a synchronization on y is cheaper than a process performing the same synchronization using x. Local channels are instead all equivalent, since any interaction, including traffic check (see Example 8), must happen inside the scope of the channel. For a more detailed description of a semantics of this kind see [11].

5   A Category of SAMs

We want to analyze now how different SAMs can be combined and interact, in order to allow interoperability among calculi based on different synchronization primitives. We use basic tools from category theory [15] to this end.

SAs form a category $\mathcal{SA}$ [19] whose objects are SAs and whose morphisms are functions $h : Act_A \to Act_B$ such that $h(\epsilon_A) = \epsilon_B$ and $(a, b, c) \in AS_A \Rightarrow (h(a), h(b), h(c)) \in AS_B$. The morphism h is called *synchronous* (strict using Winskel's terminology) if $h(a) = \epsilon_B \Leftrightarrow a = \epsilon_A$. SAs with synchronous morphisms form the subcategory $s\mathcal{SA}$ of $\mathcal{SA}$. We want to extend these definitions to SAMs.

Definition 8 (Morphism between action signatures)
Let $\mathbf{A}_A = (Act_A, ar_A, \epsilon_A)$ and $\mathbf{A}_B = (Act_B, ar_B, \epsilon_B)$ be action signatures. An asynchronous morphism $H : \mathbf{A}_A \to \mathbf{A}_B$ is a function $h : Act_A \to Act_B$ such that $h(\epsilon_A) = \epsilon_B$, together with a family of functions $h_a : ar(h(a)) \to ar(a)$ indexed by actions. Synchronous morphisms additionally require that $h(a) = \epsilon_B \Leftrightarrow a = \epsilon_A$.

Each component of identity morphisms is an identity. We define morphism composition as $(h, \{h_a\}_{a \in Act_A}); (k, \{k_b\}_{b \in Act_B}) = (k \circ h, \{h_a \circ k_{h(a)}\}_{a \in Act_A})$. Note that the functions $\{h_a\}_{a \in Act_A}$ and morphism H are in opposite directions.

Definition 9 (Morphism between SAMs)
Let $(\mathbf{A}_A, Fin_A, AS_A)$ and $(\mathbf{A}_B, Fin_B, AS_B)$ be two SAMs. A morphism H from the first to the second is a morphism $H : \mathbf{A}_A \to \mathbf{A}_B$ between the corresponding action signatures such that:

1. $a \in Fin_A \Rightarrow h(a) \in Fin_B$;
2. $(a_1, a_2, (c, \mathrm{Mob}_A, \doteq_A)) \in AS_A \Rightarrow (h(a_1), h(a_2), (h(c), \mathrm{Mob}_B, \doteq_B)) \in AS_B$
   and
   - *if* $\mathrm{Mob}_A(h_c(n)) = \mathrm{inj}_i(m)$ *then* $\exists j, m'$ *such that* $\mathrm{Mob}_B(n) = \mathrm{inj}_j(m')$ *and* $\mathrm{inj}_j(h_{a_j}(m')) \doteq_A \mathrm{inj}_i(m)$;
   - $\mathrm{inj}_i(n) \doteq_B \mathrm{inj}_j(m)$ *if and only if* $\mathrm{inj}_i(h_{a_i}(n)) \doteq_A \mathrm{inj}_j(h_{a_j}(m))$.

A SAM morphism is synchronous *iff the corresponding morphism between action signatures is synchronous.*

Essentially actions are mapped to other actions implementing them, and a mapping between parameters (in the opposite direction) is provided. Morphisms can remove parameters or add new synchronizations, but they must provide corresponding elements for the existing ones, preserving their behavior (i.e., action composition, computation of parameters and merges among them) on the remaining parameters.

Lemma 3. *SAMs with asynchronous morphisms form the category $\mathcal{ASYNC}$, SAMs with synchronous morphisms form the subcategory $\mathcal{SYNC}$ of $\mathcal{ASYNC}$.*

Processes on a SAM S_1 can be translated into processes on a SAM S_2 according to a morphism $H : S_1 \rightarrow S_2$.

Definition 10. *Given a morphism $H = (h, \{h_a\}_{a \in Act})$, we define the corresponding translation of PRISMA processes as the homomorphic extension of the prefix translation mapping $xa\vec{y}$ to $xh(a)\vec{w}$ where $\vec{w}[i] = \vec{y}[h_a(i)]$.*

In general morphisms neither preserve nor reflect process behavior, but some classes of them, such as isomorphisms, do.

Lemma 4. *An isomorphism between SAMs can only rename actions, permute their parameters, and change for each action synchronization triple the representative chosen by Mob inside a $\doteq$-equivalence class.*

Corollary 2. *Let P and Q be two processes and $H(P)$ and $H(Q)$ be their translations according to SAM isomorphism $H : S_1 \rightarrow S_2$. Then $P \approx_{S_1} Q$ iff $H(P) \approx_{S_2} H(Q)$.*

Products and coproducts exist and can be used to combine SAMs.

Lemma 5. *Let $((Act_1, ar_1, \epsilon_1), Fin_1, AS_1)$ and $((Act_2, ar_2, \epsilon_2), Fin_2, AS_2)$ be two SAMs. The product in $\mathcal{ASYNC}$, which we call* asynchronous product, *has the form $((Act_\otimes, ar_\otimes, \epsilon_\otimes), Fin_\otimes, AS_\otimes)$ where:*

- $Act_\otimes = Act_1 \times Act_2$ *with $ar_\otimes((a, b)) = ar_1(a) + ar_2(b)$;*
  - *without loss of generality, we can assume that for each (a_1, a_2), the first $ar(a_1)$ parameters correspond to the ones of a_1, and the other ones are from a_2;*
- $\epsilon_\otimes = (\epsilon_1, \epsilon_2)$;
- $Fin_\otimes = Fin_1 \times Fin_2$;
- $AS_\otimes = \{((a_1, a_2), (b_1, b_2), ((c_1, c_2), \text{Mob}_\otimes, \doteq_\otimes)) |$ *for each $i \in \{1, 2\}$ there is $(a_i, b_i, (c_i, \text{Mob}_i, \doteq_i)) \in AS_i\}$;*
  - $\text{Mob}_\otimes$ *and $\doteq_\otimes$ are defined as the union of the corresponding relations in the component objects on the respective parameters.*

The two projection maps are the obvious ones.

Proof (Sketch). If we consider just the part of morphisms that deals with actions, then we have a product in the category of sets and functions, which is cartesian product. If we fix an action and we consider its images, as far as parameters are concerned we obtain a coproduct diagram in the category of finite sets and functions, and this coproduct is the disjoint union. These diagrams can be extended to diagrams in $\mathcal{ASYNC}$ by choosing the different elements as described in the lemma. $\square$

Lemma 6. *The product in $\mathcal{SYNC}$, which we call* synchronous product, *is like the asynchronous one, but it has no actions of the form (a_A, ϵ_B) and (ϵ_A, b_B) except (ϵ_A, ϵ_B).*

Proof (Sketch). The proof is an easy modification of the one above. $\square$

Lemma 7. *Let $((Act_1, ar_1, \epsilon_1), Fin_1, AS_1)$ and $((Act_2, ar_2, \epsilon_2), Fin_2, AS_2)$ be two SAMs. The coproduct in $\mathcal{ASYNC}$ coincides with that in $\mathcal{SYNC}$ and it has the form $((Act_+, ar_+, \epsilon_+), Fin_+, AS_+)$ where:*

- $Act_+ = ((Act_1 \setminus \{\epsilon_1\}) \uplus (Act_2 \setminus \{\epsilon_2\}) \cup \{\epsilon_+\})$ *with* $ar_+(inj_i(a)) = ar_i(a)$;
- $a \in Fin_i \Rightarrow inj_i(a) \in Fin_+$, $\epsilon_+ \in Fin_+$ *iff* $\exists i \in \{1, 2\}.\epsilon_i \in Fin_i$;
- $(a, b, (c, Mob, \doteq)) \in AS_i \Rightarrow (inj_{+i}(a), inj_{+i}(b), (inj_{+i}(c), Mob, \doteq)) \in AS_+$
  where $inj_{+i}(x) = inj_i(x)$ *for each* $x \neq \epsilon_i$, $inj_{+i}(\epsilon_i) = \epsilon_+$.

The two injection maps are the obvious ones.

Proof (Sketch). Here we have as underlying diagram a coproduct diagram in the category of pointed sets and point-preserving functions (where ϵ is the point). The coproduct is the disjoint union with merged points. This diagram can be extended to diagrams in both $\mathcal{ASYNC}$ and $\mathcal{SYNC}$ by choosing the different elements as described in the lemma. $\square$

We provide now some examples on how to exploit these constructions. Products have pairs of actions with one element for each of the component SAMs as actions, with the union of parameters. For instance, the asynchronous product of two Milner SAMs is a message passing communication where at most two communications can be performed at each step. Also, the synchronous product of $Hoare_{L_1}$ and $Hoare_{L_2}$ is $Hoare_{L_1 \times L_2}$. Coproduct allows to merge two SAMs in a unique one preserving the behavior of each action, as proved by the following lemma.

Lemma 8. *Let P, Q be processes and $H(P), H(Q)$ be their translations according to SAM injection $H : S_1 \to S_1 + S_2$. Then $P \approx_{S_1} Q$ iff $H(P) \approx_{S_1 + S_2} H(Q)$.*

For instance, the SAM used in Example 6 is a coproduct of two SAMs, one isomorphic to $Milner_{\{in\}}$ and the other to $Bdc_{\{in_b\}}$. The coproduct of $Milner_{\{in_i | i \in \underline{254}\}}$ and $Bdc_{\{in_{255}\}}$ can be used to model normal TCP/IP protocol, where address 255 is used for broadcast. Clearly this is just an intuition, since far more refined techniques are needed to model TCP/IP in full details.

We conclude by presenting some interesting applications of our framework. Notice that in the examples the modeling effort is required only to choose a suitable SAM to model the desired interaction. After that, the primitives available in the model are in strict correspondence with the desired ones.

Example 8 (Introducing accounting on synchronization). Take the SAM *account* with actions $\{\epsilon, c\}$ of arity 0 with $Fin = \{c\}$ and where $(c, \epsilon, (c, \mathrm{Mob}_{0,0}, \doteq_0))$ is the only non trivial synchronization. The asynchronous product of *account* with any SAM S allows a controller process P_c to count the number of synchronizations performed by a process P. Not accounted actions can be added via a coproduct with another SAM. Let P be a process without restrictions and let x be one of its free names. Let H be the inclusion morphism mapping each action a from S to (a, ϵ). Suppose that S contains an action \$ of arity 0. Then $(x)(H(P)\|!x(\epsilon, c)\langle\rangle.y(\$, c)\langle\rangle.0)$ with the product synchronization behaves as $(x)P$ (up to translation of actions) with the synchronization specified by S, but it sends a message $(\$, c)$ on channel y for each synchronization performed by P on channel x. In fact, synchronization with (ϵ, c) is required to get a final action on x.

Example 9 (Using Fusion in a priority scenario). Consider an infrastructure built for priority communication as specified in Example 4. Suppose that one wants to run a Fusion process P_F in that framework. Suppose for simplicity that P_F uses just unary prefixes. We will show how P_F can be made to interact with the other processes (although, clearly, it will not be able to fully exploit the priority mechanism). The translation from Fusion to PRISMA can be used to have a corresponding PRISMA process P_M on the SAM $Milner_{\{in_1\}}$. In the category $\mathcal{ASYNC}$ there is a morphism $H_n : Milner_{\{in_1\}} \rightarrow Pri$ that maps in_1 to in, out_1 to (out, n) and τ to $(out+, n)$ for any statically chosen priority n. The corresponding translation allows to automatically produce a priority process $P_P = H_n(P_M)$. The process essentially has all the outputs at the fixed priority n, and it inputs the message with the highest priority as specified by the priority synchronization. Notice that to have priority communication with many different actions we can just extend the priority SAM (by considering the coproduct with other copies of itself with different actions) and then apply the same procedure.

6   Conclusion

We have presented PRISMA, a SAM-based process calculus with parametric communication patterns. This helps the modeling phase, when the desired synchronization policy can be specified directly instead of being implemented using "low-level" primitives. Different domain-specific SAMs can provide the right level of abstraction for prototyping and analysis. We have also shown that simple categorical tools allow to compare and compose SAMs. Furthermore, interoperability analysis can be easily performed, since different SAMs can be embedded in the same framework using the coproduct construction and related using morphisms. We have defined an observational semantics for PRISMA which is a congruence w.r.t. all the operators in the language, thus allowing compositional analysis of system behavior. Note that the congruence result holds for any SAM.

As future work, we want to test our model on some case studies taken from real distributed protocols. On a more theoretical side, we want to exploit PRISMA to compare processes based on different synchronization models. Furthermore, we want to see how other existing calculi can be related to PRISMA, starting from bπ-calculus [7].

References

1. Abadi, M., Fournet, C.: Mobile values, new names, and secure communication. In: Proc. of POPL'01, pp. 104–115. ACM Press, New York (2001)
2. Baeten, J.C.M., Weijland, W.P.: Process algebra. Cambridge University Press, Cambridge (1990)
3. Boreale, M., Buscemi, M.G., Montanari, U.: D-fusion: A distinctive fusion calculus. In: Chin, W.-N. (ed.) APLAS 2004. LNCS, vol. 3302, pp. 296–310. Springer, Heidelberg (2004)
4. Dal Zilio, S.: Mobile processes: A commented bibliography. In: MOVEP 2000. LNCS, vol. 2067, pp. 206–222. Springer, Heidelberg (2000)
5. Degano, P., Montanari, U.: A model for distributed systems based on graph rewriting. Journal of the ACM 34(2), 411–449 (1987)
6. Ene, C., Muntean, T.: Expressiveness of point-to-point versus broadcast communications. In: Ciobanu, G., Păun, G. (eds.) FCT 1999. LNCS, vol. 1684, pp. 258–268. Springer, Heidelberg (1999)
7. Ene, C., Muntean, T.: A broadcast-based calculus for communicating systems. In: Proc. of IPDPS'01, IEEE Computer Society, Los Alamitos (2001)
8. Fournet, C., Gonthier, G.: The reflexive chemical abstract machine and the Join calculus. In: Proc. of POPL'96, pp. 372–385. ACM Press, New York (1996)
9. Hirsch, D., Montanari, U.: Synchronized hyperedge replacement with name mobility. In: Larsen, K.G., Nielsen, M. (eds.) CONCUR 2001. LNCS, vol. 2154, pp. 121–136. Springer, Heidelberg (2001)
10. Hoare, C.A.R.: A model for communicating sequential processes. In: On the Construction of Programs, Cambridge University Press, Cambridge (1980)
11. Lanese, I.: Concurrent and located synchronizations in π-calculus. In: Proc. of SOFSEM'07, LNCS (to appear)
12. Lanese, I.: Synchronization strategies for global computing models. PhD thesis, Computer Science Department, University of Pisa, Pisa, Italy (2006)
13. Lanese, I., Montanari, U.: Synchronization algebras with mobility for graph transformations. In: Proc. of FGUC'04, ENTCS 138, pp. 43–60. Elsevier Science, North-Holland (2004)
14. Lanese, I., Tuosto, E.: Synchronized hyperedge replacement for heterogeneous systems. In: Jacquet, J.-M., Picco, G.P. (eds.) COORDINATION 2005. LNCS, vol. 3454, pp. 220–235. Springer, Heidelberg (2005)
15. MacLane, S.: Categories for the Working Mathematician. Springer, Heidelberg (1971)
16. Milner, R.: A Calculus of Communication Systems. LNCS, vol. 92. Springer, Heidelberg (1980)
17. Milner, R., Parrow, J., Walker, J.: A calculus of mobile processes, I and II Inform. and Comput. 100(1) 1–40, 41–77 (1992)
18. Parrow, J., Victor, B.: The fusion calculus: Expressiveness and symmetry in mobile processes. In: Proc. of LICS '98, pp. 176–185. IEEE Computer Society Press, Los Alamitos (1998)
19. Winskel, G.: Synchronization trees. Theoret. Comput. Sci. 34, 33–82 (1984)

On Bisimulation Proofs for the Analysis of Distributed Abstract Machines

Damien Pous

ENS Lyon, France

Abstract. We illustrate the use of recent, non-trivial proof techniques for weak bisimulation by analysing a generic framework for the definition of distributed abstract machines based on a message-passing implementation. The definition of the framework comes from previous works on a specific abstract machine; however, its new presentation, as a parametrised process algebra, makes it suitable for a wider range of calculi.

A first version of the framework can be analysed using the standard bisimulation up to expansion proof technique. We show that in a second, optimised version, rather complex behaviours appear, for which more sophisticated techniques, relying on termination arguments, are necessary to establish behavioural equivalence.

Introduction

Recently, many calculi encompassing distribution and mobility have been studied as a basis for programming languages. Examples include Join [4], Nomadic Pict [11], Kells [1], Ambients [2], Klaim [7], Seals [3]. The expressive power supplied by the primitives underlying such models raises the question of implementability in a distributed framework. In [10], a distributed abstract machine is defined, to implement the Safe Ambient Calculus [6]: the PAN. The main ingredients in the definition of this machine are *locations* – where local processes are executed – and *forwarders*, that transmit messages between locations. In [5], we defined an optimised version of this machine where useless forwarders can be garbage collected, and less messages are transmitted along the network. We proved that the resulting abstract machine is weak barbed bisimilar to the original one; however due to the lack of adequate up-to techniques or compositionality results, this proof is quite tedious, and cannot easily be used as a basis for further studies.

Motivated by these difficulties, we developed new up-to techniques for weak bisimulation [8]. These techniques improve on previously known techniques; however, they are developed in a completely abstract setting and their applicability has not yet been evaluated beyond rather simple illustrative examples.

Before focusing on behavioural equivalences and proof techniques, we present the first main contribution of this work, the definition of a framework to reason about distributed implementations of process algebras with mobility. In this

U. Montanari, D. Sannella, and R. Bruni (Eds.): TGC 2006, LNCS 4661, pp. 150–166, 2007.
© Springer-Verlag Berlin Heidelberg 2007

framework, a network is represented by a set of *locations*, or hosts, where arbitrary local processes are executed. The behaviour of local processes is specified by a given LTS, whose labels correspond to the following possible actions:

- sending arbitrary messages to other locations,
- spawning local processes, inside new locations,
- migrating to another location.

While this framework is the basis of the PAN abstract machine [10], we dropped most of the hypotheses that were related to the implementation of an Ambient-based calculus. Therefore, it should be suitable to analyse a rather wide range of calculi (this is discussed in Remark 2.1).

We then move to the analysis of this framework, which serves as support for our second main contribution: illustrating a non-trivial use of recent proof techniques to reason about a rather complex system.

A forwarder from location h to location k acts like a substitution that replaces any occurrence of h by k in the whole network: a message sent to h will actually reach k. Accordingly, we prove that a net with a forwarder *expands* the corresponding substituted net (*expansion* is the standard behavioural preorder that leads to the correct weak bisimulation up to expansion technique [9]). This result allows one to abstract over the communication framework when validating possible optimisations of local processes.

The main drawback of this framework is the creation of forwarder chains, that slow down the communications between local processes. To address this inefficiency, we introduce an optimisation, inspired from [5], that consists in defining a forwarder relocation mechanism, that contracts forwarder chains. Like in [5], this mechanism breaks the initial proof strategy, as the expansion result does no longer hold. We show in details how the techniques we developed in [8] make it possible to give nevertheless a modular proof of correctness, where the bisimulation candidates that we manipulate remain tractable and express only local properties of processes.

Being able to work with small bisimulation candidates is quite important: they are much easier to check, and when a small part of the system is refined, there is hope that only some of the proofs will need to be updated. Even more important is the fact that the relations focus on local properties, since this allows one to write explicitly the slight differences between related processes and to reason syntactically about these.

We actually allude in [8] to an example derived from [5]. It turned out that the development made in a corresponding technical report missed a crucial step in the proof, and, more importantly, contained a mistake. Moreover, the proof presented here for the optimised system is less specific and aims at giving a better illustration of the benefits given by the general techniques of [8], and of their flexibility.

Outline of the paper. In Sect. 1, we introduce our notations and the notions used in the sequel. We define the initial framework in Sect. 2, and we analyse it in Sect. 3. Section 4 is devoted to the definition of the optimisation, and to the corresponding correctness proof. We conclude with some remarks in Sect. 5.

1   LTS, Bisimilarity

We consider labelled transition systems (LTS) $\langle \mathcal{P}, \mathcal{L}, \rightarrow \rangle$, with domain $\mathcal{P}$, *labels* or *actions* in $\mathcal{L}$ and transition relation $\rightarrow \subseteq \mathcal{P} \times \mathcal{L} \times \mathcal{P}$. The elements of $\mathcal{P}$ are called *processes* and are denoted by P, Q in this section. $\mathcal{L}$ will always implicitly contain a distinguished *silent action*, noted τ. We let α, β (resp. a, b) range over actions, in $\mathcal{L}$ (resp. *visible actions*, in $\mathcal{L} \backslash \{\tau\}$).

We let $\mathcal{R}, \mathcal{S}, \mathcal{B}, \mathcal{E}$ range over binary relations (simply called *relations* in the sequel) between processes. We denote respectively by $\mathcal{R}^+, \mathcal{R}^=, \mathcal{R}^\star$ the transitive, reflexive, transitive and reflexive closures of a relation $\mathcal{R}$. $P\mathcal{R}Q$ means $\langle P, Q \rangle \in \mathcal{R}$. The composition of two relations $\mathcal{R}$ and $\mathcal{S}$, written $\mathcal{R}\mathcal{S}$, is defined by $\mathcal{R}\mathcal{S} \triangleq \{\langle P, Q \rangle / P\mathcal{R}T \text{ and } T\mathcal{S}Q \text{ for some process } T\}$. We also define the inverse of a relation: $\mathcal{R}^{-1} \triangleq \{\langle P, Q \rangle / Q\mathcal{R}P\}$. $\mathcal{I}$ is the identity relation, defined by $\mathcal{I} \triangleq \{\langle P, P \rangle / P \in \mathcal{P}\}$. We say that $\mathcal{R}$ *contains* $\mathcal{S}$ (alternatively, that $\mathcal{S}$ is contained in $\mathcal{R}$), written $\mathcal{S} \subseteq \mathcal{R}$, if $P\mathcal{S}Q$ implies $P\mathcal{R}Q$. Given an action α, the set of transitions along α induces a relation denoted by $\xrightarrow{\alpha}$: $\xrightarrow{\alpha} \triangleq \{\langle P, Q \rangle / \langle P, \alpha, Q \rangle \in \rightarrow\}$. Its inverse is written using a reversed arrow: $\xleftarrow{a} = (\xrightarrow{a})^{-1}$, and similarly for other forms of arrows, defined below.

Definition 1.1 (Termination). *A relation $\mathcal{R}$ terminates if there is no infinite sequence $(P_i)_{i \in \mathbb{N}}$ such that $\forall i, P_i \mathcal{R} P_{i+1}$.*

The definitions of behavioural equivalences and preorders will make use of the following *weak transition* relations.

Definition 1.2 (Weak transitions)

$$\xrightarrow{\hat{\alpha}} \triangleq \begin{cases} \xrightarrow{\tau}^= & \text{if } \alpha = \tau \\ \xrightarrow{a} & \text{if } \alpha = a \in \mathcal{L}\backslash\{\tau\} \end{cases} \qquad \overset{\alpha}{\Rightarrow} \triangleq \xrightarrow{\tau}^\star \xrightarrow{\alpha} \xrightarrow{\tau}^\star \qquad \overset{\hat{\alpha}}{\Rightarrow} \triangleq \xrightarrow{\tau}^\star \xrightarrow{\hat{\alpha}} \xrightarrow{\tau}^\star$$

We can remark the following properties: $\overset{\hat{\tau}}{\Rightarrow} = \xrightarrow{\tau}^\star$, $\overset{\tau}{\Rightarrow} = \xrightarrow{\tau}^+$, $\overset{\hat{a}}{\Rightarrow} = \overset{a}{\Rightarrow}$ (note in particular the difference between $\overset{\tau}{\Rightarrow}$ and $\overset{\hat{\tau}}{\Rightarrow}$).

Definition 1.3 (Evolution of relations). *Let α be an action and $\mathcal{R}, \mathcal{S}$ two relations. We say that $\mathcal{R}$ α-evolves to $\mathcal{S}$ if $P\mathcal{R}Q$, $P \xrightarrow{\alpha} P'$ implies $Q \overset{\hat{\alpha}}{\Rightarrow} Q'$ and $P'\mathcal{S}Q'$ for some Q'. We say that $\mathcal{R}$ evolves silently to $\mathcal{S}$ when $\mathcal{R}$ τ-evolves to $\mathcal{S}$, and that $\mathcal{R}$ evolves visibly to $\mathcal{S}$ when $\mathcal{R}$ a-evolves to $\mathcal{S}$ for any $a \in \mathcal{L}\backslash\{\tau\}$.*

Definition 1.4 (Simulation, Bisimulation, Bisimilarity). *Let $\mathcal{R}$ be a relation. $\mathcal{R}$ is a simulation if it evolves to itself. A bisimulation is a symmetric simulation. Bisimilarity, denoted by $\approx$, is the union of all bisimulations.*

2   A Framework for Distributed Computation

We let h, k range over a given set of *locations*. We denote by $[k/h]$ the function that replaces location h by location k. We let σ range over such substitutions, that are naturally extended to the various syntactical categories defined in the sequel. We furthermore assume two sets of *(local) processes* and *messages*, denoted respectively by P, Q and M, N. Processes may contain messages, and vice-versa. In order to represent this, we require two operations on these sets:

– the addition of a message M to a process P, denoted by "$P \,|\, \{M\}$",
– the embedding of a process P into a message, denoted by "$\texttt{reg}\ P$".

These operations are supposed to satisfy the following equations:

$$(P \,|\, \{M\}) \,|\, \{N\} = (P \,|\, \{N\}) \,|\, \{M\} \tag{1}$$
$$P \,|\, \{\texttt{reg}\ (Q \,|\, \{M\})\} = (P \,|\, \{\texttt{reg}\ Q\}) \,|\, \{M\} \tag{2}$$
$$(P \,|\, \{M\})\sigma = P\sigma \,|\, \{M\sigma\} \tag{3}$$

Nets combine localised processes and messages with a destination:

$$
\begin{array}{llll}
U ::= \ \mathbf{0} & \text{(empty net)} & |\ h[P] & \text{(process located at } h) \\
\quad |\ U \parallel U & \text{(parallel composition)} & |\ h\{M\} & \text{(pending message)} \\
\quad |\ (\nu h)U & \text{(location restriction)} & |\ h \triangleright k & \text{(forwarder located at } h)
\end{array}
$$

Definition 2.1 (Structural congruence)
Structural congruence *is the smallest congruence* $\equiv$ *such that:*

1. *parallel composition* ($\parallel$) *forms an abelian monoid, with neutral element* $\mathbf{0}$;
2. $(\nu h)U \equiv (\nu k)(U[k/h])$ *if k not free in U;*
3. $(\nu h)U \parallel V \equiv (\nu h)(U \parallel V)$ *if h not free in V;*
4. $(\nu h)(\nu k)U \equiv (\nu k)(\nu h)U$; *and* $(\nu h)\mathbf{0} \equiv \mathbf{0}$.

$\Pi_i U_i$ will denote the parallel composition of the nets U_i. The notation for tuples is $\widetilde{x}$ and $(x, \widetilde{x})$ will denote the addition of an element x to $\widetilde{x}$. Our notations are naturally extended using tuples; for example, $h\{\widetilde{M}\}$ and $\widetilde{h} \triangleright k$ will respectively denote $\Pi_i\ h\{M_i\}$ and $\Pi_i\ h_i \triangleright k$.

Definition 2.2 (Dependency relation).
Let U be a net. We call dependency relation of U *the relation* $\prec_U \triangleq \{\langle h_0, h_n \rangle\ /\ U \equiv V \parallel \Pi_{i<n}\ h_i \triangleright h_{i+1}\}$.

An *agent* is either a localised process $h[P]$, or a forwarder $h \triangleright k$. We let a, b range over an arbitrary set of *visible actions*, and we define an LTS over nets:

$$[\textsc{Loc}] \qquad \frac{P \xrightarrow{h,a,U} P'}{h[P] \xrightarrow{a} h[P'] \parallel U} \qquad\qquad \frac{P \xrightarrow{h,a,\texttt{mig}\ k} P'}{h[P] \xrightarrow{a} h \triangleright k \parallel k\{\texttt{reg}\ P'\}} \quad [\textsc{Mig}]$$

$$[\textsc{Fwd}] \quad h\{M\} \parallel h \triangleright k \xrightarrow{\tau} h \triangleright k \parallel k\{M\} \qquad\qquad h\{M\} \parallel h[P] \xrightarrow{\tau} h[P \,|\, \{M\}] \quad [\textsc{Rcv}]$$

$$[\textsc{New}] \qquad \frac{U \xrightarrow{\alpha} U' \quad h \text{ not free in } U, U'}{(\nu h)U \xrightarrow{\alpha} (\nu h)U'} \qquad\qquad \frac{U \xrightarrow{\alpha} U'}{U \parallel V \xrightarrow{\alpha} U' \parallel V} \qquad [\textsc{Par}]$$

$$[\textsc{Cong}] \qquad \frac{U \equiv U' \xrightarrow{\alpha} V' \equiv V}{U \xrightarrow{\alpha} V}$$

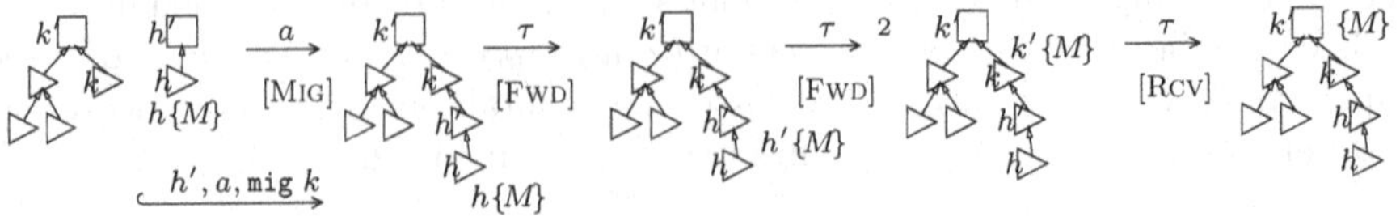

Fig. 1. Nets, Migration, Routing of Messages

This definition depends on a *localised LTS*, describing the behaviour of local processes: $P \xrightarrow{h,a,K} P'$ stands for "process P, when located at h, evolves to P' by performing a visible action a and emitting a *request K*". Such requests correspond to the primitives granted to local processes. They can be either:

- a net U (rule [LOC]), containing messages to send or new localities to spawn;
- or a migration request $\mathtt{mig}\ k$ (rule [MIG]): the local process wants to suspend its execution and to send its state to k. In that case, the local process gets replaced by a forwarder that will transmit further messages to k.

The two silent transition rules are concerned with the routing of messages: rule [FWD] defines the behaviour of forwarders: they transmit the messages; and rule [RCV] performs the actual reception of a message at its final location. A sequence of transitions is depicted in Fig. 1, where squares and triangles represent respectively localised processes and forwarders; the process located at h' migrates to k and the message $h'\{M\}$ is routed to its final destination, k'.

We assume the two properties below about the localised LTS:

$$\text{If } P \xrightarrow{h,a,K} P', \text{ then for any message } M,\ P\,|\,\{M\} \xrightarrow{h,a,K} P'\,|\,\{M\}. \quad (4)$$

$$P \xrightarrow{h,a,K} P' \quad \text{iff} \quad \text{for any substitution } \sigma,\ P\sigma \xrightarrow{h\sigma,a,K\sigma} P'\sigma. \quad (5)$$

(4) expresses the fact that an additional message should not prevent a process from doing some localised transition. (5) prevents local processes from testing the equality of two locations. In some sense, this means that local processes should not be aware of the implementation details of the framework.

Definition 2.3 (Well-formedness). *A net is well-formed if for any of its reducts U, we have $U \equiv (\nu\tilde{h})V$ for some $\tilde{h}, V$ such that:*

1. *any agent of V is located at a location mentioned in $\tilde{h}$;*
2. *for any location h in $\tilde{h}$, there is exactly one agent located at h in V; and*
3. *the dependency relation $\prec_V$ is a partial order, whose maximal elements are the locations hosting localised processes.*

In the sequel, we shall often omit the restrictions on locations that should appear in front of a well-formed net $(\nu\tilde{h})V$: they can be guessed from V.

Hypothesis 2.4. We assume that we are given only well-formed nets.

Remark 2.1 (On the expressiveness of the framework). Locations express only the *logical* distribution of processes. Hence, the second condition in our definition of well-formedness does not rule out the case where several locations are thought of as residing *physically* on the same device. Also, unlike in [10,5], the processes are not required to be distributed along a tree structure, and there is no constraint on the communication topology: since messages may contain locations, π-calculus-like mobility of links is provided by the model. Independently, migration is *subjective* in our model: the process itself decides to migrate. *Objective* migration mechanisms (like the *passivation* available in the Kell-calculus [1]) may be simulated by using messages to trigger migrations.

The main constraint imposed by the well-formedness hypothesis comes from the third point: the graph of the dependency relation is a forest whose roots are the localised processes, and no cycle of forwarders should be generated. This could happen, for example, if a process located at h migrates to some location pointing to h. We discuss the role of this hypothesis in Sect. 5. One possibility to prevent the creation of such cycles is to define a partial ordering of the local processes, and insure that all migration requests respect this ordering (this is the case in models like Ambients [2], Kells [1], or Seals [3]).

3 Reasoning Up to Forwarders

In this section, we validate the behaviour of forwarders, by showing that behavioural equivalence is not sensitive to silent transitions ($\xrightarrow{\tau} \subseteq \approx$) and to the replacement of a forwarder by a substitution.

Even though this property happens to be sufficient for our needs in the sequel (see Sect. 4.2), it does not allow one in general to reason modulo forwarders in other bisimulation proofs: it is well known that weak bisimulation up to $\approx$ is not a correct technique [9]. Therefore, we prove a stronger result using *expansion* ($\gtrsim$), the standard behavioural preorder that leads to the correct "bisimulation up to $\gtrsim$" technique. Interestingly, this allows us to use the up to transitivity technique enjoyed by expansion, so that our proof is actually easier.

Definition 3.1 (Expansion). *An* expansion relation *is a relation $\mathcal{R}$ such that for any $\alpha \in \mathcal{L}$, whenever $P\mathcal{R}Q$ we have:*

- *if $P \xrightarrow{\alpha} P'$ then $Q \xrightarrow{\hat{\alpha}} Q'$ and $P'\mathcal{R}Q'$ for some Q',*
- *if $Q \xrightarrow{\alpha} Q'$ then $P \xRightarrow{\hat{\alpha}} P'$ and $P'\mathcal{R}Q'$ for some P'.*

Expansion, *denoted by $\gtrsim$, is the union of all expansion relations.*

Theorem 3.2 (Bisimulation up to Expansion [9]). *Let $\mathcal{R}$ be a symmetric relation. If $\mathcal{R}$ evolves to $\gtrsim\mathcal{R}\lesssim$, then $\mathcal{R} \subseteq \approx$.*

Theorem 3.3 (Expansion up to Transitivity). *Let $\mathcal{R}$ be a relation. If for any $\alpha \in \mathcal{L}$, whenever $P\mathcal{R}Q$ we have:*

- if $P \xrightarrow{\alpha} P'$ then $Q \xrightarrow{\hat{\alpha}} Q'$ and $P'\mathcal{R}^\star Q'$ for some Q',
- if $Q \xrightarrow{\alpha} Q'$ then $P \xrightarrow{\hat{\alpha}} P'$ and $P'\mathcal{R}Q'$ for some P',

then $\mathcal{R} \subseteq \gtrsim$.

Notice that transitivity is allowed only on one side in the previous theorem. Nevertheless, this is sufficient for the proof of the following proposition:

Proposition 3.4. *Let U, V be two nets. If $U \xrightarrow{\tau} V$ then $U \gtrsim V$.*

Proof. We show that the following relation is an expansion up to transitivity:

$$\mathcal{R} \triangleq \xrightarrow{\tau} \cup \{\langle h\{\texttt{reg } P\} \parallel h\{M\} \parallel W, \ h\{\texttt{reg } (P \mid \{M\})\} \parallel W\rangle\}.$$

We need the up to transitivity technique to analyse the two cases below:

$$
\begin{array}{llr}
U \equiv h\{M\} \parallel h[P] \parallel W & \mathcal{R} \quad h[P \mid \{M\}] \parallel W \equiv V & [\text{Rcv}] \\
U \xrightarrow{a} h\{M\} \parallel h \triangleright k \parallel k\{\texttt{reg } P'\} \parallel W & & [\text{Mig}] \\
\mathcal{R} \ h \triangleright k \parallel k\{M\} \parallel k\{\texttt{reg } P'\} \parallel W & & [\text{Fwd}] \\
\mathcal{R} \ h \triangleright k \parallel k\{\texttt{reg } P' \mid \{M\}\} \parallel W \xleftarrow{a} V & & [\mathcal{R}, \text{Mig}]
\end{array}
$$

$$
\begin{array}{llr}
U \equiv h\{\texttt{reg } P'\} \parallel h\{M\} \parallel h \triangleright k & \mathcal{R} \quad h\{\texttt{reg } (P' \mid \{M\})\} \parallel h \triangleright k \equiv V & \\
U \xrightarrow{\tau} h\{M\} \parallel h \triangleright k \parallel k\{\texttt{reg } P'\} & & [\text{Rcv}] \\
\mathcal{R} \ h \triangleright k \parallel k\{M\} \parallel k\{\texttt{reg } P'\} & & [\text{Fwd}] \\
\mathcal{R} \ h \triangleright k \parallel k\{\texttt{reg } (P' \mid \{M\})\} \xleftarrow{\tau} V & & [\mathcal{R}, \text{Rcv}]
\end{array}
$$

The other cases are similar or straightforward. □

The smallest bisimulation relation containing $\xrightarrow{\tau}$ is $\xRightarrow{\hat{\tau}}$. Hence, proving the weaker result $\xrightarrow{\tau} \subseteq \approx$ without using this expansion-based technique would require to check that $\xRightarrow{\hat{\tau}}$ is a bisimulation, which is less tractable: while U and V differ only slightly when $U \xrightarrow{\tau} V$, this is no longer the case when $U \xRightarrow{\hat{\tau}} V$.

We now define a forwarder erasure relation, that replaces a forwarder by the corresponding substitution and we show that this relation is contained in $\gtrsim$.

Definition 3.5 (Forwarder erasure). *We call* forwarder erasure *the following relation:*

$$\mathcal{E} \triangleq \{\langle (\nu h)(h \triangleright k \parallel U), \ U[k/h]\rangle\}.$$

Proposition 3.6. *Let U, V be two nets. If $U\mathcal{E}V$, then $U \gtrsim V$.*

Proof. We check that $\mathcal{E}$ is an expansion relation: let $U = (\nu h)(W \parallel h \triangleright k)$ and $V = W[k/h]$.

- If $U \xrightarrow{\alpha} U'$, by using Hypothesis (5), we obtain $V \xrightarrow{\alpha} V'$ with $U'\mathcal{E}V'$, except in the following case, corresponding to the rule [FWD]:

$$U \equiv (\nu h)(W' \parallel h\{M\} \parallel h \triangleright k) \quad \xrightarrow{\tau} \quad (\nu h)(W' \parallel h \triangleright k \parallel k\{M\}) \equiv U',$$

  where we just check that $U'\mathcal{E}V$.
- If $V \xrightarrow{\alpha} V'$, again, by using Hypothesis (5), we obtain $U \xrightarrow{\alpha} U'$ with $U'\mathcal{E}V'$, except in the two following cases:

$$
\begin{aligned}
V \equiv{}& W'[k/h] \parallel k\{M\} \parallel k[P] \\
\xrightarrow{\tau}{}& W'[k/h] \parallel k[P \mid \{M\}] \quad \equiv \quad V' && \text{[RCV]} \\
U \equiv{}& (\nu h)(W' \parallel h\{M\} \parallel h \triangleright k \parallel k[P]) \\
\xrightarrow{\tau}{}& (\nu h)(W' \parallel h \triangleright k \parallel k\{M\} \parallel k[P]) && \text{[FWD]} \\
\xrightarrow{\tau}{}& (\nu h)(W' \parallel h \triangleright k \parallel k[P \mid \{M\}]) \quad \mathcal{E} \quad V' && \text{[RCV]}
\end{aligned}
$$

$$
\begin{aligned}
V \equiv{}& W'[k/h] \parallel k \triangleright k' \parallel k\{M\} \\
\xrightarrow{\tau}{}& W'[k/h] \parallel k \triangleright k' \parallel k'\{M\} \quad \equiv \quad V' && \text{[FWD]} \\
U \equiv{}& (\nu h)(W' \parallel h\{M\} \parallel h \triangleright k \parallel k \triangleright k') \\
\xrightarrow{\tau}{}& (\nu h)(W' \parallel h \triangleright k \parallel k\{M\} \parallel k \triangleright k') && \text{[FWD]} \\
\xrightarrow{\tau}{}& (\nu h)(W' \parallel h \triangleright k \parallel k \triangleright k' \parallel k'\{M\}) \quad \mathcal{E} \quad V' && \text{[FWD]}
\end{aligned}
$$

$\hfill\square$

$\mathcal{E}$ and $\xrightarrow{\tau}$ are confluent and terminating relations (for the termination of $\xrightarrow{\tau}$, we rely on the fact that the dependency relation of a well-formed net is a partial order). This allows us to define normal forms of nets, that will be used in Sect. 4:

Definition 3.7 (Normalisation). *We denote respectively by $U_\downarrow$ and $e(U)$ the normal forms of U w.r.t. $\xrightarrow{\tau}$ and $\mathcal{E}$. We say that a net U is normal (resp. $\mathcal{E}$-normal) if $U = U_\downarrow$ (resp. $U = e(U_\downarrow)$).*

By the two previous propositions, we have that a net expands its $\mathcal{E}$-normal form. This makes it possible to restrict to $\mathcal{E}$-normal nets in bisimulation proofs (see the proof of Theorem 4.17 for an example).

Theorem 3.8. *For any well-formed net U, we have:*

$$U \gtrsim e(U_\downarrow).$$

Proof. By definition of $U_\downarrow$ and $e(U)$, this follows from Props. 3.4 and 3.6. $\hfill\square$

Notice that $(\xrightarrow{\tau}\cup\mathcal{E})$ is terminating and confluent, and that $\mathcal{E}$ preserves $\xrightarrow{\tau}$-normal forms. In particular, we have $e(U_\downarrow) \equiv e(U)_\downarrow$. The strategy that we impose in this theorem to compute the normal form of U is hence somehow arbitrary. However, this will ease the development in Sect. 4.

4   Optimisations of the Behaviour of Forwarders

The forwarder chains that are generated along the evolution of a net are the source of inefficiencies. For example, the message $\{M\}$ in Fig. 1 will have to go trough three locations before reaching its final destination. In this section, we define an optimisation of the framework, that contracts such forwarder chains, and we prove the correctness of this optimisation, by showing that simple forwarders, as defined in the previous section, are behaviourally equivalent to the optimised ones.

4.1   Definition of the Optimisation

Optimised nets extend the syntax of nets by

- annotating pending messages with a list of locations: $h\{M\}_{\tilde{k}}$;
- introducing *blocked forwarders*: $h \triangleleft k$;
- adding a second kind of messages: *relocation messages* $h\langle\mathsf{go}_{\triangleright}\ k\rangle$.

Intuitively, the list that decorates a pending message contains the set of forwarder locations the message did pass through. Messages emitted by the underlying local processes will have an empty list, which will allow us to omit their annotation. Relocation messages are received only by blocked forwarders. Their effect is to redirect such forwarders to a destination closer to the location they indirectly point to.

We shall use the terminology *'simple net'* to denote a net as defined in Sect. 2. Structural congruence is extended to optimised nets in the obvious way. We define over this extended syntax an *optimised LTS*, written $\xrightarrow{\alpha}_{\mathsf{o}}$, by taking the rules of the initial LTS and replacing the silent transition rules ([Fwd] and [Rcv]) with the three rules below.

$$h\{M\}_{\tilde{h}}\ \|\ h \triangleright k\ \xrightarrow{\tau}_{\mathsf{o}}\ h \triangleleft k\ \|\ k\{M\}_{h,\tilde{h}} \qquad\qquad [\mathrm{OFwd}]$$

$$h\{M\}_{\tilde{h}}\ \|\ h[P]\ \xrightarrow{\tau}_{\mathsf{o}}\ h[P\,|\,\{M\}]\ \|\ \widetilde{h}\langle\mathsf{go}_{\triangleright}\ h\rangle \qquad\qquad [\mathrm{ORcv}]$$

$$h\langle\mathsf{go}_{\triangleright}\ k'\rangle\ \|\ h \triangleleft k\ \xrightarrow{\tau}_{\mathsf{o}}\ h \triangleright k' \qquad\qquad\qquad\qquad [\mathrm{OUpd}]$$

When a forwarder transmits a message, it registers its location (rule [OFwd]), and enters a *blocked* state so that it will temporarily block further potential messages. Upon reception at the final location, a relocation message is broadcasted to the locations registered in the message (rule [ORcv]). The blocked forwarders located at these locations will finally update their destination accordingly (rule [OUpd]). This behaviour is illustrated in Fig. 2, where reversed, grey triangles correspond to blocked forwarders. Notice that forwarders have to block until they receive the relocation message: otherwise, a timestamps mechanism would be required, so that a forwarder can cleverly chose between two possibly distinct relocation messages.

The definition of dependency relation is adapted by considering all forwarders uniformly, be they blocked or not. We have:

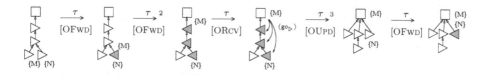

Fig. 2. Optimised Forwarder Behaviour

Proposition 4.1. *In the optimised LTS, for any reduct U of a simple, well-formed net, there exist $\tilde{h}, V$ such that $U \equiv (\nu\tilde{h})V$ and the following conditions hold:*

1. *the properties required in Def. 2.3 are satisfied;*
2. *for any blocked forwarder $h \triangleleft k$, h appears exactly once in the annotation of a pending message ($h'\{M\}_{\tilde{h}}$, with $h \in \tilde{h}$), or as the destination of a relocation message ($h\langle \mathsf{go}_{\triangleright} \, h'\rangle$); in both cases, we have $h \prec_V h'$;*
3. *any location registered in a pending message, or appearing as the target of a relocation message hosts a blocked forwarder.*

In the sequel, we shall implicitly assume that any optimised net that we manipulate satisfies these hypotheses.

4.2 Correctness of the Optimisation

Unlike in the previous section, we cannot rely on expansion-based up-to techniques: neither silent transitions, nor the erasure of forwarders are contained in expansion. This comes from the race conditions introduced by the blocking behaviour of forwarders: for example, in Fig. 2, the message $\{N\}$ has to wait for arrival of $\{M\}$. The very 'controlled' nature of expansion – the right-hand-side process has to be as fast as the left-hand-side process, at each step – cannot take into account the fact that $\{N\}$ is closer to its destination at the end.

However, by proving that in the optimised setting, a net is bisimilar to its $\mathcal{E}$-normal form (Theorem 4.16), the following restricted version of the bisimulation up to $\approx$ technique will be sufficient to prove the equivalence between the two systems (Theorem 4.17): we can restrict to $\xrightarrow{\tau}$-normal forms, so that there is no silent challenge to play.

Theorem 4.2 (Bisimulation up to Bisimilarity). *Let $\mathcal{R}$ be a symmetric relation, if $\mathcal{R}$ evolves silently to itself and visibly to $\approx \mathcal{R} \approx$, then $\mathcal{R} \subseteq \approx$.*

Like in Sect. 3, the smallest bisimulation relations containing $\xrightarrow{\tau}_o$ or $\mathcal{E}$ contain at least $\xRightarrow{\hat{\tau}}_o$, so that we need some bisimulation proof technique in order to be able to work with small and local candidate relations. We use for that the following technique from [8].

Definition 4.3 (Controlled relation). *A relation $\mathcal{B}$ is a controlled relation if the following conditions hold:*

1. $\mathcal{B}$ evolves to $\mathcal{B}^\star$,
2. $\mathcal{B}^+ \overset{\tau}{\Rightarrow}$ terminates,
3. $\mathcal{B} \subseteq \approx$.

Theorem 4.4 (Bisimulation up to a Controlled relation [8]). *Let $\mathcal{B}$ be a controlled relation, if a symmetric relation $\mathcal{R}$ evolves to $\mathcal{B}^\star \mathcal{R} \approx$, then $\mathcal{R} \subseteq \approx$.*

The following proposition will be used to prove the third point of Def. 4.3.

Proposition 4.5. *If $\mathcal{B}$ is a relation evolving to $\mathcal{B}^\star$ and such that $\mathcal{B}^+ \overset{\tau}{\Rightarrow}$ terminates, then $\mathcal{B}^\star$ is a simulation.*

We now have enough technical devices to embark in the proof of correctness. We first prove a lemma that will allow us to route messages to their destination.

Lemma 4.6. *Let $U \equiv V \parallel h_0\{M\}_{\widetilde{h}}$ be a net. Then we have:*

$$U \equiv V' \parallel h_0\{M\}_{\widetilde{h}} \parallel \Pi_{i<n} F_i(h_i, h_{i+1}) \parallel h_n[P]$$
$$U \overset{\tau}{\Rightarrow}_o V' \parallel \widetilde{h}\langle \mathsf{go}_\triangleright h_n \rangle \parallel \Pi_{i<n} h_i \triangleright h_n \parallel h_n[P \mid \{\widetilde{N}\} \mid \{M\}] \parallel \widetilde{k} \triangleright h_n$$

where $F_i(h, k)$ is either:

- *a forwarder: $h \triangleright k$, or*
- *a blocked forwarder, together with a relocation message: $h \triangleleft k' \parallel h\langle \mathsf{go}_\triangleright k \rangle$, or*
- *a blocked forwarder whose location is registered in a message blocking some other forwarders: $h \triangleleft k' \parallel k\{N\}_{h,\widetilde{k}} \parallel \widetilde{k} \triangleleft k'$.*

$\widetilde{N}$ and $\widetilde{k}$ are the messages and forwarder locations collected in $\Pi_{i<n} F(h_i, h_{i+1})$.

Proof. The decomposition of U comes from the well-formedness hypothesis. We prove the reduction by induction over n: if $n = 0$ we just apply the rule [ORCV], otherwise we reason by case analysis on the shape of $F_0(h_0, h_1)$:

- a simple forwarder: $h_0 \triangleright h_1$: we transmit the message with rule [OFWD], apply the induction hypothesis (IH), and relocate the forwarder using rule [OUPD]:

$$U \overset{\tau}{\to}_o V' \parallel h_0 \triangleleft h_1 \parallel h_1\{M\}_{h_0,\widetilde{h}} \parallel \Pi_{0<i<n} F(h_i, h_{i+1}) \parallel h_n[P] \quad \text{[OFWD]}$$
$$\overset{\tau}{\Rightarrow}_o V' \parallel h_0 \triangleleft h_1 \parallel (h_0, \widetilde{h})\langle \mathsf{go}_\triangleright h_n \rangle \parallel \Pi_{0<i<n} h_i \triangleright h_n$$
$$\parallel h_n[P \mid \{\widetilde{N}\} \mid \{M\}] \parallel \widetilde{k} \triangleright h_n \quad \text{(IH)}$$
$$\overset{\tau}{\to}_o V' \parallel h_0 \triangleright h_n \parallel \Pi_{i<n} h_i \triangleright h_n \parallel h_n[P \mid \{\widetilde{N}\} \mid \{M\}] \parallel \widetilde{k} \triangleright h_n \quad \text{[OUPD]}$$

- a blocked forwarder with a relocation message: $h_0 \triangleleft k' \parallel h_0\langle \mathsf{go}_\triangleright h_1 \rangle$: we relocate the forwarder with rule [OUPD] and fall back into the previous case.

$-\ h_0 \lhd k' \parallel h_1\{N_1\}_{h_0,\widetilde{k}_1} \parallel \widetilde{k}_1 \lhd \widetilde{k}'_1$: we apply the induction hypothesis to the message at h_1, and transmit the initial message trough the relocated forwarder:

$$U \overset{\tau}{\Rightarrow}_{\mathrm{o}}\ V' \parallel h_0\{M\}_{\widetilde{h}} \parallel h_0 \lhd h_1 \parallel h_0\langle \mathsf{go}_{\rhd}\ h_n\rangle \parallel \Pi_{0 < i < n} h_i \rhd h_n$$
$$\parallel h_n[P \,|\, \{N_1, \widetilde{N}\}] \parallel \widetilde{k}_1 \rhd \widetilde{k}'_1 \parallel \widetilde{k} \rhd \widetilde{k}' \qquad \text{(IH)}$$
$$\overset{\tau}{\rightarrow}_{\mathrm{o}}\ V' \parallel h_0\{M\}_{\widetilde{h}} \parallel \Pi_{i < n} h_i \rhd h_n \parallel h_n[P \,|\, \{N_1, \widetilde{N}\}] \parallel \widetilde{k}_1 \rhd \widetilde{k}'_1 \parallel \widetilde{k} \rhd \widetilde{k}' \qquad \text{[OUPD]}$$
$$\overset{\tau}{\rightarrow}_{\mathrm{o}}{}^3\ V' \parallel \widetilde{h}\langle \mathsf{go}_{\rhd}\ h_n\rangle \parallel \Pi_{i < n} h_i \rhd h_n \parallel h_n[P \,|\, \{N_1, \widetilde{N}\} \,|\, \{M\}]$$
$$\parallel \widetilde{k}_1 \rhd \widetilde{k}'_1 \parallel \widetilde{k} \rhd \widetilde{k}' \qquad \text{[OFWD,ORCV,OUPD]}$$

$\square$

$\overset{\tau}{\rightarrow}_{\mathrm{o}}$ does not commute with visible actions: some relocation of forwarders is involved. To handle this, we introduce the following relation, that allows one to reorganise step by step the forwarder structure of a net.

Definition 4.7. *We denote by S the* swapping relation, *defined as the symmetric closure of the following relation:*

$$\{\langle h \rhd h' \parallel h' \rhd k \parallel U,\ h \rhd k \parallel h' \rhd k \parallel U\rangle\}.$$

Our goal is to prove that $(S \cup \overset{\tau}{\rightarrow}_{\mathrm{o}})$ is a controlled relation: this entails $\overset{\tau}{\rightarrow}_{\mathrm{o}} \subseteq \approx$, but also makes it possible to give a nice proof of $\mathcal{E} \subseteq \approx$ (Prop. 4.13), by using Theorem 4.4. The three following lemmas establish progressively that $(S \cup \overset{\tau}{\rightarrow}_{\mathrm{o}})$ evolves to $(S \cup \overset{\tau}{\rightarrow}_{\mathrm{o}})^\star$, so that this relation satisfies the first point of Def. 4.3. Again, thanks to the up-to technique, we avoid manipulation of complex relations, and focus on nets that differ only slightly (as in Def. 4.7).

Lemma 4.8. *If $U \overset{\tau}{\rightarrow}_{\mathrm{o}} V$ and $U \overset{a}{\rightarrow}_{\mathrm{o}} U'$ then $U' \overset{\widehat{\tau}}{\Rightarrow}_{\mathrm{o}} S^\star \overset{\widehat{\tau}}{\Leftarrow}_{\mathrm{o}} \overset{a}{\leftarrow}_{\mathrm{o}} V$.*

Proof. It holds that $U' \overset{\tau}{\rightarrow}_{\mathrm{o}} \overset{a}{\leftarrow}_{\mathrm{o}} V$, except in the following case:

$$U \equiv W \parallel h\{M\}_{\widetilde{h}} \parallel h[P] \quad \overset{\tau}{\rightarrow}_{\mathrm{o}} \quad W \parallel h[P \,|\, \{M\}] \parallel \widetilde{h}\langle \mathsf{go}_{\rhd}\ h\rangle \equiv V \quad \text{[ORCV]}$$
$$U \overset{a}{\rightarrow}_{\mathrm{o}} W \parallel h\{M\}_{\widetilde{h}} \parallel h \rhd k \parallel k\{\mathbf{reg}\ P'\} \equiv U' \qquad \text{[MIG]}$$

where we have

$$V \overset{a}{\rightarrow}_{\mathrm{o}} W \parallel h \rhd k \parallel k\{\mathbf{reg}\ P' \,|\, \{M\}\} \parallel \widetilde{h}\langle \mathsf{go}_{\rhd}\ h\rangle \equiv V'. \qquad \text{[MIG]}$$

We reason by case analysis on the agent located at k:

$-$ a localised process $k[Q]$: by routing to k the messages exhibited in U' and V', we obtain:

$$U' \overset{\tau}{\Rightarrow}_{\mathrm{o}} W' \parallel (h, \widetilde{h}) \rhd k \parallel k[Q \,|\, \{\mathbf{reg}\ P'\} \,|\, \{M\}]$$
$$V' \overset{\tau}{\Rightarrow}_{\mathrm{o}} W' \parallel \widetilde{h} \rhd h \parallel h \rhd k \parallel k[Q \,|\, \{\mathbf{reg}\ P' \,|\, \{M\}\}]$$

(the only message to route in V' is almost at its final destination, and the relocation message has already been sent to the blocked forwarders located at $\widetilde{h}$, so that the latter gets relocated under h instead of k).

Finally, we relocate these forwarders with n applications of the swapping relation, n being the length of $\widetilde{h}$: $U' \stackrel{\widehat{\tau}}{\Rightarrow}_{\mathsf{o}} \mathcal{S}^n \stackrel{\widehat{\tau}}{\Leftarrow}_{\mathsf{o}} V'$.

- a forwarder $k \triangleright k'$: like in the previous case, we first route the available messages to their destination, say k'':

$$U' \stackrel{\tau}{\Rightarrow}_{\mathsf{o}} W' \parallel (h, k, \widetilde{h}) \triangleright k'' \parallel k''[Q \mid \{\mathtt{reg}\ P'\} \mid \{M\}],$$
$$V' \stackrel{\tau}{\Rightarrow}_{\mathsf{o}} W' \parallel \widetilde{h} \triangleright h \parallel h \triangleright k \parallel k \triangleright k'' \parallel k''[Q \mid \{\mathtt{reg}\ P' \mid \{M\}\}].$$

Here we need an additional application of the swapping relation to relocate h to k'', before being able to relocate the forwarders at $\widetilde{h}$: $U' \stackrel{\widehat{\tau}}{\Rightarrow}_{\mathsf{o}} \mathcal{S}^{n+1} \stackrel{\widehat{\tau}}{\Leftarrow}_{\mathsf{o}} V'$.

- a blocked forwarder $k \triangleleft k'$. We reason like in the previous case by first routing the message that blocks this forwarder to its destination. $\square$

Lemma 4.9. *If $U \mathcal{S} V$ and $U \stackrel{\alpha}{\rightarrow}_{\mathsf{o}} U'$ then $U' \stackrel{\tau}{\Rightarrow}_{\mathsf{o}} \mathcal{S}^\star \stackrel{\widehat{\alpha}}{\Leftarrow}_{\mathsf{o}} V$.*

Proof. It is immediate for visible challenges $\alpha = a$: we have $U' \mathcal{S} \stackrel{a}{\Leftarrow}_{\mathsf{o}} V$. When $\alpha = \tau$, the interesting cases are those where the silent transition $U \stackrel{\tau}{\rightarrow}_{\mathsf{o}} U'$ is the transmission of a message trough one of the two forwarders being swapped:

- $U \equiv W \parallel h\{M\}_{\widetilde{h}} \parallel h \triangleright h' \parallel h' \triangleright k \stackrel{\tau}{\rightarrow}_{\mathsf{o}} W \parallel h \triangleleft h' \parallel h'\{M\}_{h,\widetilde{h}} \parallel h' \triangleright k \equiv U'$.
  By routing the messages, we obtain:

$$U' \stackrel{\tau}{\Rightarrow}_{\mathsf{o}} W' \parallel h \triangleright k' \parallel h' \triangleright k' \parallel k'[Q \mid \{M\}],$$
$$V \stackrel{\tau}{\Rightarrow}_{\mathsf{o}} W' \parallel h \triangleright k \parallel h' \triangleright k' \parallel k'[Q \mid \{M\}] \equiv V'.$$

If $k = k'$, we are done. Otherwise, there is a forwarder $k \triangleright k'$, and we need one application of the swapping relation in order to relocate the forwarder located at h in V'.

- $U \equiv h \triangleright h' \parallel h'\{M\}_{\widetilde{h}} \parallel h' \triangleright k \stackrel{\tau}{\rightarrow}_{\mathsf{o}} h \triangleright h' \parallel h' \triangleleft k \parallel k\{M\}_{h',\widetilde{h}} \equiv U'$
  By routing the messages, we obtain:

$$U' \stackrel{\tau}{\Rightarrow}_{\mathsf{o}} W' \parallel h \triangleright h' \parallel h' \triangleright k' \parallel k'[Q \mid \{M\}] \equiv U'',$$
$$V \stackrel{\tau}{\Rightarrow}_{\mathsf{o}} W' \parallel h \triangleright k \parallel h' \triangleright k' \parallel k'[Q \mid \{M\}] \equiv V'.$$

If $k = k'$, we are done. Otherwise, there is a forwarder $k \triangleright k'$, and we need two applications of the swapping relation in order to relocate the forwarder located at h in both nets:

$$U'' \equiv W'' \parallel h \triangleright h' \parallel k \triangleright k' \parallel h' \triangleright k' \parallel k'[Q \mid \{M\}]$$
$$\mathcal{S}\ W'' \parallel h \triangleright k' \parallel k \triangleright k' \parallel h' \triangleright k' \parallel k'[Q \mid \{M\}]$$
$$\mathcal{S}\ W'' \parallel h \triangleright k \parallel k \triangleright k' \parallel h' \triangleright k' \parallel k'[Q \mid \{M\}] \equiv V'$$

This analysis also applies for the symmetric cases, where the silent transitions are played by the net with 'flat' forwarders. $\square$

Lemma 4.10. $\xrightarrow{\tau}_o$ *is locally confluent.*

Proof. Using Prop. 4.1, the only critical pair is $U = V \parallel h\{M\}_{\widetilde{h}} \parallel h\{N\}_{\widetilde{k}} \parallel h \triangleright k$,

$$U \xrightarrow{\tau}_o V \parallel h\{M\}_{\widetilde{h}} \parallel h \triangleleft k \parallel k\{N\}_{h,\widetilde{k}} = U_1 \qquad \text{[OFWD]}$$

$$U \xrightarrow{\tau}_o V \parallel h\{N\}_{\widetilde{k}} \parallel h \triangleleft k \parallel k\{M\}_{h,\widetilde{h}} = U_2 \qquad \text{[OFWD]}$$

By using Lemma 4.6 on U_1, we can route the message $\{N\}$ to some location k':

$$U_1 \xRightarrow{\widehat{\tau}}_o V' \parallel h\{M\}_{\widetilde{h}} \parallel h \triangleleft k \parallel (h, \widetilde{k})\langle \text{go}_\triangleright k'\rangle \parallel k'[P \mid \{N\}] \qquad \text{(Lemma 4.6)}$$

$$\xrightarrow{\tau}_o V' \parallel h\{M\}_{\widetilde{h}} \parallel h \triangleright k' \parallel \widetilde{k}\langle \text{go}_\triangleright k'\rangle \parallel k'[P \mid \{N\}] \qquad \text{[OUPD]}$$

$$\xrightarrow{\tau}_o{}^3 V' \parallel (\widetilde{k}, \widetilde{h})\langle \text{go}_\triangleright k'\rangle \parallel h \triangleright k' \parallel k'[P \mid \{N\} \mid \{M\}] \equiv U' \quad \text{[OFWD,ORCV,OUPD]}$$

The same reasoning about U_2 leads to $U_2 \xRightarrow{\tau}_o U'$.   □

Lemma 4.11. $\mathcal{S}^\star \xRightarrow{\tau}_o$ *terminates.*

Proof. We call *size* of a net U the triple $s(U) = \langle n, r, l \rangle$, where n is the number of pending messages, r the number of relocation messages, and l the number of forwarders that are not blocked. These triples are ordered lexicographically. We check that $U\mathcal{S}V$ implies $s(U) = s(V)$, and that this size strictly decreases along silent transitions (recall that $\xRightarrow{\tau}_o$ contains at least one transition).   □

Proposition 4.12. $(\mathcal{S} \cup \xrightarrow{\tau}_o)$ *is a controlled relation.*

Proof. First we check that $(\mathcal{S} \cup \xrightarrow{\tau}_o)$ satisfies the first two requirements of Def. 4.3: (1) comes from Lemmas 4.8, 4.9, and 4.10; by remarking that $(\mathcal{S} \cup \xrightarrow{\tau}_o)^+ \xRightarrow{\tau}_o = (\mathcal{S}^\star \xRightarrow{\tau}_o)^+$, Lemma 4.11 gives (2).

For (3), by Prop. 4.5, we have that $(\mathcal{S} \cup \xrightarrow{\tau}_o)^\star$ is a simulation. Moreover, $\xleftarrow{\widehat{\tau}}_o$ is a simulation (as is always the case). By combining these two results we obtain that the symmetric relation $(\mathcal{S} \cup \xleftrightarrow{\tau}_o)^\star = ((\mathcal{S} \cup \xrightarrow{\tau}_o)^\star \cup \xleftarrow{\widehat{\tau}}_o)^\star$ is a simulation, and hence a bisimulation, so that $(\mathcal{S} \cup \xrightarrow{\tau}_o) \subseteq (\mathcal{S} \cup \xleftrightarrow{\tau}_o)^\star \subseteq \approx$.   □

We now show that $\mathcal{E} \subseteq \approx$. In order to avoid confusion, we consider in the sequel bisimilarity as a relation between *rooted LTSs* that share the same set of labels: $\langle U, \rightarrow \rangle \approx \langle V, \rightsquigarrow \rangle$ will denote the fact that U with labelled transition relation $\rightarrow$, is bisimilar to V, with labelled transition relation $\rightsquigarrow$.

Notice that we do not extend the erasure relation $\mathcal{E}$ to optimised nets; like $e(.)$ it will only be used to reason about simple nets.

Proposition 4.13. *Let U, V be simple nets.*

If $U\mathcal{E}V$ then $\langle U, \rightarrow_o \rangle \approx \langle V, \rightarrow_o \rangle$.

Proof. We show that the symmetric closure of the erasure relation $\mathcal{E}$ is a bisimulation up to the controlled relation $(\mathcal{S} \cup \xrightarrow{\tau}_o)$ (Theorem 4.4).

- If $U \xrightarrow{a}_o U'$, then U' is a simple net, and we check that $V \xrightarrow{a}_o V'$ with $U' \mathcal{E} V'$.
- If $U \xrightarrow{\tau}_o U'$, the interesting case is the following, when $n > 1$:

$$U \equiv (\nu h_0)(W \parallel h_0\{M\} \parallel \Pi_{i<n} h_i \triangleright h_{i+1} \parallel h_n[P])$$

$$U \xrightarrow{\tau}_o U' \equiv (\nu h_0)(W \parallel h_0 \triangleleft h_1 \parallel h_1\{M\}_{h_0} \parallel \Pi_{0<i<n} h_i \triangleright h_{i+1} \parallel h_n[P])$$

$$U \mathcal{E} V \equiv W[h_1/h_0] \parallel h_1\{M[h_1/h_0]\} \parallel \Pi_{0<i<n} h_i \triangleright h_{i+1} \parallel h_n[P[h_1/h_0]])$$

By routing the message in both processes, we obtain:

$$U' \xrightarrow{\tau}_o U'' \equiv (\nu h_0)(W \parallel \Pi_{i<n} h_i \triangleright h_n \parallel h_n[P \,|\, \{M\}])$$

$$V \xrightarrow{\tau}_o V' \equiv W[h_1/h_0] \parallel \Pi_{0<i<n} h_i \triangleright h_n \parallel h_n[P[h_1/h_0] \,|\, \{M[h_1/h_0]\}])$$

These processes are not related by $\mathcal{E}$, we need first to relocate in U'' the forwarder located at h_0 under h_1, using a 'reversed' application of $\mathcal{S}$:

$$U' \xrightarrow{\tau}_o U'' \, \mathcal{S} \, (\nu h_0)(W \parallel h_0 \triangleright h_1 \parallel \Pi_{0<i<n} h_i \triangleright h_n \parallel h_n[P \,|\, \{M\}]) \, \mathcal{E} \, V' \xleftarrow{\tau}_o V.$$

- The cases where $V \xrightarrow{\alpha}_o V'$ are handled similarly.   □

Remark that we can also prove that $(\mathcal{E} \cup \mathcal{S} \cup \xrightarrow{\tau}_o)$ is a controlled relation. This would be useful if we had to reason up to $\mathcal{E}$ on some silent transitions.

Lemmas 4.11 and 4.10 ensure that $\xrightarrow{\tau}_o$ defines a unique normal form for any net (termination of $\mathcal{S}^*\xrightarrow{\tau}_o$ entails termination of $\xrightarrow{\tau}_o$).

Definition 4.14. *Let U be an optimised net.*
We denote by $U_{\downarrow o}$ the normal form of U w.r.t. $\xrightarrow{\tau}_o$.

Notice that $U_{\downarrow o}$ is always a simple net: it does not contain any blocked forwarder, relocation message, nor pending, annotated messages. Furthermore, we have that an optimised net U is a normal net iff $U = U_{\downarrow o}$.

The normalisation of a simple net by $\xrightarrow{\tau}$ and $\xrightarrow{\tau}_o$ does not necessarily lead to the same net: $U_{\downarrow} \neq U_{\downarrow o}$. However, these nets differ only by some rearrangement of their forwarders: they are related by $\mathcal{S}^*$. As expressed by the proposition below, in order to obtain the same net, we just need to erase all the forwarders.

Proposition 4.15. *For any simple net U, we have:*

$$e(U_\downarrow) \equiv e(U_{\downarrow o}).$$

Proof. $U \mathcal{S} V$ entails $e(U) \equiv e(V)$, therefore it is sufficient to prove that $U_\downarrow \mathcal{S}^* U_{\downarrow o}$. We proceed by well-founded induction on U, using the termination of $\xrightarrow{\tau}$:

- If U is a normal net, we have $U_\downarrow = U = U_{\downarrow o}$.
- If $U \xrightarrow{\tau} U'$, since U is simple, $U \equiv V \parallel h_0\{M\} \parallel \Pi_{i<n} h_i \triangleright h_{i+1} \parallel h_n[P]$ and:

$$U \xrightarrow{\tau} U' \xrightarrow{\tau} V \parallel \Pi_{i<n} h_i \triangleright h_{i+1} \parallel h_n[P \,|\, \{M\}] \equiv U_1$$

$$U \xrightarrow{\tau}_o V \parallel \Pi_{i<n} h_i \triangleright h_n \parallel h_n[P \,|\, \{M\}] \equiv U_2 \qquad \text{(Lemma 4.6)}$$

We check that $U_1 \mathcal{S}^n U_2$, and we have $U_1 \xrightarrow{\hat{\tau}}_o U_{1\downarrow o}$ so that from Prop. 4.12, $U_2 \xrightarrow{\hat{\tau}}_o U_2'$ with $U_{1\downarrow o}(\mathcal{S} \cup \xrightarrow{\tau}_o)^\star U_2'$. Furthermore, since $\mathcal{S}$ preserves normal forms, $U_{1\downarrow o} \mathcal{S}^\star U_2'$, and $U_2' = U_{2\downarrow o}$

Finally, by induction, $U_{1\downarrow} \mathcal{S}^\star U_{1\downarrow o}$ and $U_\downarrow = U_{1\downarrow} \mathcal{S}^\star U_{1\downarrow o} \mathcal{S}^\star U_{2\downarrow o} = U_{\downarrow o}$. □

It follows that a net is bisimilar to its $\mathcal{E}$-normal form, which leads to the final proof of correctness.

Theorem 4.16. *Let U be an optimised net, we have:*

$$\langle U, \rightarrow_o \rangle \approx \langle e(U_\downarrow), \rightarrow_o \rangle .$$

Proof. From Prop. 4.12, $\xrightarrow{\tau}_o \subseteq \approx$, and $U \approx U_{\downarrow o}$. We conclude with Props. 4.13 and 4.15: $U_{\downarrow o} \approx e(U_{\downarrow o}) \equiv e(U_\downarrow)$. □

Theorem 4.17 (Correctness of the optimisation). *For any simple net U, we have:*

$$\langle U, \rightarrow_o \rangle \approx \langle U, \rightarrow \rangle .$$

Proof. Using Theorems 4.16 and 3.8, we can suppose w.l.o.g. that U is $\mathcal{E}$-normal.

Let $\mathcal{R} \triangleq \{ \langle \langle U, \rightarrow_o \rangle, \langle U, \rightarrow \rangle \rangle \ / \ U$ is $\mathcal{E}$-normal$\}$. We show that the symmetric closure of $\mathcal{R}$ is a bisimulation up to $\approx$ (Theorem 4.2): since U is normal, there are only visible challenges to play. Suppose $U \xrightarrow{a}_o U'$. The LTSs do not differ on visible actions, hence we have $U \xrightarrow{a} U'$. U' is not necessarily $\mathcal{E}$-normal, so that $\langle U', \rightarrow_o \rangle \mathcal{R} \langle U', \rightarrow \rangle$ does not hold. However, by Theorems 4.16 and 3.8, we have: $\langle U', \rightarrow_o \rangle \approx \langle e(U'_\downarrow), \rightarrow_o \rangle \mathcal{R} \langle e(U'_\downarrow), \rightarrow \rangle \approx \langle U', \rightarrow \rangle$.

The challenges offered by $\langle U, \rightarrow \rangle$ are handled symmetrically. □

5   Concluding Remarks

The bisimilarity proof in [5]. In the GCPAN [5], which is an optimisation of the PAN [10], we actually add counters to the forwarders and garbage collect forwarders whose counter is 0, to which no message will be sent anymore.

We can build on the results presented here to give a complete correctness proof, by validating each optimisation step. Because in PAN local processes satisfy the requirement of our framework, the PAN with relocating forwarders is equivalent to the original machine. Furthermore, adding counters to the machine does not affect this. We then show that the relation that removes a forwarder with counter 0 is a strong bisimulation. Finally, correctness of the GCPAN is established by checking that the identity relation is a bisimulation up to strong bisimilarity relating the previous nets and GCPAN nets.

Forwarder cycles. In this paper, we assumed that no forwarder cycles can appear during the evolution of a net (Hyp. 2.4). However, Theorem 4.17, that states the correctness of the optimisation, holds without this assumption. Indeed, in both systems, all forwarders belonging or pointing to a cycle, and messages routed along such forwarders, will get trapped in the cycle, rendering this part of the net behaviourally equivalent to the empty net:

- In the initial system, any message trapped in a cycle will keep moving indefinitely along the cycle, producing infinitely many silent transitions (the relation $\xrightarrow{\tau}$ remains confluent, but does no longer terminate).
- In the optimised system, messages reaching the cycle will progressively block its forwarders ($\xrightarrow{\tau}_o$ still terminates, but it is no longer confluent: the shape of the final blocked cycle depends on the order of the reductions).

Furthermore, cycles can only be created by the visible rule [FWD], and we can check that the set of messages and forwarders trapped in a cycle does not depend on the setting we chose. Hence, in the proof of Theorem 4.17, we could safely remove the cycles and lost messages that appear on both sides, the same way as we normalise processes along the bisimulation game.

Acknowledgements. I would like to thank Daniel Hirschkoff, whose great help and comments have been essential during the preparation of this paper.

References

1. Bidinger, P., Stefani, J.-B.: The Kell Calculus: Operational Semantics and Type System. In: Najm, E., Nestmann, U., Stevens, P. (eds.) FMOODS 2003. LNCS, vol. 2884, pp. 109–123. Springer, Heidelberg (2003)
2. Cardelli, L., Gordon, A.: Mobile Ambients. In: Nivat, M. (ed.) ETAPS 1998 and FOSSACS 1998. LNCS, vol. 1378, pp. 140–155. Springer, Heidelberg (1998)
3. Castagna, G., Nardelli, F.Z.: The Seal Calculus Revisited. In: Agrawal, M., Seth, A.K. (eds.) FST TCS 2002: Foundations of Software Technology and Theoretical Computer Science. LNCS, vol. 2556, pp. 85–96. Springer, Heidelberg (2002)
4. Fournet, C., Le Fessant, F., Maranget, L., Schmitt, A.: JoCaml: A Language for Concurrent Distributed and Mobile Programming. In: Jeuring, J., Jones, S.L.P. (eds.) AFP 2002. LNCS, vol. 2638, pp. 129–158. Springer, Heidelberg (2003)
5. Hirschkoff, D., Pous, D., Sangiorgi, D.: In: Jacquet, J.-M., Picco, G.P. (eds.) CO-ORDINATION 2005. LNCS, vol. 3454, Springer, Heidelberg (2005)
6. Levi, F., Sangiorgi, D.: Mobile Safe Ambients. In: ACM Trans. on Progr. Lang. and Sys. vol. 25(1), pp. 1–69. ACM Press, New York (2003)
7. De Nicola, R., Ferrari, G.L., Pugliese, R.: KLAIM: A Kernel Language for Agents Interaction and Mobility. IEEE Trans. Software Eng. 24(5), 315–330 (1998)
8. Pous, D.: Up-to Techniques for Weak Bisimulation. In: Caires, L., Italiano, G.F., Monteiro, L., Palamidessi, C., Yung, M. (eds.) ICALP 2005. LNCS, vol. 3580, pp. 730–741. Springer, Heidelberg (2005)
9. Sangiorgi, D., Milner, R.: The problem of Weak Bisimulation up to. In: Cleaveland, W.R. (ed.) CONCUR 1992. LNCS, vol. 630, pp. 32–46. Springer, Heidelberg (1992)
10. Sangiorgi, D., Valente, A.: A Distributed Abstract Machine for Safe Ambients. In: Orejas, F., Spirakis, P.G., van Leeuwen, J. (eds.) ICALP 2001. LNCS, vol. 2076, Springer, Heidelberg (2001)
11. Unyapoth, A., Sewell, P.: Nomadic pict: Correct Communication Infrastructure for Mobile Computation. In: Proc. 28th POPL, pp. 116–127. ACM Press, New York (2001)

A Typed Calculus for Querying
Distributed XML Documents*

Lucia Acciai[1], Michele Boreale[2], and Silvano Dal Zilio[1]

[1] Laboratoire d'Informatique Fondamentale de Marseille (LIF),
CNRS and Université de Provence, France
[2] Dipartimento di Sistemi e Informatica, Università di Firenze, Italy

Abstract. We study the problems related to querying large, distributed XML documents. Our proposal takes the form of a new process calculus in which XML data are processes that can be queried by means of concurrent pattern-matching expressions. What we achieve is a functional, strongly-typed programming model based on three main ingredients: an asynchronous process calculus that draws features from π-calculus and concurrent-ML; a model where both documents and expressions are represented as processes, and where evaluation is represented as a parallel composition of the two; a static type system based on regular expression types.

1 Introduction

There is by now little doubt that XML will succeed as a lingua franca of data interchange on the Web. As a matter of fact, XML is a building block in the development of new models of concurrent applications, often referred to as Service-Oriented Architecture (SOA), where computational resources are made available on a network as a set of loosely-coupled, independent services.

The SOA model is characterized by the need to exchange and query XML documents. In this paper, we concentrate on the specific problems related to querying *large, distributed XML documents*. This is the case, for example, of applications interacting with distributed heterogeneous databases or that process data acquired dynamically, such as those originating from arrays of sensors (in this case, we can assume that the document is in effect infinite). For another example, consider the programs involved in the maintenance of the big Web indexes used by search engines [9]. A typical example is the computation of a *reverse web-link graph*, that is a list of web pages which contain a link to a common target URL. Distribution, concurrency and dynamic acquisition of data must be explicitly taken into account when designing an effective computational model for this kind of applications.

We most particularly pay attention to the processing model needed in this situation. Our proposal takes the form of a process calculus in which XML data are processes that can be queried by means of concurrent pattern-matching expressions. In this model, the

---

* The first and third author are supported by the French government research grant ACI TRALALA. The second author is supported by the EU within the FET-GC2 initiative, project SENSORIA.

U. Montanari, D. Sannella, and R. Bruni (Eds.): TGC 2006, LNCS 4661, pp. 167–182, 2007.

evaluation of patterns is distributed among locations, in the sense that the evaluation of a pattern at a node triggers concurrent evaluation of sub-patterns at other nodes, and actions can be carried out upon success or failure of (sub-)patterns. The calculus also provides primitives for storing and aggregating the results of intermediate computations and for orchestrating the evaluation of patterns. In this respect, we radically depart from previous works on XML-centered process calculi, see e.g. [2,6,11], where queries would be programmed as operations invoked on (servers hosting) Web Services, and XML documents would be exchanged in messages. In contrast, we view queries as code being dispatched to the locations "hosting" a document. This shift of view is motivated by our target application domain. In particular, our model is partly inspired by the *MapReduce* paradigm described in [9], that is used to write programs to be executed on Google's large clusters of computers in a simple functional style. Continuing with the "reverse web-link graph example" above (developed in Section 5), assume that the documents of interest are cached on different, perhaps replicated, servers. A query that accomplishes the aforementioned task would dispatch sub-queries to every server and create a dedicated reference cell to aggregate the partial results from each server. Sub-queries sift the local documents and transmit to the central reference cell sequences of pages with a link to the target URL, so as to eventually produce the global reverse web-link graph. To achieve reliability, sub-queries may have to report back periodically with status updates while the "master query" may decide to abort or reinstate queries in case of servers failure.

Another important feature of our model is the definition of a static type system based on *regular expression types*, an approach that matches well with Document Type Definitions (DTD) and other XML schema languages. What we achieve is a functional, strongly-typed programming model for computing over distributed XML documents based on three main ingredients: a semantics defined by an asynchronous process calculus in the style of the π-calculus [16] and proposed semantics for concurrent-ML [10]; a model where documents and expressions are both represented as processes, and where evaluation is represented as a parallel composition of the two; a type system based on regular expression types (the soundness of the static semantics is proved via a subject reduction property, Theorem 1). Each of these choices is motivated by a feature of the problem: the study of service-oriented applications calls for including concurrency and explicit locations; the need to manipulate large, possibly dynamically generated, documents calls for a streamed model of processing; the documents handled by a service should often obey a predefined schema, hence the need to check that queries are well-typed, preferably before they are executed or "shipped".

The rest of the paper is organized as follows. Section 2 presents the core components of the calculus — documents, types and patterns — and Section 3 gives the formal semantics of the calculus and an example of pattern-matching evaluation. In Section 4 we define a first-order type system with subtyping based on regular expression types and prove the soundness of our type discipline. Before concluding, we develop the example of the reverse web-link graph (Section 5) and we study possible extensions of our model (Section 6). Omitted proofs may be found in a long version of this paper [3].

2   Documents, Types and Patterns

We consider a simple language of first-order functional expressions enriched with references and recursive pattern definitions that are used to extract values from documents. Patterns are built on top of a syntax for defining regular tree grammars [8], which is also at the basis of our type system.

Documents. An XML document may be seen as a simple textual representation for nested sequences of elements <a>...</a>. In this paper, we follow notations similar to [15] and choose a simplified version of documents by leaving aside attributes among other things. We assume an infinite set of *tag names*, ranged over by a, b, ... A document is an ordered sequence of elements $a_1[v_1] \ldots a_n[v_n]$, where $v_1, \ldots, v_n$ are documents. Documents may be empty, denoted $(\,)$, and can be concatenated, denoted v, v' (the composition operator ",'' is associative with identity $(\,)$).

In the following we consider distributed documents, meaning that each element $a_j[v_j]$ is placed in a given location, say $\imath_j$. Locations are visible only at the level of the operational semantics, in which the contents of a document is represented by the index $\imath_1 \ldots \imath_n$ (the list of locations) of its elements. For simplicity, locations and indexes are the only values handled in our calculus and we leave aside atomic data values such as characters or integers.

Document Types. Applications that exchange and process XML documents rely on type information, such as DTD, to describe structural constraints on the occurrences of elements in a "valid" document. In our model, types take the form of regular tree expressions [8], which are sets of recursive definitions of the form $A := Reg(a_i[A_i])_{i \in 1..n}$, where Reg is a regular expression and $A, A_1, \ldots, A_n$ are type variables. A regular expression $Reg(\alpha_i)_{i \in 1..n}$ can be an atom α_i with $i \in 1..n$; it can be the constant All, which matches everything, or Empty, which matches the empty sequence; it can be a choice $Reg_1 \mid Reg_2$, a sequential composition Reg_1, Reg_2, or an iteration $Reg*$. For instance, the declaration below defines the type L of family trees, which are sequences of male or female people such that each person has a name element, and two elements, d and s, for the list of his daughters and sons:

$$L := (\text{man}[P] \mid \text{woman}[P])* \qquad P := \text{name}[All], d[WL], s[ML]$$
$$WL := \text{woman}[P]* \qquad\qquad ML := \text{man}[P] * \ .$$

There is a natural notion of subtyping $A <: B$ between regular expression types, meaning that every document in A is also in B. The type system is close to what is defined in functional languages for manipulating XML, see e.g. XDuce [13,14,15] or the review in [7], hence we stay consistent with actual frameworks used in sequential languages for processing XML data.

Selectors and Patterns. The core of our programming model is a system of distributed pattern matching expressions that concurrently sift through documents to extract information. Basically, patterns are types enhanced with parameters and capture variables. However, like functions, patterns are declared and have a name.

We assume a countable set of *names*, partitioned into *locations* $\imath, \jmath, \ell, \ldots$ and *variables* $x, y, \ldots$. We use the vector notation $\boldsymbol{x}$ for tuples of names. The declaration $p(\boldsymbol{x}) :=$

$(Reg(\mathtt{a}_i[p_i(\boldsymbol{y}_i)])_{i\in 1..n})$ as y defines a pattern called p, with parameters $\boldsymbol{x}$, that collects matched documents in the reference y (where y, the *capture variable* of p, should occur in $\boldsymbol{x}$). For instance, the following patterns can be used to collect the names of male and female people occurring in a document of type L (see example in the next subsection):

$$
\begin{aligned}
names(x,y) &:= \big(\mathtt{man}[p(x,y,x)] \mid \mathtt{woman}[p(x,y,y)]\big)* \\
p(x,y,z) &:= \mathtt{name}[all(z)], \mathtt{d}[names(x,y)], \mathtt{s}[names(x,y)] \\
all(z) &:= \mathtt{All \ as} \ z.
\end{aligned}
$$

In its most general form, a pattern declaration also allows $\mathtt{let}$ definitions and setting continuations to be evaluated upon success or failure of the pattern. (These optional continuations make it possible to add basic exception and transaction mechanisms to the calculus.) Hence, a pattern declaration is of the following form, where S is a *selector* $Reg(\mathtt{a}_i[p_i(\boldsymbol{y}_i)])_{i\in 1..n}$.

$$
p(\boldsymbol{x}) := \mathtt{let} \ z_1 = e_1', \ldots, z_m = e_m' \ \mathtt{in} \ \big(S \ \mathtt{as} \ y\big) \ \mathtt{then} \ e_1 \ \mathtt{else} \ e_2.
$$

An important feature of our model is that patterns may extract multiple sets of values from documents in one pass, which contrasts with the monadic queries expressible with technologies such as XPath. Also, types appears clearly as a particular kind of patterns (patterns declared without parameters, $\mathtt{let}$ definitions and continuations), and every pattern p can be associated with the type A obtained by erasing these extra information. In this case, A is exactly the type of all documents that are matched by p.

Witness and Unambiguous Patterns. It is standard in XML to restrict to expressions that denote sequences of elements unequivocally. We define formally what it means for a pattern to match an index and define a notion of *unambiguous* patterns.

Assume S is the selector $Reg(\mathtt{a}_i[p_i(\boldsymbol{v}_i)])_{i\in 1..n}$. The sequence $\mathtt{a}_{i_1} \ldots \mathtt{a}_{i_m}$ matches S if and only if it is a word in the language of $Reg(\mathtt{a}_i)_{i\in 1..n}$. This relation is denoted $\mathtt{a}_{i_1} \ldots \mathtt{a}_{i_m} \vdash_S p_{i_1}(\boldsymbol{v}_{i_1}) \ldots p_{i_m}(\boldsymbol{v}_{i_m})$ and we call the sequence $(p_{i_j}(\boldsymbol{v}_{i_j}))_{j\in 1..m}$ a *witness* for S of $\mathtt{a}_{i_1} \ldots \mathtt{a}_{i_m}$. We write $\mathtt{a}_{i_1} \ldots \mathtt{a}_{i_m} \nvdash_S$ if the sequence has no witness for S.

We say that a pattern with selector S is *unambiguous* if each sequence of tags has at most one witness for S. Assume that $(p_{i_j}(\boldsymbol{v}_{i_j}))_{j\in 1..m}$ is the witness of S for $\mathtt{b}_1 \ldots \mathtt{b}_m$. When a document $\mathtt{b}_1[v_1] \ldots \mathtt{b}_m[v_m]$ is matched against a pattern with selector S, each sub-document v_j is matched against $p_{i_j}(\boldsymbol{v}_{i_j})$. If $\mathtt{b}_1 \ldots \mathtt{b}_m$ has no witness then pattern-matching fails.

For instance, when matching the "pattern-call" $names(\imath, \ell)$ against a list of people, the contents of elements tagged $\mathtt{man}$ is matched by $p(\imath, \ell, \imath)$, which involves that the value of the $\mathtt{name}$ element inside $\mathtt{man}$ is matched by $all(\imath)$. From the capture variable in all, this results in storing the name in (the reference located at) $\imath$. More generally, a call to $names(\imath, \ell)$ stores the names of men in $\imath$ and women in ℓ. A call to $names(\ell, \ell)$ stores all the names in ℓ.

3   The Calculus

The presentation of the calculus can be naturally divided into two fragments: a language of functional expressions, or *programs*, that are used in the body of pattern and function declarations; and a language of processes, or *configurations*, that models distributed documents and the concurrent execution of programs. Typically, expressions are "program sources" that should be evaluated (they do not contain references to active locations), while a configuration represents the running state of a set of processes.

Programs. The calculus embeds a first-order functional language with references, pattern-matching and constructs for building documents. In the following, we assume that every function identifier f has an associated arity $n \geq 0$ and a unique definition $f(x) := e$ where the variables in x are distinct and include the free variables of e. We take similar hypotheses for patterns. The syntax of expressions $e, e', \ldots$ is given below:

$u, v ::=$	results
$\quad x$	name: variable or location
$\quad \imath_1 \ldots \imath_n$	index (with $n \geq 0$)
$e ::=$	expressions
$\quad u$	result
$\quad \mathsf{a}[u]$	element creation
$\quad u, v$	result composition
$\quad f(u_1, \ldots, u_n)$	function call
$\quad \mathtt{let}\ x = e_1\ \mathtt{in}\ e_2$	let
$\quad \mathtt{newref}\ u$	new reference (with initial value u)
$\quad !u$	dereferencing
$\quad u\ {+}{=}\ v$	update (adds v to the values stored in u)
$\quad \mathtt{try}\ u\ p(u_1, \ldots, u_n)$	pattern matching call
$\quad \mathtt{wait}\ u(x)\ \mathtt{then}\ e_1\ \mathtt{else}\ e_2$	wait matching

A result is either a name or an index. Expressions include results, operators for creating new elements $\mathsf{a}[u]$, for concatenating indexes u, v, and for creating, accessing and updating references. Expressions also include operators for applying a pattern to a document index ($\mathtt{try}$) and for branching on the result of pattern-matching ($\mathtt{wait}$).

Configurations. The syntax of processes $P, Q, \ldots$ is as follows:

$P, Q, R ::=$	processes
$\quad e$	expression
$\quad \mathtt{let}\ x = P\ \mathtt{in}\ Q$	let
$\quad \langle \imath \mapsto d \rangle$	location
$\quad P \upharpoonright Q$	parallel composition
$\quad (\nu \imath)P$	restriction
$d ::=$	resources
$\quad \mathtt{ref}\ u$	reference with value u
$\quad \mathtt{node}\ \mathsf{a}(u)$	node, element tagged a with index u
$\quad \mathtt{try}\ \imath\ p(u_1, \ldots, u_n)$	try matching
$\quad \mathtt{test}\ \imath\ u\ v_k$	test matching
$\quad \mathtt{ok}\ \imath$	successful match
$\quad \mathtt{fail}\ \imath$	failed match

The calculus features operators from the π-calculus: restriction $(\nu \imath)P$ specifies the scope of a name $\imath$ local to P; parallel composition $P \upharpoonright Q$ represents the concurrent evaluation of P and Q. Overall, a process is a sequence of $\mathtt{let}$ expressions, describing threads execution, and locations $\langle \imath \mapsto d \rangle$, that describes a *resource d* located in $\imath$. Hence the syntax of configurations is very expressive as it unifies the notions of expression, store, thread and processes.

The calculus is based on an abstract notion of location that is, at the same time, the minimal unit of interaction and the minimal unit of storage. Failures are not part of this model (they can be viewed as an orthogonal feature) but could be added, e.g. in the style of [4]. Locations store resources. The main resources are `ref u`, to store the current state of a reference, and `node a(u)`, to describe an element of the form $a[u]$. The calculus explicitly takes into account the distribution of document nodes and, for example, the document $a[b[\,]\,c[\,]]$ can be represented (at runtime) by the process: $(\nu \imath_1 \imath_2)(\langle \imath \mapsto \mathtt{node\ } a(\imath_1\,\imath_2)\rangle \upharpoonright \langle \imath_1 \mapsto \mathtt{node\ } b(\,)\rangle \upharpoonright \langle \imath_2 \mapsto \mathtt{node\ } c(\,)\rangle)$. The other resources arise in the evaluation of pattern-matching and correspond to different phases in its execution: scheduling a "pattern call" (`try`); waiting for the result of sub-patterns (`test`); stopping and reporting success (`ok`) or failure (`fail`).

Syntactic conventions: The operators `let`, `wait` and ν are name binders. Notions of α-equivalence and of free and bound names arise as expected. We denote $fv(P)$ the set of variables that occur free in P and $fn(P)$ the set of free names. We identify expressions and terms up-to α-equivalence. Substitutions are finite partial maps from variables to results: we write $P\{x \leftarrow u\}$ for the simultaneous, capture-avoiding substitution of all free occurrences of x in P with u. Assume σ is the substitution $\{x_1 \leftarrow u_1\}\dots\{x_n \leftarrow u_n\}$ and $\boldsymbol{u} = (u_1, \dots, u_n)$. We write $f(\boldsymbol{u}) := e'$ if $f(\boldsymbol{x}) := e$ and $e' = \sigma(e)$ and we write $p(\boldsymbol{u}) := S'$ if the selector of $p(\boldsymbol{x})$ is S and $S' = \sigma(S)$. Finally, we make use of the following abbreviations: if $u = \imath_1 \dots \imath_n$ then $(\nu u)P$ is a shorthand for $(\nu \imath_1)\dots(\nu \imath_n)P$; the term $(\nu \ell)P \upharpoonright Q$ stands for $((\nu \ell)P) \upharpoonright Q$; the term `let` $x = P$ `in` $Q \upharpoonright R$ stands for $(\mathtt{let}\ x = P\ \mathtt{in}\ Q) \upharpoonright R$; and `wait` $\ell(x)$ `then` e_1 stands for `wait` $\ell(x)$ `then` e_1 `else` `()` (and similarly for omitted `then` clause).

Reduction Semantics. The semantics of our calculus follows the chemical style found in the π-calculus [16]: it is based on structural congruence and a reduction relation. Reduction represents individual computation steps and is defined in terms of structural congruence and evaluation contexts.

Structural congruence $\equiv$ allows the rearrangement of terms so that reduction rules may be applied. It is the least congruence on processes to satisfy the following axioms:

(Struct Par Assoc)

$$\frac{}{(P \upharpoonright Q) \upharpoonright R \equiv P \upharpoonright (Q \upharpoonright R)}$$

(Struct Par Let)

$$\frac{x \notin fn(P)}{P \upharpoonright \mathtt{let}\ x = Q\ \mathtt{in}\ R \equiv \mathtt{let}\ x = (P \upharpoonright Q)\ \mathtt{in}\ R}$$

(Struct Par Com)

$$\frac{}{(P \upharpoonright Q) \upharpoonright R \equiv (Q \upharpoonright P) \upharpoonright R}$$

(Struct Res Let)

$$\frac{\ell \notin fn(Q)}{(\nu \ell)\mathtt{let}\ x = P\ \mathtt{in}\ Q \equiv \mathtt{let}\ x = (\nu \ell)P\ \mathtt{in}\ Q}$$

(Struct Res Res)

$$\frac{}{(\nu \imath)(\nu \ell)P \equiv (\nu \ell)(\nu \imath)P}$$

(Struct Res Par R)

$$\frac{\imath \notin fn(P)}{(\nu \imath)(P \upharpoonright Q) \equiv P \upharpoonright (\nu \imath)Q}$$

(Struct Res Par L)

$$\frac{\imath \notin fn(Q)}{(\nu \imath)(P \upharpoonright Q) \equiv ((\nu \imath)P) \upharpoonright Q}$$

(Struct Let Assoc)

$$\frac{x \notin \mathit{fn}(R)}{\mathtt{let}\ y = (\mathtt{let}\ x = P\ \mathtt{in}\ Q)\ \mathtt{in}\ R \equiv \mathtt{let}\ x = P\ \mathtt{in}\ (\mathtt{let}\ y = Q\ \mathtt{in}\ R)}$$

Since processes may return values, we take the convention that the result of a composition $P_1 \mathbin{\vert} \ldots \mathbin{\vert} P_n$ is the result of its rightmost term P_n. The values returned by the other processes are discarded. This entails that the order of parallel components is relevant. For this reason, unlike the situation in most process calculi, parallel composition is "left commutative" but not commutative: we have $(P \mathbin{\vert} Q) \mathbin{\vert} R$ equivalent to $(Q \mathbin{\vert} P) \mathbin{\vert} R$ but not necessarily $P \mathbin{\vert} Q \equiv Q \mathbin{\vert} P$. This choice is similar to what is found in calculi introduced for defining the semantics of concurrent-ML [10] and for concurrent extensions of object calculi [12]. An advantage of this approach is that we directly include sequential composition of processes: the term $P; Q$ can be interpreted by $\mathtt{let}\ x = P\ \mathtt{in}\ Q$, where $x \notin \mathit{fv}(Q)$. We also obtain a more direct style of programming since the operation of returning a result does not require using continuations and sending a message on a result channel, as in the π-calculus.

Reduction $\rightarrow$ is the least binary relation on closed terms to satisfy the rules in Table 1. The rules for expressions are similar to traditional semantics for first-order languages, with the difference that the resources in a configuration play the role of the store. Likewise, the rules for operators that return new values (the operators $\mathtt{newref}$, $\mathtt{a}[\,]$ and $\mathtt{try}$) yield reductions of the form $e \rightarrow (\nu\ell)(\langle \ell \mapsto d \rangle \mathbin{\vert} \ell)$, which means that new values are always allocated in a fresh location. Actually a quick inspection of the rules shows that resources are created in fresh locations and are always used in a linear way: an expression cannot discard a resource or create two different resources at the same location.

Informal Semantics. We can divide the rules in Table 1 according to the locations involved in the reduction. A location $\langle \ell \mapsto \mathtt{ref}\ w \rangle$ is a reference at ℓ with value w. Reference access, rule (Red Read), replaces a top-level occurrence of $!\ell$ with the value w. Reference update $\ell += v$, rule (Red Write), has a slightly unusual semantics since its effect is to append v to the value stored in ℓ. Actually, we could imagine that each reference is associated with an "aggregating function" (denoted op in Table 1) that specifies how the sequence of values stored in the reference has to be combined[1].

A location $\langle \imath \mapsto \mathtt{node}\ \mathtt{a}(u) \rangle$ is created by the evaluation of an element creation expression $\mathtt{a}[u]$, where u is an index, (Red Node). A location $\langle \ell \mapsto \mathtt{try}\ \imath\ p(v) \rangle$ is created by the evaluation of a $\mathtt{try}$ operator. The expression $\mathtt{try}\ u\ p(v)$ applies the pattern p to the index $u = \imath_1 \ldots \imath_n$, rule (Red Try). A $\mathtt{try}$ expression returns at once with the index ℓ of the fresh location where the matching occurs. It also creates a document node $\langle \imath \mapsto \mathtt{node}\ o(u) \rangle$ that points to the index u that is processed (we use the reserved name o for the root tag of this node). Assume that S is the selector of p, the $\mathtt{try}$ resource will trigger evaluation of sub-patterns selected from a witness of S. If there is no witness, the matching fails, rule (Red Try Error). If a witness exists, the $\mathtt{try}$ resource spawns

---

[1] For example, assume ℓ is an "integer reference" that increments its value by one on every assignment. Then, in the example of Section 2, a call to $names(\ell, \ell)$ counts the number of people in a document of type L. For the sake of simplicity, we only consider index composition in this work.

Table 1. Reductions

(Red Fun)

$$\frac{f \text{ declared as } f(\boldsymbol{x}) := e}{f(u_1, \ldots, u_n) \to e\{x_1 \leftarrow u_1\} \ldots \{x_n \leftarrow u_n\}}$$

(Red Let)

$$\mathtt{let}\ x = u\ \mathtt{in}\ P \to P\{x \leftarrow u\}$$

(Red Struct)

$$\frac{P \equiv Q, \quad Q \to Q', \quad Q' \equiv P'}{P \to P'}$$

(Red Context)$^{(\star)}$

$$\frac{P \to P'}{E[P] \to E[P']}$$

(Red Ref)

$$\frac{u = \imath_1 \ldots \imath_n}{\mathtt{newref}\ u \to (\nu \ell)(\langle \ell \mapsto \mathtt{ref}\ u \rangle \,\Gamma\, \ell)}$$

(Red Read)

$$\langle \ell \mapsto \mathtt{ref}\ u \rangle \,\Gamma\, !\ell \to \langle \ell \mapsto \mathtt{ref}\ u \rangle \,\Gamma\, u$$

(Red Write)$^{(\star\star)}$

$$\frac{w = u, v}{\langle \ell \mapsto \mathtt{ref}\ u \rangle \,\Gamma\, \ell \mathrel{+}= v \to \langle \ell \mapsto \mathtt{ref}\ w \rangle \,\Gamma\, ()}$$

(Red Node)

$$\frac{u = \imath_1 \ldots \imath_n}{\mathtt{a}[u] \to (\nu \imath)(\langle \imath \mapsto \mathtt{node}\ \mathtt{a}(u) \rangle \,\Gamma\, \imath)}$$

(Red Comp)

$$\frac{u_1 = \imath_1 \ldots \imath_k \quad u_2 = \imath_{k+1} \ldots \imath_n}{u_1, u_2 \to \imath_1 \ldots \imath_n}$$

(Red Try)

$$\frac{u = \imath_1 \ldots \imath_n \qquad \imath, \ell \text{ fresh names}}{\mathtt{try}\ u\ p(\boldsymbol{v}) \to (\nu \imath)(\nu \ell)(\langle \imath \mapsto \mathtt{node}\ \boldsymbol{o}(u) \rangle \,\Gamma\, \langle \ell \mapsto \mathtt{try}\ \imath\ p(\boldsymbol{v}) \rangle \,\Gamma\, \ell)}$$

(Red Try Match)

$$\frac{\begin{array}{c} P = \langle \imath \mapsto \mathtt{node}\ \mathtt{a}(\imath_1 \ldots \imath_n) \rangle \,\Gamma\, \prod_{l \in 1..n} \langle u_l \mapsto \mathtt{node}\ \mathtt{a}_l(w_l) \rangle \\ p(\boldsymbol{v}) := S\ \mathtt{as}\ v_k \quad \mathtt{a}_1 \ldots \mathtt{a}_n \vdash_S p_1(\boldsymbol{v}_1) \ldots p_n(\boldsymbol{v}_n) \qquad w = \jmath_1 \ldots \jmath_n \text{ fresh names} \end{array}}{P \,\Gamma\, \langle \ell \mapsto \mathtt{try}\ \imath\ p(\boldsymbol{v}) \rangle \to P \,\Gamma\, (\nu w)\big(\prod_{l \in 1..n} \langle \jmath_l \mapsto \mathtt{try}\ u_l\ p_l(\boldsymbol{v}_l) \rangle \,\Gamma\, \langle \ell \mapsto \mathtt{test}\ \imath\ w\ v_k \rangle \big)}$$

(Red Try Error)

$$\frac{P = \langle \imath \mapsto \mathtt{node}\ \mathtt{a}(\imath_1 \ldots \imath_n) \rangle \,\Gamma\, \prod_{k \in 1..n} \langle \imath_k \mapsto \mathtt{node}\ \mathtt{a}_k(w_k) \rangle \quad p(\boldsymbol{v}) := S\ \mathtt{as}\ v_k \quad \mathtt{a}_1 \ldots \mathtt{a}_n \nvdash_S}{P \,\Gamma\, \langle \ell \mapsto \mathtt{try}\ \imath\ p(\boldsymbol{v}) \rangle \to P \,\Gamma\, \langle \ell \mapsto \mathtt{fail}\ \imath \rangle}$$

(Red Test Ok)

$$\frac{P = \langle \imath \mapsto \mathtt{node}\ \mathtt{a}(\imath_1 \ldots \imath_n) \rangle \,\Gamma\, \prod_{k \in 1..n} \langle \jmath_k \mapsto \mathtt{ok}\ \imath_k \rangle \quad w = \jmath_1 \ldots \jmath_n \quad x \text{ fresh name}}{P \,\Gamma\, \langle \ell \mapsto \mathtt{test}\ \imath\ w\ v_k \rangle \to P \,\Gamma\, \mathtt{let}\ x = (v_k \mathrel{+}= (\imath_1 \ldots \imath_n))\ \mathtt{in}\ \langle \ell \mapsto \mathtt{ok}\ \imath \rangle}$$

(Red Test Fail)

$$\frac{\begin{array}{c} P = \langle \imath \mapsto \mathtt{node}\ \mathtt{a}(\imath_1 \ldots \imath_n) \rangle \,\Gamma\, \prod_{k \in 1..n} \langle \jmath_k \mapsto d_k \rangle \qquad w = \jmath_1 \ldots \jmath_n \\ \forall k \in 1..n : d_k \in \{\mathtt{ok}\ \imath_k, \mathtt{fail}\ \imath_k\} \qquad \exists j \in 1..n : d_j = \mathtt{fail}\ \imath_j \end{array}}{P \,\Gamma\, \langle \ell \mapsto \mathtt{test}\ \imath\ w\ v_k \rangle \to P \,\Gamma\, \langle \ell \mapsto \mathtt{fail}\ \imath \rangle}$$

(Red Wait Ok)

$$\frac{P = \langle \imath \mapsto \mathtt{node}\ \mathtt{a}(u) \rangle \,\Gamma\, \langle \ell \mapsto \mathtt{ok}\ \imath \rangle}{P \,\Gamma\, \mathtt{wait}\ \ell(x)\ \mathtt{then}\ e_1\ \mathtt{else}\ e_2 \to P \,\Gamma\, e_1\{x \leftarrow u\}}$$

(Red Wait Fail)

$$\frac{P = \langle \imath \mapsto \mathtt{node}\ \mathtt{a}(u) \rangle \,\Gamma\, \langle \ell \mapsto \mathtt{fail}\ \imath \rangle}{P \,\Gamma\, \mathtt{wait}\ \ell(x)\ \mathtt{then}\ e_1\ \mathtt{else}\ e_2 \to P \,\Gamma\, e_2\{x \leftarrow u\}}$$

$^{(\star)}$ where $\quad E ::= Q \,\Gamma\, E \mid E \,\Gamma\, P \mid [.] \mid (\nu \ell)E \mid \mathtt{let}\ x = E\ \mathtt{in}\ P$

$^{(\star\star)}$ in the general case we have $w = op(u, v)$, where op is some "aggregating" function

---

new `try` resources and turns into a `test`, rule (Red Try Match), waiting for the results of these evaluations. Upon termination of all the sub-patterns, a `test` resource turns into `ok` or `fail`, rules (Red Test Ok) and (Red Test Fail). The `ok` and `fail` resources are immutable.

The remaining rules are related to the evaluation of a `wait` expression. The status of a pattern evaluation can be checked with the expression `wait` $\ell(x)$ `then` e_1 `else` e_2, see rules (Red Wait Ok) and (Red Wait Fail). If the resource at ℓ is `ok` $\imath$ then the `wait` expression evaluates to $e_1\{x{\leftarrow}v\}$, where v is the index of the node located at $\imath$. If the resource is `fail` $\imath$ then the expression evaluates to $e_2\{x{\leftarrow}v\}$. In all the other cases the expression is stalled.

Remark. In rule (Red Try Match), we compute the witness for all the children of an element in one go. This is not always realistic since the size of the children's index can be very large (actually, in real applications, big documents are generally shallow and have a large number of children). It is possible to refine the operational semantics so that each sub-pattern is fired independently, not necessarily following the order of the document. For instance, we should be able to start the evaluation on an element without necessarily matching all its preceding siblings beforehand. Also, we can imagine that indexes are implemented using streams or linked lists. We have chosen this presentation for the sake of simplicity.

Example: pattern-matching evaluation. As an example of pattern-matching evaluation, consider the pattern p below, which extracts all the sub-elements tagged a and discards elements tagged b.

$$p(x) := (\mathsf{a}[p(x)] \text{ as } x \mid \mathsf{b}[p(x)])*$$

Let d be the document $\mathsf{a}[\mathsf{b}[\mathsf{a}[\,]]\,\mathsf{b}[]]$. We assume that the elements of d are stored at the indexes $(\imath_1\imath_4)$, that is d is represented by the process:

$$(\nu\imath_2\imath_3)\big(\langle \imath_1 \mapsto \mathsf{node}\,\mathsf{a}(\imath_2)\rangle\,\Gamma\langle \imath_2 \mapsto \mathsf{node}\,\mathsf{b}(\imath_3)\rangle\Gamma\langle \imath_3 \mapsto \mathsf{node}\,\mathsf{a}()\rangle\,\Gamma\langle \imath_4 \mapsto \mathsf{node}\,\mathsf{b}()\rangle\big).$$

The following expression starts the pattern-matching evaluation of p against d:

$$\mathtt{let}\ x = \mathtt{newref}\ ()\ \mathtt{in}\ \mathtt{try}\ (\imath_1\imath_4)\ p(x).$$

In what follows we show the matching evaluation step-by-step. By rules (Red Ref) and (Red Let), a new location containing a new reference (a "capture" reference) is created and substituted to x in the pattern invocation. By applying structural equivalence we obtain

$$\to (\nu\ell')\big(\langle \ell' \mapsto \mathtt{ref}\ ()\rangle\,\Gamma\,\mathtt{try}\ (\imath_1\imath_4)\ p(\ell')\big).$$

By rule (Red Try), two fresh locations are created: ℓ, where the pattern-matching is evaluated, and $\imath$, where the index of the document to analyze is stored

$$\to (\nu\imath,\ell,\ell')\big(\langle \ell' \mapsto \mathtt{ref}\ ()\rangle\Gamma\langle \imath \mapsto \mathsf{node}\,\boldsymbol{o}(\imath_1\imath_4)\rangle\,\Gamma\langle \ell \mapsto \mathtt{try}\ \imath\ p(\ell')\rangle\,\Gamma\,\ell\big).$$

Note that the "result" of the `try` evaluation is the location ℓ, which will contain `ok` or `fail` at the end of the evaluation. This location can be captured by using a `let` construct, and can be used e.g. in a `wait` expression.

Rule (Red Try Match) is now applied. Let's call S the selector of $p(\ell')$; a b $\vdash_S$ $p(\ell')$ $p(\ell')$, thus two sub-evaluations are started (between documents at $\imath_1$ and $\imath_4$ and $p(\ell')$). The **try** resource at ℓ becomes a **test** resource which waits for the sub-evaluation results

$$\rightarrow (\nu\imath, \ell, \ell', \ell_1, \ell_4)\,\big(\langle \ell' \mapsto \mathbf{ref}\,(\,)\,\rangle\,\Gamma\langle \imath \mapsto \mathbf{node}\,o(\imath_1\imath_4)\,\rangle\,\Gamma\langle \ell_1 \mapsto \mathbf{try}\,\imath_1\,p(\ell')\,\rangle$$
$$\Gamma\langle \ell_4 \mapsto \mathbf{try}\,\imath_4\,p(\ell')\,\rangle\,\Gamma\langle \ell \mapsto \mathbf{test}\,\imath(\ell_1\ell_4)\,\rangle\,\Gamma\,\ell).$$

Sub-evaluations are concurrently started. By rule (Red Try Match) applied twice, two sub-evaluations are triggered, because b $\vdash_S p(\ell')$ and a $\vdash_S p(\ell')$

$$\rightarrow^* (\nu\imath, \ell, \ell', \ell_1, \ell_2, \ell_4, \ell_5)\,\big(\langle \ell' \mapsto \mathbf{ref}\,(\,)\,\rangle\,\Gamma\langle \imath \mapsto \mathbf{node}\,o(\imath_1\imath_4)\,\rangle\,\Gamma\langle \ell_2 \mapsto \mathbf{try}\,\imath_2\,p(\ell')\,\rangle$$
$$\Gamma\langle \ell_5 \mapsto \mathbf{try}\,(\,)\,p(\ell')\,\rangle\,\Gamma\langle \ell_4 \mapsto \mathbf{test}\,\imath_4(\ell_5)\,\rangle$$
$$\Gamma\langle \ell_1 \mapsto \mathbf{test}\,\imath_1(\ell_2)\ell'\,\rangle\,\Gamma\langle \ell \mapsto \mathbf{test}\,\imath(\ell_1\ell_4)\,\rangle\,\Gamma\,\ell).$$

Note that in location ℓ_1 we take note about the reference ℓ' where the index $\imath_1$ will be stored in case of successful evaluation.

The evaluation at ℓ_5 ends, because the empty document is accepted by p, and there are no triggered sub-evaluations. While evaluation at ℓ_2 continues

$$\rightarrow^* (\nu\imath, \ell, \ell', \ell_1, \ell_2, \ell_3, \ell_4, \ell_5)\,\big(\langle \ell' \mapsto \mathbf{ref}\,(\,)\,\rangle\,\Gamma\langle \imath \mapsto \mathbf{node}\,o(\imath_1\imath_4)\,\rangle$$
$$\Gamma\langle \ell_3 \mapsto \mathbf{try}\,\imath_3\,p(\ell')\,\rangle\,\Gamma\langle \ell_2 \mapsto \mathbf{test}\,\imath_2(\imath_3)\,\rangle$$
$$\Gamma\langle \ell_5 \mapsto \mathbf{ok}\,(\,)\,\rangle\,\Gamma\langle \ell_4 \mapsto \mathbf{test}\,\imath_4(\ell_5)\,\rangle$$
$$\Gamma\langle \ell_1 \mapsto \mathbf{test}\,\imath_1(\ell_2)\ell'\,\rangle\,\Gamma\langle \ell \mapsto \mathbf{test}\,\imath(\ell_1\ell_4)\,\rangle\,\Gamma\,\ell).$$

By (Red Test Ok) evaluation at ℓ_4 ends successfully. Moreover, for evaluation at ℓ_3 we can reason as previously seen for ℓ_4, and obtain a success. Note that $\imath_3$ contains a document tagged a, thus by (Red Test Ok) location ℓ' is updated by adding $\imath_3$ to its content

$$\rightarrow^* (\nu\imath, \ell, \ell', \ell_1, \ell_2, \ell_3, \ell_4, \ell_5)\,\big(\langle \ell' \mapsto \mathbf{ref}\,(\imath_3)\,\rangle\,\Gamma\langle \imath \mapsto \mathbf{node}\,o(\imath_1\imath_4)\,\rangle\,\Gamma\langle \ell_3 \mapsto \mathbf{ok}\,\imath_3\,\rangle$$
$$\Gamma\langle \ell_2 \mapsto \mathbf{test}\,\imath_2(\imath_3)\,\rangle\,\Gamma\langle \ell_5 \mapsto \mathbf{ok}\,(\,)\,\rangle\,\Gamma\langle \ell_4 \mapsto \mathbf{ok}\,\imath_4\,\rangle$$
$$\Gamma\langle \ell_1 \mapsto \mathbf{test}\,\imath_1(\ell_2)\ell'\,\rangle\,\Gamma\langle \ell \mapsto \mathbf{test}\,\imath(\ell_1\ell_4)\,\rangle\,\Gamma\,\ell).$$

By (Red Test Ok) applied twice, evaluation at ℓ_1 ends and location ℓ' is updated:

$$\rightarrow^* (\nu\imath, \ell, \ell', \ell_1, \ell_2, \ell_3, \ell_4, \ell_5)\,\big(\langle \ell' \mapsto \mathbf{ref}\,(\imath_3)\,\rangle\,\Gamma\langle \imath \mapsto \mathbf{node}\,o(\imath_1\imath_4)\,\rangle\,\Gamma\langle \ell_3 \mapsto \mathbf{ok}\,\imath_3\,\rangle$$
$$\Gamma\langle \ell_2 \mapsto \mathbf{ok}\,\imath_2\,\rangle\,\Gamma\langle \ell_5 \mapsto \mathbf{ok}\,(\,)\,\rangle\,\Gamma\langle \ell_4 \mapsto \mathbf{ok}\,\imath_4\,\rangle$$
$$\Gamma\,\mathbf{let}\,\_ = (\ell' \mathrel{+}= \imath_1)\,\mathbf{in}$$
$$\langle \ell_1 \mapsto \mathbf{ok}\,\imath_1\,\rangle\,\Gamma\langle \ell \mapsto \mathbf{test}\,\imath(\ell_1\ell_4)\,\rangle\,\Gamma\,\ell).$$

Finally, the evaluation ends by (Red Write), (Red Let) and (Red Test Ok)

$$\rightarrow^* (\nu\imath, \ell, \ell', \ell_1, \ell_2, \ell_3, \ell_4)\,\big(\langle \ell' \mapsto \mathbf{ref}\,(\imath_3\imath_1)\,\rangle\,\Gamma\langle \imath \mapsto \mathbf{node}\,o(\imath_1\imath_4)\,\rangle\,\Gamma\langle \ell_3 \mapsto \mathbf{ok}\,\imath_3\,\rangle$$
$$\Gamma\ldots\Gamma\langle \ell_1 \mapsto \mathbf{ok}\,\imath_1\,\rangle\,\Gamma\langle \ell \mapsto \mathbf{ok}\,\imath\,\rangle\,\Gamma\,\ell).$$

4   Static Semantics

The types of document indexes are the same as the types for documents defined in Section 2. Apart from regular expressions types A, the type t of a process can also be:

the resource type $\star$ (a constant type for terms that return no values); a reference type $\texttt{ref } A$; a node type $\texttt{node a}(u)$ (the type of a location holding an element $\texttt{a}[u]$); or a try type $\texttt{loc a}(A)$ (the type of locations hosting the evaluation of a pattern of type A on the contents of an element tagged a).

$t ::=$	type
$\star$	no value
A	regular expression type
$\texttt{ref } A$	reference
$\texttt{node a}(u)$	node location
$\texttt{loc a}(A)$	try location

We can easily adapt the definition of witness to types (a type is some sort of selector). Assume A is declared as $A := Reg(\texttt{a}_\texttt{i}[A_i])_{i \in 1..n}$. We say that there is a witness for A of $\texttt{a}_{i_1} \ldots \texttt{a}_{i_m}$, denoted $\texttt{a}_{i_1} \ldots \texttt{a}_{i_m} \vdash_A A_{i_1} \ldots A_{i_m}$, if and only if the sequence of tags $\texttt{a}_{i_1} \ldots \texttt{a}_{i_m}$ is in the language of the regular expression $Reg(\texttt{a}_i)_{i \in 1..n}$. We can define the language of a type A as the set of documents that are matched by the pattern $Reg(\texttt{a}_i[A_i])_{i \in 1..n}$. Based on this definition, we obtain a natural notion of subtyping $A <: B$, meaning that the language of A is included in the language of B. We write $A \doteq B$ if the languages of A and B are equal. We write $\overline{A}$ for some chosen regular expression type whose language is the complement of A. (We will not need the type $\overline{A}$ when $A \doteq \texttt{All}$, which means that we do not need to introduce a type with an empty language.) In the case of type witness, we have $\texttt{a}_{i_1} \ldots \texttt{a}_{i_m} \nvdash_A$ if and only if there is a witness for $\overline{A}$ of $\texttt{a}_{i_1} \ldots \texttt{a}_{i_m}$.

The type system is given in Table 2. A type environment E is a finite mapping $x_1 : t_1, \ldots, x_n : t_n$ between names and types. The type system is based on a single type judgment, $E \vdash P : t$, meaning that the process P has type t under the hypothesis E. We assume that there is a given, fixed set of type declarations of the form $A := Reg(\texttt{a}_i[A_i])_{i \in 1..n}$. We assume that functions and patterns are (explicitly) well-typed, which is denoted $f : t \to t_0$ and $p : t \to A$. The types $t_1, \ldots, t_n$ in t are the types of the parameters, while t_0 is the type of the body of f and A is the type of the selector of p. The type of a selector $S = Reg(\texttt{a}_i[p_i(\boldsymbol{x_i})])_{i \in 1..n}$ is obtained from S by substituting to every pattern p_i in the selector its corresponding type A_i. Hence the type of S is equivalent to some type variable A such that $A := Reg(\texttt{a}_i[A_i])_{i \in 1..n}$. Note that if a pattern $p(\boldsymbol{x}) := S$ as x_k has type $t \to A$, then the type t_k is *compatible* with A, which means that $t_k = \texttt{ref } B$ and $B, A <: B$.

The typing rules for the functional part of the calculus are standard. In what follows, we consider that references can only hold document values (a reference can be of type $\texttt{ref } A$ but not $\texttt{ref } t$). Note that, for every assignment of a value of type B into a reference of type $\texttt{ref } A$, rule (Type Write), we check that $A, B <: A$. This is to take into account that references combine the sequence of values that are assigned to them.

The remaining typing rules are for resources and pattern-matching operators. The type of an expression $\texttt{try } u\, p(v)$ is $\texttt{loc } o(A)$ if the pattern p matches documents of type A, see rule (Type Try Doc). Indeed the effect of this expression is to return a fresh location hosting the evaluation of p on an element of the form $o[u]$. Correspondingly, a $\texttt{wait}$ expression is well typed only if it is blocking on a location of type $\texttt{loc } a(A)$,

Table 2. Typing Rules

(Type x)

$$\frac{}{E, x : t, E' \vdash x : t}$$

(Type Sub)

$$\frac{A <: B \quad E \vdash P : A}{E \vdash P : B}$$

(Type Fun)

$$\frac{f : (t_1, \ldots, t_n) \to t_0 \quad E \vdash u_i : t_i \quad i \in 1..n}{E \vdash f(u) : t_0}$$

(Type Let)

$$\frac{E \vdash P : t \quad E, x{:}t \vdash Q : t'}{E \vdash \texttt{let } x = P \texttt{ in } Q : t'}$$

(Type Doc)

$$\frac{E \vdash \imath_k : \texttt{node } \mathsf{a}_k(u_k) \quad E \vdash u_k : B_k \quad k \in 1..n}{E \vdash \imath_1 \ldots \imath_n : \mathsf{a}_1[B_1], \ldots, \mathsf{a}_n[B_n]}$$

(Type Node)

$$\frac{E \vdash u : A}{E \vdash \mathsf{a}[u] : \mathsf{a}[A]}$$

(Type Comp)

$$\frac{E \vdash u_i : A_i \quad i \in \{1, 2\}}{E \vdash u_1, u_2 : A_1, A_2}$$

(Type Ref)

$$\frac{E \vdash u : A}{E \vdash \texttt{newref } u : \texttt{ref } A}$$

(Type Read)

$$\frac{E \vdash u : \texttt{ref } A}{E \vdash !u : A}$$

(Type Write)

$$\frac{E \vdash u : \texttt{ref } A \quad E \vdash v : B \quad A, B <: A}{E \vdash u \mathrel{+}= v : \texttt{Empty}}$$

(Type Res)

$$\frac{E, \ell_1 : t_1, \ldots, \ell_n : t_n \vdash P : t \quad \{\ell_1, \ldots, \ell_n\} \cap fn(E) = \emptyset}{E \vdash (\nu \ell_1) \ldots (\nu \ell_n) P : t}$$

(Type Par)

$$\frac{E \vdash P : t' \quad E \vdash Q : t}{E \vdash P \mathbin{\vec{|}} Q : t}$$

(Type Try Doc)

$$\frac{p : (t_1, \ldots, t_n) \to A \quad E \vdash v_i : t_i \quad i \in 1..n \quad E \vdash u : B}{E \vdash \texttt{try } u\, p(v_1, \ldots, v_n) : \texttt{loc } o(A)}$$

(Type Wait)

$$\frac{E \vdash u : \texttt{loc } \mathsf{a}(A) \quad E, x : A \vdash e_1 : t \quad E, x : \overline{A} \vdash e_2 : t}{E \vdash \texttt{wait } u(x) \texttt{ then } e_1 \texttt{ else } e_2 : t}$$

(Type Loc Ref)

$$\frac{E \vdash \ell : \texttt{ref } A \quad E \vdash u : A}{E \vdash \langle \ell \mapsto \texttt{ref } u \rangle : \star}$$

(Type Loc Node)

$$\frac{E \vdash \ell : \texttt{node } \mathsf{a}(\imath_1 \ldots \imath_n)}{E \vdash \langle \ell \mapsto \texttt{node } \mathsf{a}(\imath_1 \ldots \imath_n) \rangle : \star}$$

(Type Loc Ok)

$$\frac{E \vdash \ell : \texttt{loc } \mathsf{a}(A) \quad E \vdash \imath : \texttt{node } \mathsf{a}(u) \quad u = \imath_1 \ldots \imath_n \quad E \vdash u : A}{E \vdash \langle \ell \mapsto \texttt{ok } \imath \rangle : \star}$$

(Type Loc Fail)

$$\frac{E \vdash \ell : \texttt{loc } \mathsf{a}(A) \quad E \vdash \imath : \texttt{node } \mathsf{a}(u) \quad u = \imath_1 \ldots \imath_n \quad E \vdash u : \overline{A}}{E \vdash \langle \ell \mapsto \texttt{fail } \imath \rangle : \star}$$

(Type Try Loc)

$$\frac{E \vdash \ell : \texttt{loc } \mathsf{a}(A) \quad E \vdash \imath : \texttt{node } \mathsf{a}(\imath_1 \ldots \imath_n) \quad p : (t_1, \ldots, t_n) \to A \quad E \vdash v_i : t_i \quad i \in 1..n}{E \vdash \langle \ell \mapsto \texttt{try } \imath\, p(v) \rangle : \star}$$

(Type Test Loc)

$$\frac{E \vdash \ell : \texttt{loc } \mathsf{a}(A) \quad E \vdash \imath : \texttt{node } \mathsf{a}(u) \quad E \vdash \jmath_k : \texttt{loc } \mathsf{a}_k(A_k)}{w = (\jmath_1 \ldots \jmath_n) \quad \mathsf{a}_1 \ldots \mathsf{a}_n \vdash_A A_1 \ldots A_n \quad E \vdash v_k : t_k \quad t_k = \texttt{ref } B \quad B, A <: B}{E \vdash \langle \ell \mapsto \texttt{test } \imath\, w\, v_k \rangle : \star}$$

---

that is the location of a resource that can eventually turn into ok or fail. The important aspect of this rule is that, while the continuations e_1 and e_2 of the wait expression must have the same type, they are typed under different typing environment: the expression

e_1 is typed with the hypothesis $x : A$ while e_2 is typed with the hypothesis $x : \overline{A}$. This leads to more precise types for filtering expressions.

The typing rules for locations are straightforward. Since a resource returns no value it has type $\star$. By rule (Type Try Loc), a location ℓ containing a try resource, evaluating a pattern p of type A, is well typed if ℓ is of type loc a(A) and the root tag of the evaluated document is a. Note that no assumption is made on $(\imath_1, \ldots, \imath_n)$, which might well not be of type A. Finally, the rule for node location, (Type Loc Node), states that a location containing node a(u) has only one possible type, namely node a(u) itself. Hence this rule avoids the presence of two node resources with the same location but containing different elements. Actually, we could extend our type system in a simple way to ensure that a well-typed configuration cannot have two resources at the same location: we say such a configuration is *well-formed* (see e.g. [12] for an example of how to extend the type system).

An important feature of our calculus is that every pattern is strongly typed: its type is the regular expression obtained by erasing capture variables. Likewise we can type locations, expressions and processes using a combination of regular expression types and ref types. Since we have a strongly typed language, we need to prove that well-typedness of processes is preserved by reduction.

Theorem 1 (subject reduction). *Suppose that P is well formed and contains only unambiguous patterns and t contains only unambiguous types. If $E \vdash P : t$ and $P \to Q$ then $E \vdash Q : t$.*

The proof of Theorem 1 is more involved than in "traditional proofs" for subject reduction. A reason for this is the need to take into account complement types and the fact that it is not possible to reason on a whole document at once (its content is scattered across distinct resource locations.)

We do not state a *progress theorem* in connection with Theorem 1. Indeed, there exists no notion of errors in our calculus (like e.g. the notion of "message not understood" in object-oriented languages) as it is perfectly acceptable for a pattern matching to fail or to get blocked on a wait statement. Nonetheless the subject reduction theorem is still useful. For instance, we can use it for optimizations purposes, like detecting trivial patterns (i.e. matching expressions that will always fail).

5 Example: The Reverse Web-Link Graph

We study the *reverse web-link graph* application [9], used e.g. in Google's search-engine to compute page ranks. The goal is to build a list of all pages containing a link to a given URL. We consider a calculus enriched with an atomic type for strings and a construct if $x = y$ then... to test equalities between strings, these extensions are straightforward to accommodate. We assume that web pages in the index are stored as documents of type $WP = $ pg[B], where B is the type (url[String], link[$URL*$], text[String]) and URL is a shorthand for url[String], meaning that for each page we have its location (url), a list of its hyperlinks (link) and its textual content (text). For simplicity, assume that each list contains no duplicate hyperlinks. The following patterns are used for building a reverse web-link graph:

$$revWL(t,r) \; := \; \big(\text{pg}[revWL'(t,r)]\big)*$$

$$revWL'(t,r) \; := \; \text{let } x = \text{newref } (\,) \, , \, y = \text{newref } (\,) \text{ in}$$
$$\big(\text{url}[\text{String as } x], \text{link}[URL* \text{ as } y], \text{text}[\text{String}]\big)$$
$$\text{then } \big(\text{try } !y \; sift(t, !x, r)\big)$$

$$sift(t,t',r) \; := \; \big(\text{url}[sift'(t,t',r)]\big)*$$

$$sift'(t,t',r) \; := \; \text{let } z = \text{newref } (\,) \text{ in } \big(\text{String as } z\big)$$
$$\text{then } \big(\text{if } z = t \text{ then } r \; += \text{url}[t']\big).$$

The main pattern is $revWL(t,r)$, where t is the string representing the target URL, and r is a (global) reference cell for t's reverse-index. $revWL$ visits each indexed page and invokes $revWL'$, which extracts the page's location and list of links, and stores them in two fresh references x and y. Then the pattern $sift$ is used to test whether the list of URL in y contains the target location t. If true, the result r is updated by adding to it the value of x (that is passed as the second parameter of $sift$). In each pattern, the "location" parameters t and t' have type String while the final result, held in the parameter r, is a reference holding values of type $URL*$. Hence the pattern $revWL$ has type $(\text{String}, \text{ref}\,(URL*)) \rightarrow WP*$ and $sift$ has type $(\text{String}, \text{String}, \text{ref}\,(URL*)) \rightarrow URL*$. Assume $\imath_1 \ldots \imath_n$ are the indexes of the web pages of interest, possibly stored in different physical locations, we can create a reverse index for the target location ta with the expression: $\text{let } z = \text{newref } (\,) \text{ in try } (\imath_1 \ldots \imath_n) \; revWL(ta, z)$. Note that patterns and functions are evaluated locally at each site, while the result reference z is "global" (it is local to the caller, but is accessed by every site for storing the results.).

6   Extensions

We study how to interpret two interesting programming idioms in our model: spawning an expression in a new thread, and handling user-defined exceptions.

Concurrency. We show how to model simple threads, that is, we want to encode an operator spawn such that the effect of $\text{spawn } e_1; \; e_2$ is to evaluate e_1 in parallel with e_2, yielding the value of e_2 as a result. The simplest solution is to interpret $\text{spawn } e_1; \; e_2$ by the configuration $e_1 \; \Gamma \; e_2$. A disadvantage of this solution is that it is not possible to test in e_2 whether the evaluation of e_1 has ended. Another simple approach is to rely on the pattern-matching mechanism. Let p be the pattern $p(\,) := (\text{Empty then } e_1)$. We can interpret the statement $\text{spawn } e_1; e_2$ with the expression $\text{let } x = (\text{try } (\,) \; p(\,)) \text{ in } e_2$. Indeed we have:

$$\text{let } x = (\text{try } (\,) \; p(\,)) \text{ in } e_2 \; \rightarrow^* \; (\nu\imath\ell)\big(\langle \imath \mapsto \text{node } o(\,)\rangle\,\Gamma$$
$$\big(\text{let } z = e_1 \text{ in } \langle \ell \mapsto \text{ok } \imath\rangle\big)\,\Gamma\; e_2\{x{\leftarrow}\ell\}\big).$$

In the resulting process, e_1 and e_2 are evaluated concurrently and the resource $\langle \ell \mapsto \text{ok } \imath\rangle$ cannot interact with e_2 until the evaluation of e_1 ends. Hence we can use the expression $(\text{wait } x(y) \text{ then } e)$ in e_2 to block the execution until e_1 returns a value. (We can in fact improve our encoding so that the result of e_1 is bound to z in e.) It emerges from this example that a try location can be viewed as a *future*, that is a reference to the "future result" of an asynchronous computation. More generally, we can liken a process $(\langle \imath \mapsto \mathtt{node}\ \mathtt{a}(u)\rangle \ulcorner \langle \ell \mapsto \mathtt{ok}\ \imath \rangle)$ to an (asynchronous) output action $\ell!\langle \mathtt{ok}, u\rangle$ as found in process calculi such as the π-calculus. Similarly, we can compare an expression $\mathtt{wait}\ \ell(x)$ then e_1 else e_2 with an input action.

Exceptions. We show how to model a simple exception mechanism in our calculus. Suppose we need to check that a document u of type L (the type of family trees, see Section 2) contains only women. This can be achieved using the pattern declarations $p(\,) := \mathtt{woman}[q(\,)]*$ and $q(\,) := \mathtt{name}[\mathtt{All}], \mathtt{d}[p(\,)], \mathtt{s}[\mathtt{Empty}]$ and a matching expression $\mathtt{try}\ u\ p(\,)$. A drawback of this approach is that we need to wait for the completion of all sub-patterns to terminate before completing the computation, even if the matching trivially fails because we find an element tagged $\mathtt{man}$ early in the matching. A solution is to encode a basic mechanism for handling exceptions using the following derived operators, where $\imath_e$ is a default name associated to the location $\langle \imath_e \mapsto \mathtt{node}\ o(\,)\rangle$:

$\mathtt{exception} =$	$(\nu\ell)\ell$	creates a fresh (location) exception
$\mathtt{throw}\ \ell =$	$\langle \ell \mapsto \mathtt{ok}\ \imath_e \rangle \ulcorner (\,)$	raises an exception at ℓ
$\mathtt{catch}\ \ell\ e =$	$\mathtt{wait}\ \ell(x)$ then e	catches exception ℓ and runs e $(x \notin fv(e))$.

For instance, it is possible to raise the exception in the compensation part of a pattern declaration, to catch this exception and avoid to wait the end of the pattern-matching evaluation. E.g. the pattern p above can be redefined in: $p'(x) := \mathtt{woman}[q(\,)]*$ else $\mathtt{throw}\ x$.

7   Conclusions and Related Work

We study a formal model for computing over large (even dynamic) distributed XML documents. We extend the functional approach taken in e.g. XDuce and define a typed process calculus which supports a first-order type system with subtyping based on regular expression types, a system compatible with DTD and other schema languages for XML.

This work may be compared with recent proposals for integrating XML data into π-calculus, where pattern-matching plays a fundamental role: Iota [5] is a concurrent XML scripting language with channel-based communications that relies on types to guarantee the well-formedness (not the validity) of documents; XPi [2] is a typed π-calculus extended with XML values in which documents are exchanged during communications; PiDuce [6] features asynchronous communications and code mobility and includes pattern matching expressions with built-in type checks. In all these proposals, documents are first class values exchanged in messages, which make these approaches inappropriate in the case of very large or dynamically generated data.

The goal of this paper is not to define a new programming language. We rather try to provide formal tools for the study of concurrent computation models based on service composition and streamed XML data. However our calculus could be a basis for developing concurrent extensions of strongly typed languages for XML, such as XDuce. To this end, we will also need to answer questions concerning observational equivalences that we intend to study in future work. Our approach could also be used to provide the semantics of systems in which XML documents contain active code that can be executed on distributed sites (i.e. processes and document text are mixed), like in the Active XML system for example [1]. Although, for this, it will be necessary to add an "eval/quote" mechanism, as in e.g. LISP, and to revise our static type checking approach. Finally, another avenue to investigate is the encoding of other concurrency primitives, especially channel-based synchronization and distributed transactions.

References

1. Abiteboul, S., Benjelloun, O., Milo, T., Manolescu, I., Weber, R.: Active XML: Peer-to-Peer Data and Web Services Integration. In: Proc. of VLDB (2002)
2. Acciai, L., Boreale, M.: XPi: a typed process calculus for XML messaging. In: Steffen, M., Zavattaro, G. (eds.) FMOODS 2005. LNCS, vol. 3535, Springer, Heidelberg (2005)
3. Acciai, L., Boreale, M., Dal Zilio, S.: A Typed Calculus for Querying Distributed XML Documents. LIF Research Report 29 (2006)
4. Amadio, R.: An Asynchronous Model of Locality, Failure And Process Mobility. In: Garlan, D., Le Métayer, D. (eds.) COORDINATION 1997. LNCS, vol. 1282, Springer, Heidelberg (1997)
5. Bierman, G., Sewell, P.: Iota: A concurrent XML scripting language with applications to Home Area Networking. TR 577, Computer Lab. Cambridge (2003)
6. Brown, A., Laneve, C., Meredith, G.: PiDuce: a process calculus with native XML datatypes. In: Proc. of Workshop on Web Services and Formal Methods (2005)
7. Castagna, G.: Pattern and types for querying XML documents. In: Proc. of DBPL, XSYM 2005 joint keynote talk (2005)
8. Comon, H., Dauchet, M., Jacquemard, F., Tison, S., Lugiez, D., Tommasi, M.: Tree Automata on their application (1999),
http://www.grappa.univ-lille3.fr/tata/
9. Dean, J., Ghemawat, S.: MapReduce: Simplified Data Processing on Large Cluster. In: Proc. of OSDI (2004)
10. Ferreira, W., Hennessy, M., Jeffrey, A.S.: A theory of weak bisimulation for core CML. J. Functional Programming 8(5) (1998)
11. Gardner, P., Maffeis, S.: Modelling dynamic web data. Theor. Comput. Sci. 342(1) (2005)
12. Gordon, A.D., Hankin, P.D.: A concurrent object calculus: reduction and typing. In: Proc. of HLCL. Electr. Notes Theor. Comput. Sci. 16(3) (1998)
13. Hosoya, H., Vouillon, J., Pierce, B.J.: Regular expression types for XML. ACM Transactions on Programming Languages and Systems, 27(1) (2004)
14. Hosoya, H., Pierce, B.J.: Regular expression pattern matching for XML. In: Proc. of POPL (2001)
15. Hosoya, H., Pierce, B.J.: XDuce: A Statically Typed XML Processing Language. In: Proc. of ACM Transaction on Internet Technology (2003)
16. Milner, R.: Communicating and Mobile Systems: The π-Calculus. CUP (1999)

Verification of Model Transformations: A Case Study with BPEL*

Luciano Baresi[1], Karsten Ehrig[2], and Reiko Heckel[2]

[1] Dipartimento di Elettronica e Informazione, Politecnico di Milano, Italy
baresi@elet.polimi.it
[2] Department of Computer Science, University of Leicester, United Kingdom
{karsten,reiko}@mcs.le.ac.uk

Abstract. Model transformations, like refinement or refactoring, have to respect the semantics of the models transformed. In the case of behavioural models this semantics can be specified by transformations, too, describing an abstract interpreter for the language. Both kinds of transformations, if given in a rule-based way, can formally be described as graph transformations.

In this paper, we present executable business processes, their operational semantics and refactoring, as an example of this fact. Using results from graph transformation theory about critical pairs and local confluence, we show that our transformations preserve the semantics of processes. The analysis is performed by means of the graph transformation tool AGG.

1   Introduction

Transformations of models are the key technology of Model-driven Development (MDD), an approach to software development where graphical models (rather than programs) are the focus and primary technical artefact. Model transformations can serve a variety of purposes, including the refinements of models, their mapping to implementations, consistency management, or evolution. In many of these examples, a semantic compatibility between the artefacts before and after the transformation is desired.

With the semiformal nature of most visual models, and the corresponding lack of formal semantics, this relation is often not easy to describe. And if formal semantics exist for both source and target models, they are often given in different semantic domains and using different formal techniques.

It seems that the only general solution to this problem consists in adopting a formalism powerful enough to describe both the intended semantics and the transformation of the models involved, and which provides techniques and tools

---

* Work supported in part by the IST-2005-16004 Integrated Project SENSORIA: Software Engineering for Service-Oriented Overlay Computers and by the European Community's Human Potential Programme under contract HPRN-CT-2002-00275, [SegraVis].

U. Montanari, D. Sannella, and R. Bruni (Eds.): TGC 2006, LNCS 4661, pp. 183–199, 2007.

to demonstrate the relation between them. Since we are dealing with visual models whose abstract syntax is often expressed by means of graphs, we are opting for graph transformation as one such approach.

In this paper we are demonstrating the idea by means of the transformation of executable business processes inspired by BPEL4WS, the Business Process Execution Language for Web Services [13], and presented using the notation of UML activity diagrams. Normally BPEL assumes a centralised approach, where a single entity—usually called *orchestrator*— controls the execution flow and coordinates the interactions with selected services. Centralised execution is easy to describe, but not always adequate if the system is distributed by nature, for example, in the case of inter-organisational business processes, where each party is in charge of a particular fragment of the process.

With this motivation, Baresi et al [3,4] use transformations to partition a monolithic process into a coordinated set of sub-processes. However, although the distribution is described formally by means of graph transformation rules, no verification of its semantic correctness is given. The present paper addresses this issue and discusses the conceptual and software tools required to

- formalise a notion of semantic compatibility between the distributed and the original process, taking into account that not all features of one may exist in the other;
- verify that this compatibility holds for all processes obtained through application of the proposed transformation rules.

The first aim is achieved using typed attributed graph transformation rules to define the operational semantics of centralised and distributed processes. To this end, a meta model captures the abstract syntax of executable processes, extended by information about their execution state. This meta model, formally represented as a type graph with inheritance, is the basis of a set of operational semantics rules. This approach allows us to specify the operational semantics and transformations in the same formalism, thus simplifying the analysis. The semantic relation is established by associating observations with operational rules, generating the labelled transition systems of processes, and applying the standard notion of bisimilarity modulo a suitable projection of transitions onto common labels.

The proof that the semantic relation holds for all processes obtained from each other by application of transformation rules realising the distribution is based on the idea of *mixed confluence* [8]: If transformation rules are exchangeable with operational rules, the application of a transformation does not reduce the operational semantics. Mixed confluence is shown by critical pair analysis [9] of model transformation vs. semantic rules. This allows us to establish a simulation relation between the given and the derived process. Since graph transformation rules are invertible, the same technique can be used to show bisimilarity.

The paper is organized as follows. After introducing in Section 2 those features of the BPEL language that are relevant to our model, Section 3 describes the BPEL meta model and the transformation from centralised into distributed processes. Section 4 sketches the operational semantics and Section 5 discusses the correctness of the transformation. Section 7 concludes the paper.

2   Executable Business Processes as Activity Diagrams

BPEL4WS (Business Process Execution Language for Web Services, [13]) based on WSDL (Web Services Description Language, [6]) is an XML-based language designed to enable the coordination and composition —using a workflow-based approach— of a set of Web services. BPEL defines a number of activities to describe the interaction of the process with its partners. Activities can be *basic* or *structured*. Basic activities define the interaction capabilities of BPEL processes: **invoke** activities call operations of external services and (in their synchronous version) wait for the response message to arrive, **receive** activities wait for suitable messages (invocations), **reply** activities answer invocations, etc.

Structured activities can comprise both basic and other structured activities. Examples include **switch** defining branches, **flow** allowing for parallel threads, and **pick** defining branches whose selection is based on the receipt of suitable messages.

In this paper, we consider a subset of the language, ignoring some of the control constructs and features such as asynchronous communication, fault handlers, etc., see [13] for an in-depth presentation. We illustrate the approach by means of the example in Fig. 1, using UML activity diagrams to visualise a process that manages orders received from clients in cooperation between an office and a warehouse. We assume that the **Office** receives the order through a **receive** activity and implicitly validates it. If it is acceptable, the **Warehouse invoke**s shipment, otherwise the **Office** proceeds with a **basic** (local) undo operation. The two orchestrators are distinguished by so-called swimlanes.

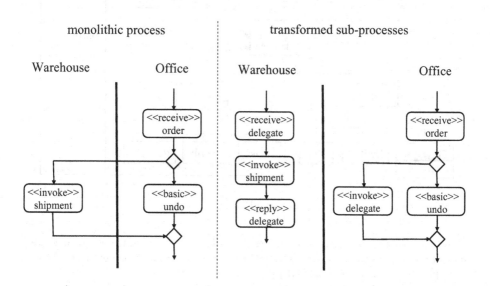

Fig. 1. Example BPEL Processes

3   Transformations

This section demonstrates the use of transformation rules to partition a process into a main process and a set of independent sub-processes. The presentation starts from a simple meta-model introducing the types of nodes and edges required to represent processes. Then, we introduce a sample transformation rule.

The presentation is based on the algebraic double-pushout approach to the transformation of typed and attributed graphs [9]. For a more compact presentation of metamodel and rules we use subtyping as well as negative application conditions.

3.1   Meta-model

The meta-model of Fig. 2, which borrows some concepts from the work proposed in [11], only comprises elements that are used by the example in this paper.

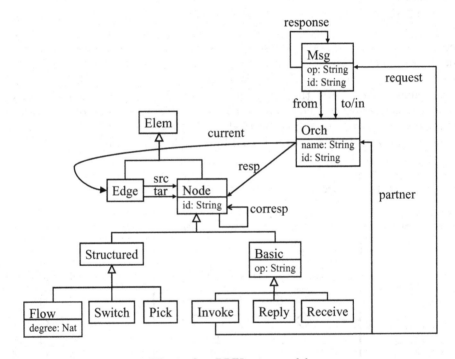

Fig. 2. Our BPEL metamodel

A business process comprises Elements, which are distinguished into Nodes and Edges, linked by means of associations source (src) and target (tar). Moreover, Nodes are further classified into

– Basic nodes corresponding to Invoke, Reply, and Receive activities[1].

---

[1] In this paper, we do not consider Assign activities since the propagation of data values is not addressed here.

- **Structured** nodes corresponding to the typical constructs of workflow languages, like **Switch**, **Flow**, and **Pick**.

Each structured activity is presented by two **Structured** nodes —related by association **corresponding**— to identify the start and the end of the composed activity. The same association is also used to relate the first and last nodes of a sequence of basic action nodes.

Each **Node** is characterised by the **Orchestrator** that is **responsible** for it (that shall execute it). Before starting the application of partitioning rules, the designer must decide how to split the process by assigning the responsibilities for the different nodes to available orchestrators.

Each **Orchestrator** has an element (currently) under execution, which is rendered using association **current** in Fig. 2. By **partner** links we point to **Orchestrator** intended as recipients of **invoke** messages. Messages (**Msg**) specify their sender (**from**), recipient (**to**), whether they are already received but not yet fully processed (**in**), or if they are the (**response**) to an earlier invocation message.

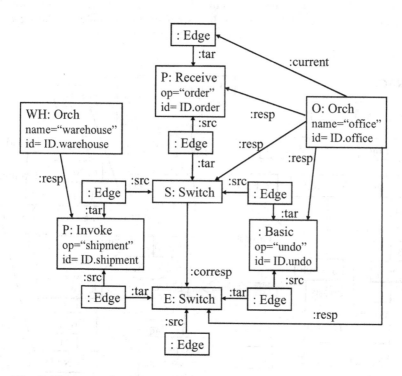

Fig. 3. The example of Fig. 1 as an instance of the metamodel of Fig. 2

The meta-model of Fig. 2 is incomplete, missing both a number of constraints and further types, but sufficient to represent the example process in Fig. 1. The corresponding metamodel instance is shown in Fig. 3.

3.2   The Partitioning Rule

The partitioning identifies parts of the original process which can be externalised and redirects the execution flow accordingly. Consider the rule in Fig. 4 delegating the execution of a block of activities that are in the domain of a different orchestrator. The part to be delegated is situated between 1:Node and 2:Node in the left-hand side of the rule. The corresp edge, removed in the transformation, represents the derived information that these two nodes are indeed connected by a workflow. It has to be set accordingly before executing the rule.

In our example model in Fig. 3 the part to be delegated consists of a single activity P:invoke only. In this case both 1:Node and 2:Node are mapped to P:invoke.

The delegation subprocess is started by the first orchestrator 8:Orch via :Invoke. The second orchestrator 3:Orch executes the process between the pair of :Receive and :Reply nodes, activated by the new :current edge. The negative application condition NAC ensures that the subprocess to be delegated is not already under execution by 3:Orch. Since it is invoked synchronously, the invoking process has to wait for a reply of the executed subprocess.

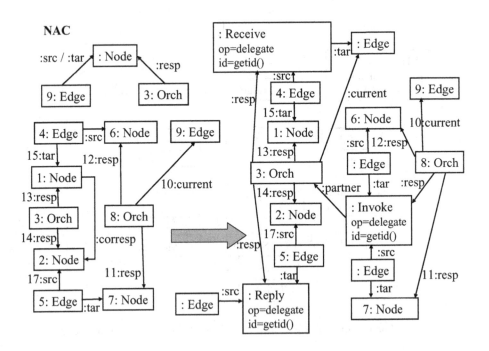

Fig. 4. Transformation rule delegate

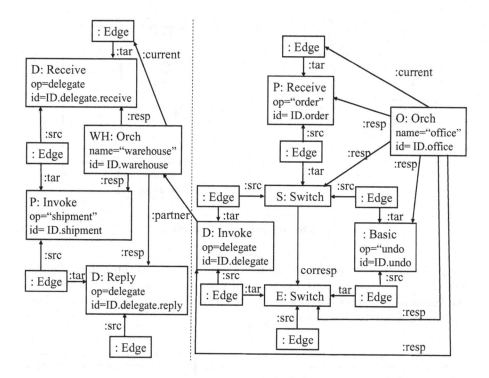

Fig. 5. Resulting subprocesses

4   Operational Semantics

Graphical operational semantics has been introduced as an extension of meta modelling (the specification of abstract syntax and/or static semantic by means of class diagrams) to deal with the dynamic aspect of modelling languages [10]. In this section we are using the approach to model the operational semantics of executable business processes, based on their graphical representation from their previous section. We focus on the rules needed for explaining the behaviour of the example (represented by the meta model instance in Fig. 1), briefly sketching the remaining rules. Then we define observations and derive a labelled transition system.

4.1   Operational Rules

Fig. 6 shows the operational rule for executing the *1:Invoke* action, sending message :Msg. The operation mentioned by the message is the same of the action node *i*, as described by the condition op = i.op in the :Msg node. A new unique identifier is supplied by getid(). As specified be the partner edge from the invoke node, the message is created by the orchestrator 3:Orch for the orchestrator 4:Orch.

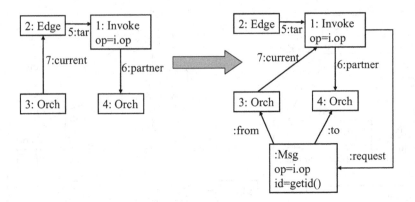

Fig. 6. Operational rule invoke

Fig. 7 shows the rule by which orchestrator 3:Orch executes the *1:Receive* action, accepting a message 4:Msg with the operation name r.op of 1:Receive. The current edge, previously pointing to the Edge before the next action Node is advanced from 2:Edge to 5:Edge.

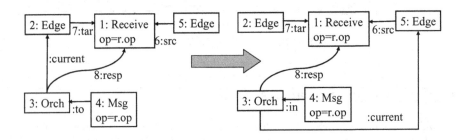

Fig. 7. Operational rule receive

Fig. 8 shows the rule by which orchestrator 3:Orch is replying to message 4:Msg with the new message :Msg which is sent to the invoking orchestrator 10:Orch.

Fig. 9 shows the rule by which orchestrator 5:Orch is handling the response of orchestrator 6:Orch by deleting the request and response messages and advancing the :current edge.

The rule switch in Fig. 10 represent an example of how the semantics of control structures are described. The rule implements both the split operation, moving the *:current* edge to one of several branches outgoing from the *1:Switch* node, and the joining of several alternative branches. Notice that split is non-deterministic because, due to the lack of data types in our model, we do not specify any guards. In practice we can expect that switches are deterministic.

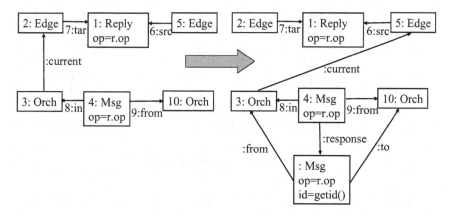

Fig. 8. Operational rule `reply`

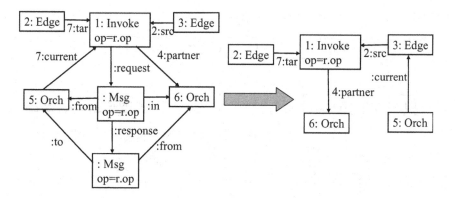

Fig. 9. Operational rule `response`

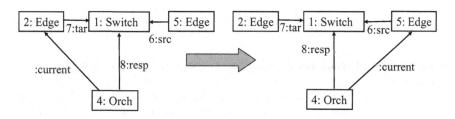

Fig. 10. Operational rule `switch`

The rule **partner** in Fig. 11 selects a partner orchestrator in a non-deterministic way. This is an under-specification of a potentially complex protocol for selecting services. Like the non-deterministic switch rule this will lead to extra transitions, which do not conflict with our aim of demonstrating the preservation of the operational semantics.

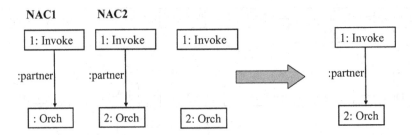

Fig. 11. Operational rule `partner`

Finally the rule `reinit` in Fig. 12 sets the `:current` edge from the end to the beginning after a subprocess has completed its execution to allow a new execution in another context.

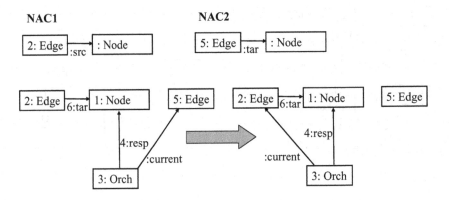

Fig. 12. Operational rule `reinit`

Additional operational rules considered in the complete version of the model include

- flow (fork and sync): the creating and synchronisation of concurrent flows of control;
- pick (split and join): like guarded/external choice in process calculi, where the incoming message determines which of a number of alternative paths is chosen;
- init and final: dealing with the start and termination of processes;

4.2   Labels and Transition System

Observations on rules define the labels of the transition system representing the operational semantics of processes. They contain the name of the rule and list the `id` attributes of some key elements. For example, `inv(i.id, m.id)` refers to the application of the rule `invoke` and observes the identity of the `invoke` action i executed and the message m created. Similarly, the remaining labels include

- `rec(r.id, m.id)` performing receive action r on message m;
- `reply(r.id, m1.id, m2.id)` replying to $m1$ with $m2$;
- `resp(i.id, m2.id)` receiving response message $m2$ for invocation i;

Control flow rules like `switch` represent internal steps and are uniformly labelled with the silent action τ.

In transformations, formal parameters from the rules are replaced by identities of the actual nodes in the graphs representing system states. Given a transformation $G \xrightarrow{p(o)} H$ with, for example rule $p = $ `invoke` (see Fig. 6) and match o, the label `inv(i.id, m.id)` produces the observation `inv(o(i).id, o(m).id)` using the values of the `id` attributes for the images of nodes `i` and `m` under occurrence o.

Given a graph transformation system $\mathcal{G} = (TG, P)$ with start graph G_0, we derive a labelled transition system $LTS(\mathcal{G}, G_0) = (S, L, \rightarrow)$ with all graphs reachable from G_0 by applications of rules as states S, observations on rules as labels L, and transformations as transitions.

The set O of observations excluding τ is potentially infinite. Those that can actually be produced by a transformation system $\mathcal{G}$ from a given graph G are limited to such expressions `rule(params)` where `params` is a list of `id` attribute values that already occur in G. We call this the *alphabet* $alph(G)$ of graph G.

5   Verification

Based on the definitions in the previous section we are now able to define a relation of semantic compatibility between processes. The idea is to require weak bisimilarity after hiding all labels that are not in the intersection of the alphabets of the two processes. On a labelled transition system, the operation of hiding replaces all occurrences of a given label by a silent action τ.

Definition 1 (semantic compatibility). *Given a graph transformation system $\mathcal{G}_{OP} = \langle TG, OP \rangle$ (specifying operational semantics), two graphs G_1 and G_2 (representing processes) are semantically compatible if they are weakly bisimilar after hiding all labels not in $alph(G_1) \cap alph(G_2)$.*

In our case O_1, the set of observations produced by a centralised process, will be a subset of O_2, the observations of the distributed process. This is because of the additional communication actions required to coordinate the different local processes. The following theorem establishes a condition for semantic compatibility. For a regular expression r, by $s \xrightarrow{r} t$ we denote a sequence of transitions $s \xrightarrow{l_1} \cdots \xrightarrow{l_n} t$ such that $l_1 \ldots l_n$ is in the language described by r.

Theorem 1 (semantic compatibility of transformations). *Assume graph transformation systems $\mathcal{G}_{OP} = \langle TG, OP \rangle$ (operational semantics) and $\mathcal{G}_T = \langle TG, T \rangle$ (model transformations) such that for all operational steps $P_1 \xrightarrow{l} Q_1$ and transformation steps $P_1 \Longrightarrow P_2$*

1. $l \in alph(P_2)$ *implies that there exist* $P_2 \xrightarrow{\tau^* l \tau^*} Q_2$ *and* $Q_1 \Longrightarrow Q_2$;
2. $l \notin alph(P_2)$ *implies that there exist* $P_2 \xrightarrow{\tau^*} Q_2$ *and* $Q_1 \Longrightarrow Q_2$;

and the same is true for the inverse of $\mathcal{G}_T$, *obtained by reversing all productions.*

$$
\begin{array}{ccc}
P_1 & \longrightarrow & Q_1 \\
\big\downarrow & & \big\downarrow \\
P_2 & \longrightarrow & Q_2
\end{array}
$$

Then, whenever there exists a transformation $G_1 \Longrightarrow G_2$ *in* $\mathcal{G}_T$, *typed graphs* G_1 *and* G_2 *are semantically compatible.*

Proof. Recall that a weak bisimulation is a relation R on states such that $P_1 \ R \ P_2$ implies

1. $P_1 \xrightarrow{l} Q_1$ implies $P_2 \xrightarrow{\tau^* l \tau^*} Q_2$ and $Q_1 \ R \ Q_2$
2. $P_1 \xrightarrow{\tau} Q_1$ implies $P_2 \xrightarrow{\tau^*} Q_2$ and $Q_1 \ R \ Q_2$

while the same is true for the inverse R^{-1}. The relation R on TG-typed graphs is defined by $G_1 \ R \ G_2$ iff $G_1 \Longrightarrow G_2$. It is easy to see that this satisfies the properties 1 and 2 above.

The inverse transformation system produces the inverse of the transformation relation R, thus making the above true for the symmetric closure of the relation.

Notice that Theorem 1 is based on a notion of local confluence, restricted by assumptions on the labels of derived transitions. Such a property, called *mixed confluence* in [8], can be verified statically by critical pair analysis and search: First we check if all pairs consisting of a model transformation rule and a semantic rule are parallel independent, i.e. there are no critical pairs between them. If this fails, we have to demonstrate confluence for all critical pairs, searching for compatible transformation sequences with the right labels that lead to a common successor state.

For our case study, this means that we have to analyse the critical pairs between **delegate** and the operational semantic rules: Critical pair analysis is supported by the attributed graph grammar tool environment AGG [22,23]. Critical pairs formalise the idea of a minimal example of a conflicting situation. From the set of all overlapping graphs the objects and links are extracted which cause conflicts or dependencies.

Fig. 13 shows the critical pair analysis in AGG where the model transformation rule **delegate** is indeed independent of all operational semantics rules (last row). The opposite is not true since we have critical pairs in the last column which are all caused by a delete-use-conflict between **10:current** in **delegate** and the semantic rules.

According to [17] two direct graph transformations $G \stackrel{(p_1, m_1)}{\Longrightarrow} H_1$ and $G \stackrel{(p_2, m_2)}{\Longrightarrow} H_2$ are in delete-use-conflict (resp. use-delete-conflict) if rule p_1 (resp. p_2) deletes part of the graph G, which is used by rule p_2 (resp. p_2) in the second (resp. first)

first \ sec...	1: receive	2: reply	3: response	4: invoke	5: switch	6: reinit	7: partner	8: delegate
1: receive	43	4	3	1	2	0	0	3
2: reply	4	64	0	2	2	0	0	6
3: response	3	3	18	0	0	0	0	0
4: invoke	1	2	0	8	1	0	0	2
5: switch	2	2	0	1	14	0	0	3
6: reinit	0	0	0	0	0	8	0	10
7: partner	0	0	0	0	0	0	1	0
8: delegate	0	0	0	0	0	0	0	?

Fig. 13. Critical Pair Analysis in AGG

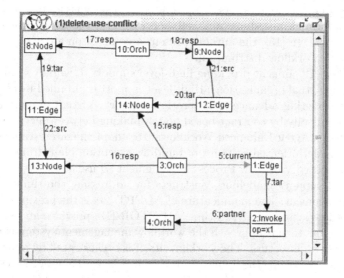

Fig. 14. Critical Pair between invoke and delegate

direct transformation. Fig. 14 shows one of these critical pairs between invoke
and delegate. (Note that the critical pairs between operational semantics rules,
or of rule delegate with itself, are not relevant for mixed confluence.)

Intuitively, the problem is that rule delegate carries an application condition
to check that the subprocess to be separated from the main one is not currently

active. Therefore it is obvious that this should be in conflict with semantic rules advancing the control flow of the process, thus potentially entering the subprocess.

The solution to this problem consists in providing additional transformation rules to deal with the delegation in the case that the subprocess is indeed active. But for its application condition, this rule coincides with `delegate`, with the additional effect that a request message would be created to represent the fact that the (then delegated) subprocess has been invoked from the main one by a message, rather than just by advancing the control flow.

Such an extension of the transformation system to deal with non-confluent cases can be seen as a variant of Knuth-Bendix completion for non-confluent critical pairs in term rewriting. With this extension, the resulting system enjoys the mixed-confluence property.

As a result we obtain mixed confluence, consequently, the compatibility of distributed process with the centralised ones they have been obtained from using rule `delegate`.

6   Related Work

The problem of workflow partitioning has been studied in the field of business process design for some ten years. It still offers interesting issues to study because of mobile information systems and web services, and the novel problems that come with them. In [15], the authors present a comparison among the different approaches to workflow distribution.

Cross-Flow [12] aims at providing high-level support to workflows in dynamically-created virtual organisations. High-level support is obtained by abstracting services and offering advanced cooperation support. Virtual organisations are created dynamically by contract-based match-making between service providers and consumers. Agent Enhanced Workflows [16] adopt the interesting approach, inspired by agent-oriented systems, of building execution plans from predefined goals. Event-based Workflow Process Management [7] use an event-based infrastructure and support modelling constructs for addressing the timing issues of process management. The main feature of ADEPT [20] is the possibility of modifying workflow instances at run-time. MENTOR [19] provides an autonomous workflow engine. In this approach the workflow management system is based on a client-server architecture. The workflow itself is orchestrated by appropriately configured servers, while the applications that invoke workflow activities are executed on the client sites. The METEOR (Managing End to End OpeRations) [2] system leverages Java, CORBA, and Web technologies to provide support for the development of enterprise applications that require workflow management and application integration. It enables the development of complex workflow applications which involve legacy information systems and that have geographically distributed and heterogeneous hardware and software environments, spanning multiple organisations. It also provides support for dynamic workflow processes, error and exception handling, recovery, and QoS management. Exotica [18] is characterised by the possibility of disconnected operations. It does not permit complete decentralisation because it maintains a central unit and all operations obey a client/server paradigm. WISE [1] exploits the Web for its engine and offers an embedded fault handler. WAWM [21] focuses on the problems related to the workflow management in wide area networks. Mobile [14] is developed to support inter-organisational workflows and is strongly based on modularity. This characteristic alleviates change management and also allows users to customise and extend aspects individually.

The analysis of presented models suggests two different and dual approaches to the problem of workflow coordination. The first approach supports the integration of autonomous and preexisting workflows and it aims mainly at the coordination of different and independent actors. The second approach supports the decomposition of single workflows to support their autonomous execution by means of different engines. Cross-Flow, Agent Enhanced Workflow, Event-based Workflow process Management, Adept, WISE and WAWM belong to the first approach; Mentor, Exotica and Mobile belong to the second one.

The systems described offer three different solutions for the definition of partitioning and allocation rules. The first solution proposes specific definition languages (Cross-Flow, Agent enhanced workflow, Mentor, Exotica). The second approach proposes the extension of workflow languages with distribution rules (Cross-Flow, ADEPT, WISE, WAWM, Mobile). The third approach does not consider the language for distribution rules (Event-based, Workflow Process Management). Cross-Flow belongs to more than one class because the distribution rules are split into several definition parts.

Our delegation model supports disconnected components like Exotica, the independence of workflow engines like MENTOR, and the possibility of modifying the workflow instance at run-time like ADEPT. Moreover, we argue that the mobile environment needs a language strongly oriented to the automatic execution like BPEL, but we do not forget the need for lightness that is a mandatory feature if the system runs on portable devices in ad-hoc networks. As far as the definition of rules is concerned, our approach defines partitioning rules, but does not define allocation rules. It defers them to the specific business process and application domain.

Many of the cited approaches do not consider web services as available instruments for decentralising business processes. An exception is made by [5], which presents an approach very similar to ours. The authors use BPEL as workflow model and use the term *Composite Web Service* to refer to a standard workflow. However, they focus on the problem of assigning workflow portions to specific orchestrators to minimise the traffic among nodes, but they do not provide any specific information about the partitioning rules and/or any proof of their validity. They introduce the concepts of *Control Flow Graph* and *Program Dependence Graph* without providing how they refer to BPEL constructs and activities.

7   Conclusion

Reporting on an application of the *mixed confluence* method to show semantic correctness of a transformation from centralised to distributed BPEL processes, the motivation of this paper was two-fold. First, the correctness of the transformation is a practical problem which arose independently and whose solution is potentially relevant to the acceptance of the idea of distributed processes for web services. Second, the problem represents an interesting case for the method of mixed confluence, whose feasibility was validated in the process.

It turns out that, specifying the operational semantics required a non-trivial refinement (and we like to believe improvement) of the meta model over the originally proposed one, which was only used to describe the transformation. Also, the importance of efficient tool support became evident, in particular with respect to the scalability to non-trivial examples.

As future work we intend to consider more transformations consisting of several steps as part of a transaction, which will allow us to consider more complex transformation scenarios.

References

1. Alonso, G., Fiedler, U., Hagen, C., Lazcano, A., Schuldt, H., Weiler, N.: WISE: Business to business e-commerce. In: RIDE, pp. 132–139 (1999)
2. Anyanwu, K., Sheth, A., Cardoso, J., Miller, J., Kochut, K.: Healthcare enterprise process development and integration. Journal of Research and Practice in Information Technology, 35(2) (2003)
3. Baresi, L., Maurino, A., Modafferi, S.: Workflow partitioning in mobile information systems. In: Kluwer, editor. In: Proc. of IFIP TC8 Working Conference on Mobile Information Systems. IFIP International Federation for Information Processing, vol. 158 (2004)
4. Baresi, L., Maurino, A., Modafferi, S.: Partitioning rules for bpel processes. Technical report, Politecnico di Milano. In preparation (2006)
5. Chafle, G.B., Chandra, S., Mann, V., Nanda, M.G.: Decentralized orchestration of composite web services. In: Proc. of the Int. World Wide Web conference on Alternate track papers & posters, pp. 134–143. ACM Press, New York, USA (2004)
6. Christensen, E., Curbera, F., Meredith, G., Weerawarana, S.: Web Services Description Language (WSDL) version 1.1. W3C (March 2001),
   http://www.w3.org/TR/wsdl
7. Eder, J., Panagos, E.: Towards distributed workflow process management. In: proc. of Workshop on cross-Organizational Workflow Management and Coordination, San Francisco, USA (1999)
8. Ehrig, H., Ehrig, K.: Overview of Formal Concepts for Model Transformations based on Typed Attributed Graph Transformation. In: Proc. International Workshop on Graph and Model Transformation (GraMoT'05). Electronic Notes in Theoretical Computer Science, vol. 152, Elsevier Science, Tallinn, Estonia (2005)
9. Ehrig, H., Ehrig, K., Prange, U., Taentzer, G.: Fundamentals of Algebraic Graph Transformation. EATCS Monographs in Theoretical Computer Science. Springer, Heidelberg (2006)

10. Engels, G., Heckel, R., Sauer, St.: Dynamic meta modeling: A graphical approach to operational semantics. In: Proc. OOPSLA'99 Workshop on Rigorous Modeling and Analysis with the UML: Challenges and Limitations, Denver, CO, USA (November 2, 1999)
11. Gardner, T., al.: Draft UML 1.4 profile for automated business processes with a mapping to the BPEL 1.0. IBM alphaWorks (2003)
12. Grefen, P., Aberer, K., Hoffner, Y., Ludwig, H.: Crossflow: Cross-organizational workflow management in dynamic virtual enterprises. International Journal of Computer Systems Science & Engineering 15(5), 277–290 (2000)
13. IBM, BEA Systems, Microsoft, SAP AG, Siebel Systems. Business Process Execution Language for Web Services version 1.1 (May 2003), http://www.ibm.com/developerworks/library/ws-bpel/
14. Jablonski, S., Bussler, C.: Workflow Management: Modeling Concepts, Architecture and Implementation. International Thomson (1996)
15. Jablonski, S., Schamburger, R., Hahn, C., Horn, S., Lay, R., Neeb, J., Schlundt, M.: A comprehensive investigation of distribution in the context of workflow management. In: proc. of International Conference on Parallel and Distributed Systems ICPADS, Kyongju City, Korea (2001)
16. Judge, D., Odgers, B., Shepherdson, J., Cui, Z.: Agent enhanced workflow. BT Technical Journal (16) (1998)
17. Lambers, L., Ehrig, H., Orejas, F.: Conflict Detection for Graph Transformation with Negative Application Conditions. In: Corradini, A., Ehrig, H., Montanari, U., Ribeiro, L., Rozenberg, G. (eds.) ICGT 2006. LNCS, vol. 4178, pp. 61–76. Springer, Heidelberg (2006)
18. Mohan, C., Alonso, G., Gunthor, R., Kamath, M.: Exotica: A research perspective of workflow management systems. Data Engineering Bulletin 18(1), 19–26 (1995)
19. Muth, P., Wodtke, D., Weisenfels, J., Kotz Dittrich, A., Weikum, G.: From centralized workflow specification to distributed workflow execution. Journal of Intelligent Information Systems 10(2), 159–184 (1998)
20. Reichert, M., Dadam, P.: Adeptflex − supporting dynamic changes of workflows without losing control. Journal of Intelligent Information Systems 10(2), 93–129 (1998)
21. Riempp, G.: Wide Area Workflow Management. Springer, London, UK (1998)
22. Taentzer, G.: AGG: A Graph Transformation Environment for Modeling and Validation of Software. In: Pfaltz, J.L., Nagl, M., Boehlen, B. (eds.) AGTIVE 2003. LNCS, vol. 3062, pp. 446–456. Springer, Heidelberg (2004)
23. Technical University of Berlin, Department of Computer Science. AGG Version 1.4.1 - (2006), http://tfs.cs.tu-berlin.de/agg

A Fuzzy Approach for Negotiating Quality of Services

Davide Bacciu, Alessio Botta, and Hernán Melgratti

IMT Lucca Institute for Advanced Studies, Italy
{davide.bacciu,alessio.botta,hernan.melgratti}@imtlucca.it

Abstract. A central point when integrating services concerns to the description, agreement and enforcement of the quality aspect of service interaction, usually known as Service Level Agreement (SLA). This paper presents a framework for SLA negotiation based on fuzzy sets. We propose (i) a request language for clients to describe quality preferences, (ii) a publication language for providers to define the qualities of their offered services, and (iii) a decision procedure for granting any client request with a SLA contract fitting the requestor requirements. We start with a restricted framework in which the different qualities of a service are handled independently (as being orthogonal) and then we propose an extension that allows clients and providers to express dependencies among different qualities.

1 Introduction

Service Level Agreement (SLA) concerns the description, negotiation and enforcement of non-functional aspects of service behaviors. Typical examples are the bounds on service response time and availability, the number of accepted requests by unit of time, and the availability of resources such as storage and bandwidth. In this context, service providers advertise their functionalities by associating different *service levels* or guaranties about the qualities of their offered services. For instance, a storage service may be published with, e.g., three different service levels, namely, *Basic*, *Gold*, and *Platinum*, associating to any of them an increasing amount of communication bandwidth. In this kind of scenario, a client (or service consumer) C is able to use (or interact with) a particular service provider P only after C and P have agreed on a particular service level. Therefore, any interaction of C with P should be preceded by a *negotiation* or *agreement creation* phase. The negotiation phase is started when the client makes a specific request to the provider containing its quality expectations. After a negotiation, if they reach an agreement, a particular contract binding the provider and the client with a particular service level is signed by both parties. After that, a second phase is started: the *utilization* phase. During the utilization phase, the client makes requests to the provider under a particular agreement or signed contract. It is assumed that the service provider will perform a service accordingly to the agreed conditions. Hence, the runtime infrastructure should provide ways for monitoring and checking whether the execution meets contract obligations, and to take corrective actions when the execution deviates from the agreed conditions.

The web services realm have gave birth to some proposals for standards, like *Web Service Level Agreement* (WSLA) [6] and *Web Service Agreement Specification* (WS-Agreement) [13], that specify the way in which services describe their quality levels (or

U. Montanari, D. Sannella, and R. Bruni (Eds.): TGC 2006, LNCS 4661, pp. 200–217, 2007.

SLA parameters), the protocols to be used for reaching agreements, how contracts are written, and how systems are monitored. As usual for these kind of specifications, they are long documents exposing the XML syntax of definitions and informally defining the semantics of the different constructs. This paper is aimed at proposing a formal approach for negotiating SLA based on *fuzzy set theory*.

Fuzzy set theory and *fuzzy logic* were introduced by Zadeh [14] to provide mathematical tools that could deal with the vagueness and the uncertainty that are typical of the human perception and reasoning process. The basic idea of the fuzzy approach is to allow an element s to belong to a set φ with degrees of membership ranging in the continuous real interval $[0, 1]$, rather than in $\{0, 1\}$. The use of fuzzy descriptions intuitively corresponds to the vagueness that can be always found in service level requests. For instance, suppose that C is looking for a FTP service with a bandwidth of "*about 5 Mbps*": what happens if the offered bandwidth is just 4.9 Mbps? If the constraint is expressed in a standard crisp way such as *Bandwidth $\geq$ 5 Mbps* (i.e. traditional non-fuzzy approach), this *almost acceptable* solution would be immediately discarded, while it could turn out that actually this is the *best* solution from a cost-similarity trade-off viewpoint. Placing a lower threshold on the minimum required bandwidth (e.g. 4.5 Mbps) does not solve the problem, since an *almost acceptable* solution could always be found (trivially, 4.4 Mbps) and since this constraint does not discriminate very good solutions like 5 Mbps from just acceptable solutions like 4.6 Mbps.

In this paper we focus on the contract creation phase, in which

1. service providers should be able to publish a description of the quality levels they may provide,
2. clients should be able to precisely describe their quality requirements,
3. a decision procedure allows clients and providers to reach agreements.

In particular, we propose a SLA framework based on fuzzy sets for supporting those activities. The proposed framework is presented by describing the following four elements:

- The *negotiation language*, called the SLA-calculus, that models the negotiation phase of the SLA and accounts for the creation and revocation of contracts. SLA-calculus is parametric with respect to the languages used for publishing services and making requests, and to the decision procedure used for reaching an agreement. Its main scope is to identify the key concepts involved in the negotiation phase.
- The *publication language* for specifying the offered service levels.
- The *request language* for specifying the quality levels desired by the user.
- The *agreement procedure* that allows a client C and service provider $\mathcal{P}$ to reach an agreement.

We remark that the negotiation language is orthogonal to the remaining elements. In particular, we provide two different instantiations of the framework. Fistly, we propose two basic languages for publications and requests in which all SLA parameters are handled independently. Then, we extend those languages (and consequently the agreement procedure) by allowing the definition of dependencies among different SLA parameters (for instance to say that the storage service never provide a low bandwidth and a large disk space).

Related works. Several approaches in the literature [7,11,5] have used the theory of fuzzy sets for studying the problem of finding suitable compositions of services (i.e., discovering appropriate services) that meet certain user-defined QoS requirements. We remark that our approach has a different aim, since it provides a mechanism that allows two specific services (i.e., the client and the provide) to negotiate a particular QoS level — a phase that takes place after the candidate provider has been identified. The work in [10] presents a process calculus accounting for QoS. The main idea is that any interaction is enriched with a constraint that describes its associated QoS. We envisage this approach as an appropriate model for the utilization phase, i.e., once the agreement has been reached. A calculus for dealing with negotiations, called cc-pi, is introduced in [2]. Differently from our approach, a client request and the offered service levels are described in cc-pi as constraints. There is an agreement when both constraints are consistent.

Paper Organization. Section 2 presents an overview of fuzzy set theory. Section 3 introduces the negotiation language, while Sections 4 and 5 describe two different instantiations for the publication and request languages and the corresponding decision procedure.

2   Background

This Section summarizes the basics of the fuzzy set theory. A fuzzy set is defined as

Definition 2.1 (Fuzzy set [14]). *Given a space of objects S ranged over by s, a fuzzy set φ in S is characterized by a membership function $\mu_\varphi(s) : S \to [0,1] \subset \mathbb{R}$. $\mu_\varphi(s)$ is the fuzzy degree of membership to which a generic element s belongs to φ.*

Given the fuzzy sets φ, ϕ, and ω defined on the same universe S, the usual concepts of set theory can be generalized by the following definitions.

Definition 2.2 (Empty fuzzy set). $\varphi = \varnothing \Leftrightarrow \forall s \in S, \mu_\varphi(s) = 0$.

Definition 2.3 (Equality). $\varphi = \phi \Leftrightarrow \forall s \in S, \mu_\varphi(s) = \mu_\phi(s)$.

Definition 2.4 (Intersection). *Let* $\omega = \varphi \cap \phi$, $\mu_\omega(s) = \min\{\mu_\varphi(s), \mu_\phi(s)\}$.

Definition 2.5 (Union). *Let* $\omega = \varphi \cup \phi$, $\mu_\omega(x) = \max\{\mu_\varphi(s), \mu_\phi(s)\}$.

The *similarity operator* $\mathrm{Sim}(\cdot, \cdot)$ measures the degree to which two fuzzy sets are equal. This operator is more powerful than the binary equality in Def. 2.3, and it will be used in the following sections to compare fuzzy sets. Intuitively, the operator $\mathrm{Sim}(\cdot, \cdot)$ is defined such that $\mathrm{Sim}(\varphi, \phi) = 0 \Leftrightarrow \varphi \cap \phi = \varnothing$ and $\mathrm{Sim}(\varphi, \phi) = 1 \Leftrightarrow \varphi = \phi$. Intermediate values in $[0,1]$ should be associated to gradually overlapping fuzzy sets. We choose the following definition for $\mathrm{Sim}(\cdot, \cdot)$:

$$\mathrm{Sim}(\varphi, \phi) = \frac{\displaystyle\sum_{s \in S} \mu_{\varphi \cap \phi}(s)}{\displaystyle\sum_{s \in S} \mu_{\varphi \cup \phi}(s)} . \tag{1}$$

Note that many similarity operators are available in the literature [12]. Likewise, there is no unique definition for intersection and union in fuzzy set theory: for the sake of simplicity, we select the most popular and simple implementation, but actually any *t-norm* $\otimes$ could be used as intersection and any *t-conorm* $\oplus$ could be used as union [3].

An important property of fuzzy sets is the possibility of extending traditional crisp functions to work on fuzzy sets, via the *extension principle* [3].

Definition 2.6 (Extension principle). *Let $f(s) : S \rightarrow T$ be a crisp function and φ a fuzzy set in S. Then, $\psi = f(\varphi)$ is a fuzzy set in T such that $\forall t \in T, \mu_\psi(t) = \sup_{s|t=f(s)} \mu_\varphi(s)$.*

Conversely, sometimes we may want to "defuzzify" fuzzy sets and to extract a crisp value that could serve as a prototype of the whole fuzzy set in crisp applications. To this aim, we need one of the many defuzzification methods that can be found it the literature. We will use the well known *center of gravity* method (defined as in [1]), which is particularly suitable for managing sets of numerical elements

$$\text{cog}(\varphi) = \frac{\sum\limits_{s \in S} s \cdot \mu_\varphi(s)}{\sum\limits_{s \in S} \mu_\varphi(s)} . \tag{2}$$

In the rest of the paper we will use the following notion of *linguistic variable*.

Definition 2.7 (Linguistic variable). *A linguistic variable is a variable whose values are linguistic terms. A linguistic variable V is a quintuple $(x, \mathbb{T}, S, G, \mathcal{M})$, where:*

1. *x is the name of the variable (e.g., Age);*
2. *$\mathbb{T}$ is the set of linguistic terms of variable x (e.g., {young, old});*
3. *S is the universe of discourse of the base variable;*
4. *G is a syntactic rule for generating composed terms of x (e.g., "very old");*
5. *$\mathcal{M} : F(S) \rightarrow \mathbb{T}$ is a semantic rule mapping a fuzzy set φ defined over the universe of discourse S of the base variable with each element $t \in \mathbb{T}$.*

Even thought we will not use the syntactic rule G in the following, we included it in Def. 2.7 for the sake of completeness. Note that this definition of linguistic variable is slightly different from the ones that can be found in the literature [15], which actually defines $\mathcal{M} : \mathbb{T} \rightarrow F(S)$. In fact, as it will be clear in Section 5.1, in some special cases we may want to associate a linguistic term with more than one fuzzy set. This anyway does not change the essence of $\mathcal{M}$, which is to capture the semantic mapping between linguistic terms and fuzzy sets.

3 SLA-**Calculus**

In this Section we provide an operational model for the agreement phase, which is parametric with respect to the languages used for describing services and for making quality requests. Its main scope is to expose the ingredients of the model, by showing how contracts are created, used and then revoked. A main assumption of this model is that the quality levels offered by a provider do not depend on the provider's internal state or, in other words, on the contracts it has already signed. For instance, the bandwidth offered by the storage server do not decrease as new contracts are signed. Moreover, we assume that providers do not revoke contracts. The following are the main entities of the model:

- *Service descriptions*, any of them declares the SLA parameters offered by a particular provider. Any service description may be thought as an entry on a UDDI registry. We rely on an infinite set S of service names ranged over by $s, s_0, \ldots$. Moreover, we assume SLA parameters to be described by a *provider descriptor* $D_{\mathcal{P}}$, which is a valid document of the publication language.
- *Service states*, we associate any service with a state. In our basic version, a service state collects the information of all active contracts signed by the provider. We assume $\mathbb{Q}$ to be the infinite set of contract names ranged over by $c, c_0, \ldots$.
- *Clients* describe the behavior of applications attempting to sign and revoke contracts with providers. As explained before, a client initiates a negotiation with a provider by sending a *request descriptor* D_C specifying the desired qualities of the service. The request descriptor is any valid document of the request language. If the requested SLA parameters can be assured by the provider, then the client will obtain a signed contract. Otherwise, the negotiation phase will fail.

Syntax. The following grammar defines the terms of the SLA-calculus:

$$
\text{(NET)} \qquad N ::= s[D_{\mathcal{P}}] \mid s\{c_0, \ldots, c_n\} \mid C \mid N|N \mid (vc)N
$$

$$
\text{(CLIENT)} \qquad C ::= 0 \mid c := s\langle D_C, A\rangle ?C : C \mid \dagger c.C \mid C|C
$$

A net (system) is either a service description $s[D_{\mathcal{P}}]$, where: (i) s is the service name and $D_{\mathcal{P}}$ is a description of the SLA parameters (the definition of provider descriptors are in the following Sections); (ii) a service state $s\{c_0, \ldots, c_n\}$, denoting that the provider s has signed the active contracts $c_0, \ldots, c_n$; (iii) a client C, (iv) the parallel composition of nets, and (iv) the declaration $(vc)N$ of a fresh contract c to be used in N.

A client is either (i) the inert process 0; (ii) a process $c := s\langle D_C, A\rangle ?C_1 : C_2$ that attempts to create a new contract c by negotiating with s for the qualities described by D_C and accepting under conditions A, if the negotiation succeeds then C_1 is executed (otherwise C_2 is activated); (iii) a process $\dagger c.C$ that revokes a signed contract c and then behaves like C; and (iv) the parallel composition $C_1|C_2$.

The only bound names are the occurrences of c in either $c := s\langle D, A\rangle ?C_1 : C_2$ or in $(vc)N$. All other occurrences are considered free. We will refer to terms up-to α-equivalence (denoted by $\equiv_\alpha$), i.e., up-to the renaming of bound names.

Operational Semantics. The reduction semantics of SLA-calculus is given up-to structural equivalence given by the the rules defining '$|$' as an associative and commutative operator with 0 as identity and the following ones.

$$
s\{c\} \mid s\{c_1, \ldots, c_n\} \equiv s\{c, c_1, \ldots, c_n\} \qquad\qquad N_1 \equiv N_2 \qquad \text{if } N_1 \equiv_\alpha N_2
$$

$$
(vc_1)(vc_2)N \equiv (vc_2)(vc_1)N \qquad\qquad N_1|(vc)N_2 \equiv (vc)(N_1|N_2) \text{ if } c \notin fn(N_1)
$$

The reduction semantics is inductively defined by the following rules.

(AGREEMENT)

$$\frac{D_{\mathcal{P}} \approx_{\mathcal{A}} D_C}{s[D_{\mathcal{P}}] \mid c := s\langle D_C, A\rangle ?C_1 : C_2 \quad \rightarrow \quad s[D_{\mathcal{P}}] \mid (vc)(C_1 \mid s\{c\})}$$

(PAR)

$$\frac{N_1 \rightarrow N_1'}{N_1 \mid N_2 \rightarrow N_1' \mid N_2}$$

(DISAGREEMENT)

$$\frac{D_{\mathcal{P}} \not\approx_{\mathcal{A}} D_C}{s[D_{\mathcal{P}}] \mid c := s\langle D_C, A\rangle ?C_1 : C_2 \quad \rightarrow \quad s[D_{\mathcal{P}}] \mid C_2}$$

(RESTRICTION)

$$\frac{N_1 \rightarrow N_1'}{(vc)N_1 \rightarrow (vc)N_1'}$$

(REVOKE) $\quad (vc)(\dagger c.C \mid s\{c\}) \quad \rightarrow \quad C$

Rule AGREEMENT stands for the creation of a contract. In this case there is a client $c := s\langle D_C, A\rangle ?C_1 : C_2$ starting a negotiation with the provider s by requiring the service level D_C and accepting the negotiation under conditions A. Since the levels $D_{\mathcal{P}}$ offered by the provider satisfy the user requirement (premise $D_{\mathcal{P}} \approx_{\mathcal{A}} D_C$), a new contract c (known only by the provider and the client) is created. Note this rule abstracts away from the actual agreed conditions, they are represented just by a contract name. Moreover, the service description $s[D_{\mathcal{P}}]$ is persistent. Rule DISAGREEMENT handles the cases in which the provided qualities $D_{\mathcal{P}}$ do not match the client requirements D_C and A. In this cases the exceptional flow C_2 is activated. Rule REVOKE handles the termination of a contract by decision of a client. Rules PAR and RESTRICTION are the standard ones.

Note the rules are parametric with respect to the relation $D_{\mathcal{P}} \approx_{\mathcal{A}} D_C$, which stands for the decision procedure. Examples of such relation are in the following Sections.

4   The Fuzzy Agreement Process (FAP)

This Section instantiates the SLA-calculus presented in the previous Section by proposing specific publication and requirement languages and a decision procedure. We called this particular instance the FAP. The aim of the FAP is to mimic the complex SLA interactions performed by humans, by means of a process in which (i) tolerance and vagueness are admitted both in request and offer specifications, and (ii) the matching of request and offers is evaluated with respect to the trade-offs between similarity metrics and cost considerations.

The following example illustrates the main ingredients of FAP. Let us assume a provider $\mathcal{P}$ offering a FTP service, which is described by a set of K qualities or resources. Any quality x_i is associated with k_i different service levels. Each service level has an associated cost, which is determined by a secret policy of the provider.

Example 4.1. The provider $\mathcal{P}$ offers a FTP service, characterized by the resources $x_1 = Storage$ and $x_2 = Bandwidth$, any of them offered with three different service levels, namely $\{Basic, Gold, Platinum\}$ for $Storage$ ($k_1 = 3$) and $\{Slow, Medium, Fast\}$ for $Bandwidth$ ($k_2 = 3$).

A *service configuration* associates a service level to any resource of the service. For the FTP example, *PlatinumStorage* $\wedge$ *FastBandwidth* is a valid service configuration for our

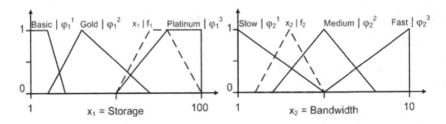

Fig. 1. Linguistic variables and fuzzy sets for the FTP service example

FTP service. In our approach, each resource is modeled by a linguistic variable, while service levels and expected qualities are expressed by using fuzzy sets defined on the universes of discourse of those linguistic variables.

Example 4.2. Fig. 1 shows the fuzzy sets describing the service levels offered by $\mathcal{P}$ (solid lines) and those corresponding to the requirements of a client C (dotted lines). All fuzzy sets are defined on the universes of discourse of the corresponding linguistic variables *Storage* and *Bandwidth*.

The following definitions formalize the publication language (i.e., the provider descriptors), the request language (i.e., the client descriptors) and the decision procedure (i.e., the relation $\approx_{\mathcal{A}}$) for the FAP instantiation.

Definition 4.1 (Provider descriptor). *A provider descriptor $D_{\mathcal{P}}$ is a pair $(\mathbb{V}, \mathbb{C})$. $\mathbb{V}$ is a set of K linguistic variables $V_1, ..., V_K$. $\mathbb{C}$ is a set of K cost functions $\Downarrow_1, ..., \Downarrow_K$, such that $\Downarrow_i \colon S_i \to U$, where S_i is the universe of discourse of the i-th linguistic variable V_i and U is the target cost universe.*

As aforementioned, linguistic variables describe resources. The name x_i of the linguistic variable V_i gives the name of the resource. We write $\Sigma = \{x_i, ..., x_K\}$ for the set of names of all linguistic variables. The service levels associated to the resource x_i are the linguistic terms $\mathbb{T}_i$ of V_i, which are associated by $\mathcal{M}_i$ to the fuzzy sets $\varphi_i^1, ..., \varphi_i^{k_i}$ defined on the corresponding universe of discourse S_i (as stated in Def. 2.7).

Example 4.3. In our FTP service, we define service levels $\mathbb{T}_1 = \{Basic, Gold, Platinum\}$ and $\mathbb{T}_2 = \{Slow, Medium, Fast\}$. Some examples of set-label associations are $\mathcal{M}_1(\varphi_1^3) = Platinum$ and $\mathcal{M}_2(\varphi_2^1) = Slow$.

Cost functions $\Downarrow_1, ..., \Downarrow_K$ are used to map each resource into a common reference universe U, and they will be used during the decision procedure to compute a global cost of a service configuration. Cost can be expressed in terms of money, time, availability or any other business-related meaningful measure. Different shapes of cost functions can represent different cost models: for instance, an important resource may have a steeper cost function than a less critical resource.

Definition 4.2 (Client descriptor). *A client descriptor D_C is a pair $(\mathbb{F}, \mathcal{A})$. $\mathbb{F}$ is a set of K pairs $\{(x_1|f_1), ..., (x_K|f_K)\}$, where f_i is a fuzzy set defined on the universe of discourse V_i of the linguistic variable named $x_i \in \Sigma$. $\mathcal{A}$ is an acceptance function $U \times [0, 1] \to \{0, 1\}$.*

$\mathbb{F}$ describes the configuration desired by the client. Indeed, a pair $(x_i|f_i)$ states that the client expects the service level described by fuzzy set f_i for the resource x_i. In this way a client C may formulate a vague request such as *"I want a bandwidth of **about** 5 Mbps"*. Note that, since fuzzy set theory extends classic set theory, it is still possible to express precise and mandatory constraints such as *"I want a bandwidth of **at least** 2 Mbps"* or *"I want a bandwidth of **exactly** 4 Mbps"*.

The acceptance function $\mathcal{A}$ is used as a classifier to discriminate acceptable from unacceptable service configurations offered by $\mathcal{P}$. In other words, $\mathcal{A}$ measures the trade-off between the cost and the similarity of the proposed configuration with respect to the original service request and decides if that solution is acceptable or not.

We remark that a client only needs the following information to be able to build a request descriptor:

1. the resource names $\Sigma = \{x_1,...,x_K\}$;
2. the universes of linguistic variable $\{S_1,...,S_K\}$;
3. the cost reference universe U.

In a real implementation, this information should be exposed by $\mathcal{P}$ in its service description, e.g., in its corresponding WSDL description. We remark that a client C needs no information about available service levels nor cost policies used by the provider. Hence, they can be kept private by the provider.

Finally, we define the decision procedure of FAP. Roughly, we say $D_C \approx_{\mathcal{A}} D_{\mathcal{P}}$ if and only if there exists (at least) a service configuration on which the client and the provider agree.

Definition 4.3 (Evaluation of $\approx_{\mathcal{A}}$). *Given $D_C = (\mathbb{F},\mathcal{A})$ and $D_{\mathcal{P}} = (\mathbb{V},\mathbb{C})$:*

Step 0. *For each resource x_i $(i = 1...K)$, and for each service level φ_i^j of x_i $(j = 1...k_i)$, let $\phi_i^j = \Downarrow_i (f_i \cap \varphi_i^j)$ be the projection on U of the overlapping between the offered level φ_i^j and the requested level f_i. Furthermore, let $s_i^j = \mathrm{Sim}(f_i, \varphi_i^j)$ be the similarity measure of the same couple of fuzzy sets.*

Step 1. *Let $\Pi = \{\pi | \pi = (\phi_1^{j_1},...,\phi_K^{j_K}), \forall i = 1...K, \forall j_i = 1...k_i \wedge s_i^{j_i} \neq 0\}$ be the set of all K-tuples representing eligible service configurations offered by $\mathcal{P}$ that have non-empty intersection with the request descriptor. Then, $\forall \pi \in \Pi$, let $\sigma(\pi) = \mathrm{cog}(\bigcup_{i=1}^K \phi_i^{j_i})$ and $\mathrm{Sim}_{\pi}(\pi) = \prod_{i=1}^K s_i^{j_i}$ be respectively the crisp global cost and the global similarity measure of π.*

Step 2. *Let $\Pi' = \{\pi \in \Pi | \mathcal{A}(\sigma(\pi), \mathrm{Sim}_{\pi}(\pi)) = 1\}$ be the set of eligible service configurations accepted by C.*

Step 3.a. *If $\Pi' \neq \varnothing$ then $D_C \approx_{\mathcal{A}} D_{\mathcal{P}}$ and let $\pi^* = \mathrm{choose}(\Pi')$ be the service configuration selected by $\mathcal{P}$'s choice function.*

Step 3.b. *If $\Pi' = \varnothing$ then $\neg(D_C \approx_{\mathcal{A}} D_{\mathcal{P}})$.*

Note that we can pass from the fuzzy sets to the linguistic description of each π at any time by simply applying $\bigwedge_{i=1}^K \mathcal{M}_i(\varphi_i^{j_i})$.

Example 4.4. We compute $\approx_{\mathcal{A}}$ for the descriptors in Fig. 1. As stated in Section 2, we use the min function as t-norm $\otimes$ and the max function as t-cornorm $\oplus$ in the implementation of $\cap$ and $\cup$, respectively (see Defs. 2.4 and 2.5).

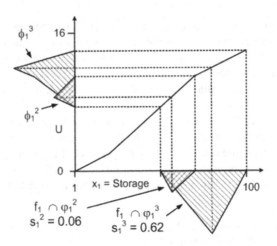

Fig. 2. The cost function of resource *Storage* and a sample application

Step 0. Fig. 2 shows the application of **Step 0** to resource *Storage*. First, fuzzy sets resulting from $f_1 \cap \varphi_1^1$, $f_1 \cap \varphi_1^2$ and $f_1 \cap \varphi_1^3$ are obtained in the original universe of discourse of *Storage* and their similarity measure is computed. Note that, as we could expect by observing Fig. 1, $f_1 \cap \varphi_1^1 = \varnothing$ and thus $s(f_1, \varphi_1^1) = 0$, while $s(f_1, \varphi_1^3) \gg s(f_1, \varphi_1^2) > 0$. Then, we use the cost function $\Downarrow_1$ and the extension principle of Def. 2.6 to project the intersections from the universe S_1 to U and thus to obtain ϕ_1^2 and ϕ_1^3 (since φ_1^1 is empty, ϕ_1^1 is also empty). The same procedure is repeated for *Bandwidth* using a very steep linear cost function $\Downarrow_2$ (i.e., *Bandwidth* is a very costly resource), obtaining $s(f_2, \varphi_2^1) = 0.34$, $s(f_2, \varphi_2^2) = 0.22$ and $s(f_2, \varphi_2^3) = 0$.

Step 1. Since $s(f_1, \varphi_1^1) = s(f_2, \varphi_2^3) = 0$, we have four eligible service configurations to include in Π: $\pi_a = (\phi_1^2, \phi_2^1)$, $\pi_b = (\phi_1^2, \phi_2^2)$, $\pi_c = (\phi_1^3, \phi_2^1)$ and $\pi_d = (\phi_1^3, \phi_2^2)$, which correspond to the linguistic descriptions *GoldStorage* $\wedge$ *SlowBandwidth*, *GoldStorage* $\wedge$ *MediumBandwidth*, *PlatinumStorage* $\wedge$ *SlowBandwidth* and *PlatinumStorage* $\wedge$ *MediumBandwidth*, respectively. We compute $\sigma(\pi_a) = \text{cog}(\phi_1^2 \cup \phi_2^1) = 9.6$ and $\text{Sim}_\pi(\pi_a) = s_1^2 \cdot s_2^1 = 0.06 \cdot 0.34 = 0.0204$, and similarly for the remaining configurations of Π.

Step 2. As shown in Fig. 3, we apply the acceptance function $\mathcal{A}(\sigma(\pi), \text{Sim}_\pi(\pi))$ provided by C to discriminate acceptable from unacceptable service configurations, thus obtaining $\Pi' = \{\pi_b, \pi_d\}$. In the figure, we can see that, for instance, π_a is discarded because its similarity with respect to the request descriptor is poor, even though it has the lowest cost. Differently, π_b falls in the acceptance region, thanks to the good trade-off between cost and similarity.

Step 3.a. Since $\Pi' \neq \varnothing$, $D_C \approx_{\mathcal{A}} D_{\mathcal{P}}$ is true. The final step is performed by $\mathcal{P}$ using its internal policies coded in the choose(Π') function to select a particular configuration π^*. For instance, $\mathcal{P}$ could alternatively select the most similar configuration (π_b), or the most costly one (π_d), or the first one in Π' (again π_b). Assuming $\mathcal{P}$ selects $\pi^* = \pi_b$, the FTP service will give to C the following service guaranties *GoldStorage* $\wedge$ *SlowBandwidth*.

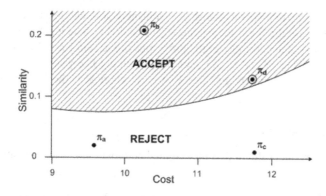

Fig. 3. Eligible configurations and the acceptance function $\mathcal{A}$

Additionally, once a configuration is selected, the provider $\mathcal{P}$ may want to fix a crisp value for each resource rather than determining only the service level, e.g., it may want to assign a *SlowBandwidth* of exactly 2 Mbps. This additional step can be performed in several ways depending on the internal policies of $\mathcal{P}$. For instance, $\mathcal{P}$ could defuzzify each $f_i \cap \varphi_i^j$ of π^*, or select a prototype point for each service level, or choose the crisp value with the highest membership degree in each $f_i \cap \varphi_i^j$ of π^*. This is a minor issue and, for the sake of simplicity, we will not enter in further details.

5   Contract Descriptors as Finite State Automata and Transducers

The FAP model cannot express complex policies such as

> Client C requests **either** a large amount of disk space with an high access throughput **or** a small amount of disk space with no particular limitation on the access throughput.

In order to describe the non-deterministic choice (**either** ... **or** ...) of quality configurations and the dependencies among the service levels of different resources, we extend the previous FAP model. In particular, we use *weighted automata* [9] to define client descriptors and *weighted transducers* [9] to define complex provider descriptors. We start by recalling the definition of semirings taken from [8], which will be used as weights in client automata and provider transducers.

Definition 5.1. *A system* $(\mathbb{K}, \oplus, \otimes, \overline{0}, \overline{1})$ *is a semiring if*

1. $(\mathbb{K}, \oplus, \overline{0})$ *is a commutative monoid with identity element* $\overline{0}$;
2. $(\mathbb{K}, \otimes, \overline{1})$ *is a monoid with identity element* $\overline{1}$;
3. $\otimes$ *distributes over* $\oplus$;
4. $\overline{0}$ *is an annihilator for* $\otimes$: $\forall e \in \mathbb{K},\ e \otimes \overline{0} = \overline{0} \otimes e = \overline{0}$.

We will write $\mathbb{K}$ as a shorthand for $(\mathbb{K}, \oplus, \otimes, \overline{0}, \overline{1})$ when the operators are clear from the context. In our framework we use the elements of fuzzy-set semiring to represent service levels. In particular, we choose the semiring whose elements are fuzzy sets and whose operators are the fuzzy intersection $\cap$ and union $\cup$. The identity and annihilator elements are chosen accordingly to the properties of the semirings. For instance, if we consider the semiring $(\mathbb{K}, \cup, \cap, \overline{0}, \overline{1})$, then $\overline{0}$ is the empty fuzzy set of Def. 2.2, while $\overline{1}$ is the fuzzy set with membership value $1 \; \forall x \in \mathbb{R}$, where $\mathbb{R}$ is the support of the fuzzy sets.

5.1 Request Descriptor

This Section introduces the notion of weighted automata and their utilization as client descriptors.

Definition 5.2. *A* client automaton *is a 6-tuple* $A_C = (\Sigma, Q, I, F, T, \mathbb{K})$ *where*

1. Σ *is the finite input alphabet;*
2. Q *is a finite set of states;*
3. $I \subseteq Q$ *is the set of the initial states;*
4. $F \subseteq Q$ *is the set of the final states;*
5. $T \subseteq Q \times \Sigma \times \mathbb{K} \times Q$ *is a finite set of weighted transitions;*
6. $\mathbb{K}$ *is a semiring over which transitions weights are defined.*

Given a transition $t_i \in T$, $p(t_i)$ denotes the origin of t_i and $n(t_i)$ the destination. For instance, let t_i be defined as follows

$$t_i = (q_i, x_i, f_i^l, q_i') \text{ with } q_i, q_i' \in Q, x_i \in \Sigma, f_i^l \in \mathbb{K} \tag{3}$$

then $p(t_i) = q_i$ and $n(t_i) = q_i'$. A path $\pi = t_1 \dots t_K \in T^*$ is defined as the composition of transitions $t_i \in T$ such that $n(t_{i-1}) = p(t_i)$ with $i = 2, \dots, K$. We extend the definitions of $p(\cdot)$ and $n(\cdot)$ to paths such that $p(\pi) = p(t_1)$ and $n(\pi) = n(t_K)$. In addition, we define a *labeling function* $\lambda : T \rightarrow \Sigma \times \mathbb{K}$ over a transition $t_i = (q_i, x_i, f_i^l, q_i')$ such that $\lambda(t_i) = (x_i | f_i^l)$. The labeling function can be extended to paths by defining $\lambda(\pi) = \lambda(t_1) \circ \dots \circ \lambda(t_K)$, where $\circ$ is the concatenation operator.

Consider the automaton in Fig. 4, where $\Sigma = \{x_1, x_2, x_3, x_4, x_5\}$, $Q = \{q_0, \dots, q_5\}$, $I = \{q_0\}$, $F = \{q_5\}$, $f_j^l \in \mathbb{K}$, and $T = \{(q_0, x_1, f_1^l, q_2), (q_0, x_2, f_1^l, q_2), \dots, (q_4, x_5, f_2^5, q_5)\}$. The labeling function applied on $\pi = t_1 t_3 t_5$ produces $\lambda(\pi) = (x_1 | f_1^1)(x_3 | f_3^1)(x_5 | f_5^1)$.

Similarly to [4], we define the acceptance set Acp for the client automaton A_C as the set of weighted strings generated by the labeling function λ on all paths π leading from an initial state $q_0 \in I$ to a final state $q_f \in F$, that is

$$Acp(A_C) = \{\lambda(\pi) | \pi \text{ is a path in } A_C, \; p(\pi) \in I, \; n(\pi) \in F\}. \tag{4}$$

In our interpretation, each automaton A_C represents a service request from a client C. The input alphabet of A_C contains the names of service qualities or resources, while $\mathbb{K}$ is the set of fuzzy sets that are used to define the service levels requested by the client. In this interpretation, the set $Acp(A_C)$ defines all the possible compositions of qualities that are acceptable for the client C together with a soft measure of the service level requested for each service.

Now, we refine the Def. 4.2 of the client descriptors as

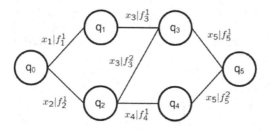

Fig. 4. A client automaton

Definition 5.3 (Client descriptor). *A client descriptor D_C is a couple $(\mathbb{F}, \mathcal{A})$. $\mathbb{F}$ is the acceptance set $Acp(A_C)$ of the acyclic weighted automaton $A_C = \{\Sigma, Q, I, F, T, \mathbb{K}\}$, having transitions $t_i \in T$ of the form (q_i, x_i, f_i^l, q_i'), where each $f_i^l \in \mathbb{K}$ is a fuzzy set defined on the universe of discourse S_i of the linguistic variable named $x_i \in \Sigma$. $\mathcal{A}$ is an acceptance function $U \times [0, 1] \rightarrow \{0, 1\}$.*

Consequently, clients may define more expressive contract descriptors in which the set $\mathbb{F}$ of alternative desired configurations is defined by a weighted automaton.

Example 5.1. Consider the automaton in Fig. 5 defining a request descriptor for the FTP service. The choice between a *BasicStorage* service and a *LargeStorage* service is expressed by the two transitions that start from the initial state q_0. Moreover, this automaton expresses that the requested level for the bandwidth depends on level offered for the storage. In particular, the client is satisfied by a large-storage service only if it is delivered together with a fast bandwidth access (path $q_0 \rightarrow q_1 \rightarrow q_3$ in Fig. 5), whereas it can accept a slow bandwidth service if it is offered in conjunction with a basic-storage service (path $q_0 \rightarrow q_2 \rightarrow q_4$). Note that the client requires different levels for the same resource depending on the path followed in the automaton. For instance, the two transitions in Fig. 5 ending in q_3 associate two different fuzzy sets (*Fast*[1] and *Fast*[2]) to the same resource *Bandwidth*.

5.2 The Provider Descriptor

In what follows we recall the definition of weighted finite state transducer (FST) of [9], which will be used for formalizing the notion of provider descriptors.

Definition 5.4. *A weighted finite state transducer is a 7-tuple*

$$FST_{\mathcal{P}} = (\Sigma_{\mathcal{P}}, C_{\mathcal{P}}, Q_{\mathcal{P}}, I_{\mathcal{P}}, F_{\mathcal{P}}, T_{\mathcal{P}}, \mathbb{K}),$$

where

1. *$\Sigma_{\mathcal{P}}$ is the finite input alphabet;*
2. *$C_{\mathcal{P}}$ is the finite output alphabet;*
3. *$Q_{\mathcal{P}}$ is a finite set of states;*
4. *$I_{\mathcal{P}} \subseteq Q_{\mathcal{P}}$ is the set of the initial states;*
5. *$F_{\mathcal{P}} \subseteq Q_{\mathcal{P}}$ is the set of the final states;*

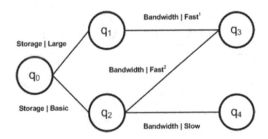

Fig. 5. Client automaton for the FTP service example

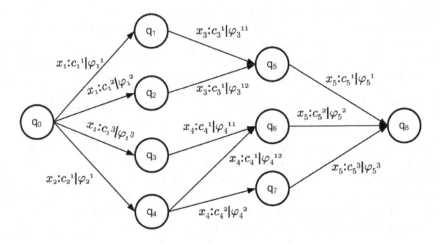

Fig. 6. A server transducer

6. $T_{\mathcal{P}} \subseteq Q_{\mathcal{P}} \times \Sigma_{\mathcal{P}} \times C_{\mathcal{P}} \times \mathbb{K} \times Q_{\mathcal{P}}$ *is a finite set of weighted transductions from the input alphabet $\Sigma_{\mathcal{P}}$ to the output alphabet $C_{\mathcal{P}}$;*

7. $\mathbb{K}$ *is a semiring over which transductions weights are defined.*

A weighted transducer is shown in Fig. 6, where the input alphabet is $\Sigma_{\mathcal{P}} = \{x_1, x_2, x_3, x_4, x_5\}$, the states are $Q_{\mathcal{P}} = \{q_0, \ldots, q_8\}$, the initial states are $I_{\mathcal{P}} = \{q_0\}$, the final states are $F_{\mathcal{P}} = \{q_8\}$ and the semiring weights are $\phi_l^{ij} \in \mathbb{K}$, where i denotes the i-th element of the input alphabet, l is the index of the l-th output symbol for a given input symbol and j (optional) is used to differentiate semiring weights for the same combination of input-output pairs.

Given a weighted FST, a path π is the composition of transitions (or transductions) $td_i \in T_{\mathcal{P}}$. We also use the operators $n(\cdot)$ and $p(\cdot)$ to refer to the origin and destination of transductions and transduction paths. The labeling function $\lambda(\cdot)$ is defined such that $\lambda(td_i) = x_i$ for a transition $td_i = (q_i, c_i^l, x_i, \phi_i^l, q_i') \in T_s$, and $\lambda(\pi) = \lambda(t_1) \circ \ldots \circ \lambda(t_K)$ for a path $\pi = t_1 \ldots t_K$. In addition, the set of the paths from q to q' is

$$\mathbb{P}(q, q') = \{\pi | p(\pi) = q, n(\pi) = q'\}, \tag{5}$$

while the set of paths from q to q' for the label $x \in \Sigma^*$ is

$$\mathbb{P}(q,x,q') = \{\pi | p(\pi) = q, n(\pi) = q', \lambda(\pi) = x\}. \tag{6}$$

Then, the provider descriptor is expressed in terms of a weighted transducer by refining the Definition 4.1.

Definition 5.5 (Provider descriptor). *A provider descriptor $D_{\mathcal{P}}$ is a couple $(FST_{\mathcal{P}}, \mathbb{C})$ where $FST_{\mathcal{P}} = (\Sigma_{\mathcal{P}}, C_{\mathcal{P}}, Q_{\mathcal{P}}, I_{\mathcal{P}}, F_{\mathcal{P}}, T_{\mathcal{P}}, \mathbb{K})$ is a weighted transducer, and where*

1. *$\Sigma_{\mathcal{P}}$ is the set containing the names x_i of the linguistic variables (or resources);*
2. *$C_{\mathcal{P}}$ is the set of linguistic terms c_i^l corresponding to service levels;*
3. *$\mathbb{K}$ is the semiring whose elements are fuzzy sets;*
4. *$\mathbb{C}$ is the set of cost projection functions $\Downarrow_i$.*

As for FAP, we have that $\forall i = 1, \ldots, K \wedge \forall l = 1, \ldots, k_i \wedge \forall j = 1, \ldots, k_i': \varphi_i^{l,j} \in \mathbb{K}$ is a fuzzy set defined on the universe of discourse S_i of the linguistic variable named $x_i \in \Sigma_{\mathcal{P}}$ and related to the linguistic term $c_i^l \in C_{\mathcal{P}}$ representing a class of service.

5.3 The Decision Procedure

In this new setting, we use the $FST_{\mathcal{P}}$ of a provider descriptor to translate the request made by a client C to the service levels offered by the provider $\mathcal{P}$. Note that any weighted string x in the request descriptor denotes a possible quality configuration desired by the client. In particular, each $(x_i | f_i) \in x$ requires the resource x_i with quality level f_i^l. Conversely, a transduction $t_i = (q_i, c_i^l, x_i, \varphi_i^j, q_i')$ describes an offer of the resource x_i with the service level c_i^l defined by the fuzzy set φ_i^j. More formally, c_i^l is a linguistic term associated to the linguistic variable x_i, on the universe S_i, such that $\mathcal{M}_i(\varphi_i^l) = c_i^l$. The provider FST translates the client requests, expressed in terms of the input alphabet $\Sigma_s = \Sigma$, to an output alphabet $C_{\mathcal{P}}$ whose elements represent the concrete service levels offered by the provider $\mathcal{P}$. Moreover, the agreement procedure calculates the degree of compliance of requested levels with the offered levels.

The translation from the input alphabet $\Sigma_{\mathcal{P}}$ to the output alphabet $C_{\mathcal{P}}$ is formalised by the following *transduction relation* $\tau : \Sigma \times T_{\mathcal{P}} \longrightarrow C_{\mathcal{P}}$ such that

$$\tau(x_i, td_i) = \begin{cases} c_i^l & \text{if } td_i = (q_i, c_i^l, x_i, \varphi_i^l, q_i') \\ \varepsilon & \text{otherwise} \end{cases} \tag{7}$$

where ε denotes the empty element of the output alphabet. The transduction relation (Equation 7) is extended to strings $x = x_1 \ldots x_K \in \Sigma^*$ and legal paths $\pi \in \mathbb{P}(q_0, x, q_f)$ as follows

$$\tau(x, \pi) = \bigcirc_{i=1}^{K} \tau(x_i, td_i) \tag{8}$$

where $\bigcirc$ denotes the concatenation operator and td_i are the transductions in π. Note that $\tau(x, \pi)$ translates a service request x to the service classes offered by the provider.

Similarly, we define a *weighting function* over strings $x = (x_1|f_i^1)\dots(x_K|f_k^l)$ and legal paths $\pi \in \mathbb{P}(q_0, x, q_f)$ as

$$\sigma(x, \pi) = \delta\left(\bigoplus_{i=1}^{K} \Downarrow_i (f_i^l \otimes \varphi_i^j)\right) \tag{9}$$

where $f_i^l \in \mathbb{K}$ is the service level requested by the client for the resource x_i, $\varphi_i^j \in \mathbb{K}$ is the weight assigning by the transduction $td_i = (q_i, c_i^l, x_i, \varphi_i^j, q_i')$, $\oplus$ and $\otimes$ are the operators on the semiring $\mathbb{K}$, $\Downarrow_i$ are the cost functions, while δ is the output function defined as the defuzzyfication operator $cog : \mathbb{K} \to U$.

Finally, the following *similarity function* calculates the similarity of the requested configuration x with the offered path π as a combination of the similarities between f_i^l and φ_i^j (i.e., the requested and offered levels) for each resource x_i. (Sim is in Equation 1)

$$\text{Sim}_\pi(x, \pi) = \prod_{i=1}^{K} \text{Sim}(f_i^l, \varphi_i^j) \tag{10}$$

The transduction relation in Equation 8 does not take into consideration the transduction weights. We extend its definition to weighted strings $x = (x_1|f_i^1)\dots(x_K|f_k^l)$ and paths $\pi \in \mathbb{P}(q_0, x, q_f)$ by using the weighting and similarity function defined so far, i.e.

$$\tau_w(x, \pi) = \begin{cases} \langle \tau(x, \pi), \sigma(x, \pi), \text{Sim}_\pi(x, \pi) \rangle & \text{if } \text{Sim}_\pi(x, \pi) \neq 0 \\ \langle \cdot \rangle & \text{otherwise} \end{cases} \tag{11}$$

where $\langle \cdot \rangle$ is the empty triplet.

Equation 11 is limited to the transduction of a single string x on a single path π. The full model takes into consideration all the requests modeled by the client automaton A_C, translating them over all eligible paths defined by the provider FST, i.e.

$$R_{FST}(Acp(A_C)) = \cup_{x \in Acp(A_C)} \cup_{\pi \in \mathbb{P}(I_\mathcal{P}, x, F_\mathcal{P})} \tau_w(x, \pi), \tag{12}$$

where $\mathbb{P}(I_\mathcal{P}, x, F_\mathcal{P})$ is the set of paths starting from an initial state $q \in I_\mathcal{P}$, ending in a final state $q' \in F_\mathcal{P}$ and labeled by $x \in \Sigma^*$, that is

$$\mathbb{P}(I_\mathcal{P}, x, F_\mathcal{P}) = \cup_{q \in I_\mathcal{P}, \, q' \in F_\mathcal{P}} \mathbb{P}(q, x, q'). \tag{13}$$

Finally, the agreement procedure is formalized as follows.

Definition 5.6 (Evaluation of $\approx_\mathcal{A}$). *Given $D_C = (Acp(A_C), \mathcal{A})$ and $D_\mathcal{P} = (FST, \mathbb{C})$:*

Step 1. *Let $\Pi = R_{FST}(Acp(A_C))$ be the set of all triplets $\langle \tau, \sigma, \text{Sim} \rangle$ representing available service configurations τ having compliance between request and offer expressed by σ and Sim.*

Step 2. *Let $\Pi' = \{\langle \tau, \sigma, \text{Sim} \rangle \in \Pi | \mathcal{A}(\sigma, \text{Sim}) = 1\}$ be the set of available service configurations accepted by the client.*

Step 3.a. *If $\Pi' \neq \varnothing$ then $D_C \approx_\mathbb{A} D_\mathcal{P}$ and let $\pi^* = \text{choose}(\Pi')$ be the service configuration selected by the provider choice function.*

Step 3.b. *If $\Pi' = \varnothing$ then $(D_C \not\approx_\mathbb{A} D_\mathcal{P})$.*

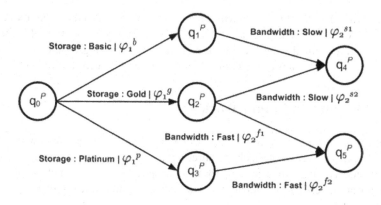

Fig. 7. Provider transducer for the FTP service example

Example 5.2. Consider the provider descriptor defined in terms of the weighted FST in Fig. 7. The provider can now express complex service allocation policies such as providing a *FastBandwidth* service only to clients requesting either a *GoldStorage* or *PlatinumStorage* service. Moreover, the provider may want to allocate *GoldStorage* clients preferentially to the *FastBandwidth* service: this can be expressed by placing a more restrictive condition on the $q_2^{\mathcal{P}} \to q_4^{\mathcal{P}}$ edge than on the $q_2^{\mathcal{P}} \to q_5^{\mathcal{P}}$ edge, that is reducing the support of φ_2^{s2} with respect to φ_2^{f1}.

Consider the client automaton described in Fig. 5, whose acceptance set is

$$Acp(A_C) = \left\{ (St|f_{large})(Bw|f_{fast^1}), (St|f_{basic})(Bw|f_{slow}), (St|f_{basic})(Bw|f_{fast^2}) \right\}$$

where we substitute *St* to *Storage* and *Bw* to *Bandwidth* to ease the notation. The client descriptor is $D_C = (Acp(A_C), \mathcal{A})$, where $\mathcal{A}$ is a suitable acceptance function.

The provider FST is defined on the signature $\Sigma_{\mathcal{P}} = \{St, Bw\}$ and on the output alphabet $C_{\mathcal{P}} = \{Basic, Gold, Platinum\} \cup \{Slow, Fast\}$, where the former set refers to the *Storage* universe and the latter to the *Bandwidth* universe. Moreover, the FST has states $Q_{\mathcal{P}} = \{q_0^{\mathcal{P}}, q_1^{\mathcal{P}}, q_2^{\mathcal{P}}, q_3^{\mathcal{P}}, q_4^{\mathcal{P}}, q_5^{\mathcal{P}}\}$, with $I_{\mathcal{P}} = \{q_0^{\mathcal{P}}\}$ and $F_{\mathcal{P}} = \{q_4^{\mathcal{P}}, q_5^{\mathcal{P}}\}$ as initial and final states, respectively. Hence, sparing the details of the transductions set $T_{\mathcal{P}}$, we obtain the provider-side contract descriptor $D_{\mathcal{P}} = (FST, \{\Downarrow_{St}, \Downarrow_{Bw}\})$, where $\Downarrow_{St}, \Downarrow_{Bw}$ are two suitable cost-projection functions on the *Storage* and *Bandwidth* universes.

By performing **Step 1** of definition 5.6, we generate the set Π of triplets containing, e.g.,

$$\tau_w(x, \pi) = \langle Basic \circ Slow, \operatorname{cog}\left(\Downarrow_{St} (\varphi_1^b \otimes f_{large}) \oplus \Downarrow_{Bw} (\varphi_2^{s1} \otimes f_{fast}^1) \right),$$

$$Sim(\varphi_1^b, f_{large}) \cdot Sim(\varphi_2^{s1}, f_{fast}^1) \rangle$$

which is obtained by considering $x = (St|f_{large})(Bw|f_{fast}^1)$ and $\pi = q_0^{\mathcal{P}} q_1^{\mathcal{P}} q_4^{\mathcal{P}}$. The operators on the fuzzy set ($\oplus$, $\otimes$), the cost-projection $\Downarrow_i$ and the defuzzyfication functions behave as described in Section 4. Therefore, after the application of **Step 1** we obtain a set of triplets whose elements are a service configuration (e.g. *BasicStorage* $\wedge$

SlowBandwidth) and two reals describing the similarity between the client request and the provider offer. These triplets are filtered by the acceptance function $\mathcal{A}$ as detailed in **Step 2** and, eventually, the provider selects a solution amongst the elements of the acceptable set Π' by means of the choice function in **Step 3** of Definition 5.6.

6   Conclusion and Future Works

This paper presents a general framework for handling SLA negotiation in which agreements rely on the fuzzy approach: required and offered quality levels are described by fuzzy sets. The described framework is at an initial phase in which many aspects deserve further investigation. In particular, we envisage the following lines:

- *Adjustment of provided service levels*: Currently, published service levels do not depend on the state of the provider. Hence, it would be interesting to resort to fuzzy theory tools for allowing the dynamic modification of the shape and position of the fuzzy sets. For instance, linguistic hedges could be used for dynamically adapting a provider descriptor when new contracts are signed, removing such adjustments when contracts are revoked by applying the corresponding inverse linguistic hedge.
- *Contract enforcement*: The SLA-calculus accounts only for SLA negotiation. We plan to extend the framework for dealing with contract enforcement, i.e., to formally explain how clients interact with providers under already signed contracts and how agreed service levels are enforced.
- *Cost models*: We plan to derive a set of off-the-shelf cost models that can help the providers in defining cost functions for their resources. For instance, cost models could be derived from usage or availability of resources. Since cost functions influence the way fuzzy sets are projected in the reference universe, each cost model should be associated with a proper aggregation and defuzzification operator.
- *Automata and transducers properties*: Our definition of weighted automata and transducers differ from the ones that can be found in the literature [9]. We plan to determine suitable composition operators, similar to those described in [9] for standard automata and FST, that can be used to define a modular approach for constructing complex client and provider descriptors by composing simpler service requests and offers.
- *Implementation*: We plan to investigate how the proposed framework can be embedded into current web service infrastructure. In particular, whether the different elements can be mapped to the de facto standards WSDL, SOAP and UDDI.

References

1. Babuska, R.: Fuzzy systems, modeling and identification. Technical report, Delft University of Technology (2001)
2. Buscemi, M., Montanari, U.: CC-Pi: A constraint-based language for specifying service level agreements. Manuscript (2006)
3. Dubois, D., Prade, H.: Fuzzy Sets and Systems - Theory and Applications. Academic Press, New York (1980)

4. Gorla, D., Hennessy, M., Sassone, V.: Security policies as membranes in systems for global computing. Logical Methods in Computer Science, 1(3) (2005)
5. Huang, C.-L., Chao, K.-M., Lo, C.-C.: A moderated fuzzy matchmaking for web services. In: CIT 2005: Proceedings fo the Fifth International Conference on Computer and Information Technology, pp. 1116–1122. IEEE Computer Society, Los Alamitos (2005)
6. Keller, A., Ludwig, H.: The WSLA framework: Specifying and monitoring service level agreements for web services. Journal of Network and Systems Management, 11(1) (2003)
7. Lin, M., Xie, J., Guo, H., Wang, H.: Solving qos-driven web service dynamic composition as fuzzy constraint satisfaction. In: EEE '05: Proceedings of the 2005 IEEE International Conference on e-Technology, e-Commerce and e-Service (EEE'05) on e-Technology, e-Commerce and e-Service, pp. 9–14. IEEE Computer Society, Washington, DC, USA (2005)
8. Mohri, M.: Semiring frameworks and algorithms for shortest-distance problems. Journal of Automata Languages and Combinatorics 7(3), 321–350 (2002)
9. Mohri, M.: Weighted finite-state transducer algorithms: An overview. In: Martín-Vide, C., Mitrana, V., Paun, G. (eds.) Formal Languages and Applications. LNCS, vol. 148, Springer, Heidelberg (2004)
10. De Nicola, R., Ferrari, G., Montanari, U., Pugliese, R., Tuosto, E.: A formal basis for reasoning on programmable qos. In: Dershowitz, N. (ed.) Verification: Theory and Practice. LNCS, vol. 2772, pp. 436–479. Springer, Heidelberg (2003)
11. Di Penta, M., Troiano, L.: Using fuzzy logic to relax constraints in GA-based service composition. In: GECCO '05: Proceedings of the 2005 Genetic and Evolutionary Computation Conference (2005)
12. Setnes, M., Babuska, R., Kaymak, U., van Nauta Lemke, H.R.: Similarity measures in fuzzy rule base simplification. IEEE Transactions on Systems, Man, and Cybernetics, Part B 28(3), 376–386 (1998)
13. Web services agreement specification (ws-agreement). version 2005/09 (2005)
14. Zadeh, L.A.: Fuzzy Sets. Information and Control 3(8), 338–353 (1965)
15. Zimmermann, H.-J.: Fuzzy set theory and its applications, 3rd edn. Kluwer Academic Publishers, Norwell, MA, USA (1996)

Scheduling to Maximize Participation[*]

Ioannis Caragiannis, Christos Kaklamanis, Panagiotis Kanellopoulos,
and Evi Papaioannou

Research Academic Computer Technology Institute &
Department of Computer Engineering and Informatics
University of Patras, 26500 Rio, Greece
{caragian,kakl,kanellop,papaioan}@ceid.upatras.gr

Abstract. We study a problem of scheduling client requests to servers. Each client has a particular latency requirement at each server and may choose either to be assigned to some server in order to get serviced provided that her latency requirement is met or not to participate in the assignment at all. From a global perspective, in order to optimize the performance of such a system, one would aim to maximize the number of clients that participate in the assignment. However, clients may behave selfishly in the sense that each of them simply aims to participate in an assignment and get serviced by some server where her latency requirement is met with no regard to the overall system performance. We model this selfish behavior as a strategic game, show how to compute equilibria efficiently, and assess the impact of selfishness on system performance. We also show that the problem of optimizing performance is computationally hard to solve, even in a coordinated way, and present efficient approximation and online algorithms.

1 Introduction

We are motivated by the following scenario where clients aim to retrieve some objects (e.g., video/audio files) from servers (each server can be thought of as an electronic store). Each client requests one object which may exist in some of the servers. In order to get serviced, the client has to connect to the server and download the object. The service time (or latency) for a client connected to a server is proportional to the number of simultaneous connections to that server. Clients may value differently the service received from each server in the sense that if the latency is high enough, the client may decide not to receive the object from that server and close the connection. A client may connect to a server and download the requested object if the current load of the server is within her valuation criterion; of course, this action could regret some other client connected to the server who will decide not to get serviced by that server and will make another choice. A client may decide not to get serviced at all if no server meets her valuation criterion.

---

[*] This work was partially supported by the European Union under IST FET Integrated Project 015964 AEOLUS.

U. Montanari, D. Sannella, and R. Bruni (Eds.): TGC 2006, LNCS 4661, pp. 218–232, 2007.

Naturally, such a scenario of selfish behavior can be modeled using the notion of a strategic game from game theory. We define a particular class of games called SMP games. In an SMP game, we have a set of clients C and a set of servers M. Each client $c \in C$ has a non-negative finite integer latency bound ℓ_c^k at each server $k \in M$. Clients are non-cooperative in the sense that each client wishes to be assigned to some server where her latency bound is satisfied; otherwise, she prefers not to be assigned to any server. Given an assignment of some of the clients to servers, an SMP game is defined by the following payoff function for each client: a client assigned to a server k together with $n_k - 1$ other clients has payoff 1 if $\ell_c^k \geq n_k$ and payoff -1 otherwise. A client that is not assigned to any server has zero payoff. We say that an assignment is *valid* if no client has payoff -1. An assignment is a *pure Nash equilibrium* (or, simply, an *equilibrium*) for an SMP game if no client has an incentive to unilaterally change her strategy. Clearly, any equilibrium is a valid assignment. The benefit of an assignment for an SMP game is the sum of the payoffs of all clients. Hence, the benefit of a valid assignment equals the number of clients accommodated in servers. We use the notion of the *price of anarchy* introduced in [20] (see also [16]) to assess the quality of equilibria of SMP games. The price of anarchy of an SMP game is defined as the ratio of the benefit of an optimal assignment for the SMP game over the benefit of the worst equilibrium.

Selfish behavior could be bypassed by having a *scheduler* which knows the load of each of the available servers, receives the requests of the clients for objects together with their latency bound for each server, and coordinates the assignment of clients to servers. Although such an approach would be inappropriate and unrealistic in a networked environment, it is important to consider it in order to compare it with the uncoordinated case and assess selfish behavior. Furthermore, it gives rise to an interesting combinatorial optimization problem which we call *scheduling to maximize participation* (SMP). Although scheduling optimization problems (focusing mainly on minimizing some function of the server latencies when all clients must be assigned to a server, e.g., see [17]) and corresponding games (such as load balancing [6,8,12,13,15,16,18] and congestion games [1,7,21]) have been extensively studied in the literature, to the best of our knowledge, SMP has not been studied before.

Our main motivating question concerns the efficient construction of equilibria in SMP games. In Section 2, we first present a Nashification technique which, starting from a valid assignment, converges to an equilibrium by making a polynomial number of client moves. This is motivated by [12] where a similar in spirit technique has been applied to a different scheduling game. We also show that the price of anarchy of any SMP game is at most 2. Hence, the Nashification technique provides an algorithm for approximating both the best and the worst equilibrium within a factor of 2; these two problems are proved to be APX-hard. An important property of our Nashification technique is that the benefit of the equilibrium computed is not smaller than the benefit of the initial assignment. So, in order to compute equilibria of large benefit, it suffices to compute valid assignments of large benefit. We use the term SMP to refer to the optimization problem that corresponds to the problem of computing a valid assignment of maximum benefit.

In Section 3, we present a $\frac{e}{e-1} \approx 1.58$-approximation SMP algorithm based on linear programming and randomized rounding. SMP can be thought of as a special case of *combinatorial auctions*. In the problem of combinatorial auctions, we have a set of players and a set of items. A feasible allocation assigns every item to at most one player. For every player, her utility function w_i is defined over the set of items that she receives. The goal is to find a feasible allocation that maximizes social welfare $\sum_i w_i(S_i)$, where S_i is the set of items allocated to player i. In SMP, the servers correspond to players and the clients correspond to items; the utility of a set of clients for a server is the maximum number of clients from this set that can be assigned to the server in any valid assignment. Recent work [9,10,11] presents $\frac{e}{e-1}$-approximation algorithms (also based on linear programming and randomized rounding) for combinatorial auctions when the utility functions have special properties (e.g., subadditivity). However, these techniques are rather impractical since they make use of the ellipsoid method in order to solve the corresponding linear programming relaxation which is of exponential size. The LP corresponding to SMP has also an exponential number of variables. In this paper, for SMP, we exploit the structure of the problem and prove that SMP is equivalent to a constrained integral flow problem whose LP relaxation is of polynomial size and, hence, it can be solved by practical linear programming algorithms. Then, randomized rounding in our case is simpler compared to [9,10,11]. On the negative side, we show that the problem is APX-hard by showing an explicit inapproximability result of $368/367$ using a reduction from multidimensional matching (this result also implies the APX-hardness of the problem of computing the best equilibrium for an SMP game).

In Section 4, we consider the online version of SMP where clients (together with their latency bound vector) appear online and an irrevocable decision has to be made when each client c appears. This means that client c can either be rejected or put in a server so that neither the latency bounds of previously assigned clients nor the latency bound of c herself is violated. This can be thought of as the problem of computing an efficient valid assignment for an SMP game when information about the game is gradually revealed to the algorithm. Here, we assess the quality of the solution in terms of the *competitive ratio* [4] (or *competitiveness*) defined as the maximum over all SMP sequences of the ratio of the optimal benefit over the expected benefit of the assignment computed by the algorithm. In general, we assume that sequences are generated by oblivious adversaries which may have knowledge of the probability distribution that may be used by the algorithm but have no access to its random choices (if any). The online version is inherently more difficult to approximate since, as we prove, no deterministic algorithm is better than T-competitive while no randomized algorithm can be better than H_T-competitive against oblivious adversaries, where T is the ratio of the maximum over the minimum non-zero latency bound over all clients and servers and H is the harmonic function. On the positive side, we show an asymptotically tight upper bound by presenting an $O(\ln T)$-competitive randomized algorithm that needs to know T in advance. In the case where no information about T is known in advance, a slightly inferior competitiveness bound is obtained. Our online algorithms are based on the *classify-and-randomly-select* paradigm (see [4]) which has been proved to be useful in other problems (e.g., call admission control in communication networks [2,3], online independent set problems [5], etc.).

2   Equilibria and Price of Anarchy

We begin by presenting our Nashification technique. We describe algorithm Nashify which starts from a valid assignment for an SMP game consisting of a set C of n clients and a set M of m servers and works as follows. It proceeds in rounds. Denote by n_k^i the number of clients assigned to server k at the beginning of round i. In each round, algorithm Nashify performs one step for each server $k \in M$. In each step of a round i, at most two moves are performed. If there exists a client c not assigned to any server which has latency bound $l_c^k > n_k^i$, c moves to server k. If there exists another client c' in server k with $l_{c'}^k = n_k^i$ (i.e., her latency bound is violated by the move of client c), then client c' moves out of server k (and is not assigned to any server). Algorithm Nashify terminates when no move is performed during a whole round. We prove the following statement.

Theorem 1 (Nashification). *For any* SMP *game with n clients and m servers, algorithm* Nashify *computes an equilibrium of benefit not smaller than the benefit of the initial assignment by performing at most $2nm$ moves.*

Proof. The assignment produced by algorithm Nashify is valid since the condition that the number of clients in any server is not greater than the latency bound of each client assigned to this server remains true after each step of the algorithm. It is also an equilibrium since, by the termination criterion, no unassigned client has an incentive to move to any server. Furthermore, during a step, a client may move out of a server only if another client moves to this server. Hence, the benefit of the final assignment is not smaller than the benefit of the initial one. In order to prove the upper bound on the total number of moves, observe that a client c that moves out of a server k at some round i has $l_c^k = n_k^i$. Since the number of clients at server k never decreases in later rounds, client c will never move to server k again. So, the total number of moves each of the n clients can make is at most $2m$ (one move in and one move out for each of the m servers).   □

Implicitly, in the proof of Theorem 1 we also prove that SMP games always have equilibria. The next result states that their benefit is fairly large.

Theorem 2. *The price of anarchy of any* SMP *game is at most 2.*

Proof. Consider an equilibrium for an SMP game on a set of servers M and an optimal assignment. We denote by o_j the number of clients that are in server j in the optimal assignment. Let n_j be the number of clients in server j in the equilibrium and R_j be the set of clients that are in server j in the optimal assignment but are not assigned to any server in the equilibrium. Consider a client $c \in R_j$ for some server j. Since c is in server j in the optimal assignment, it holds that $\ell_c^j \geq o_j$. Since c is not assigned to any server in the equilibrium, it holds that $\ell_c^j \leq n_j$, otherwise c would have an incentive to move to server j. Thus, $o_j \leq n_j$ for any server j for which $R_j \neq \emptyset$. It holds that

$$\sum_{j \in M} o_j = \sum_{j \in M: R_j = \emptyset} o_j + \sum_{j \in M: R_j \neq \emptyset} o_j \leq \sum_{j \in M: R_j = \emptyset} o_j + \sum_{j \in M: R_j \neq \emptyset} n_j$$

$$\leq \sum_{j \in M} n_j + \sum_{j \in M: R_j \neq \emptyset} n_j \leq 2 \sum_{j \in M} n_j \qquad \qquad \square$$

The above result is tight since there exists a simple matching lower bound consisting of two servers a, b and two clients x, y with $\ell_x^a = \ell_x^b = \ell_y^a = 1$ and $\ell_y^b = 0$. In the optimal solution, x is assigned to b and y is assigned to a, while the assignment where x is assigned to a and y is not assigned to any server is an equilibrium.

Algorithm Nashify is essentially a 2–approximation algorithm for computing the best equilibrium for SMP games. Starting from any initial valid assignment for an SMP game, it computes an equilibrium which (by Theorem 2) has benefit at least half the optimal benefit. In Section 3, we present an algorithm that computes a valid assignment of benefit at most 1.58 times smaller than the optimal benefit. Combined with algorithm Nashify, this yields a 1.58–approximation algorithm for computing the best equilibrium for SMP games. Clearly, algorithm Nashify is also a 2–approximation algorithm for computing the worst equilibrium for SMP games.

Concerning the hardness of approximation of the problem of computing the best equilibrium for SMP games, this follows by a statement in the next section where we show that the problem of computing the best valid assignment is APX-hard. The next theorem shows that the problem of computing the worst equilibrium is APX-hard as well.

Theorem 3. *The problem of computing the worst equilibrium for* SMP *games is APX-hard.*

Proof. We will show that there are instances of the problem which are equivalent to instances of MINIMUM MAXIMAL BIPARTITE MATCHING which is known to be APX-hard [22]. An instance of MINIMUM MAXIMAL BIPARTITE MATCHING consists of a bipartite graph $G(U, V, E)$ and the objective is to compute a maximal matching of minimum size. A matching is called maximal if we cannot obtain another matching by adding one extra edge to it. Consider such an instance consisting of a bipartite graph $G(U, V, E)$ and construct an SMP game consisting of a client for each node of U and a server for each node of V. The latency bound of a client corresponding to a node $u \in U$ is 1 to each server corresponding to a node $v \in V$ such that $(u, v) \in E$ and 0 otherwise. We will show that there exists a maximal matching in G of size K if and only if the SMP game has an equilibrium of benefit K. Consider a maximal matching in

G consisting of K edges. Then, an equilibrium for the SMP game is defined as follows. For each edge (u, v) in the matching, the client corresponding to node u is assigned to the server corresponding to node v. The fact that M is a matching guarantees that each client is assigned to at most one server and each server receives at most one client, i.e., the assignment is valid. In order to prove that it is also an equilibrium, observe that since the matching is maximal there is no edge $(u, v) \in E \backslash M$ such that neither u nor v is an endpoint of an edge in M. Hence, no client that is not assigned to any server has an incentive to move to some server. Similarly, consider an equilibrium for the SMP game. Each client is assigned to at most one server and, by the definition of the latency bounds, each server contains at most one client. Hence, the set consisting of the edges (u, v) where $v \in V$ corresponds to a server containing the client corresponding to node $u \in U$ is a matching in G. Since the assignment is an equilibrium, no client c among those not assigned to any server has an incentive to move to some server k such that $\ell_c^k = 1$ because server k already contains some other client. This implies that all edges in $E \backslash M$ are adjacent to some edge in M which means that M is maximal.   □

3 Computation of Efficient Valid Assignments

In this section, we present an algorithm that computes valid assignments for SMP instances. The algorithm is based on linear programming and randomized rounding and achieves an approximation guarantee of $\frac{e}{e-1} \approx 1.58$.

Given an instance of SMP consisting of a set C of n clients and a set M of m servers, we say that a set of clients $A \subseteq C$ is valid for server $k \in M$ if $\ell_c^k \geq |A|$ for each client $c \in A$. Hence, a valid set for server k is a set of clients which can be accommodated in server k in a solution of SMP. Now, SMP is to select one valid set of clients for each server so that the valid sets selected are disjoint and the total number of clients in valid sets selected is maximized. This is equivalent to the following integer linear program:

$$\text{(ILP)} \quad \text{maximize} \quad \sum_{k \in M} \sum_{A \in \mathcal{A}_k} x_A^k |A|$$

$$\text{subject to} \quad \sum_{k \in M} \sum_{A \in \mathcal{A}_k : c \in A} x_A^k \leq 1, \text{ for any } c \in C$$

$$\sum_{A \in \mathcal{A}_k} x_A^k \leq 1, \text{ for any } k \in M$$

$$x_A^k \in \{0, 1\}, \text{ for any } k \in M \text{ and } A \in \mathcal{A}_k.$$

where $\mathcal{A}$ denotes the set of all valid sets and $\mathcal{A}_k$ denotes the set of valid sets for server k. The variable x_A^k denotes whether the valid set A is selected at server k. The constraints guarantee that each client is assigned to at most one server (i.e., it belongs to at most one valid set) and that at most one valid set is selected for each server.

We will first show that (ILP) is equivalent to a constrained integral flow problem in a particular polynomially sized network N presented in the following. For each server $k = 1, ..., m$ the network has three nodes s_k (called the source node associated with server k), s'_k, and t_k (called the sink node associated with server k) and, for each $i = 1, ..., n$, it has two nodes u_i^k and v_i^k. For each server $k = 1, ..., m$, node s_k is connected through a directed link to node s'_k, and for each $i = 1, ..., n$, node s'_k is connected through a directed link to node u_i^k, while node v_i^k is connected through a directed link to node t_k. For each server $k = 1, ..., m$, each $i = 1, ..., n$, each $j = 1, ..., i$, and each client $c \in C$, the network has two nodes $w_i^k(c, j)$ and $z_i^k(c, j)$. For each server $k = 1, ..., m$ and each $i = 1, ..., n$, node u_i^k is connected through a directed link to all nodes $w_i^k(c, 1)$ for each client c such that $\ell_c^k \geq i$. All nodes $z_i^k(c, i)$ are connected through a directed link to node v_i^k. For each server $k = 1, ..., m$, each $i = 1, ..., n$, and each $j = 1, ..., i$, node $w_i^k(c, j)$ is connected to node $z_i^k(c, j)$. For each server $k = 1, ..., m$, we fix an ordering π_k of the clients in C (i.e., π_k assigns a distinct integer in $\{1, 2, ..., n\}$ to each client) such that $\pi_k(c') > \pi_k(c)$ implies $\ell_{c'}^k \geq \ell_c^k$. For each server $k = 1, ..., m$, each $i = 2, ..., n$, and each $j = 1, ..., i - 1$, node $z_i^k(c, j)$ is connected to nodes $w_i^k(c', j + 1)$ for all clients c' with $\pi_k(c') > \pi_k(c)$. All edges have unit capacity. The edge connecting nodes $w_i^k(c, j)$ and $z_i^k(c, j)$ (for some client $c \in C$, each server $k = 1, ..., m$, each $i = 1, ..., n$, and each $j = 1, ..., i$) belongs to the edge-set E_c of client c. Such edges are called *client edges*. An example of this construction is presented in Figure 1.

We observe that there is an $1 - 1$ correspondence between valid sets of clients and source-sink paths in N. Indeed, consider a valid set of clients $A = \{c_1, c_2, ..., c_i\}$ for server k and assume without loss of generality that $\pi_k(c_j) < \pi_k(c_{j+1})$, for $j = 1, ..., i - 1$. Then, nodes s_k and t_k are connected through the path

$$\langle s_k, s'_k, u_i^k, w_i^k(c_1, 1), z_i^k(c_1, 1), w_i^k(c_2, 2), z_i^k(c_2, 2), ..., w_i^k(c_i, i), z_i^k(c_i, i), v_i^k, t_k \rangle.$$

Similarly, consider a path p from node s_k to node t_k in network N. By the definition of the network, the path consists of the subpath $\langle s_k, s'_k, u_i^k \rangle$, a subpath

$$p' = \langle u_i^k, w_i^k(c_1, 1), z_i^k(c_1, 1), w_i^k(c_2, 2), z_i^k(c_2, 2), ..., w_i^k(c_i, i), z_i^k(c_i, i), v_i^k \rangle$$

connecting node u_i^k to node v_i^k, and the subpath $\langle v_i^k, t_k \rangle$ for some i. The client edges in subpath p' belong to different clients since an edge connecting node $z_i^k(c_j, j)$ to $w_i^k(c_{j+1}, j + 1)$ implies that $\pi_k(c_j) < \pi_k(c_{j+1})$. Consequently, it holds that $\ell_{c_j}^k \leq \ell_{c_{j+1}}^k$ for $j = 1, ..., i - 1$. Furthermore, an edge connecting node u_i^k to $w_i^k(c_1, 1)$ implies that $\ell_{c_1}^k \geq i$. So, it holds that $\ell_{c_j}^k \geq i$ for $j = 1, ..., i$, i.e., the set of clients $\{c_1, c_2, ..., c_i\}$ is valid.

Now, SMP can be thought of as the following constrained integral flow problem: the objective is to push flow f from the source nodes to the sink nodes so that the flow f_e carried by each edge e is integral, the capacity constraints are maintained (i.e., $f_e \leq 1$ for each edge e), the total flow carried by all edges in the edge-set E_c is at most 1 for each client $c \in C$, and the quantity

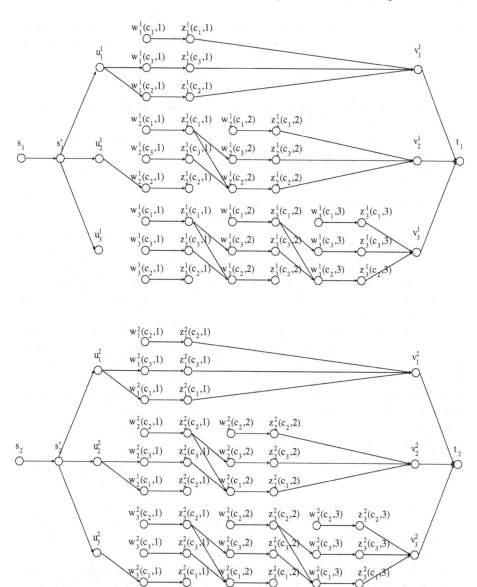

Fig. 1. The corresponding network constructed by the algorithm of Section 3 for an instance of SMP with two servers 1 and 2 and three clients c_1, c_2, c_3 with latency bounds $\ell_{c_1}^1 = 0$, $\ell_{c_1}^2 = 3$, $\ell_{c_2}^1 = 2$, $\ell_{c_2}^2 = 0$, $\ell_{c_3}^1 = 1$, and $\ell_{c_3}^2 = 2$. The ordering in each server is defined as $\pi_1(c_1) = 1$, $\pi_1(c_2) = 3$, $\pi_1(c_3) = 2$ and $\pi_2(c_1) = 3$, $\pi_2(c_2) = 1$, $\pi_2(c_3) = 2$. An optimal solution to the corresponding constrained integral flow problem consists of the paths $\langle s_1, s_1', u_1^1, w_1^1(c_2, 1), z_1^1(c_2, 1), v_1^1, t_1 \rangle$ and $\langle s_2, s_2', u_2^2, w_2^2(c_3, 1), z_2^2(c_3, 1), w_2^2(c_1, 2), z_2^2(c_1, 2), v_2^2, t_2 \rangle$ corresponding to the assignment of client c_2 to server 1 and clients c_1 and c_3 to server 2.

$\sum_{k \in M} \sum_{i=1}^{n} i \cdot f_{(v_i^k, t_k)}$ is maximized. The constraints imply that the solution to the constrained integral flow problem will consist of at most one path connecting each source node to its corresponding sink node so that the client edges in these paths belong to different clients. The quantity to be maximized equals the number of client edges that carry some flow. Equivalently, we obtain at most one valid set of clients per server so that the valid sets are disjoint and contain a maximum number of clients for the original SMP instance.

Since, as we show later in this section, SMP is APX-hard, we cannot hope to solve optimally the constrained integral flow problem. Instead, we relax the integrality constraint and solve the corresponding constrained fractional flow problem by transforming it to a linear program. Here, the variables of the linear program represent the flow f_e carried by each edge e and the constraints of the linear program are either flow conservation constraints at the network nodes, or capacity constraints at the network edges, or require that the total flow carried by the edges of the edge-set of any client is at most 1. Note that, although (ILP) has an exponential number of variables, the constrained fractional flow problem can be expressed as a linear program with polynomial number of variables and constraints since the network constructed has at most $O(n^3 m)$ nodes and $O(n^4 m)$ edges.

Once we have a solution to the constrained fractional flow problem, we can obtain a solution to the linear programming relaxation of (ILP) obtained by relaxing the integrality constraint to $x_A^k \geq 0$. This can be done by decomposing the flow into flow paths using a folklore *path stripping* technique. For $k = 1, ..., m$, we pick the edge e carrying the smallest non-zero amount of flow between nodes s_k and t_k and compute a path p from s_k to t_k that contains e and consists of edges carrying non-zero amounts of flow. We set the flow carried by the flow path p to $\hat{f}_p = f_e$ and decrease the flow on each edge in p by f_e. We repeat this procedure and decompose all flow between nodes s_k and t_k into flow paths. Note that the number of paths obtained in this way is not greater than the number of edges in the network since, in each step, the flow variable of some edge is decreased to zero. After performing path stripping, we obtain a fractional solution to the linear programming relaxation of (ILP) by setting $x_A^k = \hat{f}_p$ for each valid set of clients A corresponding to a flow path p carrying a non-zero amount of flow $\hat{f}_p$ between nodes s_k and t_k and implicitly setting all other variables to 0.

In order to obtain an integral feasible solution to (ILP), we will use randomized rounding. Due to the special structure of SMP, randomized rounding and its analysis are simpler compared to [9,10,11]. We cast a die for each server k having one face for each valid set $A \in \mathcal{A}_k$ with $x_A^k > 0$ (with probability that this face is the outcome of the die-casting equal to x_A^k) and an additional face corresponding to the fact that no client is accepted at server k (with the probability that this face is the outcome of the die-casting equal to $1 - \sum_{A \in \mathcal{A}_k} x_A^k$). After performing the die-castings for all servers, we perform a correction procedure by assigning each client c to that server k (if any) where a set containing client c is the outcome of the die-casting for server k; if more than one die-castings have outcomes containing the same client, then client c is assigned to one of the corresponding servers arbitrarily. The assignment produced is valid since the first set of constraints of (ILP) is guaranteed by the correction procedure while the second set of constraints is guaranteed by randomized rounding. Clearly, all sets produced by the correction procedure are valid since removing a client from a valid set still gives a valid set of clients.

Lemma 1. *Given an instance of* SMP, *the algorithm computes a valid assignment with expected benefit at least* $1 - \frac{1}{e}$ *times the optimal benefit.*

Proof. Denote by Y_c the $0/1$ random variable denoting whether client c is contained in some of the valid sets selected after the application of randomized rounding. The probability that a client is contained in some of the valid sets for server k selected after the randomized rounding is $\sum_{A \in \mathcal{A}_k : c \in A} x_A^k$ and, since die-castings are performed independently, the probability that a client $c \in C$ is contained in some of the valid sets selected after the randomized rounding is

$$\Pr[Y_c = 1] = 1 - \prod_{k \in M} \left(1 - \sum_{A \in \mathcal{A}_k : c \in A} x_A^k \right) \geq 1 - \exp\left(- \sum_{k \in M} \sum_{A \in \mathcal{A}_k : c \in A} x_A^k \right)$$

where the inequality follows since $\prod_{i=1}^{n} (1 - x_i) \leq \exp(-\sum_{i=1}^{n} x_i)$ when $x_i \in [0, 1]$.

Denote by $\hat{x}_A^k$ the solution obtained after the application of the correction procedure. Since a client that is contained in some valid set selected by the randomized rounding procedure also appears in exactly one valid set after the correction procedure, the benefit of the final solution is $\sum_{k \in M} \sum_{A \in \mathcal{A}_k} \hat{x}_A^k |A| = \sum_{c \in C} Y_c$. Hence, we obtain that the expected benefit of the final solution is

$$\mathcal{E}\left[\sum_{k \in M} \sum_{A \in \mathcal{A}_k} \hat{x}_A^k |A| \right] = \mathcal{E}\left[\sum_{c \in C} Y_c \right]$$

$$= \sum_{c \in C} \Pr[Y_c = 1]$$

$$\geq \sum_{c \in C} \left(1 - \exp\left(- \sum_{k \in M} \sum_{A \in \mathcal{A}_k : c \in A} x_A^k \right) \right)$$

$$\geq \sum_{c \in C} (1 - e^{-1}) \sum_{k \in M} \sum_{A \in \mathcal{A}_k : c \in A} x_A^k$$

$$= (1 - e^{-1}) \sum_{c \in C} \sum_{k \in M} \sum_{A \in \mathcal{A}_k : c \in A} x_A^k$$

$$= (1 - e^{-1}) \sum_{k \in M} \sum_{A \in \mathcal{A}_k} x_A^k |A|$$

$$\geq (1 - e^{-1}) \sum_{k \in M} \sum_{A \in \mathcal{A}_k} x_A^{*k} |A|$$

where x^* denotes the optimal integral SMP solution. The second inequality follows since $1 - \exp(-x) \geq (1 - e^{-1})x$ when $x \in [0, 1]$ and due to the constraint of the linear program. □

The algorithm can be forced to obtain a ratio which is within any constant $\epsilon > 0$ close to $\frac{e}{e-1}$ with high probability by applying the randomized rounding procedure $O(1/\epsilon)$ times; this follows by a simple application of the Markov inequality [19]. The next statement summarizes the discussion in this section.

Theorem 4. *There exists an $\frac{e}{e-1} \approx 1.58$-approximation algorithm for* SMP.

On the negative side, we show that SMP is APX-hard.

Theorem 5. *For any $\epsilon > 0$, it is NP-hard to approximate* SMP *within* $368/367 - \epsilon$.

Proof. We use a reduction from 6-dimensional matching which is known to be APX-hard. An instance of 6-dimensional matching consists of a 6-uniform 6-partite hypergraph G and the objective is to compute a matching of maximum size in G (i.e., a set of hyperedges of maximum cardinality in which no two of them share any node). In particular, [14] shows that there exist instances of 6-dimensional matching consisting of a 6-uniform 6-partite hypergraph with n nodes and $n/2$ edges for which, for any $\epsilon \in (0, 1/46)$, it is NP-hard to decide whether the maximum matching has size at least $(1-\epsilon)\frac{n}{6}$ or at most $\left(\frac{22}{23} + \epsilon\right)\frac{n}{6}$.

Given such an instance I_{6DM} of 6-dimensional matching consisting of a hypergraph G, we construct the instance I_{SMP} of SMP that contains a server for each hyperedge of G, a client for each node of G and $\frac{5n}{2}$ additional clients. Each of the additional clients has latency bound 5 at all servers while the client corresponding to node v of G has latency bound 6 at each server corresponding to hyperedges of G containing v and latency bound 5 at all other servers.

We say that a solution to I_{SMP} is maximal if it contains at least 5 clients per server. Note that given a solution to I_{SMP}, we can compute a maximal solution of at least the same benefit by accommodating additional clients to the servers that contain less than 5 clients. We observe that any solution for I_{6DM} of cardinality K can be converted to a maximal solution for I_{SMP} of benefit $\frac{5n}{2} + K$ by assigning to each server corresponding to a hyperedge in the solution of I_{6DM} the clients corresponding to nodes contained in the hyperedge and 5 of the additional clients to any other server. Similarly, any maximal solution for I_{SMP} of benefit $\frac{5n}{2} + K$ can be converted to a solution for I_{6DM} of cardinality K by simply considering the hyperedges corresponding to servers with 6 clients. Hence, if for some $\epsilon \in (0, 1/46)$ we could decide whether the optimal benefit for I_{SMP} is above $\left(\frac{368}{23} - \epsilon\right)\frac{n}{6}$ or below $\left(\frac{367}{23} + \epsilon\right)\frac{n}{6}$ then we could decide whether the maximum matching in I_{6DM} has cardinality at least $\left(\frac{368}{23} - \epsilon\right)\frac{n}{6} - \frac{5n}{2} = (1-\epsilon)\frac{n}{6}$ or at most $\left(\frac{367}{23} + \epsilon\right)\frac{n}{6} - \frac{5n}{2} = \left(\frac{22}{23} + \epsilon\right)\frac{n}{6}$. $\square$

4   Online Algorithms

In this section we consider the online version of SMP. Observe that deterministic online algorithms for SMP are at least T-competitive, where T is the ratio of the maximum over the minimum latency bound over all clients. To see this, consider an instance of SMP where a single server is available, a deterministic algorithm

A and an offline adversary $\mathcal{ADV}$ working as follows. First, the adversary presents one client of latency bound 1. If the algorithm A rejects the client, the adversary stops the sequence; in this case A has no benefit. Otherwise (i.e., if A accepts the client of latency bound 1), the adversary presents T clients each with latency bound T. In this case, the benefit of the algorithm A is 1, while the optimal benefit is T.

In what follows, using Yao's Minimax Principle (see [4,19]), we prove a lower bound on the competitive ratio of any randomized online SMP algorithm against oblivious adversaries. In our proof, we use the following lemma.

Lemma 2 (Minimax Principle [4,19]). *Given a probability distribution $\mathcal{P}$ over sequences of clients, denote by $\mathcal{E}_\mathcal{P}[B_A]$ and $\mathcal{E}_\mathcal{P}[B_{OPT}]$ the expected benefit of a deterministic algorithm A and the expected optimal benefit on sequences of clients generated according to $\mathcal{P}$. Define the competitiveness $c_A^\mathcal{P}$ of A under $\mathcal{P}$ to be*

$$c_A^\mathcal{P} = \frac{\mathcal{E}_\mathcal{P}[B_{OPT}]}{\mathcal{E}_\mathcal{P}[B_A]}$$

and let c be the minimum of $c_A^\mathcal{P}$ over all deterministic algorithms A. Then, c is a lower bound on the competitiveness of any randomized algorithm A_R against an oblivious adversary.

Our lower bound is the following.

Theorem 6. *Any (possibly randomized) online SMP algorithm has competitive ratio at least H_T against oblivious adversaries, where T is the ratio of the maximum over the minimum latency bound over all clients and servers.*

Proof. We will prove that there exists an adversary $\mathcal{ADV}$ that presents sequences of clients with latency bounds between 1 and T according to a probability distribution $\mathcal{P}$ in such way that no deterministic algorithm can be better than H_T–competitive under $\mathcal{P}$. Then, the theorem will follow by Lemma 2.

The adversary $\mathcal{ADV}$ runs at most T phases at a single server. At phase i, $1 \leq i \leq T$, it presents i clients of latency bound i. The adversary $\mathcal{ADV}$ starts with phase 1. After running phase i with $1 \leq i \leq T - 1$, $\mathcal{ADV}$ tosses a coin with probability $\Pr[\text{heads}] = \frac{1}{i+1}$. On heads, it stops the sequence; on tails, it proceeds to phase $i + 1$. After having run phase T, the adversary $\mathcal{ADV}$ stops the sequence.

Consider an algorithm and assume that the first client it accepts belongs to phase i. Since the latency bound of this client is i, the algorithm cannot accept more than $i - 1$ additional clients. So, the best the algorithm can do is to accept all clients of phase i. Thus, in order to prove the lower bound, it suffices to consider the deterministic algorithm A_t (for $t = 1, ..., T$) that waits for the first $t - 1$ phases of the sequence accepting no clients and (if phase t is run) accepts all t clients of phase t. Clearly, algorithm A_1 has benefit 1. The probability that the adversary runs phase t is $\frac{1}{t}$ (which is the probability that the adversary $\mathcal{ADV}$ continues after each of the first $t - 1$ phases). So, A_t has benefit t with probability $\frac{1}{t}$ and no benefit with probability $1 - \frac{1}{t}$. Hence, the expected benefit of A_t under $\mathcal{P}$ is 1.

The optimal benefit for a sequence produced by $\mathcal{ADV}$ is obtained by accepting all clients of the last phase of the sequence. Denote by p_i the probability that phase i is the last phase the adversary runs. It is $p_T = \frac{1}{T}$ while for $i = 1, ..., T - 1$ it is $p_i = \frac{1}{i(i+1)}$. We obtain that the expected optimal benefit under $\mathcal{P}$ is
$$\mathcal{E}_{\mathcal{P}}[B_{OPT}] = \sum_{i=1}^{T} i \cdot p_i = \sum_{i=1}^{T} \frac{1}{i} = H_T. \qquad \square$$

In the following, we present the randomized online SMP algorithm Classify. Assume that the algorithm knows in advance the values $\ell_{\min}$ and $\ell_{\max}$ of the minimum and maximum non-zero latency bounds of any client of the sequence at any server. Let $T = \ell_{\max}/\ell_{\min}$. The algorithm uses a parameter γ (to be defined later) and equiprobably selects an integer i from 0 to $\lceil \log_\gamma T \rceil - 1$. When a client appears, the algorithm checks whether her latency bound at some server is in the interval $[\ell_{\min}\gamma^i, \ell_{\min}\gamma^{i+1})$ and whether assigning the client to this server is feasible in the sense that neither the latency bound of previously accepted clients at this server nor the latency bound of the client herself at this server are violated. If such a server exists, the algorithm assigns the client to this particular server (ties are broken arbitrarily); otherwise, it rejects the client. We prove the following theorem.

Theorem 7. *Algorithm* Classify *has competitive ratio at most* $1 + \gamma + \frac{1+\gamma}{\ln \gamma} \ln T$ *against oblivious adversaries.*

Proof. Denote by OPT the optimal set of clients of the sequence. We define a partition of OPT in $\lceil \log_\gamma T \rceil$ disjoint subsets OPT_i of OPT for $i = 0, ..., \lceil \log_\gamma T \rceil - 1$. For each client c and integer $i = 0, ..., \lceil \log_\gamma T \rceil - 1$, denote by F_c^i the set of servers at which the client c has latency bound in the interval $[\ell_{\min}\gamma^i, \ell_{\min}\gamma^{i+1})$. A client c belongs to OPT_i if it is accepted at a server in F_c^i in the optimal solution.

Assume that algorithm Classify has selected integer i. Then, it considers the original sequence as a new sequence σ_i where each client c has latency bound $\ell_c'^k = \ell_c^k$ if $k \in F_c^i$ and $\ell_c'^k = 0$, otherwise. Denote by O_i the optimal set of clients for σ_i. By the definition of the sequence σ_i and the set OPT_i, it is $|O_i| \geq |OPT_i|$.

First, we show that the benefit B_i of the algorithm Classify when it selects integer i is $B_i \geq \frac{1}{\gamma+1}|O_i| \geq \frac{1}{\gamma+1}|OPT_i|$. Denote by A and R the sets of clients accepted and rejected, respectively, by the algorithm Classify when it selects integer i. For each server k, denote by A_k the set of clients accepted at server k by algorithm Classify and by O_i^k the set of clients accepted at server k in the optimal solution for σ_i. Since the latency bound of any client in A_k at server k is at most γ times smaller than the latency bound of any client in $R \cap O_i^k$ at server k and since no client from $R \cap O_i^k$ can fit in server k, it holds that $|A_k| \geq \frac{1}{\gamma}|R \cap O_i^k|$. So, for the benefit B_i we have

$$B_i = |A| \geq \frac{1}{\gamma+1}|A| + \frac{\gamma}{\gamma+1}\sum_k |A_k| \geq \frac{1}{\gamma+1}|A \cap O_i| + \frac{1}{\gamma+1}\sum_k |R \cap O_i^k|$$
$$= \frac{1}{\gamma+1}(|A \cap O_i| + |R \cap O_i|) = \frac{1}{\gamma+1}|O_i| \geq \frac{1}{\gamma+1}|OPT_i|.$$

Now, by linearity of expectation, we obtain that the expected benefit of the algorithm is

$$E[B] = \sum_{i=0}^{\lceil \log_\gamma T \rceil - 1} (\Pr[i \text{ is selected}] \cdot B_i) \geq \frac{1}{(1+\gamma)\lceil \log_\gamma T \rceil} \sum_{i=0}^{\lceil \log_\gamma T \rceil - 1} |OPT_i|$$

$$\geq \frac{1}{(1+\gamma)(1+\log_\gamma T)} |OPT|.$$

Hence, the competitive ratio of the algorithm is $1 + \gamma + \frac{1+\gamma}{\ln \gamma} \ln T$.   □

The expression in Theorem 7 is minimized to approximately $4.6 + 3.59 \ln T$ for $\gamma = 3.6$. Note that we have assumed that algorithm Classify knows the maximum and minimum over the non-zero latency bounds of all clients at all servers ℓ_{max} and ℓ_{min} in advance (and, consequently, it knows their ratio T). If it only knows T, when the first client appears, it may assume $\ell_{max} = \ell T$ and $\ell_{min} = \max\{1, \ell/T\}$ where ℓ is any non-zero latency bound of the first client appeared at some server. Then, the analysis proceeds along very similar lines to the proof of Theorem 7 and yields a competitive ratio only a constant factor worse than that of Theorem 7.

If T is not known in advance, we can adapt algorithm Classify by applying a recent technique from [5] to obtain an algorithm with slightly worse competitiveness.

Theorem 8. *There exists a randomized online* SMP *algorithm with competitive ratio at most* $O\left(\prod_{i=1}^{\log^* T} \log^{(i)} T\right)$ *against oblivious adversaries that does not require knowledge of T in advance.*

Note that function $\log^{(i)}$ is defined as $\log^{(i)} T = \log\left(\log^{(i-1)} T\right)$ for $i > 1$ and $\log^{(1)} T = \log T$ while $\log^* T$ denotes the number of times we have to apply log to T in order to get a result smaller than 2.

References

1. Awerbuch, B., Azar, Y., Epstein, A.: The price of routing unsplittable flow. In: Proc. of the 37th Annual ACM Symposium on Theory of Computing (STOC '05), pp. 57–66 (2005)
2. Awerbuch, B., Azar, Y., Fiat, A., Leonardi, S., Rosen, A.: Online competitive algorithms for call admission in optical networks. Algorithmica 31(1), 29–43 (2001)
3. Awerbuch, B., Bartal, Y., Fiat, A., Rosen, A.: Competitive nonpreemptive call control. In: Proc. of the 5th Annual ACM-SIAM Symposium on Discrete Algorithms (SODA '94), pp. 312–320 (1994)
4. Borodin, A., El-Yaniv, R.: Online computation and competitive analysis. Cambridge University Press, Cambridge (1998)
5. Caragiannis, I., Fishkin, A., Kaklamanis, C., Papaioannou, E.: Randomized online algorithms and lower bounds for computing large independent sets in disk graphs. Discrete Applied Mathematics 155(2), 119–136 (2007)

6. Caragiannis, I., Flammini, M., Kaklamanis, C., Kanellopoulos, P., Moscardelli, L.: Tight bounds for selfish and greedy load balancing. In: Bugliesi, M., Preneel, B., Sassone, V., Wegener, I. (eds.) ICALP 2006. LNCS, vol. 4051, pp. 311–322. Springer, Heidelberg (2006)

7. Christodoulou, G., Koutsoupias, E.: The price of anarchy of finite congestion games. In: Proc. of the 37th Annual ACM Symposium on Theory of Computing (STOC '05), pp. 67–73 (2005)

8. Czumaj, A., Vöcking, B.: Tight bounds for worst-case equilibria. In: Proc. of the 13th Annual ACM-SIAM Symposium on Discrete Algorithms (SODA '02), pp. 413–420 (2002)

9. Dobzinski, S., Schapira, M.: An improved approximation algorithm for combinatorial auctions with submodular bidders. In: Proc. of the 17th Annual ACM-SIAM Symposium on Discrete Algorithms (SODA '06), pp. 1064–1073 (2006)

10. Feige, U.: On maximizing welfare when utility functions are subadditive. In: Proc. of the 38th Annual ACM Symposium on Theory of Computing (STOC '06), pp. 41–50 (2006)

11. Feige, U., Vondrak, J.: The allocation problem with submodular utility functions. In: Proc. of the 47th Annual IEEE Symposium on Foundations of Computer Science (FOCS '06) (to appear)

12. Feldmann, R., Gairing, M., Lücking, T., Monien, B., Rode, M.: Nashification and the coordination ratio for a selfish routing game. In: Baeten, J.C.M., Lenstra, J.K., Parrow, J., Woeginger, G.J. (eds.) ICALP 2003. LNCS, vol. 2719, pp. 514–526. Springer, Heidelberg (2003)

13. Fotakis, D., Kontogiannis, S., Koutsoupias, E., Mavronicolas, M., Spirakis, P.: The structure and complexity of Nash equilibria for a selfish routing game. In: Widmayer, P., Triguero, F., Morales, R., Hennessy, M., Eidenbenz, S., Conejo, R. (eds.) ICALP 2002. LNCS, vol. 2380, pp. 123–134. Springer, Heidelberg (2002)

14. Hazan, E., Safra, S., Schwartz, O.: On the complexity of approximating k-dimensional matching. In: Arora, S., Jansen, K., Rolim, J.D.P., Sahai, A. (eds.) RANDOM 2003 and APPROX 2003. (Extended version as ECCC Report TR03-020) LNCS, vol. 2764, pp. 83–97. Springer, Heidelberg (2003)

15. Koutsoupias, E., Mavronicolas, M., Spirakis, P.: Approximate equilibria and ball fusion. Theory of Computing Systems 36(6), 683–693 (2003)

16. Koutsoupias, E., Papadimitriou, C.: Worst-case equilibria. In: Meinel, C., Tison, S. (eds.) STACS 99. LNCS, vol. 1563, pp. 404–413. Springer, Heidelberg (1999)

17. Leung, J.Y-T. (ed.): Handbook of scheduling: algorithms, models, and performance analysis. CRC Press, Boca Raton (2004)

18. Mavronicolas, M., Spirakis, P.: The price of selfish routing. In: Proc. of the 33rd Annual ACM Symposium on Theory of Computing (STOC '01), pp. 510–519 (2001)

19. Motwani, R., Raghavan, B.: Randomized Algorithms. Cambridge University Press, Cambridge (1995)

20. Papadimitriou, C.: Algorithms, Games and the Internet. In: Proc. of the 33rd Annual ACM Symposium on Theory of Computing (STOC '01), pp. 749–753 (2001)

21. Roughgarden, T., Tardos, E.: How bad is selfish routing? Journal of the ACM 49(2), 236–259 (2002)

22. Yannakakis, M., Gavril, F.: Edge dominating sets in graphs. SIAM Journal on Applied Mathematics 38(3), 364–372 (1980)

On the Limits of Cache-Oblivious Matrix Transposition*

Francesco Silvestri

Dipartimento di Ingegneria dell'Informazione, Università di Padova
Via Gradenigo 6/B, I-35131 Padova, Italy
francesco.silvestri@dei.unipd.it

Abstract. Intuitively, a cache-oblivious algorithm implements an adaptive strategy which runs efficiently on any memory hierarchy without requiring previous knowledge of the parameters of the hierarchy. For this reason, cache-obliviousness is an attractive feature of an algorithm meant for a global computing environment, where software may be run on a variety of different platforms for load management purposes. In this paper we present a negative result on cache-obliviousness, namely, we show that an optimal cache-oblivious algorithm for the fundamental primitive of matrix transposition cannot exist without the *tall cache* assumption, which forces the (unknown) parameters of the memory hierarchy to satisfy a certain technical relation. Our contribution specializes the result of Brodal and Fagerberg for general permutations to matrix transposition, and provides further evidence that the tall cache assumption is often necessary to attain optimality in the context of cache-oblivious algorithms.

1 Introduction

A global computer infrastructure may be employed to provide dependable and cost-effective access to a number of platforms of varying computational capabilities, irrespective of their physical location or access point. This is, for example, the case of grid environments which enable sharing, selection, and aggregation of a variety of geographically distributed resources. In such a scenario, many different platforms can be available to run applications. For load management reasons, the actual platform(s) onto which an application is ultimately run, may be not known at the time when the application is designed. Hence, it is useful to design applications which adapt automatically to the actual platform they run on.

A typical modern platform features a hierarchical cascade of memories whose capacities and access times increase as they grow farther from the CPU. In order to amortize the larger cost incurred when referencing data in distant levels of the hierarchy, blocks of contiguous data are replicated across the faster levels, either

* This work was supported in part by the EU/IST Project "AEOLUS", and by MIUR of Italy under project "ALGONEXT".

U. Montanari, D. Sannella, and R. Bruni (Eds.): TGC 2006, LNCS 4661, pp. 233–243, 2007.
© Springer-Verlag Berlin Heidelberg 2007

automatically by the hardware (e.g., in the case of RAM-cache interaction) or by software (e.g., in the case of disk-RAM interaction). The rationale behind such a hierarchical organization is that the memory access costs of a computation can be reduced when the same data are frequently reused within a short time interval, and data stored at consecutive addresses are involved in consecutive operations, two properties known as *temporal* and *spatial locality of reference*, respectively.

Many models have been proposed to explicitly account for the hierarchical nature of the memory system. A two-level memory organization, intended to represent a disk-RAM hierarchy, is featured by the *External Memory* (EM) model of Aggarwal and Vitter [1], which has been extensively used in the literature to develop efficient algorithms that deal with large data sets, whose performance is mainly affected by the number of disk accesses (see [2] for an extensive survey on external memory algorithms). In this model, operations can only be performed on data residing in RAM, and data are transfered between the RAM and the disk in blocks of fixed size, under the explicit control of the program which decides where the blocks loaded from disk are placed in RAM and chooses the eviction policy.

Another popular model featuring a two-level memory organization, intended to represent a RAM-cache hierarchy, is the *Ideal Cache* (IC) model, introduced in [3]. As in the EM model, in the IC operations can only be performed on data residing in the fast level, the cache, and data are moved in fixed-size blocks (*cache lines*) between the RAM and the cache. However, unlike the EM model, block transfers are performed automatically by the hardware whenever an operand is referenced which is not in cache, and an optimal eviction policy is assumed. Algorithm design on the IC aims at minimizing the number of RAM-cache transfers, called *misses*, and the number of operations performed. The model has received considerable attention in the literature as the base for the design of so called *cache-oblivious* algorithms, which run efficiently without knowledge of the cache parameters, namely the cache size and the cache line size. Most importantly, cache-oblivious algorithms attaining an optimal number of misses on the IC can be shown, under certain circumstances, to attain optimal number of misses at all levels of any multi-level cache hierarchy [3].

For these reasons, efficient cache-oblivious algorithms are attractive in a global computing environment since they run efficiently on platforms featuring different memory hierarchies without requiring previous knowledge of the hierarchy parameters. A number of optimal cache-oblivious algorithms [3,4] and data structures [5] have been proposed in literature for important problems, e.g. sorting, matrix transposition and searching.

In several cases, optimality of cache-oblivious algorithms is attained under the so-called *tall cache assumption* which requires that the cache size in words be at least the square of the cache line size in words. In [3] the authors raised the natural question of whether there is a gap in asymptotic complexity between cache-oblivious algorithms and algorithms which know the parameters of the memory hierarchy. Only few works in the literature have investigated this issue.

Recently, Brodal and Fagerberg [6] have proved that an optimal cache-oblivious algorithm for sorting cannot exist without the tall cache assumption, and that an optimal cache-oblivious algorithm for general permutations does not exist regardless of the tall cache assumption. Impossibility results of a similar flavor have been proved by Bilardi and Peserico [7] in the context of DAG computations on a model of memory hierarchy which does not account for the spatial locality of reference, namely the HMM [8].

In this work, we specialize the results of [6] by showing that an optimal cache-oblivious algorithm for matrix transposition cannot exist without the tall cache assumption. To this purpose we follow a similar approach as the one employed in [6]. Specifically, let $\mathcal{A}$ be a cache-oblivious algorithm for matrix transposition and consider the two sequences of misses generated by the executions of $\mathcal{A}$ on two different ICs, where one model satisfies the tall cache assumption while the other does not. We simulate these two executions on the EM model and obtain a new EM algorithm for the matrix transposition problem. By adapting the argument used in [1] to bound from below the number of disk accesses of transposition in the EM model, we conclude that $\mathcal{A}$ cannot be optimal in both ICs.

The rest of the paper is organized as follows. In Section 2 we give a formal definition of the IC and EM models, and of the matrix transposition problem. Next, Section 3 describes the simulation technique while Section 4 applies this technique to prove the limits of cache-oblivious transposition. Section 5 concludes with some final remarks.

2 Preliminaries

2.1 The Models

Two models of memory hierarchy are used in this work. The first one is the *Ideal Cache* $IC(M, B)$, introduced by Frigo *et al.* in [3], which consists of an arbitrarily large main memory and a (data) cache of M words. The memory is split into blocks of B adjacent words called *B-blocks*, or simply blocks if B is clear from the context. The cache is fully associative and organized into M/B lines of B words: each line is empty or contains a B-block of the memory. The processor can only reference words that reside in cache: if a referenced word belongs to a block in a cache line, a *cache hit* occurs; otherwise there is a *cache miss* and the block has to be fetched into a line, replacing the line's previous content. The model adopts an optimal off-line replacement policy, i.e. it replaces the block whose next access is furthest in the future. We denote as *work complexity* the running time of an algorithm in the conventional RAM model, and as *cache (miss) complexity* the number of misses.

The concept of *cache-oblivious* algorithm is also introduced in [3], as an algorithm whose specifications are independent of cache parameters (M and B); it is easy to see that a cache-oblivious algorithm is formulated as a traditional RAM algorithm. We restrict our attention to optimal cache-oblivious algorithms, which reach the best cache complexity when executed on each IC model. Most of the cache-oblivious algorithms proposed in literature are optimal only under the *tall cache* assumption, i.e. $M \geq B^2$. On the contrary, we denote a cache where $M < B^2$ as *short cache*.

The second model is the *External Memory* $EM(M, B)$ of Aggarwal and Vitter [1]; it features two levels of memory: a (fast) RAM memory of M words and a (slow) disk of unbounded size. As the memory in the IC, the disk storage is partitioned into blocks of B adjacent words called *B-blocks*, or simply blocks if B is clear from the context. The processor can only reference words that reside in memory. The movements between the memory and the disk are performed as follows: an input operation moves a B-block of the disk into B words of the memory, and an output operation moves B words of the memory into a B-block of the disk. The input/output operations (*I/Os*) are directly controlled by the algorithm through fetch and eviction operations, which is the main difference between IC and EM. We denote as *I/O complexity* of an algorithm the number of I/Os performed by the algorithm. We require an algorithm to store its output in the slow memory at the end of its execution; this will increase the I/O complexity of $O(M/B)$ I/Os, which is negligible when the input size is sufficiently large. It is easy to see that there is a relation between an I/O and a miss: a miss requires the fetching of a B-block from memory and the eviction of a B-block from cache if there is no empty line; hence a miss is equivalent to at most two I/Os in the EM, and for these reasons we will intentionally mix the two terms.

2.2   The Matrix Transposition Problem

Let G be a $p \times q$ matrix and $H = G^T$ its transpose; specifically, H is a $q \times p$ matrix where $H(j, i) = G(i, j)$, $0 \leq i < p$ and $0 \leq j < q$. Without loss of generality, we suppose the size of each entry be one machine word; therefore the overall sizes of G and H are $N = pq$ words each. Since we are only interested to the limits of cache-oblivious matrix transposition, we may safely assume that p and q are much greater than M.

Lemma 1. *Any algorithm for matrix transposition requires at least*[1]

$$\Omega\left(\frac{N \log M}{B \log(1 + M/B)}\right)$$

I/Os (resp., misses) on $EM(M, B)$ *(resp.,* $IC(M, B)$*) if* $\min\{p, q\} \geq M$.

Proof. (Sketch) The proof is presented in [1] and the same argument carries through on the $IC(M, B)$ model.

In [1] an optimal algorithm for matrix transposition is described which is parametric in B and M. Moreover, in [3] a cache-oblivious algorithm is presented, but its optimality is guaranteed only under the tall cache assumption. The interesting question arises of whether there exists an optimal cache-oblivious algorithm without the tall cache assumption, i.e. for each value of M and B. In the following sections, we will prove that such an algorithm does not exist.

---

[1] We use the following notation: log for base 2 logarithms and ln for natural logarithms.

3 The Simulation Technique

In this section we describe a technique for obtaining an EM algorithm from two executions of a cache-oblivious algorithm on two different IC models. The technique is presented in a general form and is a formalization of the *ad-hoc* one employed in [6] for proving the impossibility result for general permutations.

More precisely, consider two models $C_1 = \text{IC}(M, B_1)$ and $C_2 = \text{IC}(M, B_2)$ where $B_1 < B_2$. Let A be a cache-oblivious algorithm for an arbitrary problem and let t_1 and t_2 be its cache complexities on the two models, respectively. We define an algorithm A' for $\text{EM}(2M, B_2)$ which emulates in parallel the executions of A on both C_1 and C_2 and solves the same problem of A.

Let us regard the RAM in $\text{EM}(2M, B_2)$ as partitioned into two contiguous portions of size M each, which we refer to as M_1 and M_2, respectively. In turn, portion M_1 is subdivided into blocks of B_1 words (which we call B_1-*rows*), and portion M_2 is subdivided into blocks of B_2 words (which we call B_2-*rows*), so that we can establish a one-to-one mapping between the cache lines of C_1 and the B_1-rows of M_1, and a one-to-one mapping between the cache lines of C_2 and the B_2-rows of M_2. Algorithm A' is organized so that its I/Os occur exclusively between disk and M_2 and coincide (except for some slight reordering) with the movements of cache lines between RAM and cache performed by A in C_2; on the other hand, all operations prescribed by A are executed by A' on data in $M_1{}^2$. The movements of cache lines between RAM and cache performed by A in C_1 will be emulated by movements of B_1-rows between M_1 and M_2. (For convenience, we assume that B_2 is a multiple of B_1.)

Let us now see in detail how the execution of A' on $\text{EM}(2M, B_2)$ develops. Initially all words in both M_1 and M_2 are empty, that is, filled with NIL values, and the EM disk contains the same data of C_2 memory (or C_1 indistinguishably) with the same layout (a one-to-one relation between B_2-blocks of C_2 and B_2-blocks of the disk can be simply realized). Let α_i be the ith operation of A, $i = 1 \ldots h$. The execution of A on C_i, $1 \leq i \leq 2$, can be seen as a sequence $\mathcal{L}_i$ of operations interleaved with I/Os. Since operations in $\mathcal{L}_1$ and $\mathcal{L}_2$ are the same, we build a new sequence $\mathcal{L} = \Gamma_1^2 \Gamma_1^1 \alpha_1 \ldots \Gamma_j^2 \Gamma_j^1 \alpha_j \ldots \Gamma_h^2 \Gamma_h^1 \alpha_h \Gamma_{h+1}^2 \Gamma_{h+1}^1$. Each Γ_j^i, $1 \leq j \leq h+1$ and $1 \leq i \leq 2$, is defined as follows:

- Γ_1^i is the sequence of I/Os that precedes α_1 in $\mathcal{L}_i$.
- Γ_j^i, $1 < j \leq h$, is the sequence of I/Os which are enclosed between α_{j-1} and α_j in $\mathcal{L}_i$.
- Γ_{h+1}^i is the sequence of I/Os performed after α_h in $\mathcal{L}_i$.

Note that a Γ_j^i can be empty. The length of $\mathcal{L}$, denoted as $|\mathcal{L}|$, is the sum of the number h of operations and the size of all Γ_j^i with $1 \leq j \leq h$ and $1 \leq i \leq 2$. Let A' be divided into $|\mathcal{L}|$ phases. The behaviour of the jth phase is determined by the jth element l_j of $\mathcal{L}$:

---

[2] Note that the operations of A do not include I/Os since block movements are automatically controlled by the machine. Moreover, A's operations are the same no matter whether execution is on C_1 or C_2.

- l_j *is an operation:* $\mathcal{A}'$ executes the same operation on $\mathcal{M}_1$.
- l_j *is an input of a B_2-block (i.e. an input of $\mathcal{L}_2$):* $\mathcal{A}'$ fetches the same B_2-block from the disk and moves it into the B_2-row of $\mathcal{M}_2$ associated with the line used in $\mathcal{C}_2$.
- l_j *is an input of a B_1-block (i.e. an input of $\mathcal{L}_1$):* let x be such B_1-block and x' be the B_2-block containing x. Since there is no prefetch in the IC model, the following operation of $\mathcal{A}$ requires an element in x; thus x' must be in $\mathcal{C}_2$ cache too. For this reason, we can assume that x' was, or has just been, fetched into a B_2-row of $\mathcal{M}_2$. $\mathcal{A}'$ copies the block x in the right B_1-row of $\mathcal{M}_1$ and replaces the copy of x in $\mathcal{M}_2$ with B_1 NIL values.
- l_j *is an output of a B_2-block (i.e. an output of $\mathcal{L}_2$):* $\mathcal{A}'$ moves the respective B_2-row of $\mathcal{M}_2$ to the disk, replacing it with B_2 NIL values.
- l_j *is an output of a B_1-block (i.e. an output of $\mathcal{L}_1$):* let x be such B_1-block and x' be the B_2-block containing x. If x' is still in $\mathcal{M}_2$, then $\mathcal{A}'$ copies x from $\mathcal{M}_1$ into x' and replaces x's row with B_1 NIL values. The second possibility (i.e. x' is not in $\mathcal{M}_2$) can be avoided since no operations are executed between the evictions of x' and x. If some operations had been executed, both blocks x and x' must be kept in cache (and so in $\mathcal{M}_1$ and $\mathcal{M}_2$). Therefore, we can suppose x was removed just prior to the eviction of x'; exactly, x is moved into x', x's row is filled with B_1 NIL values, and x' is evicted from $\mathcal{M}_2$ (see previous point).

It is easy to see that every operation of $\mathcal{A}$ can be executed by $\mathcal{A}'$ on $\mathcal{M}_1$, since there is a one to one relation between cache lines and matrix rows (excluding the B_1-blocks whose evictions from cache were anticipated, see fifth point). $\mathcal{M}_2$ is a "semimirror" of C_2, in the sense that it contains the same B_2-blocks of C_2 while $\mathcal{A}$ is being executed, except for those sub B_1-blocks which are also in $\mathcal{M}_1$. By rules 2 and 4, the I/O complexity of $\mathcal{A}'$ is $\Theta(t_2)$.

Let $K = t_1 B_1 / t_2$; it is easy to see that $K \leq B_2$. Indeed, if K was greater than B_2, an algorithm for $\mathcal{C}_1$ which requires $t_2 B_2 / B_1 < t_1$ IOs would be built from the execution of $\mathcal{A}$ on $\mathcal{C}_2$; but this is a contradiction since t_1 is optimal.

$\mathcal{A}'$ can be changed so that there are at most K words exchanged between $\mathcal{M}_1$ and a B_2-block in $\mathcal{M}_2$ before this block is removed from cache. It is sufficient to insert a dummy eviction/insertion of the B_2-block: in this way the I/O complexity is increased by a constant factor: $T = \Theta(t_2) + 2t_1 B_1 / K = \Theta(t_2)$.

We define the *working set* $W(t)$ after t I/Os as the content of $\mathcal{M}_1$ plus the words in the B_2-blocks of $\mathcal{M}_2$ that will be used by $\mathcal{A}'$ (moved to $\mathcal{M}_1$) before the large blocks are evicted. When $\mathcal{A}'$ fetches a B_2-block from the disk, we can suppose that at most K elements, which will be moved between $\mathcal{M}_1$ and the block, are immediately included in the working set.

4   Matrix Transposition

In this section we prove that an optimal cache-oblivious algorithm for the matrix transposition problem does not exist without the tall cache assumption.

Let $\mathcal{A}$ be a cache-oblivious algorithm for matrix transposition and assume, for the sake of contradiction, that it attains optimal cache complexity without requiring the tall cache assumption. In particular, consider two models $\mathcal{C}_1 = \mathsf{IC}(M, B_1)$ and $\mathcal{C}_2 = \mathsf{IC}(M, B_2)$ where $B_1 < B_2$ and let t_1 and t_2 be the cache complexities of $\mathcal{A}$ on the two models, respectively. We will show that B_1 and B_2 can be suitably chosen so that the tall cache assumption holds for $\mathcal{C}_1$ but not for $\mathcal{C}_2$, and that t_1 and t_2 cannot be both optimal, thus reaching a contradiction. To achieve this goal, we apply the simulation technique described in the previous section to $\mathcal{A}$, and we obtain an algorithm $\mathcal{A}'$ for $\mathsf{EM}(2M, B_2)$ which solves the matrix transposition problem. We then apply an adaptation of the lower bound argument by [1] to $\mathcal{A}'$, and we prove the impossibility of the simultaneous optimality of $\mathcal{A}$ on the two IC models.

More precisely, let the ith target group t_i, $1 \leq i \leq N/B_2$, be the records that will ultimately be in the ith B_2-block of the output matrix H (remember that H must be in the disk at the end of $\mathcal{A}'$). We define the following convex function:

$$f(x) = \begin{cases} x \log x & \text{if } x > 0; \\ 0 & \text{if } x = 0. \end{cases}$$

Let y be a B_2-block of the disk or a B_2-row of $\mathcal{M}_2$; the *togetherness rating* of y after t I/Os is defined as:

$$C_y(t) = \sum_{i=1}^{N/B_2} f(x_{i,y}),$$

where $x_{i,y}$ denotes the number of elements in y belonging to the ith target group. These elements are not included in the working set $W(t)$ and are not NIL symbol. We also define the togetherness rating for the working set $W(t)$:

$$C_W(t) = \sum_{i=1}^{N/B_2} f(m_i),$$

where m_i is the number of elements in the working set $W(t)$ which belong to the ith target group and are not NIL symbol. The *potential function* of $\mathcal{A}'$ after t I/Os is defined as:

$$POT(t) = C_W(t) + \sum_{y \in disk} C_y(t) + \sum_{y \in \mathcal{M}_2} C_y(t).$$

At the beginning of the algorithm, $POT(0) = 0$ since $N > \min\{p, q\} > B_2$; at the end of $\mathcal{A}'$, $POT(T) = N \log B_2$, where T is the I/O complexity of $\mathcal{A}'$.

Note that the above potential function is slightly different from the one defined in [1]: there, the potential function is given by the sum of disk and memory's togetherness ratings. We cannot use such definition because the real transposition is realized only in the working set (precisely in $\mathcal{M}_1$). Actually, if a block of the disk is moved to $\mathcal{M}_2$ and then brought back to the disk without its elements have been exchanged with $\mathcal{M}_1$'s elements, the potential function does not change.

We now analyze how an I/O made by $\mathcal{A}'$ improves the potential function. Suppose the tth I/O is an input and the B_2-block x is fetched into a B_2-row of $\mathcal{M}_2$. Before the tth input, the intersection between the block x and the working set $W(t-1)$ is empty; after the input, at most K elements of x are inserted into $W(t-1)$. We use the following notation:

- m_i: number of elements in the working set $W(t-1)$ belonging to the ith target group at time $t-1$;
- x_i: number of elements in block x belonging to the ith target group at time $t-1$;
- w_i: number of elements in the (at most) K words, inserted in $W(t-1)$, belonging to the ith target group.

The m_i, x_i and w_i values are limited by the constraints below:

$$\sum_{i=1}^{N/B_2} m_i \leq 2M - K \qquad \sum_{i=1}^{N/B_2} x_i \leq B_2 \qquad \sum_{i=1}^{N/B_2} w_i \leq K.$$

The potential increases of $\nabla POT(t)$ compared to $POT(t-1)$:

$$\nabla POT(t) = POT(t) - POT(t-1) = C_W(t) + C_x(t) - C_W(t-1) - C_x(t-1)$$

$$= \sum_{i=1}^{N/B_2} f(m_i + w_i) + f(x_i - w_i) - f(m_i) - f(x_i).$$

Since $f(x_i - w_i) + f(w_i) = (x_i - w_i)\log(x_i - w_i) + w_i \log w_i \leq (x_i - w_i + w_i)\log x_i = f(x_i)$,

$$\nabla POT(t) \leq \sum_{i=1}^{N/B_2} f(m_i + w_i) - f(m_i) - f(w_i)$$

$$\leq \sum_{i=1}^{N/B_2} (m_i + w_i)\log(m_i + w_i) - m_i \log m_i - w_i \log w_i$$

$$\leq \sum_{i=1}^{N/B_2} m_i \log \frac{m_i + w_i}{m_i} + w_i \log \frac{m_i + w_i}{w_i}.$$

By a convexity argument, the increase in potential function is maximized when $m_i = (2M - K)/(N/B_2)$ and $w_i = K/(N/B_2)$, hence:

$$\nabla POT(t) \leq (2M - K)\log \frac{2M - K + K}{2M - K} + K \log \frac{2M - K + K}{K}$$

$$\leq K \log\left(1 + \frac{K}{2M - K}\right)^{\frac{2M - K}{K}} + K \log\left(\frac{2M}{K}\right)$$

$$\leq \frac{K}{\ln 2} + K \log \frac{2M}{K} \in O\left(K \log \frac{M}{K}\right).$$

Suppose now that the tth I/O is an output and the B_2-block x is evicted from a B_2-row of $\mathcal{M}_2$. Before the tth output, the intersection between the block x and the working set $W(t-1)$ contains at most K elements; after the output, at most K elements are removed from $W(t-1)$. As above, we use the following notation:

- m_i: number of elements in the working set $W(t-1)$ belonging to the ith target group at time $t-1$;
- x_i: number of elements in block x belonging to the ith target group at time $t-1$;
- w_i: number of elements in the (at most) K words, removed from $W(t-1)$, belonging to the ith target group.

The m_i, x_i and w_i values are limited by the constraints below:

$$\sum_{i=1}^{N/B_2} m_i \leq 2M \qquad \sum_{i=1}^{N/B_2} x_i \leq B_2 - K \qquad \sum_{i=1}^{N/B_2} w_i \leq K.$$

The potential increases of $\nabla POT(t)$ compared to $POT(t-1)$:

$$\nabla POT(t) = POT(t) - POT(t-1) = C_W(t) + C_x(t) - C_W(t-1) - C_x(t-1)$$

$$= \sum_{i=1}^{N/B_2} f(m_i - w_i) + f(x_i + w_i) - f(m_i) - f(x_i)$$

$$\leq \sum_{i=1}^{N/B_2} (x_i + w_i) \log(x_i + w_i) - x_i \log x_i - w_i \log w_i,$$

since $f(m_i - w_i) + f(w_i) \leq f(m_i)$. The increase in potential function is maximized when $x_i = (B_2 - K)/(N/B_2)$ and $w_i = K/(N/B_2)$, hence:

$$\nabla POT(t) \leq \frac{K}{\ln 2} + K \log \frac{B_2}{K} \in O\left(K \log \frac{B_2}{K}\right) = O\left(K \log \frac{M}{K}\right).$$

Let $\mathcal{C}_1$ and $\mathcal{C}_2$ be a tall and a short cache respectively, and let d, f, g be suitable positive constants. Since the I/Os of $\mathcal{A}'$ are $T = \Theta(t_2)$ and $t_1 = \Theta(N/B_1)$,

$$T \nabla POT \geq POT(T) \implies dt_2 K \log \frac{M}{K} \geq N \log B_2$$

$$dt_2 \frac{t_1 B_1}{t_2} \log \frac{Mt_2}{t_1 B_1} \geq N \log B_2 \implies fN \log \frac{gMt_2}{N} \geq N \log B_2$$

$$\frac{gMt_2}{N} \geq B_2^{1/f} \implies t_2 \in \Omega\left(N \frac{B_2^{1/f}}{M}\right).$$

If $B_2 = \alpha M$ for a suitable constant $0 < \alpha < 1$, the above inequality becomes

$$t_2 \in \Omega\left(\frac{N}{M^{1-1/f}}\right) \in \omega\left(N \frac{\log M}{M}\right).$$

The miss complexity in $\mathcal{C}_2$ of an optimal algorithm for matrix transposition is $\Theta\left(N\frac{\log M}{M}\right)$, thus t_2 is not optimal. However, by the initial hypothesis on $\mathcal{A}$, we can deduce that t_2 is optimal and so we have a contradiction. We can conclude that a cache-oblivious algorithm for matrix transposition does not exist without the tall cache assumption.

5 Conclusions

In this work we have presented a simulation technique to yield an EM algorithm from two executions of the same cache-oblivious algorithm on different instantiations of the IC model. Our technique can be envisaged as a formalization and a generalization of the *ad-hoc* approach employed in [6] to prove negative results on cache-oblivious permuting. Successively, we have applied the simulation technique to matrix transposition. By further using an adaptation of the potential function employed in [1] to bound the I/O complexity of matrix transposition on EM, we were able to conclude that an optimal cache-oblivious algorithm for matrix transposition cannot exist without the tall cache assumption.

Apart from the result presented in this paper, to the best of the author's knowledge the only other impossibility results in the literature on optimal cache-obliviousness concern sorting and general permuting [6]. An interesting avenue for further research would be to address other fundamental problems, such as matrix multiplication, the Discrete Fourier Transform, or the realization of rational permutations, to expose any limitation intrinsic in their cache-oblivious realization. Moreover, a more profound understanding is still required of why the tall cache assumption is so crucial to obtain optimal cache-oblivious algorithms.

Acknowledgments

This paper benefited from useful discussions with Andrea Pietracaprina, Geppino Pucci and Gianfranco Bilardi.

References

1. Aggarwal, A., Vitter, J.S.: The input/output complexity of sorting and related problems. Cacm 31(9), 1116–1127 (1988)
2. Vitter, J.S.: External memory algorithms and data structures. ACM Comput. Surv. 33(2), 209–271 (2001)
3. Frigo, M., Leiserson, C.E., Prokop, H., Ramachandran, S.: Cache-oblivious algorithms. In: Proc. of 40th IEEE Symp. on Foundations of Computer Science, pp. 285–298 (1999)
4. Demaine, E.D.: Cache-oblivious algorithms and data structures. In: Lecture Notes from the EEF Summer School on Massive Data Sets. Lecture Notes in Computer Science, BRICS, University of Aarhus, Denmark (to appear, 2002)

5. Arge, L., Brodal, G.S., Fagerberg, R.: Cache-oblivious data structures. In: Mehta, D., Sahni, S. (eds.) Handbook of Data Structures and Applications, vol. 27, CRC Press, Boca Raton (2005)
6. Brodal, G.S., Fagerberg, R.: On the limits of cache-obliviousness. In: Proc. of the 35th ACM Symp. on Theory of Computing, pp. 307–315 (2003)
7. Bilardi, G., Peserico, E.: A characterization of temporal locality and its portability across memory hierarchies. In: Orejas, F., Spirakis, P.G., van Leeuwen, J. (eds.) ICALP 2001. LNCS, vol. 2076, pp. 128–139. Springer, Heidelberg (2001)
8. Aggarwal, A., Alpern, B., Chandra, A.K., Snir, M.: A model for hierarchical memory. In: Proc. of the 19th ACM Symp. on Theory of Computing, pp. 305–314 (1987)

The KOA Remote Voting System: A Summary of Work to Date

Joseph R. Kiniry[1], Alan E. Morkan[1], Dermot Cochran[1], Fintan Fairmichael[1], Patrice Chalin[2], Martijn Oostdijk[3], and Engelbert Hubbers[3]

[1] School of Computer Science and Informatics
University College Dublin
Belfield, Dublin 4, Ireland
[2] Department of Computer Science and Software Engineering
Concordia University
Montreal, Quebec, H3G 1M8, Canada
[3] Nijmegen Institute of Information and Computing Sciences
Radboud University Nijmegen
Postbus 9010, 6500GL Nijmegen, The Netherlands

Abstract. Remote internet voting incorporates many of the core challenges of trusted global computing. In this paper, we present the Kiezen op Afstand[1] (KOA) system. KOA is a Free Software, remote voting system developed for the Dutch government in 2003/2004. In addition to being Open Source, it is also partially formally specified and verified. This paper summarises the work carried out to date on the KOA system. It charts the evolution of the system, from its initial conception by the Dutch Government, through to its current status. It also describes a roadmap of milestones towards completing its next release: a Free Software, general-purpose, formally specified and verified internet voting system, that incorporates Proof Carrying Code technology for software update and allows trustworthy voting from a mobile phone. We propose that the KOA system should be used as an *experimental platform* for research in electronic and internet voting; we are *not* saying that we have solved any of the major problems inherent in voting with computers.

1   Introduction

The Netherlands is known for its forward-thinking and progressive government, laws, and policies. Unfortunately, a government's progressiveness, particularly with respect to the adoption of new technology, is sometimes contrary to the good of its citizens.

Accordingly, in order to help avoid such a situation in the adoption of remote voting technology in the Netherlands, the Security of Systems (SoS) Group at Radboud University Nijmegen became directly involved in the evaluation and development of the KOA system in 2004.

1.1   Voting Machines in the Netherlands

The introduction of such a system was not as radical a development as it might be considered elsewhere. Electronic voting machines (EVMs) were introduced without

---

[1] "Kiezen op Afstand" is literally translated from Dutch as "Remote Voting."

U. Montanari, D. Sannella, and R. Bruni (Eds.): TGC 2006, LNCS 4661, pp. 244–262, 2007.

controversy in the Netherlands around 1998. They have been widely used in local and national elections ever since. The primary supplier of these machines is Nedap[2], the same supplier as in Ireland.

Part of the reason that EVMs were so readily accepted is historical. The Netherlands has used digital voting machines[3] since the 1980s. Therefore, Dutch citizens are comfortable with the idea of using technology for voting. The security and reliability issues of the new generation of machines was not a serious problem at the time of their introduction, much like their adoption by other governments in the late 1990s.

Unfortunately, many aspects of these systems have not been made public, contrary to the requests of concerned parties in the Netherlands. The internals of such systems are secret and are only exposed to evaluators. Each system must be examined, according to an unknown set of criteria, before being accepted by the Dutch parliament for use in elections. Evaluation reports compiled by the national reviewer, TNO[4], are also secret.

However, as attention has been focused the world over on EVMs, the Dutch parliament has begun to re-evaluate its approach. Changes to the current systems are likely to be mandated soon, particularly with respect to voter verifiable paper trails.

In keeping with this reassessment, the Dutch parliament decided to conduct experiments with the next natural step in the use of technology for voting: remote voting using both the internet and telephone. The main inspiration is that, nowadays, many personal transactions (e.g., banking), can be carried out from arbitrary locations, so why not voting?

Indeed, it is believed by some that a remote voting system will increase electoral participation by making the process more convenient. Currently, Dutch citizens must find time during the extended business hours (08:00 to 20:00) of a single day of the working week. Furthermore, each individual must vote in a particular location near their home, which may be far from their workplace.

However, given what we know about the unreliability and vulnerability of software and networks, do the risks inherent in the introduction of such a system outweigh such benefits?

These risks, together with the methods adopted in eliminating and minimising them in the KOA system form the basis for the rest of this paper. It is organised as follows. Section 2 presents some background information on the genesis of the KOA project. Past academic work on the system up to the end of 2005 is presented in Section 3. A security assessment of the KOA system is put forward in Section 4. Current work is discussed in Section 5. Related work is compared and contrasted in Section 6. Future work is considered in Section 7 and Section 8 concludes.

2   Kiezen op Afstand (KOA)

The genesis of KOA stemmed from a promise made by the Dutch government to parliament that they would investigate possible developments to the Dutch voting system.

---

[2] Nedap — http://www.nedap.com/

[3] The previous-generation systems with little-to-no software.

[4] TNO — Netherlands Organisation for Applied Scientific Research — http://www.tpd.tno.nl/tno/index.xml

This promise was fulfilled in the KOA experiment by allowing expatriates to vote in the elections to the European Parliament via the internet and by telephone.

However, Dutch national election law is quite explicit about what is permitted with respect to how votes may be cast. Therefore, in order to conduct an experiment in voting over the internet, some amendments to this general law were formulated. This formed the legal foundation for the KOA project.

Apart from the general rules governing internet voting, it also included some additional rules detailing a citizen's right to vote from a different polling booth other than the one originally appointed. However, in this paper we will refer to the KOA project as if it consisted purely as an internet voting experiment.

2.1   Internet Voting in the Netherlands

The elections to the European Parliament of June 2004 allowed remote voting via the internet and telephone. It was limited to expatriates who were required to explicitly register beforehand. It was thought that such a small-scale use (thousands of voters) would provide a useful real-world test for the technology.

The main reason why it was thought that an internet-based solution was suitable is decidedly non-technical. Essentially, by significantly constraining the remote voting problem, particularly with respect to the registration and voting process itself, it was believed that a "sufficiently secure" and reliable system could be constructed. In particular, the system needed to be at least as secure and reliable as the existing remote voting system which was based upon postal ballots.

The Remote Voting Process. When a citizen registers to use KOA, the voter chooses their own personal access code (a PIN). Some time later, a customised information packet is mailed to the voter. This packet contains general information about the vote itself (date, time, etc.), as well as voter-customised details that are known to only that voter. These details include information for voter authentication, including an identification code and the previously chosen access code.

Also included is a list of all candidates. Each candidate is assigned a large set of unique random numbers[5], and exactly one of those numbers is given to each voter. The set of codes per voter is determined randomly but is not unique.

To vote, a registered voter logs in to a web site with their voter code and access code. They then step through a series of simple web pages, typing in their candidate codes as appropriate for their choices. The system shows the voter the actual names and parties of the candidates in question to confirm the accuracy of the vote. When a voter is finished, a transaction code is provided. This code can later be used to check in a published list that the voter's choices were included correctly in the final tally.

Communication with the voting web site is secured with SSL. All votes are stored in a doubly-encrypted fashion; each vote is encrypted by a symmetric key per voter[6] and the public key of the voting authority.

---

[5] 1,000 codes were generated for each candidate for the elections to the European Parliament in 2004.

[6] This symmetric key is generated by hashing the assigned identification code.

2.2 Use and GPL Release

The trial during the elections to the European Parliament in June, 2004 was restricted to roughly 16,000 eligible Dutch expatriates. Expatriates could vote either via the internet or by telephone. The telephone votes were fed into the KOA tally system. 5,351 people used one or other system.

Subsequently, in July 2004, the Dutch Government released the majority of the source code for the KOA system under the GNU General Public License (GPL) making it the first Open Source internet voting system in the world.

3 Academic Past Work

3.1 External Security Evaluation

In late 2003 Prof. Bart Jacobs of the Security of Systems (SoS) group at Radboud University Nijmegen participated in an external review of the requirements and design of this application. One of the recommendations made by the panel was that the system should not be designed, implemented and tested all by the same company.

The system itself was designed and implemented by LogicaCMG[7]. Although eventually the government decided to make the system open source, during implementation it was not. In order to improve its quality, the Dutch company Software Improvement Group[8] performed a code review of the system. However, they were only allowed to do so after signing Non-Disclosure Agreements (NDAs). In fact, it was unexpected that the government ultimately opted for an Open Source solution.

The SoS group did not take part in the design or implementation of the system. However, the group took an active part in the final stages of the project. The group performed two tasks: it wrote an independent tally application which will be explained in detail in Section 3.2 and it performed a penetration test on the vote servers.

The penetration test was set up as a black box test. In particular the SoS group had virtually no knowledge regarding the actual hardware, software, networks or personnel involved with the server system. Indeed, the information it did possess could have been considered public information since it could easily be obtained by standard available analysis tools.

The main goal was to break into the system and try to compromise its integrity. The second goal was to test whether the system was vulnerable to denial of service attacks.

Two evaluations were conducted. The first was unsolicited and took place during a private beta test of the system. The second was requested by the government, primarily because of the results of the first evaluation.

During the first unsolicited evaluation the subnet running the service was gently probed and mapped using nmap, a more detailed evaluation of specific machines was then conducted, specifically with regards to machines running inappropriate services, weaker operating systems, etc., and finally, on the last afternoon of the test, a denial-of-service attack on the machines was conducted.

---

[7] http://www.logicacmg.com/
[8] http://www.sig.nl/

The main discovery of the first evaluation was that the system was not "tightened down" insofar as test and management machines which were running insecure versions of particular operating systems (e.g., Microsoft Windows) were on the deployed subnet, no hardware or software firewall was in place on the system, machines has likely external exploits available, and nearly all systems had inappropriate services running (e.g., unused mail servers, databases, file sharing, etc.). Also, the SoS group was able to significantly harm their service quality with our (admittedly very small) denial-of-service attack.

After the authorities realized the SoS group was responsible for this attack they asked us for a report of our findings. Given the feedback and analysis, they then asked the SoS group to perform an "official" external evaluation once they incorporated all of our suggestions and tightened-down the network.

The second evaluation found that their systems were adequately hosted, monitored and configured, their software was up-to-date, and no unnecessary services were running. Furthermore, adequate measures were in place for detecting basic probes by adversaries. Thus, in the end, the SoS group did not find any problem with the system that would have caused the Dutch Ministry to reject it for an experimental run, and the external evaluation significantly improved the security and reliability of the system.

3.2 Vote Counting System

As seen in the previous section, one of the results of the recommendation to split the responsibilities of the parties involved, was that the government decided to accept bids for the creation of a separate vote counting subsystem, to be implemented in isolation by a third party. This separate tally application would allow the vote counting to be independently verified. The SoS group put forward a proposal to write this application, and were successful in this bid. The key idea behind their tender was that the vote counting program should be formally verified using the JML [2] and ESC/Java2[9] [10] tools.

The vote counting system formed a small but important part of the whole KOA system. This provided the SoS group with a suitable opportunity to test the use of some of the formal techniques and practices that they had been developing. Given the severe time constraints placed upon them due to the impending election, the application was built by three members of the group over a barely-sufficient period of four weeks. Java was chosen as the programming language in which to implement the system so that JML could be used as the formal specification language. Due to the time constraints, verification was only attempted with the core modules.

Counting votes within KOA proceeds offline using a separate tally application. The input to this application consists of two XML files (one containing the list of candidates and their codes, and one containing the encrypted votes), and a public/private keypair used to decrypt the votes.

---

[9] ESC/Java2 is a programming tool that attempts to partially verify JML annotated Java programs by static analysis of the program code and its formal annotations. It translates the specifications into verification conditions that are modularly discharged by an automatic theorem prover.

As the informal requirements of vote-counting are obvious (for every candidate in the candidate list count the number of votes for that candidate), the functional specification [12] (in Dutch) mostly prescribes details of file formats and encryption algorithms to be used.

Nevertheless, the functional specification does impose some requirements that greatly influence the structure of the Java application and its JML specification. First, the different tasks that need to be performed in order to count the votes (reading in the two files, reading in the keys, decrypting the contents of the votes file, counting the votes, generating reports) are made explicit in this document and, more importantly, the order in which they have to be performed is specified. Second, the document provides a rough sketch of the user interface and its contents. Finally, the document gives some bounds on the data, such as the lengths of fields or the maximum number of candidates in each list, which are incorporated in the JML specifications of the data structures.

In accordance with the above high-level specification, the resulting tally application consists of some 30 classes, which can be grouped into three categories: the data structures, the user interface, and the tasks.

The data structure classes form an excellent opportunity to write JML specifications. Typical concepts from the domain of voting, such as candidate, district and municipality can be modeled with detailed JML specifications. An example invariant in Candidate.java is:

```
/*@ invariant my_gender == MALE ||
  @            my_gender == FEMALE ||
  @            my_gender == UNKNOWN;
  */
```

The different tasks associated with counting votes were mapped to individual classes. After successful completion of a task, the application state is changed. A task can only be started if the application is in an appropriate state. The life-cycle model of the application that therefore emerges is maintained in the main class of the application inside a simple integral field. This life-cycle model can be specified in JML using invariants and constraints, essentially stating that on successful completion of the application, the application went from "initial state" to "votes counted state". The state of attributes associated with the individual tasks can be linked to the application life-cycle state using invariants. For instance, such an invariant could read: 'after the application reaches the "keys imported state", the private key field is no longer null'. This is stated in MenuPanel.java as follows:

```
/*@ invariant
  @   (state >= PRIVATE_KEY_IMPORTED_STATE
  @      ==> privateKey != null);
  */
```

A graphical user interface is usually not very amenable to formal specification. Nonetheless, some light-weight specifications were written. One of the requirements defined in the original informal specification was that users should not be allowed to start certain tasks before certain other tasks are successfully completed. For instance, a user should (by means of the user interface) not be able to start decrypting votes before the votes are read in from file. In the graphical user interface, this demand is met by only enabling certain buttons when the application reaches certain states in the life-cycle model. The fact that the graphical user interface complies with the life-cycle model can be neatly specified in the GUI classes by referring to the application state.

3.3 Process

As already stated, ESC/Java2 was only used to verify the core of the tally application. This means that it was used to verify reading in the XML-files with the candidates and the votes, decryption of the votes and counting the votes. The final generation of the reports is not checked with JML.

Using JML on reading XML files is quite straightforward. Essentially, for every object that is read, some methods are called that specify that the total number of objects will be increased by exactly one. Naturally, in order to verify code that uses functionality provided in external libraries, some of the corresponding APIs must also be specified. The JML community has provided specifications for most of the APIs that come with Sun's standard edition of Java. However, APIs dealing with cryptography, XML parsing, and PDF generation, as used by the tally application had not previously been specified. These APIs were specified in a light-weight manner: the specifications mostly deal with purity and non-null references in the API methods which makes verification of client code using ESC/Java2 much easier.

Naturally, the counting process is likewise formally specified in JML, which ensures that each valid vote is counted for exactly one candidate. This also implies that specifications are easy to check to make sure that the total number of votes a party list receives is equal to the sum of votes for each candidate[10] on this party list.

The JML run-time assertion checker was also used in the development process. First, for testing the data structure classes, the checker was used to generate unit tests. Second, we ran the full application, including user interface, using the checker.

3.4 Analysis of KOA

In the Dependable Software Research Group at Concordia University, the KOA source code was used as a subject of a study in the frequency of occurrences of non-null reference type declarations [3]. This work consisted in adding nullity annotations (or constraints) and then verifying their correctness by making use of ESC/Java2. The results were similar to those of Fähndrich and Leino [13], that is to say, it was found that even a simple specification exercise of adding nullity annotations can help uncover non-trivial bugs both in the code and in the specifications.

For example, in the `sos.koa.CounterAdapter` class in the Tally Application it was found that the field named `errors` is declared nullable and yet the method `getErrors`, which uses this field, assumes that the field is non-null (i.e., a `Null-PointerException` will not be thrown).

---

[10] Including the 'blanco' or 'blank ballot' candidate.

3.5   Reverse Engineering Missing Components

The version of KOA released under the GPL was not complete. A number of pieces of functionality, constituting roughly 10% of the deployed KOA system, were proprietary and owned by LogicaCMG. Moreover, certain other changes were made for publication purposes (e.g., the length of public/private key pairs in the source code).

In addition, the released KOA system contains no high-level design documentation and very little information on how to build the system. This means that it is only possible to inspect the (partial) source, not to compile and run it. Therefore, it was necessary to perform a full analysis of the released system [14].

One of the most beneficial aspects of this analysis was that errors were found in the KOA system. One such error was found in the Java Server Pages (JSPs) whereby a button that should have guided the user back to the interface homepage had, in fact, the same action as that of the "submit" button that processed and saved a list of candidates to the database. This was due to a trivial mistake: placing the HTML tags for the "Return Home" button within the FORM tag block. This error was discovered during a trivial "click through" of the user interface followed by an examination of the code.

Such a basic mistake in the design of the user interface of a critical system is unacceptable. The fact that such a mistake could be made, remain unnoticed in the testing and evaluation phase of the software, and actually be used in the elections to the European Parliament, would suggest that there is in all likelihood further errors in this software.

Once the analysis was complete, the missing functionality was reverse engineered. 59 additional classes, together with some properties files, were added to the system. These classes carry out the base functionality of the servlets, error reporting, logging functionality, event handling, etc.

3.6   Full Open Source Foundations

One of the major goals in the redevelopment of the KOA system was that it would be entirely composed of, and dependent upon, Open Source software. The original system was developed in, deployed upon and tightly coupled to the IBM WebSphere IDE. During the reimplementation, the KOA system was ported to an Open Source alternative. This foundation consisted of a MySQL database server backend paired with a JBoss application server front-end, the latter of which incorporated the Tomcat servlet container. The other major restriction in terms of making the system fully GPL-compliant was its use of proprietary security and encryption utilities developed by IAIK and Sun. These were seamlessly replaced using the BouncyCastle Open Source alternatives.

3.7   Formal Specification and Extended Static Checking Review

As has already been stated, the Vote Counting Application of the KOA system was specified with formal methods, extensively tested and partially verified to the extent that was possible within the given time-frame. Subsequently, efforts were made to complete the specification and verification [8].

Table 1. KOA initial release system summary

	File I/O	Graphical I/O	Core
Classes	8	13	6
Methods	154	200	83
NCSS	837	1599	395
Specs	446	172	529
Specs:NCSS	1:2	1:10	5:4

When the KOA vote counting system was being designed, precedence was given to verifying the core units. These were designed by contract and as result have good specification coverage. The remaining parts, however, were only lightly annotated with JML notation.

Table 1 summarizes the size (in number of classes and methods), complexity (non-comment size of source (NCSS)), and specification coverage of the three subsystems, as measured with the JavaNCSS tool version 20.40 during the week of 24 May, 2004. This is the version of the program that was released and used in the elections to the European Parliament in June 2004.

At the time of its initial release, verification coverage of the core subsystem was good, but not 100%. Approximately 10% of the core methods (8 methods) were unverified due to issues with ESC/Java's Simplify theorem prover (i.e., either the prover did not terminate or terminated abnormally). Another 31% of the core methods (26 methods) had postconditions that could not be verified, typically due to completeness issues in ESC/Java, and 12% of the methods (10 methods) failed to verify due to invariant issues, most of which are due to suspected inconsistencies in the specifications of the core Java class libraries or JML model classes. The remaining 47% (39 methods) of the core verified completely. Since 100% verification coverage was not possible in the timeframe of the original project, to ensure the KOA application was of the highest quality level possible, a large number unit tests were generated[11] for all core classes with the jmlunit [4] tool, which is part of the JML suite. A total of nearly 8,000 unit tests were generated, focusing on key values of the various datatypes and their dependent base types. These tests cover 100% of the core code and are 100% successful.

After this analysis was completed, the specifications were gradually augmented. As an example, consider the `AuditLog` class. This class records information about the vote counting as the application proceeds. This information is then used at the end of the vote counting to help fill in the details for two of the reports that are generated. This class keeps track of the program's progress in a similar manner to that which was used for the overall program state. There were multiple invariants used to ensure the program and auditing proceeded in the correct fashion. Several corrections were required for this class, the bulk of which were modifications to the behaviours of the methods that allowed the audit log's state to change. The original specifications allowed

---

[11] The tool generates unit tests that deal with *interesting* values. Interesting values are generally boundary values for a given data type. For example, -1, 0, 1, *n* and *n+1* for an array of integers. Users are also free to handwrite their own test cases, in the case where the jmlunit tool does not test all important values.

the possibility that the variables could be changed to a state where the invariants would not hold. The changes made to this class' specifications disallowed any actions that would violate the object invariants.

3.8   Documentation Writing and Translation

The vast majority of the voting system, including high-level documentation, web interfaces, Java comments and variable names are in Dutch. Furthermore, much of the voting system is sparsely commented and unspecified. This clearly poses an obstacle to the understanding and adoption of such a system by a wider, international audience. It was therefore decided at an early stage that a complete translation of the system into an international language such as English, together with the production of additional documentation, was necessary in order to facilitate a larger number of people to carry out the necessary specification, development and testing. Consequently, the major high-level specification document and all of the JSPs have been translated from Dutch into English.

3.9   Other Voting Systems

Naturally, there are relatively considerable variations in electoral systems between countries. This is the case between the Netherlands and Ireland. Not only are these differences linguistic, but more significantly there are different vote counting procedures in the Netherlands and in Ireland. The Dutch Voting system is list based while Ireland uses Proportional Representation with a Single Transferable Vote (PR-STV).

The Irish Voting System.   The Dáil, Ireland's lower house of parliament, is composed of 166 members representing 41 constituencies. Each constituency elects multiple members to parliament. The average constituency elects four representatives with every constituency electing at least three representatives. The system used is PR-STV. This combination is considered to increase the representativeness of the Dáil.

Irish voters, by ranking the candidates, give instructions as to who should receive their support should the first choice candidate be eliminated or elected. Surplus votes are the number of votes in excess of the threshold of election a candidate receives. Surplus votes are transferred proportionally to the remaining candidates according to the indicated second preference of the voters. If the election is undecided after counting the first preferences and transferring surplus votes, then the lowest polling candidate is eliminated. The ballots cast initially in support of this candidate are now counted according to their indicated second preference. If any candidate has more than a quota of votes then he or she is elected and his or her surplus votes are transferred to the next preference candidate. If there are more candidates than seats and all surpluses have been transfered, then the candidate with least votes is excluded and his or her votes transfered to the next preference on each ballot paper. This process is repeated until the number of candidates remaining equals the number of seats remaining.

Formal Specification.   Votáil is the Irish word for voting. The Votáil specification is a JML specification for the Irish vote counting system [5]. This formal specification is derived from the complete functional specification for the Dáil election count algorithm [6,7].

Thirty nine formal assertions were identified in the Commentary on Count Rules published by the Irish Department of Environment and Local Government. Each assertion expressed in JML was identified by a Javadoc comment. In addition, a state machine was specified so as to link all of the assertions together. Java classes were specified for the vote counting algorithm, to represent the ballot papers and candidates. A concrete example of how the methodology was applied will clarify this work.

Section 7, item 3.2 on page 25 of [6] states:

> As a first step, a transfer factor is calculated, viz. the number of votes in the surplus is divided by the total number of transferable votes in the last set of votes. This transfer factor is multiplied in turn by the total number of votes in each sub-set of next available preferences for continuing candidates (note that the transfer factor is not applied to the sub-set of non-transferable votes in the set of votes).

The requirement is translated into formal natural language as follows:

> The number of votes in the surplus is divided by the total number of transferable votes in the last set of votes. This transfer factor is multiplied in turn by the total number of votes in each sub-set of next available preferences for continuing candidates.

Finally, this formal natural language is formally specified in the architecture as a JML postcondition for the method that is specifically for this requirement (the get-ActualTransfers method). The Javadoc and JML specification for this method follows.

```
/**
 * Determine actual number of votes to transfer to
 * this candidate, excluding rounding up of
 * fractional transfers
 *
 * @see requirement 25 from section 7 item 3.2
 * on page 25
 *
 * @design The votes in a surplus are transfered in
 * proportion to the number of transfers available
 * throughout the candidates ballot stack.  The
 * calculations are made using integer values
 * because there is no concept of fractional votes
 * or fractional transfer of votes, in the existing
 * manual counting system. If not all transferable
 * votes are accounted for the highest remainders
 * for each continuing candidate need to be examined.
 *
 * @param fromCandidate Candidate from which to
 *         count the transfers
 * @param toCandidate Continuing candidate eligible
 *         to receive votes
```

```
*  @return Number of votes to be transfered,
*           excluding fractional transfers
*/

//@ ensures
//@   \result ==
//@       (getSurplus(fromCandidate) *
//@        getPotentialTransfers(fromCandidate,
//@           toCandidate.getCandidateID())) /
//@        getTotalTransferableVotes(fromCandidate);
```

The Votáil specification was typechecked and checked for consistency using ESC/-Java2[12].

4 Security Assessment

Issues of security and correctness are paramount in any voting system. This is especially the case for a remote internet voting system due to the inherent vulnerabilities of the architecture. Any such system must be as secure as the system it is designed to replace. Otherwise, trust in the electoral and democratic systems of a country can be severely damaged.

The KOA system was designed to replace absentee postal ballots. It has always been accepted that postal voting is not as secure as voting in a polling booth. KOA follows all of the standard security mechanisms and also introduces some novel approaches. These security mechanisms are focused on attack prevention and, where this is impossible, on detection of intrusion. This section discusses these security mechanisms.

4.1 Data Integrity

The most significant method used in the KOA system to ensure data integrity is the use of candidate codes. 1,000 codes are generated for each candidate and only one of these is randomly assigned to each voter. Therefore, even if a malicious agent (e.g., a worm, virus or Trojan horse) can access a ballot, all the attacker can see are the encoded candidate and party IDs, which in the optimal case are unique to the voter in question. Consequently, it will be virtually impossible to substitute the ballot by choosing the appropriate code for a different candidate.

In addition, the votes are doubly-encrypted. The only way to decrypt these votes on the server side is to close the polls. Closing the polls is an irreversible action. Consequently, altering the votes at the server-side is precluded.

In the case where the voter tries to cast multiple votes at once (e.g., via both telephone and internet) there will always be one first vote. This vote will be stored. The second attempt will fail because the voter has already cast his/her vote.

---

[12] The consistency of JML specifications is checked using an experimental extension to ESC/Java2 that manipulates the JML abstract syntax tree in order to determine whether certain combinations of assertions are inherently unsatisfiable.

Finally, the KOA system has the capability to take snapshots of the candidate and voter lists called "electronic fingerprints." These fingerprints can be generated at any time to ensure that these lists have not been maliciously altered. One possible extension to the system is to automate the generation of these fingerprints at regular intervals to ensure a regular verification of data integrity.

4.2 Verifiability

Voters using the KOA system are able to verify that their vote is recorded correctly and is included in the final tally of the election using the transaction code they receive upon casting their ballot. This is possible due to the publication of a list of the transaction codes of votes for each candidate after the election. Such a check can identify any compromised PCs and in the worst case invalidate the election.

4.3 Insider Threats

The power to change the state of the system and to decrypt the votes is restricted to a small number of polling station officials. These officials hold the private key for the system and each has a PIN code to use this private key. One of these officials is designated as the current "president" or "chairman."

In order to change the state of the system (e.g., open/close the polls, decrypt the votes, etc.), the chairman and one other official must enter their PIN codes. If the role of chairman is alternated at set time intervals among random officials (or some similar mechanism), then all officials need to be in collusion in order to tamper with the system. Even then, access to the decrypted ballots is precluded, as is mentioned in Section 4.1.

In addition, an insider attack would require massive, undetectable client and/or network subversion (e.g., large numbers of client computers *and/or* network web proxies being compromised by a virus written by attacker's henchmen). Given the scale and complexity of such an attack, it is nearly inconceivable that it is possible. Such an attack would be (many) orders of magnitude more difficult to pull off than any attack on existing electronic or manual voting hardware/mechanisms due to its scale: millions of PCs versus thousands of voting machines, and millions of individuals (many of which are experts like network service providers, IT workers voting from home, etc.) participating and monitoring the election versus thousands of volunteers running the election. This is analogous to the Open Source "thousands of eyeballs" argument, but applied to voting.

4.4 Other Security Features

A part from the use of SSL, there are a couple of further noteworthy security features.

Firstly, random data is added to the votes when they are encrypted. This ensures that votes within the same voter district and for the same candidate have a different encryption result for each vote, making it impossible to interpret encrypted votes.

Secondly, the votes are decrypted in a random order in order to making tracing voters by the order in which they voted impossible.

4.5 Problems

Despite the best efforts to make KOA as secure as possible, certain security flaws still remain. These need to be addressed before further use of the system.

Firstly, if the electronic fingerprints of the system are not identical at a particular point in time, the chairman can overrule and allow the election to continue. This should not be permitted.

Like other forms of remote voting (e.g., postal voting), KOA does not provide protection for voter anonymity in the case where another person is in the vicinity of the voter during the voting process or if another person gains access to a voter's transaction code. However, due to the use of candidate codes, excluding these two scenarios, it is virtually impossible to connect a voter to his/her vote.

Denial of Service Attacks (DoS). As has already been stated in Section 3.1, the KOA system is vulnerable to DoS Attacks. This is practically impossible to prevent and is a feature of all remote internet voting systems.

One feature of the KOA system that lessens some of the problems caused by DoS attacks is that the system can be interrupted. When this state change happens, an electronic fingerprint of all the system data is taken and this can be checked against a subsequent fingerprint on system resumption. Clearly, this does not solve the problem of potential temporary disenfranchisement, but it does ensure data integrity in the face of a such an attack.

4.6 Summary

As has been described, all of the standard security mechanisms have been used together with some innovative techniques to ensure data integrity and verifiability. However, obviously the issue of security is one of the open questions of remote internet voting and there are a number of problems yet to be overcome. We believe these problems can be addressed by research and experimentation on a verified open source framework, like the one which KOA aims to provide.

5 Academic Current Work

5.1 Generalisation of System for Non-dutch Voting Systems

The Java code for Votáil was written in JML using a kind of "verification-centric" Design by Contract methodology. This means that not only are we writing each method implementation according to its JML specification, but we are checking each method's correctness with ESC/Java2 and automatically generating thousands of unit tests using JML-JUnit [4].

The KOA system has a state machine similar to that used in the Votáil specification. This allows KOA to make calls to the appropriate part of the Votáil code. The ElectionAlgorithm class in Votáil will be invoked from within the KOA system using the following four method calls: setup, which defines election parameters such as candidate list and number of seats, load, which loads all valid ballots and then calculate quota and deposit saving thresholds, count, which assign votes to candidates, distribute surpluses and exclude candidates until finished, and `report`, which reports the election results. These methods must be called in the order shown, and this fact is captured by the invariants of the state machine. Only the `report` method is called more than once for each instance of the `ElectionAlgorithm` class.

The user interface is being designed in a flexible fashion so as to present non-Dutch ballot papers to the voter. The original KOA system was designed for use with a party-list system with a single national constituency. Its user interface is being extended in line with the guidelines for the Irish voting system. The KOA system allows the voter to select a list of candidates. In the Irish system each candidate is in a list of size one. The KOA system allows only one selection by the voter. In the Irish system the voter makes multiple selections in order of preference.

6   Related Work

6.1   A Security Analysis of SERVE

The security analysis of the SERVE project [9] is one of the best known examinations of remote internet voting. It is very critical of current efforts and advises against any use of such methods given the current state of technology, due to its inherent vulnerabilities.

Two main arguments against internet voting can be distinguished in the report. Firstly, it is argued that the system allows for vote buying and selling. However, this holds for any voting system in which voters vote at home. Internet voting can only be fairly compared to postal ballots, not to voting at polling stations. If we want to introduce remote voting on a large scale, measures can be taken (technical, organisational, and legal) that make it unattractive to buy or sell votes.

A second argument against internet voting is that the technology is vulnerable to attacks. Unfortunately, despite claiming to have examined alternatives to the SERVE system, it ignores systems that have overcome some, but not all, of the problems mentioned. Although, the KOA system was not fully developed at the time of writing, the recommendations presented in 2002 by Dr. Rolf Oppliger[13] for the use of a remote internet voting system in Geneva[14], describe security mechanisms, such as code sheets, that the authors of the SERVE report do not mention.

KOA is a much more secure system than SERVE in that it uses code lists for data integrity, transaction codes for verifiability and is not closed and proprietary.

6.2   The RIES System

The RIES system was developed for elections for public water management authorities in the Netherlands. It has two main features which create confidence in the limited possibilities of attacking the system. First of all, a reference table is published before the elections, including (anonymously) for each voter the hashes of all possible votes, linking those to the candidates. It is possible to compare the number of voters in this

---

[13] *How to Address the Secure Platform Problem for Remote Internet Voting in Geneva* — available from `http://www.ifi.unizh.ch/~oppliger/Docs/sis_2002.pdf`

[14] `http://www.geneve.ch/evoting/english/welcome.asp`

table with the number of registered voters. After the elections, a document with all received votes is published. This allows for two important verifications:

1. A voter can verify his/her own vote, including the correspondence to the chosen candidate.
2. Anyone can do an independent calculation of the result of the elections, based on this document and the reference table published before the elections.

If your vote has been registered incorrectly, or not at all, it can be detected. And if the result is incorrect given the received votes, this can also be detected. The main technique that achieves this is the clever use of hash functions. Whereas the hashes of all possible votes are public, it is impossible to deduce valid votes from them without the required voter key. Of course, the relation between voter and voter key should not be stored anywhere, as is the case for bank access codes. The system has worked well in an actual election with 70,000 voters.

A disadvantage of the RIES system in comparison with the KOA system is that a voter needs to compute hash values in order to verify that a vote has been correctly recorded. This is far more complicated than simply checking a transaction code in the list of votes after the election.

7   Future Work

Several pieces of future work have been identified and some of them are currently underway by researchers at UCD.

7.1   Development of a Mobile E-Voting Application

The EU MOBIUS Project[15], of which UCD and Nijmegen are both members, focuses on several topics including the specification and verification of security properties at several levels.

As part of this work, the security properties, including a functional specification, for a MIDP-based remote voting application are in the process of being defined. An example of such a security property is: "The application must not have access to personal information (e.g., phone book) on the mobile phone".

Additionally, a MIDP-based remote voting applet has been developed at UCD. This application has been reviewed and will be refactored, including the security and functional requirements expressed in JML, for incorporation into KOA.

7.2   Full-Blown Verification

We intend to fully specify and verify critical subsystems of the KOA system as a case study for the new MOBIUS Integrated Verification Environment (IVE) that is being developed by UCD and others. This goal is much more ambitious than simply performing extended static checking on various critical classes.

---

[15] The MOBIUS Project — http://mobius.inria.fr/

7.3 Just-in-Time Deployment with PCC

One of the primary problems with electronic voting systems is that new software updates, at both operating system and application levels, are typically installed in the field without any certification [11]. One technology that can help solve this deployment issue is Proof-Carrying Code (PCC) [1,15], the primary underlying formal foundation and technology used by the MOBIUS IVE.

Using a PCC technology foundation, new system and application patches could be just-in-time deployed to the thousands of voting machines used in an election with complete assurance. Developing such a foundation is part of the MOBIUS project's mandate, so the KOA system may be used as a deployment case study in the coming years.

7.4 American Voting System

The American voting system is the focus of an intense amount of discussion and work, given the ongoing fiasco in electronic voting we have witnessed in the U.S. over the past several years.

After integrating the Votáil Irish voting subsystem, we would be interested in collaborating to formally specify and verify a voting subsystem for use in American presidential and/or congressional elections using the same verification-centric methodology we have followed thus far.

7.5 Electronic Voting Systems

An electoral-system independent, formally specified and verified remote voting system can be used in an electronic voting system, as the latter is just a trivial, non-remote version of the former. It is our intention to build and demonstrate such a system, incorporating a new formally specified and verified voter-verifiable paper trail subsystem.

7.6 Reflections and Future Plans

Many of these plans are "just" a matter of good software engineering and thus can be accomplished by undergraduate and postgraduate students as case studies, theses work, etc. Others are *much* more difficult. In particular, attempting verification in any form and incorporating PCC techniques into the system are quite difficult, time consuming, and even require new research to be conducted. This work will take several years to accomplish, and only if the number of individuals and groups working on and with the system grows over time.

8 Conclusion

The availability of an American voting subsystem will make KOA the first general-purpose, formally specified and verified remote and local voting system available in the world, and furthermore it will be available under the GPL license. Furthermore, the KOA system is being donated to the UK Grand Challenge Verified Code Repository as a major case study for the application of formal methods to critical, large-scale software development.

It is unclear how to compare such a system to the current commercial and Free/-Libre/Open Source Software (FLOSS) voting systems being proposed by others, given that none of them, to our knowledge, even write formal specifications, let alone perform verification. We hope that this work will encourage other similar projects to seriously consider the use of lightweight formal methods in such critical systems development.

While integrating the Votáil subsystem into the KOA system, and prior to/during the new full FLOSS foundation release of KOA, a number of new pieces of English documentation and functional specification must be written. Given that remote voting is a key case study in verified computing, we hope that the availability of such documentation and specification will provide additional motivation for researchers and developers to seriously consider using the KOA system as a foundation for Verified Verifiable Voting (VVV).

We propose that the KOA system should be used as an *experimental platform* for research in electronic and internet voting; we are *not* saying that we have solved any of the major problems inherent in voting with computers. We encourage researchers interested in electronic and internet voting to contact us and join this effort.

Acknowledgments

This work is being supported by the European Project Mobius within the frame of IST 6th Framework, national grants from the Science Foundation Ireland and Enterprise Ireland and by the Irish Research Council for Science, Engineering and Technology. This paper reflects only the authors' views and the Community is not liable for any use that may be made of the information contained therein.

References

1. Albert, E., Arenas, P., Puebla, G.: An Incremental Approach to Abstraction-Carrying Code. In: LPAR 2006. LNCS, Springer, Heidelberg (2006)
2. Burdy, L., Cheon, Y., Cok, D., Ernst, M., Kiniry, J., Leavens, G.T., Rustan, K., Leino, M., Poll, E.: An Overview of JML Tools and Applications. International Journal on Software Tools for Technology Transfer (February 2005)
3. Chalin, P., Rioux, F.: Non-null References by Default in the Java Modeling Language. In: Proceedings of the Workshop on the Specification and Verification of Component-Based Systems (SAVCBS 2005) (September 2005)
4. Cheon, Y., Leavens, G.T.: A Simple and Practical Approach to Unit Testing: The JML and JUnit Way. In: Magnusson, B. (ed.) ECOOP 2002. LNCS, vol. 2374, pp. 231–255. Springer, Heidelberg (2002)
5. Cochran, D.: Secure Internet Voting in Ireland using the Open Source Kiezen op Afstand (KOA) Remote Voting System. Master's thesis, University College Dublin (March 2006)
6. Department of Environment and Local Government, Commission on Electronic Voting. Count requirements and commentary on count rules, (June 2000)
7. Department of Environment and Local Government, Commission on Electronic Voting. Count requirements and commentary on count rules, update no. 7: Available surpluses and candidates with zero votes (April 2002)

8. Fairmichael, F.: Full Verification of the KOA Tally System. Final Year Undergraduate Project Thesis (March 2005)
9. Jefferson, D., Rubin, A.D., Simons, B., Wagner, D.: Analyzing Internet Voting Security. Communication of the ACM 47(10), 59–64 (2004)
10. Kiniry, J.R., Cok, D.R.: ESC/Java2: Uniting ESC/Java and JML: Progress and issues in building and using ESC/Java2 and a report on a case study involving the use of ESC/Java2 to verify portions of an Internet voting tally system. In: Barthe, G., Burdy, L., Huisman, M., Lanet, J.-L., Muntean, T. (eds.) CASSIS 2004. LNCS, vol. 3362, Springer, Heidelberg (2005)
11. Kitcat, J.: Source availability and e-voting: an advocate recants. Communications of the ACM 47(10), 65–67 (2004)
12. LogicaCMG. Kiezen op Afstand: Hertellen Stemmen. Functional specifications (2004)
13. Fähndrich, M., Rustan, K., Leino, M.: Declaring and Checking Non-Null Types in an Object-Oriented Language. In: Proceedings of the 18th Annual ACM SIGPLAN Conference on Object-Oriented Programing, Systems, Languages, and Applications (OOPSLA 2003), pp. 302–312. ACM Press, New York, USA (2003)
14. Morkan, A.E.: KOA Evaluation, Demonstration Installation and Implementation. Final Year Undergraduate Project Thesis (March 2005)
15. Necula, G.C.: Proof-Carrying Code. In: Proceedings of the 24th ACM SIGPLAN-SIGACT Symposium on Principles of Programming Languages (POPL 1997), pp. 106–119. ACM Press, New York, USA (1997)

Security Types for Dynamic Web Data*

Mariangiola Dezani-Ciancaglini[1], Silvia Ghilezan[2], and Jovanka Pantović[2]

[1] Dipartimento di Informatica, Università di Torino, Italy
dezani@di.unito.it
[2] Faculty of Engineering, University of Novi Sad, Serbia
{gsilvia,pantovic}@uns.ns.ac.yu

Abstract. We describe a type system for the $Xd\pi$ calculus, introduced in [8]. An $Xd\pi$-network is a network of locations, where each location consists of both a data tree (which contains scripts and pointers to nodes in trees at different locations) and a process, for modelling process interaction, process migration and interaction between processes and data. Our type system is based on types for locations, trees and processes, expressing security levels. The type system enjoys type preservation under reduction (subject reduction). In consequence of subject reduction we prove the following security properties. In a well-typed $Xd\pi$-network, data in a location are accessible only to processes in locations of equal or higher security level. Moreover, processes originating in a location can only go to locations of equal or less security level, with the exception of movements which are returns to the "source" location.

1 Introduction

Information systems have evolved into open distributed systems that include decentralized peer-to-peer networks. An essential role of such systems is management of data, which appear to be semi-structured and distributed. Data-sharing applications require to integrate mobile processes and semi-structured data.

As information networks become more open and dynamic, the need for security and privacy grows stronger. Systems must be able to exchange data and processes while preserving security. One solution is to ground them on typed models. In such models, a well-typed network must reduce only to well-typed networks, assuring access and movement rights.

In this paper we describe a type system for the $Xd\pi$ calculus, introduced in [8]. An $Xd\pi$-network is a network of locations, where each location consists of both a data tree (which contains scripts and pointers to nodes in trees of different locations) and of a process, for modelling process interaction, process migration and interaction between processes and data.

We decorate location names with security levels taken from a partially ordered set of security levels with a bottom element. Therefore a location in a well-formed network will be of the shape:

$$l^h[\, T \parallel P \,]$$

* This work was partly funded by the project MMIT 1438 of PSNTR, by FP6-2004-510996 Coordination Action TYPES, by MIUR Cofin'04 project McTafi, and by the project GLORA 144029 of MSEP.

U. Montanari, D. Sannella, and R. Bruni (Eds.): TGC 2006, LNCS 4661, pp. 263–280, 2007.
© Springer-Verlag Berlin Heidelberg 2007

where l is a location name, h is its security level, T is a tree of data and P is a running process. Both the tree T and the process P agree with the level h as explained below.

The tree T can contain pointers to nodes in trees at locations different from l, but only if the security levels of these locations are less than or equal to h. The tree T moreover can contain scripts, i.e. static processes, which can be activated. In turn scripts, pointers and trees can occur inside scripts and running processes, always respecting the security levels.

Processes migrate thanks to the go command. The go command can only move a process from one location to a location of equal or lower security level, unless the process is "going home", i.e. migrating to the location where it was in the initial configuration.

The security levels of the communicated data inside a location will always be less than or equal to the security level of the location itself.

Running processes can activate scripts in the local tree by the command run_p, where p is a path expression which identifies a set of nodes. In a well-typed network all scripts in a tree agree with the security level of the enclosing location, and so they can run inside the location itself without breaking the security constraints.

Running processes can also modify the local tree and use the information in that tree by means of the command update. Well-formedness assures that the so obtained trees and processes respect the security level of the enclosing location.

By means of pointers from a tree in a location to a tree in another location, running processes can also copy and activate scripts of lower security level than the level of the enclosing location, but this is safe since a process which can run at a given security level can also run at all bigger security levels (but in general not at lower or incomparable security levels).

Related Work. The X$d\pi$ calculus [8,12] models both localised, mobile processes and distributed, dynamic, semi-structured data, allowing to represent data-sharing applications. It can be seen as an extension of the Active XML model [1].

The locations and the processes of X$d\pi$ are essentially those of $d\pi$ [9] enriched with capabilities for data manipulation. The only difference is that a process in $d\pi$ can migrate to a location independently from the existence of the location itself in the current network, while in X$d\pi$ such an existence is a necessary condition for migration. The data trees of X$d\pi$ are related to those in [2,4] and the treatment of shared distributed data is inspired by [16]. We refer to [8] for further references related to the calculus design.

Many type systems controlling the use of resources and the mobility of processes have been proposed for the $d\pi$ calculus [9] and for related calculi [14,6,5]. The types discussed here are essentially inspired by the security types checking access rights for π-calculus of [10]. For simplicity we do not distinguish between reading, writing and mobility rights, but our type system can be extended to take them into account. Another simplification is to have elements of a partially ordered set with a bottom element as security levels instead of elements of a lattice as it is usual [17], this choice being justified by the fact that we do not use meets and joins. We formalise the network properties assured by our type system using the notions of network invariant and initial network as in [3].

Outline of the paper Section 2 and Section 3 introduce the syntax, the reduction rules, and the typing rules of typed $Xd\pi$, exemplified by the examples in Section 4. The properties of the calculus are stated in Section 5. Section 6 contains a few final remarks.

2 Syntax and Operational Semantics

The $Xd\pi$ calculus we consider here is essentially a typed version of the calculus introduced in [8], with two simplifications.

In order to simplify the syntax we only allow monadic instead of polyadic communication and we do not distinguish between public channels (which cannot be restricted) and session channels (which must be restricted in the scripts)[1]. These features of the original $Xd\pi$ are handled easily by our type system.

To pave the way to the type system of next section we decorate the location names with security levels and the channel names with value types. We could avoid these decorations by fixing an environment giving these mappings.

The main difference between the original $Xd\pi$ and the present one is the use of a typed matching function instead of an untyped one. In order to have type preservation under reduction the matching needs to take types into account.

2.1 Syntax

Networks A network is a parallel composition (|) of locations consisting of a tree and a process, where processes at different locations can share communication channels. In a well-formed network the locations have different names. The syntax of networks is given in Table 1. We use l, m to range over location names, and h, j, i over security levels. The location $l^h[\, T \parallel P\,]$ is well-formed if both the tree T and the process P do not contain occurrences of free variables. We use c to range over channel names and tv denotes a value type as defined in Table 7. The binder ν is, as usual, the restriction operator.

Table 1. Syntax of networks

$$\mathbf{N} ::= \mathbf{0} \mid \mathbf{N} \mid \mathbf{N} \mid l^h[T \parallel P] \mid (\nu c^{tv})\mathbf{N}$$

Trees The data model is an unordered edge-labelled rooted tree with leaves containing scripts and pointers. The syntax of trees is presented in Table 2, using a to denote an edge label.

A *script* is a static process embedded in a tree that can be activated by a process from the same location. We use Π to range over processes and variables, and a script is denoted by $\Box\Pi$.

---

[1] The distinction between public and session channels is important for implementation since otherwise one needs to alpha-convert the whole data tree of a location when a process, restricting a channel name, migrates.

A *path* identifies nodes in a tree. Table 3 gives the formation rules of paths, using p to range over paths. In a path, "a" denotes a step along an edge a, " $//$ " denotes any node, ".." a step back, "." the path from the root to the current node, x a variable and "$/$ " the path composition. We will say that a path is a *local path* if it contains ".".[2].

Table 2. Syntax of trees

$$
\begin{array}{lll}
T ::= \emptyset & & \text{empty rooted tree} \\
\quad | \;\; x & & \text{tree variable} \\
\quad | \;\; T \mid T & & \text{composition of trees, joining the roots} \\
\quad | \;\; \mathsf{a}[T] & & \text{edge labeled a with subtree } T \\
\quad | \;\; \mathsf{a}[\Box \Pi] & & \text{edge labeled a with script } \Box \Pi \\
\quad | \;\; \mathsf{a}[p@\lambda] & & \text{edge labeled a with pointer } p@\lambda
\end{array}
$$

Table 3. Syntax of paths

$$
p ::= \mathsf{a} \;\mid\; // \;\mid\; .. \;\mid\; . \;\mid\; x \;\mid\; p/p
$$

We use λ to range over variables and location names super-scripted by security levels. A *pointer* $p@\lambda$ refers to the set of nodes in the tree at location λ identified by the path p.

Processes The processes that we are concerned with are essentially $d\pi$-calculus processes [9], where the local communication modelled by π-calculus processes [13], [18] is extended with migration between locations (command go). There are two more commands for local communication between processes and data: one for updating (copy, paste, cut, etc.) the data tree (update) and the other one that activates the execution of scripts that are embedded in local data tree (run). We use P, Q, R to range over processes, and γ to range over channel names (decorated by value types) and variables.

A *value* is either a channel name super-scripted with a value type, a tree, a script, a location name super-scripted with a security level, or a path. Using v to range over values, the syntax of values is:

$$
v ::= c^{tv} \;\mid\; T \;\mid\; \Box P \;\mid\; l^h \;\mid\; p.
$$

The syntax of processes is given in Table 4.

The argument of go is a location name (super-scripted with a security level) or a variable, or the symbol $\circlearrowright$, which denotes the enclosing location.

---

[2] The path syntax allows also meaningless paths, like "./ ./ .": this could be clearly avoided either by typing or by refining the syntax.

The two arguments of the update command are respectively a pattern χ and a data term V. *Patterns* have the form

$$\chi ::= x^j \mid y^\star @ x^j \mid \Box x^j$$

where j is a security level and $\star \in \{Local, \epsilon\}$ [3] indicates whether y stands for a local path or for a path without occurrences of ".". *Data terms* can be trees, pointers, or scripts:

$$V ::= T \mid p@\lambda \mid \Box \Pi.$$

In $\text{update}_p(\chi, V).P$ the variables of χ can occur both in V and in P and they are bound. For this reason we allow variable occurrences in trees, scripts and pointers.

Table 4. Syntax of processes

$P ::=$	0	the nil process
	$\mid P \mid P$	composition of processes
	$\mid (\nu c^{tv})P$	declare new channel name c
	$\mid \bar{\gamma}\langle v \rangle$	output value v on a channel γ
	$\mid \gamma(x).P$	input parameterized by a variable x
	$\mid !\gamma(x).P$	replication of an input process
	$\mid$ go $\lambda.P$	migrate to location λ, continue as P
	$\mid$ go $\circlearrowleft .P$	migrate home, continue as P
	$\mid \text{run}_p$	run the processes identified by the path expression p
	$\mid \text{update}_p(\chi, V).P$	update command

The structural congruence for $Xd\pi$ calculus is the least equivalence relation on networks that satisfies alpha-conversion, the commutative monoid properties for $(\emptyset, \mid)$ on trees, for $(0, \mid)$ on processes and for $(\mathbf{0}, \mid)$ on networks, the scope extrusion for restricted names, and it is preserved by the calculus constructs.

2.2   Reduction Rules

The reduction relation describes three forms of interactions: communication inside a location ((com), and (com!)), process movement between locations ((stay) and (go)) and local communication between processes and data ((update) and (run)). The reduction relation is the least relation on networks which is closed with respect to structural congruence, reduction rules given in Table 5 and reduction contexts, given by

$$C ::= - \mid C \mid \mathbf{N} \mid (\nu c^{tv})C.$$

The first two rules, (com) and (com!) are the communication rules from the π-calculus [13], [18]. Processes can communicate if they are in the same location.

---

[3] Here and in the following we use ϵ to denote the empty string, so we get either $y^{Local}@x^j$ or $y@x^j$.

Table 5. Reduction rules

(com)	$l^h[\, T \parallel \bar{c}^{tv}\langle v \rangle \mid c^{tv}(z).P \mid Q \,] \to l^h[\, T \parallel P\{v/z\} \mid Q \,]$
(com!)	$l^h[\, T \parallel \bar{c}^{tv}\langle v \rangle \mid !c^{tv}(z).P \mid Q \,] \to l^h[\, T \parallel !c^{tv}(z).P \mid P\{v/z\} \mid Q \,]$
(stay)	$l^h[\, T \parallel \mathbf{go}\ l^h.P \mid Q \,] \to l^h[\, T \parallel P \mid Q \,]$
(go)	$l^h[\, T_1 \parallel \mathbf{go}\ m^j.P \mid Q \,] \mid m^j[\, T_2 \parallel R \,] \to l^h[\, T_1 \parallel Q \,] \mid m^j[\, T_2 \parallel P \mid R \,]$

$$\text{(run)}\quad \frac{p(T) \rightsquigarrow_{p,l^h,\square x^h,\square x} T, \{\{\square P_1/\square x\}, \dots, \{\square P_n/\square x\}\}}{l^h[\, T \parallel \mathbf{run}_p \mid Q \,] \to l^h[\, T \parallel P_1 \mid \dots \mid P_n \mid Q \,]}$$

$$\text{(update)}\quad \frac{p(T) \rightsquigarrow_{p,l^h,\chi,V} T', \{s_1, \dots, s_n\}}{l^h[\, T \parallel \mathbf{update}_p(\chi,V).P \mid Q \,] \to l^h[\, T' \parallel Ps_1 \mid \dots \mid Ps_n \mid Q \,]}$$

Table 6. Definition of the update function $\rightsquigarrow$

(Empty tree)	$\emptyset \rightsquigarrow_\theta \emptyset, \emptyset$
(Script)	$\square P \rightsquigarrow_\theta \square P, \emptyset$
(Pointer)	$p@l^h \rightsquigarrow_\theta p@l^h, \emptyset$

$$\text{(Node)}\quad \frac{T \rightsquigarrow_\theta T', \Theta}{a[T] \rightsquigarrow_\theta a[T'], \Theta}$$

$$\text{(Par)}\quad \frac{T \rightsquigarrow_\theta T', \Theta_1 \qquad S \rightsquigarrow_\theta S', \Theta_2}{T|S \rightsquigarrow_\theta T'|S', \Theta_1 \cup \Theta_2}$$

$$\text{(Up)}\quad \frac{\mathtt{match}(U,\chi) = s \qquad Vs \rightsquigarrow_\theta V', \Theta \qquad \theta = p, l^h, \chi, V}{a[\underline{U}] \rightsquigarrow_\theta a[V'], \{s\{l^h/\circlearrowleft, p/.\}\} \cup \Theta}$$

There are two kinds of rules for migration. Rule (go) describes migration to a distinct location, which might be the home location. The other rule, (stay), describes staying at the location where you are, being it home location or not.

The command $\mathbf{run}_p$ finds all the scripts in the local tree identified by the path p and activates their parallel execution, after replacing $\circlearrowleft$ and . by the enclosing location and the path p, respectively.

The update command $\mathbf{update}_p(\chi, V).P$ traversing top-down the local tree finds all the data terms V_k given by the path p and pattern matches these data terms with χ to obtain substitutions s_k when they exist. For each successful pattern matching it replaces the V_k with Vs_k and starts Ps_k in parallel. The $\mathtt{match}$ function, in order to check if a data term agrees with a pattern, requires not only the data term to be, respectively, a tree, a pointer or a script according to the three shapes of the pattern (as in [8]), but it requires also the data terms to satisfy the type information given by the pattern. This means that:

(1) if the pattern is x^j, then the data term must be a tree of level j in a "home" location of level j too,

(2) if the pattern is $y^\star @x^j$, then the data term must be a pointer in which the path can be a local path only if $\star = Local$ and the location must be of level j,

(3) if the pattern is $\Box x^j$, then the data term must be a script of level j in a "home" location of level j too.

These conditions are enforced by using the type assignment system of next section. If the typed match is successful the function returns a substitution which replaces the variables in the pattern by the corresponding data terms. More precisely the definition of the match function is:

(1) $\mathtt{match}(T, x^j) = \{T/x\}$ if $\vdash_j T : Tree(j)$

(2) $\mathtt{match}(p@l^j, y^\star @x^j) = \{l^j/x, p/y\}$ if $\vdash p : Path^\star$

(3) $\mathtt{match}(\Box P, \Box x^j) = \{\Box P/\Box x\}$ if $\vdash_j P : ProcLocal(j)$.

The reduction rules for $\mathtt{update}$ and $\mathtt{run}$ are based on the definition of the update function $\rightsquigarrow$, parametrized on p, l^h, χ, V, which applied to a tree or to a node label returns a data term and a set of substitutions. Table 6 defines the function $\rightsquigarrow$. The only interesting rule is (Up): it matches the selected (underlined) U in $p(T)$ with χ obtaining a substitution $\mathtt{s}$. Then it continues updating Vs obtaining the data term V' and the set of substitutions Θ. Finally it replaces U with V' and adds to Θ the substitution $\mathtt{s}\{l^h/\circlearrowleft, p/.\}$, solving in this way the references to the enclosing location and to the current path.

3   Type Assignment

The main goals of our type system are to control communication of values, access to data and migration of processes between locations. We will formalise this in Section 5.

We rely on a notion of security levels, and therefore we assume a fixed partial order $(\mathcal{L}, \leq)$ of security levels with a bottom $\bot$. As already said in Section 2 we use h, j, i to range over elements of $\mathcal{L}$.

Table 7. Syntax of types

$ch(tv)$	type of channels communicating values of type tv
$Loc(i)$	type of locations at security level i
$Script(i)$	type of scripts at security level i
$Path$	type of paths, not containing "."
$PathLocal$	type of paths, possibly containing "."
$Pointer(i)$	type of pointers, not containing local paths, at security level i
$PointerLocal(i)$	type of pointers, possibly containing local paths, at security level i
$Tree(i)$	type of trees, not containing local paths, at security level i
$TreeLocal(i)$	type of trees, possibly containing local paths, at security level i
$Proc(i)$	type of processes, not containing local paths, at security level i
$ProcLocal(i)$	type of processes, possibly containing local paths, at security level i
Net	type of networks

where $i \in \mathcal{L}$ and tv ranges over value types defined by

$$tv ::= ch(tv) \mid Loc(i) \mid Script(i) \mid Path^\star \mid Tree^\star(i)$$

The syntax of types is the content of Table 7. Clearly the types correspond to the syntactic categories of previous section. We use the suffix *Local* when we allow local paths. This distinction is useful since a run or an update command containing a local path as index cannot be executed, but it can appear inside a script.

We will use $Path^\star$ as short for $Path$ or $PathLocal$ and similarly for the other types. When more than one $\star$ appears in a typing rule we always assume that all of them are replaced either by ϵ or by *Local*.

We introduce the turnstile both with and without the decoration of a security level. This decoration gives the security level of the enclosing location and it is used only in the typing rule for the go $\circlearrowleft$ command (see rule $(procIgohome)$ in Table 10). Since channel names, location names, and paths do not contain processes, we type them using the turnstile alone, while we use the decorated turnstile in typing scripts, pointers and trees. For scripts and trees the decoration is necessary, and we choose to use it also for pointers in order to have a uniform typing judgement for data terms. For typing processes we need both turnstiles, since a process containing a go $\circlearrowleft$ command cannot be executed, but it can play the role of a script. We will say more on this introducing the typing rules for processes and networks.

An *environment* Σ gives the association between:

- variables and value types
- variables and local process types

i.e. we define:
$$\Sigma := \emptyset \mid \Sigma, x : tv \mid \Sigma, x : ProcLocal(i).$$

We distinguish two sets of types which can be predicates in environments. The first set contains $ch(tv)$, $Loc(i)$ and $Path^\star$: we use σ to range over them. For these types we have typing judgements where the turnstile has no decoration. The second set contains the remaining types, i.e. $Script(i)$, $Tree^\star(i)$ and $ProcLocal(i)$: we use τ to range over them. For these types we have typing judgements where the turnstile is decorated by a security level. To each type τ we associate in a natural way a security level (notation $|\tau|$):

$$|Script(i)| = |Tree^\star(i)| = |ProcLocal(i)| = i.$$

We get therefore two axioms for using the environment, one for each set of types:

$$\frac{}{\Sigma, x : \sigma \vdash x : \sigma} \; (axiomCLP) \qquad \frac{|\tau| \leq h}{\Sigma, x : \tau \vdash_h x : \tau} \; (axiomSTPL)$$

where the condition $|\tau| \leq h$ enforces the policy that a location at level h can only contain values at level less than or equal to h.

The typing rules for channels, locations and scripts are as expected (recall that Π ranges over processes and variables):

$$\frac{}{\Sigma \vdash c^{tv} : ch(tv)} \; (chan) \qquad \frac{}{\Sigma \vdash l^i : Loc(i)} \; (loc) \qquad \frac{\Sigma \vdash_h \Pi : Proc^\star(i)}{\Sigma \vdash_h \Box\Pi : Script(i)} \; (script)$$

Paths are typed according to the rules in Table 8: a local path always gets the type $PathLocal$ instead of $Path$.

The typing rule for pointers

$$\frac{\Sigma \vdash \lambda : Loc(i) \quad \Sigma \vdash p : Path^\star \quad i \leq h}{\Sigma \vdash_h p@\lambda : Pointer^\star(i)} \ (pointer)$$

gives a *Pointer* or a *PointerLocal* type according to the path type. The security level of the pointer is the security level of the pointed location. The security level of the enclosing location is required only to be bigger than or equal to the one of the pointer.

According to the typing rules for trees in Table 9 the security level of a tree is bigger than or equal to the security levels of all its leaves. A tree that has at least one node labelled by a local pointer will be typed by *TreeLocal*.

Table 8. Typing of paths

$$\frac{}{\Sigma \vdash \mathsf{a} : Path} \ (path\mathsf{a}) \qquad\qquad \frac{}{\Sigma \vdash \mathbin{//} : Path} \ (path\mathbin{//})$$

$$\frac{}{\Sigma \vdash \mathbin{..} : Path} \ (path\mathbin{..}) \qquad\qquad \frac{}{\Sigma \vdash \mathbin{.} : PathLocal} \ (path\mathbin{.})$$

$$\frac{\Sigma \vdash p : Path^\star \quad \Sigma \vdash p' : Path^\star}{\Sigma \vdash p \mathbin{/} p' : Path^\star} \ (path/) \qquad \frac{\Sigma \vdash p : Path}{\Sigma \vdash p : PathLocal} \ (pathL)$$

Table 9. Typing of trees

$$\frac{i \leq h}{\Sigma \vdash_h \emptyset : Tree(i)} \ (treeEmpty) \qquad \frac{\Sigma \vdash_h T_1 : Tree^\star(i) \quad \Sigma \vdash_h T_2 : Tree^\star(i)}{\Sigma \vdash_h T_1 \mid T_2 : Tree^\star(i)} \ (tree\mid)$$

$$\frac{\Sigma \vdash_h T : Tree^\star(i)}{\Sigma \vdash_h \mathsf{a}[T] : Tree^\star(i)} \ (tree\mathsf{a}) \qquad \frac{\Sigma \vdash_h \Box\Pi : Script(i) \quad i \leq h}{\Sigma \vdash_h \mathsf{a}[\Box\Pi] : Tree(i)} \ (treeScript)$$

$$\frac{\Sigma \vdash_h p@\lambda : Pointer^\star(i) \quad i \leq h}{\Sigma \vdash_h \mathsf{a}[p@\lambda] : Tree^\star(i)} \ (treePointer)$$

$$\frac{\Sigma \vdash_h T : Tree(i)}{\Sigma \vdash_h T : TreeLocal(i)} \ (treeL) \qquad \frac{\Sigma \vdash_h T : Tree^\star(j) \quad j \leq i \leq h}{\Sigma \vdash_h T : Tree^\star(i)} \ (treeUp)$$

We have two sets of typing rules for processes, with and without the security level of the enclosing location as decoration of the turnstile. We call the first rules *initial* and the second rules *ongoing*, since we use the first set of rules for typing the initial networks, while we use both sets of rules for typing the networks obtained by reducing the initial ones. Table 10 gives the initial typing rules for processes.

In typing channel restrictions, inputs and outputs we define:

- the security levels of channel types as the security levels of the transmitted values and
- the security levels of path types as $\perp$.

In rule $(procIout)$ we take into account that a value can be:

- either a channel, a location, a path, and in this case it is typed with the turnstile without decoration (i.e. $\ominus = \epsilon$)
- or a tree, a script, and in this case it is typed with the decorated turnstile (i.e. $\ominus = i$).

Rule $(procIgo)$ allows a process in a location at security level i to migrate to a location at security level j only if $j \leq i$. Rule $(procIgohome)$ instead does not compare the security levels of the source and target locations, but it requires the security level of the target location to be the decoration of the turnstile. In the sequel, we will see that the typing rule $(netIloc)$ for "initial" networks (see Table 11) assures that the target location at run time will always be the "source" location of the process (as defined at page 278).

Table 10. Initial typing of processes

$$\frac{i \leq h}{\Sigma \vdash_h 0 : Proc^\star(i)} \; (procI0) \qquad \frac{\Sigma \vdash_h P_1 : Proc^\star(i) \quad \Sigma \vdash_h P_2 : Proc^\star(i)}{\Sigma \vdash_h P_1 \mid P_2 : Proc^\star(i)} \; (procI\mid)$$

$$\frac{\Sigma \vdash_h P : Proc^\star(i) \quad |tv| \leq i}{\Sigma \vdash_h (\nu c^{tv})P : Proc^\star(i)} \; (procI\nu)$$

$$\frac{\Sigma \vdash_\ominus v : tv \quad \Sigma \vdash \gamma : ch(tv) \quad |tv| \leq i \leq h \quad \ominus \in \{\epsilon, i\}}{\Sigma \vdash_h \bar{\gamma}\langle v \rangle : Proc^\star(i)} \; (procIout)$$

$$\frac{\Sigma, x : tv \vdash_h P : Proc^\star(i) \quad \Sigma \vdash \gamma : ch(tv) \quad |tv| \leq i}{\Sigma \vdash_h \gamma(x).P : Proc^\star(i)} \; (procIinput)$$

$$\frac{\Sigma, x : tv \vdash_h P : Proc^\star(i) \quad \Sigma \vdash \gamma : ch(tv) \quad |tv| \leq i}{\Sigma \vdash_h !\gamma(x).P : Proc^\star(i)} \; (procI!input)$$

$$\frac{\Sigma \vdash_h P : Proc^\star(j) \quad \Sigma \vdash \lambda : Loc(j) \quad j \leq i \leq h}{\Sigma \vdash_h \mathbf{go} \; \lambda.P : Proc^\star(i)} \; (procIgo)$$

$$\frac{\Sigma \vdash_h P : Proc^\star(h)}{\Sigma \vdash_h \mathbf{go} \; \circlearrowleft .P : Proc^\star(i)} \; (procIgohome) \qquad \frac{\Sigma \vdash p : Path^\star \quad i \leq h}{\Sigma \vdash_h \mathbf{run}_p : Proc^\star(i)} \; (procIrun)$$

$$\frac{\Sigma \vdash p : Path^\star \quad \Sigma \cup \Sigma_0 \vdash_h P : Proc^\star(i) \quad \Sigma_0 \vdash_i V : SPT(j) \quad j \leq i}{\Sigma \vdash_h \mathbf{update}_p(\chi, V).P : Proc^\star(i)} \; (procIupdate)$$

In the typing rule for update we assume that $\chi \in \{x^j, y^\star @ x^j, \Box x^j\}$, and we add the environment Σ_0 for associating types to the variables bound by the pattern. I.e. we put

$$\Sigma_0 = \begin{cases} x : Tree(j) \text{ if } \chi = x^j, \\ x : Loc(j), y : Path^\star \text{ if } \chi = y^\star @x^j, \\ x : ProcLocal(j) \text{ if } \chi = \Box x^j \end{cases}$$

In this rule SPT stands for $Script$ or $Pointer^\star$ or $Tree^\star$.

The set of the ongoing typing rules is obtained by:

- rewriting each initial rule for processes (except the rules $(procIgo)$ and $(procIgo home)$) without the decoration on the turnstile in the process judgements and without the relative conditions and
- replacing the $(procIgo)$ and $(procIgohome)$ rules by:

$$\frac{\Sigma \vdash P : Proc^\star(j)}{\Sigma \vdash go\ l^j.P : Proc^\star(i)} \quad (procOgo)$$

Notice that we erase decorations on the turnstile only in the process judgements[4]. This implies that, in the ongoing rule for typing the update command, the judgement about the data term V preserves the decorated turnstile. The judgement about the value v in the ongoing rule for typing the output preserves the decorated turnstile too.

Clearly, the rule $(procOgo)$ could violate the security policy of process migration. For this reason we allow to use it only in running processes, where if $i < j$, then go l^j has been obtained from go $\circlearrowright$ by replacing $\circlearrowright$ with the enclosing location l^j.

One can easily check that if $\Sigma \vdash_\ominus P : Proc^\star(i)$ and $i \le j$, then $\Sigma \vdash_\ominus P : Proc^\star(j)$, with $\ominus \in \{\epsilon, h\}$, so we do not need a typing rule for increasing the security level of processes.

Table 11. Typing of networks

$$\frac{\vdash_i T : Tree(i) \quad \vdash_i P : Proc(i)}{\vdash l^i[\, T \parallel P\{l^i/\circlearrowright\}\,] : Net} \quad (netIloc)$$

$$\frac{\vdash_i T : Tree(i) \quad \vdash P : Proc(i)}{\vdash l^i[\, T \parallel P\,] : Net} \quad (netOloc)$$

$$\frac{}{\vdash \mathbf{0} : Net} \ (net0) \qquad \frac{\vdash \mathbf{N} : Net}{\vdash (\nu c^{tv})\mathbf{N} : Net} \ (net\nu)$$

$$\frac{\vdash \mathbf{N}_1 : Net \quad \vdash \mathbf{N}_2 : Net \quad \mathcal{N}(\mathbf{N}_1) \cap \mathcal{N}(\mathbf{N}_2) = \emptyset}{\vdash \mathbf{N}_1 \mid \mathbf{N}_2 : Net} \quad (net|)$$

For typing a location in a network (see Table 11) we have two typing rules: the initial rule $(netIloc)$ and the ongoing rule $(netOloc)$. Both rules require the tree and the process to have the same security level of the enclosing location. Moreover, the

---

[4] This is sound since in the initial typing rules for processes the judgements whose subjects are not processes have turnstiles decorated by the security level of the process which is the subject of the conclusion.

first rule enforces the condition that only the enclosing location can be the target of movements in which the security level of the target location is bigger than the security level of the source location. Notice that the initial and the ongoing rules for networks use respectively the initial and the ongoing rules for processes in typing P and its subprocesses which are not inside scripts, while both rules use the initial rules for processes in typing scripts occurring inside the tree T or in process P.

The function $\mathcal{N}$ associates to a network the set of its location names:

$$\mathcal{N}(\mathbf{0}) = \emptyset \qquad \mathcal{N}(l^i[\, T \parallel P\,]) = \{l\} \qquad \mathcal{N}(\mathbf{N}_1 \mid \mathbf{N}_2) = \mathcal{N}(\mathbf{N}_1) \cup \mathcal{N}(\mathbf{N}_2).$$

It is used in rule $(net|)$ to assure that each location name occurs at most once in a typed network.

4 Examples

4.1 A Simple Example

Taking naturals as security levels, let us consider the following network:

$$l^4[\, \mathsf{a}[\mathsf{b}[\Box S]] \parallel \mathsf{run}_{\mathsf{a}/\mathsf{b}} \,] \mid m^2[\, \mathsf{c}[T] \parallel 0\,]$$

where $S = \mathsf{go}\ m^2.\mathsf{update}_{/\!/}(x^2, \emptyset).\mathsf{go}\ \circlearrowleft.P$, the process P is any process with security level 4, and T is any tree with security level 2.

The process $\mathsf{run}_{\mathsf{a}/\mathsf{b}}$ at location l with security level 4 will activate the execution of process S. Since location l has greater security level than location m, then l has access to the data of m, and execution will continue at location m by cutting subtrees (which match the tree pattern with given security level) of data tree and going back home to location l. We can prove that the given network is well-typed (see Figure 1).

This network can be reduced as shown in Figure 2, where $P' = P\{l^4/\circlearrowleft, \mathsf{a}/\mathsf{b}/.\}$, $T' = T\{m^2/\circlearrowleft, /\!/\!/.\}$ and $P'' = P'\{T'/x\}$. Every network in Figure 2 is also typable. Proofs are similar to the one for the initial network, except that for typing the running processes we use the ongoing typing rules instead of the initial ones.

For example, in order to show that

$$l^4[\, \mathsf{a}[\mathsf{b}[\Box S] \parallel \mathsf{go}\ m^2.\mathsf{update}_{/\!/}(x^2, \emptyset).\mathsf{go}\ l^4.P'\,] \mid m^2[\, \mathsf{c}[T] \parallel 0\,] : Net$$

we need to prove that $\vdash \mathsf{go}\ m^2.\mathsf{update}_{/\!/}(x^2, \emptyset).\mathsf{go}\ l^4.P' : Proc(4)$. This is the content of Figure 3.

In Figure 4, we present how the command update works in this example. We may update the data in the local tree only if the data identified by a path matches the typed pattern.

4.2 Remote Voting System

The next example models a remote voting for election of a leader from a given list of candidates, inspired by [11]. In this example we allow tree nodes to contain integers, in order to represent the count of votes. A pattern too can be a variable of type $Integer$.

$\cdots$

$$x : Tree(2) \vdash_4 P : Proc(4)$$

$$\vdash \; // : Path \qquad x : Tree(2) \vdash_4 \text{go} \circlearrowleft .P : Proc(2) \qquad x : Tree(2) \vdash_2 \emptyset : Tree(2)$$

$$\vdash_4 \text{update}_{//}(x^2, \emptyset).\text{go} \circlearrowleft .P : Proc(2) \qquad\qquad \vdash m^2 : Loc(2)$$

$$\vdash_4 \text{go } m^2.\text{update}_{//}(x^2, \emptyset).\text{go} \circlearrowleft .P : Proc(4)$$

$$\vdash_4 \Box\text{go } m^2.\text{update}_{//}(x^2, \emptyset).\text{go} \circlearrowleft .P : Script(4)$$

$$\vdash_4 b[\Box\text{go } m^2.\text{update}_{//}(x^2, \emptyset).\text{go} \circlearrowleft .P] : Tree(4)$$

$$\vdash_4 a[b[\Box\text{go } m^2.\text{update}_{//}(x^2, \emptyset).\text{go} \circlearrowleft .P]] : Tree(4)$$

$$\vdash a : Path \qquad \vdash b : Path$$

$$\vdash a/b : Path$$

$$\vdash_4 a[b[\Box\text{go } m^2.\text{update}_{//}(x^2, \emptyset).\text{go} \circlearrowleft .P]] : Tree(4) \qquad \vdash_4 \text{run}_{a/b} : Proc(4)$$

$$\vdash l^4[\, a[b[\Box\text{go } m^2.\text{update}_{//}(x^2, \emptyset).\text{go} \circlearrowleft .P]] \parallel \text{run}_{a/b}\,] : Net$$

$$\vdash_2 T : Tree(2)$$

$$\vdash_2 c[T] : Tree(2) \qquad \vdash_2 0 : Proc(2)$$

$$\vdash l^4[\, a[b[\Box\text{go } m^2.\text{update}_{//}(x^2, \emptyset).\text{go} \circlearrowleft .P]] \parallel \text{run}_{a/b}\,] : Net \qquad \vdash m^2[\, c[T] \parallel 0\,] : Net$$

$$\vdash l^4[\, a[b[\Box\text{go } m^2.\text{update}_{//}(x^2, \emptyset).\text{go} \circlearrowleft .P]] \parallel \text{run}_{a/b}\,] \mid m^2[\, c[T] \parallel 0\,] \; : \; Net$$

Fig. 1. Typing of $l^4[\, a[b[\Box\text{go } m^2.\text{update}_{//}(x^2, \emptyset).\text{go} \circlearrowleft .P]] \parallel \text{run}_{a/b}\,] \mid m^2[\, c[T] \parallel 0\,]$

$$l^4[\, a[b[\Box S]] \parallel \text{run}_{a/b}\,] \mid m^2[\, c[T] \parallel 0\,] \rightarrow$$
$$l^4[\, a[b[\Box S] \parallel \text{go } m^2.\text{update}_{//}(x^2, \emptyset).\text{go } l^4.P'\,] \mid m^2[\, c[T] \parallel 0\,] \rightarrow$$
$$l^4[\, a[b[\Box S] \parallel 0\,] \mid m^2[\, c[T] \parallel \text{update}_{//}(x^2, \emptyset).\text{go } l^4.P'\,] \rightarrow$$
$$l^4[\, a[b[\Box S] \parallel 0\,] \mid m^2[\, c[\emptyset] \parallel \text{go } l^4.P''\,] \rightarrow$$
$$l^4[\, a[b[\Box S] \parallel P''\,] \mid m^2[\, c[\emptyset] \parallel 0\,]$$

Fig. 2. Reduction of $l^4[\, a[b[\Box S]] \parallel \text{run}_{a/b}\,] \mid m^2[\, c[T] \parallel 0\,]$

$\cdots$

$$x : Tree(2) \vdash P' : Proc(4)$$

$$\vdash \; // : Path \qquad x : Tree(2) \vdash \text{go } l^4.P' : Proc(2) \qquad x : Tree(2) \vdash_2 \emptyset : Tree(2)$$

$$\vdash \text{update}_{//}(x^2, \emptyset).\text{go } l^4.P' : Proc(2) \qquad\qquad \vdash m^2 : Loc(2)$$

$$\vdash \text{go } m^2.\text{update}_{//}(x^2, \emptyset).\text{go } l^4.P' : Proc(4)$$

Fig. 3. Typing of $S\{l^4/\circlearrowleft, a/b/.\} \equiv \text{go } m^2.\text{update}_{//}(x^2, \emptyset).\text{go } l^4.P'$

By assumption $\vdash_2 T : Tree(2)$ and therefore, by the definition of typed matching,
$$\mathtt{match}(T, x^2) = \{T/x\}.$$

$$\cfrac{\cfrac{\mathtt{match}(T, x^2) = \{T/x\} \quad \emptyset \leadsto_{//,m^2,x^2,\emptyset} \emptyset, \emptyset}{\mathtt{c}[\underline{T}] \leadsto_{//,m^2,x^2,\emptyset} \mathtt{c}[\emptyset], \{T'/x\}, \quad T' = T\{m^2/\circlearrowleft, ///.\}}}{m^2[\,\mathtt{c}[\underline{T}] \parallel \mathtt{update}_{//}(x^2, \emptyset).\mathtt{go}\ l^4.P'\,] \rightarrow m^2[\,\mathtt{c}[\emptyset] \parallel \mathtt{go}\ l^4.P''\,]}$$

Fig. 4. An application of the command update

The network consists of an authority location, a register location and a fixed number of voter locations. The authority and register locations have level 2, while all the voter locations have level 1.

We describe the initial configuration of the network.

The register location contains no data and one process for each voter. These processes go to the voters to collect their identifiers, then go back to communicate these identifiers to the authority.

$$register^2[\ \emptyset \parallel \ \ldots \ | \ \mathtt{go}\ voter^1.a^{Path}(x).\mathtt{go}\ register^2.\bar{a}^{Path}\langle x \rangle \ | \ \ldots \ ]$$

A voter location contains an empty candidate list and two processes: the first process communicates the voter identifier and the second process waits to receive a channel along which he will communicate his vote:

$$voter^1[\ \mathtt{candList}[\emptyset] \parallel \bar{a}^{Path}\langle \mathtt{voterId} \rangle \ | \ b^{ch(Path)}(x).Choice(y).\bar{x}^{Path}\langle y \rangle \ ]$$

When the candidate list with the candidate names is the data of the voter location, the $Choice(y)$ process is supposed to choose a candidate name, and to assign this name to the variable y.

The authority location contains as data the candidate list (of security level 1), the candidate and vote list (of security level 2), and the voter list (of security level 2). The candidate list has for each candidate an edge labelled by the candidate name pointing to the empty tree. The candidate and vote list has for each candidate an edge labelled by the candidate name pointing to an integer (the vote counter, initially 0). The voter list has for each voter an edge labelled by the voter identifier pointing to the script process $\Box P$ described below. The process in the authority location starts the elections by going to the register location, collecting the voter identifiers, going back and running the scripts corresponding to the voter identifiers.

$$authority^2[\ T \parallel \mathtt{go}\ register^2.!a^{Path}(x).\mathtt{go}\ authority^2.\mathtt{run}_{\mathtt{voterList}/x}\ ]$$

where

$$T = \mathtt{candList}[T_1] \ | \ \mathtt{candVoteList}[T_2] \ | \ \mathtt{voterList}[\ldots \ | \ \mathtt{voterId}[\ \Box P\ ] \ | \ \ldots]$$

with

$$T_1 = \ldots \ | \ \mathtt{name}[\ \emptyset\ ] \ | \ \ldots \quad \text{and} \quad T_2 = \ldots \ | \ \mathtt{name}[\ 0\ ] \ | \ \ldots$$

We assume the candidate names, voter locations and voter identifiers to be all different. In writing the process P we use the following abbreviations, already defined in [8]:

$$\text{cut}_p(x^j).Q := \text{update}_p(x^j, \emptyset).Q$$
$$\text{copy}_p(x^j).Q := \text{update}_p(x^j, x).Q$$
$$\text{paste}_p\langle T\rangle.Q := \text{update}_p(x^j, x|T).Q \qquad \text{where } x \text{ does not occur in } T, Q$$
$$\text{and} \vdash_j T : Tree(j)$$

The process P erases the edge pointing to its script, copies the candidate list, goes to the voter, pastes locally the candidate list, communicates a private channel c, receives along this channel one candidate name, goes home and increases by 1 the corresponding candidate counter.

$$P = (\nu c^{Path})(\text{cut}_{\text{voterList/voterId}}(x^2).\text{copy}_{\text{candList}}(y^1).$$
$$\text{go } voter^1.\text{paste}_{\text{candList}}\langle y\rangle.\bar{b}^{ch(Path)}\langle c^{Path}\rangle.c^{Path}(z).$$
$$\text{go } \circlearrowleft.\text{update}_{\text{candVoteList}/z}(t^{Integer}, t+1))$$

Notice that a malicious voter cannot vote more than once, since the process P destroys his identifier, and if he would send the identifier of another voter, the other voter would receive the candidate list. Moreover a malicious voter cannot change the candidate or voter lists in the authority location, since the authority location has security level 2, while the voters have security level 1. For the same reason a voter cannot modify the processes inside the register location.

A malicious voter can send to the location of another voter a process which modifies the voter list or which votes in place of the voter itself. We do not know how to avoid this kind of attacks, which model a voter stealing the position of another voter during the voting act.

5 Safety

The present section is devoted to state the properties of well-typed networks. Since reducing a well-typed network only produces well-typed networks, it is enough to formulate the access and movement rights policy assured by our type system.

Theorem 1 (Subject reduction). *If* $\vdash$ **N** : *Net and* **N** $\rightarrow$ **N**$'$*, then* $\vdash$ **N**$'$: *Net.*

More meaningful than the subject reduction theorem are the following properties of well-typed networks:[5]

P0 a channel in a location of level h can communicate only values whose security level is less than or equal to h;

P1 a pointer from a tree in a location of level h to a tree in a location of level j implies $j \leq h$;

P2 a process can migrate from a location of level h to a location of level j only if either $j \leq h$ or it "goes home" (i.e. it is the "descendent" of a process originating from that location).

Property **P0** certifies that value communication respects the security levels. Property **P1** assures that the data in a location are accessible only to processes in locations of

---

[5] Notice that **P0**, **P1** and **P2** are network invariants in the sense of [3].

equal or higher security level. Property **P2** assures that the processes originating in a location can only go to locations of equal or less security level, with the exception of movements which are returns to the "source" location. As a consequence a process that originates from a location of a certain security level will never get hold of data of higher security level. Instead a process in a location of security level h can acquire data which reside in a location of security level j with $j > h$, but only if:

- the data itself are of security level h and
- the data transfer is done by a process whose "source" location has a security level bigger than or equal to j.

This is exemplified in Subsection 4.2 by the process which copies the candidate list from the data tree of the authority location and pastes it to the tree of the voter location.

Properties **P0** and **P1** can be formalised as follows (ν is a possibly empty sequence of channel restrictions):

Proposition 2

1. *If* $\vdash \nu(l^h[\, T \parallel \bar{c}^{tv}\langle v\rangle \mid P \,] \mid \mathbf{N})$: *Net, then* $|tv| \leq h$.
2. *If* $\vdash \nu(l^h[\, T \parallel P \,] \mid \mathbf{N})$: *Net and* $p@m^j$ *is the label of a node in* T, *then* $j \leq h$.

The proof of the above proposition follows from Generation Lemmas which exploit the invertibility of the rules $(netIloc)$, $(netOloc)$, $(procIout)$, $(procOout)$, and $(treePointer)$.

In order to discuss property **P2** we need to formalise the notion of "source" location of a process, and when a process is an "ancestor" of another process. Roughly by "source" location of a process we mean the location where the process or an ancestor of the process was in the initial net or where the process or an ancestor of the process was created by a run or by an update command.

We say that a network is *initial* when its locations can be typed by means of the initial typing rules. We use $\twoheadrightarrow$ to denote the reflexive and transitive closure of $\rightarrow$. If $\mathbf{N}$ is an initial network and $\mathbf{N} \twoheadrightarrow \nu(l^h[\, T \parallel P \mid Q \,] \mid \mathbf{N}')$, then the *source* location of the process P in this reduction is defined by induction on the reduction $\twoheadrightarrow$ and by cases:

- if $\mathbf{N} \equiv \nu(l^h[\, T \parallel P \mid Q \,] \mid \mathbf{N}')$, then the source location of P is l^h;
- if $\mathbf{N} \twoheadrightarrow \nu(l^h[\, T \parallel \mathrm{run}_p \mid Q' \,] \mid \mathbf{N}') \rightarrow \nu(l^h[\, T \parallel P \mid Q \,] \mid \mathbf{N}')$ since $p(T) \rightsquigarrow_{p,l^h,\square x^h,\square x} T, \{\{\square R_1/\square x\}, \ldots, \{\square R_n/\square x\}\}$ and $R_1 \equiv P \mid R$ and $Q \equiv R \mid R_2 \mid \ldots \mid R_n \mid Q'$, then the source location of P is l^h;
- if $\mathbf{N} \twoheadrightarrow \nu(l^h[\, T' \parallel \mathrm{update}_p(\chi, V).P' \mid Q' \,] \mid \mathbf{N}') \rightarrow \nu(l^h[\, T \parallel P \mid Q \,] \mid \mathbf{N}')$ since $p(T') \rightsquigarrow_{p,l^h,\chi,V} T, \{\mathsf{s}_1, \ldots, \mathsf{s}_n\}$ and $P'\mathsf{s}_1 \equiv P \mid R$ and $Q \equiv R \mid P'\mathsf{s}_2 \mid \ldots \mid P'\mathsf{s}_n \mid Q'$, then the source location of P is l^h;
- if $\mathbf{N} \twoheadrightarrow \nu(l^h[\, T \parallel \overline{c^{tv}}\langle v\rangle \mid c^{tv}(z).P' \mid Q' \,] \mid \mathbf{N}') \rightarrow \nu(l^h[\, T \parallel P \mid Q \,] \mid \mathbf{N}')$ and $P'\{v/z\} \equiv P \mid R$ and $Q \equiv R \mid Q'$, then the source location of P is the source location of $c^{tv}(z).P'$ in the reduction without the last step;
- if $\mathbf{N} \twoheadrightarrow \nu(l^h[\, T \parallel \overline{c^{tv}}\langle v\rangle \mid !c^{tv}(z).P' \mid Q' \,] \mid \mathbf{N}') \rightarrow \nu(l^h[\, T \parallel P \mid Q \,] \mid \mathbf{N}')$ and $P'\{v/z\} \equiv P \mid R$ and $Q \equiv !c^{tv}(z).P' \mid R \mid Q'$, then the source location of P is the source location of $!c^{tv}(z).P'$ in the reduction without the last step;

- if $\mathbf{N} \twoheadrightarrow \nu(l^h[\ T\ \|\ \text{go}\ l^h.P'\ |\ Q'\ ]\ |\ \mathbf{N}') \rightarrow \nu(l^h[\ T\ \|\ P\ |\ Q\ ]\ |\ \mathbf{N}')$ and $P' \equiv P\ |\ R$ and $Q \equiv R\ |\ Q'$, then the source location of P is the source location of go $l^h.P'$ in the reduction without the last step;
- if $\mathbf{N} \twoheadrightarrow \nu(l^h[T\ \|\ Q'\ ]\ |\ m^j[\ T'\ \|\ \text{go}\ l^h.P'\ |\ R\ ]\ |\ \mathbf{N}'') \rightarrow \nu(l^h[\ T\ \|\ P\ |\ Q\ ]\ |\ \mathbf{N}')$ and $P' \equiv P\ |\ R'$ and $Q \equiv R'\ |\ Q'$ and $\mathbf{N}' \equiv m^j[\ T'\ \|\ R\ ]\ |\ \mathbf{N}''$, then the source location of P is the source location of go $l^h.P'$ in the reduction without the last step;
- if $\mathbf{N} \twoheadrightarrow \nu(l^h[\ T'\ \|\ P\ |\ Q'\ ]\ |\ \mathbf{N}'') \rightarrow \nu(l^h[\ T\ \|\ P\ |\ Q\ ]\ |\ \mathbf{N}')$, then the source location of P is the source location of P in the reduction without the last step.

The first three cases are the basic cases, in which the process P takes the current location as source location: in the first one the network is initial, in the other two the process P is generated by the last reduction step. In the last case the reduction does not modify the process P, which preserves its source location. In all other cases an action prefixing the process P (possibly in parallel with other processes and/or modulo the substitution of a value for a variable) is consumed and the source location of P is the source location of the process starting with that action in the reduction without the last step.

The proof of the following proposition follows by induction on reductions.

Proposition 3. *In every network obtained by reducing an initial network each* go *command in a process either can be typed using the rule (procIgo) or it is followed by the source location of the process.*

We are now able to show that a process can migrate without respecting the security levels of the locations only if it goes back to its source location.

Proposition 4. *If* $\mathbf{N}$ *is an initial network and* $\mathbf{N} \twoheadrightarrow \nu(l^h[\ T\ \|\ \text{go}\ m^j.P\ |\ Q\ ]\ |\ \mathbf{N}')$, *then either* $j \leq h$ *or* m^j *is the source location of the process* go $m^j.P$.

Proof. (Sketch) By Proposition 3 go $m^j.P$ can be either typed by rule $(procIgo)$, and then $j \leq h$, or the source location of go $m^j.P$ must be m^j.

6   Conclusion

We discussed a typed version of the $Xd\pi$ calculus in which the access to resources and the mobility of processes must respect a security policy. Since we used a typed pattern matching which includes a dynamic type checking we will investigate both type checking and type inference for this calculus, taking into account [7].

We plan to study modifications of our type system which allow:

- to associate different security levels to different branches in the tree,
- to regulate process migration on the basis of the source locations of processes, instead of the current locations,
- to prevent illegal flow of information [15], also in presence of dynamic flow policies [19].

We will use the behavioural equivalence studied in [12,8] in order to compare networks.

Acknowledgements. We thank Philippa Gardner and Sergio Maffeis for their careful reading of an earlier version of the paper and for many useful remarks on it. We also thank the anonymous referees for detailed and appropriate comments. The final version of the paper strongly improved due to their suggestions.

References

1. Abiteboul, S., Benjelloun, O., Cautis, B., Milo, T.: Active XML, Security and Access Control. In: Lifschitz, S. (ed) SBBD'04, pp. 13–22 (2004)
2. Abiteboul, S., Buneman, P., Suciu, D.: Data on the Web: From Relations to Semistructured Data and XML. In: Data Management Systems, Morgan Kaufmann, Seattle (1999)
3. Ahern, A., Yoshida, N.: Formalising Java RMI with Explicit Code Mobility. In: Gabriel, R.P., Johnson, R. (eds.) OOPSLA'05, pp. 403–422. ACM Press, New York (2005)
4. Cardelli, L., Ghelli, G.: A Query Language Based on the Ambient Logic. In: Sands, D. (ed.) ESOP 2001 and ETAPS 2001. LNCS, vol. 2028, pp. 1–22. Springer, Heidelberg (2004) (Invited Paper)
5. Cardelli, L., Ghelli, G., Gordon, A.D.: Types for the Ambient Calculus. Information and Computation 177(2), 160–194 (2002)
6. Castagna, G., Vitek, J., Nardelli, F.Z.: The Seal Calculus. Information and Computation 201(1), 1–54 (2005)
7. Coppo, M., Cozzi, F., Dezani-Ciancaglini, M., Giovannetti, E., Pugliese, R.: A Mobility Calculus with Local and Dependent Types. In: Middeldorp, A., van Oostrom, V., van Raamsdonk, F., de Vrijer, R. (eds.) Processes, Terms and Cycles: Steps on the Road to Infinity. LNCS, vol. 3838, pp. 404–444. Springer, Heidelberg (2005)
8. Gardner, P., Maffeis, S.: Modelling Dynamic Web Data. Theoretical Computer Science 342, 104–131 (2005)
9. Hennessy, M., Riely, J.: Resource Access Control in Systems of Mobile Agents. Information and Computation 173, 82–120 (2002)
10. Hennessy, M., Riely, J.: Information Flow vs Resource Access in the Asynchronous π-calculus. ACM Transactions on Programming Languages and Systems 5, 566–591 (2003)
11. Kiniry, J., Morkan, A., Fairmichael, F., Cochran, D., Chalin, P., Oostdijk, M., Hubbers, E.: The KOA Remote Voting System: A Summary of Work To-Date. In These Proceedings (2007)
12. Maffeis, S., Gardner, P.: Behavioural Equivalencies for Dynamic Web Data. In: Lévy, J.-J., Mayr, E.W., Mitchell, J.C. (eds.) TCS'04, pp. 541–554. Kluwer, Dordrecht (2004)
13. Milner, R., Parrow, J., Walker, D.: A Calculus of Mobile Processes, I-II. Information and Computation 100(1), 1–77 (1992)
14. De Nicola, R., Ferrari, G., Pugliese, R., Venneri, B.: Types for Access Control. Theoretical Computer Science 240(1), 215–254 (2000)
15. Sabelfeld, A., Myers, A.C.: Language-Based Information-Flow Security. IEEE Journal on Selected Areas in Communications 21(1), 5–19 (2003)
16. Sahuguet, A.: ubQL: A Distributed Query Language to Program Distributed Query Systems. PhD thesis, Penn University (2002)
17. Sandhu, R.S.: Lattice-based Access Control Models. IEEE Computer 26(11), 9–19 (1993)
18. Sangiorgi, D., Walker, D.: The π-calculus: a Theory of Mobile Processes. Cambridge University Press, Cambridge (2001)
19. Zdancewic, S.: Challenges for Information-flow Security. In: Giacobazzi, R. (ed.) PLID'04 (2004) (Invited Paper)

Anonymity Protocols as Noisy Channels*

Konstantinos Chatzikokolakis[1], Catuscia Palamidessi[1],
and Prakash Panangaden[2]

[1] INRIA and LIX, École Polytechnique, Palaiseau, France
{kostas,catuscia}@lix.polytechnique.fr
[2] School of Computer Science, McGill University, Montreal, Quebec, Canada
prakash@cs.mcgill.ca

Abstract. We propose a framework in which anonymity protocols are
interpreted as particular kinds of channels, and the degree of anonymity
provided by the protocol as the converse of the channel's capacity. We
also investigate how the adversary can test the system to try to infer the
user's identity, and we study how his probability of success depends on
the characteristics of the channel. We then illustrate how various notions
of anonymity can be expressed in this framework, and show the relation
with some definitions of probabilistic anonymity in literature.

1 Introduction

In this paper we present a general approach to measure the *degree of anonymity*
provided by an anonymity protocol. Such protocols try to hide the link between
a set $\mathcal{A}$ of *anonymous events* and a set $\mathcal{O}$ of *observable events*. Events in $\mathcal{A}$
represent the information that we want to hide from the potential attacker.
Ideally, we would like him to be totally unable to distinguish the events in $\mathcal{A}$,
that is to deduce which of them really happened in a specific execution of the
protocol. Events in $\mathcal{O}$ are the ones that the attacker actually observes. They
should model all the possible outcomes of the protocol, from the point of view of
the attacker. We assume that in each execution of the protocol one event $a \in \mathcal{A}$
and one event $o \in \mathcal{O}$ occur, and that o is disclosed to the attacker. An anonymity
system should prevent the attacker from deducing a given the information about
o and the knowledge about how the system works.

For example, a protocol could be designed to allow users to send messages to
each other without revealing the identity of the sender. In this case, $\mathcal{A}$ would
be the set of (the identities of) the possible users of the protocol, if only one
user can send a message at a time, or the powerset of the users, otherwise. On
the other hand, $\mathcal{O}$ could contain the sequences of all possible messages that the
attacker can observe, depending on how the protocol works.

Probability plays an important role in anonymity protocols. First of all these
protocols are very often probabilistic themselves. They use random primitives

* This work has been partially supported by the INRIA DREI Équipe Associée
PRINTEMPS. The work of Konstantinos Chatzikokolakis and Catuscia Palamidessi
has been also supported by the INRIA ARC project ProNoBiS.

U. Montanari, D. Sannella, and R. Bruni (Eds.): TGC 2006, LNCS 4661, pp. 281–300, 2007.
© Springer-Verlag Berlin Heidelberg 2007

and the anonymity guarantees are based on the attacker's inability of determining the outcome of probabilistic choices. Clearly, the precise analysis of such protocols requires probabilistic means. Moreover, the analysis performed by the attacker can be also probabilistic, for example by gathering statistical information about the users. The attacker might not be able to find out exactly which anonymous event happened, but he could obtain a distribution over $\mathcal{A}$ and draw conclusions of the form "user i sent a message with probability 95%".

In this paper we consider a probabilistic setting, where probability distributions can be assigned to the elements of $\mathcal{A}, \mathcal{O}$. As a consequence we will model anonymous events by a random variable A on $\mathcal{A}$ and observable events by O on $\mathcal{O}$. From the point of view of the analysis, we are only interested in the distributions of A, O. In particular, the joint distribution $p(a, o)$ provides all the information about the conjoint behavior of the protocol and of the users that we need. From $p(a, o)$ we can derive, indeed, the marginal distributions $p(a)$ and $p(o)$, and the conditional distributions $p(o|a)$ and $p(a|o)$.

Most of the times, however, one is interested in abstracting from the specific set of users and its distribution, and proving properties about the protocol itself, aiming at *universal anonymity properties* that will hold no matter how the users behave (provided they follow the rules of the protocol). To this purpose, it is worth recalling that the joint distribution $p(a, o)$ can be decomposed as $p(a, o) = p(o|a)p(a)$. This decomposition singles out exactly the contributions of the protocol and of the users to the joint probability: $p(a)$, in fact, is the probability associated to the users, while $p(o|a)$ represents the probability that the protocol produces o given that the users have produced a. The latter clearly depends only on the internal mechanisms of the protocol, not on the users.

This view of the protocol in isolation from the users brings us to consider the protocol as a device that, given $a \in \mathcal{A}$ as input, it produces an output in $\mathcal{O}$ according to a probability distribution $p(\cdot|a)$. This concept is well investigated in information theory, where such kind of device is called *channel*, and it is described by the matrix whose rows are the elements of $\mathcal{A}$, the columns the elements of $\mathcal{O}$, and the value in position (a, o) is the conditional probability $p(o|a)$. The rationale behind this view will be discussed in more details in Section 3.

1.1   Contribution

In this paper we propose a definition of the degree of anonymity of a protocol in terms of the information-theoretic notion of *capacity* of the protocol, seen as channel. We also define a more general notion, that we call *relative capacity*, which naturally models the case in which some loss of an anonymity is allowed by design.

We investigate the relation between the channel's matrix and the knowledge that an attacker can gain on the anonymous actions (the channel's inputs) from the observables (the channel's outputs). In particular, we consider attackers following the Bayesian approach to *hypothesis testing*, and we show bounds on the Bayesian probability of error regarding the probabilistic information that the attacker can acquire.

We then compare our proposal with various probabilistic notions of anonymity given in the past, in particular perfect anonymity, group anonymity, and probable innocence. Finally, we show that the condition of probable innocence corresponds to a certain information-theoretic bound.

1.2 Related Work

Probabilistic definitions of anonymity have been explored in [1,2,3,4,5]. We discuss the relation with these works in detail in Section 5.

A recent line of work has been dedicated to exploring the notion of anonymity from an information-theoretic point of view [6,7]. The main difference with our approach is that in those works the anonymity degree is expressed in terms of entropy, rather than mutual information. More precisely, the emphasis is on the lack of information that an attacker has about the distribution of the users, rather than on the capability of the protocol to conceal this information despite of the observables that are made available to the attacker. Moreover, a uniform user distribution is assumed, while in this paper we try to abstract from the user distribution and make no assumptions about it.

Channel capacity has been already used in an anonymity context in [8,9], where the ability to have covert communication as a result of non-perfect anonymity is examined. The difference with our approach is that in those works the channels are constructed by the users of the protocol using the protocol mechanisms, and the purpose is to measure the amount of information that can be transfered through these channels. In this paper, we consider the channel to be the protocol itself, as an abstraction that allows us to measure anonymity.

Another approach close in spirit to ours is the one of [10]. In this work, the authors use the notion of relative entropy to perform a metric analysis of anonymity. In our work, we use the notion of mutual information, which is a special case of relative entropy. However, the specific application of relative entropy in [10] is radically different from ours. We use it to compare the entropy of the input of an anonymity protocol before and after the observation. They use it to establish a sort of distance between the traces of an anonymity system.

In the field of information flow and non-interference there is a line of research which is closely related to ours. There have been various works [11,12,13,14,15] in which the the *high information* and the *low information* are seen as the input and output respectively of a channel. From an abstract point of view, the setting is very similar; technically it does not matter what kind of information we are trying to conceal, what is relevant for the analysis is only the probabilistic relation between the input and the output information. The conceptual and technical novelties of this paper w.r.t. the above works are explained in Section 1.1. We believe that our results are applicable more or less directly also to the field of non-interference.

The relation between the adversary's goal of inferring a secret from the observables, and the field of "hypothesis testing", has been explored in other papers in literature, see in particular [16,17,18]. To our knowledge, however, this is the first time that it is investigated in connection with the matrix of conditional probabilities determined by the protocol.

1.3   Plan of the Paper

Next section recalls some basic notions about information theory. In Section 3 we justify our view of protocols as channels and (loss of) anonymity as capacity and relative capacity, and we give a method to compute these quantities in special symmetry cases. In Section 4 we consider the tests that an attacker can make on the protocol in order to gain knowledge about the anonymous actions, and we discuss the probability of error that limits the inferences based on such tests. Finally, in Section 5, we relate our framework to other probabilistic approaches to anonymity.

The proofs of all the results can be found on line at the URL:
`www.lix.polytechnique.fr/~catuscia/papers/Anonymity/Channels/full.pdf`.

2   Preliminaries on Information Theory

Being in a purely probabilistic setting gives us the ability to use tools from information theory to reason about the uncertainty of a random variable and the information that it can reveal about another random variable. In particular the notions we will be interested in are *entropy*, *mutual information* and *channel capacity*. In this section we briefly revise these notions. We refer to [19] for more details.

In general, we will use capital letters X, Y to denote random variables and the corresponding calligraphic letters $\mathcal{X}, \mathcal{Y}$ for their set of values. We will also use small letters x, y to represent values of these variables, $p(x), p(y)$ to denote the probability of x and y respectively and $p(x, y)$ to denote the joint probability of x and y.

Let X be a random variable. The *entropy* $H(X)$ of X is defined as $H(X) = -\sum_{x \in \mathcal{X}} p(x) \log p(x)$. The entropy measures the uncertainty of a random variable. It takes its maximum value $\log |\mathcal{X}|$ when X's distribution is uniform and its minimum value 0 when X is constant. We usually take the logarithm with a base 2 and measure entropy in *bits*. Roughly speaking, m bits of entropy means that we have 2^m values to choose from, assuming a uniform distribution.

The *relative entropy* or *Kullback Leibler distance* between two probability distributions p, q on the same set $\mathcal{X}$ is defined as $D(p \parallel q) = \sum_{x \in \mathcal{X}} p(x) \log \frac{p(x)}{q(x)}$. It is possible to prove that $D(p \parallel q)$ is always non-negative, and it is 0 if and only if $p = q$.

Now let X, Y be random variables. The *conditional entropy* $H(X|Y)$ is $H(X|Y) = -\sum_{y \in \mathcal{Y}} p(y) \sum_{x \in \mathcal{X}} p(x|y) \log p(x|y)$. Conditional entropy measures the amount of uncertainty of X when Y is known. It can be shown that $0 \leq H(X|Y) \leq H(X)$. It takes its maximum value $H(X)$ when Y reveals no information about X, and its minimum value 0 when Y completely determines the value of X.

Comparing $H(X)$ and $H(X|Y)$ gives us the concept of *mutual information* $I(X;Y)$, which is defined as $I(X;Y) = H(X) - H(X|Y)$. Mutual information measures the amount of information that one random variable contains about another random variable. In other words, it measures the amount of uncertainty about X that we lose when observing Y. It can be shown that it is symmetric $(I(X;Y) = I(Y;X))$ and that $0 \le I(X;Y) \le H(X)$.

A *communication channel* is a tuple $\langle \mathcal{X}, \mathcal{Y}, p(\cdot|\cdot) \rangle$ where $\mathcal{X}, \mathcal{Y}$ are the sets of input and output symbols respectively and $p(y|x)$ is the probability of observing output $y \in \mathcal{Y}$ when $x \in \mathcal{X}$ is the input. Given an input distribution $p(x)$ over $\mathcal{X}$ we can define the random variables X, Y for input and output respectively. The maximum mutual information between X and Y over all possible distributions $p(x)$ is known as the channel's *capacity*: $C = \max_{p(x)} I(X;Y)$. The capacity of a channel gives the maximum rate at which information can be transmitted using this channel.

3 Loss of Anonymity as Channel Capacity

The notions discussed in previous section can be used to reason about the information that the adversary obtains from the protocol. The entropy $H(A)$ of A gives the amount of uncertainty about the anonymous events, before executing the protocol. The higher the entropy is the less certain we are about the outcome of A. After the execution, however, we also know the actual value of O. Thus, the conditional entropy $H(A|O)$ gives the uncertainty of the attacker about the anonymous events after performing the observation. To compare these two entropies, we consider the mutual information $I(A;O)$ which measures the information about A that is contained in O. This measure is exactly what we want to minimize. It the best case it is 0, meaning that we can learn nothing about A by observing O (in other words $H(A|O)$ is equal to $H(A)$). In the worst case it is equal to $H(A)$ meaning that all the uncertainty about A is lost after the observation, thus we can completely deduce the value of A ($H(A|O)$ is 0).

As explained in the introduction, each execution of an anonymity protocol is associated to the join probability $p(a, o)$ of the particular values taken by A, O in that execution. This probability can be written as $p(a, o) = p(a)p(o|a)$. In our view, among these two values, $p(o|a)$ can be considered as a characteristic of the protocol, while $p(a)$ depends only on the users. For instance, in a protocol for sender anonymity, A takes values on the set $\mathcal{A}$ of users, and $p(a)$ is the probability of user a being the sender. In some cases all users might have the same probability of being the sender, in other cases a particular user might send messages more often than the others. Since the design of the protocol should be independent from the particular users who will use it, the analysis of the protocol should make no assumptions about the distribution on $\mathcal{A}$. On the other hand $p(o|a)$ gives the probability of o when a is the sender, so it depends only on the internal mechanisms of the protocol, not on of how often a sends messages.

To abstract from the probabilities of the anonymous events, we view an anonymity protocol as a channel $\langle \mathcal{A}, \mathcal{O}, p(\cdot|\cdot) \rangle$ where the sets of anonymous

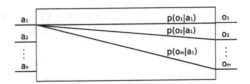

Fig. 1. An anonymity channel

events $\mathcal{A}$ and observable events $\mathcal{O}$ are the input and output alphabets respectively, and the matrix $p(o|a)$ gives the probability of observing o when a is the input. An anonymity channel is shown in Figure 1. Different distributions of the input will give different values of $I(A; O)$. We are interested in the worst possible case, so we define the *loss of anonymity* as the maximum value of $I(A; O)$ over all possible input distributions, that is the capacity of the corresponding channel.

Definition 1. *Let* $\langle \mathcal{A}, \mathcal{O}, p(\cdot|\cdot) \rangle$ *be an anonymity protocol. The* loss of anonymity C *of the protocol is defined as*

$$C = \max_{p(a)} I(A; O)$$

where the maximum is taken over all possible input distributions.

The loss of anonymity measures the amount of information about A that can be learned by observing O in the worst possible distribution of anonymous events. If it is 0 then, no matter what is the distribution of A, the attacker can learn nothing more by observing the protocol. In fact, as we will see in section 5.1, this corresponds exactly to notions of perfect anonymity in literature [1,2,3]. However, as we discuss in section 5.3, our framework also captures weaker notions of anonymity.

As with entropy, channel capacity is measured in bits. Roughly speaking, 1 bit of capacity means that after the observation A will have one bit less of entropy, in another words the attacker will have reduced the set of possible users by a factor 2, assuming a uniform distribution.

3.1 Relative Anonymity

So far, we have assumed that ideally no information about the anonymous events should be leaked. However, there are cases where *some* information about the anonymous events is allowed to be revealed by design, without this leak be considered as a flaw of the protocol. Consider, for example, the case of a simple elections protocol, displayed in figure 2. For simplicity we assume that there are only two candidates c and d, and that each user always votes for one of them, so an anonymous event can be represented by the subset of users who voted for candidate c. In other words, $\mathcal{A} = 2^V$ where V is the set of voters. The output of the protocol is the list of votes of all users, however, in order

Fig. 2. A simple elections protocol

to achieve anonymity, the list is randomly reordered, using for example some MIX technique[1]. As a consequence, the attacker can see the number of votes for each candidate, although he should not be able to find out who voted for whom. Indeed, determining the number of votes of candidate c (the cardinality of a), while concealing the vote expressed by each individual (the elements that constitute a), is the purpose of the protocol.

So it is clear that after the observation only a fraction of the anonymous events remains possible. Every event $a \in \mathcal{A}$ with $|a| \neq n$ where n is the number of votes for candidate c can be ruled out. As a consequence $H(A|O)$ will be smaller than $H(A)$ and the capacity of the corresponding channel will be non-zero, meaning that some anonymity is lost. In addition, there might be a loss of anonymity due to other factors, for instance, if the reordering technique is not uniform. However, it is undesirable to confuse these two kinds of anonymity losses, since the first is by design and thus acceptable. We would like a notion of anonymity that factors out the *intended* loss and measures only the loss that we want to minimize.

In order to cope with the intended anonymity loss, we introduce a random variable R whose outcome is the revealed information. In the example of the elections protocol, the value of R is the cardinality of a. Since we allow to reveal R by design, we can consider that R is known even before executing the protocol. So, $H(A|R)$ gives the uncertainty about A given that we know R and $H(A|R, O)$ gives the uncertainty after the execution of the protocol, when we know both R and O. By comparing the two we retrieve the notion of *conditional mutual information* $I(A; O|R)$ defined as

$$I(A; O|R) = H(A|R) - H(A|R, O)$$

So, $I(A; O|R)$ is the amount of uncertainty on A that we lose by observing O, given that R is known. Now we can define the notion of *relative loss of anonymity*.

Definition 2. *Let* $\langle \mathcal{A}, \mathcal{O}, p(\cdot|\cdot) \rangle$ *be an anonymity protocol and* R *a random variable defined by its set of values* $\mathcal{R}$ *and a probability matrix* $p(r|a, o)$. *The* relative loss of anonymity *of the protocol with respect to* R *is defined as*

$$C|R = \max_{p(a)} I(A; O|R)$$

where the maximum is taken over all possible input distributions.

---

[1] In MIX protocols an agent waits until it has received requests from multiple users and then forwards the requests in random order to hide the link between the sender and the receiver of each request.

Partitions: a special case of relative anonymity. An interesting special case of relative anonymity is when the knowledge of either an anonymous event or an observable event totally determines the value of R. In other words, both $\mathcal{A}$ and $\mathcal{O}$ are partitioned in subsets, one for each possible value of R. The elections protocol of the previous section is an example of this case. In this protocol, the value r of R is the number of votes for candidate A. This is totally determined by both anonymous events a (r is the cardinality of a) and observable events o (r is the number of c's in o). So we can partition $\mathcal{A}$ in subsets $\mathcal{A}_0, \ldots, \mathcal{A}_n$ such that $|a| = n$ for each $a \in \mathcal{A}_n$, and similarly for $\mathcal{O}$. Notice that an anonymous event $a \in \mathcal{A}_i$ produces only observables in $\mathcal{O}_i$, and vice versa.

In this section we show that such systems can be viewed as the composition of smaller, independent sub-systems, one for each value of R.

We say that R partitions a random variable X if $p(r|x)$ is 0 or 1 for all $r \in \mathcal{R}$ and $x \in \mathcal{X}$. In this case we can partition $\mathcal{X}$ as follows

$$\mathcal{X}_r = \{x \in \mathcal{X} \mid p(r|x) = 1\}$$

Clearly the above sets are disjoint and their union is $\mathcal{X}$.

Theorem 1. *Let $\langle \mathcal{A}, \mathcal{O}, p(\cdot|\cdot) \rangle$ be an anonymity protocol and R a random variable defined by its set of values $\mathcal{R} = \{r_1, \ldots, r_l\}$ and a probability matrix $p(r|a, o)$. If R partitions both A and O then the transition matrix of the protocol is of the form*

	$\mathcal{O}_{r_1}$	$\mathcal{O}_{r_2}$	$\cdots$	$\mathcal{O}_{r_l}$
$\mathcal{A}_{r_1}$	M_{r_1}	0	$\cdots$	0
$\mathcal{A}_{r_2}$	0	M_{r_2}	$\cdots$	0
$\vdots$	$\vdots$	$\vdots$	$\ddots$	$\vdots$
$\mathcal{A}_{r_l}$	0	0	$\cdots$	M_{r_l}

and

$$C|R \leq d \quad \Leftrightarrow \quad C_i \leq d, \forall i \in 1..l$$

where C_i is the capacity of the channel with matrix M_{r_i}.

3.2   Computing the Channel's Capacity

In general, there is no formula to compute the capacity of an arbitrary channel. In practice, however, channels have symmetry properties that can be exploited to compute the capacity in an easy way. In this section we define classes of symmetry and discuss how to compute the capacity for each class. Two classic cases are the *symmetric* and *weakly symmetric* channels.

Definition 3. *A matrix is* symmetric *if all rows are permutations of each other and all columns are also permutations of each other. A matrix is* weakly symmetric *if all rows are permutations of each other and the column sums are equal.*

The following result is from literature:

Theorem 2 ([19], page 189). *Let* $\langle \mathcal{A}, \mathcal{O}, p(\cdot|\cdot) \rangle$ *be a channel. If* $p(\cdot|\cdot)$ *is weakly symmetric then the channel's capacity is given by a uniform input distribution and is equal to*

$$C = \log |\mathcal{O}| - H(\mathbf{r})$$

where $\mathbf{r}$ *is a row of the matrix and* $H(\mathbf{r})$ *is the entropy of* $\mathbf{r}$.

Note that symmetric channels are also weakly symmetric so Theorem 2 holds for both classes.

In anonymity protocols, we expect all rows of the protocol's matrix to be permutations of each other since all users are executing the same protocol. On the other hand, the columns are not necessarily permutations of each other. Some symmetry is expected: if an observable o_1 is produced with probability p under user a_1, it is reasonable to assume that under a_2 there will be some other observable o_2 produced with the same probability. However, we can have observables that are produced with equal probability by all users. Clearly, these "constant" columns cannot be the permutation of a non-constant one so the resulting channel matrix will not be symmetric (and not even weakly symmetric).

To cope with this kind of channels we define a more relaxed kind of symmetry called *partial symmetry*. In this class we allow some columns to be constant and we require the sub-matrix, composed only by the non-constant columns, to be symmetric. A weak version of this symmetry can also be defined.

Definition 4. *A matrix is* partially symmetric *(resp.* weakly partially symmetric*) if some columns are constant (possibly with different values in each column) and the rest of the matrix is symmetric (resp. weakly symmetric).*

Now we can extend Theorem 2 to the case of partial symmetry.

Theorem 3. *Let* $\langle \mathcal{A}, \mathcal{O}, p(\cdot|\cdot) \rangle$ *be a channel. If* $p(\cdot|\cdot)$ *is weakly partially symmetric then the channel's capacity is given by*

$$C = p_s \log \frac{|\mathcal{O}_s|}{p_s} - H(\mathbf{r}_s)$$

where $\mathcal{O}_s$ *is the set of symmetric output values,* $\mathbf{r}_s$ *is the symmetric part of a row of the matrix and* p_s *is the sum of* $\mathbf{r}_s$.

Note that Theorem 3 is a generalization of Theorem 2. A (weakly) symmetric channel can be considered as (weakly) partially symmetric with no constant columns. In this case $O_s = O, \mathbf{r}_s = \mathbf{r}, p_s = 1$ and we retrieve Theorem 2 from Theorem 3.

4   Testing Anonymous Events

In this section we illustrate the relation between the channel's matrix and the possibility for the attacker of guessing the anonymous event from the consequent observable event. This problem is known in statistics literature as *hypothesis testing.* The idea is that we have a set of data or outcomes of an experiment, and a set of possible alternative explanations (*hypotheses*). We have to infer which hypothesis holds from the data, possibly by repeating the experiment, and try to minimize the probability of guessing the wrong hypothesis (*probability of error*).

We assume that the same hypothesis holds through the repetition of the experiment, which corresponds to allowing the attacker to force the user to redo the action. For instance, in Crowds, the attacker can intercept the message and destroy it, thus obliging the sender to resend it. We also assume that the random variables corresponding to the outcomes of the experiments are independent. This corresponds to assuming that the protocol is memoryless, i.e. each time it is reactivated, it works according to the same probability distribution, independently from what happened in previous sessions.

In statistics there are several frameworks and methods for hypothesis testing. We consider here the Bayesian approach, which requires the knowledge of the matrix of the protocol and of the *a priori* distribution of the hypotheses, and tries to infer the *a posteriori* probability of the actual hypothesis w.r.t. a given observation or sequence of observations. The first assumption (knowledge of the matrix of the protocol) is usually granted in an anonymity setting, since the way the protocol works is public. The second assumption may look too strong, since the attacker does not usually know the distribution of the anonymous actions. We show, however, that under certain conditions the a priori distribution becomes less and less relevant with the repetition of the experiment, and, at the limit, it does not matter at all.

Let us introduce some notation. Given an anonymous event a, consider the situation in which the attacker forces the users to execute the protocol n times with the same a as input event, and tries to infer a from the n observable outputs of the protocol executions. Let $O_1, O_2, \ldots, O_n$ represent the random variables corresponding to the observations made by the attacker, and let o denote a sequence of observed outputs $o_1, o_2, \ldots o_n$. As stated above, we assume that O_1, $O_2, \ldots, O_n$ are independent, hence the distribution of each of them is given by $p(\cdot|a)$, and their conjoint distribution $p : \mathcal{O}^n \to [0, 1]$ is given by

$$p(o|a) = \prod_{i=1}^{n} p(o_i|a) \tag{1}$$

Let $f_n : \mathcal{O}^n \to \mathcal{A}$ be the *decision function* adopted by the adversary to infer the anonymous action from the sequence of observables. Let $E_{f_n} : \mathcal{A} \to \mathcal{O}^n$ be the function that gives the *error region* of f_n when $a \in \mathcal{A}$ has occurred, namely:

$$E_{f_n}(a) = \{o \in \mathcal{O}^n \mid f_n(o) \neq a\}$$

Finally, let $\eta_n : \mathcal{A} \to [0, 1]$ be the function that associates to each $a \in \mathcal{A}$ the probability of inferring the wrong input event on the basis of f_n when $a \in \mathcal{A}$ has occurred, namely:

$$\eta_n(a) = \sum_{o \in E_{f_n}(a)} p(o|a)$$

We are now ready to introduce the *probability of error* associated to anonymous action testing on a given anonymity protocol, following the lines of the Bayesian approach (see for instance [19], Section 12.8).

Definition 5. *Given an anonymity protocol* $\langle \mathcal{A}, \mathcal{O}, p(\cdot|\cdot)\rangle$, *a sequence of n experiments, and a decision function* f_n, *the Bayesian probability of error* P_{f_n} *is defined as the probability weighted sum over* $\mathcal{A}$ *of the individual probabilities of error. Namely:*

$$P_{f_n} = \sum_{a \in A} p(a)\eta_n(a)$$

In the Bayesian framework, the best possible decision function is given by the so-called *maximum a posteriori rule*, which, given the sequence of observables $o \in \mathcal{O}^n$, tries to maximize the a posteriori probability of the hypothesis a w.r.t. o. The a posteriori probability of a w.r.t. o is given by Bayes theorem (aka Bayes Inversion Rule):

$$p(a|o) = \frac{p(o|a)p(a)}{p(o)}$$

We now define a class of decision functions based on the above approach.

Definition 6. *Given an anonymity protocol* $\langle \mathcal{A}, \mathcal{O}, p(\cdot|\cdot)\rangle$, *and a sequence of n experiments, a decision function* f_n *is a Bayesian decision function if for each* $o \in \mathcal{O}^n$, $f_n(o) = a$ *implies* $p(o|a)p(a) \geq p(o|a')p(a')$ *for every* $a' \in \mathcal{A}$.

The above definition is justified by the following result which is a straightforward consequence of known results in literature.

Proposition 1. *Given an anonymity protocol* $\langle \mathcal{A}, \mathcal{O}, p(\cdot|\cdot)\rangle$, *a sequence of n experiments, and a Bayesian decision function* f_n, *for any other decision function* h_n *we have that* $P_{f_n} \leq P_{h_n}$.

4.1   Independence from the Input Distribution

The definition of the Bayesian decision functions depends on the a priori probability distribution on $\mathcal{A}$. This might look artificial, since in general such distribution is unknown. We will show, however, that under a certain condition on the matrix of the protocol, for n large enough, the Bayesian decision functions and the associated Bayesian probability of error do not depend on the distribution on $\mathcal{A}$.

The following definition establishes the condition on the matrix.

Definition 7. *Given an anonymity protocol* $\langle \mathcal{A}, \mathcal{O}, p(\cdot|\cdot)\rangle$, *we say that such protocol is Bayesian-determinate iff all rows are pairwise different, i.e. the probability distributions* $p(\cdot|a)$, $p(\cdot|a')$ *are different for each pair* a, a' *with* $a \neq a'$.

We will now show that if a protocol is Bayesian-determinate, then in the definition of the decision functions the distribution on $\mathcal{A}$ eventually washes out. The intuition is that, in the comparison between $p(o|a)p(a)$ and $p(o|a')p(a')$, the factor $p(a)p(a')$ is dominated by the factor $p(o|a)p(o|a')$, for n large enough, provided that the latter is different from 1.

Proposition 2. *Given a Bayesian-determinate anonymity protocol $\langle \mathcal{A}, \mathcal{O}, p(\cdot|\cdot) \rangle$, for any distribution $p(\cdot)$ on $\mathcal{A}$, any Bayesian decision functions f_n, and any decision function $g_n : \mathcal{O}^n \to \mathcal{A}$ such that $g_n(o) = a$ implies $p(o|a) \geq p(o|a')$ for all $a' \in \mathcal{A}$, we have that g_n approximates f_n. Namely, for any $\epsilon > 0$, there exists n such that the probability of the set $\{o \in \mathcal{O}^n \mid f_n(o) \neq g_n(o)\}$ is smaller than ϵ.*

Proposition 2 allows us to define a decision function, for n sufficiently large, by comparing only the probabilities $p(o|a)$ for different a's. These probabilities are determined uniquely by the matrix and therefore no knowledge of the a priori probability on A is required.

4.2   Bounds on the Bayesian Probability of Error

In this section we discuss some particular cases of matrices and the corresponding bounds on the error that can be introduced by the Bayesian decision functions. Some more cases will be considered in the next section.

We start with the bad case (from the anonymity point of view), which is when the matrix is Bayesian-determinate:

Proposition 3. *Given a Bayesian-determinate anonymity protocol $\langle \mathcal{A}, \mathcal{O}, p(\cdot|\cdot) \rangle$, for any distribution $p(\cdot)$ on $\mathcal{A}$, and for any ϵ, there exists n such that the property*

$$g_n(o) = a \text{ implies } p(o|a) \geq p(o|a') \text{ for all } a' \in \mathcal{A}$$

determines a unique decision function g_n on a set of probability greater than $1 - \epsilon$, and the Bayesian probability of error P_{g_n} is smaller than ϵ.

Proposition 3 and its proof tell us that, in case of Bayesian-determinate matrices, there is essentially only one decision function, and it is value is determined, for n sufficiently large, by the a for which $p(o|a)$ is greatest.

Consider now the opposite case, i.e. when there are at least two identical rows in the matrix, in correspondence of a_1 and a_2. In such case, for the sequences $o \in \mathcal{O}^n$ such that $p(o|a_1)(= p(o|a_2))$ is maximal, the value of g_n is not uniquely determined, because we could choose either a_1 or a_2. Assuming that we choose arbitrarily between them, and that the probability of choosing the wrong one is uniformly distributed, we have that the Bayesian probability of error is bound from below as follows[2]: $P_{g_n} = \sum_{a \in \mathcal{A}} p(a) \eta_n(a) \geq p(a_1)1/2 + p(a_2)1/2$.

More in general, if there are k identical rows $a_1, a_2, \ldots, a_k$, the lower bound to the Bayesian probability of error is $P_{g_n} = \sum_{a \in \mathcal{A}} p(a) \eta_n(a) \geq p(a_1)(k-1)/k + p(a_2)(k-1)/k + \ldots + p(a_k)(k-1)/k$.

The situation is slightly different if we know the a priori distribution and we define the function f_n. In this case, the criterion of maximizing $p(a)p(o|a)$ reduces to maximizing $p(a)$. Hence, observing the outcome of the protocol does not add

---

[2] Note that this bound is strict. In fact, using the strong law of large numbers it is possible to prove that, when either a_1 or a_2 is the actual input, the probability of the set of the sequences $o \in \mathcal{O}^n$ for which $p(o|a_1)$ (and $p(o|a_2)$) is maximal goes to 1 as n goes to ∞.

any information to what we already know. However, the a priori knowledge can help to make a sensible guess about the most likely a. This is not the case, of course, if in addition to rows a_1 and a_2 being identical we also have $p(a_1) = p(a_2)$.

5 Relation with Existing Anonymity Notions

In this section we consider some particular channels, and we illustrate the relation with probabilistic (non information-theoretic) notions of anonymity existing in literature.

5.1 Capacity 0: Strong Anonymity

The case in which the capacity of the anonymity protocol is 0 is by definition obtained when $I(A; O) = 0$ for all possible input distributions of A. From information theory we know that this is the case iff A and O are independent (cfr. [19], page 27). Hence we have the following characterization:

Proposition 4. *Given an anonymity system* $\langle A, O, p(\cdot|\cdot) \rangle$, *the capacity of the corresponding channel is 0 iff all the rows of the channel matrix are the same, i.e.* $p(o|a) = p(o|a')$ *for all* o, a, a'.

The condition $p(o|a) = p(o|a')$ for all o, a, a' has been called *strong probabilistic anonymity* in [3] and it is equivalent to the condition $p(a|o) = p(a)$ for all o, a. The latter was considered as a definition of anonymity in [1] and it is called *conditional anonymity* in [2].

Capacity 0 is the optimal case, of course, also w.r.t. the capability of the adversary of testing the anonymous events (cfr. Section 4): All the rows are the same, hence $p(o|a_1) = p(o|a_2)$ for all $a_1, a_2 \in A$, and $o \in O^n$. Consequently the observations are of no use for the attacker to infer the anonymous event, i.e. to define the "right" $g_n(o)$, since all $p(o|a)$ are maximal. Assuming a uniform distribution in assigning a value to $g_n(o)$, the Bayesian probability of error is bound from below by $(|A| - 1)/|A|$ (cfr. Section 4.2).

An example of protocol with capacity 0 is the *dining cryptographers* in a connected graph [1], under the assumption that it is always one of the cryptographers who pays, and that the coins are fair.

5.2 Relative Capacity 0: Strong Group Anonymity

Group anonymity usually indicates the situation in which the users are divided in groups, and the protocol allows to figure out the group which the culprit belongs to, although it tries to conceal which user in the group is the culprit.

Such situation corresponds to having a partition on A and O, see Section 3.1. The case of relative capacity 0 is obtained when each M_{r_i} has capacity 0, namely when in each group r_i the rows are identical.

From the point of view of testing the anonymous events we note the following: given a $o \in O^n$, there exists exactly one group r_i of a's such that $p(o|a) > 0$, and

$p(o|a_1) = p(o|a_2)$ for all a_1, a_2 in r_i. Hence the attacker knows that the "right" value of $g_n(o)$ is an a in r_i, but he does not know exactly which one. In other words, on the basis of the observations the attacker can get complete knowledge about the group, but remains completely uncertain about the exact event a in the group, as expected. The lower bound on the Bayesian probability of error is $(|A_r| - 1)/|A_r|$ where $r \in \mathcal{R}$ determines the set of maximal cardinality in $\mathcal{A}$.

An example of protocol with relative capacity 0 is the dining cryptographers in a generic graph [1], under the assumption that the coins are fair. The groups correspond to the connected components of the graph.

The notion of strong group anonymity seems also related to the notion of equivalence classes in [20]. Exploring this connection is left for future work.

5.3 Probable Innocence: Weaker Bounds on Capacity

Probable innocence is a weak notion of anonymity introduced by Reiter and Rubin [4] for Crowds, a system based on communicating a message from the originator to the receiver through a sequence of users acting as forwarders. Probable innocence was verbally defined as "from the attacker's point of view, the sender appears no more likely to be the originator of the message than to not be the originator". In literature there are three different definitions [4,2,5] that try to formally express this notion, see [5] for details. In this section we discuss the relation between these definitions and the channel capacity.

Definition of Reiter and Rubin. In [4] Reiter and Rubin give a formalization of probable innocence for the Crowds protocol, which limits the probability of *detection*, that is the probability of a certain observable that reveals each sender. The definition requires the probability of these observables to be less than one half. A protocol satisfies RR-probable innocence if $p(o|a) \leq \frac{1}{2} \ \forall o \in \mathcal{O}, \forall a \in \mathcal{A}$. In [5] it is argued that this definition is not suitable for arbitrary protocols. We now show that RR-probable innocence imposes no bound on the capacity of the corresponding channel. Consider, for example, the protocol shown in figure 3. The protocols satisfies RR-probable innocence since all values of the matrix are less than or equal to one half. However the channel capacity is (the matrix is symmetric) $C = \log |\mathcal{O}| - H(\mathbf{r}) = \log(2n) - \log 2 = \log n$ which is the maximum possible capacity, equal to the entropy of A. Indeed, users can be perfectly identified by the output since each observable is produced by exactly one user.

Note, however, that in Crowds there are some special symmetries under which RR-probable innocence equivalent to CP-probable innocence so a bound on the capacity can be obtained.

Definition of Halpern and O'Neill. In [2] Halpern and O'Neill give a definition of probable innocence that focuses on the attacker's confidence that a particular anonymous event happened, after performing an observation. It requires that the probability of an anonymous event should be at most one half, under any observation. A protocol satisfies HO-probable innocence if $p(a|o) \leq \frac{1}{2} \ \forall o \in \mathcal{O}, \forall a \in \mathcal{A}$. This definition looks like the one of Reiter and Rubin but

	o_1	o_2	o_3	o_4	$\cdots$	o_{2n-1}	o_{2n}
a_1	1/2	1/2	0	0	$\ldots$	0	0
a_1	0	0	1/2	1/2	$\ldots$	0	0
$\vdots$	$\vdots$				$\ddots$		$\vdots$
a_n	0	0	0	0	$\ldots$	1/2	1/2

Fig. 3. A maximum-capacity channel which satisfies RR-probable innocence

its meaning is very different. It does not limit the probability of observing o. Instead, it limits the probability of an anonymous event a given the observation of o.

As discussed in [5], the problem with this definition is that it depends on the probabilities of the anonymous events which are not part of the protocol. As a consequence, HO-probable innocence cannot hold for all input distributions. If we consider a distribution where $p(a)$ is very close to 1, then $p(a|o)$ cannot possibly be less than $1/2$. So we cannot speak about the bound that HO-probable innocence imposes to the capacity, since to compute the capacity we quantify over all possible input distributions and HO-probable innocence cannot hold for all of them. However, if we limit ourselves to the input distributions where HO-probable innocence actually holds, then we can prove the following proposition.

Proposition 5. *Let $\langle \mathcal{A}, \mathcal{O}, p(\cdot|\cdot) \rangle$ be a channel and $p(a)$ a fixed distribution over $\mathcal{A}$. If the channel is symmetric and satisfies HO-probable innocence for this input distribution then $I(A; O) \leq H(A) - 1$.*

Note that we consider the mutual information for a specific input distribution, not the capacity, for the reasons explained above.

Definition of Chatzikokolakis and Palamidessi. The definition of [5] tries to combine the other two by considering both the probability of producing some observable and the attackers confidence after the observation. This definition considers the probability of two anonymous evens a, a' producing the same observable o and does not allow $p(o|a)$ to be too high or too low compared to $p(o|a')$. A protocol satisfies CP-probable innocence if

$$(n-1) \geq \frac{p(o|a)}{p(o|a')} \quad \forall o \in \mathcal{O}, \forall a, a' \in \mathcal{A} \tag{2}$$

where $n = |\mathcal{A}|$. In [5] it is shown that this definition overcomes some drawbacks of the other two definitions of probable innocence and it is argued that it is more suitable for general protocols. In this section we show that CP-probable innocence imposes a bound on the capacity of the corresponding channel, which strengthens our belief that it is a good definition of anonymity.

Since the purpose of this definition is to limit the fraction $\frac{p(o|a)}{p(o|a')}$ we could generalize it by requiring this fraction to be less than or equal to a constant γ.

Definition 8. *An anonymity protocol* $\langle \mathcal{A}, \mathcal{O}, p(\cdot|\cdot) \rangle$ *satisfies* partial anonymity *if there is a constant* γ *such that*

$$\gamma \geq \frac{p(o|a)}{p(o|a')} \quad \forall o \in \mathcal{O}, \forall a, a' \in \mathcal{A}$$

A similar notion is called *weak probabilistic anonymity* in [21].

Note that partial anonymity generalizes both CP-probable innocence ($\gamma = n - 1$) and strong probabilistic anonymity ($\gamma = 1$). The following theorem shows that partial anonymity imposes a bound to the channel capacity:

Theorem 4. *Let* $\langle \mathcal{A}, \mathcal{O}, p(\cdot|\cdot) \rangle$ *be an anonymity protocol. If the protocol is symmetric and satisfies partial anonymity with* $\gamma > 1$ *then*

$$C \leq \frac{\log \gamma}{\gamma - 1} - \log \frac{\log \gamma}{\gamma - 1} - \log \ln 2 - \frac{1}{\ln 2}$$

This bound has two interesting properties. First, it depends only on γ and not on the number of input or output values or on other properties of the channel matrix. Second, the bound converges to 0 as $\gamma \to 1$. As a consequence, due to the continuity of the capacity as a function of the channel matrix, we can retrieve Proposition 4 about strong probabilistic anonymity ($\gamma = 1$) from Theorem 4. A bound for probable innocence can be obtained by taking $\gamma = n - 1$, so Theorem 4 treats strong anonymity and probable innocence in a uniform way. Note that this bound is proved for the special case of symmetric channels, we plan to examine the general case in the future.

Concerning the testing of the anonymous events, it is interesting to note that, if the attacker has the possibility of repeating the test with the same input an arbitrary number of times, then probable innocence does not give any guarantee. In fact, condition 2 does not prevent the function $p(o|\cdot)$ from having a maximum with probability close to 1, for a sufficiently long sequence of observables o. So we can define $g_n(o)$ to be such maximum, and we have that the Bayesian error corresponding to g_n goes to 0. The only exception is when two (or more) raws a_1, a_2 are equal and correspond to maximals. Imposing this condition for all anonymous actions is equivalent to require strong anonymity. In conclusion, possible innocence maintains an upper bound on anonymity through protocol repetition only if the system is strongly anonymous. This result generalizes the one expressed by Proposition 17 in [5]: In the latter, the same conclusion is drawn, but the tests are limited to the observable sequences of the form $o, o, \ldots, o$.

6   Computing the Degree of Anonymity of a Protocol

In this section we discuss how to compute the channel matrix and the degree of anonymity for a given protocol, possibly using automated tools. We illustrate our ideas on a simple, well-known anonymity problem from the literature, namely the dining cryptographers, proposed by Chaum in [1].

In this problem three cryptographers are dining together. At the end of the dinner, the bill will be paid by either one of them or another agent called the master. The master decides who will pay and then informs each cryptographer individually about whether the latter has to pay or not. The cryptographers would like to find out whether the payer is one of them or the master. However, in the case in which one of them is the payer, they also wish to maintain anonymity over the identity of the payer. To achieve this, each cryptographer tosses a coin which is visible to himself and his neighbor to the right. Each cryptographer observes the two coins that he can see and announces *agree* if they are the same or *disagree* otherwise. However, the paying cryptographer will say the opposite. It can be proved that if the number of *disagrees* is even, then the master is paying; otherwise, one of the cryptographers is paying. Furthermore, the payer stays anonymous to both an external observer and the other cryptographers.

To measure the degree of anonymity of a system, we start by identifying the set of anonymous events, which depend on what the system is trying to hide. In protocols where one user performs an action of interest (like paying in our example) and we want to protect his identity, the set A would be the same as the set I of the users of the protocol. In the dining cryptographers, we take $A = \{c_1, c_2, c_3, m\}$ where c_i means that cryptographer i is paying and m that the master is paying. In protocols where k users can perform the action of interest simultaneously at each protocol execution, A would contain all k-tuples of elements of I. Another interesting case are MIX protocols, in which we are not interested in protecting the fact that someone sent a message (this is indeed detectable), but instead, the link between the sender and the receiver, when k senders send messages to k receivers simultaneously. In that case we consider the sets I_s, I_r of senders and receivers respectively, and take A to contain all k-tuples of pairs (a, a') where $a \in I_s, a' \in I_r$.

Then the set of observable events should also be defined, based on the visible actions of the protocol and on the various assumptions made about the attacker. In the dining cryptographers, we consider for simplicity the case where all the cryptographers are honest and the attacker is an external observer (the case of corrupted cryptographers can be treated similarly). Since the coins are only visible to the cryptographers, the only observables of the protocol are the announcements of *agree*/*disagree*. So the set of observable events will contain all possible combinations of announcements, that is $O = \{aaa, aad, \ldots, ddd\}$ where a means *agree* and d means *disagree*.

If some information about the anonymous events is revealed intentionally then we should consider using relative anonymity (see Section 3.1). In the dining cryptographers, the information about whether the payer is a cryptographer or not is revealed by design (this is the purpose of the protocol). If, for example, the attacker observes aaa then he concludes that the anonymous event that happened is m since the number of *disagree* is even. To model this fact we use relative anonymity and we take $R = \{m, c\}$ where m means that the master is paying and c that one of the cryptographers is paying.

	daa	ada	aad	ddd	aaa	dda	dad	add
c_1	0.25	0.25	0.25	0.25	0	0	0	0
c_2	0.25	0.25	0.25	0.25	0	0	0	0
c_3	0.25	0.25	0.25	0.25	0	0	0	0
m	0	0	0	0	0.25	0.25	0.25	0.25

	daa	ada	aad	ddd	aaa	dda	dad	add
c_1	0.37	0.21	0.21	0.21	0	0	0	0
c_2	0.21	0.37	0.21	0.21	0	0	0	0
c_3	0.21	0.21	0.37	0.21	0	0	0	0
m	0	0	0	0	0.37	0.21	0.21	0.21

Fig. 4. The channel matrices for probability of head $p = 0.5$ (left) and $p = 0.7$ (right)

After defining $\mathcal{A}, \mathcal{O}, \mathcal{R}$ we should model the protocol in some formal probabilistic language. In our example, we modeled the dining cryptographers in the language of the PRISM model-checker, which is essentially a formalism to describe Markov Decision Processes. Then the channel matrix of conditional probabilities $p(o|a)$ must be computed, either by hand or using an automated tool like PRISM. In the case of relative anonymity, the probabilities $p(o|r)$ and $p(o|a, r)$ are needed for all a, o, r. However, in our example, R partitions A and O, so by Theorem 1 we can compute the relative loss of anonymity as the maximum capacity of the sub-channels for each value of R individually. For $R = m$ the sub-channel has only one input value, hence its capacity is 0. Therefore the only interesting case is when $R = c$. In our experiments, we use PRISM to compute the channel matrix, while varying the probability p of each coin giving head. PRISM can compute the probability of reaching a specific state starting from a given one. Thus, each conditional probability $p(o|a)$ is computed as the probability of reaching a state where the cryptographers have announced o, starting from the state where a is chosen. In Fig. 4 the channel matrix is displayed for $p = 0.5$ and $p = 0.7$.

Finally, from the matrix, the capacity can be computed in two different ways. Either by using the general Arimoto-Blahut algorithm (see for instance [19]), or by using Theorem 3 which can be applied because the matrix is partially symmetric. The resulting graph is displayed in Fig. 5. As expected, when $p = 0.5$

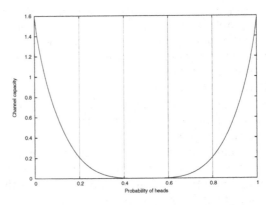

Fig. 5. The degree of anonymity in the Dining Cryptographers as a function of the coins' probability to give head

the protocol is strongly anonymous and the relative loss of anonymity is 0. When p approaches 0 or 1, the attacker can deduce the identity of the payer with increasingly high probability, so the capacity increases. In the extreme case where the coins are totally biased the attacker can be sure about the payer, and the capacity takes its maximum value of $\log 3$.

References

1. Chaum, D.: The dining cryptographers problem: Unconditional sender and recipient untraceability. Journal of Cryptology 1, 65–75 (1988)
2. Halpern, J.Y., O'Neill, K.R.: Anonymity and information hiding in multiagent systems. Journal of Computer Security 13, 483–512 (2005)
3. Bhargava, M., Palamidessi, C.: Probabilistic anonymity. In: Abadi, M., de Alfaro, L. (eds.) CONCUR 2005. LNCS, vol. 3653, pp. 171–185. Springer, Heidelberg (2005), http://www.lix.polytechnique.fr/~catuscia/papers/Anonymity/concur.pdf
4. Reiter, M.K., Rubin, A.D.: Crowds: anonymity for Web transactions. ACM Transactions on Information and System Security 1, 66–92 (1998)
5. Chatzikokolakis, K., Palamidessi, C.: Probable innocence revisited. Theoretical Computer Science 367, 123–138 (2006), http://www.lix.polytechnique.fr/~catuscia/papers/Anonymity/reportP I.pdf
6. Serjantov, A., Danezis, G.: Towards an information theoretic metric for anonymity. In: Dingledine, R., Syverson, P.F. (eds.) PET 2002. LNCS, vol. 2482, pp. 41–53. Springer, Heidelberg (2003)
7. Díaz, C., Seys, S., Claessens, J., Preneel, B.: Towards measuring anonymity. In: Dingledine, R., Syverson, P.F. (eds.) PET 2002. LNCS, vol. 2482, pp. 54–68. Springer, Heidelberg (2003)
8. Moskowitz, I.S., Newman, R.E., Crepeau, D.P., Miller, A.R.: Covert channels and anonymizing networks. In: Jajodia, S., Samarati, P., Syverson, P.F. (eds.) WPES, pp. 79–88. ACM, New York (2003)
9. Moskowitz, I.S., Newman, R.E., Syverson, P.F.: Quasi-anonymous channels. In: IASTED CNIS, pp. 126–131 (2003)
10. Deng, Y., Pang, J., Wu, P.: Measuring anonymity with relative entropy. In: Proceedings of the 4th International Workshop on Formal Aspects in Security and Trust. LNCS, Springer, Heidelberg (to appear, 2006)
11. McLean, J.: Security models and information flow. IEEE Symposium on Security and Privacy, 180–189 (1990)
12. Gray III, J.W.: Toward a mathematical foundation for information flow security. In: Proceedings of the 1991 IEEE Computer Society Symposium on Research in Security and Privacy SSP '91, Washington - Brussels - Tokyo, pp. 21–35. IEEE, Los Alamitos (1991)
13. Clark, D., Hunt, S., Malacaria, P.: Quantitative analysis of the leakage of confidential data. In: Proc. of QAPL 2001. Electr. Notes Theor. Comput. Sci, vol. 59 (3), pp. 238–251. Elsevier Science B.V., Amsterdam (2001)
14. Clark, D., Hunt, S., Malacaria, P.: Quantified interference for a while language. In: Proc. of QAPL 2004. Electr. Notes Theor. Comput. Sci, vol. 112, pp. 149–166. Elsevier Science B.V., Amsterdam (2005)
15. Lowe, G.: Quantifying information flow. In: Proc. of CSFW 2002, pp. 18–31. IEEE Computer Society Press, Los Alamitos (2002)

16. Maurer, U.M.: Authentication theory and hypothesis testing. IEEE Transactions on Information Theory 46, 1350–1356 (2000)
17. Pierro, A.D., Hankin, C., Wiklicky, H.: Approximate non-interference. Journal of Computer Security 12, 37–82 (2004)
18. Pierro, A.D., Hankin, C., Wiklicky, H.: Measuring the confinement of probabilistic systems. Theoretical Computer Science 340, 3–56 (2005)
19. Cover, T.M., Thomas, J.A.: Elements of Information Theory. John Wiley & Sons, Inc, Chichester (1991)
20. Sabelfeld, A., Sands, D.: Probabilistic noninterference for multi-threaded programs. In: Proc. of CSFW 2000, pp. 200–214. IEEE Computer Society Press, Los Alamitos (2000)
21. Deng, Y., Palamidessi, C., Pang, J.: Weak probabilistic anonymity. In: Proc. of SecCo 2005. Electronic Notes in Theoretical Computer Science, Elsevier Science Publishers, Amsterdam (2005), http://www.lix.polytechnique.fr/~catuscia/papers/Anonymity/report_wa.pdf

A Framework for Automatically Checking Anonymity with μCRL

Tom Chothia[1], Simona Orzan[2,1], Jun Pang[3], and Mohammad Torabi Dashti[1]

[1] Centrum voor Wiskunde en Informatica, Amsterdam, The Netherlands
[2] Technische Universiteit Eindhoven, Eindhoven, The Netherlands
[3] Carl von Ossietzky Universität Oldenburg, Oldenburg, Germany

Abstract. We present a powerful and flexible method for automatically checking anonymity in a possibilistic general-purpose process algebraic verification toolset. We propose new definitions of a *choice anonymity degree* and a *player anonymity degree*, to quantify the precision with which an intruder is able to single out the true originator of a given event or to associate the right event to a given protocol participant. We show how these measures of anonymity can be automatically calculated from a protocol specification in μCRL, by using a combination of dedicated tools and existing state-of-the-art μCRL tools. To illustrate the flexibility of our method we test the Dining Cryptographers problem and the FOO 92 voting protocol. Our definitions of anonymity provide an accurate picture of the different ways that anonymity can break down, due for instance to coallitions of inside intruders. Our calculations can be performed on a cluster of machines, allowing us to check protocols for large numbers of participants.

1 Introduction

Anonymity, as a security property, refers to the ability of a user to own some data or take some actions without being tracked down. This property is essential in protocols that might involve sensitive personal data, like electronic auctions, voting, anonymous broadcasts, file-sharing etc. Due to its relevance and subtle nature, anonymity has been given many definitions [3,16,17,26] and has been the subject of many theoretical studies and formal analysis [19,21]. However, automatic approaches to the formal verification of anonymity have only treated small examples of individual protocols [10,20,28,30]. We address this situation by investigating the possibility of using a powerful general-purpose explicit-state verification toolset, μCRL [4], to automatically verify anonymity properties. We define two measures of anonymity and set up a framework to calculate them from process specifications.

Our definitions of anonymity are based on a notion of secret choices for participants. These choices may signify actions (e.g., accessing a certain web server) or data (e.g., votes in a voting protocol). We represent a protocol as a composition of a number of players (participants), each given a secret choice. The two types of anonymity that we propose quantify the ability of an intruder to

U. Montanari, D. Sannella, and R. Bruni (Eds.): TGC 2006, LNCS 4661, pp. 301–318, 2007.

deduce the right association of players and choices. Consider a voting protocol with 50 candidates and 1000 voters. There are two types of questions that the intruder may ask: 1) *who* voted for a particular candidate, for instance *candidate$_3$* and 2) *what* was the vote of a particular player, for instance *player$_1$*. In the first case, a choice is fixed (*candidate$_3$*) and the originator(s) of that choice are sought, in the second case a player is fixed and determining their choice is the object of intruder's attention. The answers obtained are usually not precise, but rather in the form of a set of possibilities — the smaller the set of possibilities, the more exact the intruder's guess and therefore the smaller the degree of anonymity. Namely, there is a quantitative difference between the situation in which the intruder reaches the conclusion that the vote of *player$_1$* is in the set {*candidate$_3$, candidate$_{49}$*} and the situation in which the intruder considers all 50 candidates as possible choices of *player$_1$*. Based on these observations, we say that if the intruder considers more than one secret choice possible for a given player then the player has *choice anonymity* and the number of possible choices for the player is the *choice anonymity degree*. In a similar fashion, if the intruder considers more than one player as a possible owner of a given secret choice then that choice has *player anonymity* and the number of possible players for the choice is the *player anonymity degree*.

Our definitions allow for corrupted players that will share their information with the intruder. This means that we can measure the effect of coalitions of corrupted players and the intruder on the anonymity of honest players. We formally define these metrics in terms of bisimulation between processes and provide tool support to compute them automatically, starting from an abstract description of the protocol in the process-algebraic language μCRL. Trace equivalence has also been proposed as an equivalence for checking anonymity [22,28]. Bisimulation is a more discriminating relation than trace equivalence; while it is possible that we will detect false positives, these are better than the possible false negatives. Bisimulation also has the advantage of being more efficient to compute than trace equivalence [18].

We specify the protocols we wish to check in μCRL. This is an expressive language that comes with an extensive toolset and has a long history of successful protocol checking [5,25]. The μCRL toolset includes tools for performing state space reduction modulo bisimulation [6], which we use along with some purpose-built scripts and C programs to generate all possible cases of the model and to calculate our measures of anonymity. The μCRL toolset allows us to distribute the checking over a cluster of machines. Unlike other approaches, we support automatic generation of μCRL models for any given number of participants and any given coalition of corrupt participants.

Our verification approach is possibilistic, rather than probabilistic, i.e., we consider two processes the same if there is the possibility of them performing the same actions. We do not take into account the probability of the actions occurring. While the possibilistic approach may still allow the intruder to make a good guess at the identity of a guilty player, the metrics are much easier to calculate and it avoids the problem of combining probabilities with non-deterministic choices, such as how often a given player will use the system.

We illustrate our approach by two examples: the Dining Cryptographers problem [7] and the FOO voting protocol [13]. These systems have already been analysed with formal methods, but not within one framework. The Dining Cryptographers problem has been used as a test case for many tools; the largest protocol instance that has been verified, to the best of our knowledge, contains 8 participants, by using symbolic model checking on an epistemic specification [20]. Our approach can check more than 15 cryptographers in a few hours. In contrast, the FOO voting protocol has not previously been checked in a fully automated framework.

The contribution of this paper is threefold: 1) a framework for checking anonymity including the definitions of choice anonymity degree and player anonymity degree, with a treatment of coalitions of corrupt players, 2) demonstrating the flexibility of this framework by testing examples of two well known anonymous systems, 3) demonstrating the power of this framework by showing how we can automatically check the anonymity degrees of our examples on a single machine or on a cluster.

The structure of the paper. We discuss related work in the rest of this section. In Section 2, we define two notions of anonymity degrees, and we present our verification framework. We apply our approach to the analysis of two examples in Sections 3 and 4. The results of the experiments are gathered together in Section 5. Finally, Section 6 concludes the paper and discusses possible future extensions. The code for the examples and the scripts for calculating the anonymity degrees are available online [9].

Related work. Using process equivalences to model anonymity dates back to Meritt [23], whose work was inspired by information flow analysis. Chaum [7] uses the size of an anonymity set to indicate the degree of anonymity provided by a network based on Dining Cryptographers (DC nets). An anonymity set is defined as the set of participants who could have sent a particular message as observed by the intruder. Pfitzmann and Hansen [26] investigate a similar idea. Berthold, Pfiztmann and Standtke [2] define the degree of anonymity as $\ln(N)$, where N is the number of users of the protocols. Our metrics can be thought of as the anonymity set for players and the anonymity set for choices, defined via a behavioural equivalence.

Reiter and Rubin [27] define the degree of anonymity as the probability that an intruder can assign to a player of being the original sender of a message. This metric does not take into account the number of players in a system. Bhargava and Palamidessi [3] propose a similar definition of anonymity that makes a careful distinction between non-deterministic and probabilistic actions. Deng, Palamidessi and Pang [10] define "weak probabilistic anonymity" and use a probabilistic model checker (PRISM) to analyse the Dining Cryptographers problem. Serjantov and Danezis [29] define an information theoretic anonymity metric based entropy and Díaz et al. [11] provide a similar metric that is normalised by the number of users.

The FOO voting protocol has been analysed by Kremer and Ryan in the applied pi-calculus [19] and Chothia [8] uses bisimulation to test the anonymity of an anonymous file-sharing system. Also on the possibilistic side, Schneider and Sidiropoulos [28] use FDR to check anonymity via trace equivalence in CSP, and Garcia et al. [14] develop a formal framework for proving anonymity based on epistemic logic.

2   Anonymity Formalisation and Verification Methodology

Anonymity as a security property comes in many flavours. We take the rather general view that when participants in a protocol wish to remain anonymous they wish to hide parts of their behaviour and data. That is, an intruder should not be able to find out what choices, regarding control as well as data, that particular participant has made. We consider the environment as an active attacker that observes protocol runs, hence we need not model the intruder explicitly. We also consider the possibility of a number of corrupt insiders that may leak their observations to the attacker.

The protocol model. Group protocols can usually be written as a parallel composition of participants and an environment process:

$$\texttt{Protocol}(\mathbf{x}) = P_1(x_1)\|P_2(x_2)\|\dots\|P_n(x_n)\|Q(n) \tag{1}$$

Here $\mathbf{x} = (x_1, x_2, \dots, x_n)$ is the vector of secret choices (e.g., votes in a voting protocol). The choice x_i comes from a known domain and the anonymity refers to the link between this value and the identity of the participant using it. Each P_i ($1 \leq i \leq n$) describes the behaviour of a single player. Process $Q(n)$ represents the environment, made up from entities that 'oversee' the protocol and, by the nature of their role, do not need to be anonymous. Examples of such entities are the auction house in an auction protocol, or the ballot counter in a voting protocol. In this paper, $P_1, \dots, P_n, Q$ are models written in the process-algebraic specification language μCRL, a short description of which is given later in this section.

The possible behaviours in our model are grouped in three levels:

1. A *choice* defines the behaviour of a single player. In the Dining Cryptographers protocol, for instance, the possible choices are T, to indicate that a player is the payer, and F, to indicate that the player is not going to pay.
2. A *choice vector* is an ordered list of choices. It defines one behaviour of the entire system. The vector's ith element defines the behaviour of the ith player.
3. A *choice vector set* is a set of choice vectors that represent all possible behaviours of a system.

A short introduction to μCRL. The specification language μCRL [15] is an extension of the process algebra ACP [1] with abstract data types, which are very handy when describing real-life applications. Processes are built from atomic actions by the ACP operators for sequential composition (.), non-deterministic choice (+) and parallel compositions ($\|$). Synchronisation in ACP is governed by a communication function γ. E.g., synchronisation of actions a and b yields the action $\gamma(a, b)$. There is also an *encapsulation* operator ∂_H, that forces processes to communicate, by making the actions in the set H act exclusively in communication. The *hiding* operator τ_I turns all occurrences of actions from the set I into the internal action τ. The *renaming* operator ρ_R renames actions according to the renaming rules in R. In fact, the precise form of Equation 1 in μCRL is

$$\texttt{Protocol}(\mathbf{x}) = \tau_I \rho_R \partial_H (P_1(x_1) \| P_2(x_2) \| \ldots \| P_n(x_n) \| Q(n)) \tag{2}$$

There are two special actions: δ represents deadlock, and τ the internal action. In order to incorporate abstract data types in a specification, a signature of multiple sorts and functions can be declared, and axiomatised by equations. A number of connectives tie processes up with abstract data types. First, atomic actions can be parameterised with data elements, as in $\texttt{send}(x)$. Then, $\sum_{x:D} P(x)$ denotes alternative (possibly infinite) choice over data domain D, i.e. for any value $x_0 \in D$, the process can behave as $P(x_0)$. Finally, if b is a term of data domain *Bool* and p and q are processes, then the conditional construct $p \triangleleft b \triangleright q$ is the process 'p if b, else q'.

Groups of corrupted players. Since it is not uncommon that the intruder manages to persuade or blackmail some of the participants into revealing their secrets, our models take into account the presence of groups of corrupted players. We use Obs to denote the set of observer that join forces with an external intruder. $\texttt{Protocol}(\mathbf{x})$ specifies the behaviour of a protocol under the assumption that all participants are honest, i.e. Obs $= \emptyset$. If Obs $\neq \emptyset$, it means that the intruder has access to some extra inside information, namely all the secret choices and hidden actions of the players in Obs. Therefore, in order to obtain the behaviour corresponding to this situation, we need to cancel the effect of the action hiding and renaming applied to processes in Obs. The resulting process is denoted by $\texttt{Protocol}_{\text{Obs}}(\mathbf{x})$,

$$\texttt{Protocol}_{\text{Obs}}(\mathbf{x}) = \tau_{(I/AO)} \rho_{(R/AO)} \partial_H (P_1(x_1) \| P_2(x_2) \| \ldots \| P_n(x_n) \| Q(n)) \tag{3}$$

where AO are the actions observed by the members of Obs. We note that, $\texttt{Protocol}_\emptyset(\mathbf{x}) = \texttt{Protocol}(\mathbf{x})$.

Anonymity formalisation. We distinguish two ways to look at anonymity requirements, in a protocol specified as above, both are in terms of participants with secret choices: (1) for a given participant P, can the intruder find out its secret choice, as in "for whom did P vote?", and (2) for a given choice c, can the intruder find out which of the participants owns it, namely "who voted for c?". Following the same two-fold view, we define anonymity notions that are sensitive to quantitative nuances: (1) given a participant P, how many possibilities for the participant's secret choice will the intruder consider, and (2) given a secret choice c, how many participants will the intruder consider as possibly having taken that secret choice? These notions can be thought of as defining the anonymity degree for players in terms of choices (cad) and the anonymity degree for choices in terms of players (pad).

The equivalence used in the verification of anonymity models the observation power of the intruder. Our definitions of anonymity degree can use any equivalence relation; in our case studies we use bisimulation ($\approx$) to equate process. In particular we use branching bisimulation when we are modelling processes with hidden actions and for efficiency we use strong bisimulation when there are no hidden actions. This is in contrast to some previous work on anonymity that used trace equivalence [22,28]. While it is often possible, in an asynchronous setting, to implement processes in such a way that an intruder cannot tell the difference between two processes that are trace equivalent but not bisimilar, there also exist reasonable implementations in which the intruder can tell the difference. For instance, the two processes $a.(b + c)$ and $a.b + a.c$ are trace equivalent but not bisimilar. A reasonable implementation of these processes might use sockets for communication, in which case the first process would listen on port "a" for a message and then listen on ports "b" and "c" and accept only the first message that arrives. The second process could be implemented by either listening on port "a" and then port "b" or listening on port "a" and then port "c". All an intruder has to do to tell these processes apart is to send on port "a" and then on port "b". If the intruder then gets a message sent to port "b" rejected they may conclude that they are dealing with the second process. In this sense, using bisimulation rather than trace equivalence is a conservative decision; while it is possible for processes that are trace equivalent, but not bisimilar, to be safe, we cannot guarantee that they do not reveal information to the intruder.

A second advantage of using bisimulation is that it can be much more efficient to check. The added restrictions on bisimilar processes mean that we can reject certain paths as not bisimilar long before we could detect that they are not trace equivalent. In the most extreme cases checking a particular pair of processes for trace equivalence can take exponential time while checking the same processes for bi-simulation can take linear time.

Definition 1 (choice indistinguishability). *Let* Protocol *be the specification of a protocol,* $\mathbf{v}_1$ *and* $\mathbf{v}_2$ *two choice vectors, and* Obs *an observer set. The set of all possible choice vector is denoted by CVS. Then the relation* $\approx_{\text{Obs}} : CVS \times CVS$ *is defined as:*

$$\mathbf{v}_1 \approx_{\text{Obs}} \mathbf{v}_2 \ \text{ iff } \ \text{Protocol}_{\text{Obs}}(\mathbf{v}_1) \approx \text{Protocol}_{\text{Obs}}(\mathbf{v}_2).$$

Definition 2 (choice anonymity degree). *The choice anonymity degree* (cad) *of participant* i *w.r.t. an observer set* Obs *under the choice vector* $\mathbf{x}$ *is:*

$$\text{cad}_x(i) = |\{c \in \textit{Choices}, \exists \mathbf{v} \in \textit{CVS} \text{ such that}$$
$$v_i = c \text{ and } \mathbf{v} \approx_{\text{Obs}} \mathbf{x} \text{ and } (\forall j \in \text{Obs}.v_j = x_j)\}|$$

where $|\cdot|$ *denotes the cardinality of a set, Choices is the set of all possible choices, CVS is the choice vector set,* $\mathbf{v} = \langle v_1, \ldots, v_n \rangle$ *and* $\mathbf{x} = \langle x_1, \ldots, x_n \rangle$. *We define the choice anonymity degree of participant* i *w.r.t.* Obs *as*

$$\text{cad}(i) = \min_{\mathbf{x} \in \textit{CVS}} \text{cad}_x(i)$$

The set in the above formula for $\text{cad}_x(i)$ is the set of all choices c that could be assigned to player i, as part of a choice vector $\mathbf{v}$ that is indistinguishable from a fixed choice vector $\mathbf{x}$. The "$\exists \mathbf{v} \in \textit{CVS}$" and "$v_i = c$" conditions ensure that $\mathbf{v}$ is a choice vector which assigns choice c to player i. The choice vector $\mathbf{x}$ can be thought of as defining the observable behaviour of a particular run of the protocol and the choice vector $\mathbf{v}$ defines the observable behaviour of another run, which the observers represented by Obs, cannot distinguish from the $\mathbf{x}$-run. We look for a value of $\mathbf{x}$ that gives the smallest possible number of choices, i.e., we are looking for the worst case anonymity. Our measure of choice anonymity degree for player i is then the size of the set of possible choices that player i may have been assigned. The condition $\forall j \in \text{Obs}.v_j = x_j$ captures the fact that the choice for Obs is fixed. This is because the players in Obs share their choice values with the attacker.

Definition 3 (player anonymity degree). *The player anonymity degree (pad) of secret choice* c, *in a protocol with* n *players, w.r.t. an observer set* Obs *and the choice vector* $\mathbf{x}$ *is:*

$$\text{pad}_x(c) = |\{i \in \{1, \ldots, n\} \setminus \text{Obs}, \exists \mathbf{v} \in \textit{CVS} \text{ such that}$$
$$v_i = c \text{ and } \mathbf{v} \approx_{\text{Obs}} \mathbf{x} \text{ and } (\forall j \in \text{Obs}.v_j = x_j)\}|.$$

The player anonymity degree of secret choice c *w.r.t. an observer set* Obs *is*

$$\text{pad}(c) = \begin{cases} 0, & \text{if } \max_{\mathbf{x} \in \textit{CVS}} \text{pad}_x(c) = 0 \\ \min_{\mathbf{x} \in \textit{CVS}:\text{pad}_x(c)>0} \text{pad}_x(c), & \text{otherwise} \end{cases}$$

The set in the definition of pad_x is the set of all honest players that might, from the perspective of the intruder, have been assigned the choice c. We define the $\text{pad}(c)$ to be the lowest non-zero value assuming that such a value exists. This is because, in some systems, it is possible for a given choice vector to rule out certain choices values, so making the minimum pad value zero, while at the same time any choice vector that allows the choice to happen may allow the choice to be assigned to a number of different players. For instance, if the intruder can see the total number of messages sent then a choice c that results in four messages being sent rules out a choice vector that would only send three messages. So $\text{pad}(c)$ defines the anonymity for a choice c that results from only considering choice vectors that are compatible with c.

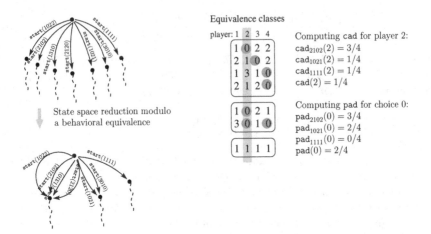

Fig. 1. Left: Computing the equivalence classes of $\approx_{Obs}$, for a Protocol$_{Obs}$. The choices come from the set $\{0,1,2,3\}$, there are 4 players and CVS is the set $\{1022, 2102, 1310, 2120, 1021, 3010, 1111\}$. The end state of every start(x) transition is the start state of Protocol$_{Obs}(x)$. After reduction modulo $\approx_{Obs}$, the transition start(x) and start(y) have the same end state iff $x \approx_{Obs} y$. The equivalence classes of $\approx_{Obs}$, listed on the right, are generated in this way. **Right:** Extracting cad and pad information from the equivalence classes, by just applying the definitions.

We believe that these measures give a good impression of the anonymity provided by a protocol. In the rest of the paper, we will write cad and pad together with the actual number of possible choices (i.e., |Choices|) and with the number of players (n), respectively. For instance, we will write cad$(2) = 3{:}5$ instead of cad$(2) = 3$, if 5 is the size of the choices' domain. Note that the maximum possible cad or pad are not always of the form $m{:}m$; in fact, this is never the case whenever we consider Obs $\neq \emptyset$, since the intruder knows whether those participants belonging to Obs have performed a certain action and what choices those participants have made.

Verification method. Our goal is to make verification of anonymity properties just as easy as verification of safety or liveness properties. Two difficulties have to be overcome. Firstly, anonymity depends on the point of view of the intruder, therefore new protocol models should be written for every new observer set. Secondly, anonymity is not a property of a single trace that can be written as a logic formula to be verified via model checking, but requires equivalence checking of several protocol instances. Note that both of these problems are specific to the general verification method of writing process specifications and then model checking temporal properties on the generated behaviour model. For instance, approaches based on epistemic logics [12,24] are able to express anonymity more naturally and do allow its verification by model checking, but they encounter other, mainly modelling, problems and are not supported by such powerful tools as we use here.

We solve these problems by automating the generation of new protocol specifications depending on the observer set and on the different protocol instances. We also support the analysis of anonymity as described above, by automatically generating the equivalence classes of $\approx_{\text{Obs}}$ and computing the anonymity degrees cad and pad.

All the tool support is available on our website [9]. We start from a base specification Protocol(x) describing the behaviour of the protocol for a parameter choice vector x. Then a .rn file will define, for a generic participant, how its actions are seen from the outside. We choose to implement ρ_R from (2) like this, rather than explicitly using it in the μCRL specification, in order to better control the effects of having a set of corrupted players Obs. The renaming is done by means of rules like assign(i,x,true)->assign(i). This example rule says that the action of i of assigning a true value to its variable x will be observed by the other players and the environment only as an assignment executed by i. Just like the modelling process itself, choosing what the appropriate renamings should be is a subjective task. The actions executed by the observing parties are not renamed, while from the actions executed by the other, honest parties, all private information should be hidden. All information for action renaming are gathered into one .rn file, which will be used to automatically generate renamings for particular protocol instances. In order to avoid interferences with this automatically generated renamings, we require the P_i processes to not contain any further renaming operators. Then the tools will generate, for this given μCRL model Protocol(x), the given set of renaming rules, a given set Obs and a given choice vector set CVS, the μCRL specification corresponding to

$$\Sigma_{v \in \text{CVS}: \forall j \in \text{Obs}. v_j = x_j} \text{ start}(v).\text{Protocol}_{\text{Obs}}(v),$$

namely the sum of all protocol instances corresponding to choice vectors which are in CVS and coincide with x on the Obs positions. After that, the μCRL toolset is used to generate the state space of this new process and reduce it modulo a behavioural equivalence. The end states of the start actions are the start states of the protocol instances compared, therefore the equivalence classes of these states are exactly the equivalence classes of the relation $\approx_{\text{Obs}}$ on choice vectors (from Definition 1). See also Figure 1 for a scheme of this procedure. Our tools will show these equivalence classes and extract the choice and player anonymity degrees according to Definitions 2 and 3.

In Sections 3 and 4, we will apply our approach to the analysis of the Dining Cryptographers problem and the FOO 92 voting protocol, respectively. Our method can also be used to check the anonymity that protocols provide over a number of rounds, by using choices that represent the behaviour of a participant over a number of rounds. We have tested a simple possibilistic version of Reiter and Rabin's Crowds protocol [27] and shown that, over a number of rounds, an external observer cannot work out which nodes have originated messages, and the observer cannot work out how many of the messages were sent by the same node. Due to page limit, we omit the detailed analysis here. The interested readers can find the μCRL specification of this example online [9].

3   The Dining Cryptographers Problem

The Dining Cryptographers protocol is probably the most well-known example of a protocol where anonymity is the main requirement [7]. The story, which is a metaphor for anonymous broadcast, starts with three cryptographers sitting down at a table to have dinner together. At the end of their meal, they learn that the bill has been paid anonymously by one of them, or perhaps by a shadowy government organisation (the National Security Agency). They respect each other's right to anonymity, but they wish to find out whether the payer was the NSA or not. To achieve this, they come up with the following protocol: each neighbouring pair of cryptographers generates a shared bit, by flipping a coin; then each cryptographer computes the exclusive or (XOR) of the two bits shared with the neighbours, then announces the result - or the opposite result, if that cryptographer was the payer. The XOR of the three publicly announced results indicates whether the payer was an insider or the NSA.

The μCRL model. We specify the behaviour of a cryptographer as a μCRL process *Crypt* and the behaviour of the whole Dining Cryptographers system as a parallel composition of *Crypt*s. With three participants, the global process looks like this:

$$DC(\mathbf{x}{:}\,ChoiceVector) = \partial_{\{\texttt{tell},\texttt{recv}\}}(Crypt_0(x_0)||Crypt_1(x_1)||Crypt_2(x_2))$$

A choice is in this case the decision to pay or not (we will call it the paying bit), represented by the Boolean values $x_i \in \{\texttt{T}, \texttt{F}\}$. A cryptographer process executes a series of actions corresponding to the three main steps of the protocol: decide whether to pay or not, flip the coins together with the neighbours, and announce the result of XOR-ing the two coins and the own paying bit. The first step is modelled as a statement $\texttt{pay}(n, i, x_i)$. In other models of this protocol [28,3], the shared coins are represented by separate processes, but we merge the behaviour of ith coin with the behaviour of the ith cryptographer, in order to keep the number of processes small. That is, process $Crypt_i$ will execute a $\texttt{flip}$ action and then share the result with the right hand neighbour, by executing an action $\texttt{tell}$ while its right hand cryptographer in the ring can get to know the result of this coin flipping by executing the action $\texttt{recv}$. The synchronisation of these two actions results into the communication action $\texttt{com}$.

$$
\begin{aligned}
Crypt_i(x_i : Bool) = {}& \texttt{pay}(n, i, x_i). \textstyle\sum_{coin\_left:Bool}(\texttt{flip}(i, coin\_left). \\
& (\texttt{tell}(next(i), coin\_left) \parallel \textstyle\sum_{coin\_right:Bool} \texttt{recv}(i, coin\_right)). \\
& CryptAnnounce(n, 0, id, ch \oplus coin\_right \oplus coin\_left))
\end{aligned}
$$

CryptAnnounce models broadcasting the result of one's computation and receiving the results from all the others. Since the broadcast implementation is not an actual part of the protocol, we do not discuss *CryptAnnounce* here. The renaming rules specifying how much of a cryptographer's actions is visible for another cryptographer or the intruder are $\{\texttt{com}(\texttt{i},\texttt{X})-> \texttt{com}(\texttt{i}), \texttt{pay}(\texttt{n},\texttt{i},\texttt{X})-> \texttt{pay}(\texttt{i})\}$. For any given observers set Obs, DC_{Obs} will be obtained from the model of DC above, by applying the renaming rules to all $Crypt_i$ processes which are not in Obs, as explained in Section 2 (verification method).

Anonymity verification. Consider an external intruder observing a run of the Dining Cryptographers protocol with 3 participants and trying to conclude who the payer was (in case one of the cryptographers paid). Let us suppose that cryptographer 0 is the payer and let us check whether their anonymity will not be broken. For this, as described in Section 2, we automatically generate the state space corresponding to $\sum_{v \in CVS} \text{start}(v).DC_0(v)$, where CVS is in this case $\Pi(\text{TFF})$, the set of permutations of the sequence TFF, since it is a publicly known fact that there is exactly one payer among the cryptographers. Therefore, the above expression becomes $\text{start}(\text{TFF}).DC_0(\text{TFF}) + \text{start}(\text{FTF}).DC_0(\text{FTF}) + \text{start}(\text{FFT}).DC_0(\text{FFT})$. Note that we exclude FFF from CVS, because there is no anonymity claim for this case. The obtained state space will then be reduced modulo strong bisimulation equivalence and one equivalence class will result: $\{\text{FFT}, \text{FTF}, \text{TFF}\}$, meaning that the intruder cannot distinguish between the three possible choice vectors and thus considers that any of the three cryptographers might have been the payer. This situation of maximum anonymity is reflected both by the **pad** measure $\text{pad}(\text{T}) = 3{:}3$, and the **cad** measure $\text{cad}(0) = 2{:}2$; the first one says that any of the three players might be the owner of the T paying bit, and the second says that any of the two values T, F might have been assigned to cryptographer 0.

For 5 participants, two of which are corrupted (1 and 3), the state space for $\sum_{v \in \Pi(\text{TFFFF}):v_1=v_3=\text{F}} \text{start}(v).DC_{\{1,3\}}(\text{TFFFF})$ will automatically be generated and reduced, resulting into the equivalence classes $\{\text{FFFFT}, \text{TFFFF}\} \{\text{FFTFF}\}$. Note that, consistent with the verification method explained in the end of Section 2, the vectors FTFFF and FFFTF are automatically excluded from this check, since it is already known to the intruder that these cannot be the case (because 1 and 3 show their secret paying bit F to the intruder). The computed anonymity degree $\text{pad}(\text{T}) = 1{:}5$, indicating that in at least one of the scenarios, the payer becomes known to the intruder (namely, when the choice vector is FFTFF). The anonymity degree restricted to the case when 0 pays $\text{pad}_{\text{TFFFF}}(\text{T}) = 2{:}5$, which is much lower than in the case of no corrupted players, indicating that, even if anonymity of 0 is not broken, the set of suspects is reduced to 2 players. The **cad** and **pad** degrees give the complete picture of the anonymity of the 3 honest cryptographers $\{0, 2, 4\}$ with respect to the coalition $\{1, 3\}$ of dishonest cryptographers, when cryptographer 0 pays. The conclusion is that 0 remains *partially* anonymous, that is the intruder doesn't know that 0 paid, but does know that one of $\{0, 4\}$ paid and 2 didn't.

4 The FOO 92 Electronic Voting Protocol

In this section, we analyse a more complex protocol, that involves choices (votes) from a larger than binary domain and elaborated cryptographic mechanisms like anonymous channels, encryption and blind signatures. These mechanisms are very naturally expressible with the abstract datatypes of μCRL.

FOO involves voters, an administrator and a collector and has four stages: registration, voting, opening and counting. During the *registration stage*, a voter id_i prepares his ballot as follows: (1) he chooses a vote v_i and creates the ballot $x_i = \xi(v_i, k_i)$ using the secure bit-commitment ξ and the randomly chosen key k_i; (2) he computes the message $e_i = \chi(x_i, r_i)$ using the blinding technique χ and a random blinding factor r_i; (3) he signs $s_i = \sigma_i(e_i)$ and sends (id_i, e_i, s_i) to the administrator , who signs it $d_i = \sigma_A(e_i)$ and sends it back to the voter as his certification, if the voter is authorised to vote, otherwise the administrator rejects the signature. In the end of the registration stage, the administrator gets to know the number of eligible voters, and publishes the list of (id_i, e_i, s_i). During the *voting stage*, a voter id_i will perform the following steps: (1) he receives d_i and obtains the desired signature y_i of the ballot x_i using the unblinding technique $y_i = \delta(d_i, r_i)$; (2) if y_i is not the administrator's signature of x_i, he claims that (x_i, y_i) is not valid; otherwise (3) he sends (x_i, y_i) to the collector using an anonymous communication channel. The collector receives (x_i, y_i) and verifies the signature y_i of x_i using the administrator's verification key. If this succeeds, the collector enters (ℓ, x_i, y_i) onto a list as the ℓ-th item. After all voters have voted, the collector publishes the list. During the *opening stage*, each voter will send the key k_i and the number ℓ to the collector using an anonymous communication channel, if his vote is on the list, Otherwise, he claims this by revealing the valid ballot x_i and its signature y_i. Finally, during the *counting stage*, the collector opens the ballot x_i, obtains the vote v_i using k_i, counts the votes, and publishes the voting result.

The μCRL model. As in the case of the Dining Cryptographers problem, we will present the μCRL model of FOO at a rather abstract level and only give details on the interesting modelling points. The complete specification is available online [9].

We chose to model the clear and encrypted votes, as well as clear or blinded or signed ballots by one data type: *Data*, with the extension to lists *DataList*. The votes come from a set $V \subseteq Data$ of size N. We model bit commitment using classical symmetric-key encryption and we use the voter's index i to model both key k_i and the blinding factor r_i. This does not introduce problems, since we encode the various laws and restrictions corresponding to k_i, r_i as equations that the functions using them: *commit, open, blind, unblind* have to satisfy. For instance, the cancelling property of the signing procedure is captured by the equation $unblind(i, sign(blind(j, x))) = $ if $eq(i, j)$ then $sign(x)$ else err.

Each voter, the administrator and the collector are modelled as parallel processes communicating by pairs of synchronising actions like (VfromA, AfromV). The *administrator* waits for blinded ballots from the voters, signs them using the function *sign* and sends them back. We assume that checks by the administrator in the registration stage are always successful.

$$Admin = \sum_{i:Nat} \sum_{m:Data} \texttt{AfromV}(i, m).\texttt{AtoV}(i, sign(m)).Admin$$

A *voter* builds the ballot $x_i = commit(v_i, i)$, blinds it as $e_i = blind(x_i, i)$, and sends (i, e_i) to the administrator. Then he receives a signed ballot m from the administrator, retrieves the desired signature of his ballot using $unblind(id_i, m)$ and sends x_i with the signature to the collector. Then the voter waits for the collector to publish the final list and finally sends k_i (i.e. i) to the collector.

$$Voter_i(v_i : Data) =$$
$$\mathtt{Vdecided}(v_i).\mathtt{VtoA}(i, blind(i, commit(i, v_i))).$$
$$\sum_{m:Data} \mathtt{VfromA}(i, m).(\mathtt{VtoC}(commit(i, v_i), unblind(i, m)).$$
$$\sum_{\ell:DataList} \mathtt{VfromClist}(\ell).\mathtt{VtoC}(find(\ell, unblind(i, m)), i).\delta$$
$$\lhd issigned(unblind(i, m)) \rhd \delta)$$

Note that the construct $\sum_{d:D} P(d) \lhd f(d) \rhd \delta$, with f being a Boolean function of d, forces choosing only the values of d that satisfy f. We model the *collector* with the knowledge of the number n of voters. The action $NVoters(n)$, below, indicates the end of the registration stage. He receives the committed votes as (x_i, y_i), adds them into a list ℓ and stops receiving when the counter ncv reaches n. Then he publishes ℓ by sending it $(CtoVlist)$ to all voters. After receiving k_i for each item in the list ℓ, he opens the vote v_i and publishes the voting result by the actions $\mathtt{numberof}(v)$ $(v \in V)$.

$$Collector = \sum_{n:Nat} \mathtt{NVoters}(n).Collecting([], n, 0)$$
$$Collecting(\ell : DataList, n : Nat, ncv : Nat) =$$
$$\sum_{x_i:Data} \sum_{y_i:Data} \mathtt{CfromV}(x_i, y_i).Collecting(add(x_i, y_i, \ell), n, ncv + 1)$$
$$\lhd ncv < n \land issigned(y_i) \rhd \delta + Opening(\ell, n, 0) \lhd ncv > n \rhd \delta$$
$$Opening(\ell : DataList, n : Nat, nv : Nat) =$$
$$\mathtt{CtoVlist}.Opening(\ell, n, nv + 1) \lhd nv < n \rhd Opening2(\ell, n, 0)$$
$$Opening2(\ell : DataList, n : Nat, nv : Nat) =$$
$$\sum_{label:Nat} \sum_{k_i:Nat} \mathtt{CfromV}(label, k_i).Opening2(openvote(\ell, label, k_i), n, nv + 1)$$
$$\lhd nv < n \rhd Counting(\ell, 0)$$
$$Counting(\ell : DataList, v : Nat) =$$
$$\mathtt{numberof}(v, count(\ell, v)).Counting(\ell, next(v)) \lhd v \in V \rhd \delta.$$

The collector waiting for all n ballots before publishing ℓ is essential for the correctness of the protocol. As noted in [19], the anonymity is broken if the collector were allowed to publish ℓ and continue interacting with the voters before actually having completed collecting all ballots. (In [19], the problem is addressed by introducing synchronisation points between voters after the registration stage. This is equivalent to forcing the collector to wait, because the voters cannot continue without the cooperation of the collector.) We reproduced this problem by modelling a bad collector, which does not wait (see the file **voting.mcrl** at [9]), but we do not insist on this modelling detail here, since our goal is rather to illustrate the anonymity measures on a correct model of the FOO protocol.

Anonymity verification. Let V be the set of possible votes. Then CVS, the allowed set of choice vectors, which is in fact the allowed set of vote outcomes, will be V^n. Note that since the outcomes become public in the end of the protocol, and thus known to the intruder, the equivalence classes of $\approx_{\text{Obs}}$ will be subclasses of the permutation equivalence relation. Note also that for an external observer, $\text{cad}(i) = 1{:}n$, because a choice vector for a unanimous election leaves no doubt as to how anyone voted. So, for this protocol, it is more informative to look at particular instances of choice vectors ($\mathbf{x}$) and evaluate $\text{cad}_\mathbf{x}(v)$ and $\text{pad}_\mathbf{x}(i)$. In the bottom table of Figure 2, a number of experiments are shown, involving various numbers of voters and various vote vectors. The votes are taken from the set $\{0, 1, 2\}$.

In the Dining Cryptographers problem, the question was "who pays?", translated to "which of the players has the choice T?"; $\text{pad}_{\text{TFF}}(\text{T})$ was in that case the appropriate anonymity measure, since it indicates the number of players (worst case: 1) who, according to the intruder, might possibly be associated with the choice T. In voting protocols however it is more relevant how many different votes the intruder might associate to a given voter, so $\text{cad}(voter)$ is a more realistic measure of anonymity. It is possible to get $\text{pad}_\mathbf{x}(v) > 1$ and $\text{cad}_\mathbf{x}(i) = 1$, for a voter i who voted v; this indicates that player anonymity is not a sensitive enough measure, while choice anonymity detects that the intruder precisely knows which candidate voter i chose. This situation is illustrated by $\mathbf{x} = 1121, \text{Obs} = \{2\}, i = 0, v = 1$.

5   Experiences with the Distributed Toolset

In order to assess the efficiency of our approach, we ran some experiments with both examples, various number of players and various coalition sizes. We generated and reduced the state spaces both with the sequential and the distributed tools. For the latter, a cluster with 16 machines (32 processors) was used.

Our initial DC specification gives a very realistic model of the protocol, allowing maximal action interleaving and including a handshake implementation of the final broadcast announcements. Unfortunately, this leads to a fast explosion of the state space, limiting the number of cryptographers that can be handled to 10. Note however, that this is already a larger instance than ever been formally analysed before; Schneider and Sidiropoulos [28] analyse four players, and the maximum we could find in the literature was 8, by means of symbolic epistemic model checking [20]. In order to deal with even larger instances in our explicit tool, we also experimented with a simpler DC model, where an order is imposed on the cryptographers' actions, and a synchronisation of all cryptographers takes place between the three protocol phases (flipping the coins, sharing the coins, broadcasting the XOR results). This requires some more computing effort during generation (and thus more time), but the state spaces resulted are much smaller, and therefore verification of instances with 17 players and more can be achieved. This simplified version occurs in Figure 2 as *DCso*.

Note also that using the distributed tool is not always more efficient. For small state spaces like DC11so, communication between the machines consuming much of the overall time and therefore the sequential tool actually performs better.

	Size	Size after red.	Time	cad(0)	pad(T)
DC3, Obs = ∅	229 469	65 112	1.5s	2:2	3:3
DC3, Obs = {1}	184 362	71 132	1.3s	2:2	2:3
DC5, Obs = {1, 3}	5189 14679	1620 4567	4.9s	2:2	2:5
DC7, Obs = ∅	185 769 695 551	27 180 85 763	8m53s	2:2	7:7
DC9, Obs = ∅	5 194 659 22 961 789	1 034 142 4 088 977	(s) - (db) 7h5m	2:2	9:9
DC10, Obs = ∅	27 436 022 130 031 220	5 002 490 21 535 547	(db) 17h20m	2:2	10:10
DC11so, Obs = ∅	33 876 41 035	6 156 7 188	(s) 6m (db) 11m	2:2	11:11
DC12so, Obs = {1, 3, 5, 7, 9, 11}	58 749 67 612	17 467 21 219	(s) 7m	1:2	1:12
DC15so, Obs = ∅	606 388 721 067	98 320 114 716	(s) 7h2m (db) 44m	2:2	15:15
DC17so, Obs = ∅	2 556 144 3 014 887	393 234 458 784	(s) - (db) 5h40m	2:2	17:17

	Size	Size after red.	Time	cad	pad
FOO4, Obs = {2}	58 749 67 612	17 467 21 219	17s	$\text{cad}_{1121}(0) = 1:3$	$\text{pad}_{1121}(1) = 3:4$
FOO6, Obs = {2}	3 423 841 10 518 810	29 451 92 835	22m36s	$\text{cad}_{010102}(0) = 3:3$	$\text{pad}_{010102}(1) = 5:6$
FOO7, Obs = {2}	65 282 690 221 299 564	3 676 249 9 628 686	(db) 4h48m	$\text{cad}_{0101022}(0) = 3:3$	$\text{pad}_{0101022}(1) = 6:7$

Fig. 2. Experiments with various protocol and coalition instances. The sizes are given as pairs (no. states, no. transitions). The times include both state space generation and reduction. *(db)* marks that the distributed toolset was used. *(s)* - marks that on a single-machine, the state-space generation ran out of memory or didn't stop within 10 hours. For the **FOO** experiments, votes are taken from the set $\{0, 1, 2\}$.

6   Conclusions

Whether a protocol satisfies an anonymity requirement depends not only on the protocol itself, but also on the particular scenarios in which the protocol is used. Namely, there are two influential factors: the strength of the intruder (that is, if/how many participants it has corrupted) and the exact data or actions that need to be protected (in DC, if the NSA pays, the intruder learns that no cryptographer paid; in voting protocols, if the vote is unanimous, there is obviously no choice anonymity). We captured these observations into two definitions of anonymity degrees, parameterised with the aforementioned factors. *Player anonymity* measures the number of participants that the intruder might consider guilty for a given event, and *choice anonymity* measures the number of different pieces of data or events that the intruder might consider as belonging to or being generated by a given participant. We have built tool support for tailoring generic protocol specifications to particular instantiations and coalitions of corrupted participants.

We demonstrated the use of a modern powerful verification toolset, μCRL, to automatically check the anonymity of the generated models. Due to the distributed state space generation and reduction tools, we were able to analyse large instances of known protocols.

Our definitions of anonymity may be based on any equivalence relation. One interesting future direction may be to attempt to model probabilistic systems using our definitions with a probabilistic bisimulation. Finding the right definition of probabilistic bisimulation would be key to making this work. We know of no tools for checking probabilistic bisimulation, so automatically calculating probabilistic anonymity degrees would not be trivial.

We model intruders by making their private communications visible to the attacker. This is done by removing the actions that the intruders see from the sets of actions that are hidden and renamed. We do not remove any actions from those that are encapsulated, i.e., those that are forced to synchronise. If we did remove names from this set too then the communications that were forced to happen with the intruder could instead happen with the outside environment. This would allow us to model active inside attackers that deviate from the protocol. However as actions can in general synchronise with a range of other actions care would have to be taken to ensure that the communications that the attacker is given access to are exactly those that are used by the intruder.

Another possible extension of our framework would be to automatically search for the worst anonymity for a fixed number of intruders. For instance, in the Dining Cryptographers protocol the intruders can be much more effective when spaced out, rather than when they are direct neighbours. We could generate all possible placements of intruders and then test each system to find the lowest anonymity degrees. Such an analysis might help to identify weak points in anonymity protocols that could be strengthen to make inside attacks harder.

The μCRL toolset includes state space optimisation tools that we haven't yet taken into account. Confluence reduction, for instance, has been successfully employed in keeping state spaces manageable [5] and might be useful in our case as well.

References

1. Bergstra, J.A., Klop, J.W.: Algebra of communicating processes with abstraction. Theoretical Computer Science 37(1), 77–121 (1985)
2. Berthold, O., Pfiztmann, A., Standtke, R.: The disavantages of free mix routes and how to overcome them. In: Federrath, H. (ed.) Proc. Workshop on Design Issues in Anonymity and Unobservability. LNCS, vol. 2009, pp. 30–45. Springer, Heidelberg (2001)

3. Bhargava, M., Palamidessi, C.: Probabilistic anonymity. In: Abadi, M., de Alfaro, L. (eds.) CONCUR 2005. LNCS, vol. 3653, pp. 171–185. Springer, Heidelberg (2005)

4. Blom, S.C.C., Fokkink, W.J., Groote, J.F., van Langevelde, I., Lisser, B., van de Pol, J.C.: μCRL: A toolset for analysing algebraic specifications. In: Berry, G., Comon, H., Finkel, A. (eds.) CAV 2001. LNCS, vol. 2102, pp. 250–254. Springer, Heidelberg (2001)

5. Blom, S.C.C., Groote, J.F., Mauw, S., Serebrenik, A.: Analysing the BKE-security protocol with μCRL. In: Proc. 6th AMAST Workshop on Real-Time Systems. ENTCS, vol. 139, pp. 49–90 (2004)

6. Blom, S.C.C., Orzan, S.M.: A distributed algorithm for strong bisimulation reduction of state spaces. Software Tools for Technology Transfer 7(1), 74–86 (2005)

7. Chaum, D.: The dining cryptographers problem: Unconditional sender and recipient untraceability. Journal of Cryptology 1, 65–75 (1988)

8. Chothia, T.: Analysing the mute anonymous file-sharing system using the pi-calculus. In: Najm, E., Pradat-Peyre, J.F., Donzeau-Gouge, V.V. (eds.) FORTE 2006. LNCS, vol. 4229, pp. 115–130. Springer, Heidelberg (2006)

9. Chothia, T., Orzan, S.M., Pang, J.: μCRL specifications.
   http://www.win.tue.nl/~sorzan/anonymity

10. Deng, Y., Palamidessi, C., Pang, J.: Weak probabilistic anonymity. In: Proc. 3rd Workshop on Security Issues in Concurrency (2005)

11. Díaz, C., Seys, S., Claessens, J., Preneel, B.: Towards measuring anonymity. In: PET 2002. LNCS, vol. 2482, pp. 54–68. Springer, Heidelberg (2002)

12. van Eijck, J., Orzan, S.M.: Epistemic verification of anonymity. In: Proc. Views On Designing Complex Architectures (VODCA'06) (2006)

13. Fujioka, A., Okamoto, T., Ohta, K.: A practical secret voting scheme for large scale elections. In: AUSCRYPT 1992. LNCS, vol. 718, pp. 244–251. Springer, Heidelberg (1992)

14. Garcia, F.D., Hasuo, I., Pieters, W., van Rossum, P.: Provable anonymity. In: Proc. 3rd ACM Workshop on Formal Methods in Security Engineering, pp. 63–72. ACM Press, New York (2005)

15. Groote, J.F., Reniers, M.A.: Algebraic process verification. In: Bergstra, J.A., Ponse, A., Smolka, S.A. (eds.) Handbook of Process Algebra, North-Holland, pp. 1151–1208 (2001)

16. Halpern, J.Y., O'Neill, K.R.: Anonymity and information hiding in multiagent systems. Journal of Computer Security, 483–514 (2005)

17. Hughes, D., Shmatikov, V.: Information hiding, anonymity and privacy: A modular approach. Journal of Computer Security 12(1), 3–36 (2004)

18. Hüttel, H., Shukla, S.: On the complexity of deciding behavioural equivalences and preorders - a survey. Technical Report RS-96-39, BRICS (1996)

19. Kremer, S., Ryan, M.: Analysis of an electronic voting protocol in the applied pi-calculus. In: Sagiv, M. (ed.) ESOP 2005. LNCS, vol. 3444, pp. 186–200. Springer, Heidelberg (2005)

20. Lomuscio, A., Raimondi, F.: MCMAS: A tool for verifying multi-agent systems. In: Hermanns, H., Palsberg, J. (eds.) TACAS 2006 and ETAPS 2006. LNCS, vol. 3920, pp. 450–454. Springer, Heidelberg (2006)

21. Mauw, S., Verschuren, J., de Vink, E.P.: A formalization of anonymity and onion routing. In: Samarati, P., Ryan, P.Y A, Gollmann, D., Molva, R. (eds.) ESORICS 2004. LNCS, vol. 3193, pp. 109–124. Springer, Heidelberg (2004)

22. Mauw, S., Verschuren, J., de Vink, E.P.: Data anonymity in the FOO voting scheme. In: Proc. Views On Designing Complex Architectures (VODCA'06) (2006)

23. Meritt, M.J.: Cryptographic Protocols. PhD thesis, Georgia Institute of Technology (1983)
24. van der Meyden, R., Su, K.: Symbolic model checking the knowledge of the dining cryptographers. In: Proc. 17th IEEE Computer Security Foundations Workshop, pp. 280–291. IEEE Computer Society Press, Los Alamitos (2004)
25. Pang, J.: Analysis of a security protocol in μCRL. In: George, C.W., Miao, H. (eds.) ICFEM 2002. LNCS, vol. 2495, pp. 396–400. Springer, Heidelberg (2002)
26. Pfitzmann, A., Hansen, M.: Anonymity, unobservability, and pseudonymity: A proposal for terminology, draft v0.23 (August 2005)
27. Reiter, M.K., Rubin, A.D.: Crowds: Anonymity for Web transactions. ACM Transactions on Information and System Security 1(1), 66–92 (1998)
28. Schneider, S., Sidiropoulos, A.: CSP and anonymity. In: Martella, G., Kurth, H., Montolivo, E., Bertino, E. (eds.) Computer Security - ESORICS 96. LNCS, vol. 1146, pp. 198–218. Springer, Heidelberg (1996)
29. Serjantov, A., Danezis, G.: Towards an information theoretic metric for anonymity. In: Dingledine, R., Syverson, P.F. (eds.) PET 2002. LNCS, vol. 2482, pp. 41–53. Springer, Heidelberg (2003)
30. Shmatikov, V.: Probabilistic model checking of an anonymity system. Journal of Computer Security 12(3/4), 355–377 (2004)

A Framework for Type Safe Exchange of Mobile Code*

Sonia Fagorzi and Elena Zucca

DISI - Università di Genova
Via Dodecaneso, 35, 16146 Genova (Italy)
{fagorzi,zucca}@disi.unige.it

Abstract. We present a simple parametric calculus of processes which exchange mobile code, where type safety is ensured by a combination of static and dynamic checks. That is, internal consistency of each process is locally verified before starting execution, by only relying on type assumptions on missing code; then, at execution time, when locally type-checked code is sent from a process to another, a run-time check based on a subtyping relation ensures that it can be successfully received, without requiring to inspect code again.

The calculus is defined in a parametric way, that is, we do not fix some ingredients which can vary depending on the specific language or system. Notably, we abstract away from the specific nature of the code to be exchanged, and of the static and dynamic checks. We formalize the notion of *type safety* in our general framework and provide sufficient conditions on the above ingredients which guarantee this property.

We illustrate our approach first on a simple lambda-calculus with records, and then on a calculus of mixin modules which generalizes the previous one.

Keywords: parametric calculus, mobile code, static and dynamic type-checking, subtyping.

Introduction

In a distributed scenario, code can be exchanged among processes, possibly running on different sites. Hence, it is not possible to perform a global static analysis; still we would like to guarantee that execution will never crash.

A convenient, modular way for doing this, advocated for instance in [7] in the context of a coordination language for mobile processes that exchange object-oriented code, is by a combination of local static checks and dynamic checks, more precisely:

- Internal consistency of each process is locally verified before starting execution, by only relying on assumptions on missing code (formally expressed by types).

---

* Partially supported by APPSEM II - Thematic network IST-2001-38957, and MIUR EOS - Extensible Object Systems.

U. Montanari, D. Sannella, and R. Bruni (Eds.): TGC 2006, LNCS 4661, pp. 319–338, 2007.

- Mobile code exchanged among processes is equipped with its type, obtained by the previous phase.
- At execution time, when locally typechecked code is sent from a process to another, it is accepted only if it satisfies the expected requirements; formally, this is expressed by a *subtyping* relation between the expected type and the provided type.
- The combination of static type system and dynamic checks via subtyping ensures that, whenever code is accepted, it can be safely composed with local code without any need of being inspected again.

Though the schema above is clearly desirable and very abstract, few attempts have been made until now of formalization and investigation of related problems in a general framework. In this paper, we give a contribution in this direction, by presenting a simple *parametric* calculus of processes which exchange mobile code in a type safe manner, relying on a combination of static and dynamic type checks. In other words, we do not present a single calculus, but a *schema* which models the above described situation abstracting from the ingredients which can vary depending on the specific language or system we are considering. These ingredients are, more in detail:

- code to be exchanged, formalized here by an underlying *core calculus*,
- static checks, formalized by a *type judgment* for the core calculus satisfying the usual subject reduction property w.r.t. to a *static subtyping* relation,
- dynamic checks, formalized by a *dynamic subtyping* relation and an associated *coercion* function, which models the fact that received code could need to be manipulated in some way before to be safely incorporated in local code.

We formalize the notion of *type safety* in our general framework and provide sufficient conditions on the above ingredients which guarantee this property.

We illustrate our approach by first taking as core calculus a simple lambda-calculus with records, and then a calculus of mixin modules which generalizes the previous one. In both cases, the key problem in guaranteeing type safe exchange of mobile code concerns conflicts due to fields (components) which were not explicitly required. We consider two different solutions which can be considered paradigmatic. The former uses simple dynamic checks based on standard subtyping, that is, a record (mixin module) can be safely received if it provides the expected fields (components), and all additional fields (components) are removed (hidden), thus avoiding conflict problems. The latter preserves the semantics (no coercion is inserted), but requires a more involved type system based on constraints, where dynamic checks prevent conflicts. Moreover, while the former solution only allows additional fields (components) at the top level of a received record (mixin module), constraints uniformly prevent conflicts at any level. Both solutions verify the conditions which guarantee type safety.

The paper is structured as follows. In Sect.1 we informally discuss the problem of guaranteeing type safety in a distributed context where mobile code is exchanged. In Sect.2 we formally define our parametric process calculus and the related notion of type safety. In Sect.3 we define two instantiations which take as core calculus a simple lambda-calculus with records, and in Sect.4 we extend both of them to a calculus of mixin modules. Finally, in 5 we summarize our contribution and briefly discuss related and further work.

1   Type Safety in a Distributed Context

In a distributed scenario, software components used by an application may be not all available from the beginning, but retrieved later during execution, possibly from another application running on a different site. Hence, local code can be typechecked only relying on type assumptions for missing code. For instance, considering a simple process calculus with standard send/receive primitives, and records as toy example of mobile code, the following process

$$p_1 = \mathsf{receive}(x\colon\{f_1\colon\mathsf{int}\}).\mathsf{send}(\{f_2 \mapsto 2\} + x).\mathsf{nil}$$

first receives a record with a field f_1 of type int, and then sends the sum[1] of the received record with another with a field f_2 having value 2. Even though record x is not statically available, assuming it has the specified type, process code can be typechecked and the type $\{f_1\colon\mathsf{int}, f_2\colon\mathsf{int}\}$ can be inferred for the sent record.

At run-time, we expect a receive action in a process $\mathsf{receive}(x\colon T).p$ to be synchronized with a send action of a process running in a parallel, which provides the required code, assumed to travel with its type.[2]

If a send/receive synchronization step is legal (that is, code can safely be accepted, see below), then both the send and the receive actions are performed and the variable x is replaced by the record sent by the other process. For instance, we can run the process p_1 in parallel with the process

$$p_2 = \mathsf{send}(\{f_1 \mapsto -1\}).\mathsf{nil}$$

and the parallel composition reduces by an internal step as follows:

$$p_1 \| p_2 \xrightarrow{\ \tau\ } \mathsf{send}(\{f_2 \mapsto 2\} + \{f_1 \mapsto -1\}).\mathsf{nil}\|\mathsf{nil}$$

since $p_1 \xrightarrow{?\{f_1 \mapsto -1\};\{f_1:\mathsf{int}\}}$ and $p_2 \xrightarrow{!\{f_1 \mapsto -1\};\{f_1:\mathsf{int}\}}$. The type annotations in the send and receive actions allow to perform a run-time check. Indeed, received code is accepted only if it provides the expected functionalities, formally expressed by its accompanying type. Note that in this way code is *never reinspected*, since dynamic checks are performed on types only.

However, requiring an exact match between required and dynamically available type, as in the above example, would be a too restrictive constraint, forcing to reject in many cases code which could be safely composed with local code. A less restrictive requirement which seems rather natural is to accept dynamically

---

[1] Also called "record concatenation" or "join" in literature. Here we prefer "sum" for uniformity with module operations later on.

[2] As discussed more in detail later, we assume here to trust the incoming type information to be correct.

available code whose type T' is a subtype, in a suitable sense, of the required type T. We will model this by a *dynamic subtyping relation* $\leq_d$.

For instance, assuming a width/depth subtyping relation on records, in the previous example one could safely run the process p_1 in parallel with the process $p_3 = \mathsf{send}(\{f_1 \mapsto 1, f_3 \mapsto 0\}).\mathsf{nil}$, which sends a record of type $\{f_1 : \mathsf{posint}, f_3 : \mathsf{posint}\}$, which is a subtype of the required type (since it has more fields and of more specific types), obtaining

$$p_1\|p_3 \xrightarrow{\tau} \mathsf{send}(\{f_2 \mapsto 2\} + \{f_1 \mapsto 1, f_3 \mapsto 0\}).\mathsf{nil}\|\mathsf{nil}$$

which is a well-typed expression.

However, assuming the simple semantics by replacement of the receive primitive described above, a dynamic check based on depth/width subtyping would not be type safe. Indeed, as it is well-known in record, object and module calculi [18,2,7,4], there is the problem of unintentional clashes. For instance, if in the example above we run the process p_1 in parallel with the process $p_4 = \mathsf{send}(\{f_1 \mapsto 1, f_2 \mapsto 0\}).\mathsf{nil}$, which also sends a record of a subtype of the required type, then we have

$$p_1\|p_4 \xrightarrow{\tau} \mathsf{send}(\{f_2 \mapsto 2\} + \{f_1 \mapsto 1, f_2 \mapsto 0\}).\mathsf{nil}\|\mathsf{nil}$$

which is not well-typed since there are two conflicting definitions for f_2.

In other words, in the static type system width/depth subtyping is not safe, in the sense that a term of a subtype cannot be safely used in a context where a supertype is expected. However, in the context of mobile code exchange it is also important, besides guaranteeing type safety, to reject communication in as few cases as possible. For instance, in our example, we can still obtain type safety if we assume to remove all fields which were not explicitly required from a received record. In general, we assume the dynamic subtyping relation to be equipped with a coercion function $[\![\_]\!]_{T' \leq_d T}$ on terms, that intuitively allows to bridge the gap between the provided type T' and the required type T.

By using this coercion function we can rewrite the previous two examples in the following way:

$$p_1\|p_3 \xrightarrow{\tau} \mathsf{send}(\{f_2 \mapsto 2\} + [\![\{f_1 \mapsto 1, f_3 \mapsto 0\}]\!]_{\{f_1 : \mathsf{posint}, f_3 : \mathsf{posint}\} \leq_d \{f_1 : \mathsf{int}\}}).\mathsf{nil}\|\mathsf{nil}$$
$$\text{where } [\![\{f_1 \mapsto 1, f_3 \mapsto 0\}]\!]_{\{f_1 : \mathsf{posint}, f_3 : \mathsf{posint}\} \leq_d \{f_1 : \mathsf{int}\}} = \{f_1 \mapsto 1\}$$

$$p_1\|p_4 \xrightarrow{\tau} \mathsf{send}(\{f_2 \mapsto 2\} + [\![\{f_1 \mapsto 1, f_2 \mapsto 0\}]\!]_{\{f_1 : \mathsf{posint}, f_2 : \mathsf{posint}\} \leq_d \{f_1 : \mathsf{int}\}}).\mathsf{nil}\|\mathsf{nil}$$
$$\text{where } [\![\{f_1 \mapsto 1, f_2 \mapsto 0\}]\!]_{\{f_1 : \mathsf{posint}, f_2 : \mathsf{posint}\} \leq_d \{f_1 : \mathsf{int}\}} = \{f_1 \mapsto 1\}$$

Note that non required fields are removed regardless of the fact they would cause conflict problems or not.

Another possible solution is to use a more sophisticated type system, with a dynamic subtyping relation which exactly detects when a conflict would arise. In this case, no coercion is needed (formally, coercion is the identity), since such a subtyping relation allows safe replacement. Both solutions will be formally presented on records and mixin modules in Sect.3 and Sect.4, respectively.

2   Formalization

In this section we define a parametric calculus of processes which formalizes type safe exchange of mobile code as described informally in the previous section. The calculus is parametric in the sense that we leave unspecified some ingredients which will depend on the specific language or system.

First of all, we assume mobile code to be formalized by an underlying *core calculus*, consisting of the following ingredients:

- *variables* $x, y, z, \ldots \in \mathsf{Var}$,
- *expressions* $e \in \mathsf{Exp}^c ::= x \mid \ldots$,
- *(capture-avoiding) substitution* $e[e'/x]$ of the free occurrences of x in e by e',
- *reduction relation* $e \xrightarrow{\;c\;} e'$.

On top of these ingredients, we can define an extended calculus modeling processes which exchange code relying on a simple coordination mechanism[3], and where type safety relies on a combination of static type system and dynamic checks.

To define the extended calculus, we need the following additional ingredients which formalize the static type system and the *exchange of mobile code*:

- *types* $t \in \mathsf{Type}^c$,
- *type judgment* $\Gamma \vdash_{\mathsf{c}} e : t$, where Γ is a *type context*, that is, a mapping from variables into types, written $x_i : t_i^{i \in I}$,
- *(static) subtyping relation* $\leq_{\mathsf{s}}$, required to be a preorder,
- *dynamic subtyping relation* $\leq_{\mathsf{d}}$,
- *coercion* family of functions $[\![\_]\!]_{t' \leq_{\mathsf{d}} t} : \mathsf{Exp}^c \to \mathsf{Exp}^c$, one for each pair $t' \leq_{\mathsf{d}} t$.

We will use the following notations for mappings (e.g., type contexts): $\mathrm{dom}(\Gamma)$ is the domain of Γ; $\Gamma[t/x]$ is the mapping obtained by updating Γ with the association from x to t.

We assume the following standard properties.

Assumption 1. *If* $\Gamma \vdash_{\mathsf{c}} e : t$, $x \notin \mathrm{dom}(\Gamma)$, *then* $e[e'/x] = e$.

Assumption 2 (SR-core). *If* $\Gamma \vdash_{\mathsf{c}} e : t$ *and* $e \xrightarrow{\;c\;} e'$, *then* $\Gamma \vdash_{\mathsf{c}} e' : t'$ *for some* $t' \leq_{\mathsf{s}} t$.

Syntax, reduction and typing rules for the extended calculus are in Fig.1.

The focus of our framework is on dynamic retrieval and typechecking, hence we consider a very simple coordination mechanism based on standard synchronous send/receive primitives. Reduction semantics of process terms is modeled by a labelled relation $p \xrightarrow{\;\lambda\;} p'$ where the label is either τ, denoting an internal step, or $!E : T$, $?E : T$, denoting, respectively, sending and dynamic retrieval of expression E of type T, where E is either a core expression or a process. An

---

[3] For simplicity, we consider here anonymous communications, but the approach could be easily adapted to named forms of communication, e.g., through channels.

$$p \in \mathsf{Proc} ::= x \mid \mathsf{nil} \mid \mathsf{send}(E:T).p \mid \mathsf{receive}(x:T).p \mid p_1 \| p_2 \qquad \textbf{process}$$
$$E \in \mathsf{Exp} ::= e \mid p \qquad\qquad\qquad\qquad\qquad\qquad\qquad \textbf{mobile code}$$
$$\lambda \qquad ::= \tau \mid !E:T \mid ?E:T \qquad\qquad\qquad\qquad\qquad\quad \textbf{label}$$
$$T \qquad ::= t \mid \diamond \qquad\qquad\qquad\qquad\qquad\qquad\qquad\quad \textbf{type}$$

$$\overline{!E:T} = ?E:T \qquad \diamond \leq_s \diamond \qquad\qquad [\![p]\!]_{\diamond \leq_d \diamond} = p$$
$$\overline{?E:T} = !E:T \qquad \diamond \leq_d \diamond$$

$$\text{(CORE)} \ \frac{e \xrightarrow{\ c\ } e'}{\mathsf{send}(e:t).p \xrightarrow{\ \tau\ } \mathsf{send}(e':t).p} \qquad \text{(SEND)} \ \frac{}{\mathsf{send}(E:T).p \xrightarrow{\ !E:T\ } p}$$

$$\text{(RCV)} \ \frac{}{\mathsf{receive}(x:T).p \xrightarrow{\ ?E:T'\ } p[\![E]\!]_{T' \leq_d T}/x]}\, T' \leq_d T \qquad \text{(PAR-LEFT)} \ \frac{p_1 \xrightarrow{\ \lambda\ } p_1'}{p_1 \| p_2 \xrightarrow{\ \lambda\ } p_1' \| p_2}$$

$$\text{(PAR-RIGHT)} \ \frac{p_2 \xrightarrow{\ \lambda\ } p_2'}{p_1 \| p_2 \xrightarrow{\ \lambda\ } p_1 \| p_2'} \qquad \text{(SYNC)} \ \frac{p_1 \xrightarrow{\ \lambda\ } p_1' \quad p_2 \xrightarrow{\ \overline{\lambda}\ } p_2'}{p_1 \| p_2 \xrightarrow{\ \tau\ } p_1' \| p_2'}$$

$$\text{(T-VAR-PROC)} \ \frac{}{\Gamma \vdash x : \diamond}\, \Gamma(x) = \diamond \qquad \text{(T-NIL)} \ \frac{}{\Gamma \vdash \mathsf{nil} : \diamond} \qquad \text{(T-SEND)} \ \frac{\Gamma \vdash E : T' \quad \Gamma \vdash p : \diamond}{\Gamma \vdash \mathsf{send}(E:T).p : \diamond}\, T' \leq_s T$$

$$\text{(T-CORE)} \ \frac{\Gamma^c \vdash_{\overline{c}} e : t}{\Gamma \vdash e : t} \qquad \text{(T-RCV)} \ \frac{\Gamma[T/x] \vdash p : \diamond}{\Gamma \vdash \mathsf{receive}(x:T).p : \diamond} \qquad \text{(T-PAR)} \ \frac{\Gamma \vdash p_1 : \diamond \quad \Gamma \vdash p_2 : \diamond}{\Gamma \vdash p_1 \| p_2 : \diamond}$$

Fig. 1. Coordination calculus

internal step occurs as effect of either a reduction step at the core level, or an exchange of code in a parallel composition of processes.

Note that core code in a $\mathsf{send}(e:t).p$ process can be either sent or further reduced, in a non deterministic way. Assuming to have a distinguished set of values among the ingredients of the core calculus, an alternative approach could be to send only (core) values; however, this would make no difference from the point of view of dynamic typechecking, so we keep here the simpler approach. In other words we do not care about where core mobile code is executed, either by the sender or the receiver, even though this will of course make a difference in practice, e.g., in case of non termination. Sending a process term, instead, intuitively means sending coordination code to be executed by the receiver. Finally, note that we keep the language as simple as possible, hence do not consider additional syntactic constructs (e.g., let-in) which could be useful in practice, but are not significant to our aim.

We denote by $\overline{\lambda}$ the complement of λ, defined in the usual way. Static and dynamic subtyping relation are extended to the process type in the trivial way.

Reduction rules are straightforward, except for (RCV), which is the key rule illustrating our approach. We denote by $p[E/x]$ the capture-avoiding substitution of the free occurrences of x in p with E, defined in the obvious way in terms of core substitution $e[e'/x]$. The side condition expresses the fact that incoming code E can be retrieved only if its type T' is compliant with the required type T, in a sense which is formally specified by the subtyping relation $\leq_d$. In this case, a coercion driven by the subtyping relation $T' \leq_d T$ is inserted before combining E with local code, to bridge the gap between provided and required type.[4]

Typing rules are straightforward as well; a context Γ now maps variables into either core types or the process type. In rule (T-SEND), $\Gamma \vdash E : T'$ can be either $\Gamma \vdash p : \diamond$, if E is a process p, or $\Gamma \vdash e : t$, as defined by rule (T-CORE), if E and T' are a core expression e and type t, respectively. We denote by Γ^c the subset of a context Γ which maps variables into core types.

We do not care here about how type annotation in $\mathsf{send}(E : T).p$ and $\mathsf{receive}(x : T).p$ are produced (that is, either written by the programmer or inferred during compilation). In practice, we expect the annotation in $\mathsf{send}(E : T).p$ to be inferred by the compiler, whereas the programmer should be totally or partially responsible for the task of writing annotation in $\mathsf{receive}(x : T).p$ (indeed, even in case the requirements on x needed to typecheck local code can be automatically inferred, the programmer should be allowed to write stronger requirements for methodological purpose).

The combination of the static type system and the dynamic checks should ensure *type safety*, that is, that internal steps can never lead to ill-formed process terms (for steps of communication with the "external world" this requires to be confident on the fact that received code complies with its accompanying type, see below).[5]

Definition 1 (Type safety). *Exchange of mobile code* $(\leq_d, \llbracket \_ \rrbracket)$ *is type safe if the following (SR) property holds:*

$$\text{If } \Gamma \vdash p : \diamond \text{ and } p \xrightarrow{\tau} p', \text{ then } \Gamma \vdash p' : \diamond.$$

We introduce now an assumption which will be shown to be a sufficient condition for type safe exchange of mobile code. Informally, the assumption states that, whenever the dynamic check on core mobile code succeeds (that is, its declared type is in the dynamic subtyping relation with the required type), this code can be safely incorporated with local code via the corresponding coercion function.

Assumption 3 (Core-$\llbracket \_ \rrbracket_{\leq_d}$-substitution). *If* $\Gamma[t_x/x] \vDash_c e : t$, $\Gamma \vDash_c e' : t''_x$, $t''_x \leq_s t'_x$, *and* $t'_x \leq_d t_x$, *then* $\Gamma \vDash_c e[\llbracket e' \rrbracket_{t'_x \leq_d t_x}/x] : t'$, *for some* $t' \leq_s t$.

Here t_x is the required type, t'_x the type declared by the mobile code and t''_x its actual type.

Lemma 1 ($\llbracket \_ \rrbracket_{\leq_d}$-substitution). *Under assumption 3, if* $\Gamma[T_x/x] \vdash E : T$, $\Gamma \vdash E' : T''_x$, $T''_x \leq_s T'_x$, *and* $T'_x \leq_d T_x$, *then* $\Gamma \vdash E[\llbracket E' \rrbracket_{T'_x \leq_d T_x}/x] : T'$, *for some* $T' \leq_s T$.

---

[4] For simplicity, here an attempt at communicating code of a wrong type corresponds to no reduction at all; a more realistic model should include reduction into a distinguished *error* term of either the receiver only or the communicating pair.

[5] Note that in distributed scenarios type safety, usually expressed by *subject reduction* (SR) and *progress* properties [11], reduces to SR (as in, e.g., [17,13]), since ensuring progress would require a sophisticated static analysis (*deadlock detection*).

Proof. By induction on typing rules. We show the most interesting cases.

(t-send) *We have that* $\Gamma[T_x/x] \vdash \mathsf{send}(E:T).p : \diamond$, $\Gamma[T_x/x] \vdash E : T'$, $T' \leq_s T$, *and* $\Gamma[T_x/x] \vdash p : \diamond$. *By inductive hypothesis we get* $\Gamma \vdash E[\![E']\!]_{T'_x \leq_d T_x}/x] : T''$, *for some* $T'' \leq_s T'$, *and* $\Gamma \vdash p[\![E']\!]_{T'_x \leq_d T_x}/x] : \diamond$. *Since* $\leq_s$ *is a preorder* $T'' \leq_s T$, *hence we get the thesis by applying typing rule* (t-send).

(t-core) *We have that* $\Gamma[T_x/x] \vdash e : t$. *Moreover, if* $T_x = \diamond$ *then* $\Gamma^{\mathsf{core}} \mid_{\overline{c}} e : t$, *hence by Assumption 1* $e[\![E']\!]_{T'_x \leq_d T_x}/x] = e$ *and the thesis follows by applying rule* (t-core). *Otherwise,* T_x *is a core type* t_x, *hence* $\Gamma^{\mathsf{core}}[t_x/x] \mid_{\overline{c}} e : t$. *Then,* T'_x *must be a core type* t'_x *as well, and* E' *a core expression* e', *and by Assumption 3 we get* $\Gamma^{\mathsf{core}} \mid_{\overline{c}} e[\![e']\!]_{t'_x \leq_d t_x}/x] : t'$, *for some* $t' \leq_s t$. *Hence, we ge the thesis by applying typing rule* (t-core).

(t-rcv) *We have that* $\Gamma[T_x/x] \vdash \mathsf{receive}(y:T).p : \diamond$, *and* $\Gamma[T_x/x][T/y] \vdash p : \diamond$. *If* $x \neq y$, *then* $\Gamma[T_x/x][T/y] = \Gamma[T/y][T_x/x]$, *by inductive hypothesis* $\Gamma[T/y] \vdash p[\![E']\!]_{T'_x \leq_d T_x}/x] : \diamond$, *and we get the thesis by applying typing rule* (t-rcv); *otherwise,* $\Gamma[T_x/x][T/y] = \Gamma[T/y]$, $(\mathsf{receive}(y:T).p)[\![E']\!]_{T'_x \leq_d T_x}/x] = \mathsf{receive}(y:T).p$, *and* $\Gamma[T/y] \vdash p : \diamond$, *and the thesis follows by applying typing rule* (t-rcv). □

Proposition 1. *If assumption 3 holds, then exchange of mobile code is type safe.*

We prove type safety as a case of the following *generalized* type safety which takes into account communication steps with the outside world. Intuitively, when receiving code E, safety is guaranteed only if E actually complies its accompanying type T. We assume here that the receiver process just trusts the incoming type information to be correct: a more sophisticated approach would require a *proof*, as in [16]. Conversely, we can prove that code sent to the external world always complies the declared type (this is inductively used to prove safety of internal steps).

We assume here for simplicity that code exchanged among processes is closed w.r.t. the current type context; in particular, considering a ground process, only ground code is exchanged. Retrieval of open code with free variables which can be dynamically bound to local code is an interesting subject of further work.

Proposition 2. *Under assumption 3:*

- *If* $\Gamma \vdash p : \diamond$ *and* $p \xrightarrow{\tau} p'$, *then* $\Gamma \vdash p' : \diamond$.
- *If* $\Gamma \vdash p : \diamond$ *and* $p \xrightarrow{!E:T} p'$, *then* $\Gamma \vdash p' : \diamond$ *and* $\Gamma \vdash E : T'$, *for some* $T' \leq_s T$.
- *If* $\Gamma \vdash p : \diamond$, $p \xrightarrow{?E:T} p'$, *and* $\Gamma \vdash E : T'$, $T' \leq_s T$, *then* $\Gamma \vdash p' : \diamond$.

Proof. By induction on reduction rules. We show the most interesting cases.

(core) *We have that* $\mathsf{send}(e:t).p \xrightarrow{\tau} \mathsf{send}(e':t).p$, $e \xrightarrow{c} e'$, *and, since we must have applied typing rules* (t-send) *and* (t-core), $\Gamma \vdash \mathsf{send}(e:t).p : \diamond$, $\Gamma^{\mathsf{core}} \mid_{\overline{c}} e : t$, *and* $\Gamma \vdash p : \diamond$. *Since SR holds for the core calculus (Assumption 2), we get that* $\Gamma^{\mathsf{core}} \mid_{\overline{c}} e' : t$, *hence by applying typing rule* (t-send) *the thesis follows.*

(send) *We have that* $\mathsf{send}(E\colon T).p \xrightarrow{!E:T} p$, *and, since we must have applied typing rule* (T-SEND), $\Gamma \vdash \mathsf{send}(E\colon t).p\colon \diamond$, $\Gamma \vdash E\colon T'$, $T' \leq_s T$, *and* $\Gamma \vdash p\colon \diamond$, *hence the thesis follows.*

(rcv) *We have that* $\mathsf{receive}(x\colon T).p \xrightarrow{?E:T'} p[\llbracket E \rrbracket_{T' \leq_d T}/x]$, $T' \leq_d T$, *and, since we must have applied typing rule* (T-RCV), $\Gamma \vdash \mathsf{receive}(x\colon T).p\colon \diamond$ *and* $\Gamma[T/x] \vdash p\colon \diamond$. *Moreover, by hypothesis* $\Gamma \vdash E\colon T''$, $T'' \leq_s T'$, *hence by Lemma 1 we get* $\Gamma \vdash p[\llbracket E \rrbracket_{T' \leq_d T}/x]\colon \diamond$. $\qquad\square$

In the next sections we will formally define instantiations of the framework on record/module calculi. We briefly mention here some other possible instantiations.

Taking as core calculus the polymorphic lambda calculus with the primitive type int and instantiation of type variables as (both static and dynamic) subtyping relation, the process $\mathsf{receive}(f\colon \mathsf{int} \to \mathsf{int}).\mathsf{send}(\ldots f(1)\ldots).\mathsf{nil}$ could receive a function $\lambda x.x$ of type $\alpha \to \alpha$, where the coercion function $\llbracket - \rrbracket_{\alpha \to \alpha \leq_d \mathsf{int} \to \mathsf{int}}$ would simply be the identity.

Another example, taken from [15], is "auto-boxing" from value types to object types as, e.g., in Java. Assume the subtyping relation to be such that $\mathsf{int} \leq_d \mathsf{Object}$. Then, the process $\mathsf{receive}(x\colon \mathsf{Object}).\mathsf{send}(\ldots x.\mathsf{toString}()\ldots).\mathsf{nil}$ could accept in input the expression 1 of type int, which would be transformed into an object by the coercion function; for instance, $\llbracket 1 \rrbracket_{\mathsf{int} \leq_d \mathsf{Object}} = \mathsf{new\ Integer}(1)$. Note that the resulting term is not required to exactly have the expected type; it is sufficient that $\mathsf{Integer} \leq_s \mathsf{Object}$ (see assumption 3).

3   A Case Study: Lambda Calculus with Records

In this section we present two different instantiations of the parametric coordination calculus introduced in the previous section, denoted by $\mathsf{MoRec}^{\mathsf{del}}$ and $\mathsf{MoRec}^{\mathsf{cnstr}}$ (for "mobile records"), respectively, which both take as core calculus a simple lambda calculus with records. These two instantiations are mainly reported as a preliminary step towards those on mixin modules which will be presented in the next section, useful to illustrate the problem and the proposed solutions in a simpler setting.

3.1   Core Calculus

The syntax of the calculus is given in Fig.2. We assume, besides variables, an infinite set Field of *field names* f. Terms of the calculus are built by (unspecified) operators of basic types, standard operators of (simply typed) lambda calculus, and *records* with three operators: *sum*, *delete* and *selection*. A record is a map from field names to expressions. Sum performs the union of fields if their sets of names are disjoint, delete removes a field (if present), selection returns an existing field. We omit standard reduction rules (see rules for corresponding operators on mixin modules in next section).

$f \in$ Field		**field name**
$e \in \mathsf{Exp}^c ::=$		**expression**
	$\cdots$	basic operators
	$x \mid \lambda x{:}t.\,e \mid e_1\,e_2$	lambda calculus operators
	$\{fs\}$	record
	$e_1 + e_2$	sum
	$e \setminus f$	delete
	$e.f$	selection
fs	$:= f_i \overset{i \in I}{\mapsto} e_i$	**fields**

Fig. 2. λ-calculus with records: syntax

3.2 Type Safety by Deleting Unexpected Fields

Types, ranged over by $t \in \mathsf{Type}^c$, include (unspecified) basic types, functional types $t_1 \to t_2$ and record types $\{\Sigma\}$, where Σ is a *signature*, that is, a map $f_i{:}t_i{}^{i \in I}$ from field names to types. We omit standard typing rules (see rules for corresponding operators on mixin modules in next section).

In Fig.3 we define the subtyping relations and the coercion functions. Both

$$\text{basic} \qquad \frac{t_1 \to t_2 \leq_{\mathsf{dpt}} t_1' \to t_2'}{t_1 \to t_2 \leq_{\mathsf{d}} t_1' \to t_2'} \qquad \frac{\Sigma_1|_{\mathsf{dom}(\Sigma_2)} \leq_{\mathsf{dpt}} \Sigma_2}{\{\Sigma_1\} \leq_{\mathsf{d}} \{\Sigma_2\}}$$
$$\text{subtyping rules}$$
$$\cdots$$

$$\frac{t_1' \leq_{\mathsf{dpt}} t_1 \quad t_2 \leq_{\mathsf{dpt}} t_2'}{t_1 \to t_2 \leq_{\mathsf{dpt}} t_1' \to t_2'} \qquad \frac{\Sigma_1 \leq_{\mathsf{dpt}} \Sigma_2}{\{\Sigma_1\} \leq_{\mathsf{dpt}} \{\Sigma_2\}} \qquad \frac{t_i \leq_{\mathsf{dpt}} t_i',\, i \in I}{f_i{:}t_i{}^{i \in I} \leq_{\mathsf{dpt}} f_i{:}t_i'{}^{i \in I}}$$

$$[\![e]\!]_{t_1 \leq_{\mathsf{d}} t_2} = \begin{cases} e \setminus (\mathsf{dom}(\Sigma_1) \setminus \mathsf{dom}(\Sigma_2)) & \text{if } t_i = \{\Sigma_i\},\, i \in \{1,2\} \\ e & \text{otherwise} \end{cases} \qquad \leq_{\mathsf{s}} \equiv \leq_{\mathsf{dpt}}$$

Fig. 3. Subtyping relations and coercion functions for MoRec^{del}

static and dynamic subtyping are defined in terms of the relation $\leq_{\mathsf{dpt}}$, which is usual subtyping on functional types (that is, contravariant in the input and covariant in the output) and depth subtyping on record types. Static subtyping $\leq_{\mathsf{s}}$ just coincides with $\leq_{\mathsf{dpt}}$, whereas dynamic subtyping $\leq_{\mathsf{d}}$ also allows width subtyping only at the top level of record types (see the premise of the left top rule). Coercion functions remove all (top level) unexpected fields on expressions of record types (that is, for pairs $\{\Sigma\} \leq_{\mathsf{d}} \{\Sigma'\}$, those fields which are in $\mathsf{dom}(\Sigma)$ but not in $\mathsf{dom}(\Sigma')$), and are the identity on expressions of other types.

For instance, if the expected type is $\{f_1{:}\{f_2{:}\mathsf{int}\}\}$, then the type $\{f_1{:}\{f_2{:}\mathsf{int}\},f{:}\mathsf{int}\}$ is accepted (and f is removed regardless it would cause conflict or not), while $\{f_1{:}\{f_2{:}\mathsf{int},f{:}\mathsf{int}\}\}$ is rejected.

Defining a dynamic subtyping relation and the associated coercion functions corresponding to hierarchical removal of fields is not trivial and will be subject of future work.

We state now that MoRec^{del} satisfies all assumptions required in Sect.2.

Theorem 1

1. If $\Gamma \vdash_{\overline{c}} e : t$, $x \notin \text{dom}(\Gamma)$, then $e[e'/x] = e$.
2. If $\Gamma \vdash_{\overline{c}} e : t$ and $e \overset{c}{\longrightarrow} e'$, then $\Gamma \vdash_{\overline{c}} e' : t'$ for some $t' \leq_s t$.
3. If $\Gamma[t_x/x] \vdash_{\overline{c}} e : t$, $\Gamma \vdash_{\overline{c}} e' : t''_x$, $t''_x \leq_s t'_x$, and $t'_x \leq_d t_x$, then $\Gamma \vdash_{\overline{c}} e[\![e']\!]_{t'_x \leq_d t_x}/x] : t'$, for some $t' \leq_s t$.

3.3 Type Safety by Detecting Conflicts

We describe now a more sophisticated type system for the simple lambda calculus with records. Before giving its formal definition, we illustrate the idea on a simple example.

Let us consider again the process $p_1 = \text{receive}(x : \{f_1 : \text{int}\}).\text{send}(\{f_2 \mapsto 2\} + x).\text{nil}$. To avoid conflicts with local code, the type of the expression to be retrieved, besides being a subtype of $\{f_1 : \text{int}\}$, should have no field named f_2. This can be formally expressed by a *constrained record type* of shape $f_2 : \text{int} \# r \Rightarrow \{f_1 : \text{int}, r\}$, where r is a *row variable* [20] which models an unknown additional signature and the constraint $f_2 : \text{int} \# r$ means that $f_2 : \text{int}$ and r have disjoint domain[6]. Consequently, the expression to be sent has type $f_2 : \text{int} \# r \Rightarrow \{f_1 : \text{int}, f_2 : \text{int}, r\}$. When receiving a record, the row variable r is replaced by the unexpected part of its signature. For instance, if we run p_1 in parallel with $p_3 = \text{send}(\{f_1 \mapsto 1, f_3 \mapsto 0\} : \{f_1 : \text{posint}, f_3 : \text{posint}\}).\text{nil}$, then r is replaced by $f_3 : \text{posint}$. This replacement is safe since the ground constraint $f_2 : \text{int} \# f_3 : \text{posint}$ is valid. On the contrary, if we run p_1 in parallel with $p_4 = \text{send}(\{f_1 \mapsto 1, f_2 \mapsto 0\} : \{f_1 : \text{posint}, f_2 : \text{posint}\}).\text{nil}$, then the synchronization step is not legal since $f_2 : \text{int} \# f_2 : \text{posint}$ is not valid. Note that no coercion is needed (formally, coercion is the identity).

Types and typing rules are given in Fig.4. Types are (unspecified) basic types, functional types and constrained polymorphic record types, consisting of a sequence of constraints and a polymorphic record type, where the signature contains a (possibly empty) sequence of row variables, conventionally written at the end. We denote by $\text{RV}(\Sigma)$ the set of row variables inside Σ, defined in the obvious way, and analogously for $\mathcal{C}$. Standard record types are obtained by taking empty constraint and row variable sequences. A constraint $\Sigma_1, \mathcal{R}_1 \# \Sigma_2, \mathcal{R}_2$ requires two polymorphic signatures to have disjoint domains. Hence, similarly to [12], the form of constraint we consider allows to express *negative* information. The condition $\text{RV}(\Sigma_1) \cap \text{RV}(\Sigma_2) = \emptyset$ prevents row variable clashes. In rule (SUM), the side-condition requires the constraints of the two arguments to imply (written $\vdash$, defined in Fig.5) that their signatures have disjoint domain.

In Fig.5 we define the subtyping relations and the coercion functions.

The relation $\leq_d^\sigma$ is the usual subtyping relation on functional types. On constrained record types, it requires constraints in the subtype to imply those in the supertype, modulo the substitution σ which maps the row variables in the

---

[6] Even though this constraints does not depend on types, we write a signature rather than just a set of names for uniformity with row variables which vary on signatures.

$$t \in \mathsf{Type} ::= \qquad \qquad \text{type}$$

	$\cdots$	basic types
	$\mid \quad t_1 \to t_2$	functional type
	$\mid \quad \mathcal{C} \Rightarrow \{\Sigma, \mathcal{R}\}$	constrained polymorphic record type
Σ	$::= f_i : t_i^{i \in I}$	signature
$\mathcal{R}$	$::= r_i^{i \in I}$	row variables
$\mathcal{C}$	$::= c_i^{i \in I}$	constraints
c	$::= \Sigma_1, \mathcal{R}_1 \,\#\, \Sigma_2, \mathcal{R}_2$	
	$\quad (\mathsf{RV}(\Sigma_1) \cap \mathsf{RV}(\Sigma_2) = \emptyset)$	constraint

$$(\text{VAR}) \; \frac{}{\Gamma \vdash_{\overline{c}} x : \Gamma(x)} \qquad (\text{LAMBDA}) \; \frac{\Gamma[t_1/x] \vdash_{\overline{c}} e : t_2}{\Gamma \vdash_{\overline{c}} \lambda x{:}t_1.\, e : t_1 \to t_2} \qquad (\text{APP}) \; \frac{\begin{array}{c} \Gamma \vdash_{\overline{c}} e_1 : t_2 \to t_1 \\ \Gamma \vdash_{\overline{c}} e_2 : t_2' \end{array}}{\Gamma \vdash_{\overline{c}} e_1 \; e_2 : t_1 \,\{\sigma\}} \; t_2' \leq_{\mathsf{s}}^{\sigma} t_2$$

$$(\text{RECORD}) \; \frac{\Gamma \vdash_{\overline{c}} e_i : t_i, \; i \in I}{\Gamma \vdash_{\overline{c}} \left\{ f_i \stackrel{i \in I}{\mapsto} e_i \right\} : \emptyset \Rightarrow \{f_i : t_i^{i \in I}\}}$$

$$(\text{SUM}) \; \frac{\Gamma \vdash_{\overline{c}} e_i : \mathcal{C}_i \Rightarrow \{\Sigma_i, \mathcal{R}_i\}, \; i \in 1,2}{\Gamma \vdash_{\overline{c}} e_1 + e_2 : \mathcal{C}_1, \mathcal{C}_2 \Rightarrow \{\Sigma_1, \Sigma_2, \mathcal{R}_1, \mathcal{R}_2\}} \; \mathcal{C}_1, \mathcal{C}_2 \vdash \Sigma_1, \mathcal{R}_1 \,\#\, \Sigma_2, \mathcal{R}_2$$

$$(\text{SEL}) \; \frac{\Gamma \vdash_{\overline{c}} e : \mathcal{C} \Rightarrow \{\Sigma, \mathcal{R}\}}{\Gamma \vdash_{\overline{c}} e.f : \Sigma(f)} \qquad (\text{DEL}) \; \frac{\Gamma \vdash_{\overline{c}} e : \mathcal{C} \Rightarrow \{\Sigma, \mathcal{R}\}}{\Gamma \vdash_{\overline{c}} e \setminus f : \mathcal{C} \Rightarrow \{\Sigma \setminus f, \mathcal{R}\}}$$

Fig. 4. Type system for $\mathsf{MoRec}^{\mathsf{cnstr}}$

supertype to the unexpected signature part of the subtype; moreover, depth subtyping is allowed on the matching part of the signatures. Intuitively, the implication $\mathcal{C} \vdash \mathcal{C}'$ holds if ground constraints in $\mathcal{C}'$ are valid and non-ground constraints are included in $\mathcal{C}$. In the last rule, the side-condition $\Sigma_1 \,\#\, \Sigma_2$ means that the two signatures have disjoint domains. Coercion functions are identities and, correspondingly, static subtyping coincides with dynamic subtyping.

Note that, differently from what happen in $\mathsf{MoRec}^{\mathsf{del}}$, here width subtyping is allowed at any level, provided that no conflicts arise. For instance, if the expected type is $\emptyset \Rightarrow \{f_1 : \emptyset \Rightarrow \{f_2 : \mathsf{int}, r_2\}, r_1\}$, then both the types $\emptyset \Rightarrow \{f_1 : \emptyset \Rightarrow \{f_2 : \mathsf{int}\}, f : \mathsf{int}\}$ and $\emptyset \Rightarrow \{f_1 : \emptyset \Rightarrow \{f_2 : \mathsf{int}, f : \mathsf{int}\}\}$ are accepted. On the other hand, the former is not a subtype of $f : \mathsf{int} \,\#\, r_1 \Rightarrow \{f_1 : \emptyset \Rightarrow \{f_2 : \mathsf{int}, r_2\}\}$ and the latter is not a subtype of $\emptyset \Rightarrow \{f_1 : f : \mathsf{int} \,\#\, r_2 \Rightarrow \{f_2 : \mathsf{int}, r_2\}, r_1\}$ (compare with the example in the previous subsection).

We now state that $\mathsf{MoRec}^{\mathsf{cnstr}}$ satisfies all assumptions required in Sect.2.

Theorem 2

1. If $\Gamma \vdash_{\overline{c}} e : t$, $x \notin \mathsf{dom}(\Gamma)$, then $e[e'/x] = e$.
2. If $\Gamma \vdash_{\overline{c}} e : t$ and $e \xrightarrow{\; c \;} e'$, then $\Gamma \vdash_{\overline{c}} e' : t'$ for some $t' \leq_{\mathsf{s}}^{\sigma} t$.
3. If $\Gamma[t_x/x] \vdash_{\overline{c}} e : t$, and $\Gamma \vdash_{\overline{c}} e' : t_x''$, $t_x'' \leq_{\mathsf{s}}^{\sigma} t_x'$, and $t_x' \leq_{\mathsf{d}}^{\sigma} t_x$, then $\Gamma \vdash_{\overline{c}} e[\![e']\!]_{t_x' \leq_{\mathsf{d}}^{\sigma} t_x} / x] : t'$, for some $t' \leq_{\mathsf{s}}^{\sigma} t$.

$$\text{basic} \quad \cfrac{t_1' \leq_d^\sigma t_1 \quad t_2 \leq_d^\sigma t_2'}{t_1 \rightarrow t_2 \leq_d^\sigma t_1' \rightarrow t_2'}$$
$$\text{subtyping rules}$$
$$\cdots$$

$$\cfrac{\Sigma_1 \leq_d^\sigma \Sigma_2}{\mathcal{C}_1 \Rightarrow \{\Sigma_1, \Sigma, \mathcal{R}_1\} \leq_d^\sigma \mathcal{C}_2 \Rightarrow \{\Sigma_2, \mathcal{R}_2\}} \quad \cfrac{\sigma(\mathcal{R}_2) = \Sigma, \mathcal{R}_1}{\mathcal{C}_1 \vdash \mathcal{C}_2 \{\sigma\}} \quad \cfrac{t_i \leq_d^\sigma t_i', \ i \in I}{f_i : t_i^{\,i \in I} \leq_d^\sigma f_i : t_i'^{\,i \in I}}$$

$$\cfrac{}{\mathcal{C} \vdash \emptyset} \quad \cfrac{\mathcal{C} \vdash \mathcal{C}_1 \quad \mathcal{C} \vdash \mathcal{C}_2}{\mathcal{C} \vdash \mathcal{C}_1, \mathcal{C}_2} \quad c ::= \Sigma \# \mathcal{R} \quad \cfrac{\mathcal{C} \vdash \Sigma_1 \# \mathcal{R}_2, \Sigma_2 \# \mathcal{R}_1, \mathcal{R}_1 \# \mathcal{R}_2}{\mathcal{C} \vdash \Sigma_1, \mathcal{R}_1 \# \Sigma_2, \mathcal{R}_2} \quad \Sigma_1 \# \Sigma_2$$
$$\mathcal{C}, c \vdash c \quad | \quad \mathcal{R}_1 \# \mathcal{R}_2$$

$$[\![e]\!]_{t \leq_d^\sigma t'} = e \qquad \leq_s^\sigma = \leq_d^\sigma$$

Fig. 5. Subtyping relations and coercion functions for MoRec^{cnstr}

4 A Calculus of Mixin Modules

In this section we present other two instantiations of the parametric coordination calculus, denoted by MoMix^{del} and MoMix^{cnstr} (for "mobile mixin modules"), respectively, which both take as core calculus the calculus of mixin modules *CMS* [2].

4.1 Core Calculus

The syntax of the calculus if given in Fig.6. Besides variables, we assume an infinite set Name of *names* $(X, Y, Z, \ldots)$. A **basic mixin** has the form $[\iota; o; \rho]$

$X, Y, Z, \ldots \in$ Name			**component name**
$e \in \text{Exp}^c$	::=		**expression**
	|	x	variable
	|	$[\iota; o; \rho]$ $\quad (\text{dom}(\iota) \cap \text{dom}(\rho) = \emptyset)$	basic mixin
	|	$e_1 + e_2$	sum
	|	$e \backslash_X$	delete
	|	$\text{freeze}_X \, e$	freeze
	|	$e.X$	selection
ι	:=	$x_i : t_i \overset{i \in I}{\mapsto} X_i \ (X_i = X_j \implies t_i = t_j)$	**input** part
o	:=	$X_j \overset{j \in O}{\mapsto} e_j$	**output** part
ρ	:=	$x_l : t_l \overset{l \in L}{\mapsto} e_l$	**local** part

Fig. 6. Mixin calculus: syntax

where: ι, the *input* part, is a map from *deferred* variables to *input* names, o, the *output* part, is a map from *output* names to expressions and ρ, the *local* part, is a map from *local* variables to expressions. Names are used to refer to a component from outside the mixin (hence they are used by module operators), while variables, which are annotated with types[7], are used to refer to a component

---

[7] We will omit type annotations when not necessary.

from the inside. A basic mixin, e.g., $[x \mapsto X, z \mapsto Z; X \mapsto 0, Y \mapsto x + y; y \mapsto 2 + z]$, declares four kinds of components: Z is *deferred*, since its name is only input; among components defined inside the mixin, X is *virtual*, since its name is both input and output; Y is *frozen*, since its name is only output; finally, y is *local*, since it has no name, hence is only internally available. Mixins can be combined by the three operators of *sum*, *delete*, and *freeze*.

The main novelties of mixin modules w.r.t. records are that they also declare input components, whose definitions must be provided from the outside (by sum and freeze) and that components can mutually refer to each other (through variables).

In Fig.7 we give the semantics of the calculus, where we omit standard contextual closure.

$$(\text{SUM}) \quad \frac{\begin{array}{l} \text{dom}(\iota_1, \rho_1) \cap FV[\iota_2; o_2; \rho_2] = \emptyset \\ \text{dom}(\iota_2, \rho_2) \cap FV[\iota_1; o_1; \rho_1] = \emptyset \\ \text{dom}(o_1) \cap \text{dom}(o_2) = \emptyset \end{array}}{[\iota_1; o_1; \rho_1] + [\iota_2; o_2; \rho_2] \xrightarrow{c} [\iota_1, \iota_2; o_1, o_2; \rho_1, \rho_2]}$$

$$(\text{DEL}) \quad \frac{}{[\iota; o; \rho] \backslash x \xrightarrow{c} [\iota; o \backslash X; \rho]}$$

$$(\text{FREEZE}) \quad \frac{\begin{array}{l} F = \{x \mid \iota(x) = X\} \\ F \neq \emptyset \implies X \in \text{dom}(o) \end{array}}{\text{freeze}_X [\iota; o; \rho] \xrightarrow{c} \left[\iota \backslash F; o; \rho, x \overset{x \in F}{\mapsto} o(X)\right]}$$

$$(\text{SEL}) \quad \frac{}{\left[; o; x_l \overset{l \in L}{\mapsto} e_l\right].X \xrightarrow{c} o(X)\left[\left[; Y \mapsto e_h; x_l \overset{l \in L}{\mapsto} e_l\right].Y \Big/ x_h^{h \in L}\right]}$$

Fig. 7. Mixin calculus: semantics

The sum operator has the effect of gluing together two mixins, performing the union of deferred components and the disjoint union of virtual, frozen and local components, see rule (SUM). Conflicts among variables are solved by α-renaming.

In rule (DEL), the delete of an output name from a mixin has the effect of removing the corresponding definition: as a consequence, a virtual component becomes deferred, whereas a frozen component just disappears.

Freezing a component means that its input name (if any) disappears, and all variables mapped into it become local, taking as defining expression the current component definition. As a consequence, a virtual component becomes frozen, see rule (FREEZE). Finally, rule (SEL) allows to access an output component of a *closed* (that is, with no input components) mixin. The result is the expression defining the selected output name where, to take into account mutual recursion, all (necessarily local) variables are replaced by their definitions.

4.2 Type Safety by Hiding Unexpected Output Components

In Fig.8 we describe a standard type system for *CMS*. Types include (unspecified) basic types and mixin types. A mixin type consists of an *input signature* π^ι and an *output signature* π^o. A signature is a map from component names into types.

$$t \in \mathsf{Type} ::= \qquad \textbf{type}$$

$$\cdots \qquad \text{basic types}$$

$$\mid \; [\pi^\iota; \; \pi^o] \qquad \text{mixin type}$$

$$\pi \quad := \; X_i \!:\! t_i^{i \in I} \qquad \textbf{signature}$$

$$\text{(VAR)} \; \overline{\Gamma \vDash x : \Gamma(x)}$$

$$\text{(BASIC)} \; \frac{\left\{ \Gamma\left[t_i / \, x_i^{\,i \in I \cup L} \right] \vDash e_h : t_h \mid h \in O \cup L \right\}}{\Gamma \vDash \left[x_i \!:\! t_i \overset{i \in I}{\mapsto} X_i; \; X_j \overset{j \in O}{\mapsto} e_j; \; x_l \!:\! t_l \overset{l \in L}{\mapsto} e_l \right] : \left[X_i \!:\! t_i^{i \in I}; \; X_j \!:\! t_j^{j \in O} \right]} \; X_i \!:\! t_i^{i \in I} \parallel X_j \!:\! t_j^{j \in O}$$

$$\text{(SUM)} \; \frac{\Gamma \vDash e_i : [\pi_i^\iota; \; \pi_i^o] , \; i \in 1,2 \quad \begin{matrix} \pi_1^\iota \parallel \pi_2^\iota \\ \pi_1^o \,\#\, \pi_2^o \\ \pi_1^\iota \parallel \pi_2^o \\ \pi_2^\iota \parallel \pi_1^o \end{matrix}}{\Gamma \vDash e_1 + e_2 : [\pi_1^\iota, \pi_2^\iota; \; \pi_1^o, \pi_2^o]} \qquad \text{(DEL)} \; \frac{\Gamma \vDash e : [\pi^\iota; \; \pi^o]}{\Gamma \vDash e \backslash x : [\pi^\iota; \; \pi^o \backslash X]}$$

$$\text{(FREEZE)} \; \frac{\Gamma \vDash e : [\pi^\iota; \; \pi^o]}{\Gamma \vDash \mathsf{freeze}_X \, e : [\pi^\iota \backslash X; \; \pi^o]} \; X \in \mathrm{dom}(\pi^\iota) \implies X \in \mathrm{dom}(\pi^o) \qquad \text{(SEL)} \; \frac{\Gamma \vDash e : [\emptyset; \; \pi^o]}{\Gamma \vDash e.X : \pi^o(X)}$$

Fig. 8. Type system for MoMix^{del}

In rules (BASIC) and (SUM) the side-condition $\pi_1^\iota \parallel \pi_2^\iota$ means that the two input signatures agree on their common domain; while $\pi_1^\iota \,\#\, \pi_2^\iota$ means that the two signatures have disjoint domains.

basic subtyping rules $\cdots$	$\dfrac{\pi_1^\iota \leq_{\mathsf{dpt}} \pi_2^\iota \quad \pi_2^o \vert_{\mathrm{dom}(\pi_1^o)} \leq_{\mathsf{dpt}} \pi_1^o}{[\pi_1^\iota; \; \pi_1^o] \leq_{\mathsf{d}} [\pi_2^\iota; \; \pi_2^o]}$	$\dfrac{\pi_2^\iota \leq_{\mathsf{dpt}} \pi_1^\iota \quad \pi_1^o \leq_{\mathsf{dpt}} \pi_2^o}{[\pi_1^\iota; \; \pi_1^o] \leq_{\mathsf{dpt}} [\pi_2^\iota; \; \pi_2^o]}$	$\dfrac{t_i \leq_{\mathsf{dpt}} t_i' , i \in I}{X_i \!:\! t_i^{i \in I} \leq_{\mathsf{dpt}} X_i \!:\! t_i'^{i \in I}}$

$$\llbracket e \rrbracket_{t_1 \leq_d t_2} = \begin{cases} (\mathsf{freeze}_H \, e) \, \backslash_H, H = \mathrm{dom}(\pi_1^o) \backslash \mathrm{dom}(\pi_2^o) & \text{if } t_i = [\pi_i^\iota; \; \pi_i^o] , i \in \{1,2\} \\ e & \text{otherwise} \end{cases}$$

$$\leq_{\mathsf{s}} \equiv \leq_{\mathsf{dpt}}$$

Fig. 9. Subtyping relations and coercion functions for MoMix^{del}

In Fig.9 we define the subtyping relations and the coercion functions. They are analogous to those given in Fig.3 for records, except for the fact that unexpected components are *hidden* rather than just deleted. The hiding operator is, as usual in module calculi [2], a combination of freeze and delete; indeed, virtual components need to be frozen before being deleted, making their definitions local, since they could be referred by other components.

Note that the classical problem in object calculi of conflict between depth subtyping and inheritance [1,6] is not present in module calculi. Assume to have objects which are like records in the previous section where fields —now called *methods*— can be mutually recursive. The conflict arises when an object, internally referring to one of its methods, say N of type t, is used in a context expecting a method N with a less specific type, say t', which then redefines N with a body of type t'. Indeed, in this case, the internal reference to N is no longer safe.

We illustrate the problem by the following example from [6], adapted to our syntax.

$$\mathsf{receive}(x\colon[M\colon\mathsf{int},N\colon\mathsf{int}]).\mathsf{send}((x \Leftarrow [N \mapsto -1]).M).\mathsf{nil}$$

Here, $\Leftarrow$ is the *overriding* operator (expressible as a combination of delete and sum), used to redefine method N in x with -1. Taking depth subtyping, an incoming object $[M \mapsto \log(N), N \mapsto 1]$ of type $[M\colon\mathsf{int},N\colon\mathsf{posint}]$ could be accepted; however, the execution of the resulting process would raise a run-time error.

The key point is that an exported method which is also internally referred acts as a virtual (both input and output) component, but this twofold role is not made explicit in the type. Differently, in module calculi, self-reference is made through *variables* rather than names, and the type indicates whether a component is input and/or output. For instance, a module analogous to the incoming object above can only be written as $[n \mapsto N; M \mapsto \log(n), N \mapsto 1;]$ of type $[N\colon\mathsf{posint}; M\colon\mathsf{int},N\colon\mathsf{posint}]$[8]. Hence, a context using this module should specify an expected input component $N\colon\mathsf{posint}$, and the analogous of the previous process

$$\mathsf{receive}(x\colon[N\colon\mathsf{posint}; M\colon\mathsf{int},N\colon\mathsf{posint}]).\mathsf{send}((x \Leftarrow [N \mapsto -1]).M).\mathsf{nil}$$

would be ill-typed. On the other hand, if the type $[N\colon\mathsf{int}; M\colon\mathsf{int},N\colon\mathsf{int}]$ was expected, making the above process well-typed, then the incoming module could not be accepted. The solution given in [6] corresponds in practice to recover what is automatically guaranteed by the type system in module calculi: that is, in [6] they specify, for each receive parameter of mixin or class type, besides the required type (that acts as an upper bound), also a "lower bound" statically inferred which records the (most general) type of all redefining methods (in the previous example $N\colon\mathsf{int}$). In our terminology, this is the expected input type of the parameter.

4.3   Type Safety by Detecting Conflicts

We now give a type system for mixin modules similar to that given in Sect.3.3 for records, which uses constraints to prevent conflicts.

Types and typing rules are in Fig.10. Types are (unspecified) basic types and *constrained polymorphic mixin types*, consisting of a sequence of constraints and a polymorphic mixin type, where the output signature contains a (possibly empty) sequence of row variables. On polymorphic signatures we use the same conventions and notations introduced in Sect.3.3. We need a new kind of constraint: $\pi_1 \parallel \pi_2, \mathcal{R}$ requires a non-polymorphic (input) signature to be compatible with a polymorphic (output) signature.

In Fig.11 we define the subtyping relations and the coercion functions. Their definitions are analogous to those seen in Sect.3.3, with the difference that here

---

[8] Recall that an input and an output component with the same name are considered as a unique (virtual) component, hence their types must agree.

$t \in$ Type ::=   **type**

$\qquad \cdots$ basic types

$\qquad |\quad \mathcal{C} \Rightarrow [\pi^\iota; \, \pi^o, \mathcal{R}]$ constrained polymorphic mixin type

$\pi \qquad := X_i : t_i^{i \in I}$ **signature**

$\mathcal{R} \qquad ::= r_i^{i \in I}$ **row variables**

$\mathcal{C} \qquad ::= c_i^{i \in I}$ **constraints**

$c \qquad ::= \pi_1 \parallel \pi_2, \mathcal{R}$

$\qquad |\quad \pi_1, \mathcal{R}_1 \, \# \, \pi_2, \mathcal{R}_2 \quad (\mathrm{RV}(\pi_1) \cap \mathrm{RV}(\pi_2) = \emptyset)$ **constraint**

$$(\text{VAR}) \frac{}{\Gamma \vdash_{\mathsf{E}} x : \Gamma(x)}$$

$$(\text{BASIC}) \frac{\left\{ \Gamma \left[t_i / x_i^{\,i \in I \cup L} \right] \vdash_{\mathsf{E}} e_h : t_h \mid h \in O \cup L \right\}}{\Gamma \vdash_{\mathsf{E}} \left[x_i : t_i \overset{i \in I}{\mapsto} X_i; \; X_j \overset{j \in O}{\mapsto} e_j; \; x_l : t_l \overset{l \in L}{\mapsto} e_l \right] : \emptyset \Rightarrow \left[X_i : t_i^{\,i \in I}; \; X_j : t_j^{\,j \in O} \right]} \; X_i : t_i^{i \in I} \parallel X_j : t_j^{j \in O}$$

$$(\text{SUM}) \frac{\Gamma \vdash_{\mathsf{E}} e_i : \mathcal{C}_i \Rightarrow [\pi_i^\iota; \, \pi_i^o, \mathcal{R}_i], \; i \in 1,2 \qquad \begin{array}{c} \pi_1^\iota \parallel \pi_2^\iota \\ \mathcal{C}_1, \mathcal{C}_2 \vdash \pi_1^o, \mathcal{R}_1 \, \# \, \pi_2^o, \mathcal{R}_2, \\ \pi_1^\iota \parallel \pi_2^o, \mathcal{R}_2, \\ \pi_2^\iota \parallel \pi_1^o, \mathcal{R}_1 \end{array}}{\Gamma \vdash_{\mathsf{E}} e_1 + e_2 : \mathcal{C}_1, \mathcal{C}_2 \Rightarrow [\pi_1^\iota, \pi_2^\iota; \, \pi_1^o, \pi_2^o, \mathcal{R}_1, \mathcal{R}_2]}$$

$$(\text{DEL}) \frac{\Gamma \vdash_{\mathsf{E}} e : \mathcal{C} \Rightarrow [\pi^\iota; \, \pi^o, \mathcal{R}]}{\Gamma \vdash_{\mathsf{E}} e \backslash x : \mathcal{C} \Rightarrow [\pi^\iota; \, \pi^o \backslash X, \mathcal{R}]} \qquad (\text{FREEZE}) \frac{\Gamma \vdash_{\mathsf{E}} e : \mathcal{C} \Rightarrow [\pi^\iota; \, \pi^o, \mathcal{R}]}{\Gamma \vdash_{\mathsf{E}} \mathsf{freeze}_X \, e : \mathcal{C} \Rightarrow [\pi^\iota \backslash X; \, \pi^o, \mathcal{R}]} \; \begin{array}{c} X \in \mathrm{dom}(\pi^\iota) \implies \\ X \in \mathrm{dom}(\pi^o) \end{array}$$

$$(\text{SEL}) \frac{\Gamma \vdash_{\mathsf{E}} e : \mathcal{C} \Rightarrow [\emptyset; \, \pi^o, \mathcal{R}]}{\Gamma \vdash_{\mathsf{E}} e.X : \pi^o(X)}$$

Fig. 10. Type system for MoMix^{cnstr}

basic   subtyping rules $\cdots$

$$\frac{\pi_2^\iota \leq_d^\sigma \pi_1^\iota \quad \pi_1^o \leq_d^\sigma \pi_2^o}{\mathcal{C} \Rightarrow [\pi_1^\iota; \, \pi_1^o, \pi^o, \mathcal{R}_1] \leq_d^\sigma \mathcal{C}' \Rightarrow [\pi_2^\iota; \, \pi_2^o, \mathcal{R}_2]} \qquad \frac{\sigma(\mathcal{R}_2) = \pi^o, \mathcal{R}_1}{\mathcal{C} \vdash \mathcal{C}' \{\sigma\}} \qquad \frac{t_i \leq_d^\sigma t_i', \; i \in I}{X_i : t_i^{i \in I} \leq_d^\sigma X_i : t_i'^{i \in I}}$$

$$\frac{}{\mathcal{C} \vdash \emptyset} \qquad \frac{\mathcal{C} \vdash \mathcal{C}_1 \quad \mathcal{C} \vdash \mathcal{C}_2}{\mathcal{C} \vdash \mathcal{C}_1, \mathcal{C}_2} \qquad \frac{}{\mathcal{C}, c \vdash c} \quad c ::= \begin{array}{l} \pi^\iota \parallel \mathcal{R} \\ \pi^o \, \# \, \mathcal{R} \\ \mathcal{R}_1 \, \# \, \mathcal{R}_2 \end{array} \qquad \frac{\mathcal{C} \vdash \pi_1^o \, \# \, \mathcal{R}_2, \pi_2^o \, \# \, \mathcal{R}_1, \mathcal{R}_1 \, \# \, \mathcal{R}_2}{\mathcal{C} \vdash \pi_1^o, \mathcal{R}_1 \, \# \, \pi_2^o, \mathcal{R}_2} \; \pi_1^o \, \# \, \pi_2^o$$

$$\frac{\mathcal{C} \vdash \pi^\iota \parallel \mathcal{R}}{\mathcal{C} \vdash \pi^\iota \parallel \pi^o, \mathcal{R}} \pi^\iota \parallel \pi^o \qquad [\![e]\!]_{t \leq_d^\sigma t'} = e \qquad \leq_s^\sigma = \leq_d^\sigma$$

Fig. 11. Subtyping relation and coercion functions for MoMix^{cnstr}

we also have contravariant subtyping on input signatures and that we have to ensure the validity of the new kind of constraint $\pi^\iota \parallel \pi^o, \mathcal{R}$.

The instantiations MoMix^{del} and MoMix^{cnstr} satisfy Assumptions 1, 2 and 3 of Sect.2; we omit the formal statements for lack of space.

5   Conclusion

The contribution of the paper is twofold. First, we have provided a simple and general formal framework for reasoning about the problem of guaranteeing type safety in a distributed context where mobile code is exchanged. The inspiration for this work has been MoMi [6,5,7,4], a coordination language for mobile processes that exchange object-oriented code (more precisely, classes or mixin classes). The framework we have presented, indeed, abstracts away from all the aspects of MoMi which are dependent on the specific language chosen for mobile code or the specific mechanism chosen for static and dynamic checks, and formalizes their key idea of ensuring type safety by a combination of static type-checking of local code and dynamic checks via subtyping (see below for a more detailed comparison).

Moreover, we have applied our general framework to a concrete case study, in which exchanged mobile code is written in a language based on records/mixin modules, and the key problem in guaranteeing type safety concerns conflicts due to fields (components) which were not explicitly required. We have defined two instantiations of the framework which solves this problem in two different ways. The former keeps dynamic checks simple, and solves interference problems by removing/hiding functionalities which were not explicitly required. The latter solution, on the contrary, preserves the semantics we would get in the static case, by means of a more involved type system based on constraints, where dynamic checks prevents conflicts. Moreover, in the latter solution width subtyping is allowed at any level, provided that no conflicts arise, while it is not trivial to generalize the former solution in order to delete/hide inner fields (components). Our aim here is not to defend either choice, but rather to show that both can be proved to be type safe in a simple way by showing that they satisfy some general assumptions. Moreover, we believe that the two presented solutions are paradigmatic in the sense that they correspond to two opposite approaches for allowing mobile code exchange as often as possible: either to introduce a more involved semantics, or a more sophisticated type system.

Compared with work on MoMi, the framework we present in Sect.1 does not consider a fixed syntax for the mobile code, but can be instantiated on an arbitrary language satisfying some natural assumptions (see the end of Sect.2 for an outline of instantiations different from those presented in this paper). In MoMi, instead, they consider a standard class-based object-oriented language SOOL supporting mixin-based class hierarchies (see, e.g., [7] Sect.3.1), which however abstracts from the nature of method bodies. Analogously, the framework we present in Sect.1 does not consider a fixed definition of static and dynamic checks, whereas in MoMi they consider a fixed type system for mixin classes which prevents mixin application in case of conflicts, and a fixed definition of dynamic checks based on hiding. In summary, the MoMi framework roughly corresponds to the first solution we present in Sect.4, with the difference that we consider mixin modules rather than mixin classes, hence we do not have the classical problem of interference between depth subtyping and inheritance (see the end of Sect.4). On the contrary, the second solution we propose is novel w.r.t. the MoMi approach.

This paper continues the work in [10], where we considered the problem of guaranteeing type safety for a calculus of mixin modules where code can be dynamically retrieved during execution. The language and the two solutions to the problem of avoiding conflicts due to unexpected components are essentially those presented in Sect.4. However, in [10] we did not allow higher-order modules. Moreover, in this paper we studied the same problem first in the more foundational context of lambda-calculus with records, what led somewhere to a cleaner formalization. The definition of an explicit process layer where code can be both sent and received and the formalization of the problem in an abstract general framework are new issues not considered in [10].

Besides the work on MoMi, an important source of inspiration has been [15], in particular for the idea of coercion driven by a subtyping relation. Other work which has directly influenced our approach is that on dynamic software updating in, e.g., [8,9,19]. However, here we consider arbitrary core calculi rather than lambda-calculi, and an explicit language for the process layer, whereas in [8,9,19] the basic primitive is an *update* primitive which when performed changes some parts of the local code in a less controlled way.

The type system based on constraints used in the latter solution is similar to that defined in [14] for getting principal typings for mixin modules. However, here we do not deal with the problem of type inference.

There are many interesting directions for further work. Concerning the general framework, we would like to investigate other properties besides type safety. For instance, we would like to formalize notions like how often code is rejected and whether the original language semantics is preserved. Moreover, we plan to study exchange of code with free variables which can be dynamically rebound in the receiver, like in [9]. On the more specific topic of interference in record/mixin calculi, a problem we did not solve in this paper is the definition of hierarchical coercion functions allowing to delete/hide inner fields/components. We also plan a more precise comparison with the type system defined in [14]. Finally, we would like to investigate implementation aspects, possibly taking as starting point the work in [3].

Acknowledgments. We warmly thank Viviana Bono for many useful discussions and suggestions, and the anonymous referees for their comments.

References

1. Abadi, M., Cardelli, L.: A Theory of Objects. Monographs in Computer Science. Springer, Heidelberg (1996)
2. Ancona, D., Zucca, E.: A calculus of module systems. Journ. of Functional Programming 12(2), 91–132 (2002)
3. Bettini, L.: A Java package for class and mixin mobility in a distributed setting. In: FIDJI 2003. LNCS, vol. 2952, pp. 12–22. Springer, Heidelberg (2003)
4. Bettini, L., Bono, V., Likavec, S.: Safe and flexible objects with subtyping. SAC 2005 10(4), 5–29 (2005) (Special Issue: OOPS Track at SAC 2005)
5. Bettini, L., Bono, V., Venneri, B.: O'Klaim: a coordination language with mobile mixins. In: De Nicola, R., Ferrari, G.L., Meredith, G. (eds.) COORDINATION 2004. LNCS, vol. 2949, pp. 20–37. Springer, Heidelberg (2004)

6. Bettini, L., Bono, V., Venneri, B.: Subtyping-inheritance conflicts: The mobile mixin case. In: Lévy, J.-J., Mayr, E.W., Mitchell, J.C. (eds.) TCS'04 - IFIP Int. Conf. on Theoretical Computer Science, pp. 451–464. Kluwer Academic, Boston (2004)
7. Bettini, L., Venneri, B., Bono, V.: MOMI: a calculus for mobile mixins. Acta Informatica 42(2-3), 143–190 (2005)
8. Bierman, G., Hicks, M.W., Sewell, P., Stoyle, G.: Formalizing dynamic software updating (extended abstract). In: USE'03 - the Second International Workshop on Unanticipated Software Evolution (2003)
9. Bierman, G., Hicks, M.W., Sewell, P., Stoyle, G., Wansbrough, K.: Dynamic rebinding for marshalling and update, with destruct-time λ. In: Runciman, C., Shivers, O. (eds.) Intl. Conf. on Functional Programming 2003, pp. 99–110. ACM Press, New York (2003)
10. Fagorzi, S., Zucca, E.: A calculus of components with dynamic type-checking. Electronic Notes in Theoretical Computer Science, Formal Aspects of Component Software (FACS'06) (to appear, 2006)
11. Felleisen, M., Friedman, D.P.: Control operators, the SECD-machine, and the lambda-calculus. In: 3rd Working Conference on the Formal Description of Programming Concepts, Ebberup, Denmark, pp. 193–219 (August 1986)
12. Harper, R., Pierce, B.C.: A record calculus based on symmetric concatenation. In: ACM Symp. on Principles of Programming Languages 1991, pp. 131–142. ACM Press, New York (1991)
13. Kobayashi, N., Pierce, B.C., Turner, D.N.: Linearity and the pi-calculus. In: ACM Symp. on Principles of Programming Languages 1996, pp. 358–371. ACM Press, New York, USA (1996)
14. Makholm, H., Wells, J.B.: Type inference, principal typings, and let-polymorphism for first-class mixin modules. In: Danvy, O., Pierce, B.C. (eds.) Intl. Conf. on Functional Programming 2005, pp. 156–167. ACM Press, New York (2005)
15. Meijer, E., Drayton, P.: Static typing where possible, dynamic typing when needed: The end of the cold war between programming languages. In: OOPSLA'04 Workshop on Revival of Dynamic Languages (2004)
16. Necula, G.C.: Proof-carrying code. In: George, C. (ed.) ACM Symp. on Principles of Programming Languages 1997, pp. 106–119. ACM Press, New York (1997)
17. Pierce, B.C., Sangiorgi, D.: Typing and subtyping for mobile processes. In: Proceedings 8th IEEE Logics in Computer Science, Montreal, Canada, pp. 376–385 (1993)
18. Riecke, J.G., Stone, C.A.: Privacy via subsumption. Information and Computation 172(1), 2–28 (2002)
19. Stoyle, G., Hicks, M.W., Bierman, G., Sewell, P., Neamtiu, I.: Mutatis mutandis: safe and predictable dynamic software updating. In: ACM Symp. on Principles of Programming Languages 2005, pp. 183–194. ACM Press, New York (2005)
20. Wand, M.: Complete type inference for simple objects. In: Proc. IEEE Symp. on Logic in Computer Science 1987, pp. 37–44, 1987. A corrigendum appeared at LICS (1988)

Author Index

Lecture Notes in Computer Science

Sublibrary 1: Theoretical Computer Science and General Issues

For information about Vols. 1– 4494
please contact your bookseller or Springer